FIFTH EDITION

CLINICAL INTERVIEWING

FIFTH EDITION

CLINICAL INTERVIEWING

John Sommers-Flanagan
Rita Sommers-Flanagan

WILEY

Library of Congress Cataloging-in-Publication Data:
Sommers-Flanagan, John, 1957–
  Clinical interviewing / John Sommers-Flanagan, Rita Sommers-Flanagan—Fifth edition.
     pages cm
  Includes bibliographical references and index.
  ISBN 978-1-118-27004-2 (pbk.)
  ISBN 978-1-118-42125-3 (e-bk.)
  ISBN 978-1-118-41956-4 (e-bk.)
  1. Interviewing in mental health.   2. Interviewing in psychiatry. I. Sommers-Flanagan, Rita, 1953– II. Title.
  RC480.7.S66 2013
  616.8900835—dc23

                                                                                    2013010134

Printed in the United States of America

10 9 8 7 6 5 4 3

To Chelsea: in honor of your excellent interviewing skills and perpetual pursuit of knowledge.
To Seth: for being able to pass Chelsea's premarital interviewing examinations and for your service to the world community.
To Rylee: for having the heart, soul, and spirit for coping with the rest of us and the ambition to become a Supreme Court justice.
To Margaret and Davis: Someday soon we'll make a video of ourselves reading you this exciting book.
We love you all and look forward to many more excellent life adventures together.

Contents

DVD Contents

DVD Chapters

- Introduction
- Basic Listening Skills
- Directive Listening Responses
- Directives & Action Responses
- Questions & Therapeutic Questions
- Intake Interview
- Mental Status Examination
- Suicide Assessment Interview

Counseling Demonstrations

- Maegan & Jessie: Basic Listening Skills
- John & Trudi: Directive Listening Responses
- John & T.J.: Directive Listening Responses
- John & Lisa: Directives & Action Responses Part I
- John & Lisa: Directives & Action Responses Part II
- Chris & Ümüt: Questions & Therapeutic Questions
- John & T.J.: Questions & Therapeutic Questions
- Rita & Michele: Intake Interview Part I
- Rita & Michele: Intake Interview Part II
- Rita & Michele: Intake Interview Part III
- John & Carl: Mental Status Examination Part I
- John & Carl: Mental Status Examination Part II
- John & Tommie: Suicide Assessment Interview Part I
- John & Tommie: Suicide Assessment Interview Part II
- John & Tommie: Suicide Assessment Interview Part III

Preface

Clinical interviewing is the cornerstone for virtually all mental health work. It involves integrating varying degrees of psychological or psychiatric assessment and treatment. The origins of clinical interviewing long precede the first edition of this text (published in 1993).

The term *interview* dates back to the 1500s, originally referring to a face-to-face meeting or formal conference. The term *clinical* originated around 1780; it was used to describe a dispassionate, supposedly objective bedside manner in the treatment of hospital patients. Although difficult to determine precisely when clinical and interview were joined in modern use, it appears that Jean Piaget used a variant of the term *clinical interview* in 1920 to describe his approach to exploring the nature and richness of children's thinking. Piaget referred to his procedure as a semi-clinical interview (see Sommers-Flanagan, Zeleke, & Hood, in press).

Our initial exposure to clinical interviewing was in the early 1980s in a graduate course at the University of Montana. Our professor was highly observant and intuitive. We would huddle together around an old cassette player and listen to fresh new recordings of graduate students interviewing perfect strangers. Typically, after listening to about two sentences our professor would hit the pause button and prompt us: "Tell me about this person."

We didn't know anything, but would offer limited descriptions like "She sounds perky" or "He says he's from West Virginia." He would then regale us with predictions. "Listen to her voice," he would say, "she's had rough times." "She's depressed, she's been traumatized, and she's come to Montana to escape."

The eerie thing about this process was that our professor was often correct in what seemed like wild predictions. These sessions taught us to respect the role of astute observations, experience, and intuition in clinical interviewing.

Good intuition is grounded on theoretical and practical knowledge, close observation, clinical experience, and scientific mindedness. Bad intuition involves personalized conclusions that typically end up being a disservice to clients. Upon reflection, perhaps one reason we ended up writing and revising this book is to provide a foundation for intuition. In fact, it's interesting that we rarely mention intuition in this text. Although one of us likes to make wild predictions of the future (including predictions of the weather on a particular day in Missoula, Montana, about three months in advance), we still recognize our limitations and encourage you to learn the science of clinical interviewing before you start practicing the art.

LANGUAGE CHOICES

We live in a postmodern world in which language is frequently used to construct and frame arguments. The words we choose to express ourselves cannot help but influence the message. Because language can be used to manipulate (as in advertising and politics), we want to take this opportunity to explain a few of our language choices so you can have insight into our biases and perspectives.

Patient or Client or Visitor

Clinical interviewing is a cross-disciplinary phenomenon. While revising this text we sought feedback from physicians, psychologists, social workers, and professional counselors. Not surprisingly, physicians and psychologists suggested we stick with the term *patient*, whereas social workers and counselors expressed strong preferences for *client*. As a third option, in the Mandarin Chinese translation of the second edition of this text, the term used was *visitor*.

After briefly grappling with this dilemma, we decided to primarily use the word *client* in this text, except for cases in which *patient* is used in previously quoted material. Just as Carl Rogers drifted in his terminology from *patient* to *client* to *person*, we find ourselves moving away from some parts and pieces of the medical model. This doesn't mean we don't respect the medical model, but that we're intentionally choosing to use more inclusive language that emphasizes wellness. We unanimously voted against using *visitor*—although thinking about the challenges of translating this text to Mandarin made us smile.

Sex and Gender

Consistent with Alfred Adler, Betty Freidan, contemporary feminist theorists, and American Psychological Association (APA) style, we like to think of ourselves as promoting an egalitarian world. As a consequence, we've dealt with gender in one of two ways: (1) when appropriate, we use the plural *clients* and *their* when referring to case examples; and (2) when necessary, we alternate our use between *she* and *he*.

Interviewer, Psychotherapist, Counselor, or Therapist

While working at a psychiatric hospital in 1980, John once noticed that if you break down the word *therapist* it could be transformed into the-rapist. Shocked by his linguistic discovery, he pointed it out to the hospital social worker, who quipped back, "That's why I always call myself a counselor!"

This is a confusing issue and difficult choice. For the preceding four editions of this text we used the word *interviewer* because it fit so perfectly with the text's title, *Clinical Interviewing*. However, we've started getting negative feedback about the term. One reviewer noted that he "hated it." Others complained "It's too formal" and "It's just a weird term to use in a text that's really about counseling and psychotherapy."

Given the preceding story, you might think that we'd choose the term *counselor*, but instead we've decided that exclusively choosing *counselor* or *psychotherapist* might inadvertently align us with one professional discipline over another. The conclusion: Mostly we use *therapist* and occasionally we leave in the term *interviewer* and also allow ourselves the freedom to occasionally use *counselor*, *psychotherapist*, and *clinician*.

WHAT'S NEW IN THE FIFTH EDITION?

As the world changes, our understanding of the world needs to change as well. In this fifth edition, we've worked to make the content accessible, culturally tuned-in, accurate, and sometimes provocative. We've made our examples more current and relevant to the technological and diagnostic changes witnessed in recent years.

Although there are too many minor changes to list, here are the 19 biggest changes:

1. All chapters have been revised and updated using feedback from over 50 graduate students and professors from various disciplines throughout the United States.

2. Chapters 1, 2, 3, 4, 7, 8, and 9 now include DVD call-outs. These call-outs provide instructors with suggestions about where material from the new accompanying Clinical Interviewing DVD might be included.

3. Chapter 1 includes a new section on developing a multicultural orientation and the three principles of multicultural competency.

4. Consistent with an evidence-based approach, there's a greater emphasis on collaborative goal setting and the client as expert beginning in Chapter 2 and throughout the text.

5. Within the context of professional attire, Chapter 2 also includes a new section on cleavage.

6. Chapter 3 includes a new multicultural highlight focusing on eye contact and including contrasting views on the subject between two professional Black or African American females, as well as new material on summarization and a new section on immediacy.

7. In response to reviewer feedback, Chapter 4 has been reorganized into two sections. Section One is Using General and Therapeutic Questions, and Section Two is Directive Interviewing Techniques. Additional content has been added on Adler's "The Question" as well as the four main questions of reality therapy. There's also a new Putting It in Practice feature titled A General Guide to Using Stages of Change Principles in Clinical Interviewing.

8. Chapter 5 has been substantially reorganized to shift its emphasis from theory-based relationship factors to research-supported evidence-based relationships.

9. In Chapter 6 we've added a section on personalismo and making cultural connections. A new Putting It in Practice on developing an informed consent form is included. There's also a new Multicultural Highlight focusing on a universal exclusion criterion for mental disorders and new content on developing case formulations.

10. Chapter 7 includes a new section on Reviewing Goals with Clients.

11. Chapter 8 includes a new section on the Dangers of Single Symptom Generalizations. There's also new content on flashbacks, memory, and on writing the mental status examination report.

12. A new Putting It in Practice on the latest acronym for suicide risk (IS PATH WARM) is featured in Chapter 9. The chapter is substantially updated with a greater emphasis on the interpersonal theory of suicide. A new Putting It in Practice designed to help beginning clinicians become more comfortable talking about suicide with clients is also included.

13. Chapter 10 has been reorganized and rewritten to correspond with *DSM-5* and now also emphasizes case formulation and treatment matching variables in addition to treatment planning.

14. The last several chapters were reordered, with Chapter 11 now becoming the Multicultural Interviewing chapter. Chapter 11 now includes a new section on professional issues.

15. Chapter 12 includes a new Table: A General Guide to Violence Assessment. It also has undergone a major rewrite to more completely clarify the nature and process of working in crisis situations, including a description of psychological first aid.

16. Chapter 13 has a new emphasis on preparation for working with youth, including a section on limit setting in the session.

17. Chapter 14 has a new Multicultural Highlight, focusing on helping new clinicians expand their comfort zone when working with sexuality issues.

18. Chapter 15 is a new chapter focusing on online and non-face-to-face interviewing formats.

19. All chapters have been updated to include the most recent research and practice as it pertains to clinical interviewing.

Using the DVD That Comes With This Text

This fifth edition of *Clinical Interviewing* has an accompanying DVD designed to bring interviewing skills described in this text to life. If you decide to use the DVD to supplement your learning, you should be aware of two things:

First, the DVD is not scripted. Instead of writing out a script to make sure we covered every possible skill in exactly the right order, we decided it would be a better learning tool for you to see us and our colleagues engaging in live and unscripted interviewing interactions. This was a judgment call, and some readers may wish for a more mechanical teaching and learning resource. However, after watching a number of other DVDs designed to help teach interviewing, counseling, and psychotherapy skills, we decided reality was more engaging than play acting. In the end, although volunteer clients and therapists were provided with guidelines and outlines about what to cover, the recorded interactions are spontaneous. The result: Sometimes specific techniques are illustrated out of sequence. For example, in the Basic Listening Skills demonstration featuring Maegan Hopkins as the counselor, Maegan demonstrates the use of an open question . . . even though basic listening skills are the focus in Chapter 3 and questions aren't covered until Chapter 4.

Second, the DVD is organized in a way that allows you to access specific content as needed. If you go to the main menu of the DVD, you'll find three options:

1. Play All
2. Chapters
3. Counseling Demonstrations

If you click on Chapters, you'll be directed to eight options. Clicking on any of these options will then take you to a place in the DVD where we're discussing a topic and introducing the upcoming counseling demonstration vignette. However, if you prefer to skip our *exciting* discussions and introductory comments, you can click on Counseling Demonstrations and then directly on any of 15 different specific demonstrations.

To help you identify places in the text that are linked to particular video content, we have two different forms of call-outs. The first type of call-out indicates where it might be beneficial to watch a specific DVD chapter in which we discuss a skill and introduce a counseling demonstration. The second type of call-out links particular text sections with specific counseling demonstrations. The Clinical Interviewing DVD can also be purchased separately (ISBN 978-1-118-39012-2). However you use it, we hope you find the DVD helpful to the teaching and learning process.

Using the Online Instructor's Manual and Ancillary Materials

The online instructor's manual and ancillary materials were designed to help make teaching clinical interviewing more pleasant and efficient. Through your John Wiley & Sons sales representative or via the Wiley website, adopting this text gives you access to the following instructional support:

- An online Instructor's Manual, coauthored with Lindsey Nichols, Ph.D., that has supplementary lecture material, discussion questions, and classroom demonstrations and activities.
- A test bank, coauthored with Emily Sidor, M.A., that has over 40 test items for each chapter.
- A downloadable set of generic PowerPoint slides geared to the textbook chapters.

Acknowledgments

Like raising children, producing a textbook requires a small village. We have many people to thank.

Thanks to our editor, Rachel Livsey: Your patience and optimism—not to mention your gentle persuasive skills—have encouraged us and helped sustain our focus. Thanks to Judi Knott for 5 A.M. e-mails, your "likes" on our Facebook page, and your consistent advocacy for our work. Thanks to Sweta Gupta whose eagle eyes and positive encouragement have been essential to the publication of this textbook. Thanks also to Amanda Orenstein whose e-mail turnaround time and efficiency is breathtaking, and to Kim Nir, Eileen Gewirtzman, and Jane Domino in production. And finally, thanks to the unknown members of the John Wiley & Sons publishing team. We know you're out there and we deeply appreciate your support.

In addition to our fabulous Wiley team, we also have had substantial support from mentors, fellow professionals, graduate students, and family members. The following list includes individuals who have either provided significant inspiration, or feedback for content in one or more chapters.

Amber Bach-Gorman, MS, North Dakota State University
Carolyn A. Berger, PhD, Nova Southeastern University
Jessica Berry, MA, Idaho State University
Philip P. Bornstein, PhD, University of Montana
Mikal Crawford, EdD, Husson University
Rochelle Cade, PhD, Mississippi College
Eric S. Davis, PhD, Argosy University-Tampa
Susan Davis, PhD, Independent Practice, Buffalo, NY
Neil Duchac, PhD, Capella University
Carlos M. Del Rio, Ph.D, Southern Illinois University Carbondal
Jennifer Fearn, MA, Chicago School of Professional Psychology
Christine Fiore, PhD, University of Montana
Kerrie (Kardatzke) Fuenfhausen, PhD, Lenoir-Rhyne University
Irene Garrick, PhD, Mental Health Counseling Group
Kristopher M. Goodrich, PhD, University of New Mexico
Elizabeth Hancock, M.S., Auburn University
Jo Hittner, PhD, Winona State University
Keely J. Hope, PhD, Eastern Washington University
Dawn Hudak, EdD, Lamar University
Eric Jett, MA, Walden University
Kimberly Johnson, EdD, DeVry University Online
David Jobes, PhD, Catholic University of America
Veronica Johnson, EdD, Winona State University
Jonathan Lent PhD, Marshall University
Charles Luke, PhD, Tennessee Tech University

Melissa Mariani, PhD, Florida Atlantic University
Doreen S. Marshall, PhD, Argosy University-Atlanta
John R. Means, PhD, University of Montana
Scott T. Meier, PhD, University at Buffalo
Ryan Melton, PhD, Portland State University
Teah L. Moore, PhD, Fort Valley State University
Michelle Muenzenmeyer, PhD, Webster University
Robert Musikantow, PhD, Adler School of Professional Psychology
Charles E. Myers, PhD, Northern Illinois University
James Overholser, PhD, Case Western Reserve University
Shawn Parmanand, PhD, Walden University
Jennifer Pereira, PhD, Argosy University, Tampa
Senel Poyrazli, PhD, Pennsylvania State University-Harrisburg
Angela S. Shores, PhD, Montreat College
Carmen Stein, PhD, Independent Practice
Kendra A. Surmitis, MA, College of William & Mary
Jacqueline Swank, PhD, University of Florida
Rebecca Tadlock-Marlo, PhD, Eastern Illinois Univeristy
Anna M. Viviani, PhD, Indiana State University
John G. Watkins, PhD, University of Montana
Janet P. Wollersheim, PhD, University of Montana
Carlos Zalaquette, PhD, University of South Florida

About the Authors

John Sommers-Flanagan, PhD, is a clinical psychologist and professor of counselor education at the University of Montana. He has been a columnist for the *Missoulian* newspaper, a local public radio show co-host of "What Is It with Men?," and is coauthor of over 50 professional publications. John is a long-time member of both the American Counseling Association and the American Psychological Association and regularly presents professional workshops at the annual conferences of both these organizations.

Photo courtesy of Todd Johnson, University of Montana.

Rita Sommers-Flanagan, PhD, has been a professor of counselor education at the University of Montana for the past 21 years. Her favorite teaching and research areas are ethics and women's issues, and she served as the director of Women's Studies at the University of Montana, as well as the acting director of the Practical Ethics Center. She is the author or co-author of over 40 articles and book chapters, and most recently authored a chapter entitled "Boundaries, Multiple Roles, and Professional Relationships" in the new *APA Handbook on Ethics in Psychology*. She is also a clinical psychologist, and has worked with youth, families, and women for many years.

John and Rita work together as the mental health consultants for Trapper Creek Job Corps. They also enjoy providing seminars and professional presentations nationally and internationally.

Together, John and Rita have coauthored nine books, including books aimed at helping mental health professionals work more effectively with their clients. These include:

- *How to Listen so Parents Will Talk and Talk so Parents Will Listen* (Wiley)
- *Tough Kids, Cool Counseling* (American Counseling Association)
- *Problem Child or Quirky Kid* (Free Spirit Press)
- *The Last Best Divorce Book* (Families First)
- *Don't Divorce Us!* (American Counseling Association; also available in Turkish, co-authored with Senel Poyralzi)

John and Rita have also written two other textbooks with John Wiley & Sons. They are:

1. *Counseling and Psychotherapy Theories: In Context and Practice, Second Edition*
2. *Becoming an Ethical Helping Professional*

John and Rita have two daughters, one son in-law, twin grandbabies, and can hardly believe their good fortune. They are deeply rooted in Montana, and in the summers, alternate writing with irrigating and haying on the family ranch. Both John and Rita enjoy professional speaking, exercising, gardening, exploring alternative energy technologies, and restoring old log cabins, old sheds, and any other old thing that crosses their path—which, given the passage of time, is now starting to include each other.

PART ONE

Becoming a Mental Health Professional

Introduction: Philosophy and Organization

CHAPTER OBJECTIVES

This chapter welcomes you to the professional field of clinical interviewing and orients you to the philosophy and organization of this book. After reading this chapter, you will understand:

- The philosophy and organization of this book.
- How becoming a mental health professional can be both challenging and gratifying.
- The authors' teaching philosophy.
- An effective learning sequence for acquiring clinical interviewing skills.
- How clinicians from different theoretical orientations approach the interviewing task.
- Why and how a multicultural orientation to interviewing can be useful.
- Advantages and disadvantages of being nondirective in your interviewing approach.
- Your potential cultural biases when interviewing.
- The goals and objectives of this book.

Imagine sitting face-to-face with your first client. You carefully chose your clothing. You intentionally arranged the seating, set up the video camera, and completed the introductory paperwork. You're doing your best to communicate warmth and helpfulness through your body posture and facial expressions. Now, imagine that your client:

- Refuses to talk.
- Talks so much you can't get a word in.
- Asks to leave early.
- Starts crying.
- Tells you that you'll never understand because of your racial or ethnic differences.
- Suddenly gets angry (or scared) and storms out.

Any and all of these responses are possible in an initial clinical interview. If one of these scenarios plays out, how will you respond? What will you say? What will you do?

From the first client forward, every client you meet will be different. Your challenge or mission (if you choose to accept it) is to make human contact with each client, to establish rapport, to build a working alliance, to gather information, to instill hope, and, if appropriate, to provide clear and helpful professional interventions. To top it off, you must gracefully end the interview on time and sometimes you'll need to do all this with clients who don't trust you or don't want to work with you.

These are no small tasks—which is why it's so important for you to remember to be patient with yourself. This is only the beginning of your developmental journey toward becoming a mental health professional.

As a prospective psychologist, professional counselor, psychiatric nurse, social worker, or psychiatrist, you face a challenging and rewarding future. Becoming a mental health professional requires persistence and an interest in developing your intellect, interpersonal maturity, a balanced emotional life, counseling/ psychotherapy skills, compassion, authenticity, and courage. Many classes, supervision, workshops, and other training experiences will pepper your life in the coming years. In fact, due to the ever-evolving nature of this business, you will need to become a lifelong learner to stay current and skilled in mental health work. But rest assured, this is an exciting and fulfilling professional path (Norcross & Guy, 2007). As Norcross (2000) stated:

> . . . the vast majority of mental health professionals are satisfied with their career choices and would select their vocations again if they knew what they know now. Most of our colleagues feel enriched, nourished, and privileged. . . . (p. 712)

The clinical interview may be the most fundamental component of mental health training (Jones, 2010). It is the basic unit of connection between the helper and the person seeking help. It is the beginning of a counseling or psychotherapy relationship. It is the cornerstone of psychological assessment. And it is the focus of this book.

WELCOME TO THE JOURNEY

This book is designed to teach you basic and advanced clinical interviewing skills. The chapters guide you through elementary listening skills onward to more advanced, complex professional activities such as intake interviewing, mental status examinations, and suicide assessment. We enthusiastically welcome you as new colleagues and fellow learners.

For many of you, this text accompanies your first taste of practical, hands-on, mental health training experience. For those of you who already have substantial clinical experience, this book may help place your previous experiences in a more systematic learning context. Whichever the case, we hope this text challenges you and helps you develop skills needed for conducting competent and professional clinical interviews.

In his 1939 classic, *The Wisdom of the Body*, Walter Cannon (1939) wrote:

> When we consider the extreme instability of our bodily structure, its readiness for disturbance by the slightest application of external forces . . . its persistence through so many decades seems almost miraculous. The wonder increases when we realize that the system is open, engaging in free exchange with the outer world, and that the structure itself is not permanent, but is being continuously broken down by the wear and tear of action, and as continuously built up again by processes of repair. (p. 20)

This observation seems equally applicable to the psyche. The psyche is also impermanent, permeable, and constantly interacting with the outside world. As most of us would readily agree, life brings many challenging experiences. Some of these experiences psychologically break us down and others build us up. The clinical interview is the entry point for most people who have experienced psychological or emotional difficulties and who seek a therapeutic experience to repair and build themselves up again.

Teaching Philosophy

Like all authors, we have underlying philosophies and beliefs that shape what we say and how we say it. Throughout this text, we try to identify our particular biases and perspectives, explain them, and allow you to weigh them for yourself.

We have several biases about clinical interviewing. First, we consider clinical interviewing to be both art and science. We encourage academic challenges for your intellect and fine tuning of the most important instrument you have to exercise this art: yourself. Second, we believe that the clinical interview should *always* be designed to facilitate positive client development. Reasons for interviews vary. Experience levels vary. But as Hippocrates implied to healers many centuries ago, we should work very hard to *do no harm*.

We also have strong beliefs and feelings about *how* clinical interviewing skills are best learned and developed. These beliefs are based on our experiences as students and instructors and on the state of scientific knowledge pertaining to clinical interviewing (J. Sommers-Flanagan & Heck, 2012; Stahl & Hill, 2008; Woodside, Oberman, Cole, & Carruth, 2007). The remainder of this chapter includes greater detail about our teaching approach, theoretical and multicultural orientation, and the book's goals and objectives.

Learning Sequence

We believe interviewing skills are acquired most efficiently when you learn, in sequence, the following skills and procedures:

1. How to quiet yourself and focus on what your client is communicating (instead of focusing on what *you* are thinking or feeling).
2. How to establish rapport and develop positive working relationships with a wide range of clients—including clients of different ages, abilities and disabilities, racial/cultural backgrounds, sexual orientation, social class, and intellectual functioning.

3. How to efficiently obtain valid and reliable diagnostic or assessment information about clients and their problems.
4. How to appropriately apply individualized counseling or psychotherapy interventions.
5. How to evaluate client responses to your counseling or psychotherapeutic methods and techniques (outcomes assessment).

This text is limited in focus to the first three skills listed. Extensive information on implementing and evaluating counseling or psychotherapy methods and techniques (items 4 and 5) is not the main focus of this text. However, we intermittently touch on these issues as we cover situations that clinicians may face.

Quieting Yourself and Listening to Clients

To be effective therapists, mental health professionals need to learn to quiet themselves; they need to rein in natural urges to help, personal needs, and anxieties. This is difficult for both beginning and experienced therapists. We still need to consistently remind ourselves to hold off on giving advice or establishing a diagnosis. Instead, the focus should be on listening to the client and on turning down the volume of our own internal chatter and biases.

Quieting yourself requires that you be fully present to your client and not distracted by your own thoughts or worries. Some students and clinicians find that it helps to arrive early enough to sit for a few minutes, clearing the mind and focusing on breathing and being in the moment.

In most interviewing situations, listening nondirectively is your first priority, especially during beginning stages of an interview. For example, as Shea (1998) noted, "...in the opening phase, the clinician speaks very little... there exists a strong emphasis on open-ended questions or open-ended statements in an effort to get the patient talking" (p. 66).

Quieting yourself and listening nondirectively will help you empower your clients to find their voices and tell their stories. Unfortunately, staying quiet and listening well is difficult because, when cast in a professional role, many therapists find it hard to manage their mental activity. It's common to feel pressured because you want to prove your competence by helping clients resolve their problems immediately. However, this can cause you to unintentionally become too directive or authoritative with new clients, and may result in them shutting down rather than opening up.

When students (and experienced practitioners) become prematurely active and directive, they run the risk of being insensitive and nontherapeutic. This viewpoint echoes the advice that Strupp and Binder (1984) gave to mental health professionals three decades ago: "...the therapist should resist the compulsion to do something, especially at those times when he or she feels under pressure from the patient (and himself or herself) to intervene, perform, reassure, and so on" (p. 41).

In a majority of professional interview situations the best start involves allowing clients to explore their own thoughts, feelings, and behaviors. When possible, therapists should help clients follow their own leads and make their own discoveries (Meier & Davis, 2011). We consider it the therapist's professional responsibility to *encourage* client self-expression. On the other hand, given time constraints commonly imposed on therapy, therapists also are responsible for *limiting* client self-expression. Whether you're encouraging or limiting client self-expression, the big challenge is to do so skillfully and professionally. It's also important to note that listening nondirectively and facilitating client self-expression is not the same as behaving passively (Chad Luke, personal communication, August 5, 2012). Listening well is an active process that requires specific skills that we'll discuss in much more detail (see Chapters 3 and 4).

Students who are beginning to learn clinical interviewing skills often struggle to stop themselves from giving premature advice. Have you ever had trouble sitting quietly and listening to someone without giving advice or sharing your own excellent opinion? To be perfectly honest, we've struggled with this ourselves and know many experienced mental health professionals who also find it hard to sit and listen without directing, guiding, or advising. For many people, it's second nature to want to give advice—even advice based solely on their own narrow life experiences. The problem is that the client sitting in front of you probably has had a very different narrow slice of life experiences and so advice, especially if offered prematurely and without an adequate foundation of listening, usually won't go all that well. Remember how you felt when your parents (or other authority figures) gave you advice? Sometimes, it might have been welcome and helpful. Other times, you may have felt discounted or resistant. Advice giving is all about accuracy, timing, and delivery. The acceptability of advice giving as a therapeutic technique is also related to your theoretical orientation and treatment goals. Focusing too much on advice giving is rarely, if ever, a wise strategy in an initial therapy session.

Developing Rapport and Positive Therapy Relationships

Before developing more advanced assessment and intervention skills, therapists must learn how to establish a positive working alliance with clients. This involves learning active listening, empathic responding, feeling validation, and other behavioral skills as well as interpersonal attitudes leading to the development and maintenance of positive rapport (Barone et al., 2005; Rogers, 1957). Counselors and psychotherapists from virtually every theoretical perspective agree on the importance of developing a positive relationship with clients before using interventions (Ackerman et al., 2001; Chambless et al., 2006; Norcross & Lambert, 2011). Some theorists refer to this as *rapport*—others use the terms "working alliance" or "therapeutic relationship" (Bordin, 1979, 1994; J. Sommers-Flanagan & Sommers-Flanagan, 2007b). In Chapters 3–5 we directly focus on the skills needed to develop positive therapy relationships.

Learning Diagnostic and Assessment Skills

After learning to listen well and develop positive relationships with clients, professional therapists should learn diagnostic and assessment skills. Although psychological assessment and psychiatric diagnosis generate great controversy (Kamens, 2011; Parens & Johnston, 2010; Szasz, 1970), initiating counseling or psychotherapy without adequate assessment is ill-advised, unprofessional, and potentially dangerous (Hadley & Strupp, 1976; R. Sommers-Flanagan & Sommers-Flanagan, 2007). Think about how you would feel if, after taking your automobile to the local repair shop, the mechanic simply began fixing various engine components without first asking you questions designed to understand the problem. Of course, clinical interviewing is much different from auto mechanics, but the analogy speaks to the importance of completing assessment and diagnostic procedures before initiating clinical interventions.

In summary, you should begin using specific counseling or psychotherapy interventions only after three conditions have been fulfilled:

1. You have quieted yourself and listened to your clients' communications.
2. You have developed a positive relationship with your clients.
3. You have identified your clients' individual needs and therapy goals through diagnostic and assessment procedures.

And of course, you should obtain professional supervision as you begin using specific interviewing and counseling techniques.

THEORETICAL ORIENTATIONS

For optimal professional development, you should obtain (a) a broad range of training experiences, (b) in a variety of settings, and (c) from a variety of theoretical orientations. Although it's good to eventually specialize, having a broad foundation is desirable. Even Freud, who's not often remembered for his openness and flexibility, is rumored to have said: "There are many ways and means of conducting psychotherapy. All that lead to recovery are good."

As instructors, we consider ourselves to be dogmatically eclectic and multiculturally sensitive. We believe therapists need to be flexible, able to sometimes change therapeutic approaches depending on the client, the problem, and the setting. Obviously, it's not the client's job to modify his or her problems, worldview, or personal preferences to fit the therapist's theoretical perspective.

When it comes to *learning* clinical skills, we advocate an approach that initially focuses on less directive interviewing skills and later on more directive skills. Therefore, in early chapters of this text, we emphasize interviewing strategies that are often, but not always, associated with person-centered and psychodynamic perspectives. By beginning less directively, we hope to emphasize the depth, richness, and potential healing power of authentic human relationships. Later, as we focus on interview assessment procedures, we emphasize more directive behavioral, cognitive-behavioral, and solution-focused approaches to interviewing.

Although person-centered and psychodynamic approaches are usually considered philosophically dissimilar, both teach that therapists should allow clients to talk about their concerns with minimal external structure and direction (Freud, 1949; Luborsky, 1984; Rogers, 1951, 1961). Both person-centered and psychodynamic therapists allow clients to freely discuss whatever personal issues or concerns they might wish to discuss. These interviewing approaches have been labeled *nondirective* and heavily emphasize listening techniques. (It would be more appropriate to label person-centered and psychodynamic approaches *less directive*, because all therapists, intentionally or unintentionally, sometimes direct their clients.)

Person-centered and psychodynamic therapists are nondirective for very different reasons. Person-centered therapists believe that when clients talk freely and openly in an atmosphere characterized by acceptance and empathy, personal growth and change occur. Carl Rogers (1961), the originator of person-centered therapy, stated this directly: "If I can provide a certain type of relationship, the other person will discover within himself the capacity to use that relationship for growth, and change and personal development will occur" (p. 33).

For Rogers, unconditional positive regard, congruence, and accurate empathy constitute the necessary and sufficient ingredients for positive personal growth and healing. We look more closely at how Rogers defines these ingredients in Chapter 5.

Psychoanalytically oriented therapists advocate nondirective approaches because they believe that letting clients talk freely allows unconscious conflicts to emerge (Freud, 1949). Eventually, through interpretation, psychoanalytic therapists bring underlying conflicts into awareness so they can be dealt with directly and consciously.

Similar to person-centered therapists, psychoanalytic therapists acknowledge that empathic listening may be a powerful source of healing in its own right: "Frequently underestimated is the degree to which the therapist's presence and empathic listening constitute the most powerful source of help and support one human being can provide another" (Strupp & Binder, 1984, p. 41). However, for psychoanalytically oriented clinicians, empathic listening is usually viewed as a necessary, but not sufficient, ingredient for client personal growth and development.

Constructive (i.e., narrative and solution-focused) approaches take the position that, although all therapists must be directive in one way or another, clients are the best experts on their own experiences (de Jong & Berg, 2008). Constructive therapists systematically focus on solutions, sparkling (positive) moments in clients' lives, and adaptive beliefs and actions that already exist within the client's behavioral repertoire. Although these approaches are intentionally directive, the position of honoring clients as the authorities of their own lives is a position we regard as crucial to effective interviewing.

In contrast, behavioral or cognitive therapists are inclined to take an expert role from the beginning of the first clinical interview. They believe in actively setting an agenda that includes focusing on maladaptive thoughts and behaviors that may be causing mental and emotional distress (J. Beck, 2011). Therefore, their main therapeutic work involves identifying and modifying or eliminating maladaptive thinking and behavioral patterns, replacing them with more adaptive patterns as quickly and efficiently as possible. About 30 years ago, Kendall and Bemis (1983) aptly described the cognitive-behavioral therapist's directive orientation:

> The task of the cognitive-behavioral therapist is to act as a diagnostician, educator, and technical consultant who assesses maladaptive cognitive processes and works with the client to design learning experiences that may remediate these dysfunctional cognitions and the behavioral and affective patterns with which they correlate. (p. 566)

Despite this description, most cognitive-behavioral clinicians also recognize the importance of empathic listening as necessary, although not sufficient, for adaptive behavior change. Notably, Wright and Davis (1994), in the inaugural issue of the journal *Cognitive and Behavioral Practice*, stated: "We find strong consensus in the conclusion that the relationship is central to therapeutic change" and "Even in specific behavioral therapies, patients who view their therapist as warm and empathetic will be more involved in their treatment and, ultimately, have a better outcome" (1994, p. 26).

We're not suggesting that person-centered, psychodynamic, constructive, or solution-focused approaches are more effective than cognitive, behavioral, or other clinical approaches. In fact, controlled studies indicate that cognitive and behavioral therapies are at least as effective as dynamic or person-centered approaches and sometimes more effective (Epp & Dobson, 2010; Luborsky, Singer, & Luborsky, 1975; Olatunji, Cisler, & Deacon, 2010; M. L. Smith & Glass, 1977; M. L. Smith, Glass, & Miller, 1980). Instead, we assert that nondirective interviewing skill development provides the best foundation for building positive therapy relationships and learning more advanced and more active/directive psychotherapy strategies and techniques. Additionally, we believe that honoring the client as the best expert on his or her own lived experiences is a solid foundation upon which to build more advanced and perhaps more directive clinical skills. A number of important facts support this assertion (see *Putting It in Practice* 1.1).

PUTTING IT IN PRACTICE 1.1

Why Learn Less-Directive Interviewing Skills?

Many famous psychotherapists began with a psychoanalytic orientation, such as Alfred Adler, Karen Horney, Aaron Beck, Fritz Perls, Carl Rogers, Nancy Chodorow, and Jean Baker Miller. These respected theorists and therapists developed their unique approaches after listening nondirectively to distressed individuals. An underlying philosophy of this book is that beginning therapists also should begin by listening nondirectively to distressed individuals. Although it's natural for beginners to feel eager to help clients, their safest and probably most helpful behavior is effective listening. As Strupp and Binder (1984) noted, "Recall an old Maine proverb: 'One can seldom listen his [or her] way into trouble'" (p. 44). Some advantages of nondirective interviewing include:

1. It's easier to begin an interview in a nondirective mode and later shift to a more directive mode than to begin in an active or directive mode and then change to a less directive approach.
2. Nondirective interviewing is an effective means for helping beginning therapists enhance their self-awareness and learn about themselves (J. Sommers-Flanagan & Means, 1987). Through self-awareness, therapists become capable of choosing a particular theoretical orientation and effective clinical interventions.
3. Nondirective approaches have less chance of offending or missing the mark with clients early in treatment (Meier & Davis, 2011). Nondirective therapists, who are there only to listen, place more responsibility on clients' shoulders and can therefore lessen their own fears (as well as the real possibility) of asking the wrong questions or suggesting an unhelpful course of action.

4. A nondirective listening stance helps clients establish feelings and beliefs of independence and self-direction. This stance also communicates respect for the client's personal attitudes, behaviors, and choices. Such respect is rare, gratifying, and probably healing (Miller & Rollnick, 2013; Rosengren, 2009).

Our belief that therapists should begin from a foundation of nondirective listening is articulated by the following excerpt from Patterson and Watkins (1996, p. 509): "Lao Tzu, a Chinese philosopher of the fifth century . . . wrote a poem titled *Leader*, which applies when *therapist* is substituted for *leader* and *clients* is substituted for *people.*"

A Leader (Therapist)

A leader is best when people hardly know he exists;
Not so good when people obey and acclaim him;
Worst when they despise him.
But of a good leader who talks little,
When his work is done, his aim fulfilled,
They will say, "We did it ourselves."
The less a leader does and says,
The happier his people;
The more he struts and brags,
The sorrier his people.
[Therefore,] a sensible man says:
If I keep from meddling with people, they take care of themselves.
If I keep from preaching at people, they improve themselves.
If I keep from imposing on people, they become themselves.

A Multicultural Orientation for Clinical Interviewing

Most of the history of counseling, psychotherapy, and clinical interviewing has involved White people of Western European descent providing services for other White people of Western European descent. We're saying this in a way to be purposely blunt and provocative. Although there are Eastern and Southern influences in the practice and provision of mental health services, the foundation of this process is distinctively Western and White.

This foundation has often served its purpose quite well. Over the years, many clients or patients have been greatly helped by mental health providers. But, beginning in the 1960s and continuing to the present, there has been increasing recognition that counseling and psychotherapy theories were sometimes (but not always) both racist and sexist in their application (J. Sommers-Flanagan & Sommers-Flanagan, 2012). There are many examples of this racism and sexism; we refer readers elsewhere for extensive information on the ways our profession has not always served minority and female clients (Brown, 2010; D. W. Sue & Sue, 2013).

Multicultural orientation and multicultural training is now a central foundational principle for all mental health practice. There are many reasons for this, including, but not exclusively the fact that the United States is growing more diverse. Based on the 2010 Census, of the 308 million people living in the United States at the time of the census, more than 85 million identified themselves as other than White (U.S. Census Bureau, 2011). Additionally, research conducted in the 1970s showed that most minority clients dropped out of therapy after only a single clinical interview (S. Sue, 1977). This finding suggested, at the very least, a poor fit between counseling or psychotherapy as traditionally practiced and the needs or interests of minority clients.

Increased diversity throughout the United States constitutes an exciting and daunting possibility for mental health professionals; exciting for the richness that a diverse population extends to our communities and for the professional and personal growth that accompanies cross-cultural interaction; daunting because of increased responsibilities linked to learning and implementing culturally relevant approaches. The good news is that empirical research indicates multicultural sensitivity training for mental health professionals significantly improves the effectiveness of service delivery for diverse clients (Constantine, Fuertes, Roysircar, & Kindaichi, 2008; L. Smith, Constantine, Graham, & Dize, 2008). In keeping with these research findings, we're placing multicultural sensitivity and competence front and center in your awareness of what's essential for your beginning and ongoing professional development.

Three Principles of Multicultural Competence

Humans are born to families or caretaking groups or individuals that are embedded within a larger community context. This community is essential to survival (Matsumoto, 2007). The membership, values, beliefs, location, and practices of this community are generally referred to as culture. In this way, culture can be understood as the medium in which all human development takes place. Everything we value, know to be real, and assume is "normal" is influenced by our past and present cultures. From a mental health perspective, answers to questions such as, "What constitutes a healthy personality?" or "What should a person strive for in life?" or "Is this person deviant?" are largely influenced by the cultural backgrounds of both clinician and client (Christopher & Bickhard, 2007). More practically, the decision of whether you should practice more or less directive interviewing strategies is also laden with cultural implications (see *Multicultural Highlight* 1.1).

MULTICULTURAL HIGHLIGHT 1.1

Pitfalls of Nondirectiveness

Most swords are double-edged, and nondirective listening is no exception. To be blunt (no pun intended), some people detest nondirective listening. For example, your friends and family may become annoyed if you try too many nondirective listening techniques with them. They'll be annoyed partly because you may be unskilled, but also because in many social and cultural settings nondirective listening is inappropriate. People want to know what you think!

As we discuss in later chapters, in some settings, and with some cultural groups, a more directive approach is warranted. This doesn't mean you must never listen nondirectively to people of certain cultural groups. Instead, it speaks to the importance of recognizing that different techniques help or hinder relationship building in different individuals who come to you seeking assistance.

Additional pitfalls of nondirectiveness include:

1. Clients may perceive nondirective therapists as manipulative or evasive.
2. Too many nondirective responses can leave clients feeling lost and adrift, without guidance.
3. If clients expect expert advice, they may be deeply disappointed when you refuse to do anything but listen nondirectively.
4. If you never offer a professional opinion, you may be viewed as unprofessional, ignorant, or weak.

When it comes to interviewing clients, often, too much of any response or technique is ill-advised. We recognize that too much nondirectiveness can be just as troublesome as too much directiveness—especially when it comes to interviewing clients outside mainstream American culture, or in settings that demand more action or input on your part.

Both the American Counseling Association and the American Psychological Association are in agreement that the basic principles of multicultural competence include three overlapping dimensions: (1) therapist self-awareness or cultural self-awareness; (2) multicultural knowledge; and (3) culture-specific expertise. We briefly define these dimensions now and return to them frequently throughout this text.

Self-Awareness

Those who have power appear to have no culture, whereas those without power are seen as cultural beings, or "ethnic." (Fontes, 2008, p. 25)

Culture pervades everything, and so, not surprisingly, culture and self-awareness interface in several ways. As Fontes (2008) noted in the preceding quotation, one dimension of cultural self-awareness is that individuals within the dominant culture tend to be unaware of their own culture while viewing others as different or ethnic. Also, individuals from the dominant culture tend to be unaware of and often resistant to becoming aware of their "invisible" culturally based privilege (McIntosh, 1998). Developing cultural self-awareness is a challenging process for everyone, but it can be especially emotionally laden for members of the dominant culture. For now, consider your awareness of yourself as a unique cultural being as well as any biases or prejudices you might hold toward minority groups, keeping in mind that minority groups might include individuals who are viewed differently on the basis of sex, age, race, sexuality, disability, religion, social class, or other factors. *Multicultural Highlight* 1.2 includes an activity to stimulate your cultural self-awareness.

MULTICULTURAL HIGHLIGHT 1.2

Exploring Yourself as a Cultural Being

The first multicultural competency for both the American Counseling Association and the American Psychological Association focuses on self-awareness. D. W. Sue, Arredondo, and McDavis (1992), expressed it this way:

> Culturally skilled examiners have moved from being culturally unaware to being aware and sensitive to their own cultural heritage and to valuing and respecting differences. (p. 482)

For this activity, you should work with a partner.

A. Describe yourself as a cultural being to your partner. What is your ethnic/cultural heritage? How did you come to know your heritage? How is your heritage manifested in your life today? What parts of your heritage are you especially proud of? Is there anything about your heritage that you're not proud of? Why?

B. What do you think constitutes a "mentally healthy" individual? Can you think of times when there are exceptions to your understanding of this?

C. Has there ever been a time in your life when you experienced racism or discrimination? (If not, was there ever a time when you were harassed or prevented from doing something because of some unique characteristic that you possess?) Describe this experience to your partner. What were your thoughts and feelings related to this experience?

D. Can you identify a time when your own thoughts about people who are different from you affected how you treated them? Would you do anything differently now? What beliefs about different cultural ethnicities do you hold now that you would consider stereotyping or insensitive? (Carolyn Berger, personal communication, August 10, 2012)

E. How would you describe the "American culture"? What parts of this culture do you embrace? What parts do you reject? How does your internalization of American culture impact what you think constitutes a "mentally healthy individual"?

At the conclusion of the activity, take time to reflect and possibly make a few journal entries about anything you may have learned about your cultural identity.

Cultural Knowledge

Cultural self-awareness is a good start, but it's not enough. Culturally competent therapists actively educate themselves regarding different cultural values, behaviors, and ways of being. It's not appropriate to remain ignorant of other cultures. This is partly because remaining ignorant is simply unprofessional, but also because when therapists are culturally uninformed they often inappropriately rely on clients to educate them about specific minority issues. We include many multicultural highlights and issues within this text, but to become multiculturally sensitive and competent you will need to explore additional sources of multicultural knowledge and experience. Outside resources focusing on multicultural knowledge are listed in the Suggested Readings and Resources section at the end of every chapter. Overall, the more diverse interviewing, supervision, and life experiences you obtain, the more likely you'll be to develop the broad, empathic perspective you need to understand clients from within their worldview and experience (D. W. Sue & Sue, 2013).

Culture-Specific Expertise

Of the many cultural skills and techniques available to clinicians, we discuss two general skills here and more specific skills later. Two essential culture-specific skills for mental health professionals that were initially described by Stanley Sue (1998; 2006) include: (1) scientific mindedness; and (2) dynamic sizing.

Scientific mindedness involves forming and testing hypotheses, rather than coming to premature and faulty conclusions about clients. Although there may be universal human experiences, you shouldn't assume you know the underlying meaning of any client's behavior, especially minority clients. As the following case example illustrates, effective therapists avoid stereotypic generalizations when working with all clients.

CASE EXAMPLE

A young woman from Pakistan was studying physics at the graduate level in the United States. She attended a graduate function and, by her description, "had an unfortunate interaction with a male graduate student." After this interaction, she came to the student counseling service for short-term counseling because she was quite upset and could not study effectively. The male counselor met her in the waiting room, introduced himself, and offered to shake hands. The Pakistani student shrank away. The counselor noted this, thinking to himself that she was either shy or had issues with men. He initially believed his hypothesis was correct as the student shared her story about the rude male student at the graduate social gathering.

Scientific mindedness requires therapists to search for alternative cultural explanations before drawing conclusions about any specific behaviors. Without utilizing scientific mindedness and exploring less commonly known and understood explanations, the therapist would

(continued)

(*continued*)

perhaps not have realized that for a Muslim woman, it's not proper to touch a male—even to shake hands. Her shrinking away had everything to do with her religious practice and nothing to do with the incident she came to talk about. The case illustrates the importance of scientific mindedness as a clinical interviewing principle and practice. If he had not practiced scientific mindedness, the therapist in this case might have inaccurately concluded, based on his initial beliefs, that his Pakistani client was either shy or had "men issues." Instead, she was behaving in a manner consistent with her religious beliefs.

Dynamic sizing is a second culture-specific skill that Stanley Sue (1998; 2006) articulated. This concept requires therapists to know when generalizations based on group membership are fit and when they don't fit.

For example, *filial piety* is often discussed as a concept associated with certain Asian cultures (Chang & O'Hara, 2013). Filial piety has to do with the honoring and caring for one's parents and ancestors. However, it would be naïve to assume that all Asian people will believe in or have their lives affected by this particular value; making such an assumption can influence your expectations of client behavior. On the other hand, you would be remiss if you were completely ignorant of the power and influence of filial piety and the possibility that it might play a large role in relationship and career decisions in many Asians' lives. When dynamic sizing is used appropriately, therapists remain open to significant cultural influences, but the pitfalls of stereotyping clients are minimized.

Another facet of dynamic sizing involves therapists' knowing when to generalize their own experiences to those of their clients. Sue (2006) explained that it's possible for a minority group member who has experienced discrimination and prejudice to use this experience to more fully understand the struggles of those in other groups who have encountered similar experiences. However, having similar experiences does not guarantee accurate empathy. Dynamic sizing requires therapists to know and understand and *not* know and *not* understand at the same time. This combination of understanding, openness, and humility is a crucial component of culturally competent interviewing.

Multicultural Humility

To this point, consistent with the literature, we've been using the term "multicultural competence." However, we have reservations about referring to cultural awareness, knowledge, and skills in a manner that implies that individuals eventually reach an endpoint or attain a particular competence level. In fact, it seems that often, as soon as we grow too confident in our abilities to relate to and work with diverse peoples, we've probably lost our competence. We strongly agree with Vargas (2012), who expressed similar concerns:

> The focus on cultural competence also worries me. I very much try to be culturally responsive to my clients. But can I say that I am "culturally competent?" Absolutely not! I am still, despite my many and genuine

efforts, "a toro (bull) in a China shop" with all the cultural implications of this altered adage intended. (p. 20)

For these and other reasons, we generally prefer the terms *multicultural sensitivity* and *multicultural humility* and only use multicultural competence somewhat grudgingly (Stolle, Hutz, & Sommers-Flanagan, 2005).

MULTICULTURAL HIGHLIGHT 1.3

Who Do You See?

Existential therapists sometimes use provocative activities to help individuals increase awareness. One such activity involves the following: People sit in pairs and repeatedly ask each other the same question. The main rule is that the same answer cannot be used twice. Many different questions can be used in this activity (e.g., "What do you want?" or "What's good about you?"), but one question we've found to be relevant to beginning therapists is "Who are you?"

The "Who are you?" question focuses squarely on identity and most of us typically respond with statements related to personal roles, vocational activities, race, culture, religion, and gender. For example, John might say, "I'm a father," "I'm a husband," "I'm a psychotherapist," "I'm on the faculty at the University of Montana," "I'm a man," and so on. Interestingly, in our experience, women and people of color often respond sooner than men and Whites with words describing their gender and racial or cultural identities (e.g., "I'm a woman" or "I'm Latina"). Recently, when doing this activity with a young Native American woman, very early in the process, she stated with clarity: "I'm a Native American" and "I'm Navajo and Salish."

When considering ourselves within the diverse array of humans in the world, an interesting variation on this questioning activity involves asking "Who do you see?" Imagine that you've just met a new client. You see someone sitting in the chair opposite you. Ask yourself, "Who do you see?" and answer. Maybe the first answer is "I see a client," because that's the context of the encounter. Ask yourself again. Remember, you can't use the same answer twice. To really get a sense of the layers of identity labels you use to construct your perception of the person you're with, keep your answers one-dimensional. In other words, stick with "I see a man" instead of doubling up identity labels (e.g., "I see a Black man").

In human encounters, most of us first notice how another person is "Like me" or "Not like me." This is a natural human tendency that's probably more or less hard-wired. But, as the existentialists and multiculturalists emphasize, whether this tendency is hard-wired or not, it's crucial that we develop an awareness of it.

When working with someone new, keep this exercise in mind. Given all you need to attend to in a beginning interview, you probably won't be able to take the time in that moment to repeatedly ask yourself,

(continued)

(*continued*)

"Who do I see?," but later, as you reflect on the interview, you can try it out. Ask yourself 5 or 10 times in succession, "Who did I see?" Write your answers down. After you've let yourself answer the "Who did I see?" question 5 to 10 times, double back and analyze your responses. Notice what labels and layers came up. Did you notice a disability? If so, what identity labels did you find yourself using to describe the disability? Did you write "I see a disabled person" or "I see a handicapped person?" Notice the valence of the labels you used. Were they common? Positive? Neutral? Pejorative? No matter what, don't be either too self-satisfied or too hard on yourself. We all make judgments. We all have residues of racist, sexist, and homophobic values and beliefs. We can all discover within ourselves unfair judgments and sources of bias. Maybe your biases focus on religious beliefs or disabilities or maybe something else. Maybe you feel special negative reactions and judgments toward middle-aged balding men named Ted because of your experiences with an abusive middle-school gym teacher. Or maybe you've dealt with all your underlying prejudices and approach each individual with grace and objectivity—although we suspect not, which is one of our biases.

The Perfect Interviewer

What if you could conduct a perfect clinical interview? Of course, this is impossible. But if you could be a perfect interviewer, you'd be able to stop at any point in a given interview and describe: (a) what you are doing (based on technical expertise); (b) why you're doing it (based on your knowledge and assessment or evaluation information); (c) whether any of your personal issues or biases are interfering with the interview (based on self-awareness); and, perhaps most importantly, (d) how your client, regardless of his or her age, sex, or culture, is reacting to the interview (based on your assessment skills).

Put another way, if you were a perfect interviewer, you could tune in to each client's personal world so completely that you would resonate with the client, similar to how a violin string begins vibrating with the same frequency as a tone played in the same room (Watkins & Watkins, 1997). You would also be able to see each client clearly and without bias (Gallardo, Yeh, Trimble, & Parham, 2011). You would be able to use this unbiased, empathic resonance to determine where every interview needed to go (refer back to *Multicultural Highlight* 1.3 to explore your potential positive and negative biases towards particular clients).

You would also assess each client's needs and situation and carry out appropriate therapeutic actions to address the client's needs and personal situation—from initiating a suicide assessment to beginning a behavioral analysis of a troublesome habit—all during the clinical interview. One can only imagine the vast array of skills and the depth of wisdom necessary to conduct a perfect clinical interview.

We readily acknowledge that perfection is unattainable. However, clinical interviewing is a professional endeavor based on scientific research and supported by a long history of supervised training (J. Sommers-Flanagan & Heck, 2012). As a consequence, it's inappropriate and unprofessional to, as an old supervisor of ours used to say, "fly by the seat of your pants" in an interview session.

In the end, as a human and imperfect therapist, you may not be able to explain your every clinical nuance or every action and reaction. You may not feel as aware and tuned in as you could be, but hopefully your interviewing behavior will be guided by sound theoretical principles, humane professional ethics, and basic scientific data pertaining to therapeutic efficacy. Additionally, once you become grounded in psychological theory, professional ethics, and empirical research, you'll be able to add intuition and spontaneity to your clinical repertoire.

DVD Clip

In the *Introduction* chapter, John and Rita discuss the purpose of the DVD as well as the importance of becoming intentional in your work with clients.

GOALS AND OBJECTIVES OF THIS BOOK

The basic objectives of this book are to:

1. Guide you through an educational and training experience based on the previously described teaching approach.
2. Provide technical information about clinical interviewing.
3. Introduce strategies for developing self-awareness, cultural awareness, and personal growth.
4. Introduce client assessment and evaluation methods (i.e., facilitate acquisition of diagnostic skills).
5. Describe procedures and suggest resources so you can develop skills in interviewing culturally diverse clients and special client populations.
6. Provide opportunities and suggestions for experiential therapist development activities.

SUMMARY

This book is organized to reflect the order in which we believe students should acquire interviewing skills and techniques. In the beginning it can be helpful to learn nondirective interviewing skills, honoring the client as expert, and gradually adding more directive strategies as you master basic listening skills. Additionally, as you begin to engage in this professional activity, you should focus on learning to: (a) quiet yourself and listen to clients, (b) develop a positive therapeutic relationship with clients, and (c) obtain diagnostic and assessment information.

As you develop, you can benefit from obtaining a broad range of training experiences. It's important to learn and practice interviewing from different theoretical perspectives, including person-centered, psychoanalytic, behavioral, cognitive, feminist, and constructive or solution-focused viewpoints. In particular, because we live in a diverse world, learning about and adopting a multicultural orientation to interviewing is essential. A multicultural orientation includes (a) self-awareness, (b) cultural knowledge, and (c) culture-specific expertise. It also helps if you have an overall attitude of multicultural humility. Although perfection is impossible, if you base your behavior on sound theoretical principles, professional ethics, and scientific research, you can become a competent and responsible mental health professional.

This book is organized into four parts, moving beginning clinicians through stages designed for optimal skill development. Because practice is needed for you to develop interviewing skills, each chapter offers suggested experiential activities to facilitate greater self-awareness, cultural sensitivity, and technical expertise.

SUGGESTED READINGS AND RESOURCES

The following textbooks, articles, and recreational readings provide a useful foundation for professional skill development.

Duncan, B., Miller, S. D., Wampold, B. E., & Hubble, D. (Eds.). (2010). *The heart and soul of change: Delivering what works in therapy* (2nd ed.). Washington, DC: American Psychological Association.

This book focuses squarely on the common factors associated with positive change in counseling and psychotherapy. It provides practical suggestions for integrating these common factors into your interviewing practice.

Goldfried, M. (2001). *How therapists change: Personal and professional recollections*. Washington, DC: American Psychological Association.

This book gives you an insider's look into how professionals have undergone personal change. It gives you a feel for how the profession of counseling and psychotherapy might affect you personally.

Hays, P. (2008). *Addressing cultural complexities in practice: Assessment, diagnosis, and therapy* (2nd ed.). Washington, DC: American Psychological Association.

Pamela Hays helps practitioners expand their awareness of cultural complexities in clinical practice. Her writing is highly accessible, and she provides many examples of cultural wisdom. Her chapter "Entering Another's World: Understanding Clients' Identities and Contexts" is the inspiration for *Multicultural Highlight* 1.2.

Kottler, J. A. (2010). *On being a therapist* (4th ed.). Hoboken, NJ: Wiley.

This book includes chapters on the therapist's journey, hardships, being imperfect, lies we tell ourselves, and many more. It offers one perspective on the road to becoming and being a therapist.

Prochaska, J., & DiClemente, C. (2005). *The transtheoretical approach*. New York, NY: Oxford University Press.

Although the transtheoretical model has both strong adherents and strong detractors, it's a change model that all helping professionals should understand. Prochaska and DiClemente integrate many theoretical perspectives into a model for determining when and how particular therapy interventions should be used.

Sommers-Flanagan, J., & Sommers-Flanagan, R. (2012). *Counseling and psychotherapy theories in context and practice: Skills, strategies, and techniques* (2nd ed.). Hoboken, NJ: Wiley.

Of the many "theories" texts out there, this is our personal favorite.

Yalom, I. (2002). *The gift of therapy*. New York: HarperCollins.

In the book, renowned therapist Irvin Yalom describes his top 85 clinical insights about conducting psychotherapy. Each insight is a very short chapter of its own.

Foundations
and Preparations

CHAPTER OBJECTIVES

When building a house, you must first define what you mean by *house*. In addition, you must prepare by gathering together your design plan, your tools, and your resources. This chapter focuses on what we mean by *clinical interviewing* and how to prepare for meeting with clients. You'll be introduced to tools and resources useful in preparing for your future work as a mental health professional.

After reading this chapter, you will understand:

- The comprehensive definition of clinical interviewing.
- The nature of a professional relationship between therapist and client.
- Common client motivations for seeking professional help.
- Basic information on establishing common goals and applying listening and psychological techniques.
- How you can both improve your effectiveness and make yourself uncomfortable by becoming more self-aware.
- How to handle essential physical dimensions of the interview, such as seating arrangements, note taking, and video and audio recording.
- Practical approaches for managing professional and ethical issues, including how to present yourself to clients, time management, discussing confidentiality and informed consent, documentation procedures, and personal stress management.

When questioned about early graduate-school memories, a former student shared:

> Probably because of too little practice and too few role plays, what I remember most about my first clinical interview is my own terror. I don't remember the client. I don't remember the problem areas, the ending, or the subsequent treatment plan. I just remember breathing deeply and engaging in some very serious self-talk designed to calm myself. All my salient memories have to do with me, not the person who came for help. Ironic, isn't it?

It's understandable and even likely that your first clinical interviews will be stressful. But we hope that by reading this book, thinking (and breathing) deeply, and practicing you'll quickly advance past self-consciousness and be able to focus on your client and your interviewing tasks.

Clinical interviews are different from ordinary conversation. This chapter delineates these differences and describes the physical surroundings as well as professional and ethical considerations essential to clinical interviewing. Nearly 80 years ago, Eleanor Roosevelt (1937/1992) articulated a major theme addressed in this chapter:

> Perhaps the most important thing that has come out of my life is the discovery that if you prepare yourself at every point as well as you can, with whatever means you have, however meager they may seem, you will be able to grasp the opportunity for broader experience when it appears. Without preparation, you will not be able to do it.
> —*Eleanor Roosevelt*, The Autobiography of Eleanor Roosevelt
> *(p. xix, 1937/1992)*

DEFINING CLINICAL INTERVIEWING

Clinical interviewing has been defined in many ways by many authors. Some prefer a narrow definition:

> An interview is a controlled situation in which one person, the interviewer, asks a series of questions of another person, the respondent. (Keats, 2000, p. 1)

Others are more ambiguous:

> An interview is an interaction between at least two persons. Each participant contributes to the process, and each influences the responses of the other. However, this characterization falls short of defining the process. Ordinary conversation is interactional, but surely interviewing goes beyond that. (Trull & Prinstein, 2013, p. 165)

Others emphasize the development of a positive and respectful relationship:

> ...we mean a conversation characterized by respect and mutuality, by immediacy and warm presence, and by emphasis on strengths and potential. Because clinical interviewing is essentially relational, it requires ongoing attention to *how* things are said and done, as well as to *what* is said and done. The emphasis on the relationship is at the heart of the "different kind of talking" that is the clinical interview. (Murphy & Dillon, 2011, p. 3)

From our perspective, the two main goals of this "different kind of talking" are to (1) conduct a clinical evaluation and/or (2) initiate counseling or psychotherapy. That said, we view an ethical clinical interview as including:

1. A positive and respectful professional relationship between therapist and client.

2. Collaborative work (more or less, depending on the situation) to establish and achieve mutually agreeable client goals focusing either on assessment or psychological treatment.
3. Verbal and nonverbal interactions during which the therapist applies active listening skills and psychological techniques to evaluate, understand, and help the client achieve goals.
4. Sensitivity, on the part of the therapist, to many factors, including culture, personality style, setting, attitudes, and goals.

The Nature of a Professional Relationship

A professional relationship involves an explicit agreement for one party to provide services to another party. This may sound awkward, but it's important to emphasize that a professional relationship includes an *agreement for service provision*. In counseling or psychotherapy, this agreement is referred to as *informed consent* (Pomerantz & Handelsman, 2004). Essentially, the informed consent process begins when clients have been given all the important information about services to be provided during the interview. Further, informed consent ensures that clients understand, and ideally, have freely consented to treatment (Anderson & Handelsman, 2010; R. Sommers-Flanagan & Sommers-Flanagan, 2007). Informed consent is discussed in detail later in this chapter.

Professional relationships are characterized by payment or compensation for services (Kielbasa, Pomerantz, Krohn, & Sullivan, 2004). This is true whether the therapist receives payment directly (as in private practice) or indirectly (as when payment is provided by a mental health center, Medicaid, or other third party). Professional therapists provide a service to someone in need—a service that should be worth its cost. Further, professional and ethical practitioners take care to provide consistent, high-quality services, even in situations in which clients are paying reduced fees (Kendra Surmitis, professional communication, September 28, 2012).

To a greater or lesser extent, professional relationships always involve power differentials (Edwards, 2003; Gilbert, 2009). This can be especially pronounced when professionals are from the dominant culture and clients are from less dominant cultural or social groups. Because clients often view themselves as coming to see an expert who will help them with a problem, they might be vulnerable to accepting unhelpful guidance, feedback, or advice. Ethical professionals continuously work to be sensitive to power dynamics both inside and outside the therapy office (Patrick & Connolly, 2009).

For some, professional relationships emphasize emotional distance and objectivity. In fact, if you look up the word *professional* in a thesaurus, you'll find the word "expert" as the first possible synonym listed. If you look up the word *clinical*, you'll find words like "scientific" and "detached." Based on these straightforward definitions, you may assume that the professional relationship a therapist establishes with clients is sterile and unemotional. However, as you reflect back on Murphy and Dillon's (2011) definition of *clinical interviewing* offered, you'll find words like *mutuality*, *respect*, and *warm*. This may make you wonder if it's possible for a therapist to establish a professional relationship based on expertise and objectivity that also includes mutuality and warmth. The answer is yes; it's possible, but not necessarily easy. Mental health professionals should be experts at being respectful, warm, and collaborative with clients, while retaining at least some professional distance and objectivity (Sommers-Flanagan, Zeleke, & Hood, 2013, in press). Maintaining this balance is both challenging and gratifying.

Some writers, perhaps cynically, have labeled psychotherapy *the purchase of friendship* (Korchin, 1976, p. 285), but there are many differences between a therapy relationship and friendship. Friendship involves a mutual intimacy with an expectation of give and take. Your friends don't regard their own personal growth and insight or the resolution of their problems as the objectives of your time together (or if they do, you may want to consider new friends). Friends usually don't carry friendship liability insurance, and although there are many benefits of friendship, the benefits aren't subjected to outcome and efficacy research, discussed in scholarly journals, or taught in graduate training programs. Finally, people don't go to friendship graduate school to become skilled and effective healers or helpers in their friend's lives.

Although there are social and friendly aspects to a professional relationship, professional therapists limit their friendliness. Part of becoming a mature professional is learning to be warm, interactive, and open with clients, while staying within appropriate professional relationship boundaries (R. Sommers-Flanagan, 2012) (see *Putting It in Practice* 2.1).

PUTTING IT IN PRACTICE 2.1

Defining Appropriate Relationship Boundaries

Although we don't often stop to think about it, boundaries define most relationships. Broken boundaries have ethical implications. Being familiar with role-related expectations, responsibilities, and limits is an important part of being a good therapist. Consider the following professional relationship boundary violations. Evaluate and discuss the seriousness of each one. Is it a minor, somewhat serious, or very serious boundary violation?

- Having a coffee with your client at a coffee shop after the interview.
- Asking your client for a ride to pick up your car.
- Offering to take your client out to dinner.
- Going to a concert with a client.
- Asking your client (a math teacher) to help your child with homework.
- Borrowing money from a client.
- Sharing a bit of gossip with a client about someone you both know.
- Talking with one client about another client.
- Fantasizing about having sex with your client.
- Giving your client a little spending money because you know your client faces a long weekend with no food.
- Inviting your client to your church, mosque, or synagogue.
- Acting on a financial tip your client gave you by buying stock from your client's stockbroker.

- Dating your client.
- Giving your client's name to a volunteer agency.
- Writing a letter of recommendation for your client's job application.
- Having your client write you a letter of recommendation for a job.

Client Motivation

Most clients come to mental health professionals for one of the following reasons:

- Subjective distress, discontent, or personal-social impairment.
- Someone, perhaps a spouse, relative, or probation officer, insisted they get counseling. Usually this means the client has misbehaved, irritated others, or broken the law.
- Personal growth and development.

When clients come to therapy because of personal distress or a functional impairment, they often feel demoralized because they've had difficulties coping with their problems independently (Frank, 1961; Frank & Frank, 1991). At the same time, the pain or cost of their problems may stimulate great motivation for change (unless they're significantly depressed, in which case their hopelessness may outweigh their motivation). This motivation can translate into cooperation, hopefulness, and receptivity to what the therapist has to say.

In contrast, sometimes clients show up for therapy with little motivation. They may have been cajoled or coerced into scheduling an appointment. In such cases, the client's primary motivation may be to terminate therapy or be pronounced "well" (J. Sommers-Flanagan & Sommers-Flanagan, 1995b; J. Sommers-Flanagan & Sommers-Flanagan, 2007b). Obviously, if clients are unmotivated, it's challenging for clinicians to establish and maintain a professional therapist-client relationship.

Clients who come to therapy for personal growth and development are usually highly motivated to engage in a therapeutic process. Because they come by choice and for positive reasons, working with these clients can be quite rewarding.

Solution-focused therapists use a similar three-category system to assess client motivation (Murphy, 2008). This system includes:

- Visitors to treatment: These clients attend therapy only when coerced. They have no personal interest in change.
- Complainants: These clients attend therapy primarily because of someone's urging. They have a mild interest in change.
- Customers for change: These clients are especially interested in change—either to alleviate symptoms or for personal growth.

Human motivation constantly influences human behavior. Within the interviewing and counseling domain, many researchers and clinicians have written about the subtle ways in which therapists can nurture client motivation (Berg & Shafer, 2004; Miller & Rollnick, 2013). Consequently, in Chapter 3 and again in Chapter 12, we go into greater detail about client motivation, readiness for change, and the stages of change in counseling and psychotherapy (Prochaska & DiClemente, 2005). Understanding these concepts is essential to effective clinical interviewing and psychotherapy.

Collaborative Goal Setting

Collaborative goal setting is a well-established evidence-based practice (Tryon & Winograd, 2011). As with all things collaborative, this finding implies complex interactive discussions between client and therapist. Although it's not perfectly clear how collaborative goal-setting influences positive treatment outcomes, this process likely involves an interactive discussion with clients not only about specific problems and worries, but also about hopes, dreams, and goals for treatment (Mackrill, 2010). Depending on theoretical orientation, this process may rely more or less on formal assessment or diagnostic procedures.

From a cognitive-behavioral perspective, collaborative goal setting is initiated when therapists work with clients to establish a problem list. This process helps illuminate client problems, provides an opportunity for empathic listening, and begins transforming problems into goals (J. Beck, 2011) provided an example of how a cognitive-behavioral therapist might initially talk with clients about goal-setting:

> Therapist: (Writes "Goals" at the top of a sheet of paper.) Goals are really just the flip side of problems. We'll set more specific goals next session, but very broadly, should we say: Reduce depression? Reduce anxiety? Do better at school? Get back to socializing? (p. 54)

J. Beck (2011) also noted that making a problem list and discussing goals with clients helps clients begin framing their goals in ways that include greater personal control.

Collaborative goal setting is a process that contributes to positive treatment outcomes regardless of therapist theoretical perspective. For example, Mackrill (2010) outlined collaborative sensitivities required from an existential perspective:

> The therapist needs to be sensitive to the isolation and perhaps vulnerability of the client who expresses goals for the first time. The therapist needs to be sensitive to the fact that considering the future may be new to the client. The therapist needs to be sensitive to the fact that focusing on goals and tasks may confront the client with his or her sense of self-worth or his or her sense of influence on the world. The therapist needs to be willing to talk about such challenges with the client, in the knowledge that this may be central to the therapy. (p. 104)

When client and therapist agree on the client's problem(s), establishing therapy goals is relatively easy and painless. On the other hand, sometimes clients and therapists may not agree on goals. These disagreements may stem from a variety of sources including, but not limited to: (a) poor client motivation or insight; (b) questionable therapist motives or insight; and (c) social-cultural differences. Historically, more prescriptive and/or authoritative approaches to psychotherapy usually considered client motivation and insight as limited or suspect, whereas therapist motivation and insight were considered relatively infallible. More recently, perhaps because of an emphasis on informed consent and accountability, most therapy approaches place greater value on the client's perspective and recognize the central importance of client motivation (Norcross, 2011).

Perhaps for dramatic effect, popular books and movies frequently portray therapists and clients as having different (and sometimes incompatible) therapy goals. In the real world, clients generally come to counseling with a reasonable amount of insight and therapists come with a reasonable amount of flexibility. This makes collaborative goal setting possible. As a therapist, it's important to value your client's perspective, while providing your professional opinion regarding appropriate goals and strategies. Striking this balance requires sensitivity, tact, and excellent communication skills.

Therapist as Expert

Therapists are designated experts in mental health and, therefore, have the responsibility to professionally evaluate clients and their situations before proceeding with treatment. A minimal first-session evaluation includes an assessment of your client's presenting problems and problem-related situations or triggers, an analysis of their expectations or goals for therapy, and a review of previous efforts at solving the problems that bring them to therapy. In most cases, if an initial assessment reveals that client and therapist goals are fundamentally incompatible, clients should be offered a referral to a different therapist.

Premature interventions based on inadequate assessment are linked to negative therapy outcomes (Castonguay, Boswell, Constantino, Goldfried, & Hill, 2010; Hadley & Strupp, 1976). If an intervention is offered before adequate assessment is conducted and mutual goals formulated, a number of negative outcomes might occur. For example:

- Therapists may choose an inappropriate approach that's potentially damaging (e.g., anxiety is increased rather than decreased).
- Clients may feel misunderstood and rushed and could conclude their problem is too severe or that the therapist isn't competent.
- Clients may follow the therapist's poor and premature guidance and become disappointed and frustrated with therapy.
- Therapists may not take time to listen to problem-solving strategies the client has already tried. A remedy the client already tried without success may be suggested and the therapist's credibility diminished.

An initial clinical interview or ongoing therapy may produce less-than-positive effects. Negative effects often result from misguided, culturally insensitive, inappropriate, or premature efforts to help. Wise and effective therapists work to establish rapport, listen carefully, evaluate client problems and strengths, and establish reasonable and mutual treatment goals before implementing specific change strategies.

Client as Expert

It's important to affirm clients as the best experts about themselves and their own experiences. This is so obvious that it seems odd to mention, but unfortunately, therapists can get wrapped up in their expertness and usurp the client's personal authority. Although idiosyncratic, and maybe even factually inaccurate, clients' stories and explanations about themselves and their lives are internally valid and therefore should be respected as such.

Therapists can intentionally or unintentionally act as an authority whose perspective is more important than their clients. Very recently, I (John) became preoccupied about convincing a client that she wasn't really "bipolar." Despite my good intentions (it seemed to me that the young woman would be better off without a bipolar label), there was something important for the client about holding onto her bipolar identity. As a "psychological expert" I thought it was unhelpful. I thought it obscured her many strengths with a label that diminished her personhood. Therefore, I tried my best to convince her to change her belief system. For better or worse, I was unsuccessful.

What's clear about the preceding example is that, despite being experts in mental health matters, as professionals we need to respect our clients' worldviews. In recent years practitioners from many theoretical perspectives have become more firm about the need for the expert therapist to take a back seat to the client's personal lived experience (J. Sommers-Flanagan & Sommers-Flanagan, 2012). This emphasis may be partly due to mental health professionals and advocates increasing awareness that clients may have very different views of themselves and the world.

In the end, how could I be certain that my client would be better off without a bipolar label? What if that label somehow offers her solace? Perhaps she feels comfort in a label that helps her explain her behavior to herself. Perhaps she never will let go of the bipolar label—and perhaps I'm the one who needs to accept that as a reasonably helpful outcome.

Whatever your theoretical orientation, you should strive to respect your client's personal expertise. You need that expertise operating in the room as much as you need your own. If clients are unwilling to collaborate and share their expertise, you'll lose at least some of your potency as a helper.

> **DVD Clip**
>
> In the Basic Listening Skills DVD chapter, John and Rita briefly discuss the continuum of listening responses, power differentials, cultural issues, and universally negative interviewer behaviors.

Applying Listening Skills and Psychological Techniques

The most concrete and common element underlying assessment and helping within mental health is sensitive and effective listening. Whether your primary role is evaluator or interventionist, you must demonstrate to your client (or your client's parents, family, or support system) that you're a good listener.

It's commonly assumed that one of the best ways to listen to clients is to ask carefully crafted questions. However, like many assumptions, this one is simplistic and incorrect—so be sure to drop that assumption immediately. Remember instead: Although asking good questions is very important to interviewing, it's also a directive activity that does *not* always allow clients to freely express themselves.

Too many questions can be disrespectful because questions guide and restrict client verbalizations. This means the information shared is what therapists think clients should share. In reality, your clients may need to tell you something much different from what you're focusing on with directive questions.

For many reasons, we should restrain ourselves from applying specific psychological techniques until we've adequately listened (nonjudgmentally) to our client's perspective. Therefore, the following guideline may be useful for you: No matter how backward it seems, begin by resisting the urge to actively help or direct your client. Instead, listen as deeply, fully, and attentively as you can. Doing so will aid your client more than if you offer premature help (Meier & Davis, 2011; Miller & Rollnick, 2002; Rogers, 1961).

CASE EXAMPLE

Jerry Fest, a therapist in Portland, Oregon, wrote of the following encounter in a manual for persons working with street youth (Boyer, 1988). One night, while he was working in a drop-in counseling center, a young woman came in obviously agitated and in distress. Jerry knew her from other visits, so he greeted her by name. She said, "Hey, man, do I ever need someone to listen to me." He showed her to an office and listened to her incredibly compelling tale of difficulties for several minutes. He then made what he thought was an understanding, supportive statement. The young woman immediately stopped talking. When she began again a few moments later, she stated again that she needed someone to listen to her. The same sequence of events played out again. After her second stop and start, however, Jerry decided to take her literally, and he sat silently for the next 90 minutes. The woman poured out her heart, finally winding down and regaining control. As she prepared to leave, she looked at Jerry and said, "That's what I like about you, Jer. Even when you don't get it right the first time, you eventually catch on."

This young woman clearly articulated her need *to be listened to, without interruption*. We offer this example not because we believe that sitting silently with clients is an adequate listening response. Instead, the case illustrates the complexity of listening, how clients who are sensitive or in crisis may need to have someone explicitly follow their directions, and how the nonverbal presence of a professional in the room can be powerfully meaningful.

Unique Interactions Between Therapist and Client

One reason clinical interviewing is so complex is that it involves two (or more) humans interacting. Human interaction nearly always results in unpredictability. Every client and therapist bring a new mix of DNA, personality traits, attitudes, and expectations into the room. This makes each interview unique. No formula for interviewing fits every situation. However, all interviews include at least three distinct variables: the client, the therapist, and their interactions. Although most of this book focuses on the client and client-therapist interactions, the following section focuses on you and your unique contribution to the interviewing process.

SELF-AWARENESS

We fondly recall an old college coach who, with great enthusiasm, discussed the difficulty of hitting a baseball. He claimed that using a round bat to make solid contact with a round ball left virtually no room for miscalculation; it required the player's body to be an instrument that can constantly respond and adjust to a small, round, spinning object traveling at varying high speeds.

The process of becoming a good hitter in baseball requires knowledge, practice, excellent body awareness, and good hand-eye coordination. We'd like to suggest that clinical interviewing also requires knowledge, practice, and self-awareness. (The good news is that the hand-eye coordination is optional.)

To stretch the analogy further, as a professional therapist, you must consistently make solid psychological, social, cultural, and emotional contact with unique individuals you're meeting for the first time. Ordinarily, you're required to accomplish this task in the short span of 50 minutes. To make contact, you must be sensitive to and tolerant of the limitless number of ways people can present themselves and be just as sensitive to and aware of your own physical, psychological, social, cultural, and emotional presence. (Upon reflection, which of these processes seems more difficult—hitting baseballs or conducting clinical interviews? One ray of hope: After a certain age, efficiency at hitting a baseball deteriorates, whereas effective interviewing enjoys a longer efficiency curve.)

Self-awareness—not to be confused with self-absorption—is a positive and important therapist trait. Self-awareness helps therapists know how their personal biases and emotional states influence and potentially distort their understanding of clients. In fact, multicultural guidelines from the American Counseling Association (ACA) and American Psychological Association (APA) emphasize cultural self-awareness as a foundation for multicultural competence. Additionally, working with clients can produce emotional reactions in you that need to be recognized and managed (e.g., anxiety, sadness, or euphoria). Good therapists work to understand themselves and their own relationships before entering into relationships with clients. Just as accomplished athletes possess high levels of body awareness to perform well, therapists must possess superior psychological, emotional, social, and cultural self-awareness to perform optimally.

Forms of Self-Awareness

Self-awareness takes many forms. These include physical self-awareness, psychosocial self-awareness, developmental self-awareness, and cultural self-awareness.

Physical Self-Awareness

Physical self-awareness involves becoming conscious of your voice quality, body language, and other physical aspects. It's important to be aware of how you affect others in the physical domain. For instance, some people have soft, warm, and comforting voices; others come across more authoritatively. Try listening to recordings of yourself or ask others to listen and give you feedback (see *Putting It in Practice* 2.2).

PUTTING IT IN PRACTICE 2.2

Dealing With Objective Self-Awareness

Objective self-awareness (OSA) is a social-psychology term that describes feelings of discomfort associated with listening to or viewing yourself on audio or video recordings (Duval & Wicklund, 1972). According to the OSA hypothesis, to watch or listen to yourself produces increased self-awareness, which also increases self-consciousness and inhibition.

Being in a high-OSA state can make people more aware of their personal behavioral standards. In fact, research has shown that individuals tend to behave more ethically when experiencing OSA (Heine, Takemoto, Moskalenko, Lasaleta, & Henrich, 2008). This means watching yourself on video may help you elevate your standards for your own interviewing behaviors to higher levels.

Although uncomfortable, facing and embracing OSA and self-consciousness experiences is encouraged. Expect to experience moderate discomfort as you review your interview recordings. Most of us hate watching images of ourselves—especially at first. As with everything, however, practice helps, so try the following:

- Record and watch your interviewing sessions as often as possible.
- Admit your discomfort. Your classmates will feel the same way and will support you for the brave act of showing a recording to the class.
- Be open to positive and negative feedback from others; but if you don't want feedback, feel free to request there be none.
- If someone gives you feedback you don't understand, ask for clarification.
- Thank people who give you feedback, even if you didn't like or agree with it. It's rare in our culture to receive direct feedback about how we come across to others. Take advantage of the opportunity and use it for personal growth.
- As Rogers (1961) and Maslow (1968) suggested, the self-actualized or fully functioning person is "open to experience" (Rogers, 1961, p. 173). Good therapists possess similar qualities. Defensiveness doesn't help you grow and develop. Try adopting an open attitude toward feedback.
- If your class or learning community feels untrustworthy, you have several choices. First, keep trying. Sometimes, persistence pays off and you'll discover someone has earned your trust. Second, find someone outside the group (friend, colleague, or therapist) in whom
(continued)

(*continued*)

you can confide, with the eventual goal of also identifying someone in your class. Third, find new people you can trust. Sometimes, pathological groups or classes form that don't provide empathy or support. If you're sure this is the case, move on to healthier surroundings. On the other hand, always scrutinize yourself before leaving a class or group. You may be able to make personal changes and stay.

• Use a relaxation or mindfulness technique. Physical and mental relaxation can help you manage the stress and anxiety that accompany self-awareness (Kabat-Zinn, 2005; Williams, Teasdale, Segal, & Kabat-Zinn, 2007).

Your physical self, including sex characteristics, race, or skin color can affect client perceptions of you. For example, male therapists may be described as rational and authoritarian and females as more warm and compassionate (Pseekos & Lyddon, 2009). Although these assumptions may reflect individual reality and cultural stereotypes, they may also be related to a specific client's history of male-female relationships. How clients perceive and judge you may have little to do with your actual behavior, but it's useful to consider how your specific physical characteristics might trigger particular perceptions in others.

As a physical and racial-ethnic dimension of self, skin color is rarely discussed directly in social situations, in therapy, or in interviewing textbooks. Tummala-Nara (2007) noted: "Initiating discussion on skin color can be uncomfortable and difficult for the client and the therapist, because its meanings are complex and varied, sometimes accompanied by deep feelings of shame" (pp. 267–268). This is unfortunate because research has shown that individuals, including people of color, often have unconscious or implicit negative associations with darker skin colors (Nosek, Greenwald, & Banaji, 2005). Surfacing and discussing these issues might help therapists and clients to overcome this potential source of racial bias (see *Multicultural Highlight* 2.2).

MULTICULTURAL HIGHLIGHT 2.2

Talking About Skin Color

No one we know over the age of 12 is very comfortable talking about skin color. Nevertheless, because research shows that many individuals have unconscious skin-color biases, some discussion of this potentially emotionally charged topic should take place within the context of graduate education. This is why we recommend some of the following activities.

1. Go to https://implicit.harvard.edu/implicit/ and take some form of the Implicit Association Test. This test is designed to evaluate your underlying and possibly unconscious attitudes toward people with various skin colors. We recommend that you take the test and then discuss your reactions to the test (and to your results) with other members of your class.

2. Teaching Tolerance.org has a website on multicultural equality. One part of this website lists a video titled "Starting Small" that shows young children with diverse racial and ethnic backgrounds comparing their skin colors (go to http://www.tolerance.org/kit/starting-small for the video). Watching the video and then engaging in the small group skin-color activity is one way for adults to start a conversation about skin color.

Although we think it's important to be able to discuss skin color and other racial, ethnic, and cultural issues directly with clients, we recommend that you do so with caution and clinical sensitivity. Frequently, beginning White counselors haven't yet examined their thoughts and feelings about their own or others' skin color (Michelle Muenzenmeyer, personal communication, August 26, 2012). Thus, skin color isn't a topic for discussion that should be initiated by a beginning White therapist working with a person of color—because White therapists should work out their own skin color issues rather than dragging clients into assisting them with their issues about race. Instead, skin color, culture, and race are issues for beginning therapists to discuss in class so you can begin to comfortably listen for these issues as they surface within interviewing sessions.

Whether therapists should discuss any ethnic, racial, or cultural concern with clients—including skin color—often comes down to individual clinical judgment and provides an excellent example of the multidimensional nature of clinical decision making. By using reflective practices and discussion with classmates and instructors, counselors increase their comfort and ability to have multicultural discussions with clients as well as each other. Eventually, counselors should be able to artfully and appropriately discuss any ethnic, racial, or cultural concern, including skin-color differences, with their clients, as needed.

Psychosocial Self-Awareness

Psychosocial self-awareness refers to how you view yourself as relating to others. As suggested by Bennett (1984), it's a slippery concept: "The social self is . . . elusive. There is no mirror in which we may actually examine interpersonal relations. Most of the feedback, most of the self-percepts come from others" (p. 276).

Not only does psychosocial self-awareness involve perceptions of and feedback about how others view us, but also our psychological, social, and emotional needs and how they influence our lives. In his oft-cited hierarchy of needs, Maslow (1970) contended that all humans have basic physiological needs; safety needs; self-esteem needs; self-actualization needs; and needs for love, acceptance, and interpersonal belongingness. Good therapists are aware of their own particular psychological and interpersonal needs and how those needs can affect their interviewing and counseling behavior. One way of enhancing your psychosocial self-awareness is to intentionally reflect on your life and career goals. Ask yourself:

1. What are my most important personal values? Do they show in the way I act, speak, dress, or live my life?
2. What are my life goals? What do I really want out of life, and why? Does my everyday behavior move me toward my life goals?
3. What are my career goals? If I want to be a counselor or psychotherapist, how will I achieve this goal? Why do I want to be a counselor or psychotherapist?
4. How would I describe myself in only a few words? How would I describe myself to a stranger? What do I particularly like and what do I especially dislike about myself?

It's also important to regularly get feedback from trusted friends and colleagues regarding how you come across to others. Having a clear sense of how others perceive you can help you avoid taking a client's inaccurate evaluation of you at face value.

CASE EXAMPLE

A client periodically accused her therapist of being too unemotional. She would say, "You never seem to have any feelings. I'm pouring my heart out to you in here, and you're just stiff as a board. Don't you care about me at all?"

To better understand his client's perceptions, the therapist asked colleagues for feedback, and they assured him that he was a kind and caring person. Additionally, at the same time, he was seeing another female client who consistently accused him of "being too emotional," complaining that he was overreacting to what she told him. Both of these clients were inpatients on a psychiatric unit and their perceptions were likely affected by their own problems. However, non-hospitalized clients also can have distorted perceptions of your physical, social, and emotional presentation; this can be disconcerting if you haven't received other feedback from peers and supervisors about your interpersonal style. We discuss this process, also known as transference or parataxic distortion, in Chapter 5.

Another way to evaluate your psychosocial self involves psychological assessment. Many graduate programs in counseling, social work, and psychology include courses in individual appraisal or psychological assessment. We recommend, when you take those courses, that you be sure to take various personality tests as one means for exploring yourself in greater detail. It can be interesting to think about how your "scores" compare to other information you have about yourself.

Developmental Self-Awareness

Although developmental self-awareness is closely linked to psychosocial self-awareness, it merits separate discussion. Developmental self-awareness refers to a consciousness of one's personal history, of specific events that significantly influenced personal development. Everyone has at least a few vivid memories that have meaning for the contemporary self (Clark, 2002).

In the tradition of psychoanalysis, we suggest you explore your own relationship history, beginning with childhood. Reviewing how you relate to others can provide insight into reaction patterns you'll have with clients. You can begin this exploration by periodically taking time to sit quietly and construct a journal or timeline about your relationship history. You may want to describe your important relationships chronologically and fashion a psychosocial developmental map of your history. Another way of exploring your developmental history is through individual or group psychotherapy (Bike, Norcross, & Schatz, 2009; Gold & Hilsenroth, 2009; Jacobs, 2011). Being in a men's or women's group also can be illuminating.

Cultural Self-Awareness

Chapter 1 included a brief discussion of self-awareness within the context of multicultural competency guidelines of awareness, knowledge, and skills. Now we return to the crossroads of self-awareness and culture.

To the extent that individuals are aware of their culture, they often tend to believe in the innate superiority or rightness of their racial-ethnic-cultural perspective. Zuckerman (1990) noted that the tendency to view one's own tribe as superior to neighboring tribes, or one's own nation or race as superior to other nations or races, is probably as old as our species. Geographical isolation and consequent inbreeding resulted in similarities among the members of human groups that laypeople refer to as *characteristics of race*. Zuckerman pointed out that these characteristics lie along a continuum and constitute only surface differences with regard to species distinction.

Most individuals (and this includes therapists) view culture from one of two major perspectives: either the *cultural universalist* or *cultural relativist* position. Cultural universalism emphasizes the commonalities and similarities among races. This might be viewed as the "we are one" perspective where cultural similarities are seen as overriding cultural distinctions (Sue & Sue, 2013).

Others have noted that differences between cultures are powerful forces in individual and group identity development. Our ideas about what is proper and improper, right and wrong, appropriate and inappropriate—even normal and abnormal—are determined by our cultural, religious, political, and gender-typed upbringing. Whether two people understand each other depends not so much on racial or cultural backgrounds, but on how strongly each of them believes in the correctness or superiority of what is personally familiar. Truly understanding someone from another culture begins with acceptance of differences as normal, interesting, and even desirable aspects of being human. This point of view—that all humans are different based on their individual culture and that these differences should be honored, respected, and valued—is more consistent with the *cultural relativist* perspective (Forsyth, O'Boyle, & McDaniel, 2008; McAuliffe & Milliken, 2009).

MULTICULTURAL HIGHLIGHT 2.3

Discovering Your Personal Biases

We suggest that you and your classmates take time to consider your own cultural, religious, and political biases. It's helpful to explore these, even among yourselves. How many in your class were raised to believe in a God referred to as masculine? How many were raised to believe that to care for the poor is a high and honorable calling in life? How many were raised to believe that being on time and standing in line are signs of weakness? How many were raised to believe that mother-in-laws and son-in-laws should not speak to one another? The list of varying beliefs and values is endless. To further complicate matters, it's not only how we were raised or even what we believe now that needs to be explored, but also the interaction of our cultural beliefs with another person's beliefs. How have we matured? How do we now respond to those who believe as we once did? There is no easy way to become culturally self-aware, but exposure, introspection, discussion, reading, and even personal therapy to uncover biases and blind spots will help you work more effectively and sensitively with people of different cultures (Fontes, 2008; D. W. Sue & Sue, 2013).

Stereotyping refers to a fixed, oversimplified, and overgeneralized belief about a particular group. Social scientists have explored stereotyping for many years and from numerous perspectives. One important finding is that stereotyping is less likely when a person has more exposure or experience with diverse individuals or groups. Although simple exposure to different cultures isn't sufficient to end stereotyping, it can increase knowledge, improve attitudes, and decrease anxiety between individuals from different racial backgrounds (Dasgupta & Asgari, 2004; Jost & Kay, 2005).

THE PHYSICAL SETTING

When therapist and client sit down together, many environmental factors influence their behavior. Although the therapist is the most important stimulus in the room affecting client behavior, other variables influence clinical interviewing process and outcome. Therapists should be conscious of these variables.

The Room

What kind of room is most appropriate for clinical interviewing?

Of course, circumstances beyond your control can determine the room you use for interviewing. Many undergraduate programs and some graduate programs don't have a therapy clinic complete with private offices. In fact, some therapists don't have a room at all; professionals who work in disaster or crisis situations conduct interviews in gyms, sitting on benches, or make do in other ways. Further, behavior therapists may take clients into environments that produce anxiety to implement exposure-based treatments (Linton et al., 2008; Seim, Willerick, Gaynor, & Spates, 2008). Therapy activities also may take place outside—while jogging, walking, dancing, or sitting in a comfortable setting, such as under a tree on a pleasant day (Malchiodi, 2005). Despite these many exceptions, we recommend you start with a room.

The minimum room requirement is privacy. A degree of professional décor is also important. People aren't inclined to reveal their deepest fears or secrets at the student union building over coffee—at least not to someone they've only just met. On the other hand, when attempting to present yourself professionally, hiding behind a massive oak desk with a background of 27 framed professional degrees is unnecessary. As is true regarding many interviewing variables, when choosing a room, it's useful to strike a balance between professional formality and casual comfort. Consider the room an extension of your professional self. In an initial interview, your major purpose is to foster *trust* and *hope*, build rapport, and help clients talk openly. Your room choice should reflect that purpose.

Control is an important issue in setting up the atmosphere in which interviews take place (see *Putting It in Practice* 2.3). The client may be given small choices such as chair selection, but overall, therapists should be in control of the surroundings.

Numerous elements distinguish counseling and psychotherapy from other social encounters. One such distinction is that time devoted to the interview is viewed as uninterruptible. An interruption not only costs time, it also disrupts the session's flow. Although interruptions during a business or social encounter may be permissible or welcome, this isn't true in therapy. At our training clinic, everyone from the janitor to the supervisors realize that professional sessions are not interrupted. The office staff would never dream of interrupting and, in fact, guard the students' client hours with a fierce loyalty to both student and client.

PUTTING IT IN PRACTICE 2.3

Staying in Control of the Interview Setting

Imagine yourself confronted with the following scenario: An interviewing student calls a volunteer interviewee:

"Hello, is Sally Sampson there?"

"Yes, this is she."

"Sally, my name is Beth McNettle, and I'm taking Interviewing 443. I believe you signed up to be interviewed for extra credit in your Psychology 101 class. I got your name, so I'm calling to set up a time."

"Oh sure. No problem . . . but it's almost finals week. I'm pretty busy."

"Uh, yeah. I wanted to do this sooner in the semester, but uh, well, let's see if we can find a time."

After much searching, they find a mutually agreeable time. Unfortunately, Beth forgot to check the room schedule and finds no rooms are available at the time chosen. She calls Sally back:

"Sally, this is Beth McNettle again. I'm sorry, but there are no rooms available at the time we decided."

(continued)

(continued)

Sally is a bit irritated, and it shows in her voice. Beth is feeling apologetic, indebted, and a little desperate. There is only one week left in the semester. They discuss their limited options. Beth suggests, "Maybe I should call someone else."

Sally counters with:

"Hey, look, I really want to do this. I need the extra credit. Why don't you just come to my room? I live in University Hall, right here on campus."

Knowing she is violating the rules, Beth reluctantly agrees to do the interview in Sally's dorm room. After all, it's just a class assignment, right? What's wrong with a nice, quiet dorm room? Who will ever know where the interview was conducted? Besides, it's better than inviting Sally to *her* house, isn't it? Beth asks Sally to make sure they will have the room to themselves. "No problem," says Sally, sounding distracted.

The next day, Beth arrives. It's late afternoon. It just happens to be the one hour designated as the time when residents can make as much noise as they please to compensate for quiet hours and finals stress. Various radio stations and raucous bursts of laughter compete for air space. Sally's friend from across the hall is getting her hair permed, which, except for the odor, should not be all that relevant, but somehow, Sally's digital clock is being used to time the perm. No one besides Beth and Sally are actually in the room, but there are numerous interruptions and Sally's cell phone buzzes five times.

Although this example is extreme, it illustrates the importance of controlling the interview setting. Loss of control can happen easily.

If you don't have access to rooms in which privacy is assured, you should place a *Do Not Disturb* or *Session in Progress* sign on the door to reduce interruptions. Additionally, phone ringers, cell phones, and answering machines should be turned down or off. The last thing you want is a cell phone vibrating just as your client begins sharing something deeply personal.

One word of caution is in order. Although therapists should take reasonable measures available to assure they're not interrupted, *do not* lock the door. There are many reasons for this. For example, if you're interviewing someone with poor impulse control and he or she gets angry, it's best to have an exit available. We hope that you'll never need to use such an exit, but you'll feel better knowing it exists. Also, a locked door conveys an intimacy that could lead some people to impute a message you didn't intend. To summarize: Quiet, comfortable, protected—yes. Locked—no.

Sometimes, despite our best efforts, an interruption occurs. There are three main types of interruptions. First, there are inadvertent and brief interruptions. For example, a new office manager may knock on the door or enter without understanding the importance of privacy. In such cases, the therapist should gently inform the intruder that the meeting is private.

Second, there are legitimate interruptions that take a few minutes to manage. For example, your 7-year-old daughter's school telephones your office, indicating your child is ill and needs to be picked up from school immediately. Your office staff person decides to interrupt you with this information. This interruption may require 5 minutes for the therapist to contact a friend or family member to pick up the child. In this situation, the therapist should inform the client that a short break is necessary, apologize, and then make the telephone calls. On returning to the session, the therapist should apologize again, offer restitution for the time missed from the session (e.g., ask the client "Can you stay an extra 5 minutes today?" or "Is it okay to make up the 5 minutes we lost at our next session?"), and then try, as smoothly as possible, to begin where the interview had been interrupted.

Third, an interruption may involve an emergency that requires your immediate presence somewhere else. If so, you should apologize for having to end the session, reschedule, and provide the rescheduled appointment at no charge (or refund the client's payment for the interrupted session). Depending on theoretical orientation, it may or may not be necessary or appropriate to disclose the nature of the emergency. Usually, a calm, explanatory statement should suffice:

> I'm sorry, but I need to leave because of an urgent situation that can't wait. I hope you understand, but we'll need to reschedule. This is very unusual, and I'm terribly sorry for inconveniencing you.

Often, giving clients general information about your leaving allays both their concern and their curiosity.

Overall, key issues for handling interruptions are (a) modeling calmness and problem-solving ability, (b) apologizing for the interruption, and (c) compensating the client for any interview time lost. In addition, if you're taking notes when an interruption occurs, you should make certain the notes are placed in a secure file or given to the office manager before leaving the counseling office.

Seating Arrangements

When we ask students and professionals how two people should sit during an interview sometimes we're surprised by the variety of responses. Some suggest face-to-face seating arrangements, others like a desk between themselves and clients, and still others prefer sitting at a 90- to 120-degree angle so client and therapist can look away from each other without discomfort. Someone usually points out that a few psychoanalytically oriented psychotherapists still place clients on a couch, with the therapist seated behind the client and out of view.

Some training clinics have predetermined seating arrangements. Our former clinic had a single, soft reclining chair along with two or three more austere wooden chairs available. Theoretically, the soft recliner provided clients with a comfortable and relaxing place from which they can freely express themselves. The recliner was also excellent for hypnotic inductions, for teaching progressive relaxation, and for free association. Unfortunately, having a designated seat for clients can produce discomfort, especially during early sessions. Not surprisingly, many clients avoided the cushioned recliners. What are some reasons you might offer for this avoidance?

Several factors dictate seating-arrangement choices, including theoretical orientation. Psychoanalysts often choose couches, behaviorists choose recliners, and person-centered therapists use chairs of equal status and comfort. You might want to try out a number of different seating arrangements to get a sense for what seems best to you. This doesn't necessarily mean your instinctive choice is best, but discovering your preference may be enlightening. You should also remain sensitive to your clients' preferences, as certain arrangements will feel better and worse to each of them.

Generally, therapist and client should be seated at somewhere between a 90- and 150-degree angle to each other during initial interviews. Benjamin (1987) stated the rationale for such a seating arrangement quite nicely:

> [I] prefer two equally comfortable chairs placed close to each other at a 90-degree angle with a small table nearby. This arrangement works best for me. The interviewee can face me when he wishes to do so, and at other times he can look straight ahead without my getting in his way. I am equally unhampered. The table close by fulfills its normal functions and, if not needed, disturbs no one. (p. 3)

The 90-degree-angle seating arrangement is safe and reasonable. Nonetheless, many therapists (and clients) prefer a less extreme angle so they can look at the client more directly but not quite face-to-face (perhaps at a 120-degree angle).

Generally, we recommend *not* insisting on given seating arrangements. Clients may sometimes disrupt your prearranged seating by moving chairs around. If a client appears comfortable with an unplanned or unusual seating arrangement, simply allow the client to choose, make a mental note of the behavior, and proceed with the interview.

An exception to this general rule can occur when a client (usually a child or adolescent) blatantly refuses to sit in an appropriate or responsive position in the therapist's office. Depending on your preferred theoretical or personal approach, you may either let the client stand or sit wherever he or she chooses or gently but firmly insist that the client choose between two or three acceptable seats. We'll return to this topic when discussing client resistance and interviewing young clients later in this text.

Office Clutter and Decor

We all have stuff that we drag around with us in our lives. Some of this stuff is disorganized, messy and unsightly. Other stuff is more interesting and pleasing to the psyche or the eye.

One of us (John) sometimes dreams that he's preparing for a therapy session and just before it begins, he notices that his office is a complete mess. There are piles of dirty laundry, books, CDs, and papers strewn around the room. At the last minute, he dashes around the room stuffing papers and clothes under his desk in anticipation of his client's arrival. Unfortunately, the cleaning never gets quite finished, and when the client comes into the room there's an obvious and embarrassing mess to explain.

Those of you inclined toward dream interpretation may quickly assume that John has excessive psychological baggage that leaks out during therapy sessions and personal needs to be addressed and de-cluttered. Although this interpretation may well be true, John also has the more concrete problem of keeping his office neat and tidy (although he strongly denies keeping dirty laundry strewn about his office). The main point is, of course, to be intentional, disciplined, and tasteful in your office décor and clutter management.

To whatever degree you wish, your office can represent your personality and values. You can consciously arrange your office more or less formally, more or less chic, and more or less self-revealing. It's important to strive for an office that a wide and diverse range of individuals may find comforting. For example, therapists working with Native American clients may want tasteful Native American art or handicrafts in their office—although multiculturally sensitive art is no substitute for adequate multicultural awareness, exposure, study, training, and supervision.

Note Taking

Many therapists and writers have discussed note taking (Benjamin, 1987; Hartley, 2002; Pipes & Davenport, 1999). Although some experts recommend that therapists take notes only after a session, others point out that therapists don't have perfect memories and thus an ongoing record of the session is desirable (Shea, 1998). In some cases, note taking may offend clients. In other cases, it may enhance rapport and therapist credibility. Clients' reactions to note taking are usually a function of their intrapsychic issues, interpersonal dynamics, previous experiences with note-taking behavior, and the therapist's tact. Because you can't predict a client's reaction to note taking in advance, providing an explanation during a session is helpful. Shea (1998) recommended:

> I frequently do not even pick up a clipboard until well into the interview. When I do begin to write, as a sign of respect, I often say to the patient, "I'm going to jot down a few notes to make sure I'm remembering everything correctly. Is that alright with you?" Patients seem to respond very nicely to this simple sign of courtesy. This statement of purpose also tends to decrease the paranoia that patients sometimes project onto note-taking, as they wonder if the clinician is madly analyzing their every thought and action. (p. 180)

We agree that when therapists take notes, they should politely introduce note taking and proceed tactfully. We also recommend practicing your interviews both with and without taking notes. It's important to explore how it feels to take notes and how it feels not to take notes during a session.

Rules for Note Taking

The following list summarizes general rules for note taking.

1. Don't allow note taking to interfere with interview flow or rapport; pay more attention to your client than you do to your notes.
2. Explain the purpose of note taking to clients. Usually a comment about not having a perfect memory suffices. Some clients are disappointed if you don't take notes; explain to them why you choose not to take notes.
3. Never hide or cover your notes or act in any manner that might suggest your clients can't have full access.
4. Never write notes that you're not okay with your client reading. This means sticking to the facts. If you write something you intend to keep to yourself, rest assured your client will want to read what you wrote. Clients with paranoid symptoms will be suspicious about what you've written and may ask to or insist on reading your notes.

5. If clients ask to see what you've written, offer to let them read your notes and explore their concerns. When clients take you up on the offer, you'll be glad you followed rule 4.

Video and Audio Recording

If you're recording a session, you should do so as unobtrusively as possible. In general, the more comfortable and matter-of-fact you are in discussing the recording equipment, the more quickly clients become comfortable. This is easier said than done because you may anticipate being closely scrutinized during supervision and, therefore, you may be even more nervous than your client about being recorded. To reassure the client (but not yourself), you might say:

> The main reason I'm recording our session is so that my supervisor can watch me working. It's to help make sure you get the best service possible and to help me improve my counseling skills.

When planning to record a session, you must obtain the client's permission before turning on the equipment. Usually, permission is obtained on a written consent form. This is important for a number of reasons. Recording clients without their knowledge is an invasion of privacy and violates their trust. It's also important for ethical and legal reasons to explain possible future uses of the recording and how it will be stored, handled, and eventually destroyed.

CASE EXAMPLE

In an effort to obtain a recording of interactions from the very beginning of a session, an intern turned on his equipment before the client entered the room (before the client had filled out her informed consent forms). He assumed that, after preserving the important initial material, he could then discuss the recording with the client. Not surprisingly, when the client discovered she was being recorded, she was angry. She refused to continue the interview. Further, she delivered to the young man a punishing tirade against which he had no defense (and, of course, this tirade was conveniently recorded as well). The student had unwittingly pinpointed one of the best ways of destroying trust and rapport early in an interview: He failed to ask permission, in advance, to make a recording.

We have one final observation about recording sessions. Invariably, when you've conducted your best interview ever, you'll discover there was a technical problem with the equipment and, consequently, your session either didn't record properly or didn't record at all. On the other hand, when you've conducted a session you'd rather forget, the equipment always seems to work perfectly and the session turns out to be the one your supervisor wants to examine closely. Because of this particular manifestation of Murphy's Law, we recommend that you carefully test the recording equipment before all sessions.

PROFESSIONAL AND ETHICAL ISSUES

Before conducting real or practice interviews, you should consider several professional and ethical issues. It can be a struggle to dress professionally, present yourself and your credentials (or lack thereof) comfortably, handle time boundaries, and discuss confidentiality. The remainder of this chapter focuses on how to deal with these professional and ethical issues comfortably and effectively.

Self-Presentation

You are your own primary instrument for a successful interview. Your appearance and the manner in which you present yourself to clients are important components of professional clinical interviewing.

Grooming and Attire

Choosing the right professional clothing can be difficult. Some students ignore the issue; others obsess about wearing just the right outfit. The question of how to dress may reflect a larger developmental issue: How seriously do you take yourself as a professional? Is it time to take off the ripped jeans, remove the nose ring, cover the tattoo, or lose the spike heels? Is it time to don the dreaded three-piece suit or carefully pressed skirt and come out to do battle with mature reality, as your parents or friends may have suggested? Don't worry. We aren't interested in telling you how you should dress or adorn your body. Our point again involves self-awareness. Be aware of how your clothes may affect others. Even if you ignore this issue, your clients—and (hopefully) your supervisor—will not. Clothing choice and grooming communicates a great deal to clients and can be a source of conflict between you and your supervisor.

We knew a student whose distinctive style included closely cropped, multicolored hair; large earrings; and an odd assortment of scarves, vests, sweaters, runner's tights, and sandals. He easily stood out in mixed crowds. Imagine his effect on, say, a middle-aged dairy farmer referred to the clinic for depression, or a mother-son dyad having trouble with discipline, or the local mayor and his wife. No matter what effect you imagined, the point is that there's likely to be an effect. Clothing, body art, and jewelry are not neutral; they're intended to communicate, and they do. An unusual fashion statement by a therapist can be overcome, but it may use up time and energy better devoted to other issues (see *Putting It in Practice* 2.4).

PUTTING IT IN PRACTICE 2.4

Dressing for Success

When it comes to fashion, everyone has an opinion and everyone (almost) has his or her particular taste. Unfortunately, the clinical interview may not be the best place to really let loose by expressing your own unique fashion statement.

(continued)

(*continued*)

Just for fun, if your professor or supervisor doesn't bring up the topic of what's appropriate and what's not appropriate to wear for a professional interview, be sure to do it yourself. Here are a few questions that might stimulate a discussion with your professor/supervisor or with your classmates.

- Are jeans appropriate to wear when providing professional therapy services? Does the brand or cost matter?
- Is it acceptable for male therapists to wear earrings or ponytails?
- When should males wear neckties?
- Are shorts ever appropriate therapeutic attire?
- Is it a problem for a male therapist to wear pants that "sag"?
- When it comes to skirts, how short is too short? How tight is too tight?
- How about women's blouses and tops—how low of a neckline is appropriate?

It's an unfortunate fact that people quickly form first impressions and that these impressions are based on and affected by many factors and may be inaccurate; your clients will judge you by the way you look and dress (Human & Biesanz, 2011, 2012). First impressions are often experienced as a vague positive or negative emotional reaction.

Your goal as a therapist is to present yourself in a way that takes advantage of first impressions. Dress and grooming that foster rapport, trust, and credibility should be your professional goal. Err on the conservative side, at least until you have a firm understanding of the effects of your presentation and the clients you'll be working with.

Straight Talk About Cleavage

For the first time ever in a textbook (and we've been writing them since 1993), we've decided to include a discussion on cleavage. Of course, this makes us feel exceptionally old, but we hope it also might reflect wisdom and perspective that comes with aging.

In recent years we've noticed a greater tendency for female counseling and psychology students (especially younger females) to dress in ways that can be viewed as somewhat provocative by certain standards. This includes, but is not limited to, low necklines that show considerable cleavage. This issue was discussed on a series of postings on the Counselor Education and Supervision listserv, which includes primarily participants who teach in master's and doctoral programs in counseling. Most of the postings included some portion of the following themes.

- Female (and male) students have the right to express themselves via how they dress.
- Commenting on how women dress and making specific recommendations may be viewed as sexist or inappropriately limiting.
- It's true that women should be able to dress any way they want.
- It's also true that specific agencies and institutions have the right to establish dress codes or otherwise dictate how their paid employees and volunteers dress.

- Despite egalitarian and feminist efforts to free women from the shackles of a patriarchal society, how women dress is still interpreted as having certain socially constructed messages that often, but not always, pertain to sex and sexuality.
- Although efforts to change socially constructed ideas about women dressing "sexy" can include activities like campus "slut-walks," the clinical interview is probably not the appropriate venue for initiating a discourse on social and feminist change.
- For better or worse, it's a fact that both middle-school males and middle-aged men (and many "populations" in between) are likely to be distracted—and their ability to profit from a counseling experience may be compromised—if they're offered an opportunity for a close up view of their therapist's breasts.
- At the very least, excessive cleavage (please don't ask us to define this phrase) is *less likely* to contribute to positive therapy outcomes and *more likely* to stimulate sexual fantasies—which we believe is probably contrary to the goals of most therapists.
- It may be useful to have young women watch themselves on video from the viewpoint of a client (of either sex) who might feel attracted to them and then discuss how to manage sexual attraction that could occur during therapy.

Obviously, we don't have perfect or absolute answers to the question of cleavage during a clinical interview. Guidelines depend, in part, on interview setting and specific client populations. At the very least, we recommend you take time to think about this dimension of professional attire, and hope you might also consider discussing cleavage and related issues with fellow students, colleagues, or your supervisor.

Presenting Your Credentials

Students sometimes have difficulty introducing themselves in a balanced and reassuring way. Referring to yourself as a student may bring forth spoken or imagined derogatory comments such as, "So, I'm your guinea pig?" Our advice is to state your full name in a warm, clear voice and offer an accurate description of your training status to your clients. For example: "My name is Hafsah Mustafa, and I'm in the graduate training program in clinical psychology," or "I'm working on my master's degree," or "I'm enrolled in an advanced interviewing course." Pause after this description to provide clients a chance to ask questions about your credentials. If your clients ask questions, answer them directly. Always represent your status clearly and honestly, whether you're working with role-play volunteers or actual clients. It's an ethical violation to misrepresent yourself by overstating your credentials. No matter how inexperienced or inadequate you feel inside, don't try to compensate through fraudulent misrepresentation.

Practicing introductory portions of the clinical interview is important. Before reading further, formulate how you want to introduce yourself in the clinical setting. You may want to write out your introduction or say it into a recorder. We also recommend practicing introductions while role-playing with fellow students. Practicing your introduction helps you to avoid making statements like: "Well, I'm just a student and um, I'm taking this interviewing course, and I have to um, practice, so . . . uh, here we are."

There's nothing wrong with being a student and no need to behave apologetically for being inexperienced. An apologetic action or attitude can erode your credibility. If you feel guilt over "practicing" your interviewing skills with real clients, try a cognitive intervention: Remind yourself that people usually enjoy a chance to talk about themselves. It's rare for people to receive 100% of someone's undivided attention. By listening well, you provide a positive experience for clients and, at the same time, learn more about interviewing.

Student therapists are usually supervised. This information should be included when you present your credentials. Say something like:

> I want you to know that my work at the clinic is supervised by Dr. Gutierrez. This means I will review what we talk about with Dr. Gutierrez to ensure you're receiving the best possible services. Dr. Gutierrez is a licensed clinical psychologist and will keep what you say confidential in the same way I will.

Time

Time is one way clinical interviews are measured. If the client is paying a fee, the fee is based on your time. Clinical interviewing is a rich, involved, and complex process and time may be the most straightforward measure of the commodity that's being offered. Therefore, you should do your best to respect time boundaries.

Clinical interviews typically last 50 minutes. This time period, though arbitrary, is convenient; it allows therapists to meet with clients on an hourly basis, with a few minutes at the end and beginning of each session to write notes and read files. Despite this customary time period, some situations warrant briefer contacts (e.g., school counseling) and other situations require longer sessions (e.g., assessment interviews). Initial intake or assessment interviews are sometimes longer than the traditional therapy hour because it's difficult to obtain all the information needed to conceptualize a case and establish treatment goals. Up to 90 to 120 minutes may be provided for an initial interview. Crisis situations also require more flexibility. Shorter but more frequent sessions may be appropriate for suicidal clients.

Start the Session on Time

Starting your interview on time is a top priority. If you're late, apologize and offer to compensate for the lost time. Say something like: "I apologize for being late; I had another appointment that lasted longer than expected. Because I missed 10 minutes of our session, perhaps we can extend this session or our next session an additional 10 minutes." Although you may not be required to collect fees, another option is to offer to prorate the fee for whatever portion of the usual interview hour remains.

You should also avoid beginning sessions early, even if you're available. Pipes and Davenport (1999) stated this succinctly: "Clients will show up early and may ask if you're free. The answer is no, unless there is a crisis" (p. 18).

Punctuality can communicate respect. Clients generally appreciate professionals who begin sessions at the scheduled time. Often, our students have discussed the contrast between the attitudes of psychotherapists and physicians (excluding psychiatrists) when it comes to punctuality. Many physicians are notoriously late for patient appointments and the lateness provides a message about physician-patient relationships. Therapists strive to show respect for clients' time and feelings and this respect is a component of the helping relationship.

When clients are late, there may be an impulse to extend the session's length or to punish the client by canceling the session entirely. Neither of these options is desirable. Clients should be held responsible for lateness and experience the natural consequences of their behavior, which is an abbreviated session. This is true regardless of the reason the client was tardy. The client may sincerely regret his or her lateness and ask you for additional time. Be empathic but firm. Say something like:

> I'm sorry this session has to be brief, but it's really important for us to stick with our scheduled appointment time. I hope we can have a full session next week.

Unless your client is in crisis, whether you have an appointment scheduled for the next hour is irrelevant; stick with your time boundaries. The key point is that clients should be held responsible for lateness (and similarly, therapists should be held responsible for *their* lateness).

One option for clients arriving late is to offer an additional appointment at another time during the week. For example, you might suggest: "If you want to make up the time we've lost today, we can try to schedule another appointment for later this week." Keep in mind, however, that when clients schedule an additional session (to make up for missed time), they sometimes complicate the problem by "no-showing" for their make-up appointment as well.

It's not unusual to feel anger or irritation toward clients who fail to keep an appointment, or who are late. As with many emotional reactions, you should notice and reflect on them, but refrain from acting on them. For example, even though you desperately want to leave the office after waiting only 10 minutes for your chronically late client, resist that impulse. Instead, clarify your policy on lateness (e.g., "If you're late, I'll wait around for 20 minutes and then I may leave the office."). If clients completely miss appointments, you must decide whether to call to reschedule, send a letter asking if they want to continue therapy, or wait for clients to call for a new appointment. Be sure to discuss various ways to handle these situations with your supervisor.

In some cases, your agency may have a policy of charging clients for a full hour if they don't cancel appointments 24 hours in advance. If so, clients should be informed of this policy up-front. Similarly, inform volunteer clients of consequences associated with missing their scheduled appointments (e.g., loss of extra credit). Also, you may not bill an insurance company for a missed hour because doing so is insurance fraud.

Ending on Time

Clinical interviews should end on time. Clinicians have many excellent excuses for consciously letting sessions run over, but rarely do these excuses justify breaking prearranged time agreements. Some reasons we have heard from our students (and ourselves) follow:

1. We were on the verge of a breakthrough.
2. She brought up a clinically important issue with only 5 minutes to go.

3. He just kept talking at the end of the hour, and I felt uncomfortable cutting in (i.e., he needed to talk more).
4. I hadn't been very effective during the hour and felt the client deserved more time.
5. I forgot my watch and couldn't see the clock from my chair.

In most of the preceding situations, the therapist should have calmly and tactfully said something like:

> I see our time is up for the day, but if you think it would be useful, we can continue with this topic at the beginning of our next session.

Additionally, always be sure to sit in a position that affords you direct visual contact with a clock. It's rude and distracting to glance at your watch—especially repeatedly—or to look over your shoulder at the clock during an interview.

There are very few situations in which it's acceptable to extend the clinical hour. These situations are usually emergencies. For example, when the client is suicidal, homicidal, or psychotic, time boundaries may be modified. A colleague of ours was once held at gunpoint by a client for about 40 minutes past the scheduled end of the session. This is certainly a situation in which time boundaries become irrelevant (although we know our friend wished he could have simply said, "Well, it looks like our time is up for today" and had the client put the gun away and leave the office).

As you read about how clinicians handle time boundaries, you may find yourself happy to be involved in a profession that is conscious and respectful of time boundaries or you may be struck by what feels like a sense of rigidity over starting and stopping on time. These different reactions are natural and may be related, in part, to your cultural roots (Trimble, 2010). For example, American Indians or First Nation peoples tend to have more flexible attitudes toward time and other cultural groups may want to engage in open-ended dialogue for as long as it takes to identify a solution to their problem. Diverse cultural attitudes toward time require professional therapists to simultaneously embrace Western time boundaries while remaining open to other cultural perspectives. Fontes (2008) recommended flexibility in this regard, but also emphasized that professionals should balance flexibility with professional standards and ethics. What this boils down to is that you may need to (a) include policies on how to handle lateness and ending sessions in your informed consent; (b) be ready to discuss time issues as needed, and (c) integrate reasonable flexibility around time boundaries into your work with clients from different cultural backgrounds.

Sometimes we've failed to uphold time boundaries, despite our best intentions. We recall a session when a colleague of ours, seated in a position where he could easily view the clock, started wondering why time seemed to be passing so slowly. In reality, his clock really was slowing down and eventually stopped because of dead batteries. Our friend ended up having a "73-minute hour."

Confidentiality

Professional counseling or psychotherapy involves helping clients talk about very personal information. This is not only a difficult task (people are often uncomfortable disclosing personal information to someone they hardly know), but also a heavy burden. Clients may be entrusting you with information they've never told anyone before. The general assumption is that whatever is shared in the therapy office stays in the therapy office.

There are legal and ethical limits of confidentiality. Some information cannot ethically and/or legally be kept secret. For example, a client could say:

> I'm very depressed and am sick and tired of life. I've decided to quit dragging my family through this miserable time with me . . . so I'm going to kill myself. I have a gun and ammunition at home and I plan to do it this weekend.

In this case, you're obligated to break confidentiality and report your client's suicidal plans to the proper authorities (e.g., police, county mental health professional, or psychiatric hospital admission personnel) and possibly family members. It's important to review the ethical standards regarding confidentiality in your professional ethics code and in your state. Laws and ethical stances change over time. This is an area in which it's essential to be clear and current.

Welfel (2013) summarized the concept of confidentiality:

> *Confidentiality* refers to the ethical duty to keep client identity and disclosures secret and a legal duty to honor the fiduciary relationship with the client. It is primarily a moral obligation rooted in the ethics code, the ethical principles, and the virtues that the profession attempts to foster. (p. 118)

Statements in the various professional codes pertaining to confidentiality are open to interpretation. To better clarify the standards, *Putting It in Practice* 2.5 provides examples of situations in which mental health professionals would be obligated or expected to break confidentiality.

After reviewing confidentiality standards associated with your profession as well as the preceding information, take time to brainstorm with your class potential situations where your need to break confidentiality might be unclear. Discuss what you should do in those situations. If you need consultation on specific ethical dilemmas consider contacting your professional insurance provider or you're the professional association of which you are a member (i.e., the American Psychological Association at 800-374-2721, the American Counseling Association at 800-347-6647, the National Association of Social Workers at 800-742-4089).

PUTTING IT IN PRACTICE 2.5

Confidentiality and Its Limits

It's important for therapists to understand the practical implications of ethics and laws pertaining to confidentiality. The following guidelines may help:

1. You must respect the private, personal, and confidential nature of client communications. This means you don't share personal client
(continued)

(*continued*)

information unless you have his or her permission. For example, if someone telephones your office and asks if you're working with Lindsay Lohan, you should simply say something like: "I'm sorry, my policy restricts me from saying whether someone by that name receives services here or not." If the person persists, you may politely add: "If you want to know if a particular person is being seen here, then you need a signed release form so I can legally and ethically provide you with information. Without a signed release form, I cannot even tell you if I've ever heard of anyone named Lindsay Lohan." Additionally, upholding confidentiality requires keeping client records in a secure place.

2. In most states, you might disclose information (or break confidentiality) in the following situations:

   a. You have the client's (or his or her legal representative's) permission.
   b. Based on your evaluation, your client is in clear danger of suicide.
   c. The client has plans to harm someone.
   d. The client is a child, and you have evidence that reasonably leads you to suspect he or she is being sexually or physically abused or neglected.
   e. You have evidence suggesting your client is abusing a minor.
   f. You have evidence suggesting elder abuse is occurring (either from working with an elderly client or because your client discloses information indicating he or she is abusing an elderly person).
   g. You have been ordered by the court to provide client information.

3. Be sure to explain these legal limits of confidentiality at the beginning of every initial session.

Note: If you're interviewing a client who tells you about having engaged in an illegal activity involving an 18- to 64-year-old (i.e., a nonchild and nonelder) in the past—even if that illegal activity involved murder—you're neither required nor allowed to disclose that information.

As stated in professional ethics codes, clinicians inform clients of the legal limits of confidentiality at the outset of the interview. This is done orally and in writing. It's important for clients to clearly understand this basic ground rule in the professional helping relationship.

Imagine a scenario where a client who wasn't initially informed of confidentiality limits begins talking about suicide. At that point, a decision whether or not to break confidentiality would have to be made. The clinician may suddenly feel compelled (and rightly so) to inform the client that he or she will be breaking confidentiality. However, informing clients *after* they begin talking about suicide that this information won't be held in confidence is like changing the rules of a game after it has begun. Clients deserve to know in advance the rules and ethics that guide your decision making. When clients understand confidentiality limitations, they may be selective in their disclosures. This is a natural side effect of the legal and ethical limits of confidentiality.

Undoubtedly, situations arise in which your ethical and/or legal responsibilities are unclear. In such cases, be sure to consult with a colleague or supervisor. For example, if the situation involves whether to report child abuse and you're unclear regarding your legal-ethical responsibilities, ask your supervisor for guidance. If you find your supervisor is unclear regarding the best course of action, contact your local child protection services and inquire, without providing specific identifying information, about your legal and ethical responsibilities. In especially tricky cases, you may want to consult an attorney for legal advice.

Informed Consent

On the surface, informed consent seems to be a simple, self-evident concept. It involves the ethical and sometimes legal mandate to inform clients about the nature of their treatment. Once clients understand the treatment they'll be receiving, they can agree to or refuse treatment.

Considered more fully, it's apparent that authentic informed consent is challenging to offer and obtain. First, for many human service, medical, and mental health providers, it can be difficult to describe client problems and available treatments in a clear and straightforward manner. Often, we speak in professional jargon (e.g., "It looks like you need some systematic desensitization for your phobia."). Additionally, clients are usually in physical or psychological pain. They may consent to anything the professional says will help, even if they don't fully understand the procedure.

As a mental health professional, you have a responsibility to explain your theoretical approach, training, techniques, and likely treatment outcomes to your clients. You must do so in plain language and must welcome interactions and questions from clients who need more time or explanation. Even if you anticipate seeing the client for only one or two interviews, the interview should be explained in a way that allows the client the right to consent to or decline participation. In longer-term therapy, informed consent needs revisiting as counseling continues (and we revisit informed consent in greater detail in Chapter 6).

At the very least, you should provide clients with two or three written paragraphs explaining your background, theoretical orientation, training, and the rationale for your usual techniques. Use of diagnosis, potential inclusion of family members (especially in the case of marital work or work with minors), consultation or supervision practices, policies regarding missed appointments, and the manner in which you can be contacted in an emergency should be included. Many professionals include a statement or two about the counseling process and emotional experiences that might accompany this process (R. Sommers-Flanagan & Sommers-Flanagan, 2007).

A single written document cannot fully satisfy the spirit of informed consent, but it does start things off on the right foot. Written informed consent gives clients the message that they have important rights in the therapy relationship. It also helps educate clients about the therapy process, which has been shown to have a positive effect on counseling outcomes (Katz et al., 2011). Finally, research

Table 2.1 Confidentiality-Related Statements From the American Psychological Association's (2010), American Counseling Association's (2005), and National Association of Social Workers (2008) Ethics Codes

From the American Psychological Association (APA)

Standard 4: Privacy and Confidentiality
4.02 Discussing the Limits of Confidentiality
  (a) Psychologists discuss with persons (including, to the extent feasible, persons who are legally incapable of giving informed consent and their legal representatives) and organizations with whom they establish a scientific or professional relationship (1) the relevant limits of confidentiality and (2) the foreseeable uses of the information generated through their psychological activities. (See also Standard 3.10, Informed Consent.)
  (b) Unless it is not feasible or is contraindicated, the discussion of confidentiality occurs at the outset of the relationship and thereafter as new circumstances may warrant.
  (c) Psychologists who offer services, products, or information via electronic transmission inform clients/patients of the risks to privacy and limits of confidentiality.

From the American Counseling Association (ACA)

Section B: Confidentiality, Privileged Communication, and Privacy
B.1.b. Respect for Privacy
Counselors respect client rights to privacy. Counselors solicit private information from clients only when it is beneficial to the counseling process.
B.1.c. Respect for Confidentiality
Counselors do not share confidential information without client consent or without sound legal or ethical justification.
B.1.d. Explanation of Limitations
At initiation and throughout the counseling process, counselors inform clients of the limitations of confidentiality and seek to identify foreseeable situations in which confidentiality must be breached. (See *A.2.b.*)
B.2. Exceptions
B.2.a. Danger and Legal Requirements
The general requirement that counselors keep information confidential does not apply when disclosure is required to protect clients or identified others from serious and foreseeable harm or when legal requirements demand that confidential information must be revealed. Counselors consult with other professionals when in doubt as to the validity of an exception. Additional considerations apply when addressing end-of-life issues. (See *A.9.c.*)
B.2.b. Contagious, Life-Threatening Diseases
When clients disclose that they have a disease commonly known to be both communicable and life threatening, counselors may be justified in disclosing information to identifiable third parties, if they are known to be at demonstrable and high risk of contracting the disease. Prior to making a disclosure, counselors confirm that there is such a diagnosis and assess the intent of clients to inform the third parties about their disease or to engage in any behaviors that may be harmful to an identifiable third party.

Table 2.1   (*continued*)

From the National Association of Social Workers (NASW)

1.07 Privacy and Confidentiality

   (a) Social workers should respect clients' right to privacy. Social workers should not solicit private information from clients unless it is essential to providing services or conducting social work evaluation or research. Once private information is shared, standards of confidentiality apply.

   (b) Social workers may disclose confidential information when appropriate with valid consent from a client or a person legally authorized to consent on behalf of a client.

   (c) Social workers should protect the confidentiality of all information obtained in the course of professional service, except for compelling professional reasons. The general expectation that social workers will keep information confidential does not apply when disclosure is necessary to prevent serious, foreseeable, and imminent harm to a client or other identifiable person. In all instances, social workers should disclose the least amount of confidential information necessary to achieve the desired purpose; only information that is directly relevant to the purpose for which the disclosure is made should be revealed.

Information in this table is excerpted from the APA, ACA, and NASW ethics codes. Their respective codes can be viewed in their entirety at: http://www.apa.org/ethics/code/index.aspx http://www.counseling.org/knowledge-center/ethics http://www.socialworkers.org/pubs/code/code.asp

suggests that well-written, readable, and personable consent forms increase the client's impression of therapist expertise and attractiveness (Wagner, Davis, & Handelsman, 1998).

Documentation Procedures

Most of us have heard the saying, "If it isn't written down, it didn't happen." (To really get the point, try imagining a grim-faced attorney shaking her head as you explain that you didn't have time to write the case notes.)

Note taking and responsible documentation aren't usually the highlights of anyone's day. On the other hand, failure to do requisite documentation can ruin your day. Professionals need to clearly and carefully record what happens in treatment. There are many positive aspects of taking good notes, including the fact that you're more likely to remember the details of what was said and planned. Reviewing progress notes can facilitate the counseling process. In addition, when asked to send your notes to another professional or if your client wishes to review the notes, having legible and coherent notes available will feel very good. If your interactions with the client take unexpected turns, you can go back through your notes and perhaps see patterns you had overlooked. Finally, on a less positive note, if things don't go well with a client and you're accused of malpractice, your notes become an essential part of your defense.

Most experienced therapists have a favorite note-taking format. Many use some rendition of the S-O-A-P acronym, which in some clinics stands for subjective, objective, assessment, and plan. S-O-A-P guides the note taker to document the following:

S: The clients' subjective descriptions of their distress.

O: The therapist's objective observations of the client's dress, presentation, and so on.

A: The therapist's assessment of progress.

P: The plan for next time, or comments regarding progress on the overall treatment plan.

The form of note taking you use is less important than regularity, inclusion of the right materials, and neutrality (see Table 2.2). Obviously, everything discussed during a session cannot be documented in the client's file. Therapists must discern important or pivotal information from each session and record it in succinct, professional ways that are neither insulting nor overly vague. A colleague of ours recommends following the ABCs of documentation—Accurate, Brief, Clear (D. Scherer, personal communication, October, 1998).

Documentation, once it exists, must be stored responsibly. At the least, it should be filed in a locking file cabinet or locked office, safe from curious perusal by those coming and going in the setting. The handling of such records is governed by federal law, as in the Health Insurance Portability and Accountability Act (HIPAA) for any services that might include health insurance billing, and the Family Education Rights and Privacy Act (FERPA) for any records related to public education.

The length of time records are kept depends on your setting, ethical guidelines, and state law. For instance, in professional practice settings, guidelines suggest that complete materials be saved from between 7 and 12 years. The file may then be reduced to a summary sheet (American Psychological Association, 2010). Because documentation has such serious clinical and legal implications, make sure

---

Table 2.2 Example of SOAP Note

S: Joyce stated: "My head hurts, my nose is stuffy, and that's why I'm so F-ing irritated." She also said, "I wouldn't be so worn out and crabby except for those Russian teachers dancing so late. I can't say no. I wanted to go home, but they were fun and cute. It's my same old pattern."

O: Joyce arrived on time but appeared tired and distracted. She was dressed in her jeans and sweater but kept a scarf wrapped around her neck the entire session. She sneezed and rubbed her nose. She spoke of wishing to have more peace and quiet in her life, but feeling unable to set limits without feeling guilty. She appeared to be sincerely distressed, both by her tiredness and her inability to set limits.

A: During the session, Joyce achieved further insight into the reasons she gives in so easily to the demands of others. She was able to begin making a schedule that gave her some free time every other day. Joyce's continued struggle with her need to please others was evident, but also, she seemed determined to gain insight and make changes.

P: Joyce will monitor her use of time in her notebook. We will analyze time use and further clarify goals for balance. She made a goal of saying no to at least one social request and will report back on this next week.

you understand the documentation, storage, and access policies and procedures of your state ethics board, professional ethics code, and agency.

Stress Management

All mental health providers are exposed to high stress and stress levels are particularly high for student clinicians (Lushington & Luscri, 2001). It's especially common for students to have fears about making mistakes and damaging clients. These fears have a basis in reality. Because you're human, you will make mistakes, and your mistakes may cause or increase client distress. The challenge is to recover from mistakes and use them for learning and growth. Sometimes, your mistakes can even be humanizing for clients, because clients realize that even their professional therapist isn't perfect.

Shea (1998), a nationally renowned psychiatrist and workshop leader, commented on mistakes he makes while conducting interviews:

> Mistakes were made, but I make mistakes every time I interview. Interviews and humans are far too complicated not to make mistakes . . . . With every mistake, I try to learn. (p. 694)

We knew one student therapist who reported high anxiety and a tendency to pick at the skin around the edges of his fingers. During his first session, he picked at his fingers until he began feeling some moisture, which prompted him to think that he was so nervous his fingers were sweating. Eventually, he peeked down at his hands and discovered that, much to his horror, one of his fingers had begun to bleed. He spent the rest of the session trying to cover up the blood and worrying that the client had seen his bleeding finger. Though this example is unusual, it illustrates how nervousness and anxiety can interfere with clinical interviewing. Managing stress effectively so that it doesn't interfere with your sessions is an important professional issue.

Therapists may be affected by stress before, during, or after the interview. Stress reactions can result in physical, mental, emotional, social, or spiritual symptoms. Developing lifelong habits of self-care that help reduce the impact of your stressful professional work is strongly recommended (Norcross & Guy, 2007; Skovholt & Trotter-Mathison, 2011). Stress management readings are included in the Suggested Readings and Resources at the end of this chapter.

SUMMARY

Clinical interviewing involves a systematic modification of normal social interactions. Although the relationship established between therapists and client is a friendly one, it's much different from friendship. Clinical interviews serve a dual function: to evaluate and to help clients.

Clinical interviewing is defined in different ways by different writers. Our definition includes the following components: (a) A professional relationship between therapist and client is established; (b) therapist and client work to establish and achieve mutually agreed on goals; (c) there are verbal and nonverbal interactions during which the therapist applies active listening skills and psychological techniques to evaluate, understand, and help clients achieve goals; and (d) sensitivity, on the part of the therapist, to many factors, including culture, personality style, setting, attitudes, and goals.

It's important for therapists to have self-awareness and insight. There are many forms of self-awareness, including physical, psychosocial, developmental, and cultural. Therapists should be aware of their preconceived biases and beliefs about themselves and others during the interviewing process.

Before meeting with clients, therapists consider a number of practical, professional, and ethical factors. Practical factors include the room, seating arrangements, office clutter and décor, note taking, and video- and audiorecording. Professional and ethical issues include self-presentation, time-boundary maintenance, confidentiality, informed consent, documentation procedures, and therapist stress management. These issues are basic and foundational; they support the interviewing activity, and without them the entire interviewing structure may suffer or collapse.

SUGGESTED READINGS AND RESOURCES

Hagedorn, W. B. (2005). *Counselor self-awareness and self-exploration of religious and spiritual beliefs: Know thyself*. Alexandria, VA: American Counseling Association.

This book is a nice resource for exploring your self-awareness of your religious or spiritual beliefs and how they might influence you in your counselor role.

Kabat-Zinn, J. (1995). *Wherever you go there you are: Mindfulness meditation in everyday life*. New York, NY: Hyperion.

Mindfulness meditation is an excellent stress management technique for clients and counselors. Kabat-Zinn writes in an easy-to-digest style that makes for relaxing reading.

Norcross, J. C., & Guy, J. (2007). *Leaving it at the office: A guide to psychotherapist self-care*. New York, NY: Guilford Press.

This is a guidebook for therapists on how to focus on the positive parts of being a psychotherapist, engage in healthy physical and cognitive self-care, and set reasonable personal boundaries on psychotherapy practice.

Skovholt, T. M., & Trotter-Mathison, M. J. (2011). *The resilient practitioner: Burnout prevention and self-care strategies for counselors, therapists, teachers, and health professionals*. New York, NY: Taylor & Francis Group.

This book is designed to help individuals in the highly interpersonal professions develop ongoing self-care skills and practice. Each chapter ends with self-reflective exercises designed to help with self-care skill acquisition.

Sommers-Flanagan, R., & Sommers-Flanagan, J. (2007). *Becoming an ethical helping professional: Cultural and philosophical foundations*. Hoboken, NJ: Wiley.

If you haven't yet had a course on ethics, it's a good idea to have a basic ethics text available to read and use for ongoing consultation.

Zeer, D., & Klein, M. (2000). *Office yoga: Simple stretches for busy people*. San Francisco, CA: Chronicle Books.

This short book provides basic yoga stretching postures for busy professionals. It includes illustrations and easy to implement stress-reducing stretching exercises.

PART TWO

Listening and Relationship Development

Basic Attending, Listening, and Action Skills

CHAPTER OBJECTIVES

For the most part, we all know a good listener when we meet one. However, it's less easy to figure out exactly what good listeners do to make it easier for others to talk openly and freely. This chapter analyzes the mechanics of effective attending and listening skills.

After reading this chapter, you will understand:

- The difference between positive and negative attending behaviors.
- How ethnocultural background and diversity can affect how clients respond to attending and listening behaviors.
- How and why therapists use nondirective listening behaviors, including: silence, paraphrasing, clarification, reflection of feeling, and summarization.
- The natural inclination many therapists have toward reassuring clients.
- How and why therapists use directive listening behaviors, including: interpretive reflection of feeling, interpretation, feeling validation, and confrontation.

Human communication involves sending and receiving information. When someone sends out information, your goal is to be a good listener, or receiver. It sounds simple enough, but very little about human communication is simple. Even if your job is to be the listener and you manage to keep your mouth shut, you're still simultaneously sending information. This is part of what makes human communication so complex. Communication professors often express this complexity by stating: *You cannot not communicate*. Human communication involves constant and interactive sending and receiving of verbal and nonverbal messages.

Think about it: No matter what you say (even if you say nothing), you're communicating something. This applies to both verbal and nonverbal communication. Recall a time when you were talking with a friend on your phone. Perhaps you said something and your statement was followed by silence. What did you think at that moment? Most of us tend to fill in the blank and conclude the pause in communication meant something. Whether that meaning was communicated intentionally may or may not be important.

> Meryt listened in stillness, watching my face as I recounted my mother's history, and the story.... My friend did not move or utter a sound, but her face revealed the workings of her heart, showing me horror, rage, sympathy, compassion.
>
> —*Anita Diamant*, The Red Tent *(1997)*

The preceding quotation aptly illustrates the power of nonverbal attending behavior. The listener doesn't move or utter a sound, but she still manages to communicate understanding and empathy (or at least the speaker interprets the listener's facial expressions as empathic).

Similarly, your clients' first impressions of you will include what they observe as they're speaking to you. Attending behavior is a message to clients—a message that, ideally, is interpreted as an invitation to speak freely. This chapter focuses not only on how to look, sound, and act like a good listener—but also on how to really hear what your clients have to say.

It may seem disingenuous to suggest that you practice *looking like* a good listener. Nevertheless, good therapists consciously and deliberately engage in specific behaviors that most clients interpret as signs of interest and concern. These behaviors are referred to in the interviewing and counseling literature as *attending behaviors* (Ivey, Normington, Miller, Morrill, & Haase, 1968).

ATTENDING BEHAVIOR

Ivey, Ivey, and Zalaquett (2010) described *attending behavior* as the foundation of interviewing. To be successful, therapists must pay attention to clients in overt ways that communicate respect and interest. If therapists fail to look, sound, and act attentive, they won't have many clients. Most clients drop out of counseling if they don't think their therapist is listening. The importance of positive attending behaviors to successful therapy is recognized across disciplines and theoretical orientations; it is spectacularly uncontroversial (Akhtar, 2007; Cormier, Nurius, & Osborn, 2012; Wright & Davis, 1994).

Attending behavior is primarily nonverbal. Anthropologist and cross-cultural researcher, Edward T. Hall (1966) claimed that communication is 10% verbal and 90% "a hidden cultural grammar" (p. 12). Others have suggested that 65% or more of a message's meaning is nonverbal (Birdwhistell, 1970). With respect to clinical interviewing, it's likely that if verbal and nonverbal messages are in conflict, the client will believe the nonverbal message. This is why being aware of and effectively using nonverbal channels is so important when communicating with clients.

Positive Attending Behavior

Positive attending behaviors open up communication and encourage free expression. In contrast, negative attending behaviors inhibit expression. When it comes to identifying positive and negative attending behaviors, there are few universals. This is because cultural background and previous experiences affect whether clients view a particular attending behavior as positive or negative. It's also due to the fact that nonverbal signals, like spoken language, vary between cultures. What works with one client may not work with the next. Therefore, the way you pay attention to clients will vary to some degree depending on each client's individual needs, personality style, and family and cultural background.

Ivey, Ivey, and Zalaquett (2010) have described four categories of attending behavior that have been studied, to some extent, cross-culturally. These behaviors are described as the three Vs + B of listening. They include:

1. Visual/eye contact
2. Vocal qualities
3. Verbal tracking
4. Body language: Attentive (Ivey, Ivey, & Zalaquett, 2010, p. 65)

Visual/Eye Contact

There is considerable variation in what different cultures define as appropriate eye contact. Individuals also vary greatly in their eye-contact patterns. For some therapists, sustaining eye contact during an interview is natural. For others, it can be difficult; there may be a tendency to look down or away from the client's eyes because of respect, shyness, or cultural dynamics. The same is true for clients; some prefer more intense and direct eye contact; others will prefer looking at the floor, the wall, or anywhere but into your eyes.

Generally, therapists should maintain eye contact most of the time with White clients. In contrast, Native American, Asian, and some African American clients may prefer less eye contact (for more information, see *Multicultural Highlight* 3.1). With most clients, it's appropriate to maintain more constant eye contact as they speak and less constant eye contact when you speak.

MULTICULTURAL HIGHLIGHT 3.1

Eye Contact!: Diverse Perspectives

In his work with the Inuit Indians of the Central Canadian Arctic, Allen Ivey, founder of the microcounseling approach, observed that clients were less comfortable with direct eye contact. This led him to use a more side-by-side seating arrangement with the Inuit people and resulted in greater comfort and rapport during interviews (Ivey, Ivey, & Zalaquett, 2010). This and similar observations have contributed to strong cautions in making interpretations about the meaning of eye contact. Never assume that minimal eye contact indicates poor self-esteem, dishonesty, disrespect, or anything other than normal cultural variation in customary eye contact.

Variable eye contact norms provide an excellent example of both cultural and individual variations in interpersonal behavior. This helps clinicians continue to develop awareness about exceptions to normative

(continued)

(*continued*)

dominant culture behavior and differences within particular cultural groups, or even subgroups. In the process of writing this new edition, we received comments from two Black/African American professors. Each of these professionals communicated different experiences with eye contact. Here's what they wrote:

Comments from Teah Moore, PhD, Assistant Professor, Fort Valley State University, Robins, GA: "I had a supervisor who would stare you right in the eyes while talking to you. Normal people glance away every once in a while but not her. It was distracting and unnerving to talk with her. As an African American I found myself looking away or finding a spot on her shirt to stare at. I heard about the same experience from other African Americans." (Teah Moore, personal communication, August 11, 2012)

Comments from Kimberly Johnson, EdD, Instructor, DeVry University Online: "As a Black female, I was taught to always look a person in the eye when speaking. To not do so displays lack of confidence, untruth, shyness, and/or uncertainty. Eye contact is requested or solicited in our culture when focus is required. Culturally we believe the eyes tell a story regarding interpretation." (Kimberly Johnson, personal communication, July 28, 2012)

Even though two people can appear very similar, based on surface characteristics, they may have experienced different subcultures and family systems. They also may have different educational and relationship experiences. Individual experiences—even within the same culture—can result in beliefs and perspectives that range from subtly to very obviously diverse.

This is also a great example of what Stanley Sue (2006) referred to as "Dynamic Sizing." Dynamic sizing involves determining whether a particular cultural characteristic applies to or "fits" for an individual member of that culture. Helping professionals must be very careful about taking cultural knowledge they have and then inappropriately generalizing it to the client(s) with whom they're working. Sue and Zane (2009) articulated this point:

> We believe that cultural knowledge and techniques generated by this knowledge are frequently applied in inappropriate ways. The problem is especially apparent when therapists and others act on insufficient knowledge or overgeneralize what they have learned about culturally dissimilar groups. (p. 5)

In conclusion: Throughout your professional life, continue to be open to the possibility that the next client you see may well surprise you in one way or another, just as we found the beliefs and perspectives of two Black/African American professional women to be both surprising and culturally enlightening.

Body Language

Body language is another important dimension of human communication. Two aspects of body language are known technically as *kinesics* and *proxemics* (Knapp, Hall, & Horgan, 2013). *Kinesics* has to do with variables associated with physical features and physical movement of any body part, such as eyes, face, head, hands, legs, and shoulders. *Proxemics* refers to personal space and environmental variables such as the distance between two people and whether any objects are between them. As you know from personal experience, a great deal is communicated through simple, and sometimes subtle, body movements. When we discussed client-therapist seating arrangements in Chapter 2, we were analyzing proxemic variables and their potential effect on the interview.

Positive body language includes the following (derived from Walters, 1980):

- Leaning slightly toward the client.
- Maintaining a relaxed but attentive posture.
- Placing your feet and legs in an unobtrusive position.
- Keeping your hand gestures unobtrusive and smooth.
- Minimizing the number of other movements.
- Matching your facial expressions to your feelings or the client's feelings.
- Sitting approximately one arm's length from the client.
- Arranging the furniture to draw you and the client together, not to erect a barrier.

These positive body language examples are based on mainstream cultural norms in Western cultures. In practice, you'll find both individual and cultural variations on these behaviors.

Mirroring, as an aspect of body language, involves synchrony or consistency between therapist and client. When mirroring occurs, the therapist's physical movements and verbal activity is in sync with the client's. Mirroring is a relatively advanced nonverbal technique that potentially enhances rapport and empathy, but when done poorly can be disastrous (Banaka, 1971; Maurer & Tindall, 1983; Rand, 2006). If mirroring is obvious or overdone, clients may think the therapist is mocking them. Therefore, intentional mirroring is best used in moderation. Generally, mirroring is more of a product of rapport and effective communication than a causal factor in establishing it.

Vocal Qualities

In Chapter 2, we recommended having friends or classmates listen to and describe your voice. If you followed this advice, your friends gave feedback on your vocal quality or paralinguistics (as it's referred to in the communication field). *Paralinguistics* consists of voice loudness, pitch, rate, rhythm, inflection, and fluency. Think about how these vocal variables might affect clients. Interpersonal influence is often determined not so much by *what* you say, but by *how* you say it.

Effective therapists use vocal qualities to enhance rapport, communicate interest and empathy, and emphasize specific issues or conflicts. As with body language, it's often useful to follow the client's lead, speaking in a volume and tone similar to the client. Meier and Davis (2011) refer to this practice as "pacing the client" (p. 9).

On the other hand, therapists can use voice tone and speech rate to lead clients toward particular content or feelings. For example, speaking in a soft, slow, and gentle tone encourages clients to explore feelings more thoroughly, and speaking with increased rate and volume may help convince them of your credibility or expertise (Ekman, 2001).

Although people perceive emotions through all sensory modalities, some research suggests that people discern emotions more accurately from auditory than from visual input (Snyder, 1974). This finding underscores the importance of vocal qualities in emotional expression and perception. Actors use their entire bodies, including their voices, when portraying various emotions. Your voice quality may influence your client's emotional expression.

Verbal Tracking

It's crucial for therapists to accurately track what clients say. Although eye contact, body language, and vocal quality are important, they do not, by themselves, represent effective listening. Therapists also demonstrate they are tracking the content of their clients' speech by occasionally repeating key words and phrases. In most cases, clients won't know if you're really hearing what they're saying unless you prove it through accurate verbal tracking.

To use Meier and Davis's (2011) terminology again, verbal tracking involves pacing the client by sticking closely with client speech content (as well as speech volume and tone, as mentioned previously). Verbal tracking involves only restating or summarizing what the client has already said. Verbal tracking doesn't include your personal or professional opinion about what your client said.

Accurate verbal tracking can be challenging, especially when clients are talkative. Also, you may become distracted by what the client is saying and drift into your own thoughts. For example, a client may mention a range of topics including New York City, abortion, drugs, AIDS, divorce, or other topics about which you may have personal opinions or emotional reactions. To verbally track effectively, internal and external personal reactions must be minimized; your focus must remain primarily on the client, not yourself. This rule is also true when it comes to more advanced verbal tracking techniques, such as clarification, paraphrasing, and summarization.

Ivey, Ivey, and Zalaquett (2010) consider verbal tracking to have three major functions.

1. *To maintain the focus on what clients are talking about.* This can help clients continue to elaborate their personal narrative.
2. *For therapists to self-reflect on what they're choosing to verbally track.* This is important because therapists and counselors tend to listen to some things and ignore others, and observing yourself can help you develop awareness of your own patterns.
3. *To selectively attend or not attend to client verbal content.* Sometimes therapists pay too much attention to unhealthy, problem-saturated client talk. Because verbal tracking involves giving attention and because giving attention often is a positive reinforcement, therapists may encourage clients to talk about positive qualities instead of negative experiences by verbally tracking positive comments and not verbally tracking negative comments.

Negative Attending Behavior

It's possible to get too much of a good thing. This is equally true with regard to positive attending behaviors. It can be disconcerting when someone listens too intensely. Therapists should avoid overusing the following behaviors:

- *Head nods.* Excessive head nods can be bothersome. After a while, clients may look away from therapists just to avoid watching their heads bob. After spending time with an overly attentive therapist, one child stated, "It looked like her head was attached to a wobbly spring instead of a neck."
- *Saying "Uh huh."* This is an overused attending behavior. Both novices and professionals can fall into this pattern. While listening to someone for 2 minutes, they may utter as many as 20 "uh huhs." Our response to excessive "uh huhs" (and the response of many clients) is to simply stop talking to force the person to say something besides "uh huh."
- *Eye contact.* Too much eye contact can cause people to feel scrutinized or intimidated. Imagine having a therapist relentlessly stare at you while you're talking about something deeply personal or while you're crying. Eye contact is crucial, but too much can be overwhelming. Of course, the exact meaning and formula varies with culture.
- *Repeating the client's last word.* Some therapists use a verbal tracking technique that involves repeating a single key word, often the last word, from what the client has said. Overusing this pattern can cause clients to feel overanalyzed, because therapists reduce 30- or 60-second statements to a single-word response.
- *Mirroring.* Excessive or awkward attempts at mirroring can be damaging. We recall a psychiatrist who used this technique with disturbed psychiatric inpatients. At times, his results were successful; at other times, the patients became angry and aggressive because they thought he was mocking them. Similarly, clients sometimes worry that counselors use secret techniques to exert special control over them. They may notice if you're trying to get into a physical position similar to theirs and wonder if you're using a psychological ploy to manipulate them. The result is usually resistance and pursuit. Clients begin moving into new positions, the therapist notices and changes position to establish synchrony, and the client moves again. If you record a session, this is especially entertaining to watch in fast-forward mode.

Additionally, research suggests that clients perceive the following therapist behaviors as negative (Cormier et al., 2012; Smith-Hanen, 1977):

- Making infrequent eye contact.
- Turning 45 degrees or more away from the client.
- Leaning back from the waist up.
- Crossing legs away from the client.
- Folding arms across the chest.

As suggested in the previous chapter, it's often difficult to know how you're coming across to others. To ensure that you and your colleagues are using primarily positive rather than negative attending behaviors, take time to give and receive constructive feedback in these areas (see *Putting It in Practice* 3.1).

PUTTING IT IN PRACTICE 3.1

Giving Constructive Feedback

Feedback regarding attending and listening skills is essential to developing counseling skills (J. Sommers-Flanagan & Heck, 2012). Specific and concrete feedback regarding eye contact, body language, vocal qualities, and verbal tracking can be obtained through in-class activities, demonstrations, role plays, and audio or video presentations. For example, feedback such as "You looked into your client's eyes with only two or three breaks, and although you fidgeted somewhat with your pencil, it didn't appear to interfere with the interview" is clear and specific (and helpful). General and positive comments (e.g., "Good job!") are pleasant and encouraging, but should be used in combination with more specific feedback; it's important to know what was good about your job.

Sometimes, class activities or role plays don't go well and negative feedback is appropriate. Give negative feedback in a constructive or corrective manner. (This means the feedback shouldn't focus so much on what you did poorly, but also identify what you could do to perform the skill correctly.) For example, constructive negative or corrective feedback might sound like this: "When you made eye contact, the interviewee seemed to brighten and become more engaged. So, at least for this client, it might be helpful to maintain your eye contact a little longer."

Getting negative feedback is a sensitive issue because it can be painful to hear that you haven't performed perfectly. General negative comments such as "Terrible job!" are unhelpful. To be constructive, negative feedback should be specific and concrete. Other guidelines for giving and receiving negative feedback include:

- Role players should evaluate themselves first.
- After a class interviewing activity, students should be asked directly whether they'd like feedback. If they say no, then no feedback should be given.
- The reason you're in an interviewing class is to improve your interviewing skills. Though hard to hear, constructive feedback is useful for skill development. Don't think of it as criticism, but as an opportunity to learn from mistakes and improve your counseling skills.
- Feedback should never be uniformly negative. Everyone engages in positive and negative attending behaviors. If you happen to be the type who easily sees what's wrong, but has trouble offering praise, impose the following rule on yourself: If you can't offer at least a little positive feedback, don't offer any at all.
- It helps to practice giving negative feedback in a positive manner. For example, instead of saying, "Your body was stiff as a board," try saying, "You'd be more effective if you relaxed your arms and shoulders more."

- Extremely negative feedback is the responsibility of the instructor and should be given during a private, individual supervision session.
- Try to remember the disappointing fact that no one performs perfectly, including the teacher or professor.

Individual and Cultural Differences

Many individual and cultural differences affect the interview. These differences include, but are not limited to: (a) gender, (b) social class, (c) ethnicity, (d) sexual orientation, (e) age, and (f) physical disabilities (Fontes, 2008). Every client is part of a distinct subculture with associated behavior patterns, social norms, and individual/collective identity (Hays, 2008, 2013). Obviously, attending behaviors that are effective with gang-affiliated youth differ from attending behaviors used with depressed middle-aged adults. A working knowledge of a different social and cultural norms helps therapists attend more effectively (see *Multicultural Highlight* 3.1).

Individual Differences

If you were to invite 20 people, one by one, into your office for an interview, you would discover that each person was optimally comfortable with slightly different amounts of eye contact, personal space, mirroring, and other attending behaviors. The guidelines discussed previously are based on averages and probabilities. For example, if you interviewed Italian American clients, you might find them, on average, desiring closer seating arrangements than clients with Scandinavian roots. However, this isn't the whole story. There also will be times when a *particular* Italian American prefers greater interpersonal distance than a *particular* Scandinavian. If you expect all Italian Americans, all Scandinavians, all African Americans, all women, and so on to be similar, you're stereotyping. Differences between individuals are often greater than the average difference among particular groups, cultural or otherwise. Therefore, although you should be aware of potential differences between members of various groups, you should suspend judgment until you've explored the issue with each individual through observation and direct discussion as needed.

Cultural Differences

Although individual differences will always be a central consideration, there are also significant cultural differences in normative attending behaviors. Further, within cultures, there are expected differences for interactions between and/or with men, women, children, and elders. Effective therapists pay close attention to client cultural signs and signals.

Sometimes, the cultural differences or preferences are obvious. A Latina counselor wouldn't need to be a sleuth to notice that she had a different cultural background than a young Chinese immigrant. Whether subtle or obvious, noticing cultural differences is just the beginning. Effective therapists adjust attending behaviors based on both knowledge of various cultures and on the clients' reactions to the attending behaviors. For example, when interviewing Mexican American clients, it may be appropriate to explicitly engage in small talk (charlar) and use a personal and friendly approach (personalismo; Gallardo, Yeh, Trimble, & Parham, 2011). It's important to take time to learn about other cultures and adjust your initial attending behaviors in ways that are likely to show cultural sensitivity (for much more on this topic, see Chapter 11).

MOVING BEYOND ATTENDING

Perhaps someday, someone will develop an authoritative guide to every potential therapist behavior, complete with a structured format for determining which behavior should be used at which time during an interview. This will then be programmed into the robot therapist who will enact the perfect clinical interview. Or maybe not. We believe that the unique relationship between therapist and client—and the interviewing process itself—is too dynamic for any such formula. Differences among clients make it impossible to reliably predict their reactions to various interviewing responses. Some clients react positively to therapist behaviors that might seem inadequate or awkward; others react negatively to what might be considered a perfect paraphrase. This next section breaks down nondirective interviewing behaviors into distinct categories, providing general guidelines regarding when and how to use these behaviors or responses. Effectively applying a particular response constitutes the artistic side of interviewing, requiring sensitivity and experience as well as other intangibles, such as having patience with yourself.

Not knowing what to say or when to say it can be disconcerting for beginning therapists, but, truthfully, no one always knows the correct response. For the most part, experienced therapists become more comfortable with long pauses resulting from not knowing what to say or do next. Meier and Davis (2011) advised: "When you don't know what to say, say nothing" (p. 11). And Luborsky (1984) noted: "Listen . . . with an open receptiveness to what the patient is saying. If you're not sure of what is happening and what your next response should be, listen more and it will come to you" (p. 91).

Margaret Gibbs (1984) expressed the distress many new therapists experience in her chapter "The Therapist as Imposter" in Claire Brody's book *Women Therapists Working with Women*:

> Once I began my work as a therapist . . . I began to have . . . doubts. Certainly my supervisors seemed to approve of my work, and my patients improved as much as anybody else's did. But what was I actually supposed to be doing? I knew the dynamic, client-centered and behavioral theories, but I continued to read and search for answers. I felt there was something I should know, something my instructors had neglected to tell me, much as cooks are said to withhold one important ingredient of their recipes when they relinquish them. (p. 22)

The missing ingredient Gibbs was seeking could have been experience. Ironically, experience doesn't make therapists sure of having the *right* thing to say. Instead, it helps take the edge off the panic associated with not knowing what to say. Experience allows therapists the confidence required to wait; they know they will eventually think of something useful to say. In addition, experience helps therapists have more confidence. Nonetheless, part of being an honest professional is to admit and tolerate the fact that sometimes you don't know what to say. Gibbs ended her chapter with the following:

> Strategies can cover up, but not resolve, the ambiguities of clinical judgments and interventions. Imposter doubts need to be shared, not suppressed, in the classroom as elsewhere. [There is] evidence to support the idea that uncertainty and humility about the accuracy of our clinical inferences is an aid to increased accuracy. I find this notion enormously comforting. (p. 32)

Being comfortable with uncertainty and developing humility is central to the process of clinical interviewing.

Generally, Robinson's (1950) organizational format is used in the following sections. We begin with therapist behaviors that are considered to be more nondirective and proceed along a continuum toward increasingly directive or therapist-centered behaviors. Therapist behaviors are categorized into three groups:

1. Nondirective listening behaviors (e.g., paraphrase; see Table 3.1).
2. Directive listening behaviors (e.g., interpretation; see Table 3.2).
3. Directive action behaviors (e.g., advice; see Table 4.2).

Table 3.1 Summary of Nondirective Listening Behaviors and Their Usual Effects

Listening Response	Description	Primary Intent/Effect
Attending behavior	Eye contact, leaning forward, head nods, facial expressions, etc.	Facilitates or inhibits spontaneous client talk.
Silence	Absence of verbal activity.	Places focus on clients to talk. Allows "cooling off" time. Allows clinician to consider next response.
Paraphrase	Reflection or rephrasing of the content of what the client said.	Assures clients you hear them accurately and allows them to hear what they said.
Clarification	Attempted restating of a client's message, preceded or followed by a closed question (e.g., 'Do I have that right?').	Clarifies unclear client statements and verifies the accuracy of what the clinician heard.
Reflection of feeling	Restatement or rephrasing of clearly stated emotion.	Enhances clients' experience of empathy and encourages further emotional expression.
Summarization	Brief review of several topics covered during a session.	Enhances recall of session content and ties together or integrates themes covered in a session.

NONDIRECTIVE LISTENING BEHAVIORS

Nondirective listening behaviors encourage clients to talk freely and openly about whatever they want to talk about. Similar to attending behaviors, these techniques are not intended to direct or lead clients. Instead, they reflect central client messages back to the client. Nondirective listening behaviors are often thought of as techniques designed to facilitate client exploration of personal issues (Hill, 2009).

Even nondirective behaviors may influence clients to talk about particular topics. There are at least two reasons for this. First, therapists may inadvertently, or purposefully, pay closer attention when clients discuss certain issues. For example, perhaps a therapist wants a client to talk about his relationship with his mother. By using eye contact, head nodding, verbal tracking, and positive facial expressions whenever the client mentions his mother, the therapist can direct the client toward "mother talk." Conversely, the therapist can look uninterested and use fewer verbal tracking responses whenever the client shifts topics and discusses something other than his mother. From a behavioral perspective, the therapist is using social reinforcement to influence the client's verbal behavior. This selective attending probably occurs frequently in clinical practice. After all, psychoanalysts are more interested in mother talk, person-centered therapists are more interested in feeling talk, and behaviorists are more interested in specific, concrete behavioral talk.

Second, clients talk about such a wide range of topics that it's impossible to pay equal attention to every issue. Selection is necessary. For example, imagine a case in which a young woman begins a session by saying:

> We didn't have much money when I was growing up and I suppose that frustrated my father. He beat us five kids all the time. He's dead now, but to this day, my mom says we needed the discipline. But I hated it then and swore I'd never be like him. Now that I'm grown and have kids of my own, I'm doing okay, but sometimes I feel I need to discipline my kids more and harder . . . do you know what I mean?

Imagine you're the therapist for this case. Which of the many issues this woman brought up would you focus on? And remember, all this—being poor, being beaten by her father, her father's death, having a mom who continues to claim that your client needed to be beaten, swearing that she never wants to be like her father, doing okay now, feeling like she needs to discipline her children more severely, and more—was expressed in the session's first 20 seconds.

Which topic did you focus on? Aside from indicating something about your personal values or theoretical orientation, selecting only one topic for a paraphrase or head nodding response is directive. To be truly nondirective, you would need to respond equally to every piece of the entire message, which is unrealistic. Therefore, because you'll selectively respond to what your client says, you should work to be aware of the powerful influence even supposedly nondirective behaviors have on what clients choose to talk about.

Silence

In some ways, silence is the most nondirective of all listening behaviors. Though simple and nondirective, silence is also a powerful therapist response. It takes time for most therapists and clients to get comfortable with silence. As the following excerpt from Edgar Allan Poe's *Silence: A Fable* (1985) suggests, silence can be frightening.

> Hurriedly, he raised his head from his hand, and stood forth upon the rock and listened. But there was no voice throughout the vast illimitable desert, and the characters upon the rock were silence. And the man shuddered and turned his face away, and fled afar off in haste so that I beheld him no more. (p. 127)

Silence can frighten both therapists and clients. Most people feel awkward about silence in social settings and strive to keep conversations alive. Lewis Thomas (1974) wrote in *The Lives of the Cell*, "Nature abhors a long silence" (p. 22).

On the other hand, when used appropriately, silence can be soothing. The Tao Te Ching states: "Stillness and tranquility set things in order in the universe" (Schwartz, 2008, p. 182). Much can be accomplished in stillness and silence. Although the primary function of silence is to encourage client talk, silence may also allow clients to recover from or reflect on what they've just said. In addition, silence allows therapists time to consider and intentionally select a response, rather than rushing into one. However, a word of caution: Therapists who begin sessions with silence and continue using silence liberally, without explaining the purpose of their silence, run the risk of scaring clients away. When therapists are silent, great pressure is placed on clients to speak and client anxiety begins to mount. Clients may wonder why they should pay to see a therapist who simply sits in silence throughout the session.

Silence is a major tool used by psychoanalytic psychotherapists to facilitate free association. Effective psychoanalytic therapists, however, explain the concept of free association to their clients before using it. They explain that psychoanalytic therapy involves primarily the client's free expression, followed by occasional comments or interpretations by the therapist. Explaining therapy or interviewing procedures to clients is always important, but especially so when therapist's are using potentially anxiety-provoking techniques, such as silence (Meier & Davis, 2011).

As a beginning therapist it can be interesting to try experimenting with silence (see *Putting It in Practice* 3.2). Consider the following guidelines:

- When a client or role-play client pauses after making a statement or after hearing your paraphrase, let a few seconds pass rather than jumping in immediately with further verbal interaction. Given the opportunity, clients can move naturally into very important material without guidance or urging.
- As you're sitting silently, waiting for your client to resume speaking, tell yourself that this is the client's time for self-expression, not your time to prove you can be useful.
- Try not to get into a rut regarding your use of silence. When silence comes, sometimes wait for the client to speak next and other times break the silence yourself.
- Avoid using silence if you believe your client is confused, experiencing an acute emotional crisis, or psychotic. Excessive silence and the anxiety it provokes can exacerbate these conditions.

- If you feel uncomfortable during silent periods, use attending skills and look expectantly toward clients. This helps them understand that it's their turn to talk.
- If clients appear uncomfortable with silence, you may give them instructions to free associate (i.e., tell them "Just say whatever comes to mind."). Or you may want to use an empathic reflection (e.g., "It's hard to decide what to say next.").
- Remember, sometimes silence is the most therapeutic response available.
- Read the published interview by Carl Rogers (Meador & Rogers, 1984) listed at the end of this chapter. It includes excellent examples of how to handle silence from a person-centered perspective.
- Remember to monitor your body and face while being silent. There is a vast difference between a cold silence and an accepting, warm silence. Much of this difference results from body language and an interior attitude that welcomes the silence.

PUTTING IT IN PRACTICE 3.2

Getting Comfortable With Silence

Dealing with silences during an interview can be uncomfortable. To help adjust to moments of silence, try some of the following activities:

1. If you're watching or listening to an interview (either live or recorded), keep track of the length of each silence. Then notice who breaks the silence. Try to determine whether the silence helped the client keep talking about something important or go into a deeper issue or whether the silence was detrimental in some way.
2. When a silence comes up during a practice interview, pay attention to your thoughts and feelings. Do you welcome silence, dread silence, or feel neutral about silence? Try thinking about silence as a tool rather than a failure to communicate.
3. Talk with friends, family, or a romantic partner about how they feel about silent moments during social conversations. You may find that people have much different feelings about silence. Your goal is to understand how others view silence and to increase your comfort level with silence as an interviewing tool.
4. Research and discuss how individuals from diverse cultures view silence.

Paraphrase (or Reflection of Content)

The paraphrase (aka reflection of content) is a cornerstone of effective communication. It lets clients know you've accurately heard what they're saying and allows clients to hear how someone else perceives them (a clarification function). This can further facilitate expression.

Paraphrasing involves restating or rewording another person's verbal communication. The paraphrase is sometimes referred to as a *reflection* or *reflection of content* (this refers to the fact that paraphrases reflect the content of what clients are saying, but not feelings or emotions). As you'll soon see, although paraphrases are typically a reflection of what clients have said, there is always room for subjectivity and so some reflections are intentionally more leading than others. A good paraphrase or reflection is usually accurate and brief.

Therapists often feel awkward when making their first paraphrases; it can feel as if you're restating the obvious. If you simply parrot back to clients what has just been said, it can come off as rigid, stilted, and, at times, offensive. You may feel you're getting nowhere (W. R. Miller & Rollnick, 2002). However, as you advance, you learn that the various forms of paraphrasing, when properly used, are flexible and creative techniques that enhance rapport and empathy and affect clients in different ways. As Miller and Rollnick (1991) noted, reflective listening is harder than it looks:

> Although a therapist skilled in empathic listening can make it look easy and natural, in fact, this is a demanding counseling style. It requires sharp attention to each new client statement, and a continual generation of hypotheses as to the meaning. Your best guess as to meaning is then reflected back to the client, often adding to the content of what was overtly said. The client responds, and the whole process starts over again. Reflective listening is easy to parody or do poorly, but quite challenging to do well. (p. 26)

Several types of paraphrases are discussed next.

The Simple Paraphrase

The simple paraphrase doesn't add meaning or direction. The therapist rephrases, rewords, and reflects what the client just said. Some examples include:

Client 1:   Yesterday was my day off. I just sat around the house doing nothing. I had some errands to run, but I couldn't seem to make myself get up off the couch and do them.

Therapist 1: You had trouble getting going on your day off.

***

Client 2:   I do this with every assignment. I wait until the last minute and then whip together the paper. I end up doing all-nighters. I don't think the final product is as good as it could be.

Therapist 2: Waiting until the last minute has become a pattern for you and you think it makes it so you don't do as well as you could on your assignments.

Each of these preceding paraphrase examples is relatively simple and straightforward. The simple paraphrase is a rephrasing of the client's core message and doesn't retain everything that was originally said. It's simple, but it's not as simple as an echo or a parrot. Simple paraphrases also don't include therapist opinion, reactions, or commentary, whether positive or negative.

As clients talk more, reflective listening can grow increasingly complex. You may notice yourself having difficulty tracking exactly what the client has said. Although it's important to do the best you can to stay accurate, sometimes reflective listening feels like a verbal dance. If you miss something important, the client will move to make a correction. Or if you include something the client didn't say, the client will make a clarification. Notice in the next exchange, the therapist misses a piece of what the client says so the client repeats a key part of his message. This gives the therapist a second chance.

Client 3:	If my goal is to lose weight, even though I don't like going to bed early, I should, and then wake up early in the morning and then I don't have an excuse to avoid exercising.
Therapist 3:	So you think it would be better for you to get up earlier in the morning.
Client 3:	But I'm a night person.
Therapist 3:	You like to stay up.
Client 3:	Yeah. I like to stay up and talk on the phone and go online and do Facebook.

Reflective listening and paraphrasing is so flexible that it can be adapted for use with all different theoretical orientations. In the next two examples, the therapists are using paraphrasing, but are including specific language that's consistent with their particular theoretical orientation. See if you can identify the theoretical orientation by reading the content of these two paraphrases.

Client 4:	A lot of times I get really nervous when I'm expected to speak up in a class. And I want to speak up but I kind of feel like I freeze.
Therapist 4:	And so in your head you would probably say, "I would like to speak up" but for some reason you feel inside some anxiety or nervousness about that
Client 4:	Definitely.
Client 4:	And then sometimes when I try to force myself to speak up when I actually don't feel ready . . . I feel like my throat's closing and I get a red face.
Therapist 4:	When you're not feeling ready it seems like the anxiety gets more physical.

***

Client 5:	I do think a lot about possible tragedies that could happen because my life has been so easy. I especially worry a lot about tragedy striking my kids. But I do have periods of time when I don't feel this way, but yeah, I have a lot of thoughts about just wanting to live like a normal person and not having all these thoughts in my head and I wonder, as we're talking now, if I'm maybe living a little anxiously all the time.

Therapist 5: Yeah, kind of this underlying anxiety, something might go wrong, something bad might happen, something that could be a tragedy. . . .

In the preceding examples, therapists use paraphrases or reflective listening in ways that fit with their underlying theoretical orientations. Therapist 4 is operating from a cognitive perspective. You can see this in the language he uses. Specifically, " . . . in your head you would probably say . . ." is focusing on self-talk or cognition and "the anxiety gets more physical . . ." is consistent with a cognitive-behavioral case formulation that distinguishes between cognitive and physical manifestations of anxiety.

Therapist 5 is using a psychodynamic approach. By repeating the anxiety-provoking words the client said, she's encouraging her client to free associate to words that produce anxiety. The therapist hopes the client will openly talk about her anxiety and fears of tragedy in a way that might uncover unconscious conflicts.

These examples give you a quick glimpse into the flexibility and sophistication of paraphrasing. They show why clinicians from all therapy orientations can and do use the clinical skill of paraphrasing.

The Sensory-Based Paraphrase

In the 1970s, Richard Bandler and John Grinder developed an approach to counseling and psychotherapy called *neurolinguistic programming* (NLP). Among other things, NLP emphasized a concept referred to as *representational systems* (Bandler & Grinder, 1975; Grinder & Bandler, 1976). Representational systems refer to the sensory system—usually visual, auditory, or kinesthetic—that individual clients use when experiencing their world. It was hypothesized that by tuning into clients' representational systems and using language that speaks to clients more directly, clinicians could have more influence. Bandler (2008) reflected on how he initially learned about language use and matching representational systems from watching great therapists, in this case, Virginia Satir:

> [A client] might say: "I just feel everything's getting on top of me and I can't move forward or back. I just don't see a way through this." She would reply: "I feel the weight of your problems is stopping you from finding your direction, and the best route you can take isn't clear yet. . . ." (2008, p. 31)

If you listen closely to your clients' words, you'll notice that some clients rely primarily on visually oriented words (e.g., "I see" or "it looks like"), others on auditory words (e.g., "I hear" or "it sounded like"), and others on kinesthetic words (e.g., "I feel" or "it moved me"). Although the research is very limited, some evidence suggests that when therapists speak through their client's representational system, empathy, trust, and desire to see the therapist again are increased (Hammer, 1983; Sharpley, 1984).

Listening for your client's sensory-related words is the key to using sensory-based paraphrases. To get more familiar with the representational system concept, we recommend doing an individual or in-class activity in which you generate as many visual, auditory, and kinesthetic words as you can. (Although clients occasionally refer to olfactory and taste experiences, it's rare that clients use these as their primary representational modality.) Examples of sensory-based paraphrases follow, with the sensory words italicized:

Client 1:   My goal in therapy is to get to know myself better. I think of therapy as kind of a *mirror* through which I can *see* myself, my strengths, and my weaknesses more *clearly*.

Therapist 1: You're here because you want to *see* yourself more *clearly* and believe therapy can really help you with that.

***

Client 2:   I just got *laid off* from my job and I don't know what to do. My job is so important to me. I *feel* lost.

Therapist 2: Your job has been so important to you, you *feel* adrift without it.

Research supporting the effectiveness of matching client representational systems is limited (Sharpley, 1984). However, we include this discussion and these examples because listening for sensory words is another way that therapists can be sensitive to the subtle communications coming from clients. Tuning into sensory words is another way of listening well.

The Metaphorical Paraphrase

Therapists can use metaphor or analogy to capture their client's central message. For instance, often clients come for therapy because of feeling stuck and not making progress in terms of personal growth or problem resolution. In such a case, a therapist might reflect, "It seems like you're spinning your wheels" or "Dealing with this has been a real uphill battle." Additional examples follow:

Client 1:   My sister is so picky. We share a room, and she's always bugging me about picking up my clothes, straightening up my dresser, and everything else, too. She scrutinizes every move I make and criticizes me every chance she gets.

Therapist 1: It's like you're in the army and she's your drill sergeant.

***

Client 2:   I'm prepared for some breakdowns along the way.

Therapist 2: You don't expect it will be smooth sailing. (From Rogers, 1961, p. 102)

This approach to paraphrasing is similar to tuning into clients' representational systems. Pomerantz (2011) commented: "Clients whose therapists literally 'speak their language' tend to feel relaxed and understood" (p. 153).

Intentionally Directive Paraphrases

Solution-focused therapists use paraphrasing in a highly selective manner. For example, O'Hanlon (1998) described a variation on reflection of content or paraphrasing that he referred to as "Carl Rogers with a Twist." He considers this technique as a means of showing empathy and compassion, while at the same time helping clients move beyond their negative or traumatic feelings from the past. Examples include:

Client 1:   I feel like cutting myself.
Therapist 1: You've felt like cutting yourself. (O'Hanlon, 1998, p. 47)
                  [In this example the therapist is validating the client, but shifting to past tense.]

***

Client 2:   I have flashbacks all the time.
Therapist 2: So you have flashbacks a lot of the time.
                  [In this example the therapist transforms the client's verbal disclosure from a global to a partial perception.]

***

Client 3:   I'm a bad person because I was sexually abused.
Therapist 3: So you've gotten the idea that you're bad because you were sexually abused.
                  [In this last example, the therapist shifts the client's words from factual to perceptual. (J. Sommers-Flanagan & Sommers-Flanagan, 2012)]

Insoo Kim Berg was famous for her ability to focus on, magnify, and paraphrase back a small positive client statement—even if the statement was surrounded by or covered up with negative content (I. K. Berg & DeJong, 2005; de Jong & Berg, 2008). For Berg, the decision regarding what to paraphrase back to her clients was simple. She believed all therapists lead their clients and so they may as well intentionally lead their clients in positive directions.

Berg's philosophy is captured by the following two quotations from other leaders in the constructive/solution-focused field.

Just as one cannot not communicate, one cannot not influence. (Weakland, 1993, p. 143)

Since we cannot avoid leading, the question becomes, "Where shall we lead our clients?" (Weiner-Davis, 1993, p. 156)

If we return to our original nondirective listening example and you focus on Berg's philosophy of leading with the positive, you might be able to identify what Insoo Kim Berg would say in response to a specific client statement. Read the following excerpt again:

We didn't have much money when I was growing up, and I suppose that frustrated my father. He beat us five kids all the time. He's dead now, but to this day, my mom says we needed the discipline. But I hated it then and swore I'd never be like him. Now that I'm grown and have kids of my own, I'm doing okay, but sometimes I feel I need to discipline my kids more . . . harder . . . do you know what I mean?

Take a moment and try to imagine what positive part of this statement Berg might choose to paraphrase.

Perhaps Berg would have said something like: "Now that you're grown and have your own kids, you see yourself as doing okay!" or "So, you swore that would never be like your father and clearly, you aren't!" Similar to Carl Rogers with a twist, these solution- or strength-focused reflections intentionally lead clients toward the positive. There are many different names for these intentionally leading responses, including: positive reconstruction, finding the exception, or focusing on sparkling moments (J. Sommers-Flanagan & Sommers-Flanagan, 2012).

Clarification

There are several forms of clarification and they all serve a common purpose: to make clear for yourself and the client precisely what has been said. The first form of clarification consists of a restatement of what the client said and a closed question, in either order. Rogers was a master at clarification:

> If I'm getting it right . . . what makes it hurt most of all is that when he tells you you're no good, well shucks, that's what you've always felt about yourself. Is that the meaning of what you're saying? (Meador & Rogers, 1984, p. 167)

The second form of clarification consists of a restatement imbedded in a double question. A double question is an either/or question including two or more choices of response for the client. For example:

- Do you dislike being called on in class—or is it something else?
- Did you get in the argument with your husband before or after you went to the movie?

Using clarification as a double question allows therapists to take more control of what clients say during an interview. Therapists try to guess a client's potential response by providing possible choices.

The third form of clarification is the most basic. It's used when you don't quite hear what a client said and you need to recheck.

- I'm sorry, I didn't quite hear that. Could you repeat what you said?
- I couldn't make out what you said. Did you say you're going home after the session?

There will be times during interviews when you don't understand what your client is saying. There also will be times when your client isn't sure what he or she is saying or why he/she is saying it. Sometimes, the appropriate response is to wait for understanding to come. Other times, it's necessary to clarify precisely what your client is talking about. There are also times when your client will need to ask you to clarify something you've said.

Brammer (1979) provided two general guidelines for clarifying. First, admit your confusion over what the client has said. Second, "[T]ry a restatement or ask for clarification, repetition, or illustration" (p. 73). Asking for a specific example can be especially useful because it encourages clients to be concrete and specific rather than abstract and vague.

There are two main factors to consider when deciding whether to use clarification. First, if the information appears trivial and unrelated to central therapeutic issues, it may be best to wait for the client to move on to a more productive area. It can be a waste of time to clarify minor details that are only remotely related to interview goals. For example, suppose a client says, "My stepdaughter's grandfather on my wife's side of the family usually has little or no contact with my parents." This presents an excellent opportunity to listen quietly. To attempt a clarification response might result in a lengthy entanglement with distant family relationships that takes the interview off course. In fact, on some occasions, the client might engage in long confusing accounts in order to avoid deeper topics. A clarification response might simply prolong or even endorse the avoidance.

Second, if the information clients discuss seems important but isn't being articulated clearly, you have two choices: Wait briefly to see if they can independently express themselves more clearly, or immediately use a clarification. For example, a client may state:

I don't know, she was different. She looked at me differently than other women. Others were missing . . . something, you know, the eyes. Usually you can tell by the way a woman looks at you, can't you? Then again, maybe it was something else, something about me that I'll understand someday.

An appropriate clarification might be: "She seemed different; it may have been how she looked at you or something about yourself you don't totally understand. Is that what you're saying?"

Reflection of Feeling

The primary purpose of a *reflection of feeling* is to let clients know, through an emotionally oriented paraphrase, that you're tuned in to their emotional state. Nondirective feeling reflections also encourage further emotional expression. Consider the following example of a 15-year-old male talking about his teacher:

Client 1:   That teacher pissed me off big time when she accused me of stealing her watch. I wanted to punch her lights out.
Counselor 1: So you were pretty pissed off.
Client 1:   Damn right.

In this example, the counselor's feeling reflection focuses only on what the client clearly articulated. This is the basic rule for nondirective feeling reflections: Restate or reflect *only* the emotional content that you *clearly* hear the client say. Do not probe, interpret, or speculate. Although we might guess at the underlying emotions causing this boy's fury, a nondirective feeling reflection doesn't address these possibilities.

Feelings are, by their very nature, personal. Any attempt at reflecting feelings is a move toward closeness or intimacy. Some clients who don't want the intimacy associated with a counseling relationship may react negatively to feeling reflections.

You minimize potential negative reactions to feeling reflections by phrasing them tentatively in the early stages of building the therapeutic relationship. Speaking from a motivational interviewing perspective, Miller and Rollnick (2002) stated:

> When using reflection to encourage continued personal exploration, which is the broad goal of reflective listening, it is often useful to understate slightly what the speaker has offered. This is particularly so when emotional content is involved. (p. 72)

Although accuracy is the ultimate goal when reflecting feelings, if you're inaccurate, understating your client's emotional intensity tends to work out better than overstating it. This is because, if you overstate emotional intensity, your client will often backtrack or deny his or her feelings. As we'll discuss in Chapter 11, there's a proper time and place for intentionally overstating client emotions. Generally, however, you should aim for accuracy while proceeding tentatively and understating rather than overstating your client's emotional intensity. Rogers (1951; 1961) would sometimes check with clients after giving a feeling reflection.

If you're tentative in your feeling reflection, your client may quickly correct you. For example:

Client 2: That teacher pissed me off big time when she accused me of stealing her watch. I wanted to punch her lights out.
Counselor 2: Seems like you were a little irritated about that. Is that right?
Client 2: Irritated, hell, I was pissed.
Counselor: You were more than irritated. You were pissed.

In this example, a stronger emotional descriptor would have been more appropriate because the client clearly expressed that he was much more than irritated. However, any adverse effect of "missing" the emotion is minimized because the counselor phrased the reflection tentatively by beginning the sentence with "Seems like . . . ." and then added a clarifying question at the end. Then, perhaps of greatest significance, when the client corrected the counselor, the counselor fixed or repaired the reflection to fit with the client's emotional experience. From a psychoanalytic perspective, the repairing of emotional mirroring or empathy may be the most important part of therapeutic listening (Kohut, 1984); see *Putting It in Practice* 3.3 to practice emotional responses to clients).

PUTTING IT IN PRACTICE 3.3

Enhancing Your Feeling Capacity and Vocabulary

There are many ways to explore and enhance your feeling capacity and vocabulary. Carkhuff (Carkhuff, 1987) recommended the following activity. Identify a basic emotion, such as anger, fear, happiness, or sadness, and then begin associating to other feelings in response to that emotion. For instance, state, "When I feel sad . . . ." and then finish the thought by associating to another feeling and stating it; for example, "I feel cheated." An example of this process follows:

When I feel joy, I feel fulfilled.
When I feel fulfilled, I feel content.
When I feel content, I feel comfortable.
When I feel comfortable, I feel safe.
When I feel safe, I feel calm.
When I feel calm, I feel relaxed.

This feeling association process can help you discover more about your emotional life and help you come up with a wide range of meaningful feeling words. Conduct this exercise individually or in dyads using each of the 10 primary emotions identified by Izard (1977; 1982):

Interest-excitement	Disgust
Joy	Contempt
Surprise	Fear
Distress	Shame
Anger	Guilt

Summarization

Summarization demonstrates accurate listening, enhances client and therapist recall of major themes, helps clients focus on important issues, and extracts or refines the meaning behind client messages. Depending on how much your clients talk, summarization can be used intermittently throughout a session and then at the end.

Therapist 1:   You've said a lot in the past 10 minutes and so I want to make sure I'm tracking your main concerns. You talked about the conflicts between you and your parents, about how you've felt angry and neglected, and about how it was a relief, but also a big adjustment, to be placed in a foster home. And you also said you're doing better than you thought you'd be doing. Does that cover the main points of what you've talked about so far?

Client 1:   Yeah. That about covers it.

Although summarization is conceptually simple, coming up with a summary can be difficult. Your memory of what your client said sometimes may fade quickly, leaving you without an accurate or complete recollection. Sometimes, therapists take on too much responsibility. For example:

You've mentioned four main issues today. First, you said your childhood was hard because of your father's authoritarian style. Second, in your current marriage, you find yourself overly critical of your wife's parenting. Third, you described yourself as controlling and perfectionistic, which you think contributes to conflicts in your marriage. And fourth, uh, fourth [long pause], uh, sorry, I forgot the fourth one—but I'm sure it will come to me.

It's usually more effective to engage clients in a collaborative summarization process. For example, you could ask your client to summarize key points of an interview or the steps to follow for a specific homework assignment. As our colleague, Carlos Zalaquett (personal communication, August 25, 2012) has pointed out, this more interactive approach will highlight your clients' perspective on what's important during an interview or serve as a check on their understanding of homework. Instead of taking on the entire responsibility of accurately summarizing everything your client said, collaboration honors your client's values and perspectives.

In summary, there are several advantages to using an interactive summary. First, doing so takes pressure off your memory. Second, it places responsibility on clients to state what *they* think is important. Third, an interactive approach models a collaborative relationship. Engaging clients to decide the therapy focus demonstrates teamwork.

Guidelines for Summarizing

Overall, when summarizing content from an interview, be informal, collaborative, supportive, and hopeful:

- Informal

    Instead of saying, "Here's my summary of what you've said," say something like, "Let's make sure I'm keeping up with the main things you talked about."

    Instead of numbering your points, simply state them one by one. That way you won't be embarrassed by forgetting a point.

- Collaborative

    Instead of taking the lead, ask clients to summarize (e.g., "What seemed most important to you during our meeting?"). This allows you to hear your client's view before offering your own. You can always add what you thought was important later.

    If you do take the lead in summarizing, pause intermittently so your client can agree, disagree, or elaborate.

    At the end of your part of the summary, ask if what you've said seems accurate (e.g., "Does that seem to fit with what you recall?").

    Using a collaborative approach can feel empowering to clients. You might say, "I'm interested in what *you* feel has been most important of all you've covered today." Or, "How would you summarize the homework we've been talking about?"

- Supportive

    It can be very supportive to acknowledge your client's efforts. For example, "You've said a lot" or "I appreciate your openness with me" are reassuring and supportive statements that help clients feel good about what they've shared. Of course, you should only make these supportive statements when you believe them.

It's also supportive to note topics that seemed difficult for your clients, stating something like, "I noticed you shared some sad events and difficult topics with me."

• Hopeful

When summarizing, it's important to consciously or intentionally decide how positive or hopeful you want your message to be. Although it's fine to be neutral and reflective, therapists who adhere to a solution-focused perspective will avoid summarizing anything negative. Instead, as described previously and discussed in more detail later, they'll highlight the positive and hopeful (e.g., "Throughout this session I heard you talking about different skills or strengths you've used to cope with the loss of your relationship partner").

Your summary focus will be tied to your theoretical orientation. Not surprisingly, psychodynamic clinicians provide summaries that emphasize early childhood developmental issues. In contrast, cognitive therapists will summarize distorted or maladaptive thinking patterns and eventually package this information into a case formulation to share with clients (Epp & Dobson, 2010). All the while, solution-focused therapists will stick with the positive. As you read this section, consider where you stand. When it comes to summarizing, what's your natural tendency? Will you be more positive and upbeat, or more focused on what's going wrong or what feels bad in your client's life? Or perhaps you'll decide it makes more sense to try and maintain a balance.

DVD Clip

In the *Maegan & Jessie* counseling demonstration, Maegan demonstrates paraphrasing, reflection of feeling, verbal tracking, summarization, clarification, and use of an open question. In this clip, after being listened to, the client naturally begins her own problem-solving process.

THE PULL TO REASSURANCE

Taken together, attending skills and nondirective listening techniques could be considered polite behaviors. They involve listening attentively to another person, indicating interest, tuning into feelings, and demonstrating a wide range of caring behaviors.

If you're listening well, you also may feel a strong pull to offer compliments or reassurance. However, it's important to know that, strictly speaking, complimenting or reassuring clients is a directive technique.

From a behavioral perspective, complimenting your client may function as a useful positive reinforcement. When you compliment, you're expressing *your* taste and *your* approval, which is a form of self-disclosure. Complimenting, or self-disclosure in any form is a *technique* to be used in moderation (Farber, 2006; Zur, 2007). Reassurance, too, is a *technique*. Clients may behave in ways that tug on your impulse to say something reassuring. They want to know if they're good parents, if they did the right thing, or if their sadness will lift. At some point you're likely to feel the pull to tell them they're doing just fine.

Premature or global reassurance is generally not recommended. When you issue blanket reassurance, you're assessing a situation and/or a person's coping abilities and declaring that things will improve or come out for the better. Even though that might be what you hope for, such an outcome cannot be guaranteed. In this sense, reassurance is misleading. In another sense, global reassurance might discount the client's difficulties. You're not in a position to know how bad things are, or how much work will be involved in making changes. It may be confusing at first, but empathy and reassurance are not interchangeable. Therapists should use reflective, empathic listening regularly, whereas reassurance should come in carefully considered, small doses.

DIRECTIVE LISTENING BEHAVIORS

To this point, this chapter has focused primarily on less-directive or client-centered therapy skills. In this section, the concept of directive listening behaviors is introduced.

Directive listening behaviors place therapists more squarely in the position of director, choreographer, or expert. Directive listening behaviors are multidimensional and used to pursue a variety of ends, but their general purpose is often to gather assessment information, deepen the therapeutic focus, and facilitate client insight (Hill, 2009).

Directive listening behaviors may be more client-centered or more therapist-centered. More client-centered directives focus in on exactly what the client is talking about, but are aimed at a deeper level. Directives that are therapist-centered typically move clients away from what they're talking about and toward what the therapist deems important. At their foundation, directive listening behaviors operate on the assumption that clients need guidance or direction from their therapists. Directives usually work better after rapport or a therapeutic alliance has been established.

DVD Clip

In the *Directive Listening Responses* DVD chapter, John and Rita briefly discuss directive listening skills and introduce the *John & Trudi* counseling demonstration.

Feeling Validation

Reflection of feeling (discussed previously) is often confused with a technique referred to as *feeling validation*. However, feeling reflections tend to be non-directive or less directive. In contrast, feeling validation occurs when a therapist acknowledges and approves of a client's stated feelings.

The purpose of feeling validation is to help clients accept their feelings as a natural part of being human. Feeling validation can be ego boosting; clients feel supported and more normal because of their therapist's validating comments. However, some theorists believe that directive and supportive techniques such as feeling validation enhance self-esteem only temporarily, based on the therapist's input rather than real or lasting client change. In addition, when therapists liberally use feeling validation, it can foster dependency. As a therapeutic technique, feeling validation contains approval and reassurance, both of which usually produce positive feelings in the recipient. This may be why friends or romantic partners offer each other frequent doses of feeling validation.

All approaches to feeling validation give clients the message: "Your feelings are acceptable and you have permission to feel them." In fact, sometimes feeling validations suggest that clients *should* be having particular feelings.

Client 1:	I've just been so sad since my mother died. I can't seem to stop myself from crying. *(Client begins sobbing.)*
Therapist 1:	It's okay for you to be sad about losing your mother. That's perfectly normal. Go ahead and cry if you feel like it.

Notice how the preceding exchange goes beyond feeling reflection to validation of feeling. This is no longer a client-centered or nondirective technique. By openly stating that feeling sad and crying is okay or healthy, the therapist takes on the role of expert.

Another way to provide feeling validation is through self-disclosure:

Client 2:	I get so anxious before tests, you wouldn't believe it! All I can think about is how I'm going to freeze up and forget everything. Then, when I get in there and look at the test, my mind just goes blank.
Therapist 2:	You know, sometimes I feel the same way about tests.

In this example, the therapist used self-disclosure to validate the client's anxiety. Although using self-disclosure to validate feelings can be reassuring, it can be risky. In this case, the client may privately wonder if the counselor can be helpful with anxiety symptoms if he/she is experiencing similar anxiety. Counselor credibility can be diminished or enhanced—depending on the client and the therapeutic relationship.

Therapists can also validate or reassure clients by using a concept Yalom and Leszcz (2005) refer to as *universality*.

Client 3:	I'm always comparing myself to everyone else—and I usually come up short. I wonder if I'll ever really feel confident.
Therapist 3:	You're being too hard on yourself. Everyone has self-doubts. I don't know anyone who feels a complete sense of confidence.

Clients may feel validated when they observe or are informed that nearly everyone else in the world (or universe) feels what they're feeling. Yalom and Leszcz (2005) provided another example:

> During my own 600-hour analysis I had a striking personal encounter with the therapeutic factor of universality . . . I was very much troubled by the fact that, despite my strong positive sentiments [toward my mother], I was beset with death wishes for her, as I stood to inherit part of her estate. My analyst responded simply, "That seems to be the way we're built." That artless statement not only offered considerable relief but enabled me to explore my ambivalence in great depth. (p. 7)

Feeling validation is common in interviewing and counseling. This is partly because people like to have their feelings validated and partly because therapists generally like validating their clients' feelings. In some cases, clients come to therapy seeking reassurance that they're normal. Alternatively, some theorists believe that open support, such as feeling validation, reduces client exploration of important issues (i.e., clients figure they must be fine if their therapist says so) and thereby diminishes the likelihood that clients will independently develop positive attitudes toward themselves.

Potential effects of feeling validation include:

- Enhanced rapport.
- Increased or reduced client exploration of the problem or feeling (this could go either direction).
- Reduction in client anxiety, at least temporarily.
- Enhanced client self-esteem or feelings of normality (perhaps only temporarily).
- Possible increased likelihood of client-therapist dependency.

Interpretive Reflection of Feeling

Interpretive feeling reflections are feeling-based statements made by therapists that go beyond the client's obvious emotional expressions. This technique is sometimes referred to as a form of advanced empathy.

The goal of an interpretive feeling reflection is to go deeper than the surface feelings or emotions that the client is expressing. This may involve working to uncover underlying emotions. Interpretive feeling reflections may produce insight (i.e., the client becomes aware of something that was previously unconscious or only partially conscious). Another way of thinking about interpretive feeling reflections is that they target buried, hidden, or deeper emotions—while nondirective feeling reflections focus on obvious, clear, and surface emotions.

Consider, again, the 15-year-old boy who was so angry with his teacher.

Client 1:   That teacher pissed me off big time when she accused me of stealing her watch. I wanted to punch her lights out.
Counselor 1:   So you were pretty pissed off. *(Reflection of feeling.)*
Client 1:   Damn right.
Counselor 1:   You know, I also sense you have some other feelings about what your teacher did. Maybe you were hurt because she didn't trust you. *(Interpretive reflection of feeling.)*

Note that the counselor's second statement is in pursuit of deeper feelings that the client didn't initially articulate. This is the essence of an interpretive reflection of feeling.

An interpretive feeling reflection may also stimulate client defensiveness. As described later, effective interpretations require good timing (Freud, 1949; Weiner, 1998). That's why, in the preceding example, the counselor initially used a nondirective feeling reflection and then, after that reflection was affirmed, used a more probing and interpretive response. Miller and Rollnick (2002) made this point in *Motivational Interviewing*:

> Skillful reflection moves past what the person has already said, though not jumping too far ahead. The skill is not unlike the timing of interpretations in psychodynamic psychotherapy. If the person balks, you know you've jumped too far, too fast. (p. 72)

Interpretive feeling reflections can have many effects, but some of the most prominent include the following:

- If offered prematurely or without a good rationale, they may feel foreign or uncomfortable to clients; this discomfort can lead to client resistance, reluctance, or denial.
- When well stated and used within the context of a positive therapy relationship, interpretive feeling reflections may feel very good to clients because the therapist is "hearing" the client on a deeper level; this can lead to enhanced therapist credibility and further strengthening of the therapy relationship.

Interpretive feeling reflections are subtle techniques that can produce significant therapeutic breakthroughs. Gestalt therapist Fritz Perls, would often engage clients in activities or experiments to help them get in touch with the feelings under their surface feelings. For example, when clients claimed feelings of guilt, he would have clients continue talking about their guilt, but have them substitute the word "resentment" for "guilt." This strategy would sometimes result in a powerful transformation of a client's guilt into underlying anger and resentment.

Keep in mind the following principles when using interpretive feeling reflections.

- Wait until:
  - You have good rapport.
  - You have shown your clients, using active listening skills, that you're able to accurately hear what they're saying.
  - You have evidence (e.g., nonverbal signals, previous client statements) that provide a rational foundation for your interpretation.
- Phrase your interpretive statement:
  - Tentatively (e.g., "If I were to guess, I'd say...")
  - Collaboratively (e.g., "Correct me if I'm wrong, but...")

The principle of phrasing your statements tentatively and collaboratively is equally true when using any form of feedback or interpretation. Many different phrasings can be used to deliver interpretive statements in ways that make them more likely to be accepted. For example:

- I think I'm hearing that you'd like to speak directly to your father about your sexuality, but you're afraid of his response.
- Correct me if I'm wrong, but it sounds like underneath your anxiety is a deeper belief that you think you're unlovable.

- If I were to guess, I'd say you're wishing you could find your way out of this relationship, but tell me if I'm wrong about that.
- This may not fit for you, but the way you're sitting seems to communicate not only sadness, but also irritation.

Interpretation

The purpose of an interpretation is to produce client insight or to help clients perceive reality more accurately. As Fenichel (1945) stated, "Interpretation means helping something unconscious to become conscious by naming it at the moment it is striving to break through" (p. 25). When therapists provide an interpretation, they're offering a form of feedback that links past relationship patterns to current relationship patterns.

Psychoanalytic or "Classical" Interpretations

According to the psychoanalytic tradition, an interpretation is based on the theoretical assumption that unconscious processes influence behavior. By pointing out unconscious conflicts and patterns, therapists help clients move toward greater self-awareness and improved functioning. This isn't to suggest that insight alone produces behavior change. Instead, insight begins moving clients toward more adaptive ways of feeling, thinking, and acting.

Consider, one last time, our angry 15-year-old student.

Client 1:	That teacher pissed me off big time when she accused me of stealing her watch. I wanted to punch her lights out.
Counselor 1:	So you were pretty pissed off. *(Nondirective feeling reflection.)*
Client 1:	Damn right.
Counselor 1:	You know, I also sense you have some other feelings about what your teacher did. Maybe you were hurt because she didn't trust you. *(Interpretive feeling reflection.)*
Client 1:	(Pauses.) Yeah, well that's a dumb idea…it doesn't hurt anymore…after a while when no one trusts you, it ain't no big surprise to get accused again of something I didn't do.
Counselor 1:	So when you respond to your teacher's distrust of you with anger, it's like you're reacting to all those times when your parents haven't trusted you. *(Interpretation.)*

In this exchange, the boy demeans the counselor's interpretive feeling reflection ("…that's a dumb idea…"), but then affirms it by noting, "it doesn't hurt anymore." With this phrase the boy gives the counselor a signal that there may be important and relevant past experiences (i.e., the word *anymore* is a reference to the past). This is consistent with psychoanalytic theory in that accurate interpretations are seen as often producing *genetic* material (i.e., material from the past). Thus, the counselor perceives the client's signal and proceeds with a more classical interpretation.

Classical interpretations work best if you have knowledge of the client and the client's past and present relationships. In the previous example, the counselor knows from earlier interviews that the boy perceived himself as being unjustly punished by his parents. The counselor could have made the interpretation after the boy's first statement, but waited until after the boy responded positively to the first two interventions. This illustrates the importance of timing when using interpretations. As Fenichel (1945) wrote, "The unprepared patient can in no way connect the words he hears from the analyst with his emotional experiences. Such an 'interpretation' does not interpret at all" (p. 25).

Much has been written about the technical aspects of psychoanalytic interpretation, what to interpret, when to interpret it, and how to interpret it (Fenichel, 1945; Greenson, 1965; Weiner, 1998). Reading basic psychoanalytic texts, enrolling in psychoanalytic therapy courses, and obtaining supervision are prerequisites to using classical interpretations. As with interpretive feeling reflections, poorly timed interpretations usually produce resistance and defensiveness.

Reframing

Practitioners from other theoretical orientations often view interpretation quite differently than psychoanalytic therapists. Instead of bringing unconscious processes into awareness, interpretation is seen as an intervention designed to help clients view their problems differently. Family systems, solution-focused, and cognitive-behavioral therapists label this approach as *reframing* or *cognitive reframing* (D'Zurilla & Nezu, 2010; de Shazer, 1985; Watzlawick, Weakland, & Fisch, 1974).

Reframing is used primarily when therapists believe their clients are viewing the world in a manner that is inaccurate or maladaptive. Consider the following exchange between two members of an outpatient group for delinquent youth and their counselor during a group session:

Peg:	He's always bugging me. He insults me. And I think he's a jerk. I want to make a deal to quit picking on each other, but he won't do it.
Dan:	She's the problem. Always thinks she's right. She's never willing to back down. No way am I gonna make a deal with her. She won't change.
Counselor:	I notice you two are sitting next to each other again today.
Peg:	So! I'd rather not be next to him.
Counselor:	You two almost always sit next to each other, and you're always sparring back and forth. I think you might actually like each other, even though you act like you hate each other.
Others:	Wow. That's it. We always thought so.

In this example, two teenagers are consistently harassing each other. The therapist suggests that, rather than mutual irritation, the two teens are expressing their mutual attraction. Although the teens deny the reframe, other group members agree the attraction is a possibility.

Effective reframing should be based on a reasonable alternative hypothesis. Other examples include:

- To a depressed client: "When you make a mistake, you tend to see it as evidence for failure, but you could also see it as evidence of effort and progress toward eventual success; after all, most successful people experience many failures before persevering and becoming successful."

- To an oppositional young girl: "You think that to say something kind or complimentary to your parents is brown-nosing. I wonder if sometimes saying something positive to your mom or dad might sometimes just be an example of you giving them honest feedback" (J. Sommers-Flanagan & Sommers-Flanagan, 2007b).
- To a socially anxious client: "When people don't say hello to you, you think they're rejecting you, when it could be that they're having a bad day or have something else on their minds."

Cognitive reframes may be met initially with denial, but having clients practice viewing their problems in a new way can reduce anxiety, anger, or sadness. Reframing promotes flexibility in perceiving or interpreting actions. Similar to all forms of interpretation, reframes work best if you have strong credibility or a positive therapeutic relationship with clients, if you can offer a reasonable rationale, and if you make the statement tentatively and collaboratively.

Confrontation

The goal of confrontation is to help clients perceive themselves and reality more clearly. Clients often have a distorted view of others, the world, and themselves. These distortions usually manifest themselves as incongruities or discrepancies. For example, imagine a client with clenched fists and a harsh, angry voice saying, "I wish you wouldn't bring up my ex-wife. I've told you before, that's over! I don't have any feelings toward her. It's all just water under the bridge." Obviously, this client still has strong feelings about his ex-wife. Perhaps the relationship is over and the client wishes he could put it behind him, but his nonverbal behavior—voice tone, body posture, and facial expression—tells the therapist that he's still emotionally involved with his ex-wife.

Confrontation works best when you have a working relationship with the client and ample evidence to demonstrate the client's emotional or behavioral incongruity or discrepancy. In the preceding example, we wouldn't recommend using confrontation unless there was additional evidence indicating the client's unresolved feelings about his ex-wife. If there was supporting evidence, the following confrontation might be appropriate:

> You mentioned last week that every time you think of your ex-wife and how the relationship ended, you want revenge. And yet today, you're saying you don't have any feelings about her. But judging by your clenched fists, voice tone, and what you said last week about her "screwing you over," it seems like you still have very strong feelings about her. Perhaps you *wish* those feelings would go away, but it sure looks like they're still there.

Notice how the therapist cites evidence to support the confrontation. In this case, the therapist has decided that the client would be better off admitting to and dealing with his unresolved feelings toward his ex-wife. Therefore, he uses confrontation to help the client see the issue. To increase the likelihood that the client will admit to the discrepancy between his nonverbal behavior and his internal emotions, the confrontation was stated gently and supported by evidence.

Confrontations can range from being very gentle to harsh and aggressive. For example, take the case of a young, newly married man who, 35 minutes into his psychotherapy session, has not yet mentioned his wife (despite the fact that she left 2 days earlier to return to school about 2,000 miles away). The young man, while discussing a general rise in his anger and frustration, was mildly confronted by his therapist, who observed, "I noticed you haven't mentioned anything about your wife leaving."

In this case, the therapist is using a reflection of content (or lack of content) to gently confront the fact that the client was neglecting to discuss his wife and the relevance of her departure on his mood. The therapist's goal is to get his client to recognize and acknowledge that he was ignoring a possible connection between his negative mood and his wife's recent departure.

Firmer confrontations are sometimes useful. However, when therapists use more aggressive confrontations, they run the risk of evoking client resistance (Miller & Rollnick, 2002). Here's an example of a moderately firm confrontation with a substance-abusing client.

Client 1: Doc, it's not a problem. I drink when I want to, but it doesn't have a big effect on the rest of my life. I like to party. I like to put a few down on the weekends, doesn't everybody?

Therapist 1: Well, you do seem to like to party. But, you've had two DUIs [tickets for driving under the influence], three different jobs, and at least a half dozen fights over the past year. It sounds to me like you've got a major problem with alcohol. If you don't start admitting it and doing something about it, you're going to continue to have legal trouble, job trouble, and relationship trouble. Do you really think that's no problem?

Unfortunately, many people believe effective confrontations must be harsh and aggressive. Especially in the substance abuse field, there is still sometimes a belief that confrontations must be an aggressive and insistent approach. This is simply not true.

> There is, in fact, no persuasive evidence that aggressive confrontational tactics are even helpful, let alone superior or preferable strategies in the treatment of addictive behaviors or other problems. (W. R. Miller & Rollnick, 1991, p. 7)

Although stronger confrontations may sometimes be needed, it's more therapeutic, sensible, and less likely to produce resistance if therapists begin with gentle confrontations, becoming more assertive later.

A final example of an incongruity worthy of confrontation involves a 41-year-old married man who is describing how he picked up a 20-year-old girl over the Internet. The client's statement is followed by three potential therapist responses, each progressively more confrontational:

Client 2: I originally met this girl in a chat room. My marriage has been dead for 10 years, so I need to do something for myself. She's only 20, but I'm set up to meet her next week in Dallas and I'm like a nervous Nellie. I've got a friend who's telling me I'm nuts, but I just want some action in my life again.

Confrontation A: Somehow, you're thinking that having a rendezvous with this young woman, rather than working on things with your wife, might help you feel better.

Confrontation B: Your plans seem a little risky. It sounds like you're valuing a possible quick sexual encounter with someone you've never met over your 20-year marriage. Have I got that right?

Confrontation C: I need to tell you that you're playing out a mid-life fantasy. You've never seen this girl, you don't know if she's really 20, whether she's got an STD, or if she plans to rob you blind. You think getting together with her will help you feel better, but you're just running away from your problems. Sooner or later, getting together with her will only make you feel worse.

A confrontation's effectiveness may be evaluated by examining your clients' responses. Clients can blatantly deny the accuracy of your confrontation, partially accept it, or completely accept its accuracy and significance.

True confrontation doesn't contain an explicit prescription for change. Instead, it implies that action is necessary (but doesn't specify or prescribe the action). In the next chapter, we review technical behaviors or responses that explicitly suggest or prescribe action.

> **DVD Clip**
>
> In the *John & Trudi* counseling demonstration, John demonstrates the use of an interpretive reflection of feeling and a confrontation.

Immediacy

Immediacy involves an integration of here-and-now self-disclosure, feedback, and confrontation. Early examples from Carl Rogers typically involved Rogers using himself and his experience in the session as a vehicle for providing feedback. For example, in one classic case, he stated to a client:

> I don't understand it myself, but when you start talking on and on about your problems in what seems to me a flat tone of voice, I find myself getting very bored. (R. C. Berg, Landreth, & Fall, 2006, p. 209)

This immediate disclosure provided the client feedback about how he was affecting Rogers and subsequently, the reasons for Rogers's feelings within the relationship could be explored.

One of the obvious problems with immediacy is not only that it involves the risk that usually accompanies confrontation, but that it can be more about the therapist and less about the client. In the preceding example, one rationale Carl Rogers used to explain why he shared his feelings of being bored was because having such feelings were very unusual for him. Depending on your background in psychology and counseling, you may recognize that immediacy can involve processing what psychoanalytic therapists refer to as countertransference as a means of exploring interpersonal dynamics emerging between therapist and client (see Chapter 5 for more on countertransference).

Like self-disclosure, immediacy is a very flexible therapist response that can be used for many different purposes. For example, it can be used as a way of expressing support:

- As I listen to you talk about the abuse you've experienced, I feel admiration for the strength I hear in your voice and in your stories.

Immediacy also can be used as a means of confrontation:

- You say you want your roommate to be neater and more respectful of you and your space and yet as you talk about it in here, it feels almost like you're a helpless child instead of the competent and resourceful adult I've come to know.

And immediacy can be used to lead clients toward specific action:

- What I hear is that you're really unhappy in your job . . . and it makes me feel dissatisfaction right along with you . . . which then makes me want to get out and explore other employment options, but I don't hear you doing that.

Based on a qualitative analysis of two case studies, Hill (2008) concluded that immediacy was a helpful therapist behavior and described three ways in which it was used productively in therapy sessions. These three ways are similar to the three purposes described previously. We include them here because they illustrate the nuanced variability in ways therapists apply immediacy. A recent empirical analysis of immediacy in a long-term psychotherapy case identified 17 categories of immediacy (Mayotte-Blum et al., 2012). However, the following three provide a sufficient glimpse into the possibilities:

1. Immediacy was used to negotiate the tasks and goals of therapy. For example: "I wonder what's working for you and not working for you in our sessions?"
2. Immediacy was used as a method for accessing "unexpressed feelings in the room or make the covert overt so that the communication would be more direct, here-and-now, and honest" (p. 324). For example: "I have a sense that you're having an emotional reaction to what I just said, but I'm not sure what it is."
3. Immediacy was used in an effort to repair ruptures. For example, "I've been asking about what you've been doing to search for a job and I'm getting the feeling that you'd rather I not ask these questions and so I think we should talk for a few minutes about what's going on between us right now."

Of all the different directive listening behaviors available to therapists, immediacy is perhaps the best illustration of how client-centered and therapist-centered behaviors are integrated into a single therapy intervention. As you can see from the preceding examples, immediacy involves relatively equal parts client

Table 3.2 Summary of Directive Listening Behaviors and Their Usual Effects

Listening Response	Description	Primary Intent/Effect
Feeling validation	Statement that supports, affirms, approves of, or validates feelings articulated by clients.	Enhances rapport. Temporarily reduces anxiety. May cause the therapist to be viewed as an expert.
Interpretive reflection of feeling	Statement indicating what feelings the therapist believes are underlying the client's thoughts or actions.	May enhance empathy and encourage emotional exploration and insight.
Interpretation	Statement indicating what meaning the therapist believes a client's emotions, thoughts, and/or actions represent. Often includes references to past experiences.	Encourages reflection and self-observation of clients' emotions, thoughts, and actions. Promotes client insight.
Confrontation	Statement that points out or identifies a client incongruity or discrepancy. Ranges from very gentle to very harsh.	Encourages clients to examine themselves and their patterns of thinking, feeling, and behaving. May result in personal change and development.
Immediacy	Statement that integrates a here-and-now therapist disclosure that can be used for confrontation, support, or guidance.	Initiates an examination or exploration of the here-and-now therapeutic relationship; focuses on how the client is affecting the therapist or being perceived by the therapist.

observation and disclosure in a way that provides both client and therapist with therapeutic grist for the mill. (See Table 3.2 for a summary of directive listening behaviors.)

SUMMARY

Attending behavior is primarily nonverbal and consists of culturally appropriate eye contact, body language, vocal qualities, and verbal tracking. Positive attending behaviors open up and facilitate client talk, whereas negative attending behaviors tend to shut down client communication.

Negative attending behavior consists of a variety of annoying behaviors, including excessive positive attending behaviors. Considerable cultural and individual differences exist among clients regarding the amount and type of eye contact, body language, vocal qualities, and verbal tracking they prefer. To improve communication and attending skills, therapists should seek feedback from peers and supervisors.

Beyond attending behaviors, therapists employ many different nondirective listening behaviors, including silence, paraphrasing (or reflection of content), clarification, reflection of feeling, and summarization. Nondirective listening behaviors are designed to facilitate client self-expression. However, even nondirective listening behaviors influence clients and have some directive qualities.

Directive interviewing behaviors are defined as responses to the client that bring the therapist's perspective into the session. Therapists can be too directive, leaving clients feeling controlled. They can also be too nondirective, leaving clients feeling lost and directionless. Generally, directive interviewing behaviors are advanced techniques that encourage clients to change their thinking or behavior patterns. Directive interviewing behaviors are used for assessment purposes, to explore issues with clients, and to facilitate insight. Directives tend to work best after a therapeutic alliance has been established.

Directive listening behaviors include feeling validation, interpretive reflection of feeling, interpretation (psychoanalytic or reframing), confrontation, and immediacy. These techniques involve therapists identifying particular issues for clients to focus on during the session.

SUGGESTED READINGS AND RESOURCES

The following textbooks and workbooks offer additional information and exercises on attending skills, as well as therapeutic techniques from different theoretical orientations.

Cormier, S., Nurius, P., & Osborn, C. J. (2012). *Interviewing strategies for helpers: Fundamental skills and cognitive behavioral interventions* (7th ed.). Monterey, CA: Brooks/Cole.
   This book includes many different activities for practicing skills such as self-disclosure, immediacy, and confrontation.
Gibbs, M. A. (1984). "The therapist as imposter." In C. M. Brody (Ed.), *Women therapists working with women: New theory and process of feminist therapy*. New York, NY: Springer.
   This chapter is a strong appeal to therapists to acknowledge their insecurities and inadequacies. It provides insights into how experienced professionals can and do feel inadequate.
Greenson, R. R. (1967). *The technique and practice of psychoanalysis* (Vol. 1). New York, NY: International Universities Press.
   This classic work provides extensive ground rules for the use of interpretation.
Hays, P. A. (2013). *Connecting across cultures: The helper's toolkit*. Thousand Oaks, CA: Sage.
   In this practical text, Pamela Hays offers many concrete examples for how clinicians can develop a strong therapy alliance with diverse clients.
Hill, C. E. (2009). *Helping skills: Facilitating exploration, insight, and action* (3rd ed.). Washington, DC: American Psychological Association.
   Chapter 14 of Hill's basic text focuses exclusively on interpretation.
Ivey, A., Ivey, M. B., & Zalaquett, C. (2010). *Intentional interviewing and counseling: Facilitating client development in a multicultural society* (7th ed.). Belmont, CA: Brooks Cole.
   Allen Ivey has been writing about microskills since the 1960s.
Meador, B., & Rogers, C. R. (1984). "Person-centered therapy." In R. J. Corsini (Ed.), *Current psychotherapies* (3rd ed.). Itasca, IL: Peacock.
   This chapter in Corsini's third edition (if you can find it) contains a fabulous excerpt of Rogers's classic interview with the "silent young man."
Messer, S. B., & McWilliams, N. (2007). *Insight in psychodynamic therapy: Theory and assessment*. Washington, DC: American Psychological Association.

This text also includes excellent advanced information on how to facilitate insight through interpretation.

Miller, J. B. (1986). *Toward a new psychology of women* (2nd ed.). Boston, MA: Beacon Press.
This book is about women (and men) and the issues they deal with in contemporary society. It helps articulate the depth and meaning of some difficulties traditionally associated with being female.

Rogers, C. R. (1951). *Client-centered therapy*. Boston, MA: Houghton Mifflin.
This text includes Rogers's original discussion of feeling reflection (Chapter 4).

Directives: Questions and Action Skills

CHAPTER OBJECTIVES

Therapists must move beyond listening and assess clients through the skillful use of questions. The interview isn't an investigation, but at times, therapists may take on an investigator role (e.g., gathering information and tracking down symptoms and/or diagnoses). In addition, therapists sometimes encourage clients to take specific actions—actions deemed helpful for creating insight or resolving a problem. In this chapter, we analyze questions and directive techniques often used in a clinical interview.

After reading this chapter, you will understand:

- The many general questions available to therapists, how to use them, and their usual effects (and side effects).
- The benefits and liabilities of using questions with clients.
- How asking some questions can be inappropriate and how asking other questions can be unethical.
- Guidelines for using questions in an interview.
- Several different theory-based assessment and therapeutic questions.
- The nature and use of directives and action skills.
- Why directives and action skills are more or less effective with different clients.
- A range of different directives and action skills, including explanation, suggestion, agreement-disagreement, approval-disapproval, advice, self-disclosure, and urging.

Questions and directives are two discrete interviewing skills that share much common ground. Keeping these skills together in one chapter emphasizes their similarities. However, we also highlight their differences by dividing this chapter into two sections. Section One is devoted to helping you understand general and theory-based questions. Section Two focuses on using directive interviewing behaviors.

SECTION ONE: USING GENERAL AND THERAPEUTIC QUESTIONS

Imagine digging a hole without a shovel or building a house without a hammer. For many therapists, conducting an interview without using questions constitutes an analogous problem: How can you complete a task without using your most basic tool?

Despite the central role of questions in an interview, we've managed to avoid discussing them until this chapter. Gathering information is not synonymous with asking questions, and believe it or not, sometimes asking questions actually gets in the way of gathering important information from your clients. Throughout this text, we hope to stimulate your creativity and help you understand the depth, breadth, and application of other listening and communication tools. Developing a complete range of interviewing skills will help you avoid depending too much on questions.

Questions are a diverse and flexible interviewing tool; they can be used to:

- Stimulate client talk
- Restrict client talk
- Facilitate rapport
- Show interest in clients
- Show disinterest in clients
- Gather information
- Pressure clients
- Focus on solutions
- Ignore the client's viewpoint

As you proceed through the section on using questions, reflect on how it feels to freely use what many of you consider your most basic tool.

> Grown-ups love figures. When you tell them that you have made a new friend, they never ask you any questions about essential matters. They never say to you, "What does his voice sound like? What games does he love best? Does he collect butterflies?" Instead, they demand: "How old is he? How many brothers has he? How much does he weigh? How much money does his father make?" Only from these figures do they think they have learned anything about him.
>
> —*Antoine de Saint-Exupéry*, The Little Prince *(1971)*

Questions are a directive and integral part of human communication. Asking questions, especially if you're interested in obtaining particular information, can be hard to resist. Unfortunately, as in the case of *The Little Prince*, there's no guarantee that the questions you ask (and their corresponding answers) will be of any value whatsoever to the person being questioned.

DVD Clip

In the *Questions and Therapeutic Questions* DVD chapter, John and Rita discuss the nature of questions and introduce the *Chris & Ümüt* counseling demonstration.

General Types of Questions

There are many forms or types of questions. Differentiating among them is important because different question types will produce different client responses. In this section, we initially organize our discussion around general question types: open, closed, swing, indirect or implied, and projective and then focus separately on therapeutic questions. Keep in mind that although we distinguish between types of general questions and therapeutic questions, all forms of questioning can be used for assessment or therapeutic purposes, depending on how the questions are used.

Open Questions

Open questions facilitate verbal output because they typically require more than a single-word response. Open questions ordinarily begin with the word *How* or *What*. Writers sometimes classify questions that begin with *Where*, *When*, *Why*, and/or *Who* as open questions, but such questions are really only partially open because they don't facilitate talk as well as *How* and *What* questions (Cormier, Nurius, & Osborn, 2012). The following hypothetical dialogue illustrates how using questions traditionally classified as open may or may not stimulate client talk:

Therapist: When did you first begin having panic attacks?
Client: In 1996.
Therapist: Where were you when you had your first panic attack?
Client: I was just getting on the subway in New York City.
Therapist: What happened?
Client: When I stepped inside the train, my heart began to pound. I thought I was dying. I just held onto the metal post next to my seat because I was afraid I would fall over and be humiliated. I felt dizzy and nauseated. Then I got off the train at my stop and I've never been back on the subway again.
Therapist: Who was with you?
Client: No one.
Therapist: Why haven't you tried to ride the subway again?
Client: Because I'm afraid I'll have another panic attack.
Therapist: How are you handling the fact that your fear of panic attacks is so restrictive?
Client: Well, frankly, not so good. I've been slowly getting more and more scared to go out. I'm afraid that soon I'll be too scared to leave my house.

As you can see, open questions vary in their degree of openness. They don't uniformly facilitate depth and breadth of talk. Although questions beginning with *What* or *How* usually elicit the most elaborate responses from clients, this isn't always the case. More often, it's the way a particular *What* or *How* question is phrased that produces specific or wide-ranging client responses. For example, "What time did you get home?" and "How are you feeling?" can be answered very succinctly. The openness of a particular question should be judged primarily by the response it usually elicits.

Questions beginning with *Why* are unique in that they commonly elicit defensive explanations. Meier and Davis (2011) stated, "Questions, particularly 'why' questions, put clients on the defensive and ask them to explain their behavior" (p. 23). *Why* questions frequently produce one of two responses. First, as in the preceding example, clients may respond with "*Because!*" and then explain, sometimes through very detailed and intellectual responses, why they're thinking or acting or feeling in a particular manner. Second, some clients defend themselves with "Why not?" or, because they feel attacked, they seek reassurance by confronting their therapist with "Is there anything wrong with that?" This illustrates why therapists usually minimize *Why* questions—they exacerbate defensiveness and intellectualization and diminish rapport. On the other hand, for cases in which rapport is good and you want clients to speculate or intellectualize regarding a particular aspect of life, *Why* questions may be appropriate and useful in helping your client take a closer, deeper look at certain patterns or motivations.

Closed Questions

Closed questions can be answered with a yes or no response. Although sometimes classified as open, questions that begin with *Who, Where,* or *When* direct clients toward very specific information; therefore, we believe they generally should be considered closed questions (see *Putting It in Practice* 4.1).

Closed questions restrict verbalization and lead clients toward specific responses. They can reduce or control how much clients talk. Restricting verbal output is useful when interviewing clients who are excessively talkative. Also, closed questions can help specify behaviors and symptoms and thereby be helpful for conducting diagnostic interviews (e.g., in the preceding example about a panic attack on the New York subway, a diagnostic interviewer might ask, "Did you feel lightheaded or dizzy?" to confirm or disconfirm the presence of panic attack symptoms).

PUTTING IT IN PRACTICE 4.1

Open and Closed Questions

The four sets of questions that follow are designed to obtain information pertaining to the same topic. As a way of comparing how clients might react to these different question types, imagine how you might answer these questions.

1. (Open) "How are you feeling about being in therapy?"
   (Closed) "Are you feeling good about being in therapy?"
2. (Open) "After you walked onto the subway and you felt your heart begin to pound, what happened next?"
   (Closed) "Did you feel lightheaded or dizzy after you walked onto the subway?"
3. (Open) "What was it like for you to confront your father after having been angry with him for so many years?"
   (Closed) "Was it gratifying for you to confront your father after having been angry with him for so many years?"
4. (Open) "How do you feel?"
   (Closed) "Do you feel angry?"

Notice and discuss with other classmates the differences in how you (and clients) are affected by open versus closed questioning.

Sometimes, therapists inadvertently or intentionally transform open questions into closed questions with a tag query. For example, we often hear students formulate questions such as, "What was it like for you to confront your father after all these years—was it gratifying?"

As you can see, transforming open questions into closed questions limits client elaboration. Unless clients faced with such questions are exceptionally expressive or assertive, they're likely to focus solely on whether they felt gratification when confronting their father (as in the *Putting It in Practice* 4.1 example). Consequently, clients may or may not elaborate on feelings of fear, relief, resentment, or anything else they've experienced.

Closed questions usually begin with words such as *Do, Does, Did, Is, Was,* or *Are.* They're very useful if you want to solicit specific information. Traditionally, closed questions are used more toward the interview's end, when rapport is already established, time is short, and efficient questions and short responses are needed (Morrison, 2007).

If you begin an interview using a nondirective approach, but later change styles to obtain more specific information through closed questions, it's wise to inform the client of this shift in strategy. For example, you might state:

> Okay, we have about 15 minutes left and I have a few things I want to make sure I've covered, so I'm going to start asking you very specific questions.

Beginning therapists sometimes are coached to avoid closed questions. This is often (but not always) good advice because closed questions are frequently interpreted as veiled suggestions. For example:

Client:	Ever since my husband came back from Afghanistan he's been moody, irritable, and withdrawn. This makes me miss him terribly, even though he's home. I just want my old husband back.
Therapist:	Have you told him how you're feeling?

In this case the client is likely to feel as though the therapist is suggesting that she open up to her husband about her feelings. Although this may (or may not) be a great idea, using a closed question instead of an open question pulls the client along in a specific direction. Instead, an open question like, "How have you been dealing with these feelings?" allows the client to tell you about what's she's been doing before a suggestion is implied or offered. Overall, closed questions are a very helpful interviewing tool—as long as they're used intentionally and in ways consistent with their purpose.

Swing Questions

Swing questions can be answered with a yes or no, but are designed to invite more elaborate discussion of feelings, thoughts, or issues (Shea, 1998). In a sense, swing questions inquire about whether the client wants to respond. Swing questions usually begin with *Could,* or *Would, Can,* or *Will.* For example:

- Could you talk about how it was when you first discovered you were HIV positive?
- Would you describe how you think your parents might react to finding out you're gay?

- Can you tell me more about that?
- Will you tell me what happened in the argument between you and your husband last night?

Ivey, Ivey, and Zalaquett (2011) wrote that swing questions the most open of all questions: "Could, can, or would questions are considered maximally open and contain some advantages of closed questions. Clients are free to say 'No, I don't want to talk about that.' Could questions suggest less interviewer control" (p. 85).

For swing questions to function effectively, you should observe two basic rules. First, avoid using swing questions unless rapport has been established. If rapport isn't adequately established, a swing question may backfire and function as a closed question (i.e., the client responds with a shy or resistant yes or no). Second, avoid using swing questions with children and adolescents. This is because children and adolescents often interpret swing questions concretely and may respond oppositionally (J. Sommers-Flanagan & Sommers-Flanagan, 2007b). The two following examples illustrate this potential problem when interviewing youth:

Counselor: Would you come with me back to my office?
Young Client: No.
Counselor: Could you tell me about how you felt when your dad left?
Young Client: No.

As you can see, using swing questions with young clients (especially if you don't have positive rapport) can produce an awkward and unhelpful situation.

Indirect or Implied Questions

Indirect or implied questions often begin with *I wonder* or *You must* or *It must* (Benjamin, 1987). They're used when therapists are curious about what clients are thinking or feeling, but don't want to pressure clients to respond. Following are some examples of indirect or implied questions:

- I wonder how you're feeling about your upcoming wedding.
- I wonder what your plans are after graduation.
- I wonder if you've given any thought to searching for a job.
- You must have some thoughts or feelings about your parents' divorce.
- It must be hard for you to cope with the loss of your health.

There are many other indirect sentence stems that imply a question or prompt clients to speak about a topic. Common examples include: "I'd like to hear about . . . " and "Tell me about. . . . "

Indirect or implied questions can be useful early in interviews or when approaching delicate topics. They're gentle and noncoercive and so they may be especially useful as an alternative to direct questions with clients who seem reticent (Chad Luke, personal communication, August 7, 2012). It should also be noted that when overused, indirect questions can seem sneaky or manipulative; after repeated "I wonder . . . " and "You must . . . " probes, clients may start thinking, "Stop all this fluff and just ask me whatever it is you want know!"

Projective or Presuppositional Questions

Projective questions help clients identify, articulate, explore, and clarify unconscious or unclear conflicts, values, thoughts, and feelings. Solution-focused therapists refer to projective questions as presuppositional questions (Murphy, 2008). These questions typically begin with some form of *What if* and invite client speculation. Often, projective questions are used to trigger mental imagery and help clients explore thoughts, feelings, and behaviors they might have if they were in a particular situation. For example:

- What would you do if you were given one million dollars, no strings attached?
- If you had three wishes, what would you wish for?
- If you needed help or were really frightened, or even if you were just totally out of money and needed some, who would you turn to right now? (J. Sommers-Flanagan & Sommers-Flanagan, 1998, p. 193)
- What if you could go back and change how you acted during that party (or other significant life event), what would you do differently?

Projective questions are also used for evaluating client values and judgment. For example, a therapist can analyze a response to the question "What would you do with one million dollars?" to indirectly glimpse client values and self-control. The million-dollar question also can be used to evaluate client decision-making or judgment. Projective questions are sometimes included in mental status examinations (see Chapter 7 and the Appendix).

Perhaps even more than with other types of questions, your use of projective questions is only limited by your creativity. One of this book's authors, John, likes to use projective questions to explore the depth or dynamics in relationships. For example, with a 15-year-old male client who was struggling in school, John asked, "If you did really well on a test, who's the first person you would tell?" The client responded, "My dad." This response was significant in this case because the boy had a very strained relationship with his father and yet, based on his response to the question, he was still very interested in getting his father's approval. Table 4.1 summarizes the various types of questions and usual client responses.

Table 4.1　Question Classification

Word Question Begins With	Type of Question	Usual Client Responses
What	Open	Factual and descriptive information
How	Open	Process or sequential information
Why	Partially open	Explanations and defensiveness
Where	Minimally open	Information pertaining to location
When	Minimally open	Information pertaining to time
Who	Minimally open	Information pertaining to a person
Do/Did	Closed	Specific information
Could/Would/ Can/Will	Swing	Diverse info, sometimes rejected
I wonder/You must/ I'd like to hear	Indirect	Exploration of thoughts and feelings
What if	Projective or presuppositional	Information on judgment and values

Benefits and Liabilities of General Questions

Therapists vary in their beliefs and habits with regard to questions. To explore this, sometimes we assign students the task of conducting a brief interview in which they only ask questions (no paraphrasing allowed!). Some students have a very positive reaction to the assignment, whereas others openly hate it. We get similar responses when the assignment is to use predominantly solution-focused questions. Student reactions have included:

- I felt more in control.
- I felt more pressure.
- It was like I was asking the same question (about positive goals) over and over again.
- The solution-focused questions really help me help the client stay positive.
- It was hard to think of questions while I was trying to listen to the client, and it was hard to listen to the client while I was thinking of what might be a good question to ask next.
- I seemed to have less patience. I just wanted to get to my next question and kept cutting in to ask more questions.
- I felt less pressure. I really liked asking questions!

As an assessment or therapeutic tool, questions have both benefits and liabilities. Whether a given question functions in a positive or negative way depends on many factors, including the therapist's skill and the client's sensitivities. Table 4.2 includes potential benefits and liabilities of questions.

Overall, although exceptions are possible, the more you emphasize questions, the more you highlight your power, responsibility, and authority within the interview. To some extent, the questioner is always in charge of the interaction, directing and controlling the interview process. Benjamin (1987) commented on excessive question use:

Yes, I have many reservations about the use of questions in the interview. I feel certain that we ask too many questions, often meaningless ones. We

Table 4.2 Potential Benefits and Liabilities of Questions

Benefit	Liability
Client discusses thoughts and feelings in greater depth.	The therapist's interests and values are the focus, not the client's.
Specific client information can be clarified and obtained more efficiently.	Clients may feel their perspective is devalued.
Clients can feel relieved when the therapist leads the interview and asks good questions.	The therapist can get set up to be the expert.
Clients can be encouraged to focus on strengths and possible positive outcomes.	Clients might feel pressured to respond to probing questions.
Specific, concrete examples of client behavior can be obtained.	Client spontaneity may be reduced or passivity may be increased.

ask questions that confuse the interviewee, that interrupt him. We ask questions the interviewee cannot possibly answer. We even ask questions we don't want the answers to, and consequently, we do not hear the answers when forthcoming. (p. 71)

Benjamin was obviously a big nondirective interviewing advocate. His concerns about questioning are well articulated, but practitioners from other theoretical orientations disagree with his conclusions. In fact, some clients prefer to be asked many questions because questions provide clear guidelines regarding what they should say. Also, less directive techniques can be disconcerting for diverse clients, partly because of trust issues (D. W. Sue & Sue, 2013). In the end, although sometimes overused, questions are very useful for gathering information, exploring client symptoms, and helping clients focus on strengths.

Therapist Curiosity and Professional Ethics

We've often noticed in ourselves and in our students a strong urge to ask inappropriate questions. These questions may be designed to satisfy our own curiosity or just be reflective of whatever is on our mind.

For example, if a client mentions he or she grew up somewhere you're familiar with, you may feel an impulse to ask questions like: "Where did you go to high school?" or "Did you ever go to that great bakery on Third Street?" These questions are more designed to satisfy your curiosity rather than help you establish a diagnosis and treatment plan. These questions also may give the interview a social, rather than therapeutic, flavor. Further, if you give in to your curiosity, you might also begin giving in to inappropriate self-disclosure ("Yeah, I remember one night I was out drinking with a couple buddies and . . . "). You can imagine where that disclosure might go. Remember, everything you do, including asking questions or using self-disclosure, should be designed to further the client's welfare (Bloomgarden & Mennuti, 2009).

Many rules have exceptions and, in fact, there may be a time, place, and purpose for therapists to let their social curiosity roam free. For example, in a qualitative study of Latino/a therapists, many of the therapists specifically spoke to the value of charlar (small talk) when providing clinical services to Latino/a clients (Gallardo, 2013). Gallardo wrote:

While the idea of "small talk" is not an "official" component in "traditional" training, in working with Latinas/os using charlar facilitates the establishment of the therapeutic relationship, while creating a foundation for future work. (p. 47)

In this and other areas, ethical and effective interviewing behaviors may involve a balancing act. If you freely follow certain impulses and ask inappropriate questions ethical problems may surface. An ethical dilemma popularized by A. Lazarus (1994) focused on whether it's acceptable, at the end of a therapy hour, for a therapist to ask the client for a ride somewhere (provided the client is going that direction anyway). Our position is that mental health professionals should get their personal needs met outside therapy, even supposedly innocuous needs—such as catching a ride or satisfying a bit of hometown curiosity. Of course, it's possible to be too rigid in your application of this principle, but we generally avoid boundary violations because they can lead to more frequent inappropriate impulses and eventual ethical violations (R. Sommers-Flanagan, Elliott, & Sommers-Flanagan, 1998).

Guidelines in Using General Questions

Both clients and therapists can have strong reactions to questions. To optimize your use of questions, we offer the following five guidelines:

1. Prepare your clients for questions.
2. Don't use questions as your predominant listening or action response (unless you're using a specific and accepted theoretical approach).
3. Make questions relevant to your clients' concerns and goals.
4. Use questions to elicit concrete behavioral examples and positive visions for the future.
5. Approach sensitive areas cautiously.

Prepare Your Clients for Questions

A simple technique that reduces negative fallout from questioning is to warn clients when intensive questioning is coming. This often helps clients be less defensive and more cooperative. You can forewarn clients by saying:

> I need to get some specific information from you. So, for a while, I'll be asking you lots of questions to help me get that information. Some of the questions may seem odd, but I promise, there's a reason behind them.

Don't Use General Questions Without Nondirective Listening

Generally speaking, questions should be combined with less directive listening skills. This is true whether the questions are used for assessment or for therapeutic purposes. Be sure to follow your client's response to your query, at least occasionally, with a listening response:

Interviewer: What happened when you first stepped onto the subway?

Client: When I got inside the train, I felt my heart begin to pound. I thought I was going to die. I just held onto the metal post as hard as I could because I was afraid I would fall over and be humiliated. Then I got off the train at my stop and I've never been back on the subway again.

Interviewer: It sounds like that was a frightening experience. You were doing everything you could to stay in control. Was anyone with you when you went through this panicky experience?

Unless listening skills are used in combination with repeated questions, clients are likely to feel bombarded or interrogated. Miller and Rollnick (2002) suggest a three-question rule: They recommend that therapists avoid asking more than three questions consecutively.

Make Your Questions Relevant to Client Concerns and Goals

Clients are more likely to view you as competent and credible if you focus on their major concerns and/or goals. Therefore, to use questions skillfully, aim your queries directly at what the client believes is important.

It may be hard for clients to understand the purpose of certain diagnostic or mental status questions. For example, when interviewing depressed clients, the following questions would be relevant:

- How has your appetite been?
- Have you been sleeping through the night?
- Have you had trouble concentrating?
- Do you find yourself interested in sex lately?

Imagine how a depressed client who is irritable, psychologically naïve, and who believes, somewhat accurately, that her bad mood is related to 10 years of emotional abuse from her domestic partner, might perceive such a series of questions. She might think, "I couldn't believe that counselor! What do my appetite, sex life, and concentration have to do with why I came to see her?" Unless clients can see the relevance of their counselor's questions, the questions can decrease rapport and reduce client interest in therapy (see Chapter 10 for more information on diagnostic interviewing).

Similarly, from a solution-focused perspective, presuppositional questions will make more sense to clients when they focus on the client's goals. For example, asking a teenage client, "What would it look like if you imagine yourself getting along great with your teacher" is more effective when the student has identified "getting along with the teacher" as a therapy goal.

Use Questions to Elicit Concrete Behavioral Examples and Positive Visions of the Future

Perhaps the best use of questions is to obtain clear, concrete, past, present, or future behavioral examples from clients. Instead of relying on abstract client descriptions, questions can be used to obtain specific behavioral examples:

Client: I have so much trouble with social situations. I guess I'm just an anxious and insecure person.

Interviewer: Could you give me an example of a recent social situation when you felt anxious and thought you were insecure?

Client: Yeah, let me think. Well, there was the party at the frat the other night. Everyone else seemed to be having a great time, and I just felt left out. I'm sure no one wanted to talk with me.

In this exchange, although the therapist asks a swing question to obtain specific information, the client remains somewhat vague. Keep in mind that it's often difficult or uncomfortable for clients to be specific when describing their problems. In this situation, reassurance may be helpful (e.g., "Sometimes it can be hard to come up with a specific example.") After offering reassurance and support, repeated open and closed questions may be needed to help clients be more specific and concrete in describing their anxiety. For example:

- What exactly was happening when you felt anxious and insecure at the party?
- Who was standing near you when you had these feelings?
- What thoughts were going through your mind?
- What would you have done differently in this situation if you could do it over again?

It's also helpful for therapists to track verbal material as clients tell their stories. For example, when clients leave gaps in a story, it's best to ask an open-ended question such as, "What happened then?" rather than a close-ended question like, "Did you go visit your mother?" Well-timed open-ended questions asked as a client tells a story about him/herself will usually keep the client talking.

From a solution-focused perspective, Sklare (2005) recommended using "What else?" questions to keep clients imagining their positive future visions. For example, questions like, "What else will happen after this miracle occurs?" (Sklare, 2005, p. 33) or "What else will you be thinking and feeling when you stay calm?" can help clients hone in on positive future visions.

Approach Sensitive Areas Cautiously

Be especially careful when questioning clients about sensitive topics. As Wolberg (1995) noted, it's important *not* to immediately question new clients in sensitive areas (e.g., appearance, status, sexual difficulties, failures). Wolberg suggested instead that clients be allowed to talk freely about sensitive topics, but if blocking occurs, questioning should be avoided until the relationship is better established; early in therapy, relationship building is a higher priority than information gathering.

Despite Wolberg's (1995) generally good advice, sometimes the therapy relationship must share the front seat with information gathering. This is especially true when conducting an intake interview, when a client is in crisis, or when the setting demands a speedy assessment. For example, if a client is suicidal or homicidal, gathering assessment data for clinical decision-making is top priority—along with relationship building (see Chapter 9). If you're in a clinical situation and unsure about whether it's acceptable to pursue a specific and sensitive area of questioning, you can always ask, "Is it okay with you if I ask you a few personal questions?" or state your intentions while giving the client permission for privacy (e.g., "I'm going to ask you some personal questions, but you don't have to answer them if you don't want to.").

DVD Clip

In the *Chris & Ümüt* counseling demonstration, Chris demonstrates not only how to use open/closed/swing/projective questions, but also skillfully integrates paraphrasing and summarization into the process.

Theory-Based Assessment and Therapeutic Questions

All questions can serve therapeutic and/or assessment purposes, but some questions are designed to elicit information or facilitate change in a manner consistent with the therapist's theoretical frame. For example, from a psychodynamic perspective, a prompt such as "Say whatever comes to mind" or questions like, "What does that bring to mind?" facilitate the free association process. When therapists use questions as interventions, they're embracing the directive quality of questions, using questions to guide clients toward thinking, feeling, and acting in certain ways. Below, we describe a number of theory-based questions. The guidance and cautions regarding general questions in the section above are relevant to these theory-driven questions as well.

The Question

Alfred Adler believed all human behavior is purposeful (Carlson, Watts, & Maniacci, 2006; Watts & Eckstein, 2009). He applied this belief to both adaptive (healthy) and maladaptive (unhealthy) behaviors. However, as discussed previously, asking clients *why* they're behaving in unhealthy or maladaptive ways is often likely to produce defensiveness and explanations for unhealthy behaviors. Ever the creative interviewer, Adler developed a projective question that he viewed as effective in uncovering the purpose of unhealthy client behaviors. Adler referred to this as "The question." It's intended to help clients articulate what they might lose if they were to give up their unhealthy behaviors. The question is phrased as: "What would be different if you were well?"

Although the goal of Adler's "The question" is somewhat different, it's often considered a precursor to the solution-focused "miracle question" (de Shazer, 1985). Both the miracle question (described in detail later in this chapter) and Adler's "The question" help clients envision themselves and their lives without their primary problem. Adler's emphasis was more on what has been termed "secondary gain" in that he was interested in understanding what underlying purpose or motive was sustaining specific unhealthy behaviors. Based on Adlerian theory, it's often likely that clients are engaging in unhealthy behaviors because of attention, power and control, revenge, or to maintain a pattern of inadequacy that ensures they're taken care of by others. Using "The question" identifies what forces make it difficult for clients to give up their maladaptive behavior patterns.

The Four Big Reality Therapy Questions

There are four essential questions associated with choice theory and reality therapy. Although these questions may or may not be asked directly, they're foundational to reality therapy. Many additional questions have been derived from these four basic, guiding questions (Wubbolding, 2011). Wubbolding has summarized the four big questions of reality therapy using the acronym WDEP (Wants, Doing, Evaluation, Planning). They include:

1. What do you want?
2. What are you doing?
3. Is it working?
4. Should you make a new plan?

Wubbolding (2011) has written extensively about these questions and many others that can be used to help clients identify goals and develop plans for attaining those goals. He emphasizes that these questions are very flexible and should be modified for different cultural populations (Wubbolding et al., 2004). For example, based on his work with Japanese clients, he suggested that, rather than asking direct questions pertaining to whether a particular behavior is working (evaluation), counselors should phrase the question differently (e.g., "Is that a plus or a minus for you?").

The work of Adler and Glasser (and now Wubbolding) emphasizes the purpose of client behavior and helps therapists focus in on whether clients are, in fact, behaving in ways that are consistent with their own best interests (Glasser, 1998, 2000). These questions have been integrated into many different therapeutic systems and even popularized in the talk-show entertainment industry. For example, when Dr. Phil asks guests on his television show, "How's that working for you?" he's using an Adlerian or choice theory approach to help them self-reflect or self-evaluate the usefulness of their behavior in attaining their own goals.

Narrative and Solution-Focused Therapeutic Questions

Solution-focused and narrative approaches rely heavily on questioning (de Jong & Berg, 2008; Madigan, 2011). de Shazer and Dolan (2007) articulated the practical and theoretical significance of questions from the solution-focused perspective:

> SFBT [Solution-Focused Brief Therapy] therapists . . . make questions the primary communication tool, and as such they are an overarching intervention. SFBT therapists tend to make no interpretation, and rarely make direct challenges or confrontations to a client. . . . The questions that are asked by SFBT therapists are almost always focused on the present or on the future. This reflects the basic belief that problems are best solved by focusing on what is already working, and how a client would like his or her life to be, rather than focusing on the past and the origin of problems. (pp. 4–5)

As noted in Chapter 3, narrative and solution-focused therapists believe that because all therapists intentionally or unintentionally lead their clients, therapists should intentionally lead their clients toward positive thoughts, feelings, and behaviors. For narrative and solution-focused therapists, there's less distinction between assessment and intervention. Consequently, you'll notice that the following therapeutic questioning strategies include questions that have both assessment and intervention qualities. These questions share a common core. They are intended to help clients focus on positive, hopeful, and constructive themes in their lives.

The Pretreatment Change Question

Research suggests that clients sometimes begin improving between the time they call for an appointment and when they initially meet with their therapist (de Vega & Beyebach, 2004). Solution-focused therapists take advantage of this tendency, and ask clients to elaborate on their self-initiated improvement. They ask a version of the following question near the beginning of the first session with nearly every client:

> What changes have you noticed that have happened or started to happen since you called to make the appointment for this session? (de Shazer & Dolan, 2007, p. 5)

If clients respond that there have been no noticeable improvements, solution-focused therapists are likely to move on and open the session by asking something like: "What would you like to have happen during our meeting that would make our time together successful today?" Or, if clients answer that "Nothing has changed," the solution-focused response might be "How have you been able to keep things from getting worse?"

If clients report any positive improvements (e.g., "Yeah, after I called I decided to get together with an old friend and we talked and had a good time."), the therapist begins asking the client questions like:

- What was good about seeing your friend?
- How did you manage to come up with the excellent idea of getting together with your friend?
- What other excellent ideas have you had since you went out with your friend?

These questions frame and highlight the client's own abilities to initiate positive change—even without the help of therapy. They also empathically acknowledge the courage and commitment it takes for clients to seek therapy (Chad Luke, personal communication, August 7, 2012). This strategy begins the process of having the client engage in "solution talk" instead of "problem talk" (de Shazer et al., 2007).

Scaling Questions

Scaling questions help clients envision their potential improvement more precisely. Here's an example:

Counselor: On a scale of 1–10, with 1 being the "very worst possible" and 10 being the "very best possible," how would you rate how well you've been handling your anger this past week?

Client: Oh, I don't know, I guess about a 4.

Counselor: Okay. Let's say next week you were able to improve your rating to a 5. What, exactly, would be different in you, if you came in next week and are able to tell me that you're handling your anger at the level of a 5?

Client: I think the biggest thing is that I'd stop yelling so much.

Counselor: What would that look like? Exactly how much would you need to stop yelling to get your rating up to a 5?

Scaling questions help clients focus on what needs to change for an improvement to be noticeable. Theoretically, from the constructive perspective, the more a therapist keeps clients focused on a vision of improvement, the more likely it is for positive change to occur.

Percentage Questions

Percentage questions are very similar to scaling questions; they direct clients to think about and define how an improvement would look, sound, feel (and even smell!).

Counselor: You've been telling me about how depressed you've been feeling and that sounds very hard. But I'm wondering, how exactly would your life be different if you were 1 percent less depressed?

Client: I might be able to get out of bed in the morning.

Counselor: Excellent. So that's what a 1% improvement would look like. How about if you were 10% less depressed? What would that look like?"

Client: I guess I'd be able to not just get up in the morning, but also be able to get out and start looking for a job.

Counselor: Great. How about if you were 50% less depressed? What would that look like?

Client: It would look pretty good.

Counselor: Exactly how good would it look, sound, feel, and even smell?

Perhaps what's most important to observe in the preceding example is how the counselor systematically keeps the client focusing on the appearance, sound, feel, and smell of success or improvement. This can be a difficult process and may require more extensive interactions than illustrated here because clients may or may not be able to articulate what small changes would look like. Also, from a cognitive therapy perspective, scaling and percentage questions provide an intervention for the black-white or dichotomous thinking often associated with depressive symptoms (J. Beck, 2011).

Unique Outcomes or Redescription Questions

Unique outcomes (sometimes referred to as unique account) or redescription questions were originally developed by renowned narrative therapist, Michael White (1988). In narrative therapy a collaborative process between therapist and client is emphasized and then the client's personal story is analyzed and reconstructed using a more positive or strength-based framework. Unique outcomes questions direct clients toward describing ways in which they've accomplished some specific positive task. Winslade and Monk (2007) described the counselor's focus while using unique outcomes questions:

> The counselor selects for attention any experience, however minute and insignificant to the client, that stands apart from the problem story. These fragments of experience are the raw material from which the new story can be fashioned. By asking questions about these "unique outcomes," the counselor inquires into the client's influence on the life of the problem. (p. 10)

Examples of unique outcomes and redescription questions include:

- How did you beat the fear and go out shopping?
- How did you manage to stay calm?

- What did you do that helped you get yourself out of bed and in here for this appointment despite the depression?
- You just stopped drinking last week cold turkey! How did you accomplish that?
- What were you telling yourself when you were feeling a little better last month? (J. Sommers-Flanagan & Sommers-Flanagan, 2012, p. 384)

Based on constructive theory, unique outcome and redescription questions can be used whenever clients report individual accomplishments, no matter how small. This question-based intervention turns the tables on traditional problem-focused interviewing approaches. Problem-focused approaches typically encourage clients to analyze their problems with questions like:

- What were you thinking when you had that panic attack?
- What usually leads to the fights and abuse in your family?

In contrast, unique outcome questions focus on strengths and successes and encourage a deeper analysis of success by asking questions like,

- What were you thinking when you were able to stay calm and fight off your anxiety?
- What helps you and your family keep the peace?

We should note that although there's great appeal in systematically and persistently focusing on client strengths, being able to do so in ways that clients are willing to accept is rather challenging. As you may already recognize, many clients strongly identify with their symptoms and would prefer talking about negative experiences more than about their personal strengths. This is one of several reasons why using solution-focused and narrative techniques isn't always simple and straightforward and consequently requires practice, supervision, and feedback.

Presuppositional Questions

Presuppositional questions are very similar to projective questions. They *presuppose* a positive change has already occurred and ask for clients to elaborate on those changes. In treatment, constructive therapists are likely to use presuppositional questions in conjunction with individualized goal setting. Similar to scaling and percentage questions, presuppositional questions orient clients toward clear visions of success or goal attainment. Examples of presuppositional questions include:

- Who will be most surprised in your family when they hear that your grades have improved? Who will be the least surprised? (Winslade & Monk, 2007, p. 58)
- What do you imagine will have changed when you start staying calm even when other students try to make you mad?
- Let's suppose 2 years have passed and now you're living your life completely free from alcohol. What exactly would you be doing every day to keep yourself sober?

The Miracle Question

The miracle question is the most famous of all solution-focused questions. It's a therapeutic question that, like most solution-focused questions, helps clients initiate and maintain a positive vision for the future and to analyze what factors might contribute to that positive future. Insoo Kim Berg initially stumbled upon the concept when a client, in apparent desperation, said that only a miracle would help (de Jong & Berg, 1998). Subsequently, the miracle question was phrased by Berg's colleague, Stephen de Shazer (1988), as:

> Suppose you were to go home tonight, and while you were asleep, a miracle happened and this problem was solved. How will you know the miracle happened? What will be different? (p. 5)

A more detailed version of the miracle question was described by Berg & Dolan (2001) and is included in John's resource blog (johnsommersflanagan.com), where we discuss the hypnotic or suggestive nature of the miracle question.

Like many solution-focused questions and techniques, the miracle question is based on positive expectations (Reiter, 2010). Many therapists have expanded on or slightly revised the miracle question to fit their work with different client populations. For example, when working with youth, Bertolino (1999) recommended substituting the word "strange" for "miracle." Similarly, Tohn and Oshlag (1996) described a slightly different version of the miracle question for use with mandated clients (see also J. Sommers-Flanagan & Sommers-Flanagan, 2012).

Externalizing Questions

Traditional diagnostic interviewing procedures typically include a series of questions designed to identify and clarify the presence or absence of specific psychiatric symptoms. These symptoms are then used to determine a diagnosis and subsequent treatment. As you know from your theories courses, there are other ways to think about the origins, location, and perpetuation of human psychological distress. From a constructive viewpoint, psychiatric conditions are socially, culturally, and individually constructed. From a narrative therapy perspective, the stories that clients tell themselves about their distress exert a great deal of influence. If individuals view their life challenges and problems as internal disorders or failures, then these problems will become more internalized and ingrained.

As a function of this constructive theoretical position, narrative and solution-focused counselors use a nontraditional approach to questioning clients about symptoms. This approach is radically different than traditional diagnostic interviewing in that it involves externalizing—placing psychiatric symptoms—outside of the self.

For example, if you're working with a young client with a reputation for being a troublemaker, instead of asking about ways he or she gets into trouble, you might ask "When did Trouble at school first come along?" and eventually follow this with "Do you think Trouble is getting more or less strong?" and "Does it interest you more to stay on the side that is trying to defeat Trouble, or would you prefer to let Trouble carry you along with it sometimes?" (Winslade & Monk, 2007, pp. 6–7, 9, 12). In this example, Winslade and Monk (2007) have transformed "trouble" from an internal character trait within the teenager to an external force that's oppressing him and that he might begin battling against.

When working with depressed clients, externalizing questions may help clients begin fighting back against depression, or depressive symptoms. For example, depression can be described in a symbolic way (e.g., as a cloud, fog, blackness, tunnel, pit, or heaviness; Corcoran, 2005). Externalizing questions for a client presenting with depressive symptoms might include:

- How might you fight back against that black cloud the next time it tries to take over your life?
- What exactly are you doing when you're free from that fog of depression?
- Who are you with when you feel lighter and happier and like you've thrown off the weight of that depression?
- How might you tell the depression thank you and good-bye?

Exception Questions

A central practice in solution-focused therapy is to ask clients questions that focus on exceptions to the problem. Guterman (2006) described this concept:

> [I]t is our job as counselors to focus on identifying and amplifying the exceptions to clients' problems rather than focus on the problems themselves. (p. 5)

Narrative therapists have a similar emphasis, but refer to positive exceptions as "sparkling moments" or "unique accounts" (J. Sommers-Flanagan & Sommers-Flanagan, 2012). In keeping with the theoretical position that only small changes are needed to instigate larger changes, exception questions seek minor evidence that the client's problem isn't always huge and overbearing. Corcoran (2005) provided a list of investigative questions for exceptions:

Who: Who is present when the exception occurs? What are they doing differently? What would they say you are doing differently?

What: What is happening before the exception occurs? What is different about the behavior during the exception period? What happens afterwards?

Where: Where is the exception occurring? What are the details of the setting that contribute to the exception?

When: What time of day does the exception occur? How often is the exception happening?

How: How are you making this exception happen? What strengths, talents, or qualities are you drawing on? (adapted from Corcoran, 2005, p. 12)

Solution-focused therapists use exception sequences to build a case for pre-existing client strengths and resources. These sequences can be helpful in reconstructing a new and more adaptive client storyline in contrast to the old and less adaptive problem-saturated storyline.

DVD Clip

In the *John & T.J.* counseling demonstration, John uses exception and presuppositional questions as he works with T.J. on anger and aggression issues.

SECTION TWO: DIRECTIVE INTERVIEWING TECHNIQUES (AKA DIRECTIVES)

Directive interviewing techniques (directives) are used to encourage clients to change the way they think, feel, or act. Similar to questions, directives are, in part, persuasion techniques, pushing clients toward specific change. However, in contrast to questions, many directives are explicit (rather than implicit) prescriptions for change.

Directives are used when therapists believe change should occur in the client's life, attitudes, or behavior. This therapist response or strategy places great responsibility on therapists for determining what client changes might be desirable. This is true even when you're working collaboratively with clients, because you're the one deciding what advice to offer and when to offer it. Of course, in the end, clients decide whether to apply your opinions, suggestions, or advice to their lives.

Directives can be used more effectively when clients are ready to change. In fact, research has shown that using directives can stimulate resistance (Beutler, 2011). Consequently, before describing specific directive techniques, we turn to a discussion of the readiness to change concept; it makes rational sense for us to look at how and why individual clients might respond differently to directives before discussing them (Miller & Rollnick, 2013).

Readiness to Change

In an ideal world (or at least an ideal therapy setting) all clients would arrive at your office filled to the brim with motivation for positive change. Even better, you'd be similarly filled with wisdom and, as you spoke, clients would listen attentively, go out into the world, and follow your sage advice. It might be a good thing that this scenario is a fantasy—because having this level of power with clients strikes us as both thrilling and frightening.

The interviewing techniques in this chapter in general and this section in particular, are explicitly designed to push clients toward making positive personal changes. But, as implied in the previous paragraph, the extent to which these techniques work depends on at least two very basic factors:

1. Your clients' motivation for change.
2. The quality of guidance you have to share with them.

There's no guarantee that clients will be motivated for positive change. (There's also no guarantee you'll have high quality guidance to offer, but we can always hope.) In fact, client motivation is usually highly variable. Some clients are exceptionally motivated and cooperative, while others won't even acknowledge the accuracy of our paraphrases and quickly dismiss our guidance. It's especially interesting that clients (and sometimes our friends and ourselves) actively resist obviously good advice (e.g., to stop smoking or to exercise more). In Chapter 12 we focus on specific interviewing strategies to use with clients who have little motivation. For now, we briefly review how your clients' readiness to change can affect how they respond to your questions and directives.

James Prochaska (1979) originally developed the transtheoretical model. This model is a complex, integrative, and multidimensional system that helps clinicians understand how clients change (Prochaska & DiClemente, 2005).

Although Prochaska's theory initially focused on how people change, he later formulated a separate but related component called, "the stages of change" (Prochaska, Norcross, & DiClemente, 1994, p. 38). This particular component of the transtheoretical model has proven very helpful and popular.

In the stages of change component of the transtheoretical model, it is hypothesized that humans approach change in five relatively distinct stages. These stages include:

1. *Precontemplation*: No particular interest in changing.
2. *Contemplation*: Occasionally thinks about making positive changes and is engaging in some self-examination or self-evaluation.
3. *Preparation*: Thinking that positive change is possible and desirable, but hasn't yet taken significant action.
4. *Action*: Actively involved in enacting a plan for positive change.
5. *Maintenance*: Adjusting to positive changes and actively practicing new skills to maintain change.

Prochaska suggested that clients will respond more positively or more negatively to the same counseling technique, depending on which stage of change they're in. As you can imagine, this concept is very important for clinical interviewing. For example, clients who are further along the readiness for change continuum (i.e., the action and maintenance stages) will be less interested in paraphrasing and summarizing and more eager for psychoeducation and advice. In contrast, clients in the precontemplative stage will often react negatively to the directive techniques covered next (e.g., advice or urging) and can even display strong negative reactions to moderately directive therapist behaviors such as interpretation. What this means is that therapists should choose techniques that match the clients "readiness" or stage of change (see *Putting It in Practice* 4.2).

DVD Clip

In the *Directive and Action Responses* DVD chapter, John and Rita discuss using directives and introduce the *John & Lisa* counseling demonstration.

PUTTING IT IN PRACTICE 4.2

A General Guide to Using Stages of Change Principles in Clinical Interviewing

Below we pose and answer basic questions about how to apply stages of change principles (Prochaska & DiClemente, 2005) to guide the techniques to use within a clinical interviewing context.

Q1: When should I use directive techniques like psychoeducation or advice?

A1: When clients are in the action or maintenance stages of change you're free to be more directive (provided you have useful information to share that fits with what the client recognizes as his or her problem).

(continued)

(*continued*)

Q2: When should I use less directive listening responses like paraphrasing, reflection of feeling, and summarization?

A2: As a general rule, if your client is in the precontemplative or contemplative stages of change, you should primarily use nondirective listening skills to help the client look at his or her own motivations for change. This would include: (a) attending behaviors, (b) paraphrasing, (c) clarification, (d) reflection of feeling, and (e) summarizing. Many questions, especially open questions and solution-focused or therapeutic questions, may be appropriate for clients who are precontemplative or contemplative. When you're with clients who present as precontemplative or contemplative, your best theoretical orientation choices will likely be person-centered, motivational interviewing, and/or solution-focused. Using more directive approaches can produce defensiveness or resistance with clients in precontemplative or contemplative stages.

Q3: How do I know what stage of change my client is in?

A3: We're tempted to suggest you'll know it when you see it . . . and there's some truth to that. If you try directly recommending a strategy for change and the client responds defensively, you may be moving forward too fast and it's advisable to retreat to using reflective listening skills. Conversely, if your client seems frustrated with your nondirective listening and expresses interest in changing now, then you've got the green light to be more directive. Also, we recommend using George Kelly's (1955) credulous approach to assessment, meaning you can always just directly ask clients what they prefer. In our work with parents we do this explicitly by stating something like:

> I want to emphasize that this is your consultation. And so if I'm talking too much, just tell me to be quiet and listen and I will. Or, if you start feeling like you want more advice and suggestions, let me know that as well. (J. Sommers-Flanagan & Sommers-Flanagan, 2011, p. 60)

There are also standardized methods for assessing clients' readiness for change. Interestingly, most of these involve asking clients very direct questions about their motivation to change, how difficult they expect change to be, and how ready they are to change (all of which seem in the spirit of George Kelly's credulous approach; for example, see (Chung et al., 2011) for a study on the predictive validity of four different measures assessing client readiness to stop smoking cigarettes).

Q4: Is the stages of change concept supported by empirical evidence?

A4: The data are mixed on whether and how much attending to and using interventions that fit your clients' stages of change makes a difference. Of course, this is true for nearly every phenomenon in counseling and psychotherapy. Overall, some studies show support for gearing your interviewing techniques to your clients' stage of change (Johnson et al., 2008). Other studies show that stages of change focused interventions do no better than interventions that don't tune into clients' particular motivational stage (Salmela, Poskiparta, Kasila, Vähäsarja, & Vanhala, 2009). We recognize this isn't the clear and decisive research outcome you might hope for, but such is the nature of our profession.

Explanation or Psychoeducation

An *explanation* is a descriptive statement used to make something plain or understandable. In an interview context, an explanation is synonymous with psychoeducation. Clients who come to therapy often need specific information. Psychoeducational targets within an interview include:

- The process of counseling.
- The meaning of a particular symptom.
- Instructions for using a specific therapeutic strategy.

Explaining the Counseling Process, Symptoms, and Strategies

Clients need to know about how counseling or psychotherapy works. Traditionally this has been called role induction or psychotherapy socialization (Luborsky, 1984). *Role induction* consists of informing or educating clients about what to expect in therapy, especially regarding the respective roles of therapist and client. Role induction is needed because many clients don't understand what a clinical interview, or counseling, entails. Research on role induction has indicated that clients benefit from knowing what to expect and how to act in therapy (Manthei, 2007; Walitzer, Dermen, & Conners, 1999).

Interviewing shouldn't be a mysterious process. That's why almost all clinical practitioners periodically stop and explain core counseling concepts. Imagine that a client tells you about her feelings of hopelessness toward the end of your first session:

> I'm not sure if I should tell you this, but I just keep thinking that none of these things we're talking about will ever change. It's nothing personal, but I think I'll never change.

This statement includes at least three possibilities:

1. The client truly doesn't know what's okay and what's not okay to talk about in therapy and needs instruction about what's important in therapy.
2. The client is exhibiting maladaptive cognitions in the session and needs to have this explained to her.
3. The client is experiencing some initial transference toward the therapist and knows what she wants to say, but is worried about how the therapist will respond.

In all three cases it's best for a therapist to begin with a statement that's supportive of client openness. The words you use may vary, but the educational message or explanation provided should be something like one of the following:

> I'm glad you shared your worries with me. That's an important part of counseling. I hope you always feel like you can speak openly here because

if you don't speak openly, I won't know what you're thinking and it will be harder for me to be helpful.

A basic rule of counseling is that when you start wondering whether you should say something or not, you should just go ahead and say it and then we can decide together whether it's important to talk about in greater depth.

Then, if you were working from a cognitive perspective, you might provide psychoeducation about the nature of automatic thoughts:

What you just said is very important. It shows me that you're having some negative automatic thoughts about counseling. This is exactly the kind of thing we'll be talking about because, although counseling may or may not be helpful, it's too soon for either of us to jump to a conclusion that your situation is hopeless and counseling won't be helpful.

It's not unusual for clients to say, "I don't know if I should talk about this" or "I'm not sure what I'm supposed to say." When they do, it often signals that some psychoeducation (or role induction) is needed. When clients are uncertain about the counseling process, it's your job to reduce the confusion.

Another possibility in the preceding situation is that, after spending 45 minutes talking about her challenging life, the client is feeling even more discouraged or demoralized than when she walked into the office. If so, the following explanation would be appropriate:

Sometimes just talking about your problems in counseling can temporarily make you feel worse. It's like when you're cleaning house and right after you get started it can feel overwhelming and hopeless. But, just like housecleaning, if you stick with counseling, it feels much better when you're finished.

A second type of explanation is needed when clients are experiencing symptoms, but are puzzled about what the symptoms mean. For example, clients with anxiety disorders often believe they're "going crazy" or "dying" despite the fact that the prognosis for most anxiety disorders is positive (Meuret et al., 2006). This is a good time to provide information because symptom explanations, even diagnosis, can be very reassuring for clients. For example:

I know you think there's something wrong with your mind, because what you're feeling is very frightening. But based on your personal history, your family history, and the symptoms you have, it's clear that you're not going crazy. The problems you're experiencing are not unusual. And they respond very well to counseling.

A third type of explanation involves giving clients information about how to apply a particular therapy technique. An example follows:

Client: I don't know what causes my anxiety. It comes out of nowhere. Is there anything I can do to get more in control over these feelings?

Therapist: The first step to controlling anxiety usually involves identifying the thoughts or situations that cause you to feel anxious. I'd like you to try the following experiment. Keep a log of your anxiety level. You can use a pocket notebook to record when you feel anxious. Write down how anxious you feel on a scale of 0 to 100, 0 being not anxious at all and 100 being the worst possible anxiety. Then, right next to your anxiety rating, list the thoughts you're thinking and the situation you're in. Bring your anxiety log to the next session and we can start pinpointing what's causing your anxiety.

In this case, a cognitive-behavioral therapist is giving instructions for a self-monitoring assignment. As a matter of course, when providing instructions, you should always ask the client if he or she has any questions to make sure your instructions are understood (i.e., "Do you have any questions about how to monitor your anxiety?").

The educational information a therapist gives is dictated, in part, by his or her theoretical orientation. Behavior therapists explain to clients the importance of behavior and self-monitoring; cognitive therapists explain how thoughts influence or cause behavior and emotions; person-centered therapists explain how sessions should consist of what clients feel is important; solution-focused therapists explain how helpful it is to talk about successes; and psychoanalytic therapists explain to their clients the importance of "saying whatever comes to mind." Whether therapists are describing free association or explaining how to engage in guided imagery, they're providing psychoeducational information.

Suggestion

Suggestion is an interesting directive action response in that, technically, it's not very directive. Although most textbooks classify suggestion as a mild form of advice, it has roots in the hypnotic literature (Erickson, Rossi, & Rossi, 1976). Although sometimes interchangeable, for our purposes we're looking at suggestion and advice as two distinct and different therapist behaviors. To *suggest* means to bring before a person's mind indirectly or without plain expression, whereas to *advise* is to give counsel to or offer an opinion worth following. Offering advice is more directive than using suggestion.

A suggestion is a therapist's statement that directly or indirectly suggests or predicts a particular phenomenon will occur. Suggestion is designed to move clients consciously or unconsciously toward engaging in a particular behavior, changing their thinking patterns, or experiencing a specific emotion. Suggestion is used much more often and by many more clinicians than most people realize. In fact, the miracle question is a form of suggestion. Additionally, nearly every relaxation or visual imagery procedure involves suggestion:

Just let yourself relax and allow your eyes to close if you like. When you let your eyes close you can let go of the stress and strain and just go inside for a break.

Although suggestions are often given when clients are in a trance state, they may also be given when clients are fully alert and awake. For example:

Client: I've never been able to stand up to my mother. It's like I'm afraid of her. She's always had her act together. She's stronger than I am.

Therapist: It might be nice for us to take a moment for you to reflect on ways you're just as strong as your mother . . . or even stronger. What comes to mind?

Another suggestion procedure occurs when the therapist suggests that the client will have a dream about a particular issue. This example is classic in the sense that psychoanalytic therapists use suggestions to influence unconscious processes:

Client: This decision is really getting to me. I have two job offers but don't know which one to take. I'm frozen. I've analyzed the pros and cons for days and just swing back and forth. One minute I want one job and the next minute I'm thinking of why that job is totally wrong for me.

Therapist: If you relax and think about the conflict as clearly as possible in your mind before you drop off to sleep tonight, perhaps you'll have a dream to clarify your feelings about this decision.

In this example, suggestion is mixed with advice. The therapist advises the client to relax and clearly think about the conflict before falling asleep and suggests that a dream will subsequently occur.

Gentle and encouraging suggestions with delinquent young clients may have a positive influence (J. Sommers-Flanagan & Sommers-Flanagan, 1998). We use the following suggestion technique when discussing behavioral alternatives with young clients:

Client: That punk is so lame. He deserved to have me beat him up.

Therapist: Maybe so. But you can do better than resorting to violence in the future. I know you can do better than that.

From an Adlerian perspective, this form of suggestion could be viewed as a method for encouraging clients (Adler, 1930).

Suggestion should be used carefully. Occasionally, it can be viewed as a sneaky or manipulative strategy. Additionally, sometimes suggestion backfires and evokes opposition. For example, each suggestion used in examples from this section could backfire, producing the following results:

- The client resists suggestions to relax and, instead, experiences irritation and animosity.
- The woman continues to insist that her mother is stronger.
- The client does not recall his dreams or is unable to make any connections between his dreams and his decision-making process.
- The delinquent boy insists that physical violence is his best behavioral option.

Agreement-Disagreement

Agreement is a very appealing interviewing response. Most of us like to be in agreement with others and to have others be in agreement with us.

Agreement occurs when a therapist makes a statement indicating harmony with a client's opinion. Agreement feels validating to both therapist and client, partly because people like to be with others who have attitudes similar to their own (Yalom & Leszcz, 2005).

As with other directives, you should explore why you feel like agreeing with your clients. Why do you want clients to know you agree with them? Is agreement being used therapeutically, or are you agreeing because it feels good to let someone else know your opinions are similar? Are you agreeing with clients to affirm their viewpoint, or yours?

Using agreement has several potential effects. First, agreement can enhance rapport. Second, if your clients think you're a credible authority, agreement can affirm the correctness of their opinion (i.e., "If my therapist agrees with me, I must be right!"). Third, agreement puts you in the expert role and your opinion is likely to be sought in the future. Fourth, agreement can reduce client exploration (i.e., "Why explore my beliefs any longer; after all, my therapist agrees with me.").

Wherever there's agreement, there can also be disagreement. Although it's simple, rewarding, and natural to express agreement, disagreeing is less socially desirable. People sometimes muffle their disagreement, either because they're unassertive or because they fear conflict or rejection.

In a clinical interview, however, you're in a position of power and authority. Consequently, you might find yourself losing your inhibition and openly expressing disagreement. Depending on the issue, the result can be devastating to clients, disruptive to therapy, and may involve abuse of power and authority. Imagine, for example, the following scenario summarized from a case involving one of our interns:

Client: I'm feeling very angry about the presidential election, but I don't suppose I should talk about that in here.
Counselor: I'd hope you feel like you can talk about whatever you like with me.
Client: I hate Obama. I'm just hoping he gets assassinated.
Counselor: Whatever your political beliefs may be, I think what you just said is completely inappropriate and it's totally unpatriotic too.

As you can see from this interaction, it's quite possible for a counselor-client interaction to deteriorate into a disagreement or argument about social or political issues. Our main point is that disagreement will often either shut down clients or escalate into conflict. Either way, the assessment or therapeutic value of the interaction is lost. For example, if the counselor is concerned that her client is expressing a threat toward the president, then it's crucial to remain neutral and to explore the client's violent impulses. In this case, expressing disagreement would interfere with the assessment function of the clinical interview. Similarly, disagreement also will interfere with the therapeutic function of interviews.

Disagreement may also be subtle. Sometimes, silence, lack of head nodding, the folding of one's arms, or therapist neutrality is interpreted as disagreement. It's good to monitor your reactions to clients so you know if you're nonverbally or inadvertently communicating disagreement (or disapproval).

The purpose of disagreement is to change client opinion. The problem with disagreement is that countering one opinion with another opinion may deteriorate into a personal argument, resulting in increased defensiveness by both parties. Therefore, the take-home message here is to avoid using personal disagreement as a therapeutic intervention. The cost is too high, and the potential benefit can be achieved through other means. Additionally, and perhaps more importantly, disagreeing with clients on values issues is simply unethical (see *Multicultural Highlight* 4.1).

Two basic guidelines apply when you feel like disagreeing with clients:

1. If you have an opinion different from a client regarding a philosophical issue (e.g., abortion, sexual behavior), remember it's not your job to change your client's opinion; it's your job to help him or her with maladaptive thoughts, feelings, and/or behaviors.
2. If, in your professional judgment, your client's belief or behavior is maladaptive (e.g., is causing stress or dangerous), then you may choose to confront the client and provide factual information to facilitate client change toward more adaptive beliefs or behaviors. (In such cases, you're better off providing psychoeducation or explanation rather than disagreement.)

A good example of a situation in which a counselor should employ an educational strategy instead of disagreement is in the area of child rearing. Clients often use ineffective or inappropriate child-rearing techniques and then support such techniques by citing their opinion or experience. Counselors should avoid bluntly rushing in and telling clients that their opinion is "wrong." Instead, clients should be encouraged to examine whether using a particular parenting strategy is helping them consistently accomplish their discipline goals:

Client: I know some people say spanking isn't good. Well, I was spanked when I was young and I turned out just fine.

Counselor: *[At this point, the counselor is strongly resisting the impulse to disagree with the client and uses a paraphrase instead]* You feel like being spanked as a child didn't have any negative effects on you.

Client: Right. I'm doing okay.

Counselor: It's true that many parents spank and many parents don't. Maybe, instead of looking at whether spanking is good or bad, we should look at your goals for parenting your son. Then, we can talk about what strategies, including spanking, might best help you accomplish your parenting goals.

In this case, empirical evidence indicates that the behavior discussed (spanking) may produce undesirable consequences (Gershoff, Lansford, Sexton, Davis-Kean, & Sameroff, 2012; Gershoff & Bitensky, 2007; Gershoff, 2002). Numerous professional groups (e.g., the American Psychological Association, American Academy of Pediatrics) have recommended that parents develop alternatives to physical punishment with children. Therefore, eventually, the counselor may discuss with the client the potential undesirable consequences of physical punishment. Generally, this discussion should focus on the client's child-rearing goals and objectives, rather than whether the counselor does or doesn't "believe in spanking." An exception to this guideline occurs when a therapist suspects the client is physically abusing a child. However, even in cases when child abuse is suspected and reported, the decision is based on violation of a legal standard, rather than therapist-client philosophical disagreements.

MULTICULTURAL HIGHLIGHT 4.1

Clashing Values: Legal Implications of Refusing to Counsel Homosexual Clients

The ethical codes of various mental health professions are clear about the fact that ethical professionals don't allow personal values to adversely affect or influence clients or the therapy process. This makes rational sense because the purpose of counseling or psychotherapy is to facilitate client personal development, and this development may or may not be consistent with the personal values of a particular therapist.

Despite this rational view, sometimes, professional therapists have emotional conflicts with client values or behaviors. In an important article, Hermann and Herlihy (2006) described a legal case where a professional counselor refused to provide counseling for a homosexual client. Here is a summary of the case of *Bruff v. North Mississippi Health Services, Inc.*:

- A Mississippi EAP counselor (Bruff) was working with a woman. After several sessions the woman disclosed that she was lesbian and asked the counselor to focus on helping her improve her romantic relationship.
- Bruff refused to help the client, citing religious values.
- Bruff further noted with the medical center vice president that her position was that she wouldn't counsel anyone in any area conflicting with her religious views.
- Bruff filed suit in federal court because she believed her employer had failed to accommodate her religious values and beliefs.
- Although a jury initially ruled in favor of Bruff, the case was over-turned upon appeal.

The legal implications of the Court's conclusions are summarized by Hermann and Herlihy (2006):

The most significant legal aspect of the Bruff case is the court's holding that an employer's legal obligation to make reason-able accommodations for employees' religious beliefs does not include accommodating a counselor's request to refer homo-sexual clients who ask for assistance with relationship issues. According to the court, providing counseling only on issues that do not conflict with a counselor's religious beliefs is an inflexible position not protected by the law. The court further acknowl-edged that homosexual clients may not seek counseling in a setting that allows counselors to refuse to work with clients on issues related to the client's sexual orientation. The court found this discriminatory result was not legally permissible either.... The court noted that a counselor who refuses to counsel a

(*continued*)

(*continued*)
homosexual client on relationship issues may cause emotional harm to the client. (p. 416)

In conclusion, this case provides an excellent example of how a client's right to mental health services overrides the therapist's personal values.

DVD Clip

In the *John & Lisa, Part One* counseling demonstration, John demonstrates psychoeducation, suggestion, and agreement/validation as he works with Lisa on her problem with insomnia.

Approval-Disapproval

Approval refers to a therapist's sanction of client thoughts, feelings, or behavior. To give your approval is to render a favorable judgment. To use approval and disapproval as interviewing techniques, therapists must have the knowledge, expertise, and sensitivity necessary for rendering judgments on their clients' ideas and behavior. Approval and disapproval are sometimes avoided (or used) because they place significant power in the therapist's hands. Therapists may prefer that clients judge, accept, and approve of their own thoughts, feelings, and behavior rather than relying on another person's external evaluation.

Many clients seek approval from their therapists. In this regard, clients are vulnerable; they need or want a professional's stamp of approval. As therapists, we must ask whether we should accept the responsibility, power, and moral authority that needy and vulnerable clients give us. In some ways, choosing to bestow approval or disapproval on clients is similar to playing God. Who are we to decide which feelings, thoughts, or behaviors are good or bad?

On the other hand, some therapists freely give approval to their clients and see it as perfectly appropriate. Many therapists will say "Good job!" when clients complete homework assignments and therapists who work with children are often quite liberal in offering high fives or bumping fists in approval. Others might claim that all therapists constantly offer approval anyway and so it may as well be provided intentionally, explicitly, and used for therapeutic purposes. The following excerpt of a single-session interview between solution-focused therapist Yvonne Dolan (de Shazer et al., 2007) and a young client offers a positive perspective on using approval for building hope and positive feelings:

> Yvonne: Um. I just want to say I really believe in you. I just have this instinct. And every once in a while I meet a young person and I kind of say to myself afterwards, and I probably wouldn't say it if I was going to see you again. Maybe I'd say it if I ran into you in a year or two. But since I am probably only going to see you once in my lifetime, I'm going to just say: There's something about you. You're one of those young people that . . . you give me hope in the next generation. I just have that feeling. I want you to know that. (p. 33)

After reading Dolan's comments, we're tempted to offer our approval or disapproval of her therapeutic strategy. Instead, our point is simply for you to be aware of your own tendencies to use approval or disapproval with clients.

Providing approval to clients can be a powerful therapeutic technique. Explicit approval can enhance rapport and increase client self-esteem. It can also foster dependent relationships. When a client's search for approval is rewarded, the client is likely to resume a search for approval when or if the insecure feelings begin again. Some clients will present as even more "needy" or as strongly seeking your approval.

As you listen to clients, sometimes you'll have feelings of disapproval. It's especially difficult to maintain professional neutrality if your client is talking about child abuse, wife battering, rape, murderous thoughts and impulses, deviant sexual practices, and so on. Keep in mind the following facts:

- Clients who engage in deviant or abusive behavior have been disapproved of before, usually by people who mean a great deal to them and sometimes by society. Nonetheless, they haven't stopped engaging in deviant or abusive behavior. This suggests that disapproval has been ineffective in changing their behavior.
- Your disapproval only alienates you from someone who needs your help to change.
- By maintaining objectivity and neutrality, you're not implicitly approving of your client's behavior. There are other techniques besides disapproval (e.g., explanation and confrontation) that show your client that you believe change is needed.
- If you cannot listen to your client's descriptions of his or her behavior without disapproval, you should consider referring the client to another qualified professional.
- Disapproval is associated with reduced rapport, feelings of rejection, and early termination of counseling.

Similar to agreement and disagreement, approval and disapproval can be communicated subtly to clients. For example, responding with the words *okay* or *right* can be interpreted by clients as approval—even when you're using these words as a verbal tracking response. Be aware that your verbal and nonverbal behavior may communicate subtle messages of approval or disapproval.

Some therapist behaviors not discussed here, such as scolding and rejection, are even more therapist-centered than approval and disapproval (see Benjamin, 1987). Others, such as humor, are difficult to place on the listening continuum. Table 4.3 is a summary of directives described in this section.

Giving Advice

All advice contains a common central message: "Here's what I think you should do." *Giving advice* is very much a therapist-centered, directive activity; it casts therapists in the expert role.

Generally, it's important to avoid advice giving early in interviews because giving advice is easy, common, and sometimes coolly received. Friends and relatives freely give advice to one another, sometimes effectively, other times less

Table 4.3   Summary of Directive Techniques and Their Usual Effects

Directive	Description	Primary Intent/Effect
Explanation or Psychoeducation	Statement providing factual information about the interview process, client problem, or implementation of a treatment strategy.	Clarifies client misconceptions. Helps client attain maximal benefit from counseling.
Suggestion	Therapist statement that directly or indirectly suggests or predicts that a particular phenomenon will occur.	May help clients consciously or unconsciously move toward engaging in a particular behavior, thinking a specific thought.
Agreement-Disagreement	Statement indicating harmony or disharmony of opinion.	Agreement may affirm or reassure a client, enhance rapport, or shut down exploration of thoughts and feelings. Disagreement can produce conflict and stimulate arguments or defensiveness.
Approval-Disapproval	Favorable or unfavorable judgment of the thoughts, feelings, or behavior of a client.	Approval may enhance rapport and foster client dependency. Disapproval may reduce rapport and produce client feelings of rejection.
Giving Advice	Recommendation given to the client by the therapist. A prescription to act, think, or feel in a specific manner.	Provides the client with ideas regarding new ways to act, think, or feel. If given prematurely, can be ineffective and can damage therapist credibility.
Self-disclosure	Sharing personal thoughts or feelings with the client.	May increase intimacy or decrease client confidence in the therapist.
Urging	Technique of pressuring or pleading with a client to engage in specific actions or to consider specific issues.	May produce the desired change or may backfire and stimulate resistance. May be considered offensive by some clients.

so. You may wonder, if advice is readily available outside therapy, why would therapists bother using it?

There are two main answers to this question: (1) People desire advice—especially expert advice, and (2) sometimes advice is a helpful therapeutic change technique (Glasser, 2000; Haley, 1976). Nonetheless, advice remains controversial; some therapists use it while others passionately avoid it (Benjamin, 1987; Rogers,

1957). Many professionals believe that Publius Syrus was correct in 42 B.C. when he claimed, "Many seek advice, few profit from it" (from Hill, 2009).

Clients will sometimes try to get quick advice from their therapists during an initial session. However, premature problem solving or advice in a clinical interview is often ineffective, partly because the client hasn't contemplated or generated the advice and therefore has less ownership or investment in the solution (Hill, 2009). An exception to this rule may occur if the counselor or psychotherapist has guru-like status—in which case, sometimes clients will, for better or worse, automatically follow the advice (Meier & Davis, 2011). A more reasonable approach for us nongurus is to thoroughly explore a specific issue with a client before offering advice. During the exploration process, often clients develop their own ideas about how to approach their problem. A good rule is to find out everything your client has tried before jumping in with advice.

Sometimes it's difficult to stop yourself from giving advice. Imagine yourself working with a client who tells you:

> I'm pregnant and I don't know what to do. I just found out 2 days ago. No one knows. What should I do?

You may have good advice for this young woman. Maybe you've gone through a similar experience or know someone who struggled with an unplanned pregnancy. The woman in this scenario may desperately *need* constructive advice (as well as basic information). However, this is speculation, because based on what she said, we still don't even know if she needs information or advice. All we know is she says she "doesn't know what to do." If she discovered she was pregnant 2 days ago, she's probably spent nearly 48 hours thinking about the options available to her. At this point, immediately telling her what she should do would likely be ineffective and inappropriate.

Giving premature advice can shut down further problem and solution exploration. We recommend starting nondirectively; you can always get more directive and provide advice later.

> So you haven't told anyone about the pregnancy. And if I understand you correctly, you're feeling maybe you should be taking a particular action, but you're not sure what.

Some clients will push hard for advice and keep asking, "But what do you think I should do?" If so, you should use psychoeducation (i.e., role induction) and an open-ended question to gain time to listen more and formulate any advice you might want to give. For example:

> Before we talk about what you should do, let's talk about what you've been thinking and feeling about your situation. Then we can talk together about options, but first, tell me what you've thought about and felt since discovering you're pregnant.

Or, in this case, an open-ended question might be adequate:

> What options have you thought of already?

When you do agree to offer advice, it should almost always be advice about how to obtain the resources or information the client needs to make a decision. In the preceding example, rather than advising the young woman to (a) get an abortion, (b) initiate an adoption process, or (c) leave an unfulfilling relationship, your advice should focus on how to analyze options and potential longer-term consequences.

PUTTING IT IN PRACTICE 4.3

A Little Advice on Giving Advice

As you might guess, we'd like to offer you advice about giving advice. Specifically, you should become aware of when and why you want to give clients advice. Review and contemplate the following questions. When you feel like giving advice, is it:

1. Just to be helpful?
2. Because you have limited sessions and feel pressured?
3. To prove you're competent?
4. Because you've had the same problem and think you know the answer?
5. Because you think you have better ideas than your client?
6. Because you think your client will never come up with any constructive ideas?

Your responses to these questions can help determine the purity of your advice-giving motives. We're not strong advocates of advice. On the other hand, we also believe that advice, when well-timed and received from the proper person, can be tremendously powerful. Timing and relationship are central.

In conclusion, when it comes to giving advice, our advice to you is: (a) be aware of why you're giving it, (b) wait for the appropriate time to deliver it, (c) avoid giving moralistic advice, and (d) avoid giving advice the client has already received from someone else.

Clients are typically more complex, thoughtful, and full of constructive solutions than we think they are (and typically more resourceful than *they* think they are). One way to honor the inner wisdom of clients is to use solution-focused questioning to emphasize client skills and resources and get clients to generate their own advice: "How did you manage to change things around?" or "What's the longest you've gone without being in trouble with the law? How did you do that?" (Bertolino, 1999, pp. 34–35).

Providing redundant advice (i.e., advice to take an action that others have previously suggested or to take an action that the client has already unsuccessfully tried) can damage your credibility and therapeutic alliance. To avoid this, you can ask clients what advice they've already received from friends, family, and past counselors (see also *Putting It in Practice* 4.3).

Self-Disclosure

Self-disclosure is a complex and flexible interviewing response that can be used for many purposes. For example, in Chapter 3 we discussed how it might be used for feeling validation and for supporting, reassuring, or complimenting clients.

Hill (2009) encourages helpers to use self-disclosure to lead clients toward greater insight. She suggests a brief self-disclosure focused on the client's central issue, followed by an indirect question ("I wonder") to check in with the client. She gives the following examples:

> Yes, I do that too. I notice that I have a tendency to regress to being dependent unless I am careful. I wonder if that's true for you? (p. 279)

> I've also struggled in thinking about my role as a professional woman and possibly having children. For me it's related to not being sure that I want both. I wonder if you experience any ambivalence about wanting both a career and a family? (p. 279)

As you can see from these examples, self-disclosure can be very leading. In each case, the therapist is suggesting a pattern that might be common for both therapist and client. This not only implies commonality, but also implies that the way the therapist thinks about or handles her own life may be a model for the client. For example, a therapist may feel good about managing his in-laws, finances, conscience, or many other inter- and intrapersonal issues and therefore believe he has just the right ideas for the client. Obviously, there are problems with this presumption—especially when it comes to working with clients with different cultural identities than your own (see *Multicultural Highlight* 4.2).

MULTICULTURAL HIGHLIGHT 4.2

Using Self-Disclosure With Culturally Diverse Clients

Most multicultural experts recommend that counselors use self-disclosure with clients from different cultures (Barnett, 2011). Self-disclosure is viewed as making you more human and real and, therefore, potentially more trustworthy. However, as with virtually all interviewing techniques, the effectiveness of self-disclosure depends on how (and why) you use it.

Self-disclosure with the purpose of joining or connecting is generally very appropriate. For example, recently, when working with a young woman from the Crow tribe, one of us shared that we might both know the same individual. This disclosure was offered in a neutral or slightly positive manner: "We have a few students in my School Counseling program from the Crow tribe. Her name is _____." The client's response was positive, and she briefly reflected on someone from her family who knew the student and then we moved on to more significant issues.

(continued)

(continued)

In contrast, when used as a means of providing advice or suggestions, self-disclosure with culturally diverse clients is risky and can damage the therapeutic relationship. Imagine, for example, a counselor from the dominant culture noting to an African American male that sometimes he feels invisible at work and wonders if the client feels the same. Given the depth and pain associated with the invisibility complex among Black men, this disclosure could further the client's belief that his counselor has no clue of what it's like to be a Black man in the workplace (Franklin, 2007).

Generally, any cross-cultural self-disclosure that implies that someone from a dominant cultural group knows the inner feelings and struggles of someone from a less-dominant cultural group is ill-advised. Instead, counselors are better off to cite research or to quote other individuals from the culture when exploring client issues. For example, instead of relying on his own personal experiences in feeling invisible, the counselor would likely be more effective if he simply notes the research and writing of Anderson Franklin about invisibility experiences of Black Americans and then checks to see if the client has had similar experiences (Franklin, 2004, 2007; Franklin, Boyd-Franklin, & Kelly, 2006;). Additionally, while interviewing a Native American woman from the Crow tribe who was separated from her children, it was better for a counselor to share what he had read about Chief Plenty Coup's view on children rather than sharing his own feelings about being apart from his children. In this case, mentioning Chief Plenty Coup stimulated an excellent exploration of the client's emotional pain of being separated from her children. Overall, although personal self-disclosure can be effective, it's rarely a substitute for cultural knowledge.

As noted in Chapter 3, self-disclosure as immediacy is a form of here-and-now communication that can facilitate therapy process or increase client defensiveness. Generally, this is an advanced-therapist response, and we recommend devoting class discussion and supervision time to explore appropriate and inappropriate uses of self-disclosure or immediacy.

Urging

Urging is a step beyond advice giving. It involves pressuring clients to take a specific action. When therapists urge clients to take a specific action, they're using a direct power approach to facilitating change.

Urging clients isn't common during clinical interviews, but there are situations when urging may be appropriate. These situations involve primarily crisis (e.g., when the client is in danger or dangerous). For example, in child abuse cases, if you are interviewing the abuser, you may urge him to report himself to the local agency responsible for protecting children. By urging the client to make the report with you present for support and encouragement, you might facilitate a better child-protection investigation process.

In domestic or intimate partner violence situations, sometimes therapists will want to urge victims or potential victims to leave an abusive partner and move to a shelter for safety. Even this seemingly rational advice may be inappropriate partly because of how important it is to respect a potential victim's own instincts and intuition about safety. In fact, urging a potential victim to leave her partner could result in escalating violence and even murder. Consequently, it's better to work collaboratively with clients to explore their options even when they're exposed to dangerous situations (Rolling & Brosi, 2010; Stover, McMahon, & Easton, 2011).

In noncrisis situations, urging is even less common. One noncrisis situation in which urging may be appropriate is in the treatment of anxiety disorders. This is because clients with anxiety disorders tend to reinforce their fears by avoiding anxiety-producing situations. They become increasingly incapacitated by fearful expectations and avoidance behaviors. A major component of treatment involves graduated exposure to previously anxiety- or fear-producing situations. People suffering from anxiety disorders often need their therapists to urge (or encourage) them to face their fears (Nayak, Powers, & Foa, 2012).

> **DVD Clip**
>
> In the *John & Lisa, Part Two* counseling demonstration, John demonstrates unskilled or poor use of reframing, disagreement, self-disclosure, and advice-giving as Lisa discusses her problems with her child and grandchildren moving into her home.

SUMMARY

This chapter is divided into two sections. Section One focuses on different types of questions, including general questions, assessment questions, and therapeutic questions. Section Two focuses on specific directive techniques.

Many types of questions are available to therapists, ranging from maximally open (*what* or *how*) to minimally open (*where*, *when*, and *who*) to closed (can be answered with yes or no) questions. Swing questions, beginning with the words *could*, *would*, *can*, or *will*, require adequate rapport but can often yield in-depth responses. Indirect questions, beginning with *I wonder* or *you must*, are implied questions that allow a client to respond or not. Projective questions usually begin with *what if* and invite client speculation.

General questions have both benefits and liabilities. Benefits include greater therapist control, potential deep exploration, efficiency in gathering information, and more. Liabilities include setting the therapist up as expert, focusing on the therapist's interests instead of the client, inhibiting client spontaneity, and so on.

To maximize the effectiveness of questions, therapists should adhere to several basic guidelines, including (a) preparing clients for liberal question use, (b) mixing questions with less directive therapist responses, (c) using questions relevant to client problems, (d) using questions to elicit concrete behavioral information, and (e) approaching sensitive areas cautiously.

All questions can serve therapeutic and/or assessment purposes, but some questions are developed within a specific theoretical framework and, therefore, designed to elicit information or facilitate change. Assessment questions based on specific theoretical perspectives include "the question" (Adlerian) and the four big questions of choice theory/reality therapy.

Narrative and solution-focused therapists use questions as their main therapeutic strategy. Examples of therapeutic questions include: (a) pre-treatment change, (b) scaling, (c) percentage, (d) unique outcomes or redescription, (e) presuppositional, (f) the miracle question, (g) externalizing, and (h) exception. Many of these questions are aimed toward both assessment and intervention.

Directive interviewing techniques encourage client action. They're based on the assumption that a particular client, for his or her personal welfare, should engage in a particular behavior. Directive action responses include explanation, suggestion, agreement-disagreement, approval-disapproval, advice, self-disclosure, and urging. Each of these techniques provides clients with guidance toward specific action. Therapists are advised to explore their motives and seek supervision as they begin using before using directive interviewing techniques.

SUGGESTED READINGS AND RESOURCES

The following books offer additional information and exercises on using questions, directive action skills, and therapeutic techniques from different theoretical orientations.

Bloomgarden, A., & Mennuti, R. B. (2009). *Psychotherapist revealed: Therapists speak about self-disclosure in psychotherapy*. New York, NY: Routledge.

    This edited volume provides a very balanced perspective on self-disclosure. The editors and authors write openly about their self-disclosure experiences and reading these honest and reflective chapters will tend to help you become more reflective and intentional with regard to your own use of self-disclosure.

de Jong, P., & Berg, I. K. (2008). *Interviewing for solutions*. Belmont, CA: Thomson.

    This book reviews, describes, and provides examples of an array of helping responses from the solution-focused perspective.

de Shazer, S., Dolan, Y., Korman, H., McCollum, E., Trepper, T., & Berg, I. K. (2007). *More than miracles: The state of the art of solution-focused brief therapy*. New York, NY: Haworth Press.

    This is the most recent solution-focused work from the late Steve de Shazer.

Farber, B. A. (2006). *Self-disclosure in psychotherapy*. New York, NY: Guilford Press.

    Farber describes the costs and benefits of self-disclosure and how therapists can use self-disclosure to strengthen the therapy relationship.

Glasser, W. (2000). *Counseling with choice theory*. New York, NY: HarperCollins.

    In this book, William Glasser, the originator of choice theory and reality therapy, describes several cases during which he uses active and directive choice theory interviewing approaches.

Welfel, E. R. (2013). *Ethics in counseling and psychotherapy: Standards, research, and emerging issues* (5th ed.). Belmont, CA: Thomson Brooks/Cole Publishing Co.

    This is another excellent ethics text.

Evidence-Based Relationships

CHAPTER OBJECTIVES

Most clinicians and researchers agree that successful therapy outcomes are more likely if clinicians establish and maintain a positive working relationship with clients. In this chapter, we examine many different dimensions of what has come to be known as evidence-based relationships.

After reading this chapter, you will understand:

- The origin and nature of the concept "evidence-based therapy relationships."
- Evidence-based relationship factors based on Carl Rogers's "core conditions" of congruence, unconditional positive regard, and accurate empathy.
- Evidence-based relationship factors derived from psychoanalytic and interpersonal theory and therapy (transference, countertransference, and the working alliance).
- Other therapy relationship factors associated with behavioral theory, social psychology, feminist theory, and constructive theories.

In 1957, Carl Rogers made a bold declaration that has profoundly shaped research and practice in counseling and psychotherapy. In an article in the *Journal of Consulting Psychology*, he proclaimed that no techniques or methods were needed, that diagnostic knowledge was "for the most part, a colossal waste of time" (1957, p. 102), and that all that was *necessary* and *sufficient* for therapeutic change to occur was a certain type of relationship between therapist and client.

Although we could go back further in time and note that Freud (of course) had originally discussed the potential value of therapeutic relationships, Rogers's revolutionary statements refocused the profession. Until Rogers, therapy was primarily about theoretically based methods, techniques, and interventions. After Rogers (1942, 1957, 1961), we began thinking and talking about the possibility that it might be the relationship between client and therapist—not necessarily the methods and techniques employed—that produced therapeutic change.

For years, a great debate has fulminated within the counseling and psychotherapy disciplines (Wampold, 2001). Norcross and Lambert (2011) refer to this debate as "The culture wars in psychotherapy" (p. 3). They describe it as a polarization or dichotomy captured by the question: "Do treatments cure disorders or do relationships heal people?" (p. 3).

As academics and professional organizations have engaged in this debate, typically there has been little room for moderation and common sense. There have been assertions about the "rape" of psychotherapy as well as strong criticisms of practitioners who blithely ignore important empirical research (Baker, McFall, & Shoham, 2008; Fox, 1995). The heat of this controversy continues, in part, because we live in a world with limited health-care dollars . . . and the fight to determine which forms of therapy are included as "valid" and, therefore, reimbursable will likely continue.

The focus of this chapter is about a part of the controversy that's really no longer considered controversial. In the past two decades, excellent research and research reviews have settled at least one dimension of the argument: Therapy relationships do contribute to positive outcomes across all forms of therapy and settings (Goldfried, 2007; Norcross & Lambert, 2011; J. Sommers-Flanagan & Sommers-Flanagan, 2007b). The question is no longer a matter of whether the relationship in counseling and psychotherapy matters, but how much it matters.

This chapter focuses on what has come to be known as "evidence-based therapy relationships" (Norcross & Lambert, 2011). Although organized around specific theories and supporting research, the chapter also provides clinical examples for how the theories and evidence translate into specific evidence-based relationships facilitating behaviors that occur in the clinical interview.

CARL ROGERS'S CORE CONDITIONS

Carl Rogers (1942) believed that the necessary and sufficient therapeutic relationship consisted of three core conditions: (1) congruence, (2) unconditional positive regard, and (3) empathic understanding. In his words:

> Thus, the relationship which I have found helpful is characterized by a sort of transparency on my part, in which my real feelings are evident; by an acceptance of this other person as a separate person with value in his own right; and by a deep empathic understanding which enables me to see his private world through his eyes. When these conditions are achieved, I become a companion to my client, accompanying him in the frightening search for himself, which he now feels free to undertake. (Rogers, 1961, p. 34)

Congruence

Congruence means that a person's thoughts, feelings, and behaviors match. Based on person-centered theory and therapy, congruence is *less a skill and more an experience*. Congruent therapists are described as genuine, authentic, and comfortable with themselves. Congruence includes spontaneity and honesty; it's usually associated with the clinical skill of immediacy and involves some degree of self-disclosure (see Chapter 4).

Congruence is complex and has been described as "abstract and elusive" (Kolden, Klein, Wang, & Austin, 2011, p. 187). The ability to be congruent includes an internal dimension that involves therapists being in touch with their inner feelings or *real self* plus an external or expressive dimension that allows therapists to articulate their internal experiences in ways clients can understand. The following excerpt from Rogers's work illustrates these internal and external dimensions of experiencing and expressing congruence:

> We tend to express the *outer* edges of our feelings. That leaves *us* protected and makes the other person unsafe. We say, "This and this (which *you* did) hurt me." We do not say, "This and this weakness of mine *made me* be hurt when you did this and this."
>
> To find this inward edge of my feelings, I need only ask myself, "Why?" When I find myself bored, angry, tense, hurt, at a loss, or worried, I ask myself, "Why?" Then, instead of "You bore me," or "this makes me mad," I find the "why" *in me* which makes it so. That is always more personal and positive, and much safer to express. Instead of "You bore me," I find, "I want to hear more personally from you," or, "You tell me what happened, but I want to hear also what it all meant to you." (1957, pp. 390–391)

Rogers also emphasized that congruent expression is important even if it consists of attitudes, thoughts, or feelings that don't, on the surface, appear conducive to a good relationship. He's suggesting that it's acceptable—and even good—to speak about things that are difficult to talk about. However, as you can see from the preceding example, Rogers expected therapists to look inward and transform their negative feelings into more positive external expressions of congruence.

Guidelines for Using Congruence

When discussing congruence, students often wonder how this concept is manifest. Common questions include:

- Does congruence mean I say what I'm really thinking in the session?
- If I feel sexually attracted to a client, should I be "congruent" and share my feelings?
- If I feel like touching a client, should I go ahead and touch?
- What if I don't like something a client does? Am I being incongruent if I don't express my dislike?

These are important questions. Greenberg, Watson, and Lietaer (1998) provided one way for determining the appropriateness of therapist transparency or congruence. They wrote: " . . . it is not necessary to share every aspect of [your] experience but only those that [you] feel would be facilitative of [your] clients' work" (p. 9). This is a good initial guideline: *Would the disclosure be facilitative?* In fact, sometimes, too much self-disclosure—even in the service of congruence or authenticity—can muddy the assessment or therapeutic focus. Perhaps the key point is to maintain balance; the old psychoanalytic model of therapist as a blank screen can foster distrust, reluctance, and resistance, whereas too much self-disclosure can distort and degrade the therapeutic focus (Farber, 2006).

Rogers (1958) also suggested limits on congruence. He directly stated that therapy wasn't a time for clinicians to talk about their own feelings:

> Certainly the aim is not for the therapist to express or talk about his own feelings, but primarily that he should not be deceiving the client as to himself. At times he may need to talk about some of his own feelings (either to the client, or to a colleague or superior) if they are standing in the way. (pp. 133–134)

Imagine that you're working with a client and you feel the impulse to congruently self-disclose in the moment. If you're not sure your comment will be facilitative or whether it will *keep the focus on the client* (where the therapy focus belongs), then you shouldn't disclose. Additionally, you should *discuss ongoing struggles with self-disclosure with your peers or supervisors* because by so doing, you'll deepen your learning about how best to be congruent with clients.

Since the 1960s, feminist therapists have strongly advocated congruence or authenticity in interviewer-client relations. Brody (1984) described the range of responses that an authentic therapist might use:

> To be involved, to use myself as a variable in the process, entails using, from time to time, mimicry, provocation, joking, annoyance, analogies, or brief lectures. It also means utilizing my own and others' physical behavior, sensations, emotional states, and reactions to me and others, and sharing a variety of intuitive responses. This is being authentic. (p. 17)

Brody is advocating many sophisticated and advanced therapeutic strategies; but keep in mind that she's an experienced clinician. *Authentic or congruent approaches to interviewing are best if combined with good clinical judgment*, which is obtained, in part, through clinical experience.

Congruence, Touch, and Sex

Sometimes during an interview you will feel an impulse to touch a client. This is natural. You may feel that impulse for a variety of reasons. Perhaps the client is crying and you want to offer your hand or a hug. Perhaps you feel curiosity. Perhaps you believe your touch will be a source of healing for your client. There are many reasons why you might feel an urge to touch a client.

Gazda, Asbury, Balzer, Childers, and Walters (1984) recommended that when counselors feel a desire to touch, they should ask themselves: "Who is it for? Am I doing this for me, the other person, or to impress those who observe?" (p. 111). This recommendation implies another guideline: *Before offering congruent touch, clinicians should explore motives underlying their behaviors.*

We tend to be very conservative about touching clients. Touch should never feel invasive or overbearing. You must also make sure your touch won't be misinterpreted—which is difficult because clients with sexual abuse histories might be inclined to interpret your touch in ways different than you intended. Consequently, if you have any doubts about how it will be interpreted, you shouldn't touch clients.

Related to touch, it's not unusual for therapists to occasionally feel sexually attracted to their clients. As Welfel (2013) stated, "Sexual attraction to clients is an almost universal phenomenon among therapists; however, most, of course, do not act on that attraction and work to handle their reactions in a responsible manner" (p. 199). One reason that touch needs to be carefully scrutinized is because your client may experience your touch as intimate, romantic, or overtly sexual . . . regardless of your intent. Also, when therapists touch clients it can move the relationship in a sexual direction and sexual relations between therapist and client are always unacceptable, unethical, and often illegal; therapist-client sex results in trauma and victimization (Sonne & Pope, 1991). We agree with Pope's (1990) terminology for sexual relations between therapists and clients. He referred to it as *sexual abuse of clients*. His terminology makes it obvious: Sexual abuse of clients cannot be therapeutic.

If you feel sexual attraction toward clients, not only is it unacceptable to act on that attraction, you also shouldn't speak of your attraction to your client. Consider this scenario: You're working with a client, you feel sexual attraction, and so you say: "I feel sexually attracted to you." How do you suppose that disclosure might be interpreted? It should be obvious that to speak of sexual attraction is nearly always laden with flirtation. And, since you're in a role with power, you're in a position to potentially exploit clients. Bottom line: When you experience sexual attraction to a client, *don't* tell the client; but *do* seek supervision and guidance (R. Sommers-Flanagan & Sommers-Flanagan, 2007).

The Evidence Base for Congruence

Kolden and colleagues (2011) reported on a meta-analysis of congruence on therapy outcomes. Their meta-analysis included 16 research studies and 863 participants. Most of the research was conducted prior to 1990. Overall, they reported an effect size (ES) of 0.24. Using Cohen's (1977) standards, this is considered a medium ES; it indicates that, for the studies reviewed, congruence accounted for about 6% of treatment variance.

This meta-analysis also included analyses based on disaggregation of the data. Specifically, studies described as client-centered, interpersonal, or eclectic had significantly higher ES ($r = 0.36$) than studies described as psychodynamic ($r = 0.04$). Further, results varied as a function of the therapy setting. They reported the following effect sizes:

- School counseling centers: ES = 0.43
- Inpatient settings: ES = 0.27
- Mixed settings: ES = 0.23
- Outpatient mental health settings: ES = −0.02

In conclusion, there's an evidence base that supports using congruence during clinical interviews. Although this is somewhat helpful information, there's little specificity about exactly how congruence should be used. Overall, based on previous discussions of self-disclosure/immediacy, recommendations from Kolden and colleagues (2011) and our own clinical experiences, we offer the following guidelines for integrating your spontaneity with good clinical judgment:

- Examine your motives for congruence and touch: Is this more about you or more about your client?
- Ask yourself: Is the disclosure likely to be facilitative?

- Ask yourself: Does the comment keep the focus on the client or will it distract from the client and his/her issues?
- Consider the possibility of a negative reaction: Is it likely that your client will respond in a negative or unpredictable manner?
- Remember: Congruence doesn't mean you say whatever comes to mind; it means that when you do speak, you do so with honesty and integrity.

Overall, authenticity or congruence should be combined with good clinical judgment. Closely supervised clinical experience is an excellent method for enhancing your clinical judgment.

Unconditional Positive Regard

Rogers (1961) defined *unconditional positive regard* as follows:

> To the extent that the therapist finds himself [herself] experiencing a warm acceptance of each aspect of the client's experience ... he is experiencing unconditional positive regard ... it means there are no conditions of acceptance no feeling of "I like you only if you are thus and so." It means a "prizing" of the person, as Dewey has used that term. ... It means a caring for the client as a separate person. (p. 98)

Unconditional positive regard implies that clients are the best authority on their own experiences. Therapist judgments are always based on inadequate information; we haven't lived with our clients, we haven't observed them very long, and we can't directly know their internal motives, thoughts, or feelings.

For Rogers, the whole idea of *unconditional positive regard* was based on an underlying belief that consistent warmth, acceptance, and prizing of clients were needed to facilitate client growth toward their potential. He stated, " ... the safety of being liked and prized as a person seems a highly important element in a helping relationship" (1961, p. 34). Here, Rogers is describing how positive or accepting feelings toward clients are what allow clients to feel safe enough to explore their self-doubts, insecurities, and weaknesses.

How to Communicate Unconditional Positive Regard

Technically, according to Rogers (1957), unconditional positive regard is an experience and not a skill. He stated: "To the extent that the therapist finds himself experiencing a warm acceptance of each aspect of the client's experience ... he is experiencing unconditional positive regard" (p. 98). Nevertheless, it's useful to discuss how unconditional positive regard might look during interactions between therapist and client. A question our students frequently ask is: "How can I express or demonstrate unconditional positive regard?"

As you can imagine, it's tempting to try expressing positive feelings directly to clients, either by touching or making statements such as: "I like (or love) you," or "I care about you," or "I will accept you unconditionally," or "I won't judge you in here." However, expressing unconditional positive regard directly to clients can backfire. Direct expressions of caring may be interpreted as phony or inappropriately intimate. Direct expressions of affection may violate ethical boundaries by implying you want a friendship or loving relationship (R. Sommers-Flanagan, 2012). Also, as humans, sooner or later you'll have negative feelings toward your clients; if you explicitly claim "unconditional acceptance," you're promising the impossible.

If it's not appropriate to make direct statements about unconditional positive regard, then, "How might you express positive regard, acceptance, and respect to clients *indirectly*?" There are many therapist behaviors from which clients can infer positive regard. Here are some general principles, followed by examples:

1. You carefully keep appointments, arrive on time, ask your clients how they like to be addressed and then remember to address them that way, and listen sensitively and compassionately.
   - "How would you like me to address you? Do you prefer Mrs., Ms., or something else?"
2. You allow clients freedom to talk about themselves in their natural manner.
   - "I've got some information about your from your physician and she said you're experiencing some troubling anxiety. I'd really like you to tell me about your personal experience of the anxiety."
3. By remembering parts of your clients' stories, you communicate interest and a valuing of what they're telling you.
   - "Earlier today you mentioned wishing your roommate respected you. And now I hear you saying again that you find her behavior disrespectful."
4. You respond with compassion or empathy to clients' emotional pain and personal conflicts without judging the content of that pain.
   - "The loss of your job really has you shaken up right now. You're feeling lost about what to do next."
5. Because clients are sensitive to your intentions, simply by making a sincere effort to accept and respect your clients, you're communicating a message that may be more powerful than any other therapy technique
   - "I know you're saying I can't really understand what you've been through, and your right about that. But I'd sure like to try to understand as much of your trauma as you're willing to tell me."
6. Although direct expression of unconditional positive regard is generally ill-advised, research suggests that direct expressions of encouragement and affirmation for specific behaviors can have a positive effect on clients.
   - "I didn't see you as submissive or weak. In fact, since showing emotion is so difficult for you, I saw it as quite the opposite." (Farber & Doolin, 2011, p. 173)
   - "I have confidence in your ability to do this."
   - "Thank you for sharing so much about yourself with me."
7. Use the concept and technique of radical acceptance from Linehan's (1993, 2000) work (see Chapters 12 and 13 for examples).

Even Rogers (1957) recognized that therapists can't constantly experience unconditional positive regard. He referred to the phrase as "an unfortunate one" (p. 98) and noted that it was more accurate to say that therapists intermittently experience unconditional positive regard. He also emphasized that therapists also sometimes experience conditional positive regard and negative regard for their clients—although when therapists feel negative regard it's likely associated with ineffective therapy.

The Evidence Base for Unconditional Positive Regard

Farber and Doolin (2011) conducted a meta-analysis on 18 treatment outcome studies involving 1,067 clients. These studies all included measures of unconditional positive regard. Their overall finding was an aggregate ES of 0.27 across all 18 studies. This indicates a medium positive effect of unconditional positive regard.

The results also showed a weak, but statistically significant tendency for studies with greater numbers of racially diverse clients to have more positive outcomes. Farber and Doolin (2011) speculated:

> . . . we tentatively hypothesize that therapists' provision of positive regard may be a salient factor in treatment outcome when non-minority therapists work with minority clients. In such cases, the possibility of mistrust and of related difficulties . . . may be attenuated by clear indications of the therapist's positive regard, in turn facilitating the likelihood of a positive outcome. (p. 182)

This interpretation of the findings is consistent with multicultural theory as Sue & Sue (2013) have articulated.

Empathic Understanding

Empathic understanding is a central concept in counseling and psychotherapy. Rogers (1980) defined empathy as:

> . . . the therapist's sensitive ability and willingness to understand the client's thoughts, feelings, and struggles from the client's point of view. [It is] this ability to see completely through the client's eyes, to adopt his frame of reference [p. 85]. . . . It means entering the private perceptual world of the other . . . being sensitive, moment by moment, to the changing felt meanings which flow in this other person. . . . It means sensing meanings of which he or she is scarcely aware. (p. 142)

Rogers's definition of empathy is complex. It includes several components.

- Therapist ability or skill
- Therapist attitude or willingness
- A focus on client thoughts, feelings, and struggles
- Adopting the client's frame of reference or perspective-taking
- Entering the client's private perceptual world
- Moment-to-moment sensitivity to felt meanings
- Sensing meanings of which the client is barely aware

A Deeper Look at Empathy

As with congruence and unconditional positive regard, the complexity of Rogers's definition has made research on empathy challenging. Many different definitions of empathy have been articulated (Batson, 2009; Clark, 2010; Duan, Rose, & Kraatz, 2002). According to Elliott, Bohart, Watson, and Greenberg (2011), recent advances in neuroscience have helped consolidate empathy definitions into three core subprocesses:

1. *Emotional simulation:* This is a process that allows one person to experientially mirror another's emotions. Emotional simulation likely involves mirror neurons and various brain structures within the limbic system (e.g., insula).
2. *Perspective taking:* This is a more intellectual or conceptual process that appears to involve the prefrontal and temporal cortices.
3. *Emotion regulation:* This involves a process of re-appraising or soothing of one's own emotional reactions. It appears to be a springboard for a helping response. Emotional regulation may involve the orbitofrontal cortex and prefrontal and right inferior parietal cortices.

Empathy is an interpersonal process that requires experiencing, inference, and action. In Chapter 1 we noted that playing a note on one violin will cause a string on another violin to vibrate as well, albeit at a lower level. In therapy, this has been referred to as resonance. Most people have had the experience of feeling tears well up at a movie or while someone talks about pain or trauma. This is the experiential component of empathy that Elliott et al. (2011) referred to as emotional simulation.

Beyond this physical/experiential resonance, one person cannot objectively know another person's emotions and thoughts. Consequently, at some level, empathy always involves subjective inference. This process has been referred to as perspective taking in the scientific literature and is considered a cognitive or intellectual requirement of empathy (Stocks, Lishner, Waits, & Downum, 2011).

Empathy—at least within the context of a clinical interview—also requires action. Therapists must cope with and process the emotions that are triggered and then provide an empathic response. Most commonly this involves reflection of feeling or feeling validation, but nearly every potential interviewing response or behavior can include verbal and nonverbal components that include empathy. The action component of empathy is likely what Elliott et al. (2011) are referring to with the term emotional regulation.

Simple guides to experiencing and expressing empathy can help you develop your empathic abilities. At the same time, we don't believe any single strategy will help you develop the complete empathy package. For example, Carkhuff (1987) referred to the intellectual or perspective-taking part of empathy as "asking the empathy question" (p. 100). He wrote:

> By answering the empathy question we try to understand the feelings expressed by our helpee. We summarize the clues to the helpee's feelings and then answer the question, How would I feel if I were Tom and saying these things? (p. 101)

Carkhuff's empathy question is a useful tool for tuning into client feelings, but it also oversimplifies the empathic process in at least two ways. First, it assumes therapists have a perfectly calibrated internal affective barometer. Unfortunately, this is not the case, because clients and therapists can have such different personal experiences that the empathy question produces completely inaccurate results; just because *you* would feel a particular way if you were in the client's shoes doesn't mean the client feels the same way. Sometimes empathic responses are a projection of the therapist's feelings onto the client. If you rely solely on Carkhuff's empathy question, you risk projecting your own feelings onto clients.

Consider what might happen if a therapist tends toward pessimism, whereas her client usually puts on a happy face. The following exchange might occur:

Client: I don't know why my dad wants us to come to therapy now and talk to each other. We've never been able to communicate. It doesn't even bother me any more. I've accepted it. I wish he would accept it too.

Therapist: It must make you angry to have a father who can't communicate effectively with you.

Client: Not at all. I'm letting go of my relationships with my parents. Really, I don't let it bother me.

In this case, asking the empathy question: "How would I feel if I could never communicate well with my father?" may produce angry feelings in the therapist. This process consequently results in the therapist projecting her own feelings onto the client—which turns out to be a poor fit for the client. Accurate empathic responding stays close to client word content and nonverbal messages. If this client had previously expressed anger or was looking upset or angry (e.g., angry facial expression, raised voice), the therapist might resonate with and choose to reflect anger. However, instead the therapist's comment is inaccurate and is rejected by the client. The therapist could have stayed more closely with what her client expressed by focusing on key words. For example:

> Coming into therapy now doesn't make much sense to you. Maybe you used to have feelings about your lack of communication with your dad, but it sounds like at this point you feel pretty numb about the whole situation and just want to move on.

This second response is more accurate. It touches on how the client felt before, what she presently thinks, as well as the numbed affective response. The client may well have unresolved sadness, anger, or disappointment, but for the therapist to connect with these buried feelings requires a more interpretive intervention. Recall from Chapter 3 that interpretations and interpretive feeling reflections must be supported by adequate evidence.

To help with the intellectual process of perspective taking, instead of focusing exclusively on what you'd feel if you were in your client's shoes, you can expand your repertoire in at least three ways:

1. Reflect on how other clients have felt or might feel.
2. Reflect on how your friends or family might feel and think in response to this particular experience.
3. Read and study about experiences similar to your clients'.

Based on Rogers's writings, Clark (2010) referred to intellectual approaches to expanding your empathic understanding as objective empathy. *Objective empathy* involves using "theoretically informed observational data and reputable sources in the service of understanding a client" (Clark, 2010, p. 349). Objective empathy is based on the application of external knowledge to the empathic process—this can expand your empathic responding beyond your own personal experiences.

Rogers (1961) also emphasized that feeling reflections should be stated tentatively so clients can freely accept or dismiss them. Elliott et al. (2011) articulated the tentative quality of empathy very well: "Empathy should always be offered with humility and held lightly, ready to be corrected" (Elliott et al., 2011, p. 147).

From a psychoanalytic perspective, it's possible to show empathy not only for what clients are saying, but also for their defensive style (e.g., if they're using defense mechanisms such as rationalization or denial, show empathy for those):

Client: I don't know why my dad wants us to come to therapy now. We've never been able to communicate. It doesn't even bother me any more. I've accepted it. I wish he would.

Therapist: Coming into therapy now doesn't make much sense to you. Maybe you had feelings about your lack of communication with your dad before, but it sounds like you feel pretty numb about the whole situation now.

Client: Yeah, I guess so. I think I'm letting go of my relationships with my parents. Really, I don't let it bother me.

Therapist: Maybe one of the ways you protect yourself from feeling anything is to distance yourself from your parents. Otherwise, it could still bother you, I suppose.

Client: Yeah. I guess if I let myself get close to my parents again, my dad's pathetic inability to communicate would bug me again.

This client still has feelings about her father's poor communication. One of the functions of accurate empathy is to facilitate the exploration of feelings or emotions (Greenberg, Watson, Elliott, & Bohart, 2001). By staying with the client's feelings instead of projecting her own feelings onto the client, the therapist is more likely to facilitate emotional exploration.

A second way in which Carkhuff's (1987) empathy question is simplistic is that it treats empathy as if it had to do *only* with accurately reflecting client feelings. Although accurate feeling reflection is an important part of empathy, as Rogers (1961) and others have discussed, empathy also involves *thinking* and *experiencing* with clients (Akhtar, 2007). Additionally, Rogers's use of empathy with clients frequently focused less on emotions and more on meaning. Recall that in his original definition, Rogers wrote that empathy involved: "... being sensitive, moment by moment, to the changing felt meanings which flow in this other person..." (p. 142). And so empathic understanding is not simple, it involves feeling with the client, thinking with the client, sensing felt meanings, and reflecting all this and more back to the client with a humility that acknowledges deep respect for the validity of the client's own experiences.

Misguided Empathic Attempts

It's surprisingly easy to try too hard to express empathy, to completely miss your client's emotional point, or otherwise stumble in your efforts to be empathic. Classic statements that beginning therapists often use, but should avoid, include (J. Sommers-Flanagan & Sommers-Flanagan, 1989):

1. "I know how you feel" or "I understand."
   In response to such a statement, clients may retort: "No. *You* don't understand how I feel" and would be absolutely correct. "I understand" is a

condescending response that should be avoided. However, saying "I want to understand" or "I'm trying to understand" is acceptable.

2. "I've been through the same type of thing."

   Clients may respond with skepticism or ask you to elaborate on your experience. Suddenly the roles are reversed: The interviewer is being interviewed. If true, such a statement would also entail self-disclosure, which is a technique that requires serious consideration before use.

3. "Oh my God, that must have been terrible."

   Clients who have experienced trauma sometimes are uncertain about how traumatic their experiences really were. To hear a professional exclaim that what they lived through and coped with was "terrible" might be too negative. The determination you need to make is whether you are leading or tracking the client's emotional experience. If clients give you a clear indication that they sense the "terribleness" of their experiences, reflecting that an experience "must have been terrible" is empathic. However, a better empathic response would remove the judgment of "must have" and get rid of the "Oh my God" (i.e., "Sounds like you feel terrible about what happened.").

The Evidence Base for Empathy

There's a substantial body of empirical research addressing the relationship between empathy and treatment process and outcomes. This research strongly supports the central role of empathy in facilitating positive treatment outcomes.

In a meta-analysis of 47 studies including over 3,000 clients, Greenberg and colleagues (2001) reported a correlation of .32 between empathy and treatment outcome. Although this is not a large correlation, they noted, "empathy... accounted for almost 10% of outcome variance" and "Overall, empathy accounts for as much and probably more outcome variance than does specific intervention" (p. 381).

Elliott and colleagues (2011) also conducted a more recent meta-analysis. This sample included: "224 separate tests of the empathy-outcome association" (p. 139) from 57 studies including 3,599 clients. They concluded (based on a weighted r of 0.30) that empathy accounts for about 9% of therapy outcomes variance.

Based on their 2001 meta-analysis and an analysis of various theoretical propositions, Greenberg et al., identified four ways in which empathy contributes to positive treatment outcomes:

1. Empathy improves the therapeutic relationship. When clients feel understood, they're more likely to stay in therapy and be satisfied with their therapist.

2. Empathy contributes to a corrective emotional experience. A corrective emotional experience occurs when the client expects more of the same pain-causing interactions with others, but instead, experiences acceptance and understanding. Empathic understanding tends to foster deeper and more trusting interactions and disclosures.

3. Empathy facilitates client verbal, emotional, and intellectual self-exploration and insight. Rogers (1961) emphasized this: "It is only as I see them (your feelings and thoughts) as you see them, and accept them and you, that you feel really free to explore all the hidden nooks and frightening crannies of your inner and often buried experience" (p. 34).

4. Empathy moves clients in the direction of self-healing. This allows clients to take the lead in their own personal change—based on a deeper understanding of their own motivations.

Although it's difficult to prove causal relationships in psychotherapy research, it appears that empathy contributes to positive treatment outcomes (Duan, Rose, & Kraatz, 2002; Elliott et al., 2011; Greenberg et al., 2001). In fact, some authors suggest that empathy is the basis for all effective therapeutic interventions: "Because empathy is the basis for understanding, one can conclude that there is no effective intervention without empathy and all effective interventions have to be empathic" (Duan et al., 2002, p. 209).

PUTTING IT IN PRACTICE 5.1

What and How to Validate: Empathic Responding to Trauma and Abuse

Empathy often includes validation of client emotional experiences. But sometimes clients have ambivalent feelings about their own experiences that makes empathic validation complicated. This is especially possible in cases of trauma and abuse, in which victims can and do experience victim guilt—feeling as though they caused their own abusive experiences. For example, take the following therapist-client interaction:

Therapist: Can you think of a time when you felt unfairly treated? Perhaps punished when you didn't deserve it?

Client: No, not really. *(15-second pause)* Well, I guess there was this one time. I was supposed to clean the house for my mother while she was gone. It wasn't done when she got back, and she broke a broom over my back.

Therapist: She broke a broom over your back? *(stated with a slight inflection, indicating possible disapproval or surprise with the mother's behavior)*

Client: Yeah. I probably deserved it, though. The house wasn't cleaned like she had asked.

In this situation, the client seems to have mixed feelings about her mother. On the one hand, the mother treated her unfairly; on the other hand, the client felt guilty because she saw herself as a bad girl who didn't follow her mother's directions. The therapist was trying to convey empathy through voice tone and inflection. This technique was chosen due to concerns that focusing too strongly on the client's guilt or indignation and anger might prematurely shut down exploration of the client's ambivalent feelings. Despite the therapist's minimal expression of empathy, the client defends her mother's punitive actions. This suggests that the client had already accepted (by age 11, and still accepted at age 42) her mother's negative evaluation of her. From a person-centered or psychoanalytic perspective, a stronger supportive statement such as "That's just abuse, mothers should never break

(continued)

(*continued*)

brooms over their daughters' backs" may have closed off any exploration of the client's victim guilt about the incident.

Alternatively, this is a situation in which gentle, open and empathic questioning might help deepen the therapist's understanding of the client's unique personal experience and help her explore other feelings, like anger, that she might feel in response to her mother's abuse. For example, the therapist could have asked:

> I hear you saying that maybe you feel you deserved to be hit by your mother in that situation, but I also can't help but wonder... what other feelings you might have?

Or, the therapist might use a third-person or relationship question to help the client engage in empathic perspective-taking herself:

> What if you had a friend who experienced something like what you experienced? What would you say to your friend?

From a nondirective perspective, sensitive nondirective responses that communicate empathy through voice tone, facial expression, and feeling reflection are usually more advantageous than open support and sympathy. There's always time for open support later, after the client has explored both sides of the issue.

In the first version of this interaction, the therapist used a nondirective model, expressing only nonverbal empathy for the client's abuse experience. He didn't openly criticize or judge the mother's violence. Do you think the therapist might have been too nondirective—in some ways aligning with the part of the client that felt her mother was justified in abusing her? Is it possible that the client actually might have been more able to explore her anger toward her mother if the therapist had led her in that direction with an empathic self-disclosure like:

> When I imagine myself in your situation, I can feel the guilt you feel, but also, a part of me feels angry that my mother would care so much about housecleaning and so little about me.

This self-disclosure is both empathic and leading. Do you think it's too leading? Or do you think it's a better response than the neutrality often emphasized in psychoanalytic therapies? Discuss this possibility with your classmates or colleagues.

Concluding Thoughts on Empathy

Empathy is a vastly important, powerful, and complex interpersonal phenomenon. People express themselves on multiple levels, and due to natural human ambivalence, can simultaneously express conflicting meanings and emotions. Rogers believed that the desire to judge clients or respond to them out of his own need was greatly reduced through empathy. He found that the interrelatedness of empathy, unconditional positive regard, and congruence modified the spontaneity associated with congruence. Accurate empathy also diminishes the tendency to judge clients and thus enhances unconditional positive regard. Empathy, unconditional positive regard, and congruence are not competing individual constructs; they complement and influence one another.

Greenberg and associates (2001) captured the challenges of being empathic with individual clients when they wrote:

> Certain fragile clients may find expressions of empathy too intrusive, while highly resistant clients may find empathy too directive; still other clients may find an empathic focus on feelings too foreign. Therapists therefore need to know when—and when not—to respond empathetically. Therapists need to continually engage in process diagnoses to determine when and how to communicate empathic understanding and at what level to focus their empathic responses from one moment to the next. (p. 383)

The preceding description of how it is necessary to constantly attune your empathic responding to your individual client probably sounds daunting . . . and it should. When we add cultural diversity to the empathic mix, the task becomes even more daunting. Nevertheless, we encourage you to embrace the challenge with hope, optimism, and patience. It's only by sitting with people as they struggle to express their emotional pain and suffering that we can further refine our empathic way of being. Like everything, empathic responding takes practice, something Rogers (1961) recommended over 50 years ago.

EVIDENCE-BASED PSYCHOANALYTIC AND INTERPERSONAL RELATIONSHIP CONCEPTS

The following theoretically and empirically supported relationship factors are derived from psychoanalytic, object relations, and interpersonal or attachment-based theoretical perspectives. A closer look at these factors adds to our understanding of the power of the therapeutic relationship.

Transference

Transference is a relational concept associated with psychoanalytic theory and practice. Sigmund Freud (1949) defined *transference* as a process that occurs when " . . . the patient sees in his analyst the return—the reincarnation—of some important figure out of his childhood or past, and consequently transfers on to him feelings and reactions that undoubtedly applied to this model" (p. 66). Transference is an important relational concept because in psychoanalytic therapy—as well as other therapies—a major goal is to help clients gain awareness of repeating maladaptive relationship patterns in their lives. By gaining greater awareness or insight into their deeply ingrained interpersonal patterns, clients can begin changing those patterns. Awareness or insight is viewed as a necessary prerequisite to intentional change in interpersonal relationship patterns.

Transference is generally characterized by inappropriateness; a client responds to a therapist with actions, thoughts, or feelings that are too intense, too extreme, too capricious, and that are held onto with tenacity (Greenson, 1967). Freud (1912/1958) noted that transference "exceeds anything that could be justified on sensible or rational grounds" (p. 100). Sometimes, but not always, intense and obvious transference issues can surface early in an interview. For example, an angry young man had a negative reaction to his female counselor and became verbally aggressive during an initial screening interview. He repeatedly stated, "You f---ing women can't understand where I'm coming from. No way. Women just don't get me. You don't get me." Because the counselor's behavior hadn't warranted a strong reaction, it's likely this client was displacing "feelings, attitudes, and behaviors" based on previous interactions he had experienced with females (Gelso & Hayes, 1998, p. 51).

Examples of Transference

More commonly, transference is abstract, vague, and elusive. To notice it, you have to pay close attention to idiosyncratic ways in which your clients interact with you; for example, clients may subtly respond to you in ways that are more emotional than the situation warrants, they may make assumptions about you that have little basis in reality, or they may express unfounded and unrealistic expectations regarding you or therapy.

One common old map on new terrain (transference) occurs when clients expect their therapists are judging them negatively. For example, a client with whom we worked expressed anxiety regarding her performance on a psychological test and her out-of-session homework. She stated tentatively,

> Um . . . you know, I think some things that personality test says about me don't seem accurate. I must have done something wrong when I took the test.

This comment is revealing. Usually when clients are provided with inaccurate psychological test feedback, they question the test's validity, rather than their own performance. In a similarly tentative way, she later stated, "I did the assignment, but I'm not sure I had the right idea." She made this statement despite the fact that she'd turned in the most thorough homework assignment we'd ever seen. She did exactly as instructed, but her self-doubt was likely triggered because she viewed her therapist as an authority figure who might evaluate her negatively. Her expectation of criticism suggested, based on the psychoanalytic perspective, that she may have experienced harsh and inappropriate criticism in the past. In this sense, her reaction is similar to a child who flinches when approached by an adult whose arm is extended. The child may flinch because of previous physical abuse; the flinch may be an automatic and unconscious response. Similarly, clients who have been exposed to excessive criticism may have automatic and unconscious tendencies to prepare themselves (or flinch) when exposed to evaluative situations. This is an example of transference.

As Freud (1949) wrote, "Transference is ambivalent" (p. 66). Transference may manifest itself in positive (e.g., affectionate, liking, loving) or negative (hostile, rejecting, cold) attitudes, feelings, or behaviors. It can be productive to work through either form of transference as therapy progresses. However, during initial stages, the wisest course is for therapists to be astute observers, noticing patterns of client responses that seem interpersonally inappropriate and may stem from old terrain and past relationships in the client's life. Commenting on these patterns should wait for later.

Noticing and Exploring Transference

Adequate rapport and a working relationship should precede transference interpretation (Meissner, 2007). Further, working directly with transference as part of therapy requires advanced skills and firm theoretical grounding obtained from specialized texts and professional supervision. However, that doesn't mean you should ignore transference. In the beginning of counselor or psychotherapist training it's important to notice attitudes, emotions, or behaviors directed at you that are repeated and seem unwarranted or exaggerated. Keep these three principles and practices in mind:

1. Be aware of the possibility that repeating inappropriate transference reactions may occur during an interview.
2. Notice repeating patterns internally and then when a pattern is very clear, notice it with an explicit comment:
   - "I've noticed you seem to get angry when we talk about your father."
   - "It's just an observation, but you've said very negative things about yourself—I think you've even used the word pathetic three times to describe yourself."
3. Explore repeating patterns that may be significant:
   - "When have you felt similar feelings in the past?"
   - "What do you make of your tendency to get angry when we talk about your father?"

Transference gives you a special opportunity to glimpse the converging nature of your client's past, present, and in-session relationships.

The Empirical Base for Transference

Research suggests that transference reactions during sessions can be reliably and validly measured (Kivlighan, 2002). There is also evidence that measures of transference (e.g., the core conflictual relationship theme or CCRT) in therapy are highly similar to contemporary relationship patterns observed outside therapy (Kivlighan, 2002; Luborsky & Crits-Christoph, 1998). Finally, empirical research indicates that working directly with transference using various psychoanalytic or dynamic models can produce positive treatment outcomes (Jarry, 2010; Shedler, 2010). For example, in a meta-analysis of 10 studies focusing on long-term psychoanalytic treatment, an ES of 0.78 was reported (Driessen et al., 2010). As a comparator, a meta-analysis of medications for major depression produced an ES of 0.31 (Turner, Matthews, Linardatos, Tell, & Rosenthal, 2008).

These findings have implications for even the beginning clinical interview. It's possible that during initial and follow-up interviews, clients will display behaviors representing transference. Although dealing with these behaviors therapeutically requires extensive training, beginning therapists can benefit from gently commenting on and exploring relationship patterns that emerge in an interview and also cause clients distress outside of therapy.

Countertransference

Freud (1910/1957) originally defined *countertransference* as a phenomenon:

> ...which arises in the physician as a result of the patient's influence on his [the physician's] unconscious feelings, and have nearly come to the point of requiring the physician to recognize and overcome this countertransference in himself (pp. 144–145)

As you can sense from the quotation, Freud had a negative view of countertransference (CT). He also wrote: "...no psychoanalyst goes further than his own complexes and internal resistances permit" (1957, p. 145).

Contemporary definitions of CT have been divided into four categories (Gelso & Hayes, 2007):

1. *Classical*: This is Freud's view. Client transference triggers the analyst's unresolved childhood conflicts. This triggering results in the analyst acting out in a way consistent with the unresolved conflicts. This form of CT is negative and should be "overcome."
2. *Totalistic*: This CT refers to all reactions the therapist has toward the client. These reactions are meaningful, should be studied, understood, and consequently used to benefit therapy process and outcome.
3. *Complementary*: This CT emanates from specific client interaction patterns that "pull" therapists to respond in ways that others (outside therapy) respond to the client. Good therapists inhibit their reactive impulses, seek to understand the nature of the transaction, and then use this knowledge to frame interventions designed to modify the client's maladaptive relational style.
4. *Relational*: This CT is constructed from the combination or integration of the unmet needs and conflicts of both client and therapist.

Most contemporary theorists and therapists have moved beyond Freud's negative view of CT and adopt one or more of the other perspectives. What this means is that most therapists now view CT as a natural and valuable source of information that can contribute to positive treatment outcomes (see *Putting It in Practice* 5.2).

Examples of Countertransference

Client behavior is the trigger for CT. Sometimes clients treat their therapists with such open hostility or admiration that therapists are quickly caught up in transference-countertransference dance. This can result in therapists behaving in ways that are very unusual for them. For example, at a psychiatric hospital, a patient unleashed an unforgettable accusation against her therapist:

> You are the coldest, most computer-like person I've ever met. You're a robot! I talk and you just sit there, nodding your head like a machine. I bet if I cut open your arms, I'd find wires, not veins!

This accusation might be considered pure transference. Perhaps the client was responding to her therapist in this way because she had experienced significant male figures from her past as emotionally unavailable. On the other hand, as the saying goes, it takes two to tango; the therapist also needed to examine his contributions to this particular interaction.

Taking a hard look at his reactions to this patient, the therapist consulted with colleagues and a supervisor, engaged in self-reflection, and came to several conclusions. First, he realized he was behaving cooler and less emotionally with her than he generally did with clients. Second, he became aware that he was frightened of her intense demands for emotional intimacy. He began recognizing that he had been protecting himself by becoming more inhibited and robotic. Third, his supervisor reassured him that he wasn't the first clinician to experience CT; finally, he worked to respond to the client more therapeutically, rather than reacting with his own fears of intimacy.

There are an unlimited number of potential CT behaviors, considering that nearly any behavior or emotional response may represent CT. For example,

- Reaching out and touching a client/drawing back away from a client who is seeking to shake your hand or give you a hug.
- Talking too much in a session; feeling inhibited and unable to speak freely in a session.
- Feeling bored; feeling aroused.
- Joking too much; feeling unable to shake negative and depressive thoughts and feelings.
- Offering to give your client a ride home; refusing to give your client a ride home.
- Dreaming about your client; dreading your client's arrival.

Clinicians from various theoretical orientations have acknowledged the reality of CT. Speaking from a behavioral perspective, Goldfried and Davison (1976, 1994), the authors of *Clinical Behavior Therapy*, offered the following advice: "The therapist should continually observe his own behavior and emotional reactions, and question what the client may have done to bring about such reactions" (p. 58). Similarly, Beitman (1983) suggested that even technique-oriented counselors may fall prey to CT. He wrote: "any technique may be used in the service of avoidance of CT awareness" (p. 83). For example, clinicians may repetitively apply a particular technique to clients (e.g., progressive muscle relaxation, mental imagery, or thought stopping) without realizing they're applying the techniques to address their own needs, rather than the needs of their clients (see *Putting It in Practice* 5.2 and *Multicultural Highlight* 5.1).

PUTTING IT IN PRACTICE 5.2

Coping With Countertransference

Most broadly (using the totalistic CT definition), CT is defined as therapist emotional and behavioral reactions to clients. As an example, imagine a therapist who lost his mother to cancer as a child. His father's grief was very severe. As a consequence, the father offered little emotional support when the therapist was a child. The situation eventually

(continued)

(*continued*)

improved, his father recovered, and the therapist's conscious memory consists of a general sense that losing his mother was very difficult. Now, years later, he's a graduate student, conducting his first interviews. Things are fine until a very depressed middle-aged man comes in because he recently lost his wife. What reactions might you expect from the therapist? What reactions might catch him by surprise?

CT reactions may be more or less conscious, more or less out of the therapist's awareness. These reactions, if unmanaged, can have a negative effect on therapy. The following guidelines are provided to assist you in coping with CT reactions:

- Recognize that CT reactions are normal and inevitable. If you experience strong emotional reactions, persistent thoughts, and behavioral impulses toward a client, it doesn't mean you are a "sick" person or a "bad" therapist.
- You should also recognize that CT could be a sign that you need to do some personal work. This work can begin on a personal level with you engaging in activities that will help foster your psychological well-being and with you taking time to develop greater self-awareness or insight.
- If you're having strong reactions to a client, consult with a colleague or supervisor.
- Do additional CT reading. It's especially useful to obtain reading materials pertaining to problems your clients are manifesting (e.g., eating disorders, depression, antisocial behavior).
- If your CT persists despite efforts to deal with it, consider: (a) Referring your client to another therapist and/or (b) getting personal psychotherapy. As Hayes, Gelso, and Hummel (2011) noted: "Personal therapy for the therapist seems especially important when dealing with chronic CT problems." (p. 255)

MULTICULTURAL HIGHLIGHT 5.1

Coping With Cultural Countertransference

Potential CT can lurk everywhere. Imagine you're a veteran who served in Iraq and a Sunni Muslim refugee comes to see you for counseling. Imagine that you were sexually assaulted by a very tall, red-haired man with an Irish brogue, and a very tall red-haired man with a similar accent arrives in your waiting room. Unless you've done your personal work previously, you're likely to have significant reactions (perhaps both conscious and unconscious) and issues to work through, based on cultural and physical cues emanating from your new client. Racial and cultural stereotypes are imbedded in all of us, even if we haven't had difficult experiences with people from specific ethnic backgrounds.

CT is omnipresent (and tricky) because it can be triggered by so many different factors. Not only can you succumb to a client who behaves in ways similar to your domineering sister, but you can also overreact to clients who sound whiney or who are particularly handsome or particularly unattractive by a given set of cultural standards. CT doesn't discriminate: We all can and will be affected by it.

The renowned group psychotherapist Irvin Yalom (1989) wrote eloquently about his negative CT toward an obese client:

> Of course, I am not alone in my bias. Cultural reinforcement is everywhere. Who ever has a kind word for the fat lady? But my contempt surpasses all cultural norms. Early in my career, I worked in a maximum security prison where the least heinous offense committed by any of my patients was a simple, single murder. Yet I had little difficulty accepting those patients, attempting to understand them, and finding ways to be supportive.
>
> But when I see a fat lady eat, I move down a couple of rungs on the ladder of human understanding. I want to tear the food away. To push her face into the ice cream. "Stop stuffing yourself! Haven't you had enough, for Chrissakes?" I'd like to wire her jaws shut! Poor Betty—thank God, thank God—knew none of this as she innocently continued her course toward my chair, slowly lowered her body, arranged her folds and, with her feet not quite reaching the floor, looked up at me expectantly. (p. 95)

Your client's cultural background (or physical appearance) may trigger CT reactions. These reactions may range from traditional discrimination ("I shouldn't expect much educational ambition from my American Indian or African American clients.") to guilt and pity ("I need to be especially nice to minority clients because they've been so mistreated over the years.") to competition ("Women and minorities are taking all the best jobs and now I'm stuck working with this militant Sri Lankan woman who's filing a sexual harassment suit against her employer.").

There are many examples of cultural CT in the research literature. For example, mental health professionals from the United States have been found to overdiagnose psychotic disorders in patients of African American descent (Zuckerman, 2000).

As you read this section, you may find yourself wondering: "What's the difference between CT and racism?" That's an excellent question. What do you think the differences (and similarities) might be?

The Empirical Base for Countertransference

Research suggests that CT reactions can teach therapists about their own important underlying conflicts as well as about client interpersonal dynamics (Betan, Heim, Conklin, & Westen, 2005; Mohr, Gelso, & Hill, 2005; Schwartz & Wendling, 2003). For example, based on a survey of 181 psychiatrists and clinical psychologists, Betan et al. (2005) reported

> . . . patients not only elicit idiosyncratic responses from particular clinicians (based on the clinician's history and the interaction of the patient's and the clinician's dynamics) but also elicit what we might call average expectable countertransference responses, which likely resemble responses by other significant people in the patient's life. (p. 895)

This conclusion is consistent with contemporary views that CT is now widely considered a natural phenomenon and useful source of information that can contribute to therapy process and outcome (Luborsky & Barrett, 2006).

Hayes, Gelso, and Hummel (2011) conducted a meta-analysis on 10 quantitative studies that measured CT and outcomes. They reported a small, negative overall effect for CT on outcomes (weighted $r = 0.16$). Based on their meta-analysis it appears that CT tends to be associated with slightly poorer treatment outcomes.

Hayes et al. (2011) also conducted a meta-analysis focusing on whether CT management reduced negative outcomes. Their study rationale was stated as: "A fundamental concept in this literature is that if CT is to be a help rather than a hindrance, the therapist must do something to, with, or about CT" (p. 251). They identified 11 quantitative studies where an effort was made to manage or control CT. Overall, they again reported a small effect, suggesting that efforts to manage CT were associated with reduced manifestations of CT (weighted $r = -0.14$).

In a third meta-analysis, Hayes et al. (2011) examined the relationship of CT management and treatment outcomes. Their question was whether or not CT management might contribute to improved outcomes. Based on seven quantitative studies, they reported a "significant and large" effect (weighted $r = 0.56$). Their results suggest that when therapists actively manage their CT reactions to clients it can contribute to more positive treatment outcomes.

Therapeutic Alliance or Working Alliance

The idea that therapist and client collaborate in ways that sustain the therapy process originated with Freud (1912/1958). Later, psychoanalytic theorists introduced the terms *therapeutic alliance* and *working alliance* (Greenson, 1965; Zetzel, 1956). Greenson (1965, 1967) distinguished between the two, viewing the working alliance as the client's ability to cooperate with the analyst on psychoanalytic tasks and the therapeutic alliance as the bond between client and analyst.

Bordin (1979, 1994) introduced a pantheoretical version that he referred to as the working alliance. Bordin's model consists of three alliance dimensions:

1. Goal consensus or agreement
2. Collaborative engagement in mutual tasks
3. Development of a relational bond

Bordin's model is somewhat dominant today, but there are many different models and measures of the therapeutic or working alliance.

The working alliance has become one of the most frequently studied concepts in counseling and psychotherapy. Horvath, Re, Fluckiger, and Symonds (2011) noted that when searching electronic research databases for keywords *alliance, helping alliance, working alliance,* and *therapeutic alliance* in 2010, they obtained over 7,000 hits. In summarizing the research literature, Constantino and associates offered this conclusion:

> ... it seems reasonable to say that regardless of the treatment approach (psychodynamic, cognitive-behavioral, gestalt, interpersonal, eclectic, drug counseling, or management), the length of therapy, the type of problems presented by clients (depression, bereavement, anxiety, substance abuse, and so on), and the type of change aimed at (specific target complaints, symptom reduction, interpersonal functioning, general functioning, intrapsychic change and so on), therapists should make deliberate and systematic efforts to establish and maintain a good therapeutic alliance. (Constantino, Castonguay, & Schut, 2002, pp. 111–112)

Strupp and Binder (1984), among others, pointed out that a client's ability to establish a therapeutic or working alliance is predictive of his or her potential to grow and change as a function of psychotherapy. In other words, if clients cannot or will not engage in a working alliance with a therapist, there's little hope for change. Conversely, the more completely clients enter into such a relationship, the greater their chances for positive change (Hardy, Cahill, & Barkham, 2007). Many researchers and theorists agree that people's abilities to enter into productive relationships are determined in large part by the quality of their early interpersonal relations. Ironically and unfortunately, it appears those most in need of a curative relationship may be those least able to enter into one.

The Empirical Base for the Working Alliance

Research has indicated that therapists vary in their ability to form a working alliance (Baldwin, Wampold, & Imel, 2007). In a meta-analysis, Ackerman and Hilsenroth (2003) identified characteristics of therapists who were effective at forming strong working alliances. Those able to form and sustain the alliance had personal attributes that included warmth, flexibility, experience, and trustworthiness. They also used reflective and affirming techniques that facilitated emotional expression and focused directly on their client's experiences.

Horvath et al. (2011) conducted a meta-analysis on alliance in psychotherapy. Based on "190 independent alliance-outcome relations representing over 14,000 treatments," (p. 47) they reported a medium ES ($r = 0.275$). These results indicated that across many different therapies, higher alliance ratings are related to better treatment outcomes. Further, these results are consistent with previous reviews (Horvath & Bedi, 2002; Martin, Garske, & Davis, 2000).

Bordin's working alliance model includes collaboration and goal consensus components. Tryon and Winograd (2011) conducted a meta-analysis on the relationship between these two alliance dimensions and treatment outcomes. They reviewed 15 studies with an overall sample of 1,302 clients. Results indicated a medium ES ($r = 0.34$). Results were similar for collaboration. Tryon and

Winograd also analyzed 19 collaboration studies with 2,260 clients and reported an ES of $r = 0.33$.

In recent years it has been suggested that therapy outcomes might improve if therapists collect feedback from clients about the therapy alliance and treatment progress (Lambert, 2010; Miller & Donahey, 2012). Conceptually, the idea is that therapists should be asking clients "How am I doing?" or "How are we doing?" and then make adjustments based on the feedback clients provide. Given that clients are consumers, empowering them to provide guiding feedback seems to be a very reasonable strategy and as it turns out, empirical research supports the efficacy of feedback monitoring. Specifically, Lambert and Shimokawa (2011) conducted a meta-analysis on collecting client feedback and reported a variety of effect sizes, depending on the particular feedback measure employed. Overall, all measures showed a positive relationship to outcome, with effect sizes ranging from $r = 0.23$ to $r = 0.54$.

Developing a positive treatment alliance and the associated activities of collaboration, goal consensus, and feedback or progress monitoring are clearly associated with positive treatment outcomes. The strength of association between these variables and outcomes are greater than any specific therapy techniques. This fact led Horvath and colleagues to write: "The magnitude of this correlation makes it one of the strongest and most robust predictors of treatment success that research has been able to document" (p. 56). There's little doubt that integrating this knowledge into your repertoire is likely to improve the quality of your clinical work.

Recommendations for Developing and Using a Positive Working Alliance

Although Freud started the conversation, he might not recognize contemporary models of the working alliance. This is because Freud advocated analyst emotional distance and a detached psychoanalytic stance, whereas today's working alliance involves therapists initiating a process of collaborative engagement with clients.

Therapists who want to develop a positive working alliance (and that should include all therapists) will integrate strategies for doing so during initial interviews and beyond. Based on Bordin's (1979) model, alliance-building strategies would focus on (a) collaborative goal setting; (b) engaging clients on mutual therapy-related tasks; and (c) development of a positive emotional bond. Additionally, feedback monitoring within clinical interviews is recommended.

- Initial interviews and early sessions appear especially important to developing a working alliance. Many clients who enter your office will be naïve about what will be happening in their work with you. This makes including role inductions or explanations of how you work with clients essential. Here's an example from a cognitive-behavioral perspective:

  > For the rest of today's session, we are going to be doing a structured clinical interview. This interview assesses a range of different psychological difficulties. It is a way to make sure that we "cover all of our bases." We want to see if social anxiety is the best explanation for your problems and also whether you are having any other difficulties that we should be aware of. (Ledley, Marx, & Heimberg, 2010, p. 36)

- Asking direct questions about what clients want from counseling and then listening to them and integrating that information into your treatment plan is also important: In cognitive therapy this is often referred to as making a problem list (J. Beck, 2011).

Therapist:	What brings you to counseling and how can I be of help?
Client:	I've just been super down lately. You know. Tough to get up in the morning and face the world. Just feeling pretty crappy.
Therapist:	Then we definitely want to put that on our list of goals. Can I write that down? [Client nods assent] How about for now we write, "Find ways to help you start feeling more up?"
Client:	Sounds good to me.

- Engaging in a collaborative goal-setting process—and not proceeding with therapy tasks until it's clear that mutual goals (even temporary mutual goals) have been established

Therapist:	So far I've got three goals written down: (1) Find ways to help you start feeling more up, (2) Help you deal with the stress of having your sister living with you and your family, and (3) Improving your attitude about exercising. Does that sound about right?
Client:	Absolutely yes. If we can climb those three mountains it will be great.

- Soliciting feedback from clients during the initial session and ongoing in an effort to monitor the quality and direction of the working alliance. Although there are a number of instruments you can use for this, you can also just ask directly:

> We've been talking for 20 minutes now and so I just want to check in with you on how you're feeling about talking with me today. How are you doing with this process?

- Making sure you're able to respond to client anger or hostility without becoming defensive or launching a counterattack is essential to establishing and maintaining a positive working relationship. In our work with challenging young adults, we apply Linehan's (1993) "radical acceptance" concept. For example, an initial session with an 18-year-old male started like this:

Therapist:	I want to welcome you to therapy with me and I hope we can work together in ways you find helpful.
Client:	You talk just like a shrink. I punched my last therapist in the nose (client glares at therapist and awaits a response) (J. Sommers-Flanagan & Bequette, 2013, p. 15).
Therapist:	Thanks for telling me about that. I definitely want to avoid getting punched in the nose. And so if I accidentally say anything that offends you I hope you'll tell me, and I'll try my best to stop.

In this case the therapist accepted the client's aggressive message and tried to transform it into a working concept in the session.

- Having specific therapy tasks (no matter your theoretical orientation) that fit well with the mutually identified therapy goals. For example, if illuminating unconscious processes is a mutually identified goal, then using free association can be a task that makes sense to the client. On the other hand, if you've agreed to work toward greater self-acceptance and greater acceptance of frustrating people in the client's life, then engaging in intermittent mindfulness tasks will feel like a reasonable approach.

ADDITIONAL THEORETICAL- AND EVIDENCE-BASED CONCEPTS RELATED TO THE THERAPEUTIC RELATIONSHIP

In this section we briefly review additional theoretically based relational concepts that are likely linked to therapy success. These relationship factors also have empirical support, although the evidence may not be as direct or as extensive as the relationship factors we've just reviewed. However, as many meta-analytic reviewers have acknowledged, variations in how specific concepts are defined and measured, imply that empirical support for relational factors is more broad than narrow (Horvath et al., 2011; Kolden et al., 2011; Tryon & Winograd, 2011). As we review these additional relational factors, you'll notice linkage and overlap with the relational factors discussed previously.

Role Modeling: AKA Identification and Internalization

Modeling is a powerfully ubiquitous force in contemporary psychology. The fact that humans learn through modeling was articulated in Mary Cover Jones's early work with phobic children and later became a cornerstone of Bandura's social-learning theory. Modeling is a form of treatment in its own right. Specifically, modeling is empirically supported and used extensively in the treatment of anxiety disorders and skill deficits (Spiegler & Guevremont, 2010). However, for the purposes of this chapter, modeling is viewed as a phenomenon that occurs within the therapist-client relationship.

Psychoanalytic and object relations theorists use the terms *identification* and *internalization* to describe what behaviorists consider modeling (Forester, 2007; Safran, Muran, & Eubanks-Carter, 2011; Safran, Muran, & Rothman, 2006). Individuals *identify* with others whom they love, respect, or view as similar. Through this identification process, individuals begin to incorporate or internalize unique and specific ways in which that loved or respected person thinks, acts, and feels.

No one knows the precise psychological dynamics that cause people to imitate or model their behavior after someone else. It could occur as a function of self-efficacy, it could involve the identification-internalization process, or it could be caused by other factors. Imagine the following scenario: A young adult's probation officer refers him to a mental health professional after several minor criminal convictions. The client arrives for the initial clinical interview, but is reluctant to talk openly with the therapist. Eventually the client begins to like the therapist and enjoys spending time with him. They talk about specific triggers that have gotten the client in trouble in the past as well as how to stop and reflect before acting impulsively. Therapy is very successful and in the final session the therapist asks the client what he found most helpful. Although they've worked together on cognitive-behavioral strategies such as problem-solving and consequential thinking, the client described his success as based on something else.

> I guess I think it was two things, Doc. You're a good guy and at some point in my time with you I started thinking I'd like to be more like you. And then, when I faced situations where I would usually make a bad decision, it was like your voice popped into my head and then I thought, hmm, I wonder what the doc would do? And then I did what I thought you would do instead of what I would have usually done.

According to psychoanalytic theory, identification is the precursor to internalization. Object-relations theorists hypothesize that as we develop we internalize components of various caretakers and others in our early environment. These internalizations serve as the basis for how we feel about ourselves and how we interact with others (Fairbairn, 1952). If we internalize "bad objects" (i.e., abusive parents, neglectful caretakers, vengeful siblings), we may experience disturbing self-perceptions and interpersonal relationships. Based on a psychoanalytic model, psychotherapy involves a relationship that can replace maladaptive internalizations with adaptive or good internalizations, derived from a relatively healthy psychotherapist. Strupp (1983) stated, "[I have] stressed the importance of the patient's identification with the therapist, which occurs in all forms of psychotherapy. Since the internalization of 'bad objects' has made the patient 'ill,' therapy succeeds to the extent that the therapist becomes internalized as a 'good object'" (p. 481).

Clients may improve because of psychoanalytic dynamics of identification and internalization, or they may improve because of a more simplified observational learning process. Either way, it seems that therapists have a chance to contribute to positive outcomes just by being a positive, respectful, and reflective person with whom clients can identify.

Expertness (Credibility), Attractiveness, and Trustworthiness

Social psychology research has focused on a variety of different relationship factors (e.g., influence, conformance, etc.) that are relevant to clinical practice. In 1968, Stanley Strong published an article that described how three characteristics from opinion change research could be applied to counseling. These characteristics were expertness, attractiveness, and trustworthiness.

Expertness

Therapy is all about change. Based on social psychology principles, communicators with greater expertness are more likely to influence listeners in ways that lead to changes in beliefs or opinions (Strong, 1968). Within the interviewing and counseling domain, expertness has also been described as credibility or competence.

Based on research findings and clinical observations, there are many ways therapists can *look* credible (Goates-Jones & Hill, 2008; Yuar & Chen, 2011).

- Displaying your credentials (e.g., certificates, licenses, diplomas) on office walls.
- Keeping shelves of professional books and journals in the office.
- Having an office arrangement conducive to open dialogue.
- Being professionally groomed and attired.
- Using language that is at least as sophisticated as the client's.
- Explaining to clients that their problems, although unique, are similar to problems other clients have had that were successfully treated.
- Sharing your general knowledge about a particular disorder.
- Dealing effectively with clients' distrust; you can also express empathy for the distrust and gently explore it with your client—which is a very expert thing to do.

Attractiveness

As the saying goes, beauty is in the eye of the beholder. However, there are some standard features that most people view as attractive. Because of its subjective nature and the fact that it's good to cultivate your self-awareness, we refer you to the activity in *Multicultural Highlight* 5.2. This activity helps you explore behaviors and characteristics you might find attractive if you went to a therapist. Note that when we speak of what's attractive, we're referring not only to physical appearance but also to behaviors, attitudes, and personality traits.

MULTICULTURAL HIGHLIGHT 5.2

Defining Therapist Attractiveness

Attractiveness is an elusive concept. But being aware of how we appear to others is invaluable in therapist development. Reflect on the following questions:

1. How you would like your therapist to look? Would your ideal therapist be male or female? How would he or she dress? What type of facial expressions would you like to see? Lots of smiles? Do you want an expressive therapist? One with open body posture? A more serious demeanor? Imagine all sorts of details (e.g., amount and quality of makeup, type of shoes, length of hair).
2. Now, think about what racial or ethnic or other characteristics you'd like your therapist to have? Do you want someone whose skin color is the same as yours? Do you want someone whose accent is just like yours? Would you wonder, if you had a counselor with an ethnic background different from your own, if that person could really understand you? How about your counselor's age or sexual orientation; would those characteristics matter to you?

3. What types of technical interviewing responses would your ideally attractive therapist use? Would she use plenty of feeling reflections or be more directive (e.g., using confrontations and psychoeducation)? Would he use lots of eye contact and "uh-huhs," or express attentiveness some other way?

4. How would an attractive therapist respond to your feelings? For example, if you started crying in a session, how would you like the therapist to act and what would you like him or her to say?

5. Would an attractive therapist touch you, self-disclose, call you by your first name, or stay more distant and focus on analyzing your thoughts and feelings?

Ask these questions of a fellow student or friend or family member. Although you may find you and your friends or family don't have specific criteria for what constitutes therapist attractiveness, after discussion, people usually discover that they have stronger opinions than they originally thought. Be sure to ask fellow students of racial/ethnic backgrounds, ages, and sexual orientations different from yours about their ideally attractive therapist.

Trustworthiness

Trust is defined as confidence in or reliance on the integrity, strength, ability, surety of a person or thing. Establishing trust is crucial to effective interviewing. Strong (1968) emphasized the importance of clients perceiving their therapists as trustworthy. When therapists are perceived as trustworthy, clients are more likely to believe what they say and follow their recommendations or advice.

It's not appropriate to express trustworthiness directly in an interview. Saying "trust me" to clients isn't recommended, lest someone mistake you for an automobile salesperson. Like empathy and unconditional positive regard, trustworthiness is a therapist characteristic that is best cultivated indirectly.

Perceptions of therapist trustworthiness begin with initial client-therapist contacts. These contacts may be over the telephone or during an initial greeting in the waiting room. The following therapist behaviors are associated with trust:

- Courteous, gentle, and respectful initial introductions.
- Clear and direct explanations of confidentiality and its limits.
- Acknowledgment of difficulties associated with coming to a professional therapist.
- Sharing of information you have about the client.
- Manifestations of congruence, unconditional positive regard, and empathy.
- Punctuality and general professional behavior.

With clients who are mandated to counseling, it can be helpful to state outright that the client may have trouble trusting the therapist. For example:

I can see you're not happy to be here. That's often true when people are forced to attend counseling. So right from the beginning, I want you to know I don't expect you to trust me or to like being here. It's up to you to decide how much trust to put in me and in this counseling. Also, just because you're required to be here doesn't mean you're required to have a bad time.

Clients will periodically test their therapists (Fong & Cox, 1983). In a sense, clients will "set you up" to determine whether you're trustworthy. For example, children who have been sexually abused often behave seductively when they meet a therapist; they may sit in your lap, rub up against you, or tell you they love you. You might be asked to undress. These behaviors can be viewed as blatant tests of therapist trustworthiness (i.e., the behaviors ask, "Are you going to abuse me, too?"). It's important to recognize tests of trust and to respond, when possible, in ways that enhance the trust relationship.

Mutuality

Feminist theory and psychotherapy emphasize the importance of establishing an egalitarian relationship between client and therapist (Worell & Remer, 2003). The type of egalitarian relationship preferred by feminist therapists is one characterized by mutuality and empowerment. Although they share common ground with the core relationship components identified by Carl Rogers, feminists take into account the social location, gender, and power differentials that impact the way clients experience themselves and their worlds (Brown, 2010).

Mutuality refers to a sharing process; it means that power, decision making, goal selection, and learning are shared. Although various psychotherapy orientations (especially person centered) consider treatment a mutual process wherein clients and therapists are open and human with one another, nowhere are egalitarian values and the concept of mutuality emphasized more than in feminist theory and therapy.

The following case example illustrates this concept:

CASE EXAMPLE

Cammy, a 25-year-old graduate student, came for an initial interview. The therapist's supervisor urged the therapist to stay neutral and to resist impulses to self-disclose. The therapist says to Cammy, "Tell me about what brings you in at this time." Cammy begins crying immediately and says, "My mother is dying of cancer. She lives 200 miles away but wants me there all the time. I'm finishing my PhD in chemistry and my dissertation chair is going on sabbatical in 3 months. I have two undergraduate courses to teach, and my husband just told me he's thinking of leaving me. I don't know what to do. I don't know how to prioritize. I feel like I'm disappearing. There's hardly anything left of me. I'm afraid. I feel like a failure being in therapy, but . . . " Cammy cries a while longer.

The therapist feels the overwhelming sadness, fear, and confusion of these situations. She is tempted to cry herself. She works hard, internally, to think of something appropriately neutral to say. After just a slight pause, in a kind voice, she says, "All these things leave you feeling diminished, afraid, perhaps like you're losing a sense of who you are. Being in therapy adds to the sense of defeat." Cammy says, "Yes, my mother always said therapists were for weak folks. Her term was addle-brained. My husband refuses to see anyone. He thinks if I stay home and drop this education thing, we could be happy together again. Sometimes I feel my dissertation chair would be happier if I just gave it up."

The therapist responds, "The important people in your life somehow want you to do things differently than you are doing."

Although the preceding interactions are acceptable, if both Cammy and the therapist stay with this modality, Cammy would finish knowing very little about her therapist and she would feel, generally, that the therapist was the provider of insight, and she, Cammy, was the provider of problems.

In a more mutuality-oriented interaction, when the therapist feels overwhelming sadness, fear, and confusion, she might say, "Wow, Cammy. Those are some very difficult situations. Just hearing about all that makes me feel a little sad and overwhelmed. Is that what you're feeling?" Cammy might then say, "Yes. I feel both. It's nice to have you glimpse that. See, my mom says counseling is a waste of time. My husband thinks I'm too busy outside the home . . . and I even get the same message from my dissertation chair."

The therapist, aware of the power and gender dynamics that are part of Cammy's struggles, might then say, "Yeah. It's hard to decide to get into therapy, or to even keep going when those close to you disapprove of your choices, and when as women, we've been taught to value this approval so much."

The differences in responses may not seem huge, but the underlying framework of the therapist-client relationship in mutuality-oriented therapies contrasts sharply with traditional frameworks. The therapist shares her emotional reactions. The therapist uses mutual empathy to resonate with power issues her client is experiencing. Groundwork is laid for a relationship that includes honest self-disclosure on the therapist's part and that may, later in therapy, even include times when the client observes and comments on patterns in the therapist's behavior (Jordan, 2010).

When therapists engage in mutuality, they do so to empower and resonate with their clients. Although mutuality doesn't alter the fact that a certain amount of authority rests with the counselor, feminist therapists actively work to teach clients to respond to authority with assertiveness, a sense of personal worth, and with their own personal authority. Feminist therapists believe respectful, reciprocal interactions can result in a growing sense of personal power in clients; empirical data support this claim (Neff & Harter, 2003).

The Client Is the Expert

Person-centered, feminist, gestalt, solution-focused, and narrative therapists view clients as the best experts on their own lives. In particular, solution-focused therapists make this concept explicit and constantly emphasize it during the therapy process. De Shazer and Dolan (2007) wrote:

> It is rare for an SFBT therapist to make a suggestion or assignment that is not based on the client's previous solutions or exceptions. It is always best if change ideas and assignments emanate from the clients, at least indirectly during the conversation, rather than from the therapist, because the client is familiar with these behaviors. (p. 5)

Through this stance, solution-focused therapists honor the client's way and utilize existing strengths and resources emanating from the client and his or her life.

CONCLUDING COMMENTS

There is general, if not unanimous, consensus that therapeutic relationships facilitate positive therapy outcomes. If he were alive, Rogers might say they're necessary, and unlike back in 1957, nearly everyone would agree with him because research supports this idea. In fact, relationship factors are so ubiquitous that they even exert an influence on telephonic or online therapy outcomes (Hanley, 2009; Jain, 2011).

SUMMARY

In his early work, Carl Rogers (1942, 1951, 1957) articulated the importance of relationship variables in psychotherapy. Similarly, clinical interviewing is characterized, to some degree, by the formation of a special type of relationship between therapist and client. Based on Rogers's foundational ideas, contemporary researchers and practitioners have begun referring to therapeutic relationship factors in counseling and psychotherapy as "evidence-based relationships" (Norcross, 2011).

Rogers identified three core conditions he believed were necessary and sufficient for personal growth and development to occur: congruence, unconditional positive regard, and accurate empathy. Congruence is synonymous with genuineness or authenticity and generally means the therapist is open and real with clients. However, it is inappropriate for therapists to be completely congruent or authentic with clients all of the time because the purpose of counseling is to facilitate the client's (and not the therapist's) growth. Similar to congruence, unconditional positive regard and accurate empathy are complex relationship variables that, for the most part, must be communicated indirectly to clients. Empirical research indicates that Rogers's original core conditions contribute to positive therapy outcomes.

Several relationship variables derived from psychoanalytic and interpersonal theories also have been linked to positive therapy outcomes. These include transference, countertransference, and the working alliance. Transference occurs when clients begin viewing and reacting to therapists as if the therapist were a significant figure from the past. Countertransference has been defined in many ways, but most broadly, it refers to the reactions that therapists have toward clients. The working alliance includes three main dimensions: (a) collaborative identification of goals, (b) working together on tasks related to the identified goals, and (c) the bond established between client and therapist.

Other theoretically based relationship concepts also appear to have a positive influence on treatment outcomes. Behavioral role-modeling or psychoanalytic identification and internalization seem to encourage clients to behave in ways similar to their therapists. Social psychology factors of expertness, attractiveness, and trustworthiness also have empirical support as potential contributors to therapist influence. Feminist theory, practice, and research suggest that mutuality in therapy relationships is a positive factor. Finally, person-centered, feminist, gestalt, solution-focused and narrative therapies all emphasize that treating clients as the best experts of their situations is an essential relational factor in therapy.

SUGGESTED READINGS AND RESOURCES

de Shazer, S., Dolan, Y., Korman, H., McCollum, E., Trepper, T., & Berg, I. K. (2007). *More than miracles: The state of the art of solution-focused brief therapy*. New York, NY: Haworth Press.

   This book, published after Steve de Shazer's death, provides case examples and detailed explanations for how to practice solution-focused brief therapy.

Enns, C. Z. (2004). *Feminist theories and feminist psychotherapies: Origins, themes, and diversity* (2nd ed.). New York, NY: Haworth Press.

   This is a great primer for understanding the history and application of feminist theory and therapy.

Freud, S. (1949). *An outline of psychoanalysis*. New York, NY: Norton.

   This relatively quick read provides a succinct description of psychoanalytic principles in Freud's own words.

Jordan, J. (2010). *Relational-cultural therapy*. Washington, DC: American Psychological Association.

   Jordan is a prominent feminist therapist and author. In this book, she articulates a feminist approach to therapy that emphasizes relational mutuality as a healing force.

Norcross, J. (2011). *Psychotherapy relationships that work: Evidence-based responsiveness*. New York, NY: Oxford University Press.

   This book is the compilation of task forces from Divisions 12 (Clinical Psychology) and 29 (Psychotherapy) of the American Psychological Association. It includes 21 chapters that report data on the contribution of relationship factors to psychotherapy outcomes.

Rogers, C. R. (1961). *On becoming a person*. Boston, MA: Houghton-Mifflin.

   This text contains much of Rogers's thinking regarding congruence, unconditional positive regard, and empathy.

PART THREE

Structuring and Assessment

An Overview of the Interview Process

CHAPTER OBJECTIVES

Every interview has a flow and pattern. Even if therapists are completely nondirective and allow clients to free associate for 50 minutes, there's still a beginning, middle, and end to the interview process. In this chapter, we examine the structure of a typical clinical interview; we take a close look at how interviews begin, proceed, and end, and how you can smoothly integrate many essential activities into a single clinical hour.

After reading this chapter, you will understand:

- The stages or structure of a typical clinical interview.
- How to handle the introduction stage of an interview, including phone contact, initial meetings, building rapport, putting clients at ease, the utility of small talk (charlar), and clarifying expectations during an interview.
- How to handle the interview's opening stage, including your opening statements and the client's opening response.
- How to handle information-gathering and assessment tasks associated with the body of an interview.
- General methods for evaluating client psychopathology.
- How to handle the closing stage of an interview, including how to: support clients, summarize crucial issues and themes, instill hope, guide, and empower clients, and tie up loose ends before ending a session.
- How to handle the termination stage of an interview, including time boundaries, termination, and dealing with feelings about the end of the session.

The clinical interview cannot and should not be an interaction that runs along a prescribed path from point A to point B. True, we can dissect the interview into components, but in the end, each interview involves unique human beings, interacting with and responding to each other.

Learning to conduct a clinical interview is similar to learning other new skills, such as juggling or dancing. You can read about how to juggle or tango and when you first start trying to take the steps required to perform the skill, you feel awkward and need to keep reminding yourself of what comes next.

Like juggling or dancing, the clinical interview has a more or less mechanized format (but the guidebook for learning to do interviews is somewhat longer than the instructions that came with your juggling set). After reading this and other chapters, you may find yourself worrying about engaging in the proper interviewing step at the proper time. You might catch yourself thinking, "I need to establish rapport here.... Now it's time to elicit information.... Time to prepare for closing." In contrast, experienced therapists, like tango aficionados, find their flow and gather information, maintain rapport, and begin dealing with closure at the same time, without specifically thinking about it ... but they didn't begin their careers with this ability (Skovholt & Jennings, 2004).

In this chapter the rhythm and rules of the clinical interview are clarified. Our purpose is to provide a map for conducting interviews so you become comfortable with the continuity of this unique 50-minute hour. When you're comfortable with these rules, you'll spend less energy contemplating what's next and more energy on understanding, evaluating, and helping your clients.

The interviewing structure presented here primarily illustrates how typical assessment interviews proceed. However, it also pertains to psychotherapy or counseling sessions. Therapy sessions proceed in a similar manner. The major difference is that the *body* of a therapy interview involves the application of therapy interventions, rather than information gathering.

STRUCTURAL MODELS

Just as professional and social interactions have a predictable, implicit sequence, ritual, or stages, so does the clinical interview. Shea (1998) identified these stages as

1. The introduction.
2. The opening.
3. The body.
4. The closing.
5. The termination.

Shea's model is generic and atheoretical and may be applied to virtually all interviewing situations. This chapter outlines and discusses tasks and potential pitfalls associated with each interview stage.

Although we've adopted Shea's (1998) language for interviewing stages, we recognize that other stage models exist. For example, Foley and Sharf (1981) identified five sequential tasks common to interviews:

1. Putting the patient at ease.
2. Eliciting information.
3. Maintaining control.
4. Maintaining rapport.
5. Bringing closure.

Most interviewing models are quite similar. Foley and Sharf's model has many commonalities to Shea's model, but the language in Foley and Sharf's model gives you a clearer glimpse of what they view as the interviewer's general tasks.

Allen E. Ivey (1971) has written about clinical interviewing for many years. In the most recent edition of his *Essentials of Intentional Interviewing* he and his colleagues described a five-stage model with a positive and constructive theoretical emphasis (Ivey, Ivey, Zalaquett, & Quirk, 2012, p. 10):

1. *Relationship:* Establishing rapport and making a connection.
2. *Story and strengths:* Exploring client strengths and personal narrative.
3. *Goals:* Identifying and formulating counseling goals.
4. *Restory:* Reformulating or reconstructing client narratives in a more positive frame.
5. *Action:* Helping clients take action to make life changes.

As you compare the models described in this section, be sure to notice the similarities and the differences. In contrast to Shea's model (which is very generic and atheoretical) and Foley and Sharf's (which focuses on general tasks), Ivey's model is more process oriented and theoretical (with an emphasis on narrative or constructive theory). These are not competing models and can easily be integrated together to provide common flow and rhythm to the 50-minute hour.

Ideally, therapists guide clients through interview stages, allowing them to rush or linger in a given place as needed. This is the nature of an unstructured or less structured clinical interview (Jones, 2010). As a clinician, you're responsible for managing the hour, for smoothly integrating interview elements, for staying within time limits, and for covering the essentials, given your setting. However, the less rigidly you exercise this responsibility, the better.

THE INTRODUCTION: FIRST CONTACT

Shea (1998) defined the introduction stage:

> The introduction begins when the clinician and the patient first see one another. It ends when the clinician feels comfortable enough to begin an inquiry into the reasons the patient has sought help. (p. 58)

The introduction stage primarily involves initiating the helping relationship. This includes your first contact with clients and involves putting the client at ease in a way that facilitates open discussion of a wide range of personal information.

Telephone Contact

The introduction stage may begin on the telephone or Internet *before* you see the client. Whether you do this yourself or a receptionist makes a phone call, the therapy relationship begins with initial contact. Done well, the phone call, the paperwork, and the clarity and warmth with which clients are greeted can put them at ease. Done thoughtlessly or poorly, these same elements can confuse and intimidate. This is also true for online counseling (see Chapter 15).

The important point is that first contact, whether via mail, e-mail, telephone, questionnaire, online, or in person, directly affects your relationship with clients.

The following transcript illustrates an initial telephone contact:

Therapist:	Hello, I'm trying to reach Bob Johnson.
Client:	That's me.
Therapist:	Bob, this is Chelsea Brown. I'm a therapist at the University Counseling Center. I understand you're interested in counseling. I'm calling to see if you'd like to set up an appointment.
Client:	Yeah, I filled out a questionnaire.
Therapist:	Right. If you're still interested in counseling, we should set up a time to meet. Do you have particular days and times that work best for you?
Client:	Tuesday or Thursday is best for me . . . after 2 . . . but before 6.
Therapist:	How about this Thursday, the 24th, at 4?
Client:	That's fine with me.
Therapist:	Do you know how to find the center?
Client:	Yep. I was there to fill out the questionnaire.
Therapist:	Good. If you could come at 10 minutes before 4 P.M. and check in that would be great. The receptionist will give you a few forms to fill out and that way you can finish them before we start our meeting at 4. Is that okay?
Client:	Sure, no problem.
Therapist:	Great. I look forward to meeting you Thursday, the 24th, at 4 P.M.
Client:	Okay, see you then.

Note several points in this dialogue. First, scheduling the initial appointment is a collaborative process. This activity begins the working alliance (described in Chapter 5). It can be difficult to schedule an appointment with some clients, perhaps because of the problem of finding a meeting time for two busy people. The preceding dialogue illustrates a simple, straightforward scheduling experience. Such is not always the case. It's important to be clear about your available times for meeting with clients before initiating the phone call.

Second, the therapist identifies herself, her status (i.e., therapist), and her place of employment. You may want to be even clearer about these facts. For example, when students in our upper-level interviewing courses contact volunteers, they say something like, "I'm a graduate student in Psych 555, and I received your name and number from the extra credit sign-up sheet."

Third, the therapist checks to make sure the client knows how to get to the interview location. Even though many clients will obtain a map to your location via the Internet, you should be prepared to provide clear directions before making the call. For some clients, it may be helpful for the agency to provide a map with directions or instructions for public transportation.

Fourth, the therapist asks the potential client what days and times work best. This is a reasonable question only if the therapist has a flexible schedule. If your schedule is very busy, you should begin by identifying your open times. Whatever the case, it's not necessary to disclose specific information about why you cannot meet at a particular time. For example, during an initial phone call it would be inappropriately self-disclosing to say, "Oh, I can't meet then because I have to pick up my daughter from school" or "I'm in class then."

Fifth, the therapist closes by repeating the appointment time and noting that she's looking forward to meeting the client. She also clarifies exactly what the client should do when arriving at the center (i.e., check in with the receptionist). Avoid saying things like, "Check in with the receptionist and I'll be right out to meet you," because you don't know when the client will arrive. If he arrives 25 minutes early, you're stuck—either you meet him 25 minutes early or you end up not following through with what you said on the phone.

You may want to practice telephone conversations in class or with a supportive friend or family member. Invite them to throw you a few curves, so you can practice handling a question or two you weren't prepared for. If you've practiced, you'll be more able to focus on how clients present themselves and on the task of working together to schedule an appointment.

Initial Face-to-Face Meeting

Privacy is an important initial consideration. Most agencies have public waiting rooms. It's more difficult to keep a client's identity anonymous in these settings than it is for single clinicians in private practice. Therefore, it's incumbent on therapists who work in public settings to consider how to respect client privacy. One option is to have the receptionist point out or describe a new client so you can walk up and say the client's name in a quiet, friendly voice, not easily overheard by others in the room and introduce yourself. A handshake may or may not be appropriate (more on this later). It's best to say something like, "It's nice to meet you" and "Come back this way" and then lead the client to your private office.

First impressions are especially important in the world of therapy and mental health assessment (Human & Biesanz, 2011; Human & Biesanz, 2012). You need to be aware of how much hinges on first impressions and how much information you gain by observing client behavior during the first moments of your meeting. Some clients will be nervous, although others may be eager to meet you, angry, nonchalant, or challenging.

As you observe your client, your client is simultaneously sizing up the situation and you. To increase the consistency of client perceptions, some professionals follow an introductory ritual that includes some or all of the following:

1. Shaking hands (this can be culturally inappropriate, for example, with Muslim women or Orthodox Jewish women and men who have religious reasons for not shaking hands with the opposite sex).
2. Offering something to drink.
3. Chatting about a neutral topic while walking to the interviewing room.

A standard greeting ritual can be comforting and frees you to be more observant. Standardization strengthens your ability to make inferences from your observations (see *Putting It in Practice* 6.1). You can design your greeting ritual to reflect a warm, welcoming, professional image. However, many therapists never establish an exact routine; they like to size up clients individually and offer whatever seems called for. Lazarus (1996) referred to this as being an *authentic chameleon*. Sometimes, this is a firm handshake and/or comforting social banter. In other situations, no handshake and less banter is wiser. Our advice is for you to begin with a relatively standard routine and then learn to vary it as needed.

PUTTING IT IN PRACTICE 6.1

Standardized Introductions

In some ways, it's best to use a standardized introduction procedure with all clients, because the more consistent you are, the more certain you can be that individual differences in how clients present themselves reflect actual client differences and not different reactions to your different behaviors. For example, if you vary your introduction routine based on your mood, whatever you observe will be more about you than about your clients. Standardization is a part of good psychological science (Groth-Marnat, 2009). If you have a standard approach, you increase the reliability, and potential validity, of your observations.

On the other hand you don't want to be inflexible and come across as inauthentic or detached. Similarly, it's important to respond not only to each client's unique individual characteristics, but also to typical differences found in social or cultural groups. For example, the same approach wouldn't be equally appropriate or effective with male adolescents and female senior citizens. Individuals in these two groups typically have different relational styles. To treat them identically during an introduction is a mistake. Also, excess standardization may adversely affect rapport. When dealing with different individuals in the introductory stage of an interview, you should follow two general guidelines:

1. Go with the base rates: Greet people in a manner consistent with their basic demographics, including culture, age, and sex.
2. Choose the least offensive alternative: If you make a mistake, make a minor mistake.

Some beginning therapists are put off by standardization and routine. Shouldn't we give each client a unique and human response? Our answer to that question is no and yes. No, it's not necessary to give each client a unique or different response just for the sake of avoiding routine. And yes, we should give each client a human response.

For example, we usually begin first sessions with a description of confidentiality and a comment on how initial interviews are a chance for us to get to know each other. Although this is part of a standardized introduction, we sincerely mean what we're saying every time: we genuinely want each client to understand confidentiality and its limits. Just because we've said the same statement to hundreds of clients doesn't mean we're operating on autopilot.

The final point is to be intentional. For example, if you don't want your session to begin in the waiting room, you shouldn't greet your client with the usual and socially spontaneous, "How are you?" The whole process of greeting clients involves an extension of the intentionality you want to display when you're conducting a clinical interview.

This leads to the issue of how to address your clients. The first rule is to be polite, but politeness depends on your setting and population. In some situations it will be best to use first names. In other situations it will be best to use Mr., Ms., Mrs., or Dr. It can be difficult to tell which title to use with which person. If you're comfortable with Spanish and working with a Latino client, it may be best to begin with Señor or Señora or Señorita. Overall, when in doubt, go with the clients first and last name while making eye contact, but not too much eye contact. Later, if you're not sure whether you addressed your client properly, you can ask "How would you like me to greet you in the waiting room?" If you sense you used the wrong greeting strategy, check with your client, correct yourself, and apologize ("Would you prefer I call you Mrs. Rodriguez? Okay. Sorry about that. I wasn't sure how you wanted to be greeted."). The effort to address clients as they want to be addressed communicates respect (respeto) and acceptance.

Establishing Rapport

Rapport is a generic relationship variable. Therapists of all theoretical orientations acknowledge the importance of having a positive rapport with clients. Positive *rapport* is defined as having an especially harmonious connection; this connection may occur immediately or may require extended interactions. Many technical responses discussed in Chapter 3 are associated with developing rapport (e.g., paraphrase, reflection of feeling, and feeling validation). When working across cultures or with young clients, rapport building may depend on acceptance of diverse communication styles, language use, and personal values (Hays, 2013). The following factors contribute to positive rapport.

Having Sensitivity to Common Client Fears

Clients naturally have many fears and doubts about therapy. Being aware of these can help you with the rapport building process. Common concerns include:

- Is this therapist competent?
- More importantly, can this person help *me?*
- Will this therapist understand me, my culture, my values, my religion, and my problems?
- Am I going crazy?
- What will this therapist think of me?
- Can I trust this person to be honest with me?
- Will I be pressured to say things I don't want to say?
- Will this counselor think I'm a bad person?

To some extent, all professional therapists are perceived as authority figures. Power and authority reside in the mental health professional role and denial of this power can result in you abusing your power.

Clients may believe they should treat you like they treat other authority figures, such as physicians and teachers. They may expect you to behave like previous authority figures in their lives have behaved. This can range from warm, caring, wise, and helpful to harsh, cold, and rejecting. Because clients come to counseling with both conscious and unconscious assumptions about authority figures, you may need to help your client view you as a partner in the therapeutic process. Consequently, it's a good idea to say something very clear, straightforward, and informative about the developing collaborative partnership between you and your client during your initial meeting. Examples include:

- I'm looking forward to working with you today.
- Since we don't really know each other, counseling can feel awkward at first, but hopefully we'll start getting comfortable together today.
- Because this is our time to start getting to know each other, I may ask more questions today than I usually do.
- I hope you'll feel free to ask me any questions you want as we talk together today.

In addition to statements implying partnership, it's also important to provide clients with support and reassurance. However, generic reassurance ("Don't worry, everything will be okay") or premature reassurance ("I'm sure you don't have any serious problems") can be viewed as inaccurate, patronizing, and false. Instead, as suggested by Carl Rogers over 70 years ago, we should use reassurance to promote a sense of universality. He stated, " . . . the only type of reassurance which has any promise of being helpful is that which relieves the client's feeling of peculiarity or isolation" (1942, p. 165). It's also important to refrain from reassurance unless or until you see or hear evidence that reassurance might be appropriate. Examples of appropriate reassurance include:

- Lots of people who come for counseling feel uncomfortable at first, but it usually gets more comfortable as we get to know each other.
- Many of my clients have concerns similar to yours, and they usually find counseling is very helpful.

Putting the Client at Ease

After explaining confidentiality (see Chapters 2 and 5), you may wish to use a statement similar to the following:

> Counseling is a unique situation. This first meeting is a chance for us to get to know each other. My goal is to understand your concerns. Sometimes I'll just listen. Other times I'll ask questions. This first session is also a chance for you to see how I work in counseling. If you have any questions, feel free to ask them.

This introduction, stated in your own words, can help put clients at ease. It acknowledges the fact that therapist and client are "getting to know each other" and gives clients permission to ask questions about therapy.

Conversation and Small Talk

Conversation and initial informal chatting are common methods to help put clients at ease. These efforts may involve the following:

- You must be Steven Green. (Initial greeting)
- Do you like to be called Steven, Steve, or Mr. Green? (Clarifying how the client would like to be addressed, or how to pronounce his name)

- Were you able to find the office (or a place to park) easily? (Small talk and empathic concern)
- How was the traffic on the way here? (Acknowledgment of challenges associated with transportation)
- (With children or adolescents) I see you've got a Miami Heat hat on. You must be a Heat fan. (Small talk; an attempt to connect with the client's world)

Chatting may or may not be important with adult clients. On the other hand initial casual conversation can easily make or break an interview with a child or adolescent or with a client from a different culture (see Chapters 11 and 13). Many interviews with young people succeed partly because, at the beginning of the first session, you take time to discuss the client's favorite music, television shows, video games, toys, foods, sports teams, and so on. Similarly, in interviews with adolescents or preadolescents, we sometimes discuss what slang words are "in" and how to use them appropriately (e.g., Recently we had a Latino client tell us that other boys were upset with him because they thought he was "macking" on the girls. The ensuing discussion about the definition of macking—which we'll leave for you to discover—had a very positive effect on the interview's outcome).

Personalismo and Cultural Connections

When working with clients from diverse cultures it's very important to remember the Latino principle and practice of personalismo. This principle emphasizes informal social connection and can be crucial for rapport with clients from many different cultures. For African Americans, this informal personal interaction has been referred to as "person-to-person connection," and American Indians sometimes refer to it as "respect and reciprocity" (Hays, 2008).

To create personalismo, therapists need to speak casually and informally about social commonalities (Ayón & Aisenberg, 2010). This may involve conversations about the weather, recent news, traffic, parking availability, sports teams, jewelry, clothing, and other topics. However, even comments about the weather may not be without baggage and so we recommend caution. (Believe it or not, John regularly gets himself in trouble when expressing his idiosyncratic views on the weather forecast.)

Engaging in personalismo helps transform the therapist from an authority figure within a dominant cultural setting into a real person who deals with traffic and is curious or observant about clothing and other issues. In certain cross-cultural situations, it also creates a connection to share that you have (or don't have) children, depending on the situation and purpose of your disclosure. Because self-disclosure is considered to be a technique, it's important to be thoughtful and purposeful in these disclosures.

Striking a Balance

In many cases it may seem natural to share and compare children's ages, marital status, food preferences, exercise, political figures, common places of origin, and other information. You may feel an urge, on seeing the husband of your client holding a baby, to say something like, "We have a little one at home, too" or "Our little girl likes that same book." If your client is carrying a bike helmet, you may feel tempted to say, "I commute on my bike, too." Unfortunately, interviewing is not a simple social situation and so the decision about how much to self-disclose can feel daunting. It's best to strike a balance and be aware that your self-disclosure is to build rapport, rather than to build a social friendship. Beginning an interview with too much self-disclosure or small talk can misguide clients into thinking the interview is a social encounter. We encourage you to engage in reasonable and limited self-disclosure under the guidance of your supervisor. Following through on every social urge or impulse is not the best approach (see *Putting It in Practice* 6.1). For example, Weiner (1998) stated:

> Just as a patient will have difficulty identifying the real person in a therapist who hides behind a professional facade and never deviates from an impersonal stance, so too he will see as unreal a therapist who ushers him into the office for a first visit saying, "Hi, my name is Fred, and I'm feeling a little anxious because you remind me of a fellow I knew in college who always made me feel I wasn't good enough to compete with him." (p. 28)

Educating Clients and Evaluating Their Expectations

Another introductory stage activity is client education. This activity sets the interview frame or boundaries. We sometimes say something like:

> Before we officially get started, we've got some housekeeping [or paper-work or red tape or whatever word seems to work for you and your clients] to take care of.

This interview activity is a continuation of the informed consent process and several issues need to be addressed. First, clients should be informed of confidentiality and its limits. This process should be simple, straightforward, and interactive—and it should occur even if your client already signed a lengthy informed consent form (see *Putting It in Practice* 6.2 for an informed consent assignment). Remember: No mound of paperwork is a substitute for a conversation about therapy (J. Sommers-Flanagan & Sommers-Flanagan, 2007b).

PUTTING IT IN PRACTICE 6.2

Developing an Informed Consent Form

Purpose: to help you develop an intentional informed consent form that you like and believe is a good reflection of your personality and practice style.

Gathering What You Know: You may already be familiar with using informed consent forms. You also may have one in your possession that your University uses in your training program. For this activity you should gather together hard copies of informed consent forms to which you have access.

Conducting an Internet Search: Go online. Using your favorite search engine, find additional sample informed consent forms. You might want to try a variety of search terms and alternate between counseling, psychotherapy, and social work. You can also use a variety of search engines to get a more comprehensive sense of what's out there.

Conducting a Focused Internet Search: Go to http://kspope.com/consent/index.php to access Kenneth Pope's excellent ethics-related website. On Dr. Pope's site you'll find several links to useful informed consent samples.

Creating Your Own Informed Consent Form: This might be the hard part; but if you like to express yourself in your own unique voice, it also might be the easy part. Take what you've learned and create your own unique informed consent form designed for you to use in your particular setting. Be sure to include legal items as well as a more personable description of the type of counseling or psychotherapy you'll be offering. Also, think about how you want your "voice" to sound in your own informed consent. Although you can use ideas from the informed consents you've gathered, you shouldn't plagiarize someone else's form.

Getting Feedback: Either turn your finished product into your professor or ask one of your classmates to read it and provide you with feedback. It's good to get an outside perspective on how others perceive your newly created consent form.

A conversation similar to the following is recommended:

Counselor: Have you heard the term *confidentiality* before?

Client: Uh, I think so.

Counselor: Let me briefly describe what counselors mean by confidentiality. Basically, it means *what you say in here stays in here*. It means what you talk about with me is private; I won't discuss our conversations with other people. But there are limits to confidentiality. For example, if you talk about harming yourself or someone else or if you talk about child or elder abuse, then I have to break confidentiality and inform the proper authorities. Also, if you want me to provide information about you to another person, such as an attorney, insurance company, or physician, I can do that if you give me your written permission. So, although there are some limits, basically what you say in here is private. Do you have any questions about confidentiality?

In some cases after a confidentiality explanation, clients will make a joke—usually an awkward joke—to lighten up the situation (e.g., "Well, I'm not planning to kill my mother-in-law or anything."). Other times they'll respond with specific questions (e.g., "Will you be keeping records about what I say to you?" or "Who else has access to your files?"). When clients ask questions about confidentiality, they may just be expressing curiosity or they may be especially conscious of trust issues. They may have suicidal or homicidal thoughts and want to clarify the limits of what they should and shouldn't say. Whatever the case, it's best to respond to questions directly and clearly: "Yes, I'll be keeping records of our meetings, but only my office manager and I have access to these files. And the office manager will also keep your records confidential."

Finally, if you're being supervised and your supervisor has access to your case notes and recordings, make that clear as well. For example:

> Because I'm a graduate student I have a supervisor who checks my work. Sometimes we discuss my work with a small group of other graduate students. However, in each of these situations, the purpose is to enable me to provide you with the best services possible. Other than the exceptions I mentioned, no information about you will leave this clinic without your permission.

The second issue concerning client education and client expectations is to inform clients of the interview's purpose. When I (John) am working with adolescents or young adults, I generally say something like, "I see my job as partnering with you to help you accomplish your goals in life . . . as long as your goals are legal and healthy." Some young clients laugh at my explicit limitation to the legal and healthy, but years ago after introducing myself to a young male and offering to help him be successful, he countered with: "My goal is to get damn good at selling drugs so I can be rich." When I refused to help with his drug-selling ambitions he swore at me and stormed out of my office. Based on this lesson, I decided to add limits to my explanation of my role in helping young clients.

Obviously, the explanation you provide to clients varies depending on the type of interview you're conducting. A general statement regarding the interview's purpose helps put clients at ease by clarifying their expectations about what will happen during the session. It can also help clarify client and therapist roles and behaviors. For example, a psychologist who routinely conducted assessment interviews of prospective adoptive parents made the following statement:

> The purpose of this interview is for me to help the adoption agency evaluate what you might be like as adoptive parents. I like to start this interview in an open-ended way by having you describe why you're interested in adoption and having each of you talk about yourselves, but eventually I'll get more specific and ask about your childhoods. Finally, toward the end of the interview, I'll ask very specific questions about your approach to parenting. Do you have any questions before we begin?

In our work as mental health consultants at Job Corps, we often interview new students with emotional or behavioral issues. Many of these youth are perhaps a bit unhappy to be meeting with a mental health professional. Consequently, we have to be very clear about our role and the purpose of the interview:

> Before we start, let me tell you what I've been told about you and why you're here. Your counselor asked me to meet with you because he said you have a history of depression and he wanted me to check in with you on how you're adjusting here. So, I'm going to spend some time getting to know you and then I'll ask you questions about depression and other stuff. Also, just so you know, my job is to help you be successful here.

	Table 6.1 Checklist for Introduction Stage	
	Therapist Task	**Evidence-Based Relationship Factors**
☐	1. Schedule a mutually agreed upon meeting time.	Working alliance, positive regard, mutuality
☐	2. Introduce yourself.	Congruence, attractiveness, positive regard
☐	3. Identify how the client likes to be addressed.	Positive regard, empowerment
☐	4. Engage in conversation or small talk.	Empathy, rapport
☐	5. Direct client to an appropriate seat (or let the client choose).	Expertness, empathy, rapport
☐	6. Present your credentials or status (as appropriate).	Expertness
☐	7. Explain confidentiality.	Trustworthiness, working alliance
☐	8. Explain the purpose of the interview.	Working alliance, expertness
☐	9. Check client expectations of interview for similarity to and compatibility with your purpose.	Working alliance, mutuality, empowerment
☐	10. Clarify time limits as needed.	Working alliance, expertness

You're not in any trouble. I meet with lots of students. Even though I'll ask you lots of questions today, I hope you'll feel free to ask me whatever you want to ask.

The third issue concerning client education is time. Early in the interview clients should be informed or reminded of the session's length.

Personal note: We must admit that sometimes we've forgotten to set the interview's frame or boundaries in the manner discussed here. We usually have excellent excuses, such as the client was agitated, or eager to start, or in crisis. In the end, we always end up wishing we had remembered to explicitly deal with informed consent, client expectations, and basic educational information about therapy. (See Table 6.1 for a checklist of the introduction tasks.)

THE OPENING

The opening begins with a therapist's first questions about the client's current concerns and ends when the therapist begins determining the focus by asking questions about specific topics. In Shea's (1998) model, the opening is a nondirective interview stage lasting about five to eight minutes. During this stage, you use basic attending skills and nondirective listening responses to encourage client disclosure. Another way of thinking of your task during this stage is that it involves staying out of the way so clients can tell their stories.

CASE EXAMPLE

You arrive in your office. You allow the client to choose a seat. (We've had clients choose our usual chair, even when the chair is sitting behind a desk!) Your client shifts frequently in her chair, keeps her coat on, and grips a large purse tightly. Her smile appears strained. You have the informed consent and intake forms she filled out. You ask if she has any questions. She shakes her head. You review confidentiality. She nods. You sense both nervousness and sadness; she appears frightened, is blinking rapidly, and her eyes appear misty.

In the multicultural literature, Stanley Sue wrote of several concepts that are helpful during an initial interview (S. Sue, 1998, 2006). He recommended that clinicians maintain an attitude of scientific mindedness (see also Chapter 11). Scientific mindedness involves forming tentative hypotheses about clients, and then, during initial and subsequent contacts, maintaining an open mind about clients, culture, and problems. You must be willing to modify old hypotheses and, if necessary, disregard them.

To apply Sue's approach to the preceding situation, you might ask yourself: What initial impressions or hypotheses am I forming about the client and what are these hypotheses based on? For example, what hypotheses come into your mind about her "keeping her coat on" or "blinking rapidly?" Maintaining an attitude of scientific mindedness is very important to clinical interviewing. The client may be keeping her coat on because of feeling chilled or feeling unsafe or forgetfulness or for some other reason. Sue's scientific mindedness concept reminds us to formulate hypotheses tentatively and carefully sift through client information, while eschewing premature conclusions.

The Therapist's Opening Statement

The therapist's opening statement signals to the client that small talk, introductions, and informed consent procedures are over and it's time to begin the interview. An opening statement is the first direct inquiry into the client's personal concerns. The statement is delivered in a calm, easy manner, so it doesn't feel like an interruption in the interview flow. However, occasionally, you'll need to assertively cut in to officially start the interview.

Most counselors and psychotherapists develop a standard opening statement. This usually consists of an open question or prompt designed to get clients to share their concerns. One of the most common openings is: "What brings you here?" A more detailed version of this is: "Tell me what brings you to counseling (or therapy) at this time." The elements of import include:

- *Tell Me:* The therapist is expressing interest in hearing what the client has to say and makes it clear that the client will be doing the telling.
- *What Brings You:* This is more specific than "Tell me about yourself," yet it's open to the client's interpretation regarding which areas of life to begin sharing with the therapist.

- *To Counseling:* This phrase acknowledges that coming for counseling is a distinct goal-oriented behavior. It suggests the client tell you about events that prompted the decision to seek counseling.
- *At This Time:* This helps clients direct their comments to the pertinent factors leading up to the decision to come in. The decision to seek help is based not only on causes but on timing. Sometimes a problem existed for years, but the time to seek help was never quite right until now.

You may or may not be comfortable with these particular words. The point is for you to consciously decide exactly what you want to say to open your session.

Many alternative opening statements are possible. You can say whatever you like, but it's helpful if your opening statement includes either an open question (i.e., a question beginning with *what* or *how*) or a gentle prompt. The opening statement described at the beginning of this section is an example of a gentle prompt—a directive that usually begins with the words "Tell me." Other opening statements include:

- What brings you here?
- How can I be of help?
- Maybe you could begin by telling me things about yourself, or your situation, that you believe are important.
- So, how's it been going?
- What are some of the stresses you have been coping with recently? (Shea, 1998)

As you look over these openings, think about how you would respond to each one as a client. You may have noticed that the first openings were very wide open, while the next series of openings were more focused. You may want to experiment with different openings in practice interviews and you may discover certain clients respond better to more focused openings.

Your opening statement guides how clients begin talking about themselves or their problems. For example, if you want to hear about stressors and coping responses, you could use the sample opening provided by Shea (1998). It's likely that if you ask about it, you might get it. Consequently, if you ask "How's it going?" you might get a more casual social report, and if you ask, "How has your week been?" you'll get a description of the past week. "How can I be of help?" communicates an assumption that the client needs help and that you'll be functioning as a helper. No opening is completely nondirective. In general, the opening statement's purpose is to help clients talk freely about personal concerns that caused them to seek professional assistance.

The Client's Opening Response

Immediately after your opening statement, the spotlight is on the client. Will he or she take your opening and run with it, or hesitate, struggle for the right words, and ask for more direction or structure? As noted, some clients come for professional help expecting authoritative guidance; they may be surprised by an open question. Their first response provides a clue about how they respond to less structured situations. Psychodynamic or interpersonally oriented clinicians consider this initial behavior crucial in understanding client personality dynamics

(Teyber & McClure, 2011). For example, Cabaniss, Cherry, Douglas, and Shwartz (2011) described why openings should be . . . open:

> Openings should be just that—open—and should generally consist of open-ended questions. The beginning of the session is a time for the patient to speak freely and your opening should encourage this. Let the patient speak in his/her own way for a little while—perhaps 5 minutes or so. This will help you to hear the patient's speech pattern and thought process. It will also let you see where the patient begins and what he/she prioritizes. (p. 100)

Rehearsed Client Responses

The way clients begin may suggest they've rehearsed for their part in the interview. For example, we've heard clients begin with:

- Well, let me begin with my childhood.
- Currently, my symptoms include . . .
- There are three things going on in my life right now that I'm having difficulty with.
- I'm depressed about . . .

There are advantages and disadvantages to working with clients who begin interviews in a straightforward and organized manner. The advantages are that these clients have thought about their personal problems and are getting to the point as quickly as possible. If they're insightful and have a good grasp of why they want help, the interview should proceed smoothly.

Client openings that are overly organized may indicate what Shea (1998) referred to as a "rehearsed interview" (p. 76). In such cases, clients may provide stock interview responses as a defense. They may offer emotionally distant accounts of their problems, and in fact, emotional distance may be a part of their problem (e.g., the client has trouble emotionally connecting in relationships).

Helping Clients Who Struggle to Express Themselves

Clients struggle to express themselves for many reasons. It could be the therapist's fault (i.e., lack of clarity in an opening statement). It could be an unstructured opening was the last thing the client expected. It could be related to cultural issues. Or it could be that taking the initiative and engaging in self-expression is or will emerge as a central therapy issue for the client.

How therapists handle clients who struggle with an opening often depends on theoretical orientation. For now, consider the following evidence-based relationship guidelines.

> *Express empathy and positive expectations:* If your client says, "I don't know what I'm supposed to talk about," respond with something like, "It can be very hard to decide what to talk about right at the beginning, but that's okay . . . give yourself a moment to think of where you'd like to begin."

Articulate positive expectations about the helpfulness of therapy: When your client falters, consider saying, "It can be very hard to talk about some things in therapy, but like lots of parts of life, facing up to and talking about the hard things can be very helpful."

Encourage the client take the lead: If your client asks, "What should I talk about?" begin nondirectively with something like, "I'll be asking you questions later, but to start, whatever you'd like to talk about is fine with me." It's useful to let clients pick where to start because they're the best experts on their own lives.

Emphasize collaboration: Let clients know that you're open to working with them in ways that work for them: "Sometimes it's good to start our session very open-ended, with you saying whatever you like. Other times it's good for me to ask specific questions. I can either be quiet and listen or ask you questions or a combination of listening and questioning. Which way would you like to start?"

Make adaptations as needed: Clients may need or want a more structured opening for many reasons. One reason might be related to culture. Research on culture in counseling and psychotherapy suggests that culturally competent therapists make cultural adaptations as needed (Griner & Smith, 2006). Cultural adaptations might include having an interpreter, inviting the family for an initial interview, serving tea, spending more time with small talk, self-disclosure, and other variations on the traditional clinical interview (Hays, 2008). For example, you might offer a self-disclosure (family therapists would refer to this as "joining") and combine it with increased structure: "I often find the beginning of a session can be challenging because it's hard to know what to talk about first. How about if we start by drawing a family tree (genogram)? That way I can get to know a bit more about your family background."

Every client will arrive at your office with different needs and goals. Some clients are uncomfortable talking about the past and unable or unwilling to talk about how they're feeling in the here-and-now. In these cases it can help to be both structured and casual by beginning with a question that's relatively easy to answer: "How about if you begin by telling me how your day has been going so far?"

Other Client Responses to the Therapist's Opening Statement

On occasion, clients will begin interviews in odd ways that give you concerns about their current functioning. For example, imagine the following client statements:

- I have come because the others told me to come. You will be my witness.
- You're the doc, you tell me what's wrong with me.
- It's by the grace of God that I'm sitting before you right now. May I pray before we begin?
- I have this deep ache inside of me. It comes over me sometimes like a wave. It's not like I have been a wellspring of virtue and propriety, but then . . . I ask myself constantly, do I deserve this?

Evaluating client functioning based on unusual presentations such as these is a difficult task requiring clinical judgment. We discuss evaluation procedures in more detail later in this chapter and in Chapter 8.

Ideal client responses to your opening statement usually reflect thoughtfulness and the initiation of a working alliance. For example:

> I'm not sure of all the reasons I'm here or why I chose to come right now. I've been pretty overwhelmed with stress at work lately, and it's affecting my family life. I guess I'll start by telling you about work and family and as I go along maybe you can tell me if I'm talking about the things you need to know about me.

Evaluating Client Verbal Behavior During the Opening

As clients begin talking during the opening stage, ideally you'll observe their responses and then modify your approach accordingly. With clients who are very verbal, you may need to interject yourself into the interview when you get a chance. For example, toward the end of the opening, you might feel the need for more control in a session when a client is rambling. You could choose to:

1. Progressively ask more closed questions to interrupt the client's monologue.
2. Use an explanation or psychoeducation to explain that you'll be interrupting on occasion to make sure you're tracking accurately.
3. Avoid all open-ended or exploratory questions.

Another client style you might notice is the tendency to use an internal frame of reference when describing problems. For example:

> I feel anxious all the time . . . like someone's watching me and evaluating me, but I know that's not the case. And I feel depressed. Nothing I do turns out right. I'm underemployed. I can't seem to get involved in a good relationship. I pick the wrong type of women, and I can't figure out why anyone who has anything going for them would want to go out with me anyway.

Clients who use an internal frame tend to self-criticize and self-blame. They may begin criticizing themselves and not stop until the session ends. They're sometimes referred to as *internalizers* because they describe their problems as having internal causes. Internalizing clients seem to be saying, "There's something wrong with me."

On the other hand, some clients are more aptly described as *externalizers*. They communicate the message, "I'm fine! It's just that everybody else in my life has a problem." A client who tends to externalize might say:

> My problem is that I have a ridiculous boss. He's rude, stupid, and arrogant. In fact, men in general are insensitive, and my life would be fine if I never had to deal with another man again. And my daughter thinks I'm rude to people, but she has no idea how many jerks I have to be around. I even have jerks as neighbors.

MULTICULTURAL HIGHLIGHT 6.1

Where Does the Problem Reside: Exploring Society's Contributions to Client Problems

Although everyone is ultimately responsible for their behaviors, client problems also should be viewed in a social and cultural context. For example, just prior to publishing this text, a man entered a school in Connecticut and shot and killed 27 people. This man was 100% responsible for his behavior. However, in this and all cases of human behavior, it's useful to examine other factors—factors outside the individual—that might have contributed to his behavior. Another way of thinking about this is to ask the question: Where does the "problem" reside? Is it centered in the person, in the person's culture, or somewhere else?

Several decades ago, renowned family therapist Salvador Minuchin (Minuchin, Rosman, & Baker, 1978) began accumulating research and clinical data on eating disorders and asthma in children and adolescents. He found that successful interventions for these physical problems could involve the entire family, rather than just the afflicted individual. His research and practice in family therapy led him to the conclusion that the locus of pathology was not *in the individual*, but instead centered within families (Goldenberg & Goldenberg, 2012).

Minuchin argued the importance of seeing individual client symptoms from a family systems perspective. In contrast, for many decades, the *DSM* has narrowly defined mental disorders as residing within the individual (American Psychiatric Association, 2000, 2013).

If you were aware of only the *DSM*'s perspective and Minuchin's perspective, you might conclude that they're polar opposite ends of a conceptual continuum. In reality, both the *DSM* and Minuchin represent what might be considered "moderate" etiological perspectives. A more extreme view has been articulated by biological psychiatry—where the cause of mental disorders is not only within the individual, but genetically predestined in some ways (Horwitz & Wakefield, 2007).

On the other extreme, therapists operating from a feminist, multicultural, or constructive theoretical perspective tend to view individual problems as caused by oppressive or maladaptive social and cultural factors (Brown, 2010; D. W. Sue & Sue, 2013). In other words, a psychiatric diagnosis isn't something residing within the genes or families of individuals, but instead is caused by and manifests itself due to disturbed and disturbing social factors.

Overall, it's possible to identify at least four points on a continuum examining the causes of mental disorders. The biological psychiatrists might even claim the words *mental disorder* are inaccurate (and *mental illness* more accurate), while someone like Thomas Szasz (1970) or William Glasser (2003) would claim there's no such thing as mental illness. The following table briefly describes four viewpoints on causal factors in mental/behavioral problems.

(continued)

(*continued*)

Biological Psychiatry	*DSM-5*	Minuchin	Feminist or Multicultural
Client problems are a product of individual genetic and biological make-up.	Client problems reside in the individual, but are sometimes provoked or maintained by social or cultural factors.	Client problems are primarily a function of family and environmental contexts.	Client problems are caused by social, gender, cultural, and political contexts.

As with many issues in psychology and counseling, your beliefs about where the problem lies will influence your interactions with clients. Be sure to discuss your thoughts about this continuum of client responsibility.

Clients with externalizing tendencies tend to believe their troubles stem from other people. Although there may be truth to this, it can be difficult to get them to accept responsibility and constructively focus on their own feelings, thoughts, and behavior.

Realistically, client problems usually stem from a combination of personal (internal) and situational (external) factors. It's useful, especially during the opening stage, to listen for whether your clients seem to be taking too much or too little responsibility for their problems (see *Multicultural Highlight* 6.1).

It takes more than one piece of evidence to conclude—even tentatively—something about a client from a brief opening statement. Recall again the concept of scientific mindedness (S. Sue, 2006). Opening responses provide an initial glimpse of how clients perceive themselves and their problems. As you consider your clients' openings, ask yourself the following questions:

• Does the client express himself or herself in a rational/coherent manner?
• Is the opening response overly structured and perhaps rehearsed?
• Does the client struggle with lack of structure?
• If the client does struggle with lack of structure, what is the nature of the struggle (e.g., Does he or she ask you directly for more structure, become angry or scared in the face of low structure, digress into a disordered or confusing communication style)?
• Is the client's speech characterized by oddities?
• Does the client's response focus on external factors (other people or situations causing distress) or internal factors (ways the client may have contributed to his or her own distress)?
• Does the client seem especially oriented toward a particular cultural group or to have very specific and strong religious beliefs?

Table 6.2 lists therapist tasks for the opening stage of the interview.

Table 6.2 Checklist for Opening Stage	
Therapist Task	**Technical Approaches**
☐ 1. Continue working on rapport.	Nondirective listening
☐ 2. Focus on client's view of life and problems.	Open-ended questioning, gentle prompting
☐ 3. Provide structure and support if necessary.	Feeling reflections, clarify purpose of opening stage, narrow the focus of opening question
☐ 4. Help client adopt an internal, rather than external, frame of reference, if culturally appropriate.	Nondirective listening, therapeutic questioning
☐ 5. Evaluate how the interview is proceeding and think about what approaches might be most effective during the body.	Paraphrasing, summarization, role induction, therapeutic questioning

THE BODY

The body of an initial interview primarily involves information gathering or a therapy intervention. The quality and quantity of information gathered and the type of therapy intervention depends almost entirely on the interview's purpose and the therapist's theoretical orientation. For instance, if the purpose of a particular interview is something specific—for example, to determine whether the client will make a good candidate for psychoanalytic psychotherapy—then the body of the interview will include asking questions and listening for information that will help you judge, among other things, whether the client is psychologically minded, motivated, and capable, both financially and psychologically, to seek such treatment (Levenson, 2010). More typically, the purpose of a clinical interview is, at least in part, to determine a client's clinical diagnosis and formulate a treatment plan. If so, data gathered during the interview body will focus primarily on diagnostic clues and criteria (see Chapter 10). However, in all cases, the focus of the interview body may change, depending on information shared by the client during the course of the interview. For example, in either of the scenarios just described, if you discover your client is contemplating suicide, your goal will shift to suicide assessment (see Chapter 9).

Sources of Clinical Judgment: Making Inferences

During the body stage, you'll gather information to make professional inferences about the client. Depending on the interview's purpose, the inferences will relate to some of the following:

- The client's personality style, acculturation, or stress level.
- Recommendations on whether therapy is needed.
- Recommendations regarding the most appropriate therapy approach.
- The client's mental status and/or psychiatric diagnosis.

- Estimates of client intellectual or cognitive functioning.
- Parenting ability, attitudes, and adequacy.
- Suicide or violence potential.
- Addictions, past criminal behavior, past employment, and relationship and educational experiences.

Making statements, recommendations, estimates, or predictions based on a single clinical interview is risky. Describing, explaining, and especially predicting human behavior is challenging and often fraught with error (Hilton, Harris, & Rice, 2006; Loeber et al., 2005). Nonetheless, after conducting an assessment interview, you may need to make tentative statements or definitive decisions about your client. The next section provides you with a general foundation for thinking about client psychopathology. In later chapters we focus specifically on mental status examinations, suicide assessment, and psychiatric diagnosis.

Defining Psychological and Emotional Disorders

A central task of all clinical interviews is to make distinctions between normal/ healthy functioning and deviant/disordered functioning. The *Diagnostic and Statistical Manual of Mental Disorders (DSM-5)* is the standard reference in the United States for diagnoses of mental disorders (American Psychiatric Association, 2013). However, the *International Classification of Diseases*, 10th edition (World Health Organization, 2004) is the global standard for classification of mental disorders and can be used instead of the *DSM-5* in many settings. Please note that U.S. insurance companies will accept either *DSM* or *ICD* diagnostic codes for billing purposes.

Before you use these manuals to identify specific clinical diagnoses, it can be useful to think more generally about how to judge whether a client's behavior is diagnosable. What follows are general standards for determining whether clients might be experiencing psychological disorders. These are not diagnostic criteria. Instead, they're guidelines to help you further develop your clinical judgment and thinking about normal and abnormal behavior (in Chapter 10, the American Psychiatric Association's *Diagnostic and Statistical Manual's* approach to defining mental disorders is reviewed).

Unusual Behaviors That Deviate From the Statistical Norm

Behaviors that deviate from the statistical norm are, by definition, abnormal. These behaviors are different or unusual. For example, if a college-age friend of yours reports he sleeps 10–12 hours a night, his behavior would be considered unusual because most college students average about 8 hours. However, that particular abnormal behavior isn't necessarily bad or dysfunctional—it may even be desirable. Your friend may be perfectly happy with his 10–12 hours of sleep; his sleeping patterns may not interfere with other important activities in his life; and there may be many days when you wish you could switch places with him and spend more time snoozing.

The fact that we're suggesting that abnormal behavior is neither bad nor undesirable may make you wonder why a discussion of unusual behaviors that deviate from the statistical norm is included here. The reason is simple. Most humans—therapists included—naturally notice and are inclined to negatively judge statistically unusual behaviors. Consequently, this discussion is designed to make three key takeaway points:

1. It's easy for clinicians to reflexively assume that abnormal (unusual) behavior is undesirable or problematic. This can be dangerous because historically this assumption has led to tragic judgments and treatment of people who are racially, sexually, or spiritually different.
2. The fact is: Abnormal (unusual) behavior is NOT necessarily undesirable or problematic.
3. Clinicians need to be especially careful not to fall into the trap of judging an individual's behavior as bad or problematic just because it's unusual or "different" behavior.

There has been a long and continuing struggle over how to best judge and define mental health problems. This struggle is intermittently political—as illustrated in the roiling controversies associated with publication of the 5th edition of the American Psychiatric Association's *Diagnostic and Statistical Manual* (Frances & Widiger, 2012). A basic question deeply imbedded in the psychiatric diagnostic process is: "How can we best judge whether an individual is experiencing a mental disorder?" Put another way, "If unusual or abnormal behavior isn't a good criterion for judging an individual's mental health, then what is?" To answer this we explore three possible alternative criteria for determining the presence or absence of a mental disorder and one universal exclusion criterion:

1. Is the behavior maladaptive or dysfunctional?
2. Does the behavior cause significant personal distress?
3. Is the behavior consistently disturbing to others?
4. Is the behavior rationally or culturally justifiable, or caused by a medical condition? (See *Multicultural Highlight* 6.2)

The Dysfunction or Impairment Criterion: Is the Behavior Maladaptive or Disabling?

Most people would agree that some individuals engage in consistently maladaptive behaviors; they may also experience maladaptive thoughts and emotions. But what is maladaptive? The key feature of a maladaptive behavior is that it's self-destructive. It's a behavior or behavior pattern that, instead of being self-enhancing, repeatedly gets in the way of an individual's personal development, health, or success.

For instance, a parent may sincerely want a teenager to keep her room clean, but constant screaming and arguing about it may end up damaging the parent-child relationship and not achieve a clean room. In fact, personal observations and developmental research both indicate that screaming, yelling, and striking teenagers are maladaptive behaviors; not only are they ineffective for attaining desired goals, they're also destructive. Similarly, a man may want to be in an intimate relationship, but his overly enthusiastic behavior could alarm potential partners and scare them away. The man's intent is positive, but his approach is maladaptive; it results in increased loneliness.

More formally, based on *DSM-5* criteria, a behavioral, thinking, or emotional pattern is maladaptive or disabling when it "causes…impairment in social, occupational, or other important areas of functioning" (American Psychiatric Association, 2013, p. 21). In *DSM-5* and *ICD* nomenclature, this is sometimes referred to as the impairment or disability criterion. It's important to note that individuals may not be aware of the dysfunctional or maladaptive nature of their behavior and they may deny that their behavior is interfering with their ability to function effectively. Perhaps the best example of this is when someone is abusing substances; often others can easily see the destructive consequences, while the substance user seems unable or unwilling to recognize how using substances is a problem.

The Distress Criterion: Does the Behavior Cause Significant Personal Distress?

In contrast to the dysfunction or impairment criterion, clients are nearly always aware of whether their behavior, thoughts, or emotions fulfill the distress criterion. Some people might sleep 12 hours nightly and drink large quantities of beer and feel just fine about that behavior. Others might feel extreme personal distress after sleeping more than nine hours two nights in a row or because they drank to excess on a single occasion. It's difficult to predict what behaviors will produce personal distress in particular individuals. Therefore, you should ask clients if they feel distress linked to their own behaviors (which may feel beyond their control).

The *DSM-5* now uses a "generic diagnostic criterion" that combines the impairment and distress criteria discussed separately here (American Psychiatric Association, 2013, p. 21). The emphasis is that either impairment or personal distress can characterize a mental disorder.

An example of a mental disorder that may involve more distress than impairment is panic disorder. Specifically, panic symptoms are often experienced in public settings. These attacks include extremely distressing physical sensations and cognitions. However, in some cases, no one else in the room is aware that an individual is experiencing a panic attack. This is a great example of a condition in which clients' experience intense internal distress, but this distress doesn't necessarily cause a functional impairment (it can, but some people just bear through it). And unless the person with panic symptoms confides in others, his or her panic symptoms are unlikely to be experienced as disturbing to others.

The Disturbing Criterion: Is the Behavior Consistently Disturbing to Others?

Many behaviors associated with mental disorders are much more disturbing to others than they are to the person engaging in them. Prominent examples include: (a) drug and alcohol abuse or dependency; (b) under eating and over exercising (i.e., anorexia); (c) interpersonally antagonistic behaviors (e.g., aggression, abuse, lying, and theft are behaviors linked to some of the *DSM-5* personality disorders); and (d) autism spectrum disorder.

As you may know from personal experience, the people who live or work with family or friends who are exhibiting alcohol abuse, anorexia symptoms, aggression, autistic symptoms, or other similar conditions are usually highly distressed. Eventually they may insist the person get treatment. Therefore, when evaluating clients, it's helpful to ask if anyone in their immediate environment is especially bothered by their behavior or encouraging them to seek treatment.

MULTICULTURAL HIGHLIGHT 6.2

The Three-Dimensional Universal Exclusion Criterion: Is the Behavior Rationally or Culturally Justifiable or Caused by a Medical Condition?

Let's say you meet with a client for an initial interview. During the interview the client describes an unusual belief (e.g., she believes she is possessed because someone has given her the "evil eye"). This belief is clearly dysfunctional or maladaptive because it has caused her to stop going out of her house due to fears that an evil spirit will ovetake her and she will lose control in public. She also acknowledges substantial distress and her staying-at-home-and-being-anxious behavior is disturbing her family. In this case it appears you've got a solid diagnostic trifecta—her belief-behavior is (a) maladaptive, (b) distressing, and (c) disturbing to others. How could you conclude anything other than that she's suffering from a psychiatric disorder?

This situation illustrates why diagnosis (see Chapter 10) is a fascinating part of mental health work. In fact, if the client has a rational justification for her belief-behavior...or if there's a reasonable cultural explanation...or if the belief-behavior is caused by a medical condition—then it would be inappropriate to conclude that she has a mental disorder. One source of support for a universal exclusion criterion is the DSM-5. It includes the statement: "The level of severity and meaning of the distressing experiences should be assessed in relation to the norms of the individual's cultural reference groups" (American Psychiatric Association, 2013, p. 750).

To explore this three-dimensional "universal" exclusion principle in greater depth, partner up with one or more classmates and discuss the following questions:

Can you think of any rational explanations for the client's belief-behavior?

Can you think of any reasonable cultural explanations for the client's belief-behavior?

Can you think of any underlying medical conditions that might explain her belief-behavior?

After you've finished discussing the preceding questions, see how many new examples you can think of where a client presents with symptoms that are (a) dysfunctional/maladaptive, (b) distressing, and (c) disturbing to others. Then discuss potential rational explanations, cultural explanations, and medical conditions that could produce the symptoms (e.g., you could even use something as simple as major depressive symptoms and explore how rational, cultural, or medical explanations might account for the symptoms, thereby causing you to defer the diagnosis).

Applying the Four Principles

These four principles can be applied to almost any clinical observation that takes place during an interview. For example, if a client exhibits symptoms of depression or sadness, you could consider the following questions:

- Is the sadness adversely affecting the client's ability to function at work, in interpersonal relationships, or enjoyment of recreational activities?
- Is the sadness disturbing or upsetting to the client?
- Is the sadness particularly disturbing to other people in the client's environment?
- Is there a rational or cultural or medical explanation for the client's sadness? For example, was there an event that's logically associated with your client's sadness (e.g., the death of a loved one or a series of failures)?

We offer the preceding guidelines to help you think about psychopathology or mental disorders in a systematic way. These guidelines also can help with identifying client goals or the focus of therapy. Of course, you shouldn't rely solely on any one of these criteria to determine the presence or absence of a mental disorder. Each criterion—especially when applied in isolation—has its shortcomings.

Applying Interventions

The body of the interview is when therapists use interventions to facilitate client change. Ideally, most interventions will be applied after a suitable assessment has been completed. However, in many cases, assessments and interventions happen simultaneously.

From a solution-focused or constructive perspective, assessments and interventions are inseparable. This is because of the underlying philosophy that all change is founded on linguistic construction. Consequently, when constructive theorists say, "therapists are not just taking history, they're making history" they're referring to the likelihood that change begins based on the way the therapist and client talk about the client's lived experiences and future trajectory.

Whatever your theoretical orientation, the body of the interview is where you'll actively work for change. Behavior therapists will use reinforcement, response cost, participant modeling, and exposure during this stage. Cognitive therapists will question maladaptive thoughts and explore core client schemata. Person-centered therapists will use the therapeutic relationship to enable clients to engage in deeper encounters with the self. Psychoanalytic therapists will listen and interpret. Constructive therapists will use therapeutic questions. Feminist therapists will focus on how power and social forces are linked to client distress. The body of the interview is where the therapeutic action resides. However, of equal importance is the transition out of the body and into the closing . . . and regardless of your theoretical orientation, you will move into the closing stage (Tasks for the body stage of the interview are listed in Table 6.3.)

THE CLOSING

As time passes during an interview, both therapist and client may begin feeling pressure. The therapist may be tempted to fire a few more pertinent questions

Table 6.3   Checklist for Body Stage

	Therapist Task	Therapist Tools
☐	1. Transition from nondirective to more directive listening.	Role induction; explain this shift of style to the client.
☐	2. Gather information.	Open and closed questions (see Chapter 4).
☐	3. Obtain diagnostic information.	Use the *DSM*, *ICD-10*, or the four guiding principles discussed in this chapter to formulate useful questions.
☐	4. Apply appropriate interventions	Use interpretation, confrontation, therapeutic questions, or other interventions depending upon your theoretical orientation.
☐	5. Shift from information gathering or intervention to preparation for closing.	Acknowledge that time is passing; explain and discuss the need to summarize major issues.

at the client; it can start to feel like a race to see if you can fit everything into a 50- or 90-minute session. Our colleague, Chad Luke (personal communication, August 10, 2012) suggests that a key to a smooth closing is to begin a process of reflecting on the session about halfway through with a question like, "We're about halfway through our session and I'm wondering how you're feeling about our time together so far today?" This gives clients an opportunity to provide the therapist with feedback and serves as a marker for gauging the passing of time (Lambert & Shimokawa, 2011). Another key to a smooth closing is to consciously and skillfully stop gathering new information somewhere between 5 and 10 minutes before your interview time is over. Shea (1998) noted, "One of the most frequent problems I see in supervision remains the over-extension of the main body of the interview, thus forcing the clinician to rush through the closing phase" (p. 130).

Clients also may feel increasing tension as time passes. They may wonder whether they've expressed themselves adequately and whether they can be helped. Clients also may feel worse than when the interview started because they've discussed their problems too graphically or because reflecting on problems makes them feel worse. Because clients often feel worried or stressed toward the interview's end, therapists should leave ample time for closure.

Reassuring and Supporting Your Client

Clients need to be reassured and supported in at least two main areas. First, they need to have their expressive capabilities noticed and supported. Nearly all clients who voluntarily seek professional assistance do the best they can during an initial interview. The first contact in a mental health counseling experience can be challenging and sometimes anxiety provoking. Comments such as the following can help:

- You covered lots of ground today.
- I appreciate your efforts in telling me about yourself.

- First sessions can be difficult because there's so much to cover and so little time.
- You did a nice job describing yourself in a very short time period.
- Thanks for being open and sharing so much about yourself with me.

These comments acknowledge that interview situations can be difficult and commend clients for their expressive efforts.

Second, most clients have ambivalent feelings about therapy; they have both hope and fear about coming to therapy. Therefore, the therapist should support the client's decision to seek professional services, siding with the hope evidenced by that decision. For example:

- You made a good decision when you decided to come for an appointment.
- I want to congratulate you for coming here today. Coming for help can be hard. Some people might think otherwise, but I believe getting help is a sign of strength.

These statements acknowledge the reality of how difficult it can be to seek professional help and may help clients feel good about choosing to get help.

Sometimes, clients behave defensively and avoid disclosing information during an interview. Even in these cases you should recognize and acknowledge that clients are doing their best to interact with you on any given day. It can help to note the task's difficulty or to comment on how the client seemed to be reluctant to talk much. Expressing anger or disappointment toward clients should be avoided. If your client was defensive, remain optimistic:

I know it was hard for you to talk with me today. That's not surprising; after all, we're basically strangers. Usually, it gets easier over time and as we get to know each other.

Summarizing Crucial Themes and Issues

Perhaps the most important task of the closing is "solidifying the patient's desire to return for a second appointment or to follow the clinician's referral" (Shea, 1998, p. 125). One of the best methods for enhancing a client's likelihood of returning is to identify why the client has come for professional assistance. This can be difficult because often clients themselves aren't exactly sure why they've come. Variations on the following statement may be useful:

Based on what you've said today, it seems you're here because you want to feel less self-conscious when you're in social situations. You'd like to feel more positive about yourself. I think you said, 'I want to believe in myself,' and you also talked about how you want to figure out what you're feeling inside and how to share your emotions with others you care about.

Most clients come to professionals because they hope their lives can improve. If you can summarize how they would like to improve their lives, clients are more likely to return to see you or follow your recommendations. Providing this sort of summary also shows the client that you've heard and understood them.

Providing an Initial Case Formulation

Case formulation or case conceptualization is a cornerstone of effective counseling and psychotherapy (Persons, 2008; J. Sommers-Flanagan & Sommers-Flanagan, 2012). This process involves integrating assessment information with a theoretically supported or evidence-based approach to guide subsequent therapeutic work.

Case formulation involves laying out a therapeutic plan. Nearly a century ago Alfred Adler emphasized that client insight enhances client motivation. More recently, it has become clear that collaborative formulation of a treatment plan is an empirically supported therapy component (Tryon & Winograd, 2011). If therapists can describe the client's central problem and explain how they'll address this problem in therapy, the client will often experience (a) insight, (b) the sense of being known or understood, (c) enhanced motivation, and (d) hope for change.

It's too much to expect beginning therapists to smoothly articulate a comprehensive case formulation or treatment plan at the end of an initial session. Experienced therapists sometimes wait until their second or third session before providing a clear treatment plan (Ledley, Marx, & Heimberg, 2010). However, for now, it's important to recognize that case formulation can occur very quickly and when it does it fits well into the closing stage of the interview.

At the very least, you should try to provide a summary of the client's problem combined with a brief and tentative explanation of the likely treatment approach (and how it fits well with the presenting problem). Prior to offering this information it can be helpful to ask for clients' permission:

> Is it okay with you if I just go ahead and share with you my thoughts about your main concerns and how we might address these concerns in counseling?

In virtually every case, clients will respond affirmatively to this collaboration request.

After obtaining your client's permission, you can offer an initial case formulation. Do it clearly, politely, and directly—but tentatively. For example, during a closing with a client with anger and aggression issues, the following case formulation was offered (J. Sommers-Flanagan & Sommers-Flanagan, 2004):

> We've been talking a lot about anger today. I've been struck by how much of the time your anger seems related to your high standards for yourself and for others. If I were to try to describe it in a word, I think I might say you seem perfectionistic. It seems like your perfectionism is often underneath your anger. And so as we work together, I think it could be very helpful for us to focus on not just on your anger, but also on your high standards and how they set you up to become angry in different situations. How does that sound to you?

Or, with a client who presents with depressive symptoms, you might offer the following initial case formulation.

> You've told me about your depressive symptoms and how miserable you feel sometimes. Is it okay with you if I share with you some of what I'm

thinking about you and your tendency to feel depressed? [Client responds affirmatively].

One thing that seems to increase your down feelings is that you have an automatic thought process that comments, very often, very quickly, and very negatively, on you and your behavior. For example, when you're in social situations, those thoughts flood right into your head and you think negatively about what you're wearing, you believe you're saying stupid things, and you tell yourself no one would ever like you. It's no big surprise that you don't enjoy yourself and then feel miserable after the social event. Does this make sense to you? [Client says, "Absolutely it does."]

Good. I'm glad this makes sense. One part of our plan, if it's okay with you, will be to work together to develop strategies to interrupt these automatic thoughts. We might do it with mindfulness activities or with gentle questioning of the validity of your thoughts or with specific behaviors that help you get that negative voice out of your head. How does that sound? [Client says, "That works for me."]

Initial case formulations should be simple, straightforward, and jargon-free. They also should be brief, based on what you've been talking about, and not especially deep. If your initial session goes well, there will be chances to go deeper later.

Instilling Hope

As noted previously, accurately summarizing why your client has sought professional assistance and making an initial case formulation statement can implicitly instill hope in clients. However, because hope has long been shown to be a central force in treatment outcomes, it also makes sense to explicitly make hopeful or positive statements about counseling (Frank & Frank, 1991; J. Sommers-Flanagan, Richardson, & Sommers-Flanagan, 2011). These hopeful statements can be very brief. For example, "You've made a wise decision to try counseling. I think this will help."

They can also be integrated into your initial case formulation:

This anger has been troubling you for some time and you've made valiant efforts to deal with it. But I think if we dig down into your perfectionism and then build a concrete plan for how you can deal with both the perfectionism and the anger that we'll be successful in our work together.

If you believe therapy can be helpful (and we hope you do), part of your job is to communicate that belief. Most clients are somewhat naïve about the potential benefits (and detriments) of psychotherapy. Of course, you should only make positive and hopeful statements if you actually believe them.

Guiding and Empowering Your Client

You've spent 40 to 45 minutes with someone you've never met before and listened to fears, pain, confusion, and problems. You hope you've listened well, summarized along the way and, when necessary, guided your client to talk about especially important material. Regardless of how accepting you've been, your client may be worried about being judged. No matter how collaborative you've tried to be, your client may still feel the experience was one-sided; after all, you know a fair amount about your client, but your client knows very little about you. Therefore, it's often useful to explicitly give your client more power and control as the interview closes. What follows are a few methods for empowering clients:

- I've done all the questioning here. Do you have questions for me?
- Has this interview been as you expected it to be?
- Are there any areas that you feel we've missed or that, if we meet again, you'd like to discuss at greater length?
- What do you want to remember from our time together today?

Although it's important to maintain control toward the end of an interview, it's also important to share that control. Depending on your theoretical orientation, you may have been explicitly sharing power and control from the beginning, but it's good to do so again as the interview closes. In most cases, clients won't jump in with lots of questions or comments; however, offering the opportunity is a collaborative and empowering act. Questions and comments from clients also can augment your professional growth.

Tying Up Loose Ends

The final formal task of the therapist is to clarify whether there will be further professional contact. This involves specific and concrete steps such as scheduling additional appointments, dealing with fee payment, and handling administrative issues associated with working in your particular setting. Tasks associated with the closing stage are presented in Table 6.4.

Table 6.4 Checklist for Closing Stage

	Therapist Task	Therapist Tools
☐	1. Reassure and support the client.	Feeling reflection, validation; openly appreciate your client's efforts at expression.
☐	2. Summarize crucial themes and issues.	Summarization; use interpretation to determine client's insight and ability to integrate themes and issues.
☐	3. Provide an initial case formulation	Questions; summarization; psychoeducation
☐	4. Instill hope.	Suggestion; explanation of counseling process and how it is usually helpful.
☐	5. Guide and empower your client.	Questions; ask client for comments or questions of you.
☐	6. Tie up loose ends.	Questions; clarification; collaboratively schedule next appointment.

TERMINATION

Some professionals believe that the termination of each session is an unconscious reminder of all things that end, including our own mortality. Although comparing an interview's end with death is a bit dramatic, it does point out how important endings are in our lives. For many people, saying goodbye is difficult. Some of us bolt away, avoiding the issue altogether; others linger, hoping it won't happen; still others have emotional responses such as anger, sadness, or relief. The way clients cope with a session's end may foreshadow the eventual termination of therapy. It may also represent our own or our clients' conflicts in the areas of separation and individuation. Termination is an essential and often overlooked component of clinical interviewing.

Watching the Clock

Therapists shouldn't literally watch the clock, at least not overtly. However, they should promote timely session endings which means being very aware of the time. If there isn't adequate time and you rush through the closing, the termination stage may be negatively affected. If your client is from a culture that has a less linear conception of time, it may be necessary to acknowledge those differences and apologize for the fact that your clinical situation requires observing formal time boundaries (Hays, 2013).

The ideal is to finish with all clinical business on time so the client's termination behavior can be observed. When it's time to end the session, clients often begin thinking, feeling, and behaving in ways that give the sensitive clinician clues regarding therapeutic issues, psychopathology, and diagnosis (see *Putting It in Practice* 6.3). Some client behaviors at the end of the session require immediate attention, whereas others simply require a firm, but kind statement, such as "I'm glad you thought of that. It will give us an excellent place to begin next week."

Guiding or Controlling Termination

Therapists need control over session termination. Termination occurs as both parties acknowledge the meeting is over. This may involve escorting clients out along with a comfortable farewell gesture or ritual. One of our colleagues always says "Take care" in a kind voice but with a tone of finality. Some therapists like to set up the next appointment and finish by saying "See you then." We also recall, with some chagrin, a colleague who would peek her head out of her office as the client was leaving and say, "Hang in there!"

It's worth thinking—in advance—about how you'd like to end your sessions. It's also wise to practice various endings ahead of time with colleagues. Find a comfortable method of bringing about closure firmly and gently.

PUTTING IT IN PRACTICE 6.3

Interpreting and Understanding Doorknob Statements

Statements made by clients at the very end of their sessions, as they're getting up to leave or as they walk out the door, are commonly referred to as *doorknob statements*. Review the following doorknob statements and actions and then discuss their potential clinical significance in a small group or with a partner.

- "Thank you so much for your time today." (Accompanied by a handshake or an attempt to give you a hug at the end of every session.)
- "By the way, my thoughts about killing myself have really intensified these past few days." (Clients sometimes wait until the final minute of a session to mention suicidal thoughts.)
- "Maybe sometime we could get together for coffee or something."
- "That was great! Almost as good as a massage. I feel lots better now."
- "So that's it? When will I start feeling better?"

In some cases, clients will try to control termination. A client may keep an eye on the clock and then, 2, 5, or even 15 minutes before time is up, stand up abruptly, and say something like, "I'm done talking for today." Obviously, at some point, you will want to explore what motivates such clients to terminate sessions early. As a rule, interview sessions have a designated ending time, and clients shouldn't be excused early (although certain clients, such as adolescents, commonly claim that they have nothing else to talk about and request to be "let out" early). When adult clients want to leave early, it may be a sign of anxiety; the desire to leave may be a defense—conscious or otherwise—designed to avoid experiencing and talking about something. In can also be an indirect way of expressing anger or disappointment in the process or in you.

You should be prepared for clients who want to leave early, as well as clients who want to stay late. Following are several strategies that may be used alone or in combination when you encounter a client who wants to terminate an interview early.

- Use the time to solicit feedback from the client on his/her perception of the session and of your work with him/her.
- Use an indirect question: "I wonder if you could tell me why you want to leave early today."
- Ask if your client usually ends relationships or says goodbye quickly.
- Gently ask the client to "say whatever comes to mind" right now.
- Explicitly consult your notes or an outline to check whether you've covered all the issues you wanted to cover during the interview (e.g., "Let me take a look through my notes to see if there's anything to check back in on.")
- Let the client know there's no hurry by saying something like, "We still have plenty of time left," and then continue to go about the business of closure (see the previous discussion about closing).

In rare cases, your client may be desperate to leave early. Engaging in a power struggle to keep the client in the room is a bad idea. Instead, accept the client's choice, making a note to explore leaving early the next time you meet. If it appears the client is leaving early, and seems to have no intention of ever coming back, you can make a statement suggesting that, sometime in the future, your client may decide to come back for another meeting or visit a different professional. For example:

> I can see you really want to leave right now, even though we still have plenty of time remaining. It could be that you've talked about everything you wanted to talk about today or it could be that you don't want to go deeper into personal issues. Obviously, I'm not interested in forcing you to stay and talk. But I hope you'll come back and meet with me, or maybe someone else, in the future if or when you want to talk again.

Facing Termination

Often, our own issues affect the way we terminate with clients. If we're characteristically abrupt and hurried, it can show in the way we say goodbye. If we're unsure of ourselves or not convinced we did a good job, we may linger and "accidentally" go overtime. If we're typically assertive, and the client keeps trying to share just "one more thing," we may hurry the client out of the room.

Time limits are important from both a practical and an interpretive perspective. For your own professional survival, you should stay in bounds with regard to beginning and ending on time. At a deeper level, sticking with time boundaries models for your clients that therapy, too, is bound in time, place, and real-world demands. You're not omniscient; you're not the all-good parent, and you can't give clients extra time to compensate for the difficult lives they've had. Your time with clients, no matter how good, must end. You must stand firm when clients push time boundaries.

In our experience, students sometimes feel guilty for firmly ending sessions on time. They allow clients to go on and break the rules just a little. This doesn't really serve clients well in the end, even though they may feel special or believe they got a little extra for their money. In fact, wishing for or demanding special status may be what they most need to face and work on. Limitations imposed by the real world aren't easy, and neither is closing an interview or therapy session. By doing so in a kind, timely, professional manner, the message you give your client is: "I play by the rules, and I believe you can, too. I'll be here next week. I hold you in positive regard and am interested in helping you, but I can't work magic or change reality for you."

The list of tasks for this final stage of the interview is in Table 6.5.

Table 6.5 Checklist for Termination Stage

	Therapist Task	Therapist Methods
❏	1. Watch the clock.	Place a clock where you can see it without straining. Paraphrase. Make feeling reflections.
❏	2. Observe for client's significant doorknob statements.	Explain that time is nearly up.
❏	3. Guide or control termination.	Use a standardized ending. Make a warm and comfortable termination statement. Discuss termination and time boundaries with your client.
❏	4. Face termination.	Evaluate your own response to ending sessions. Stay within time boundaries.

SUMMARY

Researchers and clinicians have developed many models to describe the temporal and process structure of what occurs during a clinical interview. A generic model described by Shea (1998) is used in this chapter as a means of highlighting the events and tasks in the typical interview.

The introduction stage begins with the client's first contact with the therapist. This may involve telephone or face-to-face contact. It's important that therapists plan how to handle first contacts with prospective clients. Some therapists follow a standard procedure when first meeting clients, which may be perceived as artificial or sterile. A balance between standardization and flexibility is recommended. During the introduction, therapists should educate clients on key issues such as confidentiality and the interview's purpose.

All theoretical orientations emphasize the need for establishing rapport with clients. There are many different tactics or strategies therapists use to establish rapport. Some of these strategies address client fears about therapy through education, reassurance, courteous introductions, light conversation, and flexibility. When working with clients with diverse cultural backgrounds a personal approach with friendly small talk can be helpful.

The opening stage of an interview begins when the therapist first makes an open-ended inquiry into the client's condition. The opening stage typically consists of several activities, including the therapist's opening statement, the client's opening response, and the therapist's silent evaluation of the client's expressive abilities. The opening stage ends when the therapist has listened carefully to the main reasons why the client has sought professional assistance.

The body of an interview focuses primarily on information gathering. Information to be gathered during an interview depends in part on the interview's purpose and in part on what clinical material is revealed during the interview. An important clinical interviewing component that occurs during the body of an interview is diagnosis and assessment of mental, behavioral, and emotional problems or disorders. During a psychotherapy interview, the body focuses primarily on application of psychological interventions.

The closing interview stage consists of a shift from information gathering to activities that prepare clients for interview termination. Often, both clients and therapists feel pressured during this part of the interview because time is running short, and there's usually much more information that could be obtained or additional feelings that could be discussed. Therapists should summarize key issues discussed in the session, instill hope for positive change, and empower clients by asking them if they have questions or feedback for the therapist.

Interview termination sometimes brings important separation or loss issues to the surface in both clients and therapists. Clients may express anger, disappointment, relief, or a number of other strong emotions at the end of an interview. These emotions may reflect unresolved feelings that the client has concerning previous separations from important people in his or her life. It's important that therapists plan how they can most effectively end their interviews.

SUGGESTED READINGS AND RESOURCES

This chapter contains numerous topics woven together to form the structure and sequence of the clinical interview. The following readings may help further your understanding of these issues.

Carlson, J., Watts, R. E., & Maniacci, M. (2006) *Adlerian therapy: Theory and practice.* Washington, DC: American Psychological Association.

This text will orient you to stages of interviewing and counseling from an Adlerian theoretical perspective.

Gladwell, M. (2005). *Blink: The power of thinking without thinking.* New York, NY: Little, Brown.

Gladwell's book is really about the power of first impressions and how we make instant judgments without thinking.

O'Donohue, W. T., & Cucciare, M. (2008). *Terminating psychotherapy: A clinician's guide.* New York, NY: Routledge.

In this edited book a variety of authors drill down into the nuts and bolts of termination. Chapters include: "Managed care and termination" and "Terminating psychotherapy therapeutically."

Shea, S. C. (1998). *Psychiatric interviewing: The art of understanding.* Philadelphia, PA: W. B. Saunders.

Chapter 2 of Shea's book is titled "The Dynamic Structure of the Interview" and provides a thorough and practical discussion of the temporal structure typical of most diagnostic clinical interviews.

Sue, S. (2006). Cultural competency: From philosophy to research and practice. *Journal of Community Psychology. Special Issue: Addressing Mental Health Disparities through Culturally Competent Research and Community-Based Practice*, 34(2), 237–245.

Stanley Sue is a leader in writing about cultural competency. His concepts of scientific-mindedness and dynamic sizing are essential for developing culturally sensitive approaches.

Teyber, E., & McClure, F. H. (2011). *Interpersonal process in therapy: An integrational model* (6th ed.). Belmont, CA: Brooks/Cole.

This text spells out the basic ways in which interpersonal process—the dynamics between therapist and client—can be used to facilitate therapist and client insights.

Intake Interviewing and Report Writing

CHAPTER OBJECTIVES

In most mental health settings, treatment begins with an intake interview. During an intake interview, you're faced with the seemingly insurmountable task of gathering a large amount of information about the client and his or her situation while establishing and maintaining rapport. In this chapter, we review the nuts and bolts of conducting an intake interview. Information is also provided on preparing intake reports.

After reading this chapter, you will understand:

- The definition, nature, and objectives of a typical intake interview.
- Strategies for identifying, evaluating, and exploring client problems and goals.
- Strategies for obtaining background or historical information about clients, for evaluating their interpersonal styles, and for assessing their current level of functioning.
- How agency or institutional policy, theoretical orientation, and other factors might affect your intake interview process.
- A brief intake interviewing procedure for working with clients in managed care or time-limited models.
- How to write a professional, but client-friendly intake report.

WHAT IS AN INTAKE INTERVIEW?

The intake interview is primarily an assessment interview. Before initiating counseling, psychotherapy, or psychiatric treatment, it's usually necessary and always wise to conduct an intake interview. Intake interviews are designed to answer a number of critical questions, which typically include:

- What is the client's presenting problem or psychiatric diagnosis?
- Is the client motivated for treatment?

- What is the optimal treatment plan for this client and this problem?
- Who should provide the treatment and in what setting?

Over the past two decades, managed health care and limits imposed by third-party payers have dramatically changed the nature of psychological help available to most people. Ages ago, back when we had to walk five miles through the snow to get to our graduate classes, our supervisors emphasized that several 50-minute interviews were needed before enough assessment information could be obtained to diagnose the client, develop an adequate treatment plan, and initiate treatment. This was true even in the case of traditionally shorter therapies such as cognitive or behavioral therapy.

Despite the fact that research data indicate longer-term treatment is more efficacious (Lambert, 2007), many employee assistance programs and managed care insurance plans set strict limits on the number of therapy sessions available per year. This means practitioners must be faster and more efficient in identifying client problems, establishing treatment goals, and outlining an expected treatment course. For now, speed and brevity are the order of the day. In addition, treatment goals are typically more modest in depth and breadth.

Although it's reasonable for therapists to become more efficient in making treatment decisions, efficiency isn't always enhanced by speed or brevity. For example, when individuals are pressured to work faster, it doesn't matter whether they're baking cakes, building cabinets, repairing automobiles, or doing intake interviews—the outcome is similar: Quality can be compromised.

As we discuss intake-interview procedures in this chapter, be aware that we're describing an intake procedure that's more comprehensive and lengthy than is usually expected, or even tolerated, when session numbers have an absolute limit. We do so for several reasons. First, it's important to learn what *can* be accomplished in the context of an intake-interview assessment, even though it may not accurately reflect what ordinarily *will* be accomplished. Second, insurance companies are profit-driven organizations that regulate therapy services; they don't provide therapy, and it would be incorrect to assume they have expertise for determining how mental health professionals should conduct intake interviews or formulate treatment plans (Schoenholtz, 2012). Third, it would be unethical to educate prospective mental health professionals using exclusively a "bare bones" intake-assessment approach; trimming back and becoming more efficient is best done from a broad and thorough understanding of the process. However, we must be pragmatic; if you're in graduate school today, chances are you will, at some point in your career, work in settings that limit your counseling sessions. Therefore, toward the end of this chapter, we provide an outline and checklist for conducting brief intake interviews.

OBJECTIVES OF INTAKE INTERVIEWING

DVD Clip

In Chapter 7, the intake interview DVD chapter, John and Rita briefly discuss the nature of the intake interview and introduce the *Rita & Michelle* counseling demonstration.

Broadly speaking, the three basic objectives of an intake interview are: (1) identifying, evaluating, and exploring the client's chief complaint and associated therapy goals; (2) obtaining data related to the client's interpersonal style, interpersonal skills, and personal history; and (3) evaluating the client's current life situation and functioning.

Thus, the intake interviewer gathers information about:

1. The problem or problems.
2. The person.
3. The client's current functioning.

This information is used to determine a working diagnosis (or problem formulation) and treatment plan.

An additional objective associated with intake interviewing involves communicating the results of your intake interview—most often to other professionals, but sometimes to other interested parties. In mental health settings, you not only conduct the intake interview, but also write or dictate the *intake report* following your session (Zuckerman, 2010).

Identifying, Evaluating, and Exploring Client Problems and Goals

Your first objective is to find out about your client's chief complaint or main problem. This begins with your opening statement (e.g., "What brings you here?" or "How can I be of help?"; see Chapter 6). After the opening statement, at least 5 to 15 minutes should be spent tracking the client and trying to understand why he or she has come to see you. In some cases, clients quickly identify their reasons for seeking professional assistance; in other cases, they're vague about why they're in your office. As clients articulate problems, nondirective listening responses are used to facilitate rapport. After an initial impression of primary concerns is obtained, questions are used more liberally.

Client problems are intrinsically linked to client goals (Jongsma, Peterson, & Bruce, 2006). Unfortunately, many clients who come to therapy are unable to see past their problems. Often, it's up to you to help clients orient toward goals or solutions early in counseling (Berg & DeJong, 2005; de Shazer et al., 2007; J. Sommers-Flanagan & Barr, 2005). Remember that behind (or in front of) every client problem (or complaint) is a client goal.

Common problems presented by clients include anxiety, depression, and relationship conflicts. Other problems include eating disorders, alcoholism or drug addiction, social skill deficits, physical or sexual abuse, stress reactions, vocational confusion, and sexual dysfunction. Because of the wide range of client symptoms or problems, it's crucial that therapists have at least a general knowledge of psychopathology and the *DSM-5* (American Psychiatric Association, 2013). However, as noted, every problem has an inherent goal. Early in the intake, therapists can help clients reframe problem statements into goal statements. For example, problems with anxiety can be reframed as goals of calmness:

> I hear you talking about feelings of nervousness and anxiety. If I understand you correctly, you'd like to feel calm and in control more often. So, one of your therapy goals might be to feel calm more often and to be able to bring on those calm feelings yourself. Do I have that right?

By reframing client problems into goal statements, therapists help clients feel hopeful and begin a positive goal-setting process (Taylor, 2005). Goal-setting reframes also provide useful assessment information; clients will be more or less open to setting realistic therapy goals.

Prioritizing and Selecting Client Problems and Goals

Often, we wish clients would come to their intake interview with a single, easily articulated problem and associated goal. For example, it might be nice (though a bit intimidating) if a new client in the first session stated:

> I have a social phobia. When in public, I worry about being scrutinized and negatively judged. My anxiety about this is manifest through sweating, worries about being inadequate, and avoidance of most, but not all, social situations. What I'd like to do in therapy is build my self-confidence, increase my positive self-talk, and learn to calm myself down when I'm starting to get upset.

Unfortunately, most clients come to their intake interview with either a number of interrelated complaints or with general vague symptoms. They usually use problem-talk (verbal descriptions of what's wrong) to express concerns about their lives. Sometimes during an initial interview, clients will share a real, but lower emotional-cost concern to "test out" how the therapist responds. Later, if you pass the test, you may begin hearing about deeper concerns or problems (Charlie Myers, personal communication, October 14, 2012).

After the initial 5 to 15 minutes of an intake interview your job is to begin establishing a list of primary problems and goals identified by the client. Usually, when a therapist begins helping a client identify problems and goals, it signals a transition from general nondirective listening to a more structured, collaborative, and/or directive approach. Transitioning from client free expression to more structured interactions has a dual purpose. First, it allows the therapist to check for any additional problems that the client has not yet talked about. Second, the transition begins the process of problem prioritization, selection, and goal setting:

Therapist: So far, you've talked mostly about how you've been feeling so down lately, how it's so hard for you to get up in the morning, and how most things that are usually fun for you haven't been fun lately. I'm wondering if you have any other major concerns or distress in your life right now.

Client: As a matter of fact, I do. I get big butterflies. I feel so scared sometimes. Mostly I feel scared about my career . . . or maybe lack of career.

During problem exploration, therapists help clients identify their problems or concerns. This process is truly exploratory; therapists listen closely to problems that clients discuss, paraphrase or summarize what problems have been identified, and inquire about the existence of additional significant concerns.

In the preceding exchange, the therapist used an indirect question to continue exploring for problems. After several problems were identified, the therapist moved to problem prioritization. Because all problems can't be addressed simultaneously, therapist and client choose together which problem(s) need attention during an intake. This collaborative activity is an ethical responsibility associated with initial treatment planning (R. Sommers-Flanagan & Sommers-Flanagan, 2007).

Therapist:	I guess so far we could summarize your major concerns as your depressed mood, anxiety over your career, and shyness. Which of these would you say is currently most troubling to you?
Client:	Well, they all bother me, but I guess my mood is worst. When I'm in a really bad mood and don't get out of bed all day, I end up never facing those other problems anyway.

This client has identified depression as his biggest concern. Of course, an alternative formulation of the problem is that social inhibition and anxiety produce the depressed mood and, therefore, should be dealt with first. Otherwise, the client will never get out of bed because of his strong fears and anxieties. However, it's usually (but not always) best to follow client leads and explore their biggest concerns first (psychiatrists refer to what the client considers the main problem as the *chief complaint*). In this example, all three symptoms may eventually be linked anyway. Exploring depression first still allows the clinician to integrate the anxiety and shyness symptoms into the picture.

Even if you want to explore a different issue than the client identified (e.g., alcoholism), it's best to wait and listen carefully to what the client thinks is the main problem (chief complaint). Acknowledging, respecting, and empathizing with the client's perspective helps you be effective, gain trust, and keep the client in counseling. From a motivational interviewing perspective, this process of coming alongside clients as they discuss their concerns is essential for managing resistance and facilitating an alliance (Miller & Rollnick, 2013). Miller and Rollnick (2013) also warned against labeling the client's concern as a "problem" if the client doesn't define it as such (e.g., with substance abuse). In time-limited circumstances (e.g., managed care), nondirective empathic responses are usually brief and intermittent because there needs to be a quick transition from problems to goal setting. This is reasonable given that goal setting has a positive effect on treatment outcome (Latham & Locke, 2006, 2007). In Chapter 10, goal setting is discussed more thoroughly, in the context of treatment planning.

Analyzing Symptoms

Once you have identified a primary problem, in collaboration with your client, attention should turn to a thorough analysis of that problem, including emotional, cognitive, and behavioral aspects. Using a list of questions similar to the following may be helpful. As you read the questions, think about different client problems (e.g., panic attacks, low self-esteem, unsatisfactory personal relationships, binge eating or drinking, vocational indecision) that you might be exploring through the use of such questions:

- When did the problem or symptoms first occur? (In some cases, the symptom is one that the client has experienced before. If so, explore its origin and more recent development and maintenance.)
- Where were you and what exactly was happening when you first noticed the problem? (What was the setting, who was there, etc.?)

- How have you tried to cope with or eliminate this problem?
- What have you done that was most successful?
- What else has been helpful?
- Are there any situations, people, or events that usually precede your experience of this problem?
- What exactly happens when the problem or symptoms begin?
- What thoughts or images go through your mind when it's occurring?
- Do you have any physical sensations before, during, or after the problem occurs?
- Where and what do you feel in your body? Describe it as precisely as possible.
- How frequently do you experience this problem?
- How long does it usually last?
- How does it usually end (or what do you do that makes it finally stop)?
- Does the problem affect or interfere with what you usually do at work, at home, or when recreating?
- In what ways does it interfere with your work, relationships, school, or recreational pursuits?
- Describe the worst experience you've had with this symptom. When the symptom is at its worst, what thoughts, images, and feelings come up?
- Describe the best experience you've had with this problem, a time when you handled it very well.
- Have you ever expected the symptom to occur and it did not occur, or it occurred only for a few moments and then disappeared?
- If you were to rate the severity of your problem, with 1 indicating no distress and 100 indicating so much distress that it's going to cause you to kill yourself or die, how would you rate it today?
- What rating would you have given your symptom on its worst day ever?
- What's the lowest rating you would ever have given your symptom? Has it ever been completely absent?
- As we've discussed your symptom during this interview, have you noticed any changes? (Has it gotten any worse or better as we've focused on it?)
- If you were to give this symptom and its effects on you a title, like the title of a book or play, what title would you give it?

These questions are listed in an order that flows well in many interview situations. However, these particular questions and their order aren't standard, and you don't need to use this list. Some practitioners might take issue with the fact that the preceding approach to analyzing the client's problem primarily uses internalizing or problem-saturated language (Gonçalves, Matos, & Santos, 2009). For example, solution-focused or narrative therapists would use questions specifically designed to facilitate problem externalization or questions emphasizing problem exceptions—when the client's problems are absent. Although the list does include some positive-focused or constructive questioning, it's generally more problem-focused.

Before conducting an intake interview, you might want to review the preceding question list. You can always reword them to fit your style. New questions can be added and others deleted until you have a set of questions that meets your needs. We encourage you to continually revise your list so that you can become increasingly efficient and sensitive when questioning clients. Through practice, you can develop a sense of how many questions you can fit reasonably into a single interviewing session, and you may end up memorizing a list of questions that flows well for you.

Sometimes even best-laid plans fail. Clients can be skillful at drawing therapists off track. And at times, it may be important to be drawn off track because shifting from your planned menu of questions can lead to a different and perhaps more significant area (e.g., reports of sexual or physical abuse or suicidal ideation). While focusing on your planned task, use empathic statements such as paraphrases, feeling validation, and nondirective reflection of feeling. Remain flexible to avoid overlooking important clues clients give about other significant problem areas.

Using Problem Conceptualization Systems

Some authors recommend using problem conceptualization systems when analyzing client problems (Cormier, Nurius, & Osborn, 2012). Usually, these systems are theory-based, but some are more eclectic. Most conceptualization systems guide therapists by analyzing and conceptualizing problems with strict attention to predetermined, specified domains of functioning. For instance, Lazarus (1976) developed a "multimodal" behavioral-eclectic approach. Lazarus used the acronym *BASIC ID* to represent his seven-modality system:

B: *Behavior.*   Specific, concrete behavioral responses are analyzed in Lazarus's system. He particularly attends to behaviors that clients engage in too often or too infrequently. These include positive or negative habits or reactions. A multimodal therapist might ask: "Are there some things you'd like to stop doing?" and "Are there some things you'd like to do more often?" as a way of determining what concrete behaviors the client might like to increase or decrease through therapy.

A: *Affect.*   Lazarus's definition of *affect* includes feelings, moods, and other self-reported and self-described emotions. He might ask, "What makes you happy or puts you in a good mood?" or "What emotions are most troubling to you?"

S: *Sensation.*   This modality refers to sensory processing of information. For example, clients often report physical symptoms associated with high levels of anxiety (e.g., choking, elevated temperature, heart palpitations). The multimodal therapist might ask, "Do you have any unpleasant aches, pains, or other physical sensations?" and "What happens to cause you those unpleasant sensations?"

I: *Imagery.*   Imagery consists of internal visual cognitive processes. Clients often experience powerful pictures or images of themselves or of future events. A multimodal therapist could query, "When you're feeling anxious, what images or pictures pop into your mind?"

C: *Cognition.*   Lazarus closely evaluates client thinking patterns and beliefs. This process usually includes an evaluation of distorted or irrational thinking patterns that lead to emotional distress. For example, a therapist could ask, "When you meet someone new, what thoughts go through your mind?" and "What are some positive things you say to yourself during the course of a day?"

I: *Interpersonal Relationships.*   This modality concerns variables such as communication skills, relationship patterns, and assertive capabilities as manifest during role-play and as observed in the client-therapist relationship.

Possible relevant questions include, "What words would you use to describe the positive or healthy relationships that you have?" and "Who would you like to spend more time with, and who would you like to spend less time with?"

D: *Drugs*.   This modality refers to biochemical and neurological factors that can affect behavior, emotions, and thinking patterns. It includes physical illnesses and nutritional patterns. Questions might include, "Are you participating in any regular physical exercise?" and "Do you take any prescription drugs?"

Lazarus's (1976) model is broad-based, popular, and useful to therapists of different theoretical orientations. If you're interested in learning more about his model, his latest book is *Brief but comprehensive psychotherapy: The multimodal way* (Lazarus, 2006).

Lazarus's model slightly overemphasizes cognitive processes (two separate cognitive modalities exist in his seven-modality system: cognition and imaging) while neglecting or deemphasizing spiritual, cultural, and recreational domains. As suggested previously, similar to every system designed to aid in problem identification, exploration, and conceptualization, the multimodal system has its imperfections. It's important to be familiar with numerous systems so, as a competent professional therapist, you can flex your questioning and conceptualizing to your setting and individual client problems and needs.

Behavioral and cognitive theorists and practitioners emphasize the importance of antecedents and consequences in problem development and maintenance. This approach is founded on the belief that analyzing clients' environments and their interpretation of environmental stimuli allows counselors to explain, predict, and control specific symptoms. Behaviorists have called this model of conceptualizing problem behavior the *ABC model* (Thoresen & Mahoney, 1974): behavioral *A*ntecedents, the *B*ehavior or problem itself, and *C*onsequences. Although this model has been criticized (Goldfried, Greenberg, & Marmar, 1990), it's useful to explore—at minimum—the following ABCs with their clients:

- What events, thoughts, and experiences precede the identified problem?
- What is the precise operational definition of the problem (i.e., what behaviors constitute the problem)?
- What events, thoughts, and experiences follow the identified problem?

When following the ABC model, therapists can be meticulous in their search for potential behavioral antecedents and consequences. For example, behavioral antecedents and consequences could be assessed using all modalities identified by Lazarus (1976):

Behavior: What behaviors precede and follow symptom occurrence?
Affect: What affective experiences precede and follow symptom occurrence?
Sensation: What physical sensations precede and follow symptom occurrence?
Imagery: What images precede and follow symptom occurrence?
Cognitions: What specific thoughts precede and follow symptom occurrence?
Interpersonal: What relationship events or experiences precede or follow symptom occurrence?
Drugs: What biochemical, physiological, or drug-use experiences precede or follow symptom occurrence?

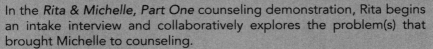

DVD Clip

In the *Rita & Michelle, Part One* counseling demonstration, Rita begins an intake interview and collaboratively explores the problem(s) that brought Michelle to counseling.

Obtaining Background and Historical Information

In an intake interview, three general information sources are used to assess the client's personality or interpersonal style and mental condition:

1. The client's personal history.
2. The client's manner of interacting with others.
3. Formal evaluation of client mental status.

The remainder of this section discusses methods and issues related to obtaining a client's personal history and evaluating a client's interpersonal style (evaluating mental status is the focus of Chapter 8).

Shifting to the Personal or Psychosocial History

After spending 15 to 25 minutes exploring the presenting complaint, you should have a reasonable idea of the primary reasons the client is seeking counseling. A useful bridge from problem exploration to personal or psychosocial history is the *why now* question. Say to the client something like:

> I'm pretty clear on the main reasons you've come for counseling, but one thing I'd like to know more about is *why* you've chosen to come for counseling *now*.

This question helps determine what specific factors, or precipitating events, convinced the client to seek professional help at this *particular time* in his or her life. The client's response can also shed light on whether the client is a willing participant in the interview or perhaps was coerced by friends or family to come for assistance. If the client balks at your *why now* question, simply continue to pursue the question, perhaps through alternative approaches, such as:

- Why didn't you come in a few weeks ago when you were first jilted by your girlfriend?
- You've had these symptoms so long, I'm a little puzzled over exactly what prompted you to seek counseling now. Why not before? And why didn't you choose to wait and 'tough it out' as you have in the past?

After your client has responded to the *why now* question (and after you've summarized or paraphrased his or her response), you can formally shift the interview's focus from the *problem* to the *person*. This shift can be made with a statement similar to the following:

> So far, we've spent most of our time discussing the concerns that led you to come for counseling. Now I'd like to try to get a better sense of you. One of the best ways for me to do that is to ask you some questions about your past.

Nondirective Historical Leads

Immediately following your shift to psychosocial history, in most cases, you should again become nondirective. This is because you're moving away from analyzing specific symptoms and entering a new domain:

- How about if you begin by telling me some of your childhood memories?
- Maybe it would be easiest if you started with where you were born and raised and then talk about whatever significant details come to mind.
- Tell me what you remember about growing up.

For assessment purposes, your first inquiry into psychosocial history should be nondirective or open. Clients reveal significant information simply by what they choose to focus on and by what they choose to avoid. After a brief nondirective period (perhaps 2 to 5 minutes), you can provide clients with more structure and guidance and begin asking specific questions about their past.

As discussed in Chapter 6, clients may be hesitant to talk freely about their childhood experiences; they may ask for more structure and guidance. For a few minutes during history taking, we believe it can be useful to avoid giving structure and guidance. If you immediately provide structure and ask specific questions, you may never know what the client would have spontaneously chosen to talk about. If your client presses you on this issue, you can state directly:

I'll ask you some specific questions about your childhood in a few minutes, but right now I'm interested in whatever past experiences and memories come into your mind. Just tell me a few memories that seem important to you.

At times, clients may be anxious and uncomfortable, and may resist delving into their personal history. Personal histories are sometimes traumatic and disturbing. Significant historical events may be hard to recall or purposely not considered or remembered very often. In our experience, clients frequently claim, "I really can't remember much of my past" or "My childhood is mostly a blank." If this happens, provide supportive and reassuring psychoeducation:

Memory is a funny thing. Sometimes bits will come back to you as we discuss it. Of course, most of us have memories we'd rather not recall because they're painful or unpleasant. My job isn't to force you into talking about difficult past experiences but to let you talk about whatever past events you want to talk about.

Obtaining a psychosocial history is a delicate and sensitive process. For the most part, intake interviews don't involve direct questioning about specific trauma experiences. On the other hand, opening up and sharing about traumas can be a therapeutic and emotionally ventilating experience (Goodman & Epstein, 2008; Simha-Alpern, 2007). Effective intake therapists give clients an opportunity to appropriately disclose past traumatic events, but they don't encourage disclosure of details until an adequate therapy relationship has been established.

It's important to be able to shift back to nondirective listening if the client reveals significant traumatic memories or events. Many times, our students have asked, "What if my client has been sexually abused?" or "What if my client's parents died when she was a young child; what do I do then?" When you delve into a client's personal history, you should anticipate the possibility of hearing emotionally charged material. When this happens, the best thing you can do is simply listen well. You cannot fix the memories or change the past. When clients first disclose traumatic experiences, mostly they need a supportive and empathic ear. Comments that track your client's experience, such as "Sounds like that was an especially difficult time" or "That was a time when you were really down (or angry, or anxious)," might be the most important type of response you can offer.

Some clients may have trouble pulling themselves out of emotionally distressing memories. In such cases, clear distinctions can be made between what happened then and what's happening now. Explore with clients how they managed to handle the trying times in their lives. Solution-focused approaches that involve exploring, identifying, and emphasizing how clients coped and survived during a difficult past situation can be very helpful. In fact, you may be able to point out ways your clients were strong during their most difficult times. For example:

> You've been through some very hard times, there's no doubt about that. And yet, it's also clear, as I listen to you, that back then, when things were at their worst, you reached out and got help and got yourself back on your feet again.

It's also helpful to gradually lead clients back to the present as you gather historical information. You can make comments or ask questions that lead from the past to the present, such as, "When your daughter was born, your family wasn't very supportive. How old is she now?" As you move into the present, your clients may be able to gain distance from painful past experiences. On rare occasions, a client will remain consumed with negative emotions. Sometimes, this happens because of the powerful nature of traumatic memories. Other times, clients get stuck because they don't view the present as an improvement over bad times in the past. Whatever the case, when clients get stuck in negative or traumatic memories, it can be disheartening or frightening. We write about strategies for assessing and managing clients who are overwhelmed by negative or suicidal thoughts in Chapter 9 and specific approaches for moving clients to a more positive emotional state are illustrated in *Putting It in Practice* 7.1.

Directive Historical Leads

After briefly allowing clients to freely discuss whatever they feel is significant in their past, you should initiate another transition in the interview and become a more directive explorer of your client's past. You can potentially obtain literally a lifetime of historical material from a client. Because you have limited time in a typical intake, you must choose your areas of focus. A good place to begin a directive exploration of a client's past is with an early memory (Clark, 2002):

Counselor:	What's your earliest memory—the first thing you can remember from your childhood?
Client:	I remember my brothers trying to get me to get into my dad's pickup. They wanted me to pretend I was driving it. They were laughing. I got into the cab and somehow got the truck's brake off,

> because it started to roll. My dad got pretty mad, but my brothers were always trying to get me to do these outrageous things.

Counselor: How old were you?

Client: I suppose about 4, maybe 5.

Memories clients report can hold significance for their present lives; the memories represent major themes or issues the client is currently struggling with (Carlson, Watts, & Maniacci, 2006; Sweeney, 2009). For example, the client who revealed the preceding memory reported that his life was characterized by performances that he put on for others. He admitted having strong urges to do outrageous things to get attention and approval.

When clients reveal memories that are either strikingly positive or strikingly negative, it's useful to follow up with questions that seek an opposite type of memory. Virtually everyone has both positive and negative childhood memories. A good practice is to assess whether your client can produce a balanced report of positive and negative childhood experiences. Clients who remember mostly negative childhood experiences may be suffering from a depressive disorder, whereas clients who never mention negative experiences may be using defense mechanisms of denial, repression, or dissociation (Mosak, 1989):

Client: I remember breaking a pipe down in the basement of my house. I had gotten into my dad's tools and was striking an exposed pipe with a hammer. It started leaking and flooded the basement. I was in big trouble.

Counselor: It sounds like that memory was mostly of negative times when you got in trouble. Can you think of an early memory of something with a more positive flavor?

Client: Oh yeah, my memories of playing with my next-door neighbor are great. My mom used to have him over and we would play with every game and toy in the house.

Counselor: Do you remember a specific time when he came over and you played?

Client: Uh . . . yeah. He always wanted to play army, but I liked dinosaurs better. We got in a fight, and I ended up throwing all the army men out into the front yard. Then we stayed in and played dinosaurs.

Sometimes, even when you ask for a positive client memory, you will get a response with negativity and conflict. On the other hand, some clients deny any negative memories. There is probably no use in pointing out to clients, unless they note it themselves, the fact that they reported another largely negative (or positive) event. Instead, merely take note of the quality of their memories and move on.

Another method for exploring childhood or, more specifically, parent-child relationships is to ask clients to provide three words to describe their parents.

Counselor: Give me three words to describe your mother.

Client: What do you mean?

Counselor: When you think of your mother and what she's like, what three words best describe her?

Client: I suppose . . . clean, . . . and proper, and uh, intense. That's it, intense.

As noted, there is a high likelihood of stumbling into strong, affectively charged memories when exploring your clients' psychosocial history. This is especially true when exploring parent-child relationships. Words used by clients to describe their parents may require follow up. You can do so by asking clients to provide specific examples:

> You said your mother was intense. Can you give me an example of something she did that fits that word?

A natural flow while history taking is: (a) first memories, (b) memories of parents and siblings (if any), (c) school and peer relations, (d) work or employment, and (e) other areas (see Table 7.1). Psychosocial history information that might be covered in a very thorough intake interview is listed in Table 7.1. Note that this is a fairly comprehensive list. In a typical clinical intake, you'll need to be selective regarding history taking. It's impossible to cover everything in the 15 to 20 minutes you have to devote to personal history taking. In fact, even in a 50-minute interview exclusively dedicated to history taking, judicious selection from the areas listed in Table 7.1 is necessary.

Table 7.1 provides an array of areas to explore in psychosocial history-taking. Other interviewing guides are available for many of the content areas (or domains) listed in the table (see Suggested Readings and Resources at the end of the chapter).

Because it's often difficult to choose which domains to explore during a brief intake interview, agencies and individual clinicians often use registration forms or intake questionnaires for new clients. These forms provide therapists with client information before they see the client for the first time so they can select which domains to emphasize with a new client. Some research has examined the effects of computer-administered intake interviews and mental status examinations. Although this approach is impersonal, it has some advantages: Computers don't forget to ask particular questions, and some clients actually feel more comfortable disclosing their drug abuse history, sexual history, or other sensitive facts (e.g., HIV status) to a computer rather than to an therapist (DiLillo, DeGue, Kras, Di Loreto-Colgan, & Nash, 2006; Garb, 2007).

> **DVD Clip**
>
> In the *Rita & Michelle, Part Two* counseling demonstration, Rita explores the possible contributions of Michelle's personal history to the main problem that she's brought to counseling.

Evaluating Interpersonal Style

The claim that individuals have personality traits resulting in consistent or predictable behavior patterns is more or less controversial, depending on your theoretical orientation (Bem & Allen, 1974). Psychoanalytic and interpersonal psychotherapists base their therapy approaches on the assumption that individuals behave in highly consistent ways (Fairbairn, 1952). In contrast, cognitive and behavioral psychotherapists are more likely to reject the concept of personality and claim that behavior is a function of the situation or a person's cognitions about the situation (Beck, 1976; Mischel, 1968; Ullman & Krasner, 1969).

Table 7.1 Personal History Interview Sample Questions

Content Areas	Questions
1. First memories	What is your first memory? How old were you then? Do you have any very positive (or negative) early memories?
2. Descriptions and memories of parents	Give me three words to describe your mother (or father). Who did you spend more time with, Mom or Dad? What methods of discipline did your parents use with you? What recreational or home activities did you do with your parents?
3. Descriptions and memories of siblings	Did you have any brothers or sisters? (If so, how many?) What memories do you have of time spent with your siblings? Who was your closest sibling and why? Who were you most similar to in your family? Who were you most dissimilar to in your family?
4. Elementary school experiences	Do you remember your first day of school? How was school for you? (Did you like school?) What was your favorite (or best) subject in school? What subject did you like least (or were you worst at)? Do you have any vivid school memories? Who was your favorite (or least favorite) teacher? What made you like (or dislike) this teacher so much? Were you ever suspended or expelled from school? Describe the worst trouble you were ever in when in school. Were you in any special or remedial classes in school?
5. Peer relationships (in and out of school)	Do you remember having many friends in school? What kinds of things did you do for fun with your friends? Did you get along better with boys or girls? What positive (or negative) memories do you have from relationships you had with your friends in elementary school?
6. Middle school, high school, and college experiences	Do you remember having many friends in high school? What kinds of things did you do for fun with your friends? Did you get along better with boys or girls? What positive (or negative) memories do you have from high school? Do you remember your first day of high school? How was high school for you? (Did you like high school?) What was your favorite (or best) subject in high school? What subject did you like least (or were you worst at)? Do you have any vivid high school memories? Who was your favorite (or least favorite) high school teacher? What made you like (or dislike) this teacher so much? Were you ever suspended or expelled from high school? Describe the worst trouble you were ever in when in high school.

Table 7.1 (*continued*)

Content Areas	Questions
	What was your greatest high school achievement (or award)? Did you go to college? What were your reasons for going (or not going) to college? What was your major field of study in college? What is the highest degree you obtained?
7. First employment and work experience	What was your first job or the first way you ever earned money? How did you get along with your coworkers? What kinds of positive and negative job memories do you have? Have you ever been fired from a job? What is your ultimate career goal? How much money would you like to make annually?
8. Military history and experiences	Were you ever in the military? Did you volunteer, or were you drafted? Tell me about your most positive (or most negative) experiences in the military. What was your final rank? Were you ever disciplined? What was your offense?
9. Romantic relationship history	Have you ever had romantic feelings for someone? Do you remember your first date? What do you think makes a good romantic or loving relationship? What do you look for in a romantic (or marital) partner? What first attracted you to your spouse (or significant other)?
10. Sexual history (including first sexual experience)	What did you learn about sex from your parents (or school, siblings, peers, television, or movies)? What do you think is most important in a sexual relationship? Have you had any traumatic sexual experiences (e.g., rape or incest)?
11. Aggressive history	What is the most angry you have ever been? Have you ever been in a fight? Have you ever been hit or punched by someone else? What did you learn about anger and how to deal with it from your parents (or siblings, friends, or television)? What do you usually do when you get angry? Tell me about a time when you got too angry and regretted it later. When was your last fight? Have you ever used a weapon (or had one used against you) in a fight? What is the worst you have ever hurt someone physically?

(*continued*)

Table 7.1 *(continued)*

Content Areas	Questions
12. Medical and health history	Did you have any childhood diseases? Any medical hospitalizations? Any surgeries? Do you have any current medical concerns or problems? Are you taking any prescription medications? When was your last physical examination? Do you have any problems with eating or sleeping or weight loss or gain? Have you ever been unconscious? Are there any major diseases that seem to run in your family (e.g., heart disease or cancer)? Tell me about your usual diet. What kinds of foods do you eat most often? Do you have any allergies to foods, medicines, or anything else? What are your exercise patterns? How often do you engage in aerobic exercise?
13. Psychiatric or counseling history	Have you ever been in counseling before? If so, with whom and for what problems, and how long did the counseling last? Do you remember anything your previous counselor did that was particularly helpful (or particularly unhelpful)? Did counseling help with the problem? If not, what did help? Why did you end counseling? Have you ever been hospitalized for psychological reasons? What was the problem then? Have you ever taken medication for psychiatric problems? Has anyone in your family been hospitalized for psychological reasons? Has anyone in your family had significant mental health problems? Can you remember that person's problem or diagnosis?
14. Alcohol and drug history	When did you have your first drink of alcohol (or pot, etc.)? About how much alcohol do you consume each day (or week or month)? What is your drink/drug of choice? Have you ever had any medical, legal, familial, or work problems related to alcohol? Under what circumstances are you most likely to drink? What benefits do you believe you get from drinking?
15. Legal history	Have you ever been arrested or ticketed for an illegal activity? Have you been issued any tickets for driving under the influence? Have you been given any tickets for speeding? How many or how often? Have you ever declared bankruptcy?

Table 7.1 (continued)	
Content Areas	**Questions**
16. Recreational history	What is your favorite recreational activity?
	What recreational activities do you hate or avoid?
	What sport, hobby, or leisure time pursuit are you best at?
	How often do you engage in your favorite (or best) activity?
	What prevents you from engaging in this activity more often?
	Whom do you do this activity with?
	Are there any recreational activities that you'd like to do, but you've never had the time or opportunity to try?
17. Developmental history	Do you know the circumstance surrounding your conception?
	Was your mother's pregnancy normal?
	What was your birth weight?
	Did you have any significant health or medical problems?
	When did you sit, stand, and walk?
18. Spiritual or religious history	What is your religious background?
	What are your current religious or spiritual beliefs?
	Do you have a religious affiliation?
	Do you attend church, pray, meditate, or otherwise participate in religious activities?
	What other spiritual activities have you been involved in previously?

For the purposes of this section, we assume that people engage in consistent behavior patterns, but recognize that these patterns may vary greatly depending on particular persons and situations.

Interpersonal Styles

People tend to assume specific roles in their interpersonal relationships. Some behave in dominant ways; others are more submissive and self-effacing. Other individuals adopt a hostile or aggressive stance in interpersonal relationships; still others prefer to be warm and affiliative when relating to others. Some people seem to stay consistently in one role; others behave much differently depending on the situation and people involved. This interplay between consistency and variance can be informative and useful in assessing clients' interpersonal problem areas.

During an intake interview, three primary sources of data help therapists evaluate client interpersonal style. These include:

1. Client descriptions of how he or she has related to others in the past (e.g., during childhood, adolescence, and young adulthood).
2. Information about how your client relates to others in his or her contemporary relationships.
3. Client behavioral interactions that occur with you during the interview session.

Some psychotherapy approaches place great importance on evaluating a client's interpersonal style. Luborsky (1984) referred to a client's "core conflictual relationship theme" (p. 98). He believed psychotherapy involves helping clients recognize the consistency in the troubles that emerge in their interpersonal relationships and begin to have greater conscious choice regarding their interpersonal behavior. To help clients develop greater freedom from their old interpersonal relationship patterns, awareness of such patterns or *interpersonal style* is needed.

It's not necessary and often not possible, to have a precise sense of a client's interpersonal style after a single interview. The goal, instead, is to have a few working hypotheses about how your client generally relates to others. Further, as noted by Teyber and McClure (2011), therapists should attend to feelings elicited by clients. For example, some clients may cause you to feel bored, aroused, depressed, or annoyed. Of course, it's important to evaluate how much of the reaction is a result of your client's behavior, and how much is simply your own. As noted previously, personal and emotional reactions you have toward clients are a sign of countertransference (Luborsky & Barrett, 2006). Teyber and McClure (2011) suggested that if the reactions that the client evokes in you are also evoked in others, it's likely that the client's behavior is causing those reactions. However, if your reactions are unique, then the reactions might reflect countertransference on your part.

Evaluating a client's personal history and interpersonal style are formidable tasks that could easily take several sessions. However, contemporary limits on psychotherapy usually don't allow for lengthy assessment procedures. Traditionally, the main purpose of exploring interpersonal and historical issues during an intake has been to formulate hypotheses and not to provide definitive treatment plans.

Assessment of Current Functioning

After exploring historical and interpersonal issues, therapists should make one more major shift and focus on current functioning. It's important to end the intake interview with a focus on the present and future—not the past. The shift to current functioning provides both a symbolic and a concrete return to the present. The end of the interview is also a time to encourage clients to focus on personal strengths and social or environmental resources.

Questions during this last portion should focus on current client involvements or activities. The following statements and questions help clients talk about areas of current functioning:

- We've talked about your major concerns and a bit about your past. I'd like to shift back to what's happening in your life right now.
- What kinds of activities fill up your usual day?
- Describe a typical day in your life.
- How much time do you spend at work?
- About how much time do you spend with your partner (spouse)?
- What do you and your partner do together? How often do you do these activities?
- Do you spend much time alone?
- What do you most enjoy doing all by yourself?

Some clients have difficulty shifting from talking about their past to talking about the present. This can be especially true with clients who had difficult or traumatic childhoods. In such cases, you can use two primary strategies so clients can view their intake interviewing experience in an appropriate and realistic context. When clients become upset during an intake interview, respond by (1) validating the client's feelings and (2) instilling hope for positive change. For example, in a case of a mother who comes to counseling shortly after losing her child to a tragic accident, you might state:

> I can see that losing your son has been terribly painful. You probably already know that your feelings are totally normal. Most people consider losing a child to be the most emotionally painful experience possible. Also, I want you to know how smart it is for you to come and talk with me so openly about your son's death and your feelings. It won't make your sad and horrible feelings magically go away, but in almost every case, talking about your grief is the right thing to do. It will help you move through the grieving process.

Feeling validation, as discussed in Chapter 3, involves acknowledgment and approval of a client's feelings. This technique is generally reassuring to clients and is an appropriate tool toward the end of an intake when a client is experiencing painful or disturbing feelings. Another more general example of what a therapist might say to a client who is in emotional pain or distress toward the end of an intake follows:

> I can't help but notice that you're still feeling pretty sad about what we've talked about today. I want you to know that it's very natural to have sad or upset feelings. Many people who come in to talk to a counselor leave with mixed feelings. That's because it's hard to talk about your childhood or your personal problems without having uncomfortable feelings, but sort of good at the same time. What you're feeling is natural.

It's normal to feel bad when talking about sad, disappointing, or traumatic events. Therapists should provide this factual information to clients in a reassuring, validating manner. Reassurance and support are essential parts of an effective closing (see *Putting It in Practice* 7.1).

PUTTING IT IN PRACTICE 7.1

Helping Clients Regain Emotional Control

It's not unusual for clients to experience emotional distress during an intake interview. Generally, this is a natural process and clients also naturally pull themselves together and are in decent emotional shape by the interview's end. However, sometimes, toward the end of an interview, your client may still be emotionally distraught and you will need to help him/her regain emotional control before leaving your office. Although there are no strategies that guarantee emotional
(continued)

(*continued*)

reconstitution, the following techniques may be helpful. Of course, these strategies or techniques should be prefaced with empathic comments.

[Focus or refocus on the present and immediate future] What are your plans for the rest of the day? What will you do right after you leave here? Is there anything in particular that you might want to do that would be emotionally comforting?

[Ask the client about what s/he usually does for emotional soothing] When you feel upset at home or outside therapy, what do you usually do to help yourself feel better?

[Change the subject back to a more positive issue] Earlier when we were talking I was very impressed with how you've been handling your work stress.

[Give a compliment and suggestion] It takes lots of strength to be as open as you've been with me today. I hope you recognize that and can give yourself a pat on the back.

[Acknowledge the negative reality and then have the client review some positives] Sometimes it's hard to get refocused on the positive, and so I'm going to ask you some questions that will take some thought and help move you in that direction. What were the most positive things you would say you'll take from our meeting today?

Reviewing Goals and Monitoring Change

Another issue toward the end of the intake is the future. Clients come to counseling or therapy because they want change, and change involves the future.

Many therapists pose some form of the following question toward the end of the intake: "Let's say that therapy is successful and you notice some major changes in your life. What will have changed?" Other future-oriented questions may also be appropriate, including "How do you see yourself changing in the next several years?" or "What kind of personal (or career) goals are you striving toward?" Discussing therapy goals during an intake interview or in early therapy sessions provide a foundation for termination (J. Sommers-Flanagan & Sommers-Flanagan, 2007b). Through establishing clear definitions of desired change, clients and therapists can jointly monitor the progress of therapy and together determine when the end of therapy is approaching. Client goals should be formulated from client problems at the beginning of an intake interview. It's also important to review client goals in a positive and upbeat manner toward the interview's end.

DVD Clip

In the *Rita & Michelle, Part Three* counseling demonstration, Rita closes the intake with Michelle, tries an initial or early interpretation, and begins planning for future sessions.

FACTORS AFFECTING INTAKE INTERVIEW PROCEDURES

To conduct an intake interview that thoroughly covers each area described in this chapter within a traditional 50-minute period is impossible. As a professional, you must make choices regarding what to emphasize, what to deemphasize, and what to ignore. Several factors affect your choices.

Client Registration Forms

Some agencies and practitioners rely on client registration forms or intake questionnaires for information about clients. This practice is especially helpful for obtaining detailed information that might unnecessarily extend the clinical hour. For example, registration forms that include space for listing names of previous therapists, names and telephone numbers of primary care physicians, and basic biographical information (e.g., date of birth, age, birthplace, educational attainment) are essential.

Although intake questionnaires are acceptable in moderation, when used excessively, they may offend or intimidate clients. For example, some agencies use 10- to 15-page intake questionnaires to screen potential clients. These question-naires contain many extremely personal questions, such as "Have you experienced sexual abuse?" and "Describe how you were punished as a child." This type of questionnaire can be offensive and should not be used without first thoroughly explaining its purpose to clients. It also may be appropriate, depending on your setting, to include standardized symptom checklists or behavioral inventories as a part of a pretherapy questionnaire battery (although the purpose of these questionnaires should be explained to clients before administering them).

Institutional Setting

Often, information obtained in an initial interview is partly a function of agency or therapist policy. Some institutions, such as psychiatric hospitals, require diagnostic or historical information; other settings, such as health maintenance organizations, place greater emphasis on problem or symptom analysis, goal setting, and treat-ment planning. Your intake approach will vary depending on your employment setting.

Theoretical Orientation

The therapist's theoretical orientation can strongly influence both *what* infor-mation is obtained during an intake session and *how* it's obtained. Specifically, behavioral and cognitively oriented therapists tend to focus on current prob-lems, and psychoanalytic therapists downplay current problem analysis in favor of historical information. Person-centered therapists focus on the current situ-ation and how clients are feeling (e.g., whether any discrepancies exist between clients' real and ideal selves). Solution-oriented therapists focus on the future and dwell on potential solutions rather than laboriously examining past or current problems. Psychoanalytic, person-centered, and feminist therapists are also less likely to make use of detailed client registration forms, computerized interviewing procedures, or standardized questionnaires.

Professional Background and Professional Affiliation

Your professional background and professional affiliation can have a strong influence on what information is obtained in an intake interview. Before writing this book, we asked professionals from different backgrounds for their opinions about what was most needed in an interviewing textbook. The correlation between response content and respondents' areas of professional training was strikingly high. Psychiatrists emphasized the importance of mental status exam and diagnostic interviewing, based on the *DSM-IV-TR or DSM-5*. Clinical psychologists were interested in assessment and diagnosis as well, but they also emphasized problem assessment and behavioral and cognitive analysis. Counselors and counseling psychologists focused less on formal assessment and more on listening skills and helping strategies; clinical social workers expressed interest in psychosocial history taking, treatment planning, and listening skills. Marriage and family therapists stressed the importance of understanding the family and social systems and milieu of the client. Actually, addressing all these areas is important. Your training, theoretical orientation, and professional affiliations influence the major focus and proportion of attention paid in certain areas, but in reality, none of these areas should be systematically neglected.

BRIEF INTAKE INTERVIEWING

Given the current cost containment climate in health care, it's essential for therapists to be trained to conduct abbreviated intake interviews. Intake interview objectives remain the same when operating under a limited session philosophy. Obtaining information about clients' problems and goals, the clients themselves, and clients' current situation is essential. However, three primary modifications are necessary for obtaining this information within the usual employee assistance or managed care guidelines. First, therapists must rely more extensively on registration forms and questionnaire data obtained from clients before an initial meeting. Second, therapists must use more questions and permit less time for client-directed self-expression. Third, therapists must reduce time spent obtaining personal history and interpersonal style information. Because using registration forms and questionnaires and asking more questions are both relatively straightforward modifications, the following discussion focuses on how to briefly obtain personal history and interpersonal style information. We also provide an outline for conducting brief intake interviews (see Table 7.2).

Obtaining Historical and Interpersonal Style Information

Time-limited mental health philosophy involves placing responsibility for client well-being back on the client (Hoyt, 1996). In some ways this model empowers clients to make greater contributions to their own mental health. To stay within this model, when reviewing a client's history, you might say:

> We have only a few minutes to discuss your childhood and things that have happened to you in the past. So, very briefly, tell me, what are the most essential things I need to know about your past?

Often, when given this assignment, clients can successfully identify a few critical incidents in their developmental history. As an alternative, if therapists see clients for a second or follow-up session, they can ask for a one- to two-page biographical summary. This offers clients an opportunity to communicate essential historical information in a time-sensitive manner.

Information pertaining to client interpersonal style is minimally relevant when total sessions available are very limited. Therefore, although gathering information associated with client interpersonal dynamics may be a part of a time-limited intake, little or none of the therapist's time can be directly devoted to this task. Several approaches to dealing with this issue may be employed. First, interpersonal information may be ignored unless clients exhibit *DSM-5* personality disorder characteristics. In such cases, counselors can use a checklist to indicate whether a client exhibits interpersonal behaviors consistent with one or more of the three personality disorder clusters. If the presence of a personality disorder is suspected, further and more definitive assessment may be pursued, depending on the particular managed care policy.

Second, therapists may employ an abbreviated mental status examination format. In such cases, notes or reports about the client would briefly state the nature and quality of a client's "attitude toward the interviewer" (see Chapter 8 for detailed information regarding mental status examinations).

Third, therapists may reflect, after the session, on how they were affected by their client. After this reflection, some hypotheses can be generated and written down to assure that, if necessary, attention can be paid to further understanding of interpersonal dynamics during the next session.

A Brief Intake Checklist

A managed care or limited-session intake outline is included in Table 7.2. We recommend that you practice full-scale intake interviews as well as abbreviated intake interviews (see *Putting It in Practice* 7.2).

PUTTING IT IN PRACTICE 7.2

Prompting Clients to Stick With Essential Information

Using the limited-session intake-interviewing checklist provided in Table 7.2, work with a partner from class to streamline your intake interviewing skills. Therapists working in a managed care environment must stay focused and goal-directed throughout the intake interview. To maintain this crucial focus, it may be helpful to:

1. Inform your client in advance that you have only a limited amount of time and therefore must stick to essential issues or key factors.
2. If your client drifts into some less-essential area, gently redirect him or her by saying something such as:

"You know, I'd like to hear more about what your mother thinks about global warming (or whatever issue is being discussed), but
(continued)

> *(continued)*
> because our time is limited, I'm going to ask you a different set of questions. Between this meeting and our next meeting, I want you to write me an autobiography—maybe a couple of pages about your personal history and experiences that have shaped your life. If you want, you can include some information about your mom in your autobiography and get it to me before our next session."
>
> Often, clients are willing to talk about particular issues at great length, but when asked to write about those issues, they're much more succinct.
>
> Overall, the key point is to politely prompt clients to only discuss essential and highly relevant information about themselves. Either before or after practicing this activity with your partner, see how many gentle prompts you can develop to facilitate managed care intake interviewing procedures.

THE INTAKE REPORT

Report writing constitutes a unique challenge to clinicians. You must consider at least five dimensions:

1. Determining your audience.
2. Choosing the structure and content of your report.
3. Writing clearly and concisely.
4. Keeping your report confidential.
5. Sharing the report with your client.

Before discussing these dimensions, it should be emphasized that therapists have a responsibility to keep and maintain client records. Although this responsibility varies depending on your professional affiliation and theoretical orientation, failure to maintain appropriate records is unethical and, in some cases, illegal. The American Psychological Association's (2010) ethical code includes the following statement:

> Psychologists create, and to the extent the records are under their control, maintain, disseminate, store, retain, and dispose of records and data relating to their professional and scientific work. (p. 1067)

The American Counseling Association (2005) has an almost identical statement in its ethical code:

> Counselors maintain records necessary for rendering professional services to their clients and as required by laws, regulations, or agency or institution procedures. (p. 4)

The guidelines as written by the American Counseling Association and American Psychological Association imply a balancing act; they suggest, but don't

---

Table 7.2 A Brief Intake Checklist

When necessary, the following topics may be covered quickly and efficiently within a time-limited model.

☐ 1. Obtain presession or registration information from the client in a sensitive manner. Specifically, explain: "This background information will help us provide you with services more efficiently."

☐ 2. Inform clients of session time limits at the beginning of their session. This information can also be provided on the registration materials. All policy information, as well as informed consent forms, should be provided to clients prior to meeting with their therapist.

☐ 3. Allow clients a brief time period (not more than 10 minutes) to introduce themselves and their problems to you. Begin asking specific diagnostic questions toward the 10-minute mark, if not before.

☐ 4. Summarize clients' major problem (and sometimes a secondary problem) back to them. Obtain agreement from them that they would like to work on their primary problem area.

☐ 5. Help clients reframe their primary problem into a realistic long-term goal.

☐ 6. Briefly identify how long clients have had their particular problem. Also, ask for a review of how they have tried to remediate their problem (e.g., what approaches have been used previously).

☐ 7. Identify problem antecedents and consequences, but also ask clients about problem exceptions. For example: "Tell me about times when your problem isn't occurring. What happens that helps you eliminate the problem at those times?"

☐ 8. Tell clients that their personal history is important to you, but that there is obviously not time available to explore their past. Instead, ask them to tell you two or three critical events that they believe you should know about them. Also, ask them about (a) sexual abuse, (b) physical abuse, (c) traumatic experiences, (d) suicide attempts, (e) episodes of violent behavior or loss of personal control, (f) brain injuries or pertinent medical problems, and (g) current suicidal or homicidal impulses.

☐ 9. If you will be conducting ongoing counseling, you may ask clients to write a brief (two- to three-page) autobiography.

☐ 10. Emphasize goals and solutions rather than problems and causes.

☐ 11. Give clients a homework assignment to be completed before they return for another session. This may include behavioral or cognitive self-monitoring or a solution-oriented exception assignment.

☐ 12. After the initial session, write up a treatment plan that clients can sign at the beginning of the second session.

---

directly state, that written documents must meet standards set by more than one entity. This leads us to a discussion of the first challenge of report writing: Determining your audience.

Determining Your Audience

Consider this question: When you write an intake report, are you writing it for yourself, another professional, your client, your supervisor, and/or your client's insurance company? As you write, who might be looking over your shoulder?

Having a diverse audience may be the hardest part of report writing. For example, imagine giving your report to a supervisor. Depending on your supervisor, you might emphasize your diagnostic skills through a sophisticated discussion of your client's psychopathology or you might try using behavioral jargon such as "consequential thinking, response cost, and behavioral rehearsal." On the other hand, if you imagine your client reading your report, you may choose to avoid the behavioral jargon—and certainly you will deemphasize complex discussions of psychopathology (see *Multicultural Highlight* 7.1).

MULTICULTURAL HIGHLIGHT 7.1

Using Person-First and Constructive Language

For at least two decades there has been a strong movement within education, rehabilitation, and psychology toward using *person-first language*. This linguistic approach emphasizes the person first and his or her disability second. For example, instead of referring to an individual as "a visually impaired man," using person-first language we would say, "a man with a visual impairment."

Of course, like all new ideas or movements, person-first language has strong supporters and dissenters. For example, Jeanette Lim of the Office of Civil Rights (OCR) of the U.S. Department of Education issued a memorandum in support of person-first language in 1992, stating:

> the preference of individuals with disabilities to use phraseology that stresses the individuality of all children, youth, and adults, and then the incidence of a disability. In all our written and oral communications, care should be given to avoid expressions that many persons find offensive. (quoted in Bickford, 2004, pp. 120–121)

In contrast, the National Federation of the Blind wrote:

> We believe that it's respectable to be blind, and although we have no particular pride in the fact of our blindness, neither do we have any shame in it. To the extent that euphemisms are used to convey any other concept or image, we deplore such use. We can make our own way in the world on equal terms with others, and we intend to do it. (quoted in Bickford, 2004, p. 121)

To make matters even more complex, preliminary research indicates that people with disabilities often have either no preference for person-first versus disability-first language and sometimes report preferring disability-first language (Bickford, 2004).

As professionals who wish to be advocates for individuals in need of mental health services, we find this debate fascinating on many levels. Although we believe language has the potential to shift attitudes and increase consciousness, we also believe individuals with disabilities

(AKA: disabled individuals) have a right to reject a movement that some see as representing political correctness.

From another perspective, the domain of professional publications, our mandate is clearly articulated in the American Psychological Association's Publication Manual, which states: "[t]he guiding principle for 'nonhandicapping' language is to maintain the integrity of individuals and human beings. Avoid language that equates persons with their condition . . . ." (American Psychological Association, 2010, p. 69)

Somewhat surprisingly, we find that within the field of mental health, this issue may be less controversial. For example, we find it very important—and not particularly politically correct—to use terms like "the boy with ADHD" rather than "the ADHD boy." Somehow, at least for us, we consider it very important to always lead with the person when referring to individuals with mental disorders, even though it may be easier to speak using mental-disorder-first language.

Recently, we found a "case study" in a textbook that helped clarify our position on this issue. The case study was written using what we consider to be old-fashioned positivistic language that we tend to associate with medicine and psychiatry. For example, the following words and language were used: "Lois Carter, a chronically depressed European American woman, was torn with guilt over her perceived failure to rear a child who could function adequately at home and in school . . . Mrs. Carter's mother was a passive aggressive woman who turned to religion for comfort in her later years . . . . His mother was a pleasant though ineffectual woman . . . ."

For us, the language in this case study was too judgmental, too pejorative, and too conclusive. After reading this language we were able to clearly identify our position on person-first language. We find it very important to speak about clients and write reports about clients in ways that are respectful and that honor possibilities for change and growth and possibilities that we may be incorrect in our conclusions. When referring to mental health issues and diagnoses, we avoid "label-first" language and try to write and speak in all formal communications with enough respect that we wouldn't mind if the client or patient were to overhear our communication. Further, we believe it's inappropriate to give lifelong labels to individuals with mental health issues, when, given the longstanding problems of reliability and validity associated with psychiatric diagnosis, the lifelong labels may well be inappropriate (and limiting). On the other hand, although we lean toward using person-first language with individuals who have physical disabilities, we also remain open to respecting their views on how they prefer to be addressed or described.

After contemplating these issues, some beginning therapists throw up their hands in frustration and consider writing two versions of the same report. This solution might be fine, except that it requires too much extra work and, in the end, your client has a right to read whatever you write about him or her anyway (even the version of the report solely aimed at impressing your supervisor).

In the end, the answer to the question posed earlier, "Who's looking over your shoulder?" is this: Just about everybody. As you write, include the following list of people and agencies in your imagined audience:

- Your client
- Your supervisor
- Your agency administrator
- Your client's attorney
- Your client's insurance company
- Your professional colleagues
- Your professional association's ethics board
- Your state or local ethics board

After the preceding discussion, you should feel either motivated to write a carefully crafted intake report or flagrantly paranoid. We hope it's the former. For additional guidance regarding intake report writing, see *Putting It in Practice* 7.3: The Intake Report Outline, as well as the case example at the end of this chapter.

PUTTING IT IN PRACTICE 7.3

The Intake Report Outline

Use the following outline as a guide for writing a thorough intake report. Keep in mind that this outline is lengthy and, therefore, in practical clinical situations, you will need to select what to include and what to omit in your client reports.

Confidential Intake Report

NAME:	DATE OF BIRTH:
AGE:	DATE OF INTAKE:
INTAKE INTERVIEWER:	DATE OF REPORT:

I. Identifying Information and Reason for Referral
   A. Client name
   B. Age
   C. Sex
   D. Racial/Ethnic information
   E. Marital status
   F. Referral source (and telephone number, when possible)
   G. Reason for referral (why has the client been sent to you for a consultation/intake session?)
   H. Presenting complaint (use a quote from the client to describe the complaint)

II. Behavioral Observations (and Mental Status Examination).
   A. Appearance upon presentation (including comments about hygiene, eye contact, body posture, and facial expression)

B. Quality and quantity of speech and responsivity to questioning

C. Client description of mood (use a quote in the report when appropriate)

D. Primary thought content (including presence or absence of suicide ideation)

E. Level of cooperation with the interview

F. Estimate of adequacy of the data obtained

III. History of the Present Problem (or Illness)

A. Include one paragraph describing the client's presenting problems and associated current stressors.

B. Include one or two paragraphs outlining when the problem initially began and the course or development of symptoms.

C. Repeat, as needed, paragraph-long descriptions of additional current problems identified during the intake interview (client problems are usually organized using diagnostic—*DSM*—groupings, however, suicide ideation, homicide ideation, relationship problems, etc., may be listed).

D. Follow, as appropriate, with relevant negative or rule-out statements (e.g., with a clinically depressed client, it's important to rule out mania: "The client denied any history of manic episodes.").

IV. Past Treatment (Psychiatric) History and Family Treatment (Psychiatric) History

A. Include a description of previous clinical problems or episodes not included in the previous section (e.g., if the client is presenting with a problem of clinical anxiety, but also has a history of treatment for an eating disorder, the eating disorder should be noted here).

B. Description of previous treatment received, including hospitalization, medications, psychotherapy or counseling, case management, and so on.

C. Include a description of all psychiatric and substance abuse disorders found in all blood relatives (i.e., at least parents, siblings, grandparents, and children, but also possibly aunts, uncles, and cousins).

D. Also include a list of any significant major medical disorders in blood relatives (e.g., cancer, diabetes, seizure disorders, thyroid disease).

V. Relevant Medical History

A. List and briefly describe past hospitalizations and major medical illnesses (e.g., asthma, HIV positive, hypertension).

B. Include a description of the client's current health status (it's good to use a client quote or physician quote here).

C. Current medications and dosages.

(continued)

(*continued*)
      D. Primary care physician (and/or specialty physician) and telephone numbers.
  VI. Developmental History (This section is optional and is most appropriate for inclusion in child/adolescent cases.)
 VII. Social and Family History
      A. Early memories/experiences (including, when appropriate, descriptions of parents and possible abuse or childhood trauma)
      B. Educational history
      C. Employment history
      D. Military history
      E. Romantic relationship history
      F. Sexual history
      G. Aggression/Violence history
      H. Alcohol/Drug history (if not previously covered as a primary problem area)
      I. Legal history
      J. Recreational history
      K. Spiritual/Religious history
 VIII. Current Situation and Functioning
      A. A description of typical daily activities
      B. Self-perceived strengths and weaknesses
      C. Ability to complete normal activities of daily living
  IX. Diagnostic Impressions (This section should include a discussion of diagnostic issues or a listing of assigned diagnoses.)
      A. Brief discussion of diagnostic issues
      B. Diagnostic code and label from *ICD-10* or *DSM-5*
   X. Case Formulation and Treatment Plan
      A. Include a paragraph description of how you conceptualize the case. This description will provide a foundation for how you will work with this person. For example, a behaviorist will emphasize reinforcement contingencies that have influenced the client's development of symptoms and that will likely aid in alleviation of client symptoms. Alternatively, a psychoanalytically oriented therapist will emphasize personality dynamics and historically significant and repeating relationship conflicts.
      B. Include a paragraph description (or list) of recommended treatment approaches.

Choosing the Structure and Content of Your Report

The structure of your intake report varies based on your professional affiliation, professional setting, and personal preferences. For example, psychiatrists are more likely to emphasize medical history, mental status, and diagnosis, while social workers are more inclined to include lengthier sections on social and developmental history. The following suggested structure (and accompanying outline in *Putting It in Practice* 7.3) won't please everyone, but it can be easily modified to suit your particular needs and interests. Also, keep in mind that the following structure errs on the side of being thorough; abbreviated intake reports may be preferred.

Identifying Information and Reason for Referral

After listing client name, date of birth, age, date of the intake session, date of the report, and interviewer's name and professional credentials, most intake reports begin with a narrative section to orient the reader to the report. This section is typically one or two short paragraphs and includes identifying information and a summary of the reasons for referral. Psychiatrists usually label this initial section *Identifying Information and Chief Complaint*, but the substance of the section is essentially the same as described here. It might read something like:

> John Smith, a 53-year-old married Caucasian male, was referred for psychotherapy by his primary care physician, Nancy Jones, MD (509-555-5555). Dr. Jones described Mr. Smith as "moderately depressed" and as suffering from "intermittent anxiety, insomnia, and general distress associated with his recent job loss." During his initial session, Mr. Smith confirmed these problems and added that "troubles at home with the wife" and "finances" were furthering his overall discomfort and "shame."

Behavioral Observations (and Mental Status Examination)

The intake report begins with concrete, objective data and eventually moves toward more subjective therapist judgments. After the initial section, the intake report turns to specific behavioral observations. Depending on your institutional setting, these specific observations may or may not include a complete mental status report (i.e., if you're in a medical setting, inclusion of a mental status examination is more likely, and possibly required). However, because we discuss mental status examinations in the next chapter, the following example includes a basic description of the therapist's behavioral observations, with only minor references to mental status.

> Mr. Smith presented as a short and slightly overweight man who looked approximately his stated age. His hair looked greasy and unkempt and he had slight body odor. Mr. Smith's eyes were sometimes downcast and sometimes focused intensely on the therapist. He engaged in frequent hand wringing, and his crossed legs bounced continuously. He spoke deliberately, answering interview questions briefly and to the
> *(continued)*

> (*continued*)
> point; he responded directly to all therapist questions. He described himself as feeling "pathetic" and "hyper." He acknowledged suicidal ideation, but denied suicidal intent, stating, "I've thought about ending my life, but I'm the kind of person who would never do it." Mr. Smith was cooperative with the interview process; the following information is likely an accurate representation of his past and present condition.

History of the Present Problem (or Illness)

Traditionally, psychiatrists include a section in the intake report entitled, History of the Present Illness. This terminology reflects a medical model orientation and may or may not be a good fit for nonphysicians or appropriate for nonmedical settings. This section is for stating the client's particular problem in some detail, along with its unique evolution. The history and description of several problems may be included.

> Mr. Smith reported that he's been feeling "incredibly down" for the past 6 weeks, ever since being laid off from his job as a millworker at a local wood products company. Initially, after losing his job, Mr. Smith indicated he was "angry and resentful" at the company. For about two weeks, he aggressively campaigned against his termination and, along with several coworkers, consulted an attorney. After it became apparent that he would not be rehired and that he had no legitimate claim against the company, he went for two job interviews, but reported "leaving in a panic" during the second interview. Subsequently, he began having difficulty sleeping, started snacking at all hours of the day and night, and quickly gained 10 pounds. He also reported difficulty concentrating, feelings of worthlessness, suicide ideation, and minimal constructive activity during the course of a typical day. He stated: "I've lost my confidence. I got nothing to offer anybody. I don't even know myself anymore."
>
> When asked if he had previously experienced deep sadness or anxiety, Mr. Smith responded with, "Never." He claimed that this is the "first time" he's ever had any "head problems." Mr. Smith denied experiencing recurrent panic attacks and minimized the significance of his "panic" during the job interview by claiming "I was just getting in touch with reality. I don't have much to offer an employer."

Past Treatment (Psychiatric) History and Family Treatment (Psychiatric) History

For many clients, this section is brief or nonexistent. For others, it's extensive, and you may need to reference other records you've reviewed regarding the client. For example, you might simply make a summary statement such as: "This client has been seen previously by a number of mental health providers for the treatment of posttraumatic stress disorder, substance abuse, and depression" unless there is something in particular about the treatment that warrants specification (e.g., a particular form of treatment, such as "dialectical behavior therapy" was employed and associated with a positive or negative outcome). In this section, we also include information on any family history of psychiatric problems (although some report writers devote a separate section to this topic).

Mr. Smith has never received mental health treatment previously. In the referral note from his primary physician, it was acknowledged that he was offered antidepressant medications at his outpatient appointment, but refused to take them in favor of a trial of psychotherapy.

Initially, Mr. Smith reported that no one in his family had ever seen a mental health professional, but later admitted his paternal uncle suffered from depression and received "shock therapy" back in the 1970s. He denied the existence of any other mental problems with regard to both himself and his family.

Very little information was provided by Mr. Smith's primary care physician regarding his medical history. During the interview, Mr. Smith described himself as in generally good health. He denied having major illnesses or hospitalizations during his childhood or teen years. He noted that he rarely "gets sick" and that his employment attendance was exceptionally good. To the best of his recollection, his only major medical problems and associated treatments were for kidney stones (1996) and removal of a benign polyp from his colon (1998). He reported taking vitamins and glucosamine sulfate (for general health and joint pain), but currently does not take any prescription medications. Mr. Smith's primary care physician is Dr. Emil Rodriquez.

Mr. Smith was born and raised in Kirkland, Washington, a suburb of Seattle. He was the third of five children born of Edith and Michael Smith. His parents, now in their late 70s, have remained married and still live in the Seattle area, although they're beginning to experience significant health problems. Mr. Smith remains close to them, visiting several times a year and expressing concern about their well-being. He reported no significant conflicts or problems in his relationships with his parents or siblings.

Early childhood memories were characterized by Mr. Smith as "normal." He described his parents as "loving and strict." He denied any experiences or knowledge of sexual or physical abuse in his family of origin.

(continued)

(continued)

Mr. Smith attended school in his hometown and graduated from high school in 1977. He described himself as "an average student." He had some minor disciplinary problems, including numerous detentions (usually for failing to turn in his homework) and one suspension (for fighting on school grounds).

Following high school graduation, Mr. Smith moved to Spokane, Washington, and briefly attended Spokane Falls Community College. During this time, he met his eventual wife and decided to seek employment, rather than pursue college. He worked briefly at a number of jobs, including as a service-station attendant and roofer, eventually obtaining employment at the local wood-products plant. He reported working at the plant for 31 years. He emphasized that he has always been a hard worker and has never been fired from a job. Mr. Smith never served in the military.

In terms of overall demeanor, Mr. Smith indicated that he has always been (until recently) "friendly and confident." He dated a number of young women in high school and continued to do so after moving to Spokane. He met Irene, the woman he married, in 1977, shortly before turning 20 years old. He described her as "the perfect fit" and described himself as a happily married man. He denied any sexual difficulties, but acknowledged diminished sexual interest and desire over the past month or so. He stated that his "pathetic condition" following his job loss had put a strain on his marriage, but he believed his marriage is still strong.

Mr. Smith and his wife have been married for 37 years. They have three children (two sons and one daughter; ages 28 to 34), all of whom live within 100 miles of Mr. and Mrs. Smith. According to Mr. Smith, all of his children are doing fairly well. He reported regular contact with his children and seven grandchildren.

Mr. Smith occasionally got in "fights" or "scuffles" during his school years, but emphasized that such behavior was "normal." He denied ever using a weapon in a fight and reported that his most recent physical altercation was just after quitting college, "back when I was about 20."

Alcohol and drugs have never been a significant problem for Mr. Smith. He reported drinking excessively a number of times in high school and a number of times in college. He also noted that he went out with his buddies for "some beers" every Friday after work and that he also would have a few beers on Tuesdays, associated with his and his wife's participation in a bowling league. He briefly experimented with marijuana while enrolled in college, but claimed, "I didn't like it." He's never experimented with any "harder" drugs and denied any problems with prescription drugs, stating: "I avoid 'em when I can."

Other than a few speeding tickets (usually on the drive from Spokane to Seattle), Mr. Smith denied legal problems. His only nonvehicular-related citation was in his "college days" when he was cited for "disorderly conduct" while "causing a ruckus" outside a bar with a group of his "drinking buddies." He was required to pay a small fine and write a letter of apology to the business owner.

Mr. Smith reported that his favorite recreational activities include bowling, fishing, and duck hunting. He also acknowledged that he and his wife enjoy traveling together and gambling small amounts of money at casinos. He denied ever losing more money than he could "afford to lose" and said he does not consider his small-scale gambling to be a problem. He admitted that recently he has not been interested in "having any fun." Consequently, his involvement in recreational activities has been curtailed.

Mr. Smith was raised Catholic and reported attending church "off and on" for most of his life. He said he is currently in an "off" period, as he has not attended for about nine months. His wife attends regularly, but he indicates that his irregular attendance has not really been a problem in their relationship. He considers himself a "Christian" and a "Catholic."

Relevant Medical History

Depending on how much information you have obtained from your client's physician and on how closely you have covered this area during the intake, you may or may not have much medical history to include. At minimum, ask your client about (a) his or her general health, (b) any recent or chronic physical illnesses or hospitalizations, (c) prescription medications, and (d) when he or she last had a physical. Additionally, if you have the name (and telephone number) of your client's primary physician, include that information as well.

Developmental History

The developmental history begins before birth and focuses primarily on the achievement of specific developmental milestones. A developmental history is most appropriate when working with child or adolescent clients. We discuss the developmental history in Chapter 11.

Social and Family History

Writing a social and family history about your client can be like writing a full-length novel. Everyone's life takes many twists and turns; your goal, as a historian, is to condense the client's life into a tight narrative. Be brief, relevant, organized, and whenever possible, summarize or present highlights (or low spots) of the client's history. Once again, the depth, breadth, and length of your social/developmental history depend on the purpose of your intake and your institutional setting (topics to be covered are listed in *Putting It in Practice* 7.3).

Current Situation and Functioning

This section of the intake report focuses on three main topics: (1) usual daily activities, (2) client self-perception of personal strengths, and (3) apparent ability to adequately perform usual age-appropriate activities of daily living. Depending on your setting and preference, it's also possible to expand on this section by including a description of the client's psychological functioning, cognitive functioning, emotional functioning, or personality functioning. This provides the therapist with an opportunity to use more of a subjective appraisal of current client functioning in a variety of areas.

Currently, during a typical day, Mr. Smith rises at about 7 A.M., has coffee and breakfast with his wife, reads the newspaper, and then moves to the living room to watch the morning news. He indicated that he usually reads the "classified" section closely for job opportunities, circling the positions he may be interested in. However, after moving into the living room, he reports doing everything he can to avoid having to go out and seek employment. Sometimes he watches television, but he reports being too "pent up" to sit around too long, so he goes out to the garage or into his backyard and "putters around." He usually makes himself a sandwich or a bowl of soup for lunch and then continues his puttering. At about 5:30 P.M., his wife returns home from her job as an administrator at a local nonprofit corporation. Occasionally, she reminds him of his plans to get a new job, but Mr. Smith indicated that he usually responds with irritation ("It's like I try to bite her head off.") and then she retreats to the kitchen and makes dinner. After dinner with his wife, he "continues to waste time" by watching television until it's time to retire. His usual routine is interrupted on the weekends, often by visits from his children and grandchildren and sometimes when he and his wife venture out to a local casino to "spend a few nickels" (however, he indicated their weekend activities are diminishing because of tightening finances).

Mr. Smith sees himself as ordinarily having numerous personal strengths, although he needed prompting to elaborate on these. For example, he considers himself an honest man, a hard worker, and a devoted husband and father. He further believes he is a good buddy to several friends and fun to be around ("back when I was working and had a life"). In terms of intelligence, Mr. Smith claimed he is "no dummy" but that he is having some trouble concentrating and "remembering anything" lately. When asked about personal weaknesses, Mr. Smith stated, "I hope you got lotsa ink left in that pen of yours, Doc," but primarily focused on his current state of mind, which he described as "being a problem of not having the guts to get back on that horse that bucked me off."

Despite his poor hygiene and general lack of productiveness, Mr. Smith seems capable of adequately performing most activities of daily living. He reported occasionally cooking dinner, fixing the lawnmower, and taking care of other household and maintenance tasks. His perception, and it may be accurate, is that he is less efficient with most tasks because of distractibility and intermittent forgetfulness. His interpersonal functioning appears somewhat limited, as he described relatively few current outside involvements.

Diagnostic Impressions

For good reason, students are often reluctant to assign a diagnosis to clients. Nonetheless, most intake reports should include some discussion of diagnostic issues, even if you discuss only broad diagnostic categories, such as depression, anxiety, substance use, eating disorders, and so on. In some cases, clients will need a diagnosis in order to access their insurance benefits. Although simply listing your diagnostic considerations is acceptable in some circumstances and including a single psychiatric diagnosis is preferred by managed care companies, our preference is for a brief discussion of diagnostic issues followed by a *DSM-5* diagnosis. The brief discussion orients the reader to how you conceptualized your diagnosis, and it can even include an explanation of why you chose one particular diagnostic label over another. In the following case, we use Morrison's (2007) guidelines of assigning the least severe label that adequately explains the symptom pattern.

This 53-year-old man is suffering from an adjustment disorder. Although he meets the diagnostic criteria for major depression, I'm reluctant to assign this diagnosis because his depressive symptoms are associated with recent life changes and he has no personal and minimal family history of a mood disorder. Mr. Smith is also experiencing numerous significant anxiety symptoms, which may actually be more central than his depressive symptoms in interfering with his ability to seek new employment. Similarly, a case could also be made for assigning him an anxiety disorder diagnosis, but again, the abrupt onset of these symptoms is in direct association with his job loss suggests that his current mental state is better accounted for with a less severe diagnostic label.

His provisional ****DSM-5** diagnosis follows:

Axis I:	309.28 (DSM) or F43.23 (ICD) Adjustment Disorder with Mixed Anxiety and Depressed Mood (Provisional)
Rule Out (R/O)	296.21 (DSM) or F32.0 (ICD) Major Depressive Disorder, Single Episode, Mild

Note that in the preceding diagnosis we used a number of procedures provided by the *DSM* for indicating diagnostic uncertainty. Specifically, we used the "provisional" tag and included a "rule out" diagnostic possibility (major depression).

Case Formulation and Treatment Plan

For this section, include a paragraph description of how you conceptualize the case. This description provides you an opportunity to describe how you view the case and how you're likely to proceed in working therapeutically with this client. Not surprisingly, behaviorists describe their cases in behavioral terminology, while psychoanalytically oriented therapists describe their cases using psychoanalytic terminology. Generally, keep your theoretical jargon to a minimum, in case your client requests a copy of your intake report.

Mr. Smith is a stable and reliable individual who is currently suffering from severe adjustment to sudden unemployment. It appears that, for many years, much of his identity has been associated with his work life. Consequently, he feels depressed and anxious without the structure of his usual workday. Furthermore, his depression, anxiety, and lack of perceived constructive activities have considerably shaken his confidence. For a variety of reasons, he feels unable to go out and pursue employment, which, especially because of his strong values of normality and employment, further reduces his confidence in and respect for himself.

Psychotherapy with Mr. Smith should focus on two simultaneous goals. First, although it's impossible to provide him with new employment, it's crucial that Mr. Smith begin making a consistent effort to seek and obtain employment. It seems unrealistic to simply suggest to him (after 31 years of employment) that he reconstruct his identity and begin valuing himself as an unemployed person. The treatment objectives associated with this general goal include:

1. Analyze factors preventing Mr. Smith from following through on his daily job searches.
2. Develop physical anxiety coping strategies (including relaxation and daily exercise).
3. Develop and implement cognitive coping strategies (including cognitive restructuring and self-instructional techniques).
4. Develop and implement social coping strategies (including peer or spousal support for job-seeking behaviors).
5. Develop and implement social-emotional coping strategies. (Mr. Smith needs to learn to express his feelings about his personal situation to close friends and family without pushing them away through irritable or socially aversive behaviors).

The second general goal for Mr. Smith is to help him expand his identity beyond that of a man who is a long-term employee at a wood products company. Objectives associated with this second goal include:

1. Helping Mr. Smith recognize valuable aspects of relationships and activities outside an employment situation.
2. Helping Mr. Smith identify how he would talk with a person in a similar situation, and then have him translate that attitude and "talk" into a self-talk strategy with himself.
3. Exploring with Mr. Smith his eventual plans for retirement.

Although Mr. Smith's therapy will be primarily individually oriented treatment, it's recommended that his spouse accompany him to some sessions for assessment and support purposes. As he noted, there have been increasing conflicts in their relationship, and it should prove beneficial for them to work together to help him cope more effectively with this difficult and sudden life change.

Overall, it's important to encourage Mr. Smith to use his already-existing positive personal skills and resources to address this new challenge in his life. If, after 8 to 10 sessions using this approach, no progress has been attained, I will discuss the possibility of medication treatment and/or an alternative change in approach to his treatment.

Writing Clearly and Concisely

Writing a clear and concise intake report takes time and effort. Don't expect to sit down and write the report perfectly the first time. It may take several drafts before you get it to the point where you want anyone else to see it. We have several recommendations for making the writing process more tolerable.

- Write the report as soon as possible (immediately following the session is ideal; the longer you wait, the harder it's to reconstruct the session in your mind and from your notes).
- Write an immediate draft without worrying about perfect wording or style; then store it in a confidential location and return to it soon for editing.
- Closely follow an outline; although we recommend the outline in *Putting It in Practice* 7.3, following virtually any outline is better than simply rambling on about the client.
- Try to get clear information from your supervisor or employer about what's expected. If a standard format is available, follow it.
- If your agency has sample reports available, look them over and use them as a model for your report.
- Remember, like any skill, report writing becomes easier with practice; many seasoned professionals dictate a full intake report in 20 to 30 minutes—and someday you may do so as well.

Another issue associated with writing concisely involves choosing what information to put into your intake report. How brief and how detailed should you be? How much deeply personal information should be included in the report? Our position is to be only as detailed as is necessary and as can be accomplished while remaining respectful (see *Multicultural Highlight* 7.1).

Keeping Your Report Confidential

It's hard to overemphasize confidentiality. We all need to be reminded that our clients are disclosing personal information about their lives, and we need to treat that information like precious jewels. To help assure intake report confidentiality, we always type or stamp the word *CONFIDENTIAL* on our reports. This is no guarantee of confidentiality, but it's a step in the right direction.

Be sure to have an adequately secure place for storing client records. Don't leave your report on your desk or open on your computer where clients and unauthorized colleagues might accidentally discover it. Keeping your records stored securely is simpler if you keep paper records (a locked file drawer in a locked office should suffice).

Organizations and individuals relying on electronic systems for maintaining confidential records face unique problems and must closely adhere to the Health Insurance Portability and Accountability Act of 1996 (HIPAA). Information about HIPAA compliance is available widely on the Internet, in many books/journals, and addressed briefly in Chapter 15.

Sharing the Report With Your Client

Although clients have a legal right to access their medical-psychological-counseling records, its good practice to be careful when releasing a report directly to a client. Once again, it's a balancing act. Because of consumer rights, clients have a right to their records. On the other hand, some clients may misunderstand or misinterpret what you've written—meaning you can get yourself in trouble by releasing the information.

In most cases, we follow these guidelines:

- Inform clients at the outset of counseling that you will keep records and that they have access to them.
- When appropriate, inform clients that some portions of the records are written in language designed to communicate with other professionals; consequently, the records may not be especially easy to read or understand.
- If clients request their records, tell them you would like to review the records with them as you release the records, so as to minimize the possibility that the records are misinterpreted—you can even say that such a practice is suggested in your professional ethical guidelines.
- When clients request records, schedule an appointment (free of charge) with them to review the records together.
- If clients are no longer seeing you, are angry with you, or refuse to meet with you, you can (a) release the records to them without a meeting (and hope the records are not misinterpreted), or (b) agree to release the records *only* to another licensed professional (who will review them with the client).
- Whatever the situation, always discuss the issue of releasing records with your supervisor, rather than acting impulsively on your client's request.

When clients request to see their records, it's important to remain calm and acknowledge their rights. It's also important to have a procedure for sharing the records and to follow that procedure closely. Most clients will be satisfied if you treat them with compassion and respect *and* if your records about them are written in a compassionate and respectful manner (see *Multicultural Highlight* 7.1).

SUMMARY

The intake interview is probably the most basic type of interview that mental health professionals conduct. It involves obtaining information about a new client to identify what type of treatment, if any, is most appropriate. The intake is primarily an assessment interview, and usually involves the liberal use of questions.

The three major objectives of intake interviewing involve evaluating the client's: (1) current problems (perhaps psychiatric diagnosis) and goals, (2) personality, personal history, and mental condition, and (3) current situation.

Evaluating a client's problems and goals requires that therapists identify the client's main source of personal distress as well as the range of other problems contributing to the discomfort. Problems and goals need to be prioritized and selected for potential therapeutic intervention. Many theory-based assessment systems are available to help therapists analyze and conceptualize client symptoms. Usually, these systems involve identifying the factors or events that precede and follow occurrence of client symptoms.

Obtaining personal history information about clients is a sensitive and challenging process. Personal history flows from early memories to descriptions of parents and family experiences to school and peer relationships to employment. Therapists must be selective and flexible regarding the historical information they choose to obtain from their clients; there's always way too much historical information than can be covered in a single interview.

The last focus in an intake is the client's current functioning. Therapists should focus on current functioning toward the interview's end because it helps bring clients back in touch with their current situation, both liabilities and assets. The end of the interview should emphasize client personal strengths and social-environmental resources and focus on the future and on goal setting.

Client registration forms and intake questionnaires can help therapists determine in advance some of the areas to cover in a given intake. The therapist's theoretical orientation, therapeutic setting, and professional background and affiliation also guide the focus of intake interviews. An approach to providing an initial interview within managed care guidelines is outlined.

Writing the intake report is a major challenge for most therapists. When preparing an intake report, consider your audience, the structure and content of your report, how to write clearly and concisely, how you will keep the report confidential, and how you might share it with your client.

SUGGESTED READINGS AND RESOURCES

American Psychiatric Association. (2013). *Diagnostic and statistical manual of mental disorders* (5th ed.). Washington, DC: Author.

   The *DSM-5* was published in mid-May, 2013. Either the *DSM-5* or the World Health Organization's (WHO) *International Classification of Diseases, 9th Edition*, Clinical Modification (ICD-9-CM) should be used as a guide to formulating psychiatric diagnoses.

Davis, S. R., & Meier, S. T. (2001). *The elements of managed care: A guide for helping professionals*. Belmont, CA: Thomson Brooks/Cole.

   Davis and Meier provide counselors and psychotherapists with excellent guidance for navigating the often-turbulent seas of managed care and third-party payers.

Lazarus, A. A. (1976). *Multimodal behavior therapy*. New York, NY: Springer.

   This is Lazarus's classic text on multimodal behavior therapy in which he details his . BASIC ID model.

Lazarus, A. A. (2006). *Brief but comprehensive psychotherapy: The multimodal way*. New York, NY: Springer.

   This text is the most recent description of Lazarus's multimodal assessment and treatment model.

The Mental Status Examination

CHAPTER OBJECTIVES

Your professional identity as a mental health professional requires that you have skills to evaluate and communicate about client mental status. In this chapter, we focus on the basic components of a mental status examination (MSE).

After reading this chapter, you will understand:

- The definition of a mental status examination.
- Individual and cultural issues to consider during MSEs.
- Basic components of a mental status examination, including client appearance; behavior; attitude; affect and mood; speech and thought; perceptual disturbances; orientation and consciousness; memory and intelligence; and client reliability, judgment, and insight.
- When you do and don't need to administer a complete MSE.
- How to write brief MSE reports.

Historically, the mental status examination (MSE) has held a revered place in psychiatry and medicine. In recent years, professional competence in conducting MSEs has expanded to include all mental health professionals, especially those who work within medical settings. For example, the latest accreditation standards for professional counselors require coverage of MSE concepts and skills within master's level counseling programs (Council for Accreditation of Counseling and Related Educational Programs, 2009). Overall, the MSE offers physicians, psychotherapists, and counselors a unique method for evaluating the internal mental condition of patients or clients.

To assume we can quickly discern another human's mental status is both exciting and presumptuous. The excitement comes from being able to objectively analyze and rate another person's mental status in a wise and helpful way. On the other hand, the idea of quickly and accurately evaluating and articulating the mental functioning of someone (other than yourself) is a bit presumptuous.

There are some who make a point of trying to investigate the world we live in with full scientific rigour without becoming estranged from it. This is never easy: is it possible?

—R. D. Laing, *The Voice of Experience*

As Laing implies, complete detachment and emotional objectivity in the service of scientific investigation—especially investigation of the mind—is impossible. Why then, devote an entire chapter to the mental status examination?

Like it or not, mental health professionals sometimes must make judgment calls in situations that don't allow for long-term relationship development. It can be helpful and sometimes essential to have a structured or semi-structured interview protocol for evaluating clients and a standard format for communicating your evaluation results to other professionals. A system that's both objective and compassionate is needed for evaluating, rating, and understanding mental status.

OBJECTIVITY

Total objectivity requires complete emotional neutrality. Fritjof Capra in *The Tao of Physics* (Capra, 1975) articulated why neither total objectivity nor emotional neutrality is possible:

A careful analysis of the process of observation in atomic physics has shown that the subatomic particles have no meaning as isolated entities, but can only be understood as interconnections between the preparation of an experiment and the subsequent measurement.... In atomic physics, we can never speak about nature without at the same time speaking about ourselves. (p. 19)

Even in subatomic physics, human emotion and idiosyncratic beliefs influence and give meaning to what's observed. Mental status examiners are simultaneously participant and observer. It's impossible to completely detach yourself and objectively observe and evaluate clients. As an example, we're certain you can recall a time when someone's mood, or something someone said to you, affected you emotionally or even physically. Such is the nature of human interaction.

Objectively evaluating clients becomes even more complex when considering this: Not only can your mood or beliefs interfere with objective mental status evaluations—your mood or beliefs can also help you be a better evaluator! This is because it's possible to *use* your emotional connection and emotional reactions to help you more completely understand the person with whom you're working. Understanding how and why clients affect you (also known as countertransference) can be illuminating and helpful (Tryon & Winograd, 2011). The challenge of mental status evaluations is to balance emotional sensitivity with appropriate objective detachment.

WHAT IS A MENTAL STATUS EXAMINATION?

The mental status examination is a method of organizing and evaluating clinical observations pertaining to mental status or mental condition. The primary purpose of the MSE is to evaluate current cognitive processes (Strub & Black, 1977; Zuckerman, 2010). The MSE described in this chapter is a generic psychiatric model that focuses more on possible psychiatric diagnoses and less on neurological functioning. Other chapters in this text are devoted to the related topics of psychosocial history (Chapter 7), suicide assessment (Chapter 9), and diagnosis and treatment planning (Chapter 10).

For psychiatrists, the MSE is similar to the physical examination in general medicine (Siassi, 1984). In hospital settings, it's not unusual for admitting psychiatrists to request or administer daily MSEs for acutely disturbed patients. The results are reported in concise descriptions of approximately one medium-length paragraph per patient (see *Putting It in Practice* 8.1). Anyone seeking employment in the medical mental health domain should be competent in communicating client or patient mental status. This is why physician, psychotherapist, and counselor training all now include MSE skills. For example, Talley and Littlefield (2009) reported devoting about five instructional hours per medical student to teaching the MSE. Short mental status reports are used to communicate important information in a format commonly understood among professionals.

PUTTING IT IN PRACTICE 8.1

Mental Status Examination Reports

A good report is brief, clear, concise, and addresses all the areas described in this chapter. The following reports are provided as samples.

Mental Status Report 1

Gary Sparrow, a 48-year-old White male, was disheveled and unkempt upon arriving at the hospital emergency room. He wore dirty khaki pants, an unbuttoned golf shirt, and white shoes. He appeared slightly younger than his stated age. He displayed behaviors suggesting agitation, frequently changing seats. He was impatient and sometimes rude during this examination. Mr. Sparrow reported that today was the best day of his life, because he had decided to join the professional golf circuit. His affect was labile, but appropriate to the content of his speech (i.e., he became tearful when reporting he had "bogeyed number 15"). His speech was loud, pressured, and overelaborative. He exhibited loosening of associations and flight of ideas; he intermittently and unpredictably shifted the topic of conversation from golf, to the mating habits of geese, to the likelihood of extraterrestrial life. Mr. Sparrow described grandiose delusions regarding his sexual and athletic performances. He reported auditory hallucinations (God had told him to quit his job to become a professional golfer). He was oriented to time and place, but claimed he was the illegitimate son of Jack Nicklaus. He denied suicidal and homicidal ideation. He refused to participate in intellectual- or memory-related portions of the examination. Mr. Sparrow was unreliable and had poor judgment. Insight was absent.

(continued)

(*continued*)
Mental Status Report 2

Ms. Rosa Jackson, a 67-year-old African American female, was evaluated during routine rounds at the Cedar Springs Nursing Home. She was about 5 feet tall, wore a floral print summer dress, held tight to a matching purse, and appeared approximately her stated age. Her grooming was adequate and she was cooperative. She reported her mood as "desperate" because she had recently misplaced her glasses. Her affect was characterized by intermittent anxiety, generally associated with having misplaced items or with difficulty answering the examiner's questions. Her speech was slow, halting, and soft. She repeatedly became concerned with her personal items, clothing, and general appearance, wondering where her scarf "ran off to" and occasionally inquiring about whether her appearance was acceptable (e.g., "Do I look okay? You know, I have lots of visitors coming by later."). Ms. Jackson was oriented to person and place, but indicated the date as January 9, 1981 (today is July 8, 2009). She was unable to calculate serial sevens and after recalling zero of three items, became briefly anxious and concerned, stating "Oh my, I guess you pulled another one over on me, didn't you, sonny?" She quickly recovered her pleasant style, stating "And you're such a gem for coming to visit me again." Her proverb interpretations were concrete. Judgment, reliability, and insight were significantly impaired.

THE GENERIC MENTAL STATUS EXAMINATION

DVD Clip

In the *Mental Status Examination* DVD chapter, John and Rita briefly discuss components of a mental status examination and introduce the *John & Carl* MSE demonstration.

The main categories covered in a basic MSE vary slightly among practitioners and settings. This chapter includes the following categories:

1. Appearance
2. Behavior/psychomotor activity
3. Attitude toward examiner (interviewer)
4. Affect and mood
5. Speech and thought
6. Perceptual disturbances
7. Orientation and consciousness
8. Memory and intelligence
9. Reliability, judgment, and insight

During a mental status examination, observations are organized to establish hypotheses about the client's *current mental or cognitive functioning*. Although MSEs provide important diagnostic information and research on the reliability and validity of specific MSE protocols exist, administration of the exam is not primarily or exclusively a diagnostic procedure, nor is it considered a formal psychometric assessment process (Polanski & Hinkle, 2000; Zuckerman, 2010). Technically, MSEs are best classified as semistructured assessment interviews.

Individual and Cultural Considerations

Like all assessment procedures, MSEs are vulnerable to error. This is especially the case if an examiner lacks multicultural knowledge, sensitivity, or openness toward human diversity. To claim that client mental states are partly a function of culture is an understatement; culture can determine an individual's mental state. As captured by the following excerpt from Nigerian novelist Chinua Achebe (1994), perceptions of madness depend on cultural perspective:

> After the singing the interpreter spoke about the Son of God whose name was Jesu Kristi. Okonkwo, who only stayed in the hope that it might come to chasing the men out of the village or whipping them, now said:
> "You told us with your own mouth that there was only one god. Now you talk about his son. He must also have a wife, then." The crowd agreed.
> "I did not say He had a wife," said the interpreter, somewhat lamely . . .
> The missionary ignored him and went on to talk about the Holy Trinity. At the end of it Okonkwo was fully convinced that the man was mad. He shrugged his shoulders and went away to tap his afternoon palm-wine. (pp. 146–147)

Sometimes specific cultural beliefs, especially spiritual beliefs, sound like madness (or delusions) to outsiders. The same can be said about beliefs and behaviors associated with physical illness, recreational activities, and marriage and family rituals. In some cases, fasting might be considered justification for involuntary hospitalization, whereas in other cases, fasting—even for considerable time periods—is associated with spiritual or physical practices (Polanski & Hinkle, 2000). Overall, mental status examiners must sensitively consider individual and cultural issues before coming to conclusions about a client's mental state (for more on this, see *Multicultural Highlight* 8.2 toward the end of this chapter).

The Danger of Single Symptom Generalizations

As you read this chapter and gain knowledge about the potential diagnostic meaning of specific symptoms, you may find yourself tempted to make sweeping judgments about clients based on very little information. This is a natural and human temptation, and, like most temptations, it should be resisted. There are many examples in the professional literature of clinicians making idiosyncratic and inaccurate generalizations. In a book titled *The Mental Status Examination and Brief Social History in Clinical Psychology*, Smith (2011) stated:

> A Fu-Manchu mustache suggests the wearer doesn't mind being thought of as "bad," whereas a handlebar mustache tells you the person may be somewhat of a dandy or narcissist. (p. 4)

After reading the preceding excerpt, John decided to conduct a small research study by surveying men in Montana with Fu-Manchu mustaches. Whenever he saw men sporting a Fu-Manchu, he asked them to rate (on a 7-point Likert scale) whether they minded being thought of as "bad." In contrast to Smith's (2011) observations, John found that most men with Fu-Manchu's actually thought they looked good and reported wearing the mustache in an effort to be more attractive. Of course John didn't really conduct this survey, but the fact that he *thought* about doing it and *imagined* the results carries about the same validity as the wild assumption that a mental status examiner can quickly "get into the head of" all clients with Fu-Manchu (or handlebar) mustaches and accurately interpret their underlying personal beliefs or intentions or, even worse, assign a personality disorder diagnosis.

Although we're poking fun at Smith's (2011) overgeneralizations, our intent is to note how easy it is to grow overconfident when conducting MSEs. Like Smith, we've sometimes found ourselves making highly speculative assumptions about the psychopathological meaning of very specific behaviors (John reluctantly admits to developing his own personalized theory about "tanning" behaviors and narcissism years ago). The key to dealing with this natural tendency toward overconfidence is to use Stanley Sue's (2006) scientific-mindedness concept. A single symptom should be viewed as a sign that the sensitive and ethical mental status examiner considers as a hypothesis to explore.

Another example from Smith (2011) further illustrates the dangers of over-interpreting single symptoms. He stated: "If the person is unshaven, this may be a sign of depression, alcoholism, or . . . poor ability at social adaptation" (p. 4).

Smith may be correct in his hypotheses about unshaven clients. In fact, if a research study were conducted on diagnoses or symptoms commonly associated with unshaven-ness, it might show a small correlation with depressive symptoms, partly because poor hygiene can be associated with depression. However, in the absence of additional confirming evidence, an unshaven client is just an unshaven client. And when it comes to social adaptation, we should note that we know many young men (as well as a variety of movie stars) who consider the unshaven look as either desirable, sexy, or both. This could lead to an equally likely hypothesis that an unshaven client is particularly cool or has an especially high level of social adaptation.

In your own MSE work we encourage you to adopt the following three guidelines to avoid making inappropriate overgeneralizations based on minimal symptoms:

1. When you spot a single symptom or client feature of particular interest, begin the scientific-mindedness process.
2. Remember that hypotheses are hypotheses and not conclusions; this is why hypotheses require additional supporting evidence.
3. Don't make wild inferential leaps without first consulting with colleagues and/or supervisors; it's easier to become overconfident and to make inappropriate judgments when working in isolation.

Keep these preceding guidelines in mind as you review the nine generic mental status examination domains.

Appearance

When conducting MSEs, you should take note of your clients' general appearance. Observations are limited primarily to physical characteristics, but some demographic information is also included.

Physical characteristics commonly noted on a mental status exam include personal grooming (including the presence of particular mustache styles), dress, pupil dilation/contraction, facial expression, perspiration, make-up, body piercing, tattoos, scars, height, weight, and physical signs possibly related to nutritional status (Daniel & Gurczynski, 2010). Examiners should closely observe not only how clients look, but also how they physically react or interact. For example, Shea (1998) wrote: "The experienced clinician may note whether he or she encounters the iron fingers of a Hercules bent upon establishing control or the dampened palm of a Charlie Brown expecting imminent rejection" (p. 9).

A client's physical appearance is at least partially a manifestation of his or her mental state. Physical appearance also may be linked to psychiatric diagnosis. For example, dilated pupils are sometimes associated with drug intoxication and pinpoint pupils, with drug withdrawal. Of course, dilated pupils shouldn't be considered conclusive evidence of drug intoxication, but as one piece of the puzzle. Additional data are needed to confirm intoxication.

Client sex, age, race, and ethnic background are also concrete variables to note during a mental status exam. These factors can be related to psychiatric diagnosis and treatment planning. As Othmer and Othmer (2002) noted, the relationship between appearance and biological age may have significance. There are many reasons why clients might appear older than their stated age. An older appearance could be related to drug or alcohol abuse, severe depression, chronic illness, or a long-term mental disorder.

In a mental status report, a client's appearance might be described with the following narrative:

> **Sample Appearance Description:** Maxine Kane, a 49-year-old single, self-referred, Australian American female, appeared much younger than her stated age. She was very tall and thin and arrived for the evaluation wearing sunglasses, a miniskirt, spike heels, heavy makeup, and a contemporary bleached-blonde hairstyle.

A client's physical appearance may also be a manifestation of his or her environment or situation (Paniagua, 2010). In the preceding example, it would be important to know that Ms. Kane came to her evaluation appointment directly from her place of employment—the set of a television soap opera.

Behavior or Psychomotor Activity

Mental status examiners watch for excessive or limited body movements as well as physical movements, such as absence or excessiveness of eye contact (keeping cultural differences in mind), grimacing, excessive eye movement (scanning), odd or repeated gestures, and posture. Clients may deny experiencing particular thoughts or emotions (e.g., paranoia or depression), although their body movements suggest otherwise (e.g., vigilant posturing and scanning or slowed psychomotor activity and lack of facial expression).

Excessive body movements may be associated with anxiety, drug reactions, or the manic phase of bipolar disorder. Reduced movements may represent an organic brain condition, catatonic schizophrenia, or drug-induced stupor. Depression can manifest either via agitation or psychomotor retardation, although severe depression is more likely to include psychomotor retardation (Buyukdura, McClintock, & Croarkin, 2011; Iverson, 2004). Clients with paranoid symptoms may scan their visual field to be on guard against external threat. Repeated motor movements (such as dusting off shoes) may signal the presence of obsessive-compulsive disorder. Similarly, repeated picking of imagined lint or dirt off clothing or skin can indicate delirium or toxic reactions to drugs/medications.

As noted previously, each of the single symptoms or observations just described may or may not be linked to psychopathology. Many contextual factors, including the interview itself, can contribute to behaviors that look like they could represent a diagnostic condition. Another example from Smith (2011) helps illustrate the importance of considering symptom context.

> ...I have noticed, for example, that virtually every patient who has a rapid bob of the foot when she is in the exam, has a high degree of pathology. (p. 5)

In this situation the client could be nervous simply because her therapist has an unusually large handlebar mustache.

Sample Behavior/Psychomotor Activity Description: The client was grimacing and rocking throughout the interview. When asked about her rocking movements, the client responded, stating, "Really? I hadn't noticed."

Attitude Toward Examiner (Interviewer)

Attitude toward the examiner refers to how clients *behave* in relation to the interviewer. *Attitude* is defined as behavior that occurs in an interpersonal context. Attitudes also have affective components that may be tied to the client's evaluation of the situation or the examiner. When you think of the range of attitudes clients can exhibit during an interview (e.g., hostile, smug, ingratiating, etc.) it gives a "feel" to the complex cognitive, affective, and interpersonal components of an attitude.

Physical characteristics and movements provide a foundation for evaluating client attitude. Also, observations regarding client responsiveness to interviewer questions, including nonverbal factors such as voice tone, eye contact, and body posture, as well as verbal factors such as response latency and directness or evasiveness of response, all help interviewers determine their clients' attitude (n.b., speech and voice qualities are discussed later in this chapter).

Judgments about client attitude are particularly susceptible to interviewer subjectivity. For example, a male interviewer may infer seductiveness from the behavior of an attractive female because he wishes her to behave seductively, rather than actual seductive behavior. What's judged as seductive by an examiner may not be considered seductive by a client. Different individual or cultural backgrounds can cause differences in perception and judgment.

When describing client attitude, it's especially helpful to identify the observations supporting your description. In mental health settings, clinicians may be encouraged to use the concept of "as evidenced by" to support their statements (AEB; J. Swank, personal communication, August 7, 2012).

> **Sample Attitude Toward the Examiner Description:** The client's attitude toward the interview was hostile as evidenced by repeated eye-rolls, sarcastic comments, and intermittent use of the word "duh."

Words for describing client attitude toward the examiner are in Table 8.1.

Affect and Mood

Affect is the visible moment-to-moment emotional tone observed *by the examiner*. Observations of affect are typically based on nonverbal behavior. Affect is also referred to as an individual's outward expression of emotion (K. Hope, personal communication, October 7, 2012). In contrast, *mood* is the client's internal, subjective, verbal *self-report* of mood state (Serby, 2003).

Affect

Affect is usually described in terms of its (a) content or type, (b) range and duration (also known as variability and duration), (c) appropriateness, and (d) depth or intensity (Buyukdura et al., 2011; Iverson, 2004). Each of these descriptive terms is discussed further.

Affective Content. This involves identifying the client's affective state. Is it sadness, euphoria, irritability, anxiety, fear, anger, or something else? Affective content indicators include facial expression, body posture, movement, and voice tone. For example, if you see tears, accompanied by a downcast gaze and minimal movement (psychomotor retardation), you'll likely conclude your client has a "sad" affect. In contrast, clenching fists, gritted teeth, and strong language suggests an "angry" affect.

Although people use a wide range of feeling words in conversation, affect content usually can be accurately described using one of the following:

Angry	Guilty or remorseful
Anxious	Happy or joyful
Ashamed	Irritable
Euphoric	Sad
Fearful	Surprised

Table 8.1 Descriptors of Client Attitude Toward the Examiner

Aggressive: The client attacks the examiner physically or verbally or through grimaces and gestures. The client may "flip off" the examiner or simply say to an examiner something like, "That's a stupid question" or "Of course I'm feeling angry, can't you do anything but mimic back to me what I've already said?"

Cooperative: The client responds directly to interviewer comments or questions. There is a clear effort to work with the interviewer to gather data or solve problems. Frequent head nods and receptive body posture are common.

Guarded: The client is reluctant to share information. When clients are mildly suspicious they may appear guarded in terms of personal disclosure or affective expression.

Hostile: The client is indirectly nasty or biting. Sarcasm, rolling of the eyes in response to an interviewer comment or question, or staring off into space may represent subtle, or not so subtle, hostility. This behavior pattern can be more common among young clients.

Impatient: The client is on the edge of his seat. The client is not very tolerant of pauses or of times when interviewer speech becomes deliberate. She may make statements about wanting immediate answers to her concerns. There may be associated hostility and competitiveness.

Indifferent: The client's appearance and movements suggest lack of concern or interest in the interview. The client may yawn, drum fingers, or become distracted by irrelevant details. The client could also be described as apathetic.

Ingratiating: The client is overly solicitous of approval and interviewer reinforcement. He may try to present in an overly positive manner, or may agree with everything the interviewer says. There may be excessive head nodding, eye contact, and smiles.

Intense: The client's eye contact is constant, or nearly so; the client's body leans forward and listens closely to the interviewer's every word. Client voice volume may be loud and voice tone forceful. The client is the opposite of indifferent.

Manipulative: The client tries to use the examiner for his or her own purpose. Examiner statements may be twisted to represent the client's best interests. Statements such as "His behavior isn't fair, is it Doctor?" are efforts to solicit agreement and may represent manipulation.

Negativistic: The client opposes virtually everything the examiner says. The client may disagree with reflections, paraphrases, or summaries that appear accurate. The client may refuse to answer questions or be completely silent. This behavior is also called oppositional.

Open: The client openly discusses problems and concerns. The client may also have a positive response to examiner ideas or interpretations.

Passive: The client offers little or no active opposition or participation in the interview. The client may say things like, "Whatever you think." He may simply sit passively until told what to do or say.

Seductive: The client may move in seductive or suggestive ways. He or she may expose skin or make efforts to be "too close" to or to touch the examiner. The client may make flirtatious and suggestive verbal comments.

Suspicious: The client may repeatedly look around the room (e.g., checking for hidden microphones). Squinting or looking out of the corner of one's eyes also may be interpreted as suspiciousness. Questions about the examiner's notes or about why such information is needed may signal suspiciousness.

Range and Duration. Range and duration of affect varies depending on the client's current situation and the subject under discussion. Generally, emotional expression is associated with positive mental health (Nyklíček, Vingerhoets, & Denollet, 2002; Tsuchida, 2007). However, in some cases, affective or emotional expression can be too variable. For example, clients with mania or histrionic traits may show an excessively wide range of emotions, from happiness to sadness and back again, rather quickly. Clients with this emotional pattern are described as having a *labile affect*.

Sometimes clients exhibit little or no affect during the course of a clinical interview, as if their emotional life has been turned off. This absence of emotional display is commonly described as having a *flat affect*. The term is used to describe clients who seem unable to relate emotionally to other people. Flat affect may be present in clients diagnosed with schizophrenia, severe depression, or a neurological condition such as Parkinson's disease.

When clients take antipsychotic medications, they may show diminished affect. This condition, similar to flat affect, is often described as a *blunted affect* because an emotional response appears present under the surface, but is displayed in a restricted or minimal manner. In contrast, the term *constricted affect* is usually used when individuals appear to be constricting their own affect. For example, some individuals with compulsive personality traits may intentionally constrict their emotions because they don't like feeling or expressing emotion.

Appropriateness. The appropriateness of clients' affect is judged in the context of their speech content and life situation. Most often, inappropriate affect is observed in very disturbed clients suffering from severe mental disorders such as schizophrenia or bipolar disorder. Clients diagnosed with autism spectrum disorder also may exhibit inappropriate affect.

Determining appropriateness of client affect is subjective and can be more or less straightforward. For example, if a client is speaking about a tragic incident (e.g., the death of his child) and giggling and laughing without rational justification, the examiner would have evidence for concluding the client's affect was "inappropriate with respect to the content of his speech." However, some clients have idiosyncratic reasons for smiling or laughing or crying in situations where it seems inappropriate to do so. For example, when a loved one dies after a long and protracted illness, it may be appropriate to smile or laugh, for reasons associated with relief or religious beliefs. Similarly, clients from diverse cultures may be uncomfortable expressing emotion in a professional's presence and may appear unemotional. Caution is required when judging appropriateness of client affect, especially when interviewing clients with diverse cultural backgrounds (Hays, 2013).

Some clients exhibit a striking emotional indifference to their physical or personal situation. This condition, in which clients speak about profound physical problems with the emotional intensity that college students feel when reading textbooks, is referred to as *la belle indifférence* (French for "lofty indifference"). La belle indifference is most commonly associated with conversion disorder, somatization disorder, or dissociative disorder. Although research suggests this condition can be reliably identified, it may not accurately distinguish clients with mental disorders from clients with neurological deficits (Stone, Smyth, Carson, Warlow, & Sharpe, 2006).

Depth or Intensity. Examiners also describe client affect in terms of depth or intensity. Some clients appear profoundly sad, whereas others seem to experience a more superficial sadness. Determining the depth of client affect can be difficult, because many clients make strong efforts to "play their affective cards close to their vest." However, through close observation of client voice tone, body posture, facial expressions, and ability to quickly move (or not move) to a new topic, examiners can obtain at least some evidence regarding client affective depth or intensity. Nonetheless, we recommend limiting affective intensity ratings to situations when clients are deeply emotional or incredibly superficial.

When describing client affect in mental status reports, it's not necessary to discuss every possible affective dimension. It's common to describe affect content. The next most common dimension included is affective range and duration, with affective appropriateness and affective intensity included somewhat less often. A typical mental status report of affect in a client who is experiencing depression who exhibited sad affective content, a narrow band of expression, and speech content consistent with sad life circumstances, might be stated in this way:

> **Sample Affect Description I:** Throughout the examination, Ms. Brown's affect was occasionally sad, but often constricted. Her affect was appropriate with respect to the content of her speech.

In contrast, a client (Mr. Brown) who presents with manic symptoms might display the following affective signs:

Euphoric (content or type): referring to behavior suggestive of mania (e.g., the client claims omnipotence, exhibits agitation or increased psychomotor activity, and has exaggerated gestures).

Labile (range and duration): referring to a wide band of affective expression over a short time (e.g., the client shifts quickly from tears to laughter).

Inappropriate with respect to speech content and life situation (appropriateness): (e.g., the client expresses euphoria over job loss and marital separation; client's affective state is not rationally justifiable).

Shallow (depth or intensity): referring to little depth or maintenance of emotion (e.g., the client claims to be happy because "I smile" and "smiling always takes care of everything").

> **Sample Affect Description II:** Throughout the examination, Mr. Brown exhibited a labile, primarily euphoric affect with a tendency toward being inappropriate and shallow as evidenced by him moving from tears to laughter several times during the session.

Mood

Mood is defined as the client's self-report regarding his or her prevailing emotional state (Serby, 2003). Mood should be evaluated directly through a simple open-ended question such as, "How have you been feeling lately?" or "Would you describe your mood for me?" rather than a closed and leading question that suggests an answer: "Are you depressed?"

When asked about their emotional state, some clients respond with a description of their physical condition or a description of their current life situation. If so, simply listen and then follow up with, "And how about emotionally? How are you feeling about (the physical condition or life situation)?"

Verbatim recording of your client's response to your mood question is desirable. This makes it easier to compare a client's self-reported mood on one occasion with self-reported mood on another occasion. In addition, it's important to compare self-reported mood with client affect, especially because although mood is a more prevailing emotional state, many clients will note that their mood shifts somewhat rapidly. Self-reported mood should also be compared with self-reported thought content, because thought content may account for the predominance of a particular mood (this is discussed in the next section).

Mood can be distinguished from affect on the basis of several features. Mood tends to last longer than affect. Mood changes less spontaneously than affect. Mood constitutes the emotional background. Mood is reported by the client, whereas affect is observed by the interviewer (Othmer & Othmer, 2002). Put another way (for you analogy buffs), mood is to affect as climate is to weather.

In mental status reports, client mood is typically included as a client quote.

Sample Mood Description I: The client reported, "I feel miserable, unhappy, and angry most of the time."

Mood also can be evaluated in greater detail using a scaling technique (see the Appendix). After obtaining a general description of mood, clients are asked to rate their (a) current mood, (b) their normal mood, (c) their lowest mood in the past two weeks, and (d) their highest mood in the past 2 weeks. To initiate the scaling process, you might ask: "On a scale from 0 to 10, where 0 is the worst possible mood you could experience and 10 is the best possible mood, what would you rate your mood *right now*?" Specific follow-up questions consistent with DSM-5 (APA, 2013) depressive disorder diagnoses can be integrated into this portion of the MSE.

After obtaining mood ratings, additional follow-up questions may be asked, such as, "What's going on right now that makes you rate your mood as a 4?" or "What's happening that makes you so happy (or sad) right now?" Despite the fact that the purpose of these questions is to rate client mood, effective mental status examiners will take time to respond empathically. When writing the mental status section on mood, it also may be appropriate (depending on your setting, the client's symptoms, and your inclination) to include a more detailed description of client mood as in the example below.

Sample Mood Description II: The client's current mood rating was a 4 on a 0–10 scale. His reported his 2-week low as a 3 and his 2-week high as a 5 and noted this range of 3 to 5 is pretty normal for him. He described experiencing significant irritability most of the time rather than sadness.

> **DVD Clip**
>
> In the *John & Carl, Part One* MSE demonstration, John introduces the MSE and evaluates Carl's orientation and consciousness, his immediate memory, and his affect and mood.

Speech and Thought

In mental status exam formulations, speech and thought are intimately linked. This is partly because mental status examiners observe and evaluate thought process and content primarily through observing client speech. There are, however, other ways for interviewers to observe and evaluate thought processes. Nonverbal behavior, sign language (in deaf clients), and writing also provide valuable information about thinking processes. Speech and thought are evaluated both separately and together.

Speech

Speech is ordinarily described in terms of rate and volume. *Rate* refers to the observed speed of a client's speech. *Volume* refers to how loud a client talks. Both rate and volume can be categorized as:

High (fast or loud)
Normal (medium or average)
Low (slow or soft)

Client speech is usually described as pressured (high speed), loud (high volume), slow or halting (low speed), or soft or inaudible (low volume). When client speech is judged as within normal limits, it's generally written, "The client's speech was of normal rate and volume."

Speech that occurs without much direct prompting or questioning is usually described as spontaneous. Clients with *spontaneous* speech provide easy access to their internal thought processes. However, some clients are naturally less verbal or may resist speaking openly. When clients provide little verbal material they're described as exhibiting *poverty of speech*. Clients who respond slowly to questions may be described as having increased response *latency*. Although increased speech rate and volume may be associated with mania or aggressive tendencies and decreased speech rate and volume may be linked to depression or passivity, there are many other possible explanations as well. For example, both age (e.g., older client's may process questions more slowly) and language fluency (e.g., clients speaking a second or third language) can reduce speech rate and volume.

Distinct speech qualities or speech disturbances also should be noted. These may include accents, high or low pitch, and poor or distorted enunciation. Specific speech disturbances include:

- *Dysarthria*: Problems with articulation (e.g., mumbling) or slurring of speech.
- *Dysprosody*: Problems with rhythm, such as mumbling or long pauses or latencies between syllables.
- *Cluttering*: Rapid, disorganized, and tongue-tied speech.
- *Stuttering*: Halting speech with frequent repetition of sounds.

Dysarthria, dysprosody, and cluttering can be associated with specific brain disturbances or drug toxicity; for example, mumbling may occur in patients with Huntington's chorea and slurring of speech in intoxicated patients. Many other distinctive deviations from normal speech are possible, including a rare condition referred to as "foreign accent syndrome." This syndrome, thought to be caused by brain damage, causes individuals to speak with a non-native accent. There is some question about whether the individual really has adopted a "foreign" accent or whether the individual's pitch and prosody have been affected in ways that lead others to perceive a particular foreign accent (Kanjee, Watter, Sévigny, & Humphreys, 2010).

Thought Process

Observation and evaluation of thought is usually divided into two broad categories: thought process and thought content. *Thought process* refers to *how* clients express themselves. In other words, does thinking proceed in an organized and logical manner? It's useful to obtain a verbatim sample of client speech to capture psychopathological processes. The following sample is from a client's letter to his therapist, who was relocating to seek further professional education.

> Dear Bill:
> My success finally came around and I finally made plenty of good common sense with my attitude and I hope your sister will come along just fine really now and learn maybe at her elementary school whatever she may ask will not really develop to bad a complication of any kind I don't know for sure whether you're married or not yet but I hope you come along just fine with yourself and your plans on being a doctor somewhere or whatever or however too maybe well now so. I suppose I'll be at one of those inside sanitariums where it'll work out ... and it'll come around okay really, Bye for now.

This client's letter illustrates a thought process dysfunction. His thinking is disorganized and minimally coherent. Initially, his communication is characterized by a loosening of association. Interestingly, after writing the word *doctor*, the client decompensates into complete incoherence or word salad (see Table 8.2 for common MSE thought process descriptors).

Sometimes clients from nondominant cultures have difficulty responding to MSE questions. For example, as noted by Paniagua (2001), "Clients who are not fluent in English would show thought blocking" (p. 34). If interviewers ignore culture and language issues, they might incorrectly conclude that response latency indicates anxiety, schizophrenia, or depressive symptoms. This conclusion would be inaccurate for many cultural groups including

> African American clients who use Black English in most conversational contexts [and who] would ... spend a great deal of time looking for the construction of phrases or sentences in Standard American English when they feel that Standard American English is expected. (Paniagua, 2001, p. 34)

Table 8.2 Thought Process Descriptors

Blocking: Sudden cessation of speech in the midst of a stream of talk. There is no clear reason for the client to stop talking and little explanation. Blocking may indicate that the client was about to associate to an uncomfortable topic. It also can indicate intrusion of delusional thoughts or hallucinations.

Circumstantiality: Excessive and unnecessary detail provided by the client. Very intellectual people (e.g., college professors) can become circumstantial; they eventually make their point, but don't do so directly and efficiently. Circumstantiality or overelaboration may be a sign of defensiveness and can be associated with paranoid thinking styles. (It can also simply be a sign the professor was not well-prepared for the lecture.)

Clang Associations: Combining unrelated words or phrases because they have similar sounds. Usually, this is manifest through rhyming or alliteration; for example: "I'm slime, dime, do some mime" or "When I think of my dad, rad, mad, pad, lad, sad." Some clients who clang are also perseverating (see below). Clanging usually occurs among very disturbed clients (e.g., schizophrenics). As with all psychiatric symptoms, cultural norms may prompt the behavior (e.g., clang associations among rappers is normal).

Flight of Ideas: Speech in which the client's ideas are fragmented. Usually, an idea is stimulated by either a previous idea or an external event, but the relationship among ideas or ideas and events is weak. In contrast to loose associations (see below), there are logical connections in the client's thinking. However, unlike circumstantiality (see above), the client never gets to the point. Clients who exhibit flight of ideas often appear overactive or overstimulated (e.g., mania or hypomania). Many normal people exhibit flight of ideas after excessive caffeine intake—including one of the authors.

Loose Associations: Minimal logical connections between thoughts. The thinking process is nearly, but not completely random; for example: "I love you. Bread is the staff of life. Haven't I seen you in church? I think incest is horrible." In this example, the client thinks of attraction and love, then of God's love as expressed through communion, then of church, and then of an incest presentation he heard in church. It may take effort to track the links. Loose associations may indicate schizotypal personality disorder, schizophrenia, or other psychotic or prepsychotic disorders. Extremely creative people also regularly exhibit loosening of associations, but are able to find a socially acceptable vehicle through which to express their ideas.

Mutism: Virtually total unexpressiveness. There may be signs the client is in contact with others, but these are usually limited. Mutism can indicate autism or schizophrenia, catatonic subtype. Mutism may also be selective in that young clients will be able to speak freely at home, but become mute and apparently unable to speak at school or with professionals.

Neologisms: Client-invented words. They're often spontaneously and unintentionally created and associated with psychotic disorders; they're products of the moment rather than of a thoughtful creative process. We've heard words such as "slibber" and "temperaturific." It's important to check with the client with regard to word meaning and origin. Unusual words may be taken from popular songs, television shows, or a product of combining languages.

> **Table 8.2   (Continued)**
>
> *Perseveration*: Involuntary repetition of a single response or idea. The concept of perseveration applies to speech and/or movement. Perseveration is often associated with brain damage and psychotic disorders. After being told no, teenagers often engage in this behavior, although normal teenagers are being persistent rather than perseverative; that is, if properly motivated, they're able to stop themselves voluntarily.
>
> *Tangential speech*: Tangential speech is similar to loose associations, but connections between ideas are even less clear. Tangential speech is different from flight of ideas because flight of ideas involves pressured speech.
>
> *Word Salad*: A series of unrelated words. Word salad indicates extremely disorganized thinking. Clients who exhibit word salad are incoherent. (See the second half of the preceding "Dear Bill" letter for an example of word salad.)

Thought Content

Thought content refers to what clients talk about. *Thought process* constitutes the *how* of client thinking. What clients talk about can give interviewers valuable information about mental status.

Clients can talk about an unlimited array of subjects during an interview. However, during a mental status exam, several specific content areas should be explored. These include delusions, obsessions, and suicidal or homicidal thoughts or plans. Because we cover suicide assessment in Chapter 9, the remainder of this section focuses on evaluating for delusions and obsessions.

Delusions are defined as false beliefs. They're not based on facts or real events or experiences and thus represent a break from reality. For a particular belief to be a delusion it must be outside the client's cultural, religious, and educational background. Examiners should not directly dispute delusional beliefs. Instead, a question that explores a client's belief may be useful: "How do you know this [the delusion] is the case?" or "I was wondering how you first began to notice this voice speaking to you" (Robinson, 2007, p. 239).

Clients can develop different types of delusions. *Delusions of grandeur* are false beliefs pertaining to a person's ability or status. Clients with delusions of grandeur believe they have extraordinary mental powers, physical strength, wealth, or sexual potency. They're usually unaffected by discrepancies between their beliefs and objective reality. Sometimes grandiose clients believe they're a specific historical or contemporary figure (Napoleon, Jesus Christ, and Joan of Arc are common historical figures).

Clients with *delusions of persecution* or *paranoid delusions* hold false beliefs that others are out to get them. Clients may falsely believe their home or telephone is bugged or that they're under FBI surveillance. Clients with paranoid delusions often have *ideas of reference*, which involves an erroneous belief that unrelated events are referring to them. Cognitive therapists sometimes refer to this as personalization. For example, paranoid clients sometimes believe the television, newspaper, or radio is referring to them. One hospitalized patient with whom we worked complained bitterly that the television news was broadcasting his life story every night and humiliating him in front of the rest of the patients.

Clients who believe they're under the control or influence of an outside force or power are experiencing *delusions of alien control*. Symptoms usually involve a disowning of personal volition. A client might report feeling as if he or she is a puppet, passive and unable to assert personal control. In years past, it was popular to report being controlled by the Russians or Communists; in recent years, the Russians are out and we've observed a greater frequency of delusions about being possessed, abducted by aliens, having body doubles, or being controlled by supernatural or alien forces.

Somatic delusions involve false beliefs about medical conditions. Somatic delusions may involve a traditional illness or condition (e.g., AIDS or pregnancy) or an idiosyncratic physical condition. A case reported in the literature involved a man who "believed that his internal organs were not functioning, that his heart stopped beating, and that his heart was displaced to the right side of his chest" (Kotbi & Mahgoub, 2009, p. 320). Like all delusions, somatic delusions can incorporate current events or recent medical discoveries (Hegarty, Catalano, & Catalano, 2007).

About 25% of hospitalized patients with depression and 15% of outpatients diagnosed with depression report delusions (Maj, 2008). These often include *delusions of self-deprecation*. Clients with depression may hold tightly to the belief that they're the "worst case ever" or that their skills and abilities are grossly impaired (even when they're not impaired). Common self-deprecating comments include statements about sinfulness, ugliness, and stupidity.

It may or may not be important to seek factual evidence to determine the validity of a client's apparent delusions. Whether such information is sought depends primarily on the clinical and diagnostic situation. However, clients with somatic delusions should be examined by a physician to rule in or rule out the presence of a medical condition.

Exploring delusional beliefs can help mental status examiners develop hypotheses about psychodynamics underlying client symptoms. For example, a client who claims "alien forces" are making him shout obscenities at his parents may feel controlled by them and finds it less threatening to disown his angry impulses. Similarly, a grandiose client may feel unimportant and may compensate by developing a belief (delusion) of having special importance (e.g., "I am Jesus Christ"). Interpersonal dynamics combined with a client's particular genetic and biological predisposition may combine to produce unique delusional content.

On the other hand, we must also entertain the possibility that client delusions are primarily a function of bio-genetic factors rather than psychological dynamics. For example, the young man who believes the aliens are forcing him to shout obscenities at his parents may have Tourette's disorder (APA, 2013) and an otherwise positive relationship with his parents.

Obsessions

Obsessions are recurrent and persistent ideas, thoughts, and images. True obsessions are experienced as involuntary, cause distress or impairment, and are viewed as excessive or irrational *even by those who are experiencing them.*

Clients may worry or intentionally ruminate about a wide variety of issues, but obsessions are beyond normal worry or neurotic rumination. One obsessive-compulsive client with whom we worked had intrusive obsessive thoughts that his car would roll away even when parked in a flat parking lot. To deal with these thoughts he developed ritualistic *compulsions* wherein he would check and reset his parking brake seven times before leaving his car.

More typically individuals with compulsions exhibit either *washing* or *checking* behaviors. Clients who engage in compulsive washing are usually responding to thoughts or fears of infection or contamination. Clients who engage in compulsive checking behavior are usually responding to thoughts or fears about an intruder, gas leak, kitchen fire, etc. Obsessions are often characterized by a sense of doubt. Clients with obsessive-compulsive disorder often wonder:

- Are my hands clean?
- Have I been contaminated?
- Did I remember to lock the front door?
- Did I remember to turn off the oven (lights, stereo, etc.)?
- Is anyone under my bed?

Although everyone experiences obsessive thoughts on occasion, such thoughts may or may not be clinically or diagnostically significant. Information is of *clinical* significance if it contributes to the treatment process; information is of *diagnostic* significance if it contributes to the diagnostic process. During a mental status exam, it's important to evaluate obsessions because they reveal what the client spends time thinking about. Such information may be clinically significant; it may enhance empathy and treatment planning. However, the same obsessions may or may not be diagnostically significant. For example, if a client describes occasional obsessions or compulsions—such as always feeling compelled to count the number of stairs climbed—that don't interfere with his or her ability to function at work, school, home, or play, they may not be diagnostically significant. These are referred to as "normal obsessions" (Rassin, Cougle, & Muris, 2007; Rassin & Muris, 2007).

Questions that can be used to assess for obsessive thoughts include:

- Do you ever have repeated thoughts that you find are very difficult to get out of your mind?
- Do you ever engage in repeated behavior to calm your anxiety, such as checking the locks of your house or washing your hands?
- You know how sometimes people get a song or tune stuck in their head and they can't stop thinking about it? Have you ever had that kind of experience?"

Anxiety is at the heart of obsessive-compulsive disorder as well as many other psychiatric diagnoses. Anxiety, followed by obsessive and compulsive behavior may or may or may not indicate obsessive-compulsive disorder. For example, a client who experienced trauma (e.g., sexual assault) may also display obsessive anxiety and engage in compulsive behavior in efforts to assure her safety. In this case, the client may (or may not) experience a significant reduction of anxiety as a function of her compulsive behaviors. The point is that the client is likely experiencing post-traumatic stress and not an obsessive-compulsive disorder.

> **Sample Speech and Thought Description:** The client's speech was loud and pressured. Her communication was sometimes incoherent; she exhibited flight of ideas and neologisms as evidenced by her inability to stay on topic and use of words such as "Whaddingy" and "Ordinarrational." She didn't respond coherently to questions about obsessions, but appeared preoccupied with the contents of a small notebook.

Perceptual Disturbances

Perceptual disturbances involve difficulties in the perception and interpretation of sensory input. Understanding the nature of clients' perceptual disturbances can be helpful in establishing a diagnosis. Three major perceptual disturbances (i.e., hallucinations, illusions, and flashbacks) are described next.

Hallucinations

Hallucinations are false sensory impressions or experiences that exist in the absence of external sensory stimuli. Hearing voices in the absence of auditory sensory input is the most common hallucination type. Hallucination content may be diagnostically relevant. For example, clients experiencing depression may have hallucinations that come in the form of voices repeatedly offering insulting commentary (e.g., "You're nothing but worthless scum. You should just die.").

Hallucinations may occur in any of the five major sensory modalities: visual, auditory, olfactory, gustatory, and tactile. Auditory hallucinations are most common and usually associated with a mood disorder (i.e., extreme mania; severe depression) or schizophrenia. However, auditory hallucinations also may be linked to chemical intoxication or acute traumatic stress. In less severe cases clients may report having especially good hearing or they may report listening to their own "inner voice." Although such reports are worth exploring, they're not necessarily perceptual disturbances.

Visual or tactile hallucinations are usually linked to organic conditions (Tombini et al., 2012). These conditions may include drug intoxication or withdrawal, brain trauma, Parkinson's, or other brain diseases. Clients in acute delirious states may pick at their clothes or skin in an effort to remove objects or organisms. They may believe insects are crawling on them and producing their sensory experiences. Similarly, clients may reach out or call out for people or objects that don't exist. When clients report these experiences or you observe these perceptual disturbances, the disorder is usually of a very serious nature.

Some clients will report having odd perceptual experiences while falling off to sleep or upon awakening. A common example involves seeing someone at the foot of the bed when falling asleep, sometimes accompanied by feelings of paralysis. Although frightening, these perceptual disturbances are naturally occurring phenomena during the hypnogogic (sleep onset) or hypnopompic (sleep termination) sleep stages (Cheyne & Girard, 2007). When evaluating for hallucinations, you should determine *when* such experiences usually occur. If they're linked to sleep onset or termination, they're less diagnostically relevant.

Illusions

Illusions are perceptual distortions. They're based on sensory input and technically involve misperceptions. For example, if you misperceive a coat hanging on the back of a door for an intruder, you're experiencing an illusion. Illusions can be more persistent or more transient—as in the case when you quickly realize the feared intruder isn't actually an intruder, but instead a harmless coat hanging on the door.

Although auditory hallucinations are typically associated with mood disorders or schizophrenia, illusions are more difficult to link with specific mental disorders. This might be because many people within the normal range of functioning have unusual beliefs and experiences that involve their creative imaginations.

Flashbacks

Flashbacks are a core symptom of post-traumatic stress disorder (PTSD). They consist of sudden and vivid sensory-laden recollections of previous experiences. Flashbacks are typically triggered by current sensory input (Kroes, Whalley, Rugg, & Brewin, 2011; Muhtz, Daneshi, Braun, & Kellner, 2010). For example, it's not unusual for war veterans to have flashbacks triggered when they hear or see firecrackers or fireworks. Similarly, sexual-abuse survivors may experience flashbacks in response to certain forms of touch, smells, or voice tones. Flashbacks may be fleeting and mild; but they also may be lengthy, dissociative episodes wherein an individual acts as if he or she were reliving the traumatic experience for "several hours or even days" (see *DSM-5*, p. 275).

Flashbacks are typically related to trauma, so distinguishing between flashbacks and other perceptual disturbances (illusions or hallucinations) is diagnostically important. Flashbacks are commonly associated with other PTSD symptoms, such as nightmares, hyperarousal, emotional numbing, avoidance of triggering stimuli, and high anxiety levels.

Asking Clients About Perceptual Disturbances

Clients can be reactive to inquiries about delusions, hallucinations, or flashbacks. Be especially sensitive and gentle when asking about these experiences. Robinson (2007) suggested a three-part approach that includes:

1. *Greasing the wheels* to help the patient feel comfortable sharing information.
2. *Uncovering the logic* associated with the delusional material.
3. *Determining the client's insight* and how much distance he/she has from the symptom.

Robinson (2007) provided sample questions for exploring delusions:

- I'm interested in what you just said; please tell me more. (Greasing the wheels)
- How did this all start? (Greasing the wheels)
- What has happened so far? (Uncovering the extent and logic)
- Why would someone want to do this to you? (Uncovering the extent and logic)
- How do you know that this is the situation? (Determining distance)

- How do you account for what has taken place? (Determining distance) (Robinson, 2007, pp. 239–240)

The following interview dialogue provides an example of how you might help a client talk about unusual or bizarre experiences:

Interviewer:	I'm going to ask a few questions about experiences you may or may not be having. Some of these questions may seem odd, but others may fit personal experiences you've had but haven't yet spoken about.
Client:	Okay.
Interviewer:	Sometimes radio broadcasts or television newscasts or programming can feel very personal, as if the people in them were speaking directly to you. Have you ever thought a particular program was talking about you or to you on a personal basis?
Client:	That program the other night was about my life. It was about me and Taylor Swift.
Interviewer:	You know Taylor Swift?
Client:	I sure do; she's my woman.
Interviewer:	And how did your relationship with her start?
Client:	She wrote a song about me, and I got in touch with her.

This next portion models an evaluation for auditory perceptual disturbances, with a similar check for visual hallucinations or illusions:

Interviewer:	I've noticed you seem to be a pretty observant person. Is your hearing especially good?
Client:	Yes, as a matter of fact, I have better hearing than most people.
Interviewer:	Really? What can you hear that most people can't hear?
Client:	I can hear voices right now, coming through the wall.
Interviewer:	Really. What are the voices saying?
Client:	They're talking about me and Taylor . . . about our sex life.
Interviewer:	How about your vision? Do your eyes ever play tricks on you?

The next dialogue models methods for exploring client flashbacks:

Interviewer:	It's not unusual for individuals who have been through very difficult circumstances, like you, to sometimes have thoughts or images from the past come into the present. Have you noticed this happening?
Client:	It's terrible. Sometimes it's just like I was there all over again with my buddy and we're getting jumped and shot and stabbed.
Interviewer:	Sometimes it feels like you're back in your gang days. Does that just come out of nowhere or are there certain triggers that take you back there?
Client:	Mostly it starts if somebody's talking smack to me. I get pissed and scared and ready to go on the attack.

Notice how the interviewer in these examples normalizes the pathology by saying things like, "you seem observant" or "It's not unusual" and then inquiring about the symptoms present. These are techniques similar to Robinson's (2007) "greasing the wheels" approach and illustrate the importance of approaching what may be considered unusual perceptual experiences delicately. Similarly, with regard to visual hallucinations, Jefferis and colleagues (Jefferis, Mosimann, Taylor, & Clarke, 2011) reported that 50 consecutive patients responded openly and 26% reported visual hallucinations when asked the question, "Do your eyes ever play tricks on you?"

Table 8.3 Characteristics of Different Perceptual Disturbances

	Hallucinations	Illusions	Flashbacks
Definition	False sensory experiences	Perceptual distortions	Sudden and vivid sensory-laden recollections of previous experiences
Diagnostic Relevance	Auditory hallucinations are most common and usually associated with schizophrenia, bipolar disorder, or a severe depressive episode	Illusions are more common among clients who have vivid imaginations, who believe in the occult, or have other schizotypal personality disorder symptoms	Flashbacks are most common among clients with post-traumatic stress disorder
Useful Questions	Do you ever hear or see things that other people can't see or hear? When and where do you usually see or hear these things (checking for hypnogogic or hypnopompic experiences)? Does the radio or television ever speak directly to you? Has anyone been trying to steal your thoughts or read your mind?	What was happening in your surroundings when you saw (or experienced) what you saw (or experienced)? Did the vision (or image or sounds) come out of nowhere, or was there something happening?	Have you had any similar experiences before in your life? Sometimes when people have had very hard or bad things happen to them, they keep having those memories come back to them. Does that happen to you? Was there anything happening that triggered this memory or flashback to the past?

> **Sample Perceptual Disturbances Description:** The client sponta-
> neously reported hearing voices in a variety of different settings. These
> voices usually tell him to "crawl" or "get to your knees" because he has
> been "bad." He did not report illusions or flashbacks.

Orientation and Consciousness

Mental status examiners routinely evaluate whether clients are oriented to person,
place, time, and situation. You can ask four simple questions:

1. What is your name?
2. Where are you (i.e., what city or where in a particular building)?
3. What is today's date?
4. What's happening right now? Or Why are you here?

If a client answers these queries correctly, you might write that the client was
"Ox4" (oriented times four). Evaluating client orientation is a direct way to assess
confusion or *disorientation*. There are many reasons why clients may not be able
to respond accurately to one or more of these questions. For example, questions
about the date or day of the week may be irrelevant to individuals who are long
retired or living in extended care settings (J. Winona, personal communication,
September 16, 2012).

In some cases, resisting (or refusing to answer) questions about orientation
imply disorientation. In the following example, a hospital patient with a recent
head trauma was interviewed regarding orientation:

Interviewer: I'm going to ask you a few questions. Just do the best you can in
answering them. Tell me, what day is it today?

Client: They told me I was riding my bike and that I didn't have my
helmet on.

Interviewer: That's right. I'm still curious, though. What day is it today?

Client: Could I get a glass of water?

Note that the examiner began with a very simple orientation to time question
(i.e., a question about the day of the week instead of a question about the date,
which is more difficult). In this case, after several more questions, the client
continued to evade the question about orientation to time. When clients avoid
answering orientation questions, it may signal some level of disorientation.

Orientation can be pursued in greater or lesser depth. For example, clients
can be asked what county they're in, who the governor of the state is, and the
name of the mayor or local newspaper. They also can be asked if they recognize
hospital personnel, visitors, and family. However, these additional questions
may be confounded by factors such as the client's socioeconomic status, social
awareness, or cultural background.

Common causes of disorientation include drug intoxication, recent brain
trauma, and dementia (e.g., Alzheimer's). It's not the mental status examiner's task
to determine the cause of a client's disorientation, but to accurately and briefly
document presence or absence of disorientation.

Elderly clients, particularly those in acute and chronic care settings, may experience delirium. *Delirium* consists of diurnally shifting consciousness, attention, perception, and memory, typically lasting from a few minutes to several days (Moraga & Rodriguez-Pascual, 2007). Several formal mental status assessment tools are available for evaluating delirium, including the Mini-Mental State (Edlund et al., 2006), the Organic Brain Syndrome Scale (Edlund et al., 2006), and the Richmond Agitation-Sedation Scale (Peterson et al., 2006). With delirium, acutely disoriented clients may experience a gradual clearing of consciousness. When clients become disoriented, they usually lose awareness of the situation first, then their sense of time, then their sense of place, and finally their identity. Orientation is recovered in reverse order (person, place, time, situation).

Fully oriented clients may view questions about their orientation as offensive. They may feel belittled by having to answer these simple questions. Cognitively impaired clients may also act indignant, perhaps from embarrassment or to cover their disorientation. It helps to inform clients that orientation questions are routine and to express empathy with the client's uncomfortable feelings.

Questions on the following list can be used in combination with more chatty questions or statements to assess client orientation.

- Self/Person
  What is your full name? Where are you from?
  Where do you currently live?
  Are you employed? (If so) What do you do for a living?
  Are you married? (If so) What is your spouse's name?
  Do you have any children?

- Place
  There's been a lot happening these past few days (or hours); I wonder if you can describe for me where you are?
  What city are we in?
  What's the name of the building we're in right now?

- Time
  What's today's date? (If client claims not to recall, ask for an estimate; estimates can help assess level of disorientation.)
  Do you know what day of the week it is?
  What month (or year) is it?
  How long have you been here?
  Do you know what holiday is coming soon?

- Situation
  Do you know why we're here?
  How did you get here?
  What's your best guess as to what we'll be doing next?

Consciousness is usually evaluated along a continuum from alert to comatose. Although consciousness and orientation are related, they're not identical. As examiners observe clients' responses and behaviors during an interview, they select a descriptor of consciousness. Descriptors include:

- Alert
- Confused

- Clouded
- Stuporous
- Unconscious
- Comatose

After evaluating a client who's relatively cognitively intact, a mental examiner might write, "The client was alert and Ox4."

Sample Perceptual Disturbances Description: The client's consciousness was clouded; she was oriented to person (Ox1), but incorrectly identified the year as "1999" instead of 2013 and was unable to identify our location or the purpose of the interview.

Memory and Intelligence

MSEs include a cursory assessment of advanced client cognitive abilities. This includes assessments of memory, abstract reasoning, and general intelligence.

Memory

A mental status exam can provide a quick memory screening, but it doesn't provide definitive information about specific memory impairments. Formal neuropsychological assessment is needed to specify the nature and extent of memory impairments.

Memory is broadly defined as the ability to recall experiences. Three types of memory are typically assessed in a mental status examination: remote, recent, and immediate. *Remote memory* refers to recall of events, information, and people from the distant past. *Recent memory* refers to recall of events, information, and people from the prior week or so. *Immediate memory* refers to retention of information or data to which one was just exposed.

Some clinicians weave remote memory questions into the history-taking portion of the intake interview. This involves questioning about time and place of birth, names of schools attended, date of marriage, age differences between client and siblings, and so forth. The problem with basing an assessment of remote memory on self-report of historical information is that the examiner is unable to verify the accuracy of the client's report. This problem reflects the main dilemma in assessment of remote memory impairment: the possibility of confabulation.

Confabulation refers to spontaneous and sometimes repetitive fabrication or distortion of memories (Gilboa & Verfaellie, 2010). Confabulation often occurs during recall and typically involves problems with memory retrieval and evaluation of whether a retrieved memory is accurate (Metcalf, Langdon, & Coltheart, 2007). To some extent, confabulation is normal (Gilboa & Verfaellie, 2010). In fact, we've found that intense marital disputes can occur—for some couples, but of course, not ourselves—when memories of key events fail to jibe. Human memory is imperfect and, as time passes, events are subject to reinterpretation. This is especially the case if an individual feels pressured into responding to specific questions and is one reason why coercive questioning techniques are contraindicated when interviewing witnesses in legal situations (Stolzenberg & Pezdek, 2013). For example, a client may be able to recall only a portion of a specific memory, but when pressured to elaborate, confabulation can occur. Here's an example of confabulation on a simple test of remote memory.

Interviewer:	I'm going to ask you a few questions to test your memory. Ready?
Client:	Yeah, I guess.
Interviewer:	Name five U.S. presidents since 1950.
Client:	Right. There was, uh Obama . . . and Ronald Reagan . . . uh, yeah there's uh, Bush and Bush again. I've got another one on the tip of my tongue.
Interviewer:	You're doing great. Just one more.
Client:	Yeah, I know. I can do it.
Interviewer:	Take your time.
Client:	Washington. That's it, William Washington.

In this case, the examiner's support and enthusiasm may be perceived as pressure on the client to perform. When pressuring occurs, through either positive or coercive means, humans tend to make things up to relieve the pressure.

The preceding example pertains to a client's memory for historical fact. In contrast, when it comes to personal history confirming or disconfirming your client's memories may be impossible. For example, if a client claims to have been "abducted" as a child, it may be difficult to judge the accuracy of that claim.

Client responses to personal history questions nearly always contain minor inaccuracies or confabulation. That's how memory works. It's the examiner's responsibility, within reason, to determine whether a client is accurately reporting personal history events. Pursuing truth can be a challenging experience!

When confabulation or memory impairment is suspected, it may be helpful to ask clients about objective past events. This usually involves inquiring about significant and memorable social or political events (e.g., Who was president when you were growing up? What countries were involved in World War II? What were some popular recreational activities during your high school years?). Asking social and political questions may be unfair to cultural minorities, so caution should be exercised when using such strategies.

If the accuracy of a client's historical report is questionable, it may be useful (or necessary) to call on friends or family of the client to confirm historical information. Such a procedure can be complicated because legal documents must be signed to release client information. In addition, friends and family members may not be honest with you or may themselves have impaired or confabulated memories. Although verification of client personal history is recommended, it's not a problem-free strategy.

Clients may acknowledge memory problems. This is sometimes referred to as subjective memory complaints (Kurt, Yener, & Oguz, 2011) and doesn't necessarily constitute evidence of memory impairment. In fact, clients with brain injury or damage may be more likely to deny memory problems and try to cover them up through confabulation. Conversely, depressed clients may exaggerate the extent to which their cognitive skills have diminished, complaining to great lengths that something is wrong with their brain (Othmer & Othmer, 2002).

Clients with depression sometimes experience cognitive impairment. This phenomenon is called *pseudodementia* (Dunner, 2005). In other words, depressed clients may have no organic impairment but still suffer from emotionally based memory problems. Once the depression is alleviated, memory problems are often resolved. However, the presence of reversible pseudodementia tends to be a positive predictor of later dementia (Sáez-Fonseca & Walker, 2007).

Evaluating recent and immediate memory is simpler than evaluating remote memory because experiences of the recent past are more easily verified. If the client has been hospitalized, questions can be asked pertaining to reasons for hospitalization, treatments received, and hospital personnel with whom the client had contact. Clients may be asked what they ate for breakfast, what clothes they wore the day before, and whether they recall the weather of the prior week.

Immediate memory requires sustained attention and concentration. There are several formal ways to evaluate immediate memory. The most common of these are serial sevens, recall of brief stories, and digit span (Folstein, Folstein, & McHugh, 1975).

To administer *serial sevens* clients are asked to "begin with 100 and count backward by 7" (Folstein et al., 1975, p. 197). Clients who can sustain attention (and who have adequate math skills) should be able to perform serial sevens without difficulty. However, excessive anxiety—sometimes associated with clients who have an anxiety disorder, but also associated with clients who have a history of difficulty with math or performance-based tasks—may interfere with concentration and impair performance. Clients of diverse cultural backgrounds also struggle with this task, partly because of difficulty comprehending and lack of experience participating in such activities (Paniagua, 2001). The research on using serial sevens to evaluate cognitive functioning is weak (Hughes, 1993). Anxiety level, cultural and educational background, distractibility, and potential invalidity of the procedure should all be considered when evaluating a client's memory or attention span using serial sevens.

Digit span is a subtest on the Weschler intelligence scales, but is often administered separately by stating, "I'm going to say a series of numbers. When I finish, repeat them back to me in the same order." A series of numbers is then read to the client at one-second intervals. Using a very standardized procedure when administering digit span tests has been shown to be important to reliability and validity of the test (Woods et al., 2011). Examiners begin with a short series of numbers and then proceed to longer lists. For example:

Interviewer:	I want to do a simple test with you to check your ability to concentrate. First, I'll say a series of numbers. Then, when I'm finished, you repeat them to me. Okay?
Client:	Okay.
Interviewer:	Here's the first series of numbers: 6–1–7–4.
Client:	6 . . . 1 . . . 7 . . . 4.
Interviewer:	Okay. Now try this one: 8–5–9–3–7.
Client:	Um . . . 8 . . . 5 . . . 9 . . . 7 . . . 3.
Interviewer:	Okay, here's another set: 2–6–1–3–9. (Notice that the examiner does not point out the client's incorrect response but simply provides another set of five numbers to give the client another opportunity to respond correctly. If a client gets one of two trials correct, he or she can proceed to the next higher level, until both trials are incorrect.)

After completing digit span forward, it's common to administer digit span backward.

Interviewer: Now I'm going to have you do something a little different. I'll read another short list of numbers, but this time when I'm finished I'd like you to repeat them to me in reverse order. For example, if I said: 7–2–8, what would you say?

Client: Uh . . . 8 . . . 2 . . . 7. That's pretty hard.

Interviewer: That's right, I think you've got it. Now try this: 4–2–5–8.

Clients may become sensitive about their performance on specific cognitive tasks. Their responses may range from overconfidence (e.g., "Sure, no problem, what a silly question.") to excuse making (e.g., "Today's not a good day for me!") to open acknowledgment of performance concerns (e.g., "I'm afraid I got that one wrong. I'm just horrible at this."). The way clients respond to cognitive performance tests may reveal important clinical information, such as grandiosity, rationalizing or making excuses for poor performance, or a tendency toward self-deprecation. However, as always, these observations provide only tentative hypotheses about client behavior patterns. Digit span performance, like all cognitive assessments, may be strongly affected by education level, native language, and cultural background (Ostrosky-Solís & Lozano, 2006).

When clients are referred specifically because of memory problems, an initial MSE is appropriate, but it should always be followed by further clinical assessment. To obtain more comprehensive information pertaining to a client's current memory functioning, it's highly recommended that you obtain appropriate legal releases so you can interview family members or other knowledgeable parties. In particular, you should ask family members specific questions about their perceptions of the onset, duration, and severity of memory problems.

There are many other forms of memory that have been studied extensively. These include *episodic memory* (i.e., memory for events), *semantic memory* (i.e., memory for facts), *skill memory* (i.e., memory for activities), and *working memory* (i.e., holding multiple pieces of information in memory at one time). The study of memory is fascinating and worth additional reading (Gluck, Mercado, & Myers, 2013).

Intelligence

Evaluation of intellectual functioning is a controversial subject, perhaps especially so when evaluation takes place during a brief clinical interview (Mackintosh, 2011). Despite this controversy, general statements about intellectual functioning are usually made following a mental status exam. However, caution is advisable when judging intelligence after a brief mental status examination. Statements about intellectual functioning should be phrased tentatively.

Few people agree on a single definition of *intelligence*. Wechsler (1958) defined it as a person's "global capacity . . . to act purposefully, to think rationally, and to deal effectively with his environment" (p. 35). Though general, this definition is still useful. Put as a question, it might be "Is there evidence that the client is resourceful and functions adequately in a number of life domains?" or "Does the client make mistakes in life that appear due to limited 'intellectual ability' rather than clinical psychopathology?"

Some writers have suggested that it may be more reasonable to view intelligence as a composite of several specific abilities rather than as a general adaptive tendency (Sternberg, 1985, 2005; Sternberg & Wagner, 1986). Using this construct, an individual might be evaluated as having strong intellectual skills in one area but deficiencies in another.

Sternberg and Wagner (1986) described a triarchic theory of intelligence. They identified three forms of intelligence:

1. Academic problem solving
2. Practical intelligence
3. Creative intelligence

Using the triarchic intelligence concept, a mental status examiner might conclude that a client has excellent practical and creative intellectual skills, as exemplified by social competence, good street survival skills, and the ability to come up with creative solutions to mechanical problems. However, the same individual might lack formal education and appear unintelligent if evaluated strictly from the perspective of academic problem-solving abilities.

Gardner's (1983, 1999) theory of multiple intelligences posits that human intelligence can be divided into seven or eight different forms. However, the whole idea of multiple intelligences has been widely criticized, due to lack of empirical support (Waterhouse, 2006). Nevertheless, for the purposes of MSEs, the lack of empirical evidence supporting Gardner's (1999) and Sternberg's (2005) theories is less important than the reminder that people can express intellectual abilities in different ways. This reminder may prevent us from prematurely or inappropriately concluding that minority clients or clients from lower socioeconomic backgrounds are unintelligent based on a single intellectual dimension (e.g., language/vocabulary use).

During a mental status exam, intelligence is usually measured using several methods. First, native intelligence is inferred from a client's education level. This method overvalues academic intelligence. Second, intelligence is assessed by observing a client's language comprehension and use (i.e., vocabulary or verbal comprehension). It has been shown that vocabulary is the single strongest IQ predictor. Again, this method is biased in favor of the formally educated over cultural minorities (Ortiz & Ochoa, 2005). Third, intelligence is inferred from client responses to questions designed to determine fund of knowledge. Fund of knowledge is often a by-product of a stimulating educational background and questions used to assess knowledge are culturally biased. Fourth, intelligence is measured through client responses to questions designed to evaluate abstract thinking abilities. Fifth, questions designed to measure social judgment are used to evaluate intellectual functioning. Sixth, intelligence is inferred from observations of responses to tests of other cognitive functions (e.g., orientation, consciousness, and memory). Based on these procedures, statements about intellectual functioning should be phrased tentatively, especially when they pertain to minority clients. (See *Multicultural Highlight* 8.1 for sample questions that test fund of knowledge, abstract thinking, and social judgment.)

Sample Memory and Intelligence Description: This client's intellectual ability is probably at least in the above-average range. He completed serial sevens and other concentration tasks without difficulty. His remote, recent, and immediate memory appeared intact.

Reliability, Judgment, and Insight

Reliability

Reliability refers to a client's credibility and trustworthiness. Reliable informants carefully present their life histories and current personal information honestly and accurately. In contrast, some clients may be highly unreliable; for one reason or another, they distort, confabulate, or blatantly lie about their life circumstances and personal history.

It's often difficult to determine when clients are being untruthful. Over the years we've had clients tell us they don't use substances (when they do), that they have children who passed away (when there's no evidence a child ever existed), that they recently won a lawsuit for a million dollars (when they're essentially homeless), that they've captured the spirit of a demon in a crystal (when they don't own a crystal), and that their 9-month-old child knows martial arts and speaks in complete sentences (despite the developmental impossibility of those behaviors).

Perhaps what's most interesting about these situations is not so much that lies were told, but that the clients may have had good reasons to tell their lies. Dishonesty and unreliability may be manifest during a mental status exam due to distrust in the process or distrust in the examiner. Unreliability may also occur due to a longstanding pattern of compulsive lying or other unknown factors. Because it's so difficult to sort out the truth from fiction, statements about client reliability should be phrased tentatively.

Reliability may be estimated based on a number of observable factors. Clients with good attention to detail and who give spontaneous and elaborate responses to your questions are likely to be reliable informants. In contrast, clients who answer questions in a vague or defensive manner or who appear to be obviously exaggerating or storytelling have a greater probability of being unreliable. In some cases, you will have a clear sense that clients are intentionally omitting or minimizing parts of their history.

If a client behaves in ways that are guarded or defensive, it can be helpful to address the issue directly by stating something like, "You seem uncomfortable with this process. Is there anything I can do to help you feel more comfortable?" When you suspect a client is unreliable, it's useful to contact family, employers, or other client associates to corroborate the client's story. This step involves obtaining the client's consent, but it's often recommended to verify facts. If no one is available with whom you can discuss the client's story, it's advisable to proceed cautiously with your client's care while observing his or her behavior closely. You should note reservations about the client's reliability in your mental status report.

Judgment

People with good judgment consistently make adaptive decisions that affect their lives in positive ways. Client judgment can be evaluated by exploring their activities, relationships, and vocational choices. Consistent participation in illegal activities, destructive relationships, and life-threatening activities constitutes evidence that an individual is exercising poor judgment regarding relationship or activity choices.

Adolescent clients frequently exercise poor judgment. For example, a 17-year-old with whom we worked impulsively quit his job as a busboy at an expensive restaurant simply because he found out an hour before his shift that he was assigned to work with an employee whom he did not like and viewed as lazy. Six months later, still complaining about lack of money and looking for a job, he continued to defend his impulsive move, despite the fact that it appeared to be an example of shortsightedness and poor judgment.

Some clients, especially impulsive adolescents or adults in the midst of a manic episode, may exhibit grossly impaired judgment. They may profoundly overestimate or underestimate their physical, mental, and social prowess. For example, manic patients often exhibit extremely poor judgment in their financial affairs, spending large amounts of money on sketchy business ventures or gambling schemes. Similarly, driving while intoxicated, engaging in unprotected sex, or participating in poorly planned criminal behavior are all behavior patterns usually considered as evidence of poor judgment.

In addition to evaluating judgment on the basis of clients' reports of specific behaviors, judgment can be assessed by having clients respond to hypothetical scenarios. Sample scenarios are provided in *Multicultural Highlight* 8.1, under the "judgment" category.

MULTICULTURAL HIGHLIGHT 8.1

Sample Mental Status Exam Questions Used to Assess Intelligence

Part One

Many questions used to assess intelligence during a mental status exam are taken from standardized tests and copyrighted. The following questions are similar in content to typical questions used by mental status examiners, but used only for illustration purposes.

Fund of Knowledge

Name six large U.S. cities.
What is the direction you go when traveling from New York to Rome?
Who was president of the United States during the Vietnam War?
Which president "freed the slaves"?
What poisonous chemical substance is in automobile emissions?
What is Stevie Wonder's profession?
What does the phrase "macking on the girls" mean?

Abstract Thinking

In what way are a pencil and a typewriter alike?
In what way are a whale and a dolphin alike?
What does this saying mean: People who live in glass houses shouldn't throw stones?
What does this saying mean: A bird in the hand is worth two in the bush?

Judgment

> What would you do if you discovered a gun hidden in the bushes of a local park?
> If you won a million dollars, what would you do with it?
> How far would you estimate it is from Los Angeles to Chicago?
> If you were stuck in a desert for 24 hours, what measures might you take to survive?
> How would you handle it if you discovered that your best friend was having an affair with your boss's spouse?

Part Two

After reviewing this list of "intelligence questions," gather in small groups and discuss potential individual or cultural biases associated with each question. For example, some questions are clearly biased against younger clients, others against older clients, and still others are biased against clients who were not born in the United States. In many cases, mental health professionals show bias against individuals who respond poorly to "fund of knowledge" by judging such individuals as having intellectual deficits even though these individuals simply have lacked educational opportunities and so you should discuss this issue as well. Also, analyze each question with your group and try to come up with better questions for briefly assessing client intelligence. Are there any perfect intellectual assessment questions?

Note: These items were developed for illustrative purposes. Therapists should consult published, standardized testing materials when conducting formal evaluations of intelligence. It's inappropriate to make conclusive statements about client intellectual functioning based on just a few interview questions.

Insight

Insight refers to clients' understanding of their problems. Take, for example, the case of a male client who presented with symptoms of exhaustion. During the interview, he was asked if he sometimes experienced anxiety and tension. He insisted, despite shallow breathing, flushing on the neck, and clenched fists, that he had no problems with tension, so learning to relax would be useless. On further inquiry about whether there might be, in some cases, a connection between his chronically high levels of tension and his reported exhaustion, his response was a terse "No, and anyway I told you I don't have a problem with tension." This client displayed no insight into a clear problem area.

It can be useful to ask clients to speculate on the cause or causes of their symptoms. Some clients respond with powerfully insightful answers, while others will begin discussing a physical illness they may have contracted (e.g., "I don't know, maybe I have mono?"). Still others have no ideas about potential underlying causes or dynamics.

Clients who are insightful are generally able to intelligently discuss the possibility of emotional or psychosocial factors contributing to their symptoms; they're open to considering and addressing nonbiological factors. In contrast, clients with little or no insight become defensive when faced with possible psychosocial or emotional explanations for their condition; in many cases, clients without insight will blatantly deny they have any problems.

Four descriptors are used to describe client insight:

Absent: Clients with a lack of insight usually don't admit to having any problems. They may blame someone else for their treatment or hospitalization. These clients show no evidence of grasping a reasonable explanation for their symptoms because they deny that they have any problematic symptoms. If an examiner suggests that a problem may exist, these clients usually become very defensive.

Poor: Clients with poor insight may admit to having minor problems, but primarily rely on physical, medical, or situational explanations for their symptoms. These clients will deny personal responsibility for their problems. If they admit a problem exists, they're likely to rely on medications, surgery, or getting away from people they blame for their problems as treatment for their condition.

Partial: Clients with partial insight may have a problem warranting treatment; however, this insight can pass and such clients often leave treatment prematurely. These clients occasionally articulate how situational or emotional factors contribute to their condition and how their own behavior may contribute to their problems, but they're reluctant to focus on such factors. Gentle reminders can motivate them to work with nonmedical treatment approaches.

Good: Clients with good insight readily admit to having problems for which psychological treatments may be required. These clients are likely to take personal responsibility for modifying their life situation. They articulate and use psychosocial treatment approaches independently. These clients may be exceptionally creative in formulating ways to address their problems through nonmedical methods.

Sample Reliability, Judgment, and Insight Description: Overall, this client appeared forthright and reliable. He was open about his drug abuse history and expressed interest in obtaining help. His responses to questions pertaining to social judgment were positive; he described social relationships based on empathy and rational decision making. His insight and judgment were good.

DVD Clip

In the *John & Carl, Part II* MSE demonstration, John assesses Carl's intermediate memory, obsessive and psychotic thoughts, including hallucinations, delusions, and ideas of reference. He also evaluates Carl's abstract thinking and social judgment.

Table 8.4 Mental Status Examination Checklist		
Category	**Observation**	**Hypothesis**
Appearance		
Behavior/Psychomotor Activity		
Attitude Toward Examiner		
Affect and Mood		
Speech and Thought		
Perceptual Disturbances		
Orientation and Consciousness		
Memory and Intelligence		
Judgment, Reliability and Insight		

WHEN TO USE MENTAL STATUS EXAMINATIONS

Formal MSEs are not appropriate for all clients. Here's a good basic guideline: MSEs become more necessary as client psychopathology increases. If clients appear well adjusted and you aren't working in a medical setting, it's unlikely you'll conduct a full mental status evaluation. However, if you have questions about diagnosis or client psychopathology and are working in a medical setting, a formal MSE is usually recommended (see Table 8.4 for an MSE checklist).

Some practitioners have suggested that it's nearly always inappropriate to use a traditional MSE with cultural minority clients (Paniagua, 2001). The is because the evaluative judgments made during a mental status exam can be culturally insensitive or culturally biased (to help mitigate this potential problem, see *Multicultural Highlight* 8.2 as a method for sensitizing you to potentially invalid conclusions you might reach when using mental status exams with culturally diverse clients).

MULTICULTURAL HIGHLIGHT 8.2

Cultural Differences in Mental Status

Part One: Cultural norms must be considered when evaluating mental status. In the following table, read through the MSE category, the MSE observation, and then contemplate the "invalid conclusion" along with the "explanation." The purpose of this activity is to illustrate how cultural background and context can affect the meaning of specific client symptoms.

(continued)

(continued)

Category	Observation	Invalid Conclusion	Explanation
Appearance	Numerous tattoos and piercings	Antisocial tendencies	Comes from region or area or subculture where tattoos and piercings are the norm
Behavior/ psychomotor activity	Eyes downcast	Depressive symptom	Culturally appropriate eye contact
Attitude toward examiner	Uncooperative and hostile	Oppositional-defiant or personality disorder	Has had abusive experiences from dominant culture
Affect and mood	No affect linked to son's death	Inappropriately constricted affect	Expression of emotion about death is unaccepted in client's culture
Speech and thought	Fragmented and nearly incoherent speech	Possible psychosis	Speaks English as third language and is under extreme stress
Perceptual disturbances	Reports visions	Psychotic symptom	Visions are consistent with Native culture
Orientation and consciousness	Inability to recall three objects or do serial sevens	Attention deficit or intoxication	Misunderstands questions due to language problem
Memory and intelligence	Cannot recall past presidents	Memory impairment	Immigrant status
Reliability, judgment, and insight	Lies about personal history	Poor reliability	Does not trust White examiner from dominant culture

Part Two: For each category addressed in a traditional MSE, try to think of cultures that would behave very differently but still be within "normal" parameters for their cultural or racial group. Examples include differences in cultural manifestations of grief, stress, humiliation, or trauma. In addition, persons from minority cultures who have recently been displaced may display confusion, fear, distrust, or resistance that is entirely appropriate to their situation.

Work with a partner to generate possible MSE observations, in addition to those listed in Part One of this Multicultural Highlight and using the table below, that might lead you to an inappropriate and invalid conclusion regarding client mental status.

Category	Observation	Invalid Conclusion	Explanation

All evaluation procedures, including MSEs, are culturally biased in one way or another. Examiners must use caution when applying the procedures described in this chapter to clients from diverse cultural backgrounds. As is the case with all interviewing procedures, respect for client individuality, cultural background, other identity factors, and significant recent events (e.g., stressors or trauma) should be factored into your conclusions.

SUMMARY

Mental status examinations (MSEs) are a way of organizing clinical observations to evaluate current mental status. Administration of an examination is common in medical settings. Although mental status information is useful in the diagnostic process, MSEs are not primarily diagnostic procedures.

Complete MSEs require therapists to observe and/or query client functioning in nine areas: appearance; behavior or psychomotor activity; attitude toward examiner (therapist); affect and mood; speech and thought; perceptual disturbances; orientation and consciousness; memory and intelligence; and reliability, judgment, and insight. The validity of clinical observations in a mental status examination can be compromised when clients come from diverse individual or cultural backgrounds and so adaptations are essential. Although it can be tempting for examiners to leap to conclusions based on single client symptoms, such temptations should be resisted.

Appearance refers to client physical and demographic characteristics, such as sex, age, and race. *Behavior or psychomotor activity* refers to physical movements made by clients during an interview. Movements may be excessive, limited, absent, or bizarre. Documentation of client movement during an interview is important evidence that may support your mental status conclusions.

Client *attitude toward the evaluator* is assessed primarily as interpersonal behavior toward the examiner or therapist. Since determination of attitude may be affected by your emotional reactions during an interview, you should exercise caution when labeling client attitude.

Affect refers to the examiners observation of a client's prevailing emotional tone; *mood* refers to the client's self-reported emotional state. Affect may be described in terms of its content or type, range or variability, and duration, appropriateness, and depth or intensity. In contrast, mood consists simply of the client's response to questions such as "How are you feeling today?" or "What's your mood like today?"

Speech, thought, and *perceptual disturbances* are interrelated aspects of client functioning evaluated during a mental status examination. Evaluation of thought is divided into two categories: thought process and thought content. *Thought process* is defined as *how* a client thinks and includes process descriptors such as circumstantiality, flight of ideas, and loose association. In contrast, *thought content* is defined as *what* a client thinks and includes delusions and obsessions. Suicidal or homicidal thought content is also routinely noted on MSEs. Perceptual disturbances include hallucinations and illusions. *Hallucinations* are false or inaccurate perceptual experiences. *Illusions* are distorted perceptual disturbances.

Client *orientation, consciousness, memory,* and *intelligence* are cognitive functions evaluated during a mental status exam. Intellectual and memory assessments involve only surface evaluations during a mental status exam; more formalized assessments should follow if potential problems are identified. Examiners should take care to avoid cultural biases when making such assessments.

Reliability, judgment, and insight are higher-level interpersonal/cognitive functions evaluated in the mental status exam. *Reliability* refers to the degree to which a client's reports about self and situation are believable and accurate. *Judgment* refers to the presence or absence of impulsive activities and poor decision making. *Insight* refers to the degree to which a client is aware of the emotional or psychological nature of his or her problems. Various procedures can be used to assess reliability, judgment, and insight.

MSEs are usually administered in cases in which psychopathology is suspected. If clients are getting help on an outpatient basis for problems associated with daily living, a mental status evaluation is less important. As in all evaluation procedures, client cultural background, age, significant events, and other identity and situational factors should be considered and integrated into evaluation reports.

SUGGESTED READINGS AND RESOURCES

Folstein, M. E., Folstein, S. E., & McHugh, P. R. (1975). "Mini-mental state": A practical method for grading the cognitive state of patients for the clinician. *Journal of Psychiatric Research, 12,* 189–198.

This now-classic article presents a quick and commonly used method for evaluating client mental state. The mini-mental state is a popular technique in psychiatric and geriatric settings.

Gluck, M., Mercado, E., & Myers, C. E. (2013). *Learning and memory: From brain to behavior.* New York, NY: Worth.

See Chapter 3 for an excellent review of "Episodic and Semantic Memory."

Morrison, J. (2007). *The first interview: A guide for clinicians* (3rd ed.). New York, NY: Guilford Press.

This text includes two chapters discussing the mental status exam. It's especially helpful in giving guidance regarding potential diagnostic labels associated with specific mental status symptoms.

Othmer, E., & Othmer, S. C. (2002b). *The clinical interview using DSM-IV-R* (Vol. 1, Fundamentals). Washington, DC: American Psychiatric Press.

Chapter 4 of this text, "Three Methods to Assess Mental Status," is recommended as it contains very useful information about mental status evaluation.

Paniagua, F. A. (2001). *Diagnosis in a multicultural context*. Thousand Oaks, CA: Sage Publications.

Paniagua provides many examples of appropriate and inappropriate diagnostic and assessment procedures and conclusions with multicultural patients.

Polanski, P. J., & Hinkle, J. S. (2000). The mental status examination: Its use by professional counselors. *Journal of Counseling and Development*, 78, 357–364.

This brief article, published in a major counseling journal, illustrates the central place MSEs have taken with regard to client assessment in all mental health professions.

Robinson, D. J. (2001). *Brain calipers: Descriptive psychopathology and the psychiatric mental status examination* (2nd ed.). Port Huron, MI: Rapid Psychler Press.

This book provides an overview of the MSE with examples, sample questions, and discussions of the relevance of particular findings. It uses an entertaining approach complete with illustrations, humor, mnemonics, and summary diagrams. It also has a helpful chapter on the mini-mental-state exam.

Strub, R. L., & Black, W. (1999). *The mental status examination in neurology* (4th ed.). Philadelphia, PA: F. A. Davis.

This is a very popular and classic MSE training text for medical students. It provides excellent practical and sensitive methods for determining client mental status along with some norms for evaluating patient performance on specific cognitive tasks.

Zuckerman, E.L. (2010). *The clinician's thesaurus: The guide to conducting interviews and writing psychological reports* (7th ed.). New York, NY: Guilford Press.

This comprehensive resource includes three chapters focusing on the MSE.

Suicide Assessment

CHAPTER OBJECTIVES

Suicide is an issue many people don't like to talk or think about. For better or worse, talking about suicide can be a central focus of clinical interviewing. In this chapter, we outline and discuss practical suggestions for conducting a suicide assessment interview.

After reading this chapter, you will understand:

- The importance of examining your own personal and philosophical reactions to suicide
- Suicide statistics
- Suicide risk factors
- Procedures for conducting a suicide risk assessment
- How to conduct a thorough suicide assessment interview
- The difference between traditional suicide assessment approaches and contemporary, constructive, and collaborative approaches
- Differential activation theory and its implications for how to use negatively and positively worded questions with depressed and potentially suicidal clients
- Suicide intervention methods and safety planning
- Essential methods for working professionally with suicidal clients

Working with clients who are suicidal is one of the most stressful tasks mental health professionals face (Fowler, 2012; Juhnke, Granello, & Granello, 2011; Roberts, Monferrari, & Yeager, 2008). It takes little imagination to conjure up a small dose of this stress. Just think of the following scenario: *Your new client tells you he plans to kill himself . . . you try to develop a treatment plan to keep him safe . . . he assures you that he'll be fine and thanks you for your concern . . . but, during the subsequent week, he follows through and ends his life.* This sequence of events can be devastating both personally and professionally. Scenarios like this make it easy to understand why working with clients who are suicidal can be so anxiety provoking.

When mental health professionals discover a client is suicidal, the law is clear: Our professional responsibility includes a *duty to protect*. Jobes and O'Connor (2009) wrote:

> [A]ll states . . . have explicit expectations of a duty to protect that requires clinical recognition of the severity of clients' emotional and behavioral problems when these struggles pose an imminent danger to self. (p. 165)

The duty to protect is an ethical and legal mandate (*Tarasoff v. Board of Regents of California*, 1974; *Tarasoff v. Regents of the University of California*, 1976). If you determine a client is a danger to him or herself, you become legally responsible for initiating communications to ensure your client's safety (Pabian, Welfel, & Beebe, 2009).

Because it's not possible to know in advance if your next client will be suicidal, all clinicians should prepare to work with distressed and suicidal clients (J. Sommers-Flanagan & Sommers-Flanagan, 1995a). This preparation is a basic component of every human service training program, including professional counseling, psychology, social work, psychiatry, and medicine (Hung et al., 2012; McNiel et al., 2008). In this chapter, professional and personal issues linked to working with suicidal clients are explored. We also outline state-of-the-art suicide assessment interviewing approaches that all prospective therapists should master.

PERSONAL REACTIONS TO SUICIDE

Suicide, both as a concept and as an act, often evokes strong feelings. This is one good reason to start this chapter with an historical anecdote designed to help provide a more intellectual focus on suicide.

In 1949, Edwin Shneidman, a suicidology pioneer, was working at the Los Angeles Veteran's Administration. He was asked to write condolence letters to two widows of soldiers who had killed themselves and stumbled upon a vault of suicide notes at the L.A. County Coroner (Leenaars, 2010). In retrospect, he wrote:

> The fulcrum moment of my suicidological life was not when I came across several hundred suicide notes in a coroner's vault while on an errand for the director of the VA hospital, but rather a few minutes later, in the instant when I had a glimmering that their vast potential value could be immeasurably increased if I did not read them, but rather compared them, in a controlled blind experiment, with simulated suicide notes that might be elicited from matched nonsuicidal persons. My old conceptual friend, John Stuart Mill's Method of Difference, came to my side and handed me my career. (Leenaars, 1999, p. 247)

Shneidman's career focused almost exclusively on understanding the suicidal mind. He became an immense advocate for saving individuals who were experiencing what he came to refer to as "psychache," a condition captured in his vivid descriptions of the inner world of individuals who came to contemplate and sometimes act on suicidal thoughts and impulses:

> In general, it is probably accurate to say that suicide always involves an individual's tortured and tunneled logic in a state of inner-felt, intolerable emotion. In addition, this mixture of constricted thinking and unbearable anguish is infused with that individual's conscious and unconscious psychodynamics (of hate, dependency, hope, etc.), playing themselves out within a social and cultural context, which itself imposes various degrees of restraint on, or facilitations of, the suicidal act. (Leenaars, 2010, p. 8)

Insights from Shneidman's work are sprinkled throughout this chapter.

Whether it occurs from a distance, as in the much-publicized suicides of renowned director Tony Scott, professional football player Junior Seau, movie star, Marilyn Monroe, or grunge rocker Kurt Cobain, or more locally, people are sometimes affected so profoundly that suicide rates increase (Gould, Jamieson, & Romer, 2003; Hacker, Collins, Gross-Young, Almeida, & Burke, 2008). This phenomenon is referred to as *suicide contagion*. Individuals with a previous history of depression appear especially vulnerable to suicide contagion (Cheng et al., 2007).

As you read this chapter and begin practicing suicide-assessment interviewing, you may experience challenging emotions. These reactions are especially likely if you've had someone close to you attempt or complete suicide, or if you, like many people, have contemplated suicide at some point in your life. We recommend that you discuss your reactions to this chapter with colleagues, instructors, or with a personal counselor. At the chapter's end, we turn again to a discussion of suicide and its emotional ramifications for the professional clinical interviewer.

DVD Clip

In the *Suicide Assessment Interview* DVD chapter, Rita very briefly introduces the suicide assessment interview and the upcoming *John & Tommie* counseling demonstration.

SUICIDE STATISTICS

The Centers for Disease Control reported that 38,364 Americans died by suicide in 2010 (Centers for Disease Control and Prevention & National Center for Injury Prevention and Control, 2012). This compares with 36,909 reported in 2009. Although this number usually changes only slightly from year to year, at 12.4 deaths per 100,000 people, the 2010 rates are the highest in recent history (2009 rates were 12.0 per 100,000). For comparison, rates were lower in 2004 (11.0 per 100,000) 1999 (10.0 per 100,000), and 1995 (11.91 per 100,000) (Anderson, Kochanek, & Murphy, 1997; Anderson, 2001; Heron, 2007). Suicide is currently the 10th leading cause of death in the United States. However, due to issues related to the stigma of reporting suicides, true rates of death by suicide may be even higher (Amber Bach Gorman, personal communication, September 13, 2012).

Although completed suicides are rare and difficult to predict, efforts to assess suicide risk during clinical interviews are justifiable on many grounds. First, suicide occurs more frequently in clinical populations than in the general population (e.g., clients with mood and/or substance disorders, schizophrenia, and personality disorders are at significantly greater risk; (Schneider, 2012)). Second, suicide attempts occur much more frequently than completed suicides and are relatively common among clinical populations (Snarr, Heyman, & Slep, 2010; Thompson & Light, 2011). The clinician's goals are to reduce the incidence not only of completed suicides, but also of suicide attempts—partly because repeated attempts are associated with later death by suicide (Andover, Morris, Wren, & Bruzzese, 2012; Beghi & Rosenbaum, 2010). Finally, from clinical, ethical, and legal standpoints, it's better to err in assuming the possibility that your client may be suicidal (and proceed with a thorough assessment and safety plan) than to err by dismissing the possibility your client is suicidal.

SUICIDE RISK FACTORS

A *suicide risk factor* is a measurable demographic, trait, behavior, or situation that has a positive correlation with suicide attempts and/or death by suicide. Not surprisingly, given the immense number of variables involved in human decision-making, the science of predicting suicide risk is challenging and complex. For example, in 1995 a renowned suicidologist wrote:

> At present it is impossible to predict accurately any person's suicide. Sophisticated statistical models...and experienced clinical judgments are equally unsuccessful. When I am asked why one depressed and suicidal patient commits suicide while nine other equally depressed and equally suicidal patients do not, I answer, "I don't know." (Litman, 1995, p. 135)

Since Litman's 1995 statement, research on suicide risk has accumulated. This is good news in that research potentially aids in the prediction and prevention of death by suicide. However, as researchers have increased their focus, the number and range of potential suicide risk factors have multiplied and when considered in the context of a practical suicide assessment, can feel overwhelming. To help clinicians deal with so many possible suicide-related variables, researchers and practitioners have developed various acronyms to use as a guide to risk factor assessment (see *Putting It in Practice* 9.1).

As you read this next section, keep in mind that although knowledge of suicide risk factors is useful, developing a positive working alliance with potentially suicidal clients is of far greater import. Additionally, at the end of this risk factor frenzy, we will step back and look at two general models for anticipating suicide. Finally, always remember that *an absence of risk factors in an individual client is no guarantee that he or she is safe from suicide.*

PUTTING IT IN PRACTICE 9.1

Risk Factors, Acronyms, and the Evidence Base

In 2003, the American Association of Suicidology brought together a group of suicidologists to examine existing research and develop an evidence-based set of near-term signs or signals of immediate suicide intent and risk. These suicidologists came up with an acronym to help professionals and the public better anticipate and address heightened suicide risk. The acronym is: IS PATH WARM and it's detailed below:

I = Ideation
S = Substance Use
P = Purposelessness
A = Anxiety
T = Trapped
H = Hopelessness
W = Withdrawal

A = Anger
R = Recklessness
M = Mood Change

IS PATH WARM is typically referred to as evidence-based and, in fact, it was developed based on known risk factors and warning signs. Unfortunately, reminiscent of other acronyms used to help providers identify clients at high risk for suicide, in the only published study we could find that tested this acronym, IS PATH WARM failed to differentiate between genuine and simulated suicide notes (Lester, McSwain, & Gunn, 2011). Although this is hardly convincing evidence against the use of this acronym, it illustrates the inevitably humbling process of trying to predict or anticipate suicidal behavior. In conclusion, we encourage you to use the acronym in conjunction with the comprehensive and collaborative suicide assessment interviewing process described in this chapter.

Mental Disorders and Psychiatric Treatment

In general, psychiatric diagnosis is considered a risk factor for suicide. However, some diagnostic conditions (e.g., bipolar disorder and schizophrenia) have higher suicide rates than others (e.g., specific phobias and oppositional-defiant disorder). Several diagnostic conditions associated with heightened suicide risk are discussed in this section.

Schizophrenia

Schizophrenia is a good example of a mental disorder that has a complex association with increased suicide risk. As you may realize, many individuals diagnosed with schizophrenia are unlikely to attempt suicide or die by suicide. Some individuals with a schizophrenia diagnosis are at higher suicide risk than others.

In 2010, Hor and Taylor conducted a research review of risk factors associated with suicide among individuals with a diagnosis of schizophrenia. They initially identified 1,281 studies, eventually narrowing their focus to 51 with relevant schizophrenia-suicide data. Overall, they reported a lifetime suicide risk of about 5% (Hor & Taylor, 2010). Given that the annual risk in the general population is about 12 in 100,000 and assuming a life expectancy of 70 years the general lifetime risk is likely about 840 in 100,000 or 0.84%. This suggests that suicide risk among individuals diagnosed with schizophrenia is about 6 times greater than suicide risk within the general population.

However, there are unique predictive factors within the general population of individuals diagnosed with schizophrenia that further refine and increase suicide prediction. Hor and Taylor (2010) reported the following more specific suicide risk factors within the general population of individuals with a schizophrenia diagnosis:

- Age (being younger)
- Sex (being male)

- Higher education level
- Number of prior suicide attempts
- Depressive symptoms
- Active hallucinations and delusions
- Presence of insight into one's problems
- Family history of suicide
- Comorbid substance misuse (p. 81)

If you're working with a client diagnosed with schizophrenia, the lifetime suicide prevalence for that client is predicted to be higher than in the general population. Presence of any of the preceding factors further increases that risk. This leaves a "highest risk prototype" among clients with schizophrenia as:

A young, male, with higher educational achievement, insight into his problems/diagnosis, a family history of suicide, previous attempts, active hallucinations and delusions, along with depressive symptoms and substance misuse.

Given what's known about suicide unpredictability, it's also important to remember that someone who fits the highest risk prototype may not be suicidal, whereas a client with no additional risk factors may be actively suicidal.

Depression

The relationship between depression and suicidal behavior is very well established (Bolton, Pagura, Enns, Grant, & Sareen, 2010; Holikatti & Grover, 2010; Schneider, 2012). Some experts believe depression is always associated with suicide (Westefeld and Furr, 1987). This close association has led to the labeling of depression as a lethal disease (Coppen, 1994).

It's also clear that not all people with depressive symptoms are suicidal. In fact, it appears that depression by itself is much less of a suicide predictor than depression combined with another disturbing condition or conditions. For example, when depression is comorbid (occurring simultaneously) with anxiety, substance use, post-traumatic stress disorder, and borderline or dependent personality disorder, risk substantially increases (Bolton et al., 2010). Earlier research also supports this pattern, with suicidality increasing along with additional distressing symptoms or experiences, including:

- Severe anxiety
- Panic attacks
- Severe anhedonia
- Alcohol abuse
- Substantially decreased ability to concentrate
- Global insomnia
- Repeated deliberate self-harm
- History of physical/sexual abuse
- Employment problems
- Relationship loss
- Hopelessness (Fawcett, Clark, & Busch, 1993; Marangell et al., 2006; Oquendo et al., 2007)

Given this pattern it seems reasonable to conclude that when clients are experiencing greater depression severity and/or additional distressing symptoms, suicide risk increases. Van Orden and colleagues offered a similar conclusion:

> ...data indicate that depression is likely associated with the development of desire for suicide, whereas other disorders, marked by agitation or impulse control deficits, are associated with increased likelihood of acting on suicidal thoughts. (Van Orden et al., 2010, p. 577)

Bipolar Disorder

Research has repeatedly shown that individuals diagnosed with bipolar disorder are at increased risk of suicide. Similar to schizophrenia and depression, there are many specific risk factors that predict increased suicidality among clients with bipolar disorder.

In a large-scale French study, eight risk factors were linked to lifetime suicide attempts (Azorin et al., 2009). These included:

- Multiple hospitalizations
- Depressive or mixed polarity of first episode
- Presence of stressful life events before illness onset
- Younger age at onset
- No symptom-free intervals between episodes
- Female sex
- Greater number of previous episodes
- Cyclothymic temperament (p. 115)

These findings are consistent with the research on unipolar depression; it appears that severity of bipolar disorder and accumulation of additional distressing experiences increase suicide risk. Another study identified (a) White race, (b) family suicide history, (c) history of cocaine abuse, and (d) history of benzodiazepine abuse were associated with increased suicide attempts (Cassidy, 2011).

Post-Traumatic Stress

In 2006, renowned psychologist Donald Meichenbaum reflected on his 35-plus years of working with suicidal clients. He wrote:

> In reviewing my clinical notes from these several suicidal patients and the consultations that I have conducted over the course of my years of clinical work, the one thing that they all had in common was a history of victimization, including combat exposure (my first clinical case), sexual abuse, and surviving the Holocaust. (Meichenbaum, 2006, p. 334)

Clinical research supports Meichenbaum's reflections. For example, in a file review of 200 outpatients, child sexual abuse was a better predictor of suicidality than depression (Read, Agar, Barker-Collo, Davies, & Moskowitz,

2001). Similarly, data from the National Comorbidity Survey ($N = 5,877$) showed that women who were sexually abused as children were 2 to 4 times more likely to attempt suicide, and men sexually abused as children were 4 to 11 times more likely to attempt suicide (Molnar, Berkman, & Buka, 2001). Overall, research over the past two decades points to several stress-related experiences as linked to suicide attempts and death by suicide (Wilcox & Fawcett, 2012). These include general trauma, stressful life events, and childhood abuse and neglect. Characteristics of these experiences that are most predictive of suicide are:

- Assaultive abuse or trauma.
- Chronicity of stress or trauma.
- Severity of stress or trauma.
- Earlier developmental stress or trauma. (Wilcox & Fawcett, 2012)

These particular life experiences appear related to suicidal behavior across a variety of populations—including military personnel, street youth, and female victims of sexual assault (Black, Gallaway, Bell, & Ritchie, 2011; Cox et al., 2011; Hadland et al., 2012; Snarr et al., 2010; Spokas, Wenzel, Stirman, Brown, & Beck, 2009).

Substance Abuse

Research is unequivocal in linking alcohol and drug use to increased suicide risk (Sher, 2006). Suicide risk increases even more substantially when substance abuse is associated with depression, social isolation, and other suicide risk factors.

One way that alcohol and drug use increases suicide risk is by decreasing inhibition. People act more impulsively when in chemically altered states and suicide is usually considered an impulsive act. No matter how much planning has preceded a suicide act, at the moment the pills are taken, the trigger is pulled, or the wrist is slit, some theorists believe that some form of disinhibition or dissociation has probably occurred (Shneidman, 1996). Mixing alcohol and prescription medications can further elevate suicide risk.

Several other specific mental disorders have clear links to death by suicide. These include:

- Anorexia nervosa
- Borderline personality disorder
- Conduct disorder (see Van Orden et al., 2010)

Post-Hospital Discharge

For individuals admitted to hospitals because of a mental disorder, the period immediately following discharge carries increased suicide risk. This is particularly true of individuals who have additional risk factors such as previous suicide attempts, lack of social support, and chronic psychiatric disorders. Overall, suicide ideation and attempts are predictably high. In one study 3.3% completed suicide within 6 months of discharge, whereas 39.4% had self-harm behaviors or suicide attempts (Links et al., 2012). Another study reported "3% of patients categorized as being at high risk can be expected to commit suicide in the year after discharge" (Large, Sharma, Cannon, Ryan, & Nielssen, 2011, p. 619).

Selective Serotonin Reuptake Inhibitors (SSRIs)

Over the past two decades, empirical data linking SSRI medications to suicidal impulses has accumulated to the point that recent administration of SSRI medications should be considered a possible suicide risk factor (Breggin, 2010; Valenstein et al., 2012). This is true despite the fact that some research also shows that SSRI antidepressants reduce suicide rates (Kuba et al., 2011; Leon et al., 2011). Overall, it appears that in a minority of clients (2–5%) SSRI antidepressants may increase agitation in a way that contributes to increased risk for suicidal behaviors (J. Sommers-Flanagan & Campbell, 2009).

In September 2004, an expert panel of the U.S. Food and Drug Administration (FDA) voted 25–0 in support of an SSRI-suicide link. Later, the panel voted 15–8 in favor of a "black box warning" on SSRI medication labels. The warning states:

> Antidepressants increased the risk compared to placebo of suicidal thinking and behavior (suicidality) in children, adolescents, and young adults in short-term studies of Major Depressive Disorder (MDD) and other psychiatric disorders. Patients of all ages who are started on antidepressant therapy should be monitored appropriately and observed closely for clinical worsening, suicidality, or unusual changes in behavior. Families and caregivers should be advised of the need for close observation and communication with the prescriber.

In 2006, the FDA extended its SSRI suicidality warning to adult patients aged 18–24 years (United States Food and Drug Administration, 2007).

There's no doubt that debate about whether SSRI medications increase suicide risk will continue. In the meantime, prudent practice dictates that mental health providers be alert to the possibility of increased suicide risk among clients who have recently been prescribed antidepressant medications (Sommers-Flanagan & Campbell, 2009).

Social and Personal Factors

There are a number of social and personal factors linked to increased suicide risk. Many of these factors have been reviewed and integrated into Thomas Joiner's interpersonal theory of suicide (Joiner & Silva, 2012; Van Orden et al., 2010).

Social Isolation/Loneliness

In a review of the literature, 34 research studies were identified that include support for social isolation as a suicide risk factor (Van Orden et al., 2010). These findings provide support for Joiner's (Joiner & Silva, 2012) attachment-informed interpersonal theory of suicide. Van Orden et al. (2008) described the two primary dimensions of Joiner's interpersonal theory:

> The theory proposes that the needs to belong and to contribute to the welfare of close others are so fundamental that the thwarting of these needs (i.e., thwarted belongingness and perceived burdensomeness) is a proximal cause of suicidal desire. (p. 72)

Interpersonal theory explains why a number of social factors, such as unemployment, social isolation, reduced productivity, and physical incapacitation are associated with increased suicide risk. Specifically, research indicates that divorced, widowed, and separated people are in a higher suicide-risk category and that single, never-married individuals have a suicide rate nearly double the rate of married individuals (Van Orden et al., 2010). Based on interpersonal theory, an underlying reason that these factors are linked to suicidality is because they involve thwarted belongingness and a self-perception of being a burden to family and friends, rather than contributing in a positive way to the lives of others.

In a fairly recent study, the suicide notes of 98 active duty U.S. Air Force (USAF) members were analyzed. Using Joiner's interpersonal theory, results indicated strong themes of hopelessness, perceived burdensomeness, and thwarted belongingness. Overall, interpersonal risk factors were communicated more often than intrapsychic risk factors (Cox et al., 2011).

Physical Illness

Many decades of research have established the link between physical illness and suicide. Specific illnesses that confer suicide risk include brain cancer, chronic pain, stroke, rheumatoid arthritis, hemodialysis, and HIV-AIDS (e.g., Lin, Wu, & Lee, 2009; Martiny, de Oliveira e Silva, Neto, & Nardi, 2011). Overall, although physical illness is a major predictor, several social factors appear to mediate the relationship between illness and death by suicide. In particular, Joiner's concept of becoming a social burden seems a likely contributor to suicidal behavior, regardless of specific diagnosis (Van Orden et al., 2010). Similar to previously hospitalized psychiatric patients, medical patients also exhibit higher suicidal behavior shortly after hospital discharge (McKenzie & Wurr, 2001).

Previous Attempts

Over 27 separate studies have indicated that suicide risk is higher for people who have previously attempted (Beghi & Rosenbaum, 2010). Van Orden et al. (2010) refer to previous attempts as "...one of the most reliable and potent predictors of future suicidal ideation, attempts, and death by suicide across the lifespan" (p. 577).

As one example, in a 15-year prospective British study of deliberate self-harm, repeated self-harm was a strong predictor of eventual suicide, especially in young women (Zahl & Hawton, 2004). By the study's end, 4.7% of women who had repeatedly engaged in deliberate self-harm committed suicide as compared to 1.9% in the single episode group. In this study, deliberate self-harm was defined as intentionally poisoning or self-injuring that resulted in a hospital visit. The study concluded that repeated deliberate self-harm increases suicide risk in males and females, but is a particularly salient predictor in young females. This is the case despite the fact that many clients use cutting, burning, or other forms of self-harm to aid in emotional regulation. Overall the research suggests that self-harm that rises to the level of hospitalization is likely beyond that which enhances self-regulation and instead constitutes practicing or successive approximation toward suicide.

Unemployment

Individuals who have suffered any form of recent, significant personal loss should be considered higher suicide risk (Hall, Platt, & Hall, 1999). However, in particular, unemployment is a life situation that repeatedly has been linked to suicide attempts and death by suicide. Joiner's (2005) interpersonal theory of suicide posits that unemployment confers suicide risk at least partly because of individuals experiencing an increased sense of themselves as a burden on others. Other losses that can increase risk include (a) status loss, (b) loss of a loved one, (c) loss of physical health or mobility, (d) loss of a pet loss, and (e) loss of face through recent shameful events (Beghi & Rosenbaum, 2010; Packman, Marlitt, Bongar, & Pennuto, 2004).

Sexual Orientation

Over the years the data have been mixed regarding whether gay, lesbian, bisexual, or transgender individuals constitute a high suicide risk group. More recently, a 2011 publication in the *Journal of Homosexuality* reported there is no clear and convincing evidence that GLBT individuals die by suicide at a rate greater than the general population (Haas et al., 2011).

Although this is good news, the data also show that GLB populations have significantly higher suicide attempt rates. Haas et al. (2011) wrote:

> Since the early 1990s, population-based surveys of U.S. adolescents that have included questions about sexual orientation have consistently found rates of reported suicide attempts to be two to seven times higher in high school students who identify as LGB, compared to those who describe themselves as heterosexual. (p. 17)

Overall, it's likely that transgender people and youth questioning their sexuality may be at increased risk for suicide attempts or death by suicide. Additionally, GLBT youth who have experienced homosexual-related verbal abuse and parental rejection for their behaviors related to gender and sexuality are more likely to engage in suicidal behaviors (D'augelli et al., 2005).

Demographics: Sex, Age, Race, and Religion

Suicide rates vary based on demographics. Although age, sex, and race are not strong predictors of suicide, having knowledge about higher and lower risk groups based on demographic variables is generally important and helpful information. *Multicultural Highlight* 9.1 includes specific information about demographic variables and their relationship to suicide.

MULTICULTURAL HIGHLIGHT 9.1

Sex, Age, and Race as Suicide Predictors

Historically, various client demographics have been used to estimate suicide risk. For example, because males, in general, commit suicide at approximately three to four times the rate of females, boys and men are usually considered a higher risk for suicide than girls and women.

Unfortunately, most demographic variables include moderating and mediating factors that increase uncertainty when trying to predict suicide risk. To return to the example of sex as a suicide predictor, it also happens to be true that females attempt suicide at approximately three times the rate of males. Although there are many potential explanations for these apparently contradictory trends, no one really knows why these patterns exist and persist. However, preventing suicide attempts (primarily among females) is nearly as important as preventing death by suicide (primarily among males). Consequently, every male and female who enters your office should receive equal care, attention, and *if appropriate*, a suicide assessment interview and intervention. Similarly, just because Black females have extremely low suicide base rates and older Asian women have somewhat elevated suicide base rates doesn't mean that we should always conduct a suicide assessment interview with Chinese American women, while never conducting one with Black American women. Obviously, whether a suicide assessment interview is conducted and how extensive that interview is, depends on the characteristics of the specific client in the consulting room.

Generally, suicide risk increases with age among most client groups. However, close analysis of suicide data suggests a less clear and linear picture.

Despite these unique patterns of suicide potential associated with sex, age, and race, there are some trends in the data worth committing to memory. Based on 2005– 2009 mortality data from the Centers for Disease Control, these include:

- White males over 65 have very high suicide rates (32.4/100.000).
- Alaskan Native and American Indian males, ages 10 to 24 have very high suicide rates (31.3/100,000).
- White males from 25 to 64 years old and American Indian/Alaskan Native males have similarly high suicide rates (slightly over 29/100,000)
- The lowest suicide rates seem to consistently be among Black females at less than 2/100,000.
- Across all ages and races, males are about 4 times more likely to commit suicide than females.
- Although suicide rates typically increase with age, rates among Alaskan Native and American Indian males typically decrease with age.

To get a sense of how difficult it is to predict suicide even in the highest risk demographic group, the percent of completed suicides among White males over 65 is 0.032 percent or approximately 1 per every 3,125. The good news is that suicide continues to be a rare event, even in high-risk populations. The bad news is that it remains highly improbable that we can efficiently predict, in advance, which one White male over 65 out of a group of over 3,000 will commit suicide.

Race and religion may sometimes function as suicide protective factors. For example, African American women have exceedingly low suicide rates and speculation suggests that these rates may be associated with a high sense of familial responsibility, which in turn may be associated with specific religious beliefs or convictions (C. L. Davidson & Wingate, 2011).

PUTTING IT IN PRACTICE 9.1

Using a Comprehensive Checklist for a Thorough Suicide Assessment

After practicing and gaining familiarity with risk factors, the following checklist can be used in practice sessions and role plays to help you conduct a thorough suicide assessment in almost any circumstance. It's important to practice actually obtaining the information from different types of clients because the energy, setting, time allotted, and so forth, can make for interesting challenges when it comes to getting this information.

Either in pairs in class or with a willing friend or colleague set up a suicide assessment role play. Using the following checklist, identify which risk factors fit your client. It might also be helpful to try role plays without the list in front of you to see how many you remember on your own.

General Suicide Assessment Risk Factor Checklist

- ❏ 1. The client is in a vulnerable group because of age/sex characteristics.
- ❏ 2. The client has made a previous suicide attempt.
- ❏ 3. The client is using alcohol/drugs excessively or abusively.
- ❏ 4. The client meets *DSM-5* diagnostic criteria for a specific mental disorder (major depression, bipolar disorder, schizophrenia, substance abuse or dependence, borderline personality disorder, anorexia nervosa).
- ❏ 5. The client is unemployed.
- ❏ 6. The client is unmarried, alone, or isolated.
- ❏ 7. The client is experiencing a physical illness.

(continued)

(*continued*)

☐ 8. The client recently experienced a significant personal loss (of ability, objects, or persons).

☐ 9. The client is a youth and is struggling with sexuality issues.

☐ 10. The client was a victim of childhood sexual abuse or is a current physical or sexual abuse/assault victim.

☐ 11. If depressed, the client also is experiencing one or more of the following symptoms:
- Panic attacks
- General psychic anxiety
- Lack of interest or pleasure in usually pleasurable activities
- Alcohol abuse increase during depressive episodes
- Diminished concentration
- Global insomnia

☐ 12. The client reports significant hopelessness, helplessness, or excessive guilt.

☐ 13. The client reports presence of suicidal thoughts.
- Note in your evaluation:
  - Frequency of thoughts (How often do these thoughts occur?)
  - Duration of thoughts (Once they begin, how long do the thoughts persist?)
  - Intensity of thoughts (On a scale of 0 to 10, how likely are you to act on these thoughts or how easy is it for you to distract yourself from the thoughts?)

☐ 14. The client reports presence of a suicide plan that has specificity, lethality, availability, and there's little proximity of social support.

☐ 15. The client reports diminished self-control and/or has a history of impulsive behavior.

☐ 16. The client reports distressing family conflict.

☐ 17. The client reports a moderate to high intent to kill self (or has made a previous lethal attempt).

☐ 18. The client was recently discharged from a psychiatric facility.

☐ 19. The client was recently prescribed an SSRI and has associated disinhibition or agitation.

☐ 20. The client has access to firearms.

SUICIDE ASSESSMENT INTERVIEWING

Although there are a variety of scales and questionnaires available for evaluating suicide risk, the professional gold standard is a suicide assessment interview. A comprehensive suicide assessment interview includes the following components:

- Gathering information about suicide risk factors.
- Asking directly about suicidal thoughts and plans.
- Gathering information about suicide intent and client self-control.

- Consultation with one or more professionals.
- Implementation of one or more suicide interventions.
- Collaboratively developing a safety plan.
- Provision of safety resources (e.g., telephone numbers) to clients.
- Documentation of your assessment and decision-making process.

In the past decade leading writers and practitioners have advocated for a shift away from medical model suicide assessment and intervention procedures. Specifically, Jobes (2006) developed a model he refers to as the "collaborative assessment and management of suicidality" (CAMS). The CAMS approach emphasizes the development of a therapeutic alliance as the foundation for effective suicide assessment and intervention. This approach has both empirical and theoretical support (Jobes, Wong, Conrad, Drozd, & Neal-Walden, 2005).

A Reformulation of Suicide Assessment Interviewing and Intervention

Historically, suicidal thoughts and behaviors have been viewed as representing a deviant mental state, addressed primarily through medical or psychiatric intervention. This has led, on some occasions, to expert-oriented medical-psychiatric evaluation and subsequent medical intervention. In particular, Jobes (2006) and others (Edwards & Sachmann, 2010; Rudd, Mandrusiak, & Joiner, 2006) have criticized the use of "coercive" no-suicide contracts. These contracts are extracted from suicidal patients without an empathic and alliance-building interpersonal context. This medical model approach has emphasized a medical authoritative approach to keeping the patient alive and medical liability management. An authentic concern for and alignment with the patient has been lacking. The CAMS approach as described by Jobes (2006) reformulates the assessment and intervention process into a more seamless and humane encounter that emphasizes the client as the expert regarding his or her emotional state and suicide ideation. Jobes, Moore, & O'Connor (2007) stated:

> Philosophically speaking, CAMS emphasizes an intentional move away from the directive "counselor as expert" approach that can lead to adversarial power struggles about hospitalization and the routine and unfortunate use of coercive "safety contracts." (p. 285)

Further, CAMS works to equalize and strengthen the therapist-client relationship by viewing the client's suicidal thoughts and behaviors as "an effort to cope or problem-solve" with personal problems related to legitimate personal needs for control, power, communication of pain, and ending of suffering (Jobes, 2006). Using the CAMS model, therapist and client collaborate to develop an individualized treatment plan to address the client's suicide ideation and impulses (Jobes et al., 2004).

A Constructive Critique

The CAMS approach is consistent with a constructive perspective that views psychiatric diagnosis and medicalization of human suffering as having the potential to inadvertently facilitate an iatrogenic process (Horwitz & Wakefield, 2007;

Overholser, 2006; J. Sommers-Flanagan & Campbell, 2009). There's a distinct possibility that the manner in which therapists speak with clients and obtain historical and suicide ideation-related information can, in some cases, increase depressive symptoms and associated suicidal thoughts and impulses. This possibility is based on the post-modern constructivist and social constructionist theoretical perspectives (also known as the constructive perspective). We review this perspective prior to providing information on how to conduct formal suicide assessment and intervention interviews. A classic quotation from Freud helps articulate the constructive perspective:

> Words were originally magic and to this day words have retained much of their ancient magical power. By words one person can make another blissfully happy or drive him to despair.... Words provoke affects and are in general the means of mutual influence among men. (Freud, 1963, p. 17)

Freud was suggesting that, simply by using particular words with clients, we can provoke or produce specific emotional states. In the next section, we discuss contemporary research supporting this observation about the power of words.

Differential Activation Theory

Based on differential activation theory, when individuals who were previously depressed and/or suicidal experience a negative mood, they may have their former negative information processing biases reactivated. The original theory stated:

> [T]hat during a person's learning history—and particularly during episodes of depression—low mood becomes associated with patterns of negative information processing (biases in memory, interpretations, and attitudes). Any return of the mood reactivates the pattern, and if the content of what is reactivated is global, negative, and self-referent (e.g., "I am a failure; worthless and unlovable."), then relapse and recurrence of depression is highly likely. (Lau, Segal, & Williams, 2004, p. 422)

This theory and supporting empirical research suggests that during a clinical interview, certain questioning procedures may move a client who was previously depressed toward a more negative mood state with an accompanying increase in negative information processing and suicide ideation. In fact, researchers have reported that individuals with or without depressive symptoms can be quickly and powerfully affected by mood inductions (Lau, Segal, & Williams, 2004; Mosak, 1985; Teasdale & Dent, 1987; Williams, Van der Does, A. J. W., Barnhofer, Crane, & Segal, 2008).

In one study, participants were divided into three groups: (1) previously depressed with suicide ideation; (2) previously depressed without suicide ideation; and (3) no history of previous depression (Lau et al., 2004). Following a mood challenge in which participants spent eight minutes listening to a depressive Russian opera at half speed while reading 40 negative statements such as, "There are things about me that I do not like," participants generally experienced worsening mood and performed more poorly on a cognitive problem-solving test than prior to the mood challenge. Additionally, participants with a history of depression and suicide ideation exhibited significantly greater impairment in problem solving than comparison groups. The authors concluded: " . . . when mood has returned to normal, cognitive variables may return to normal, but those who have been depressed and suicidal in the past are vulnerable to react differently to changes in mood—with greater deterioration in problem-solving ability" (p. 428). This deterioration in problem solving is consistent with Shneidman's (1980) mental constriction concept, addressed later in this chapter.

Overall, research indicates that all individuals, depressed or not and suicidal or not, can have their mood quickly and adversely affected through simple experimental means. Additionally, it appears that individuals with a depression history may experience differential activation and therefore also have increases in negative cognitive biases about the self, others, and the future. Further, individuals with a history of suicidality may be especially vulnerable to deterioration in problem-solving skills when experiencing a negative mood state.

Depressogenic Social, Cultural, and Interview Factors

In addition to the preceding research findings, contemporary social and cultural factors may predispose or orient individuals toward depressive and suicidal states. More than ever, the U.S. media is involved in defining depressive states and promoting medical explanations for depression and suicidality. Many books, magazine articles, and Internet sites encourage individuals to examine themselves to determine if they might be suffering from depression, bipolar disorder, anxiety disorder, AD/HD, or other mental disorders. In particular, pharmaceutical advertisings encourage individuals to consult with their doctor to determine whether they might benefit from a medication to treat their emotional and behavioral symptoms. Unfortunately, as most of us know from personal experience and common sense, it's very easy to move into a negative mood in response to suggestions of personal defectiveness (which, over time, certainly may be as potent as eight minutes of a slow Russian opera). Consequently, it wouldn't be surprising to find that continually rising depression rates and accompanying pharmaceutical treatments are, in part, related to increased awareness of depressive conditions.

Even more relevant to the suicide assessment interviewing process, therapists who focus predominantly or exclusively on the presence or absence of negative mood states may inadvertently increase such states. This possibility is consistent with constructive theory and relational frame theory in that, whatever we consciously focus on, be it relaxation or anxiety or depression or happiness, tends to shape individual reality (Gergen, 2009; Hayes, 2004). It's also consistent with anecdotal data from our students who report feeling surprisingly down and depressed after conducting and role-playing suicide assessment interviews.

Our concern is that depression and suicide assessment interviewing based on the medical model may sometimes inadvertently contribute to underlying depressive cognitive and emotional processes. Consequently, in the following sections we guide you toward balancing negatively oriented depression and suicide questions with an equal or greater number of questions, along with prompts designed to focus on more positive client experiences and emotional states. This interviewing approach serves two functions. First, including positive questions and prompts may help clients focus on positive experiences and therefore improve their current mood state and problem-solving skills. Second, if clients are unable to focus on positive personal experiences or display positive affect, it may indicate a more chronic or severe depressive and suicidal condition.

Adopting a Client and Suicide-Friendly Therapist Attitude

Consistent with the CAMS approach as well as other more recent treatment perspectives (e.g., action and commitment therapy, dialectal behavior therapy), we want to encourage you to adopt a fresh new attitude toward clients with depressive and suicidal symptoms. Consider these attitudinal statements:

- Depression and suicidality are natural conditions that arise, in part, from normal human suffering. Just because a client arrives in your office with depressive symptoms and suicidal features, this doesn't necessarily indicate deviance—or even a mental disorder.
- Given that depressive and suicidal symptoms are natural and normal, it's helpful for you to validate and normalize these feelings if they arise. This validation is especially important because many suicidal individuals feel socially disconnected, emotionally invalidated, and as if they're a social burden (Joiner, 2005). There's no danger in accepting and validating client emotions. The point is not to minimize the importance of suicidal thoughts or feelings, but to accept them and then partner with clients to work toward a positive outcome.

In the spirit of the CAMS approach, we encourage you to listen to your clients' suicidal thoughts and impulses nonjudgmentally; these thoughts and impulses represent your clients' unique efforts to cope with their interpersonal and life problems. Also, rather than continually drilling down into your clients' depressive and suicidal symptoms, be sure to balance your clinical interview with questions focusing on the positive and your clients' unique reasons for living. Forgetting to ask your client about positive experiences is like forgetting to go outside and breathe fresh air (see *Putting It in Practice* 9.2 for an activity to continue your development toward greater comfort working with clients who have suicide impulses).

PUTTING IT IN PRACTICE 9.2

Increasing Your Comfort in Working With Potentially Suicidal Clients

For many beginning therapists, it's difficult to get past the idea that suicidal thinking is dangerous and deviant. To help with this challenge, it can be useful to review positive evidence to the contrary. Here are a few facts:

- Most people think about suicide at one point or another; this suggests it's statistically normal for clients to think about or to have thoughts about suicide
- Consider this: Most clients who come to counseling want to live. This means that even when your client begins talking about suicide,

they're often bringing it up so they can talk through their feelings, develop coping strategies, and continue living—albeit less miserably and more happily.

- Although many students worry that if they ask about suicide, it might make suicide more likely. In fact, the opposite is more likely true; if you fail to ask clients about suicide, they may think they shouldn't talk about suicide with you. Not talking about active suicidal thoughts—when such thoughts exist—is more dangerous than asking about suicidal thoughts when they're not present.

Asking directly about suicide is another big challenge for beginning therapists. We've heard all sorts of substitute language, but the most common is: "Have you thought about hurting yourself?" Although this is a nice question and may be helpful if you're working with clients who engage in self-harm (e.g., cutting, burning, etc.), it's not the same as asking about suicide. As a consequence, we've developed an activity to practice using the words "suicide" or "kill yourself."

Practicing: For this activity, pair up with a partner and practice asking directly about suicide. You can do this very quickly, but it's important for you to hear the words coming out of your mouth. Ask something like: "In the past 2 weeks have you had any thoughts about killing yourself?" Then try it a different way: "Have you ever thought about committing suicide?" And another: "Have you ever made a suicide attempt?" And then ask a series of questions about suicide ideations, suicide plans, suicide attempts, etc. You don't have to have the words flow perfectly, but you should practice saying them, hearing them, and responding empathically to whatever your partner says.

Warning: As you can imagine, engaging in this activity may provoke strong emotions. If you or someone you care about has been close to someone who died from suicide or who attempted it, it can be especially difficult. In some ways we'd prefer avoiding this topic altogether so that we'd never provoke sad or bad feelings in any of our students. However, because as professionals we have to get comfortable working with all clients and we have to prepare ourselves to work with clients who are suicidal, we consider practice as essential. Although we insist on doing this practice, we also think it's crucial for you to talk about whatever feelings come up—either in class or with a friend or counselor as you continue on your path of personal and professional development.

Assessing for Depression

Despite our aforementioned reservations about how depression assessments can contribute to depressed moods, suicide assessment interviewing always includes an assessment of depression. Depression is both a significant suicide predictor and strongly associated with other suicide risk factors (e.g., substance abuse, poor health).

According to the *DSM-5* (APA, 2013), there are two primary forms of depression:

1. Major depressive disorder (a more acute form of depression).
2. Persistent depressive disorder (previously dysthymic disorder; a more chronic form of depression).

To receive a major depressive disorder or persistent depressive disorder diagnosis, specific *DSM-5* criteria must be met. However, for the purposes of our discussion, we focus less on the specific diagnostic criteria and more on general depressive symptoms. These symptoms include:

1. Mood-related symptoms
2. Physical or neurovegetative symptoms
3. Cognitive symptoms
4. Social/interpersonal symptoms

Mood-Related Symptoms

Because depression is a mood disorder, it makes sense to begin depression assessments with mood questions derived from the mental status examination. For example, questions such as "How have you been feeling lately?" or "Would you describe your mood for me?" constitute a good beginning. After asking these questions, you can listen for the client's quality of mood. Then, be sure to use a paraphrase to make sure you have heard the client correctly (e.g., "It sounds like what you're saying is you're feeling sad and hopeless right now.")

Clients usually won't be aware of the fact that in the *DSM-5* a *depressive mood* symptom for major depressive disorder is defined as: "Depressed mood most of the day, nearly every day, as indicated by either subjective report (e.g., feels sad, empty, or hopeless) or observation made by others (e.g., appears tearful). Children and adolescents may have an irritable mood" (American Psychiatric Association, 2013, p. 160). Consequently, rather than reporting "sadness, emptiness, hopelessness, or irritability," your client may say something like "I've just been feeling really nasty lately." If that's the case, respond with language similar to your client's (instead of the *DSM's*) in your paraphrase. Later, you can use *DSM* diagnostic language in your interview.

After you obtain a sense of the *quality* of a client's mood, it can be helpful to get a *quantitative* mood rating. For example:

Therapist: You said you've been feeling totally down and nasty. What I want to know next is how nasty or how bad you're feeling right now, how you usually feel, and how down you feel when you're at your very worst. So, on a scale of 0 to 10, with 0 being the worst possible—totally depressed and suicidal—and with 10 being absolute perfect happiness, how would you rate how sad or how "nasty" you're feeling right now?

Client: I don't know. I guess I'm at about a 3.

Therapist: Okay, now how about recently, for the past 2 weeks or so, on that same scale, what's the very worst you've felt?

Client: I think last weekend I was at about a 2. That was the worst I've ever felt.

Therapist: That sounds miserable. How about your normal mood, when you're not feeling down or depressed, what rating would you give your normal mood, outside of this past two weeks or this particular down time?

Client: Usually I'm a pretty happy person. My normal mood is about a 6 or 7.

In this exchange, the therapist obtained valuable assessment information. Using a simple rating scale, she now has a sense of her client's mood. Although this isn't the level of statistical analysis we recommend for research reports or dissertation defenses, it's an effective method for quantifying subjective distress.

As noted previously, it's important to remain balanced when assessing mood. In addition to evaluating for sadness, emptiness, hopelessness, and irritability, the following positive mood questions may be appropriate:

- What's happening in your life when you feel happy or joyful?
- When have you felt especially good?
- Some people feel especially good when they do something nice for someone else . . . does that help put you in a good mood, too?

Major depressive disorder in adults also can involve a loss of interest or pleasure in usually enjoyable activities. Typically, when clients no longer experience joy, interest, or pleasure, it's not surprising that life begins feeling less worthwhile. This mood symptom is known as *anhedonia* (without pleasure) and is typically evaluated during depression assessments. It's important to evaluate whether your clients are obtaining gratification from their social, recreational, sexual, or other usually pleasurable activities. However, questions about anhedonia and other depressive symptoms can be asked with a positive valence and with an expectation that the client will be able to identify what he or she does for enjoyment:

- What recreational activities do you enjoy?
- What do you do for fun?
- Who do you most look forward to spending time with?

Keep in mind that clients who are experiencing severe depressive symptoms, including anhedonia, may be unable to respond to the preceding questions.

Lack of positive mood reactivity is another mood-related symptom that may help distinguish between depressive subtypes. Although this mood symptom is similar to anhedonia, it's usually evaluated via observation, rather than direct questioning. Specifically, when interviewing clients with depression, mood reactivity is evaluated by observing whether client mood seems to brighten when discussing positive experiences. Alternatively, when you interject hope or other positive factors into a session, clients without a reactive mood don't smile or otherwise exhibit a brighter mood. For instance, although John likes to evaluate mood reactivity by observing whether clients laugh at his jokes, Rita reports having greater concerns about clients' mental health when they do laugh at John's jokes.

Guilt and hopelessness are also emotional states associated with depression. However, rather than discuss them here, we include them in the section on cognitive symptoms, because these particular emotional states are often generated or moderated by specific and powerful cognitions.

Physical or Neurovegetative Symptoms

Clients with depression frequently experience physical symptoms. Psychiatrists often refer to these symptoms as neurovegetative signs and consider them cardinal features of biological depression. In fact, insomnia is considered a suicide risk factor (McCall, 2011). Perhaps what's most fascinating about these physical signs/symptoms of depression is that most of them are bidirectional. Clients suffering from depression often report:

- Significant unintentional weight loss *or* weight gain.
- A decrease *or* increase in appetite nearly every day.
- Insomnia *or* hypersomnia nearly every day.
- Symptoms of agitation (excessive and unnecessary movement) *or* psychomotor retardation (less movement than usual).

These first three physical symptoms can be assessed through direct questioning about client weight loss/gain patterns, appetite, and sleep patterns. Although direct questioning about psychomotor agitation/retardation is also possible, this symptom is primarily evaluated via direct observation.

Another important physical depression symptom is fatigue. Clients with depression commonly experience diminished energy, sometimes staying in bed all or most of the day because of persistent fatigue. Again, this symptom is generally assessed via questioning, with a particular emphasis on whether client energy levels have changed from a previously higher level. On a related note, sexual disinterest, often considered a symptom of anhedonia, may be caused or exacerbated by client fatigue.

Queries into physical symptoms should include open-ended questioning as well as questions phrased to encourage or require positive responses. For example:

- How is your energy level?
- When do you find yourself sleeping well?
- What comforting thoughts help you get to sleep?
- What disturbing thoughts keep you awake?
- What sorts of foods do you find most appealing?
- When was the last time you had your normal appetite?

Cognitive Symptoms

When clients are depressed, they typically experience negative cognitions. These negative beliefs often center around Beck's cognitive triad—which includes negative thoughts about the self, others, and the future.

Common negative cognitive factors include worthlessness, guilt, and hopelessness. Potentially useful questions for evaluating worthlessness include:

- How are you feeling about yourself?
- Tell me about a time when you were feeling good about yourself.
- What sorts of negative (or positive) thoughts about yourself do you usually have?

Clients with severe depression may exhibit a symptom referred to as *preoc-cupation*. This symptom occurs when clients are mentally consumed by negative thoughts, usually thoughts about worthlessness or guilt. When clients have an obsessive preoccupation with negative thoughts, it can be difficult to get them to focus on anything else. You may almost be able to observe this process directly. For example, a client might look downward and seem stuck processing and repro-cessing a past event where they disappointed themselves or a loved one. It's not unusual for clients with severe depressive symptoms to experience persistent or recurrent thoughts and feelings of worthlessness or guilt.

Depending on your affinity for numbers and your client's response to the mood-rating task (described previously), you can obtain additional ratings later in your depression assessment. One especially important cognitive symptom linked with suicidality is hopelessness (Van Orden et al., 2010). You could repeat the rating task by asking:

> On that same scale from 0 to 10 that we talked about before, this time with 0 meaning you have no hope at all that your life will improve and 10 being you're totally full of hope that things in your life will improve and you'll start feeling better, what rating would you give?

Getting a sense of your client's hopelessness is a good idea because specific hopelessness may be a better predictor of suicide risk than overall depression (Ellis, 2006). Clients who express interest and hope in their personal short- and long-term life plans have lower suicide risk than clients who report few interesting hopes, plans, or dreams.

Hopelessness may be expressed in a variety of statements, such as "I don't see how things will ever be any different" or "I've felt like this for as long as I can remember, and I'll probably always feel this way." Client ability to make constructive or pleasurable future plans is an important gauge of hopefulness and is more likely in clients who are less depressed. Future-oriented questions are helpful when evaluating hopefulness. For example:

- What plans do you have for tomorrow?
- What do you think you'll be doing 5 years from now?
- Do you think you'll start feeling better soon . . . or ever?
- What would help you feel hopeful again? (Carlos del Rio, personal commu-nication, August 15, 2012)

Also, it can be helpful to ask questions that require clients to reflect on past successes or third-person questions to see if hopefulness can be stimulated:

- I know you've been down before. What have you done in the past that helped you bring yourself back up?
- What advice would you give to a good friend going through the very same experience as you? [To set this question up well, it's important to have clients identify a close friend and build up a more concrete and personal scenario.]

Helplessness is another important feature associated with depressive thinking. From the clients' perspective, helplessness may indicate a feeling or belief that they are generally incapable of positive change. Expressions of helplessness may be an indirect request for help from the therapist. Although clients may believe they're unable to help themselves, they may still retain some hope for you as a positive change agent.

Clients with depression exhibit additional cognitive symptoms that can be the focus of questioning, including: (a) difficulty concentrating ("What helps you concentrate?"), (b) recurrent thoughts about death or suicide ("Have you had some thoughts of death?" "Have you had some thoughts about what makes life worth living?"), (c) difficulty making decisions and/or problem solving ("When do you feel mentally sharp?" "When do you feel less sharp?"), and (d) mental constriction ("What options have you thought of for feeling better?").

Social/Interpersonal Symptoms

The most common interpersonal manifestation of depression is withdrawal from friends, family, and usual social activities. Therapists should listen for signs of social withdrawal because, at times, depressed persons aren't fully aware of their isolation and/or how they contribute to their own isolation. If you believe you don't have the full picture, you may need a release of information so you can speak with family or friends. With regard to social symptoms, it's helpful to listen for statements indicating the client has changed and become more distant, hard-to-reach, despondent, or exceptionally touchy or irritable.

Exploring Suicidal Ideation

If you're concerned that your client may be at risk for suicide, you should directly and calmly ask about the presence or absence of suicidal thoughts. This may feel awkward or difficult, but we encourage gentle directness. Graduate student therapists often tell us that the most difficult areas to ask about are suicide and sex. Learning to ask difficult questions in a deliberate, compassionate, professional, and calm manner requires practice for most people (so go ahead and practice saying the words *sex* and *suicide* with your colleagues). It also may help to know that, in a study by Hahn and Marks (1996), 97% of previously suicidal clients were either receptive or neutral about discussing previous suicide attempts with their therapists during intake sessions.

We believe it's best to ask about suicide with a standard question that makes it easier for clients to admit to suicide ideation. Here are some examples:

- I make it a practice to ask nearly everyone I meet with about suicide and so I'm going to ask you: Have you had thoughts about death or suicide?
- I've read that somewhere between 10 and 20% of teenagers have thought about suicide . . . is that true for you?
- Sometimes when people are down or depressed or feeling miserable, they think about suicide and reject the idea or they think about suicide as a solution. Have you had either of these thoughts about suicide?

As noted earlier, a common fear is that asking directly about suicide will put suicidal ideas in the client's head. There's no evidence to suggest this phenomenon occurs (Jobes, 2006). Instead, clients may be relieved to talk about their suicidal thoughts. The invitation to share self-destructive thoughts also reassures clients that you're comfortable with the subject, in control of the situation, and capable of dealing with the problem.

Many clients who feel suicidal will readily admit self-destructive thoughts when asked about them. Others will deny suicidal thoughts. If denial occurs and yet depressive symptoms or other risk factors are fueling your concern, don't just heave a sigh of relief and immediately drop the subject. Try to make it easier for the person to admit such thoughts. Wollersheim (1974) provided a classic example:

> Well, I asked this question since almost all people at one time or another during their lives have thought about suicide. There is nothing abnormal about the thought. In fact it is very normal when one feels so down in the dumps. The thought itself is not harmful. (p. 223)

When a client admits to suicide ideation, the onset, frequency, antecedents, intensity, and duration of suicidal thoughts should be explored. These qualities should be explored collaboratively. However, keep in mind that some research indicates that variability in suicide ideation—ideation that comes and goes—may be more predictive of eventual suicide than ideation frequency (Busch & Fawcett, 2004). Additional research is needed to understand this observation more completely, but it may be that intermittent and intense suicide ideations are more lethal than frequent or ongoing ideation.

Assessing Suicide Plans

Once an initial rapport is established and the client has talked about suicide ideation, it's appropriate to explore suicide plans. Exploration of suicide plans can begin with a paraphrase and a question:

> You've talked about how you sometimes think it would be better for everyone if you were dead. Some people who have similar thoughts also have a plan in their head for committing suicide. Have you planned how you would kill yourself if you decided to follow through on your thoughts?

Many clients respond to questions about suicide plans with reassurance that indeed they're not really thinking about acting on their suicidal thoughts; they may cite religion, fear, children, or other reasons for staying alive. Typically, clients say something like: "Oh yeah, I think about suicide sometimes, but I'd never do it." After hearing clients' reasons for living, you may be adequately reassured and decide you don't need to further assess their suicide plan. They also may deny or lie about an existing plan to preserve their "right" to use it if they so choose. However, if clients are open with you and identify a potential suicide plan, further exploration of that plan is essential.

When exploring and evaluating a client's suicide plan, assess four areas (Miller, 1985): (1) *specificity* of the plan; (2) *lethality* of the method; (3) *availability* of the proposed method; and (4) *proximity* of social or helping resources. These four areas of inquiry are easily recalled with the acronym SLAP.

Specificity

Specificity refers to the details of a client's suicide plan. Has the person thought through details necessary to die by suicide? Some clients outline a clear suicide method, others avoid the question, and still others say something like, "Oh, I think would be easier if I were dead, but I don't really have a plan."

If your client denies a suicide plan, you have two choices. First, if you have a good working relationship, you may decide the client is being completely honest and drop your pursuit of specific suicide plan information. Alternatively, you may still suspect your client has a plan but is reluctant to speak with you about it. If so, you may choose to use Wollersheim's (1974) question for making it easier for clients to answer in the affirmative:

> You know, most people who have thought about suicide have at least had passing thoughts about how they might do it. What kinds of thoughts have you had about how you would commit suicide if you decided to do so? (p. 223)

From a constructive perspective and based on differential activation theory research, Wollersheim's approach may pull the client deeper into a negative mood state and simultaneously increase suicide ideation and diminish problem-solving ability. On the other hand, traditional suicide assessment models emphasize that a complete evaluation of suicide thoughts and plans is essential.

An important question to address is whether exploring the client's previous attempts and current suicide plans in great depth is useful. Although obtaining detailed information is important from a medical-diagnostic-predictive perspective, it's much less important from a constructive perspective. Whether to explore past attempts or stay focused on the positive is a dialectical problem in suicide-assessment protocols. On the one hand, as Clark (1998) and others (Packman et al., 2004) noted, suicide scheduling, rehearsal, experimental action, and preoccupation indicate greater risk and, therefore, is valuable information. On the other hand, to some extent, detailed focus on suicide plans may be experienced as deepening preoccupation and a rehearsal of suicide-planning cognitions.

To address this thorny issue we again recommend therapist balance, with a clear focus on a collaborative relationship (Jobes, 2006). If you believe obtaining the information is essential, do so collaboratively. Additionally, as you proceed, integrate positively oriented questions into your protocol. For example, be sure to ask questions like:

- How do you distract yourself from your thoughts about suicide?
- As you think about suicide, what other thoughts spontaneously come into your mind that make you want to live?
- Now that we've talked about your plan for suicide, can we talk about a plan for life?
- What strengths or inner resources do you tap into to fight back those suicidal thoughts?

Lethality

Lethality refers to how quickly a suicide plan could result in death. Greater lethality is associated with greater risk. Lethality varies depending on the way a particular method is used. If you believe your client is a very high suicide risk, you might inquire not simply about your client's general method (e.g., firearms, toxic overdose, razor blade), but also about the way the method will be employed. For example, does your client plan to use aspirin or cyanide? Is the plan to slash his or her wrists or throat with a razor blade? In each of these examples, the latter alternative is, of course, more lethal.

Availability

Availability refers to availability of the means. If the client plans to overdose with a particular medication, check whether that medication is available. (Keep in mind this sobering thought: Most people keep enough substances in their home medicine cabinets to complete a suicide.) To overstate the obvious, if the client is considering suicide by driving a car off a cliff and has neither car nor cliff available, the immediate risk is lower than if the person plans to shoot himself or herself and keeps a loaded gun in the bedroom (Hawton, 2007).

Proximity

Proximity refers to proximity of social support. How nearby are helping resources? Are other individuals available who could intervene and rescue the client if an attempt is made? Does the client live with family or roommates? Does the client live alone with no friends or neighbors nearby? Is the client's day spent mostly alone or around people? Generally, the further a client is from helping resources, the greater the suicide risk.

If you're working on an ongoing basis with a client, you should check in periodically regarding his or her plan. As one guideline, Jobes and colleagues (Jobes, Moore, & O'Connor, 2007) recommended collaborative reassessment at every session until suicide thoughts, plans, and behaviors are absent in three consecutive sessions.

> **DVD Clip**
>
> In the *John & Tommie, Part One* counseling demonstration, John begins with a cultural check-in and then initiates a depression assessment and eventually asks directly about suicide ideation and Tommie's potential suicide plans.

Assessing Client Self-Control and Past or Familial Attempts

Client safety and suicide risk are related to self-control. Clients who fear losing control of suicidal impulses are at high risk. Asking directly about the clients' self-control is important. If you want to focus on the positive, you can ask something like:

What helps you stay in control and stops you from killing yourself?

In contrast, if you want to explore the less positive side, you could ask:

Do you ever feel worried that you might lose control and try to kill yourself?

Exploring either or both sides of self-control (what helps with maintaining self-control and what triggers a loss of self-control) can be therapeutic. What's important is that either exploration track be nested in a collaborative working relationship. The point is that you're exploring this together or alongside your client in an effort to more clearly understand the client's perceptions of self-control in the face of suicidal impulses. When clients express doubts about self-control it may be necessary to consider hospitalization so that external control is available until the client feels more internal control.

Here's an example of a discussion that includes both a focus on the fear of losing control as well as an indirect question focusing on what helps prevent the client from acting on suicidal impulses.

Client: Yes, I often fear losing control late at night.
Therapist: Sounds like night is the roughest time.
Client: I hate midnight.
Therapist: So, late at night, especially around midnight, you're sometimes afraid you'll lose control and kill yourself. But, so far, I wonder what has helped keep you from doing it.
Client: Yeah. I think of the way my kids would feel when they couldn't get me to wake up in the morning. I just start bawling my head off at the thought. It always keeps me from really doing it.

A brief verbal exchange, such as the previous, isn't sufficient to determine a client is safe *or* that the client needs hospitalization. However, the point is that mitigating factors, such as this client's love for her children, may work against a loss of self-control.

Determining if clients have a history of impulse-control problems can aid in determining client self-control. For instance, if the client has a tendency toward explosive verbal outbursts or physical altercations, it may indicate a problem with impulse control and increased suicide risk. In addition, clients who are emotionally overcontrolled most of the time but who, on rare occasions, *completely* lose control may be at greater risk. Because making this kind of judgment call is very stressful, when you have a client who reports fear of losing control, you should seek immediate supervision or consultation.

Clients who have made previous suicide attempts are at higher risk for suicide than those who haven't. That's why it's important to ask questions about previous attempts, including assessing past stressors that may have precipitated previous attempts as well as the outcome (e.g., hospitalization, medical intervention; Doreen Marshall, personal communication, September 30, 2012). You also will want to assess what was helpful and what was less helpful during previous suicidal crises.

Assessing Suicide Intent

Suicide intent is essentially defined as how much an individual wants to or is determined to die by suicide. Formally, suicide intent is evaluated following a suicide attempt (Hasley et al., 2008; Horesh, Levi, & Apter, 2012). Higher suicide intent is associated with more lethal means, more extensive planning, reaction to surviving the act, and other variables. In a small, longitudinal research study, suicide intent, as measured by the Beck Suicide Intent Scale (BSIS), was a moderately strong predictor of death by suicide (Stefansson, Nordström, & Jokinen, 2012).

Assessing suicide intent prior to a potential attempt is more challenging and less well researched. The question can be placed on a scale and asked directly: "On a scale from 0 to 10, with 0 being you're absolutely certain you want to die and 10 is you're absolutely certain you want to live, how would you rate yourself right now?" It's also possible to infer intent based on the S-L-A-P assessment. This has some evidence base as suicide-planning items on the BSIS appear to be the strongest predictors of death by suicide (Stefansson et al., 2012).

> **DVD Clip**
> In the *John & Tommie, Part Two* counseling demonstration, John explores Tommie's previous attempts and tries to assess her suicide intent.

SUICIDE INTERVENTION

The following guidelines provide basic ideas about suicide intervention options during a suicide crisis. These guidelines are consistent with Shneidman's (1996) excellent advice for therapists working with suicidal clients: "Reduce the pain; remove the blinders; lighten the pressure—all three, even just a little bit" (p. 139).

Listening and Being Empathic

The first rule of working therapeutically with suicidal clients is to listen closely to their thoughts and feelings. Often, suicidal clients feel isolated, and, therefore, it's imperative to establish an empathic connection. Your clients may have never openly discussed their suicidal thoughts and feelings with another person. Basic attending behaviors and listening responses (e.g., paraphrasing and reflection of feeling) are your tools for expressing empathy for the depth of your clients' emotional pain (Jobes, 2006; Shneidman, 1980, 1996).

When clients discuss suicide, you may feel scared or nervous on the inside, but outward expressions of shock or surprise should be avoided. We're suggesting you let your competence and poise rise to the surface and take the lead over your internal anxiety. As we've noted before, it's important for you to prepare yourself for working with suicidal clients through role plays and practice. The more you've practiced, the more you'll feel comfortable and natural using your basic counseling skills to show empathy and eventually provide suicide interventions.

Establishing a Therapeutic Relationship

A positive therapy relationship is foundational to suicide assessment and effective treatment. In a crisis situation (e.g., suicide telephone hotline) there's less time for establishing a therapeutic relationship and more focus on applying suicide prevention interventions. However, whether you're working in a crisis setting or a therapy setting, you should still use relationship-building counseling responses as much as possible given the constraints of your setting.

Within the CAMS approach, the assessment is designed to help the therapist understand "the idiosyncratic nature of the client's suicidality, so that both parties can intimately appreciate the client's suicidal pain and suffering" (Jobes et al., 2007, p. 287). The purpose of the assessment process is to collaborate and empathize in a way to facilitate a positive working relationship. At some point after you've "intimately appreciated" your client's suicidality, you may then make an empathic statement designed to facilitate hope:

> I hear you saying it doesn't feel like your life is worth much. But, despite those feelings, it's important for you to know that most people who get depressed get over it and eventually feel better. The fact that we're meeting today and developing a plan to help you deal with your emotional pain is a big step in the right direction.

As noted previously, differential activation research indicates that people who are depressed, or in a mood characterized by psychological or emotional discomfort, may have difficulty remembering positive events or emotions (Lau et al., 2004). Therefore, although you can help clients focus on positive events and past positive emotional experiences, you also need to have empathy with the fact that it isn't easy for most clients who are suicidal to recall anything positive. Also, suicidal clients may find it difficult to attend to what you're saying. Therefore, it's important to speak slowly and clearly, occasionally repeating key messages.

Suicide Prevention Contracts

Suicide prevention contracts usually involve a time-limited verbal or written "no suicide" agreement between therapist and client. In the past, a statement like the following was used: "I promise to stay alive and not attempt suicide until our next therapy meeting."

Suicide prevention contracts were initially introduced to the suicide literature in the 1970s (Drye, Goulding, & Goulding, 1973). Following this original publication and until about the turn of the century, suicide prevention contracts (or no-suicide contracts) were viewed favorably and considered the usual standard of care (M. W. Davidson, Wagner, & Range, 1995; Descant & Range, 1997; Weiss, 2001). However, more recently, experts in suicide assessment and treatment have questioned and strongly criticized suicide assessment contracts (Edwards & Sachmann, 2010; D. A. Jobes, Rudd, Overholser, & Joiner, 2008; Rudd et al., 2006). For example, in their review, Rudd and colleagues (2006) concluded that suicide prevention contracts not only have no empirical basis, but also may increase clinician liability. Consequently, we don't recommend their use in clinical practice unless they're integrated into a positive safety plan and situated in the context of a collaborative therapeutic relationship.

Safety Planning

> The primary thought disorder in suicide is that of a pathological narrowing of the mind's focus, called constriction, which takes the form of seeing only two choices; either something painfully unsatisfactory or cessation of life. (Shneidman, 1984, pp. 320–321)

Helping clients develop a thoughtful and practical plan for coping with and reducing psychological pain is a central component in suicide interventions. This plan can include relaxation, mindfulness, traditional meditation practices, cognitive restructuring, social outreach, and other strategies that increase self-soothing, decrease social isolation, and decrease the sense of being a social burden (Joiner, 2005).

Instead of the traditional approach of implementing no-suicide contracts, contemporary approaches emphasize obtaining a commitment to treatment statement from the client (Rudd et al., 2006). These treatment statements or plans go by various names including, "Commitment to Intervention," "Crisis Response Plan," "Safety Plan," and "Safety Planning Intervention" (Jobes et al., 2008; Stanley & Brown, 2012); they're more comprehensive and positive in that they describe activities that clients will do to address their depressive and suicidal symptoms, rather than focusing narrowly on what the client will not do (i.e., commit suicide). These plans also include ways for clients to access emergency support after hours (such as the national suicide prevention lifeline 1(800) 273-TALK or a similar emergency crisis number; Doreen Marshall, personal communication, September 30, 2012).

As a specific safety-planning example, Stanley and Brown (2012) developed a brief treatment for suicidal clients, called the Safety Planning Intervention (SPI). This intervention was developed from evidence-based cognitive-therapy principles and can be used in hospital emergency rooms as well as inpatient and outpatient settings (Brown et al., 2005). The SPI includes six treatment components:

1. Recognizing warning signs of an impending suicidal crisis.
2. Employing internal coping strategies.
3. Utilizing social contacts as a means of distraction from suicidal thoughts.
4. Contacting family members or friends who may help to resolve the crisis.
5. Contacting mental health professionals or agencies.
6. Reducing the potential use of lethal means. (Stanley & Brown, 2012, p. 257)

Stanley and Brown (2012) noted that the sixth treatment component, reducing lethal means, isn't addressed until the other five safety-plan components have been completed. Component six also may require assistance from family members or a friend, depending on the situation.

Identifying Alternatives to Suicide

Suicide is a possible alternative to life. Engaging in a debate about the acceptability of suicide or whether with clients with suicidal impulses "should" seek death by suicide can backfire. Sometimes suicidal individuals feel so disempowered that the threat or possibility to take their own lives is perceived as one of their few sources of control. Consequently, our main job is to help identify methods for coping with suicidal impulses and to identify life alternatives that are more desirable than death by suicide—rather than taking away clients' rights to consider suicide.

Suicidal clients often suffer from mental constriction and problem-solving deficits; they're unable to identify options to suicide. As Shneidman (1980) suggested, clients need help to improve their mood, regain hope, take off their constricting mental blinders, and "widen" their view of life's options.

Shneidman (1980) wrote of a situation in which a pregnant suicidal teenager came to see him in a suicidal crisis. She said she had a gun in her purse. He conceded to her that suicide was an option, while pulling out paper and a pen to write down other life options. Together, they generated 8 to 10 alternatives to suicide. Even though Shneidman generated most of the options and she rejected them, he continued writing them down, noting they were only options. Eventually, he handed the list over to her and asked her to rank order her preferences. It was surprising to both of them that she selected suicide as her third preferred option. As a consequence, together they worked to implement options one and two and happily, she never needed to choose option three.

This is a practical approach that you can practice with your peers and implement with suicidal clients. Of course, there's always the possibility that clients will decide suicide is the best choice (at which point you've obtained important assessment information). However, it's surprising how often suicidal clients, once they've experienced this intervention designed to address their mental constriction symptoms, discover other, more preferable, options that involve embracing life.

DVD Clip

In the *John & Tommie, Part Three* counseling demonstration, John explores with Tommie her reasons for living and discusses a safety plan with her.

Separating the Psychic Pain From the Self

Rosenberg (1999; 2000) described a helpful cognitive reframe intervention for use with suicidal clients. She wrote, "The therapist can help the client understand that what she or he really desires is to eradicate the feelings of intolerable pain rather than to eradicate the self" (p. 86). This technique can help suicidal clients because it provides much needed empathy for the clients' psychic pain, while helping them see that their wish is for the pain to stop existing, not for the self to stop existing.

Similarly, Rosenberg (1999) recommended that therapists help clients reframe what's usually meant by the phrase *feeling suicidal*. She noted that clients benefit from seeing their suicidal thoughts and impulses as a communication about their depth of feeling, rather than an "actual *intent to take action*" (p. 86). Once again, this approach to intervening with suicidal clients can decrease clients' needs to act, partly because of the elegant cognitive reframe and partly because of the therapist's empathic message.

Becoming Directive and Responsible

When clients are a clear danger to themselves, in our culture and by our laws, it becomes the therapist's responsibility to intervene. For many counselors and psychotherapists, this mandate means taking a more directive role than usual. You may have to tell the client what to do, where to go, whom to call, and so forth. It also may involve prescriptive therapeutic interventions, such as strongly urging the client to get involved in daily exercise, consistent recreational activity, church activities, or whatever seems preventative based on the client's unique individual needs. When a client is acutely suicidal, addressing suicidality becomes the primary focus of the session.

Clients who are acutely suicidal may require hospitalization. However, due to a number of issues, including reduced hospital stays associated with insurance cost containment, many professionals view hospitalization as a less than optimal option. Nonetheless, if you have a client with acute suicide ideation, hospitalization may still be the best alternative. If so, be positive and direct regarding the need for and potential benefit of hospitalization. Clients may have stereotyped views of what life is like inside a psychiatric hospital. Statements similar to the following may help you begin the discussion.

- I wonder how you feel (or what you think) about the possibility of staying in a hospital until you feel safer and more in control?
- I think being in the hospital may be just the right thing for you. It's a safe place where you can work on developing coping skills and on any medication adjustments you may need or want.

Linehan (1993) discussed a number of directive approaches for reducing suicide behaviors based on dialectical behavior therapy. For example, she advocated:

- Emphatically instructing the client not to commit suicide.
- Repeatedly informing the client that suicide isn't a good solution and that a better one will be found.
- Giving advice and telling the client what to do when/if he or she is frozen and unable to construct a positive action plan.

Hopefully, these suggestions give you a sense of how direct you may need to be when working with clients who are suicidal.

Making Decisions About Hospitalization and Referral

The first question to be addressed in the decision-making process is, "How suicidal is the client?" Suicidality can be measured along a continuum from nonexistent to extreme. Clients with mild to moderate suicide potential can usually be managed on an outpatient basis. Obviously, the more frequent and intense the ideation and the more clear the plan (assess using SLAP), the more closely the client should be monitored. We also recommend developing a collaborative treatment plan, discussing suicide as one of many alternatives, separating the suicidal pain from the self and other aforementioned interventions.

Some clients with mild-to-moderate suicide ideation might be treated as though they're more severely suicidal. For example, imagine a 55-year-old depressed male who presents with highly variable suicide ideation, a vague plan, and sense of purposelessness. These symptoms might be classified as mild or moderate, but he also may have additional risk factors; if he's socially isolated, having panic attacks, and has increased alcohol use, he probably needs to commit to a safety plan or be considered for hospitalization.

Clients who fall into the severely and extremely suicidal category warrant swift and directive intervention. These clients shouldn't be left alone while you consider intervention options. Instead, inform them in a supportive but directive manner that it's your professional responsibility to ensure their safety. Actions may include contacting the police or a county/municipal mental health professional. Unless you have special training and it's the policy of your agency, *never* transport a severely or extremely suicidal client to a psychiatric facility on your own. Suicidal clients have jumped from moving vehicles, attempted to drown themselves in rivers, and thrown themselves into freeway traffic to avoid hospitalization. Regardless of whether they die during such an attempt, the attempt itself is traumatic for everyone.

There are several reasons why hospitalization may not be the best option for moderately or severely suicidal clients (although it's probably always the best option when clients are extremely suicidal and you believe they're an imminent risk). For some clients, hospitalization itself is traumatic. They experience deflated self-esteem, may regress to lower functioning, and potentially become cut off from more socially acceptable support networks. Severely suicidal clients who are employed and have adequate social support networks may, in some instances, be better off without hospitalization. In such cases, you might increase client contact, perhaps even meeting for brief sessions every working day and collaboratively establish an individualized and comprehensive treatment plan. In all instances, you should consult with supervisors and colleagues regarding actions taken with a client who is suicidal and document those actions and consultation.

PROFESSIONAL ISSUES

Many important professional issues are associated with suicide assessment. Some of these issues are personal; others emphasize professional or legal issues. It's sometimes difficult to disentangle the personal from the professional-legal. These issues are discussed briefly.

Can You Work With Suicidal Clients?

Some therapists aren't well suited to regular work with suicidal clients. Depressed and suicidal clients are often angry and hostile toward those who try to help. However, it remains your responsibility to maintain rapport and not become too irritated, even with hostile clients. Avoid taking the comments of irate or suicidal clients personally.

If you're prone to depression and suicidal thoughts yourself, you may want to avoid regular work with suicidal clients. Working with suicidal clients may trigger your depressive thoughts and add to your tendency to become depressed and/or suicidal.

Strong values about suicide can be an important professional consideration. Some people strongly believe that suicide is a viable choice and that clients shouldn't be prevented from committing suicide (Szasz, 1986):

> All this points toward the desirability of according suicide the status of a basic human right (in its strict, political-philosophical sense). I do not mean that killing oneself is always good or praiseworthy; I mean only that the power of the state should not be legitimately invoked or deployed to prohibit or prevent persons from killing themselves. (p. 811)

If you have strong philosophical or religious beliefs either for or against suicide, these beliefs could impede your ability to be objective and helpful when working with clients who are suicidal (Neimeyer, Fortner, & Melby, 2001). You may still be able to conduct suicide assessment interviews and do so professionally and supportively. However, if your beliefs predispose you to negatively judge clients, consider referring suicidal clients to other professionals who can work more supportively and effectively with them. It isn't a failure to have certain groups of people or problem areas that you don't work with. It *is* a failure to have such areas and not recognize them.

Consultation

As mental health professionals and instructors, we believe ongoing peer consultation is essential to competent, ethical practice (R. Sommers-Flanagan & Sommers-Flanagan, 2007). Consultation with peers and supervisors serves a dual purpose. First, it provides therapists with much-needed professional support; dealing with suicidal clients is difficult and stressful, and input from other professionals is helpful. For your health and sanity, you shouldn't do work with suicidal clients in isolation.

Second, consultation will provide you with feedback about appropriate practice standards. If you have to defend your actions (or lack thereof) during a post-suicide trial, you'll need to demonstrate that you functioned in the usual and customary manner with regard to professional standards; consultation is one way to review your professional competency.

Documentation

Professional therapists should always document contact with clients (Miret, Nuevo, & Ayuso-Mateos, 2009). It's especially important when working with suicidal clients to document the rationale underlying your clinical decisions. For example, if you're working with a severely or extremely suicidal client and decide against hospitalization, you should outline in writing exactly why you made that decision. You might be justified choosing not to hospitalize your client if a collaborative safety plan has been established and your client has good social support resources (e.g., family or employment).

When you work with suicidal clients, keep documentation to show you:

1. Conducted a thorough suicide risk assessment.
2. Obtained adequate historical information.
3. Obtained records regarding previous treatment.
4. Asked directly about suicidal thoughts and impulses.
5. Consulted with one or more professionals.
6. Discussed limits of confidentiality.
7. Implemented suicide interventions.
8. Developed a collaborative safety plan.
9. Gave safety resources (e.g., telephone numbers) to the client.

Remember, the legal bottom line with regard to documentation is that if an event wasn't documented, it didn't happen (see *Putting It in Practice* 9.3).

Dealing With Completed Suicides

In the unfortunate event that one of your clients dies by suicide, it's important to be aware of several personal and legal issues (McGlothlin, 2008; Roberts et al.,

2008). First, seek professional and personal support. Sometimes, therapists need psychotherapy or counseling to deal with feelings of grief and guilt. In other cases, post-suicide discussion with supportive colleagues is sufficient. Some professionals conduct "psychological autopsies" in an effort to identify factors that contributed to the suicide (Pouliot & De Leo, 2006; Shneidman, 2004). Psychological autopsies are especially helpful for professionals who regularly work with suicidal clients; autopsies may help prevent future deaths by suicide.

Second, depending on your circumstances, you may want to consult an attorney immediately. It's helpful to know the nature of your legal situation and how to best protect yourself (McGlothlin, 2008; Roberts et al., 2008). Legal assistance may be available through your professional organization or state association.

Unless your attorney is adamantly against it, you probably should be available to your deceased client's family. They may want to meet with you personally or simply discuss their loss over the telephone. At the legal level, if you refuse to discuss the situation with a client's family, you risk their anger; obviously, angry families are more likely to prosecute than are families who feel you've been open and fair. Realize that anything you say to a deceased client's family can be used against you, but also realize that if you say nothing, you may be viewed as cold, distant, and unfeeling.

Your attitude toward the family may be more important than what you disclose about your client's case. Avoid saying, "My attorney recommended that I not answer that question." Make efforts to be open about your own sadness regarding the client's death, but avoid talking about your guilt or regrets (e.g., don't say, "Oh, I only wish I had decided to hospitalize him after our last session."). At the therapeutic level, talking with the family can be important for both them and you. In most cases, they will regard you as someone who was trying to help their loved one get better. They will appreciate all that you tried to do and will expect that, to some degree, you share their grief and loss. Each case is different, but don't let legal fears to overcome your professional concern and your humanity.

PUTTING IT IN PRACTICE 9.3

Assessing Your Assessment Procedures: Documentation Guidelines

For this exercise, have two brave individuals volunteer to role-play a suicide assessment in front of the class using the checklists from the earlier boxes. Have the entire class observe and evaluate the assessment, including the following important aspects.

Suicide-Assessment Documentation Checklist

Check off the following items to ensure that your suicide-assessment documentation is up to professional standards.

❐ 1. The limits of confidentiality and informed consent were discussed.

❏ 2. A thorough suicide assessment was conducted, including:
  ❏ Risk factor assessment.
  ❏ Suicide assessment instruments or questionnaires.
  ❏ Assessment of suicidal thoughts, plan, client self-control, and suicidal intent.
❏ 3. Relevant historical information from the client regarding suicidal behavior (e.g., suicidal behaviors by family members, previous attempts, lethality of previous attempts, etc.) was obtained.
❏ 4. Previous treatment records were requested/obtained.
❏ 5. Consultation with one or more licensed mental health professionals was sought.
❏ 6. An appropriate safety plan was established.
❏ 7. The patient was provided with information regarding emergency/crisis resources.
❏ 8. In cases of high suicide risk, appropriate and relevant authority figures (police officers) and/or family members were contacted.
❏ 9. Appropriate suicide interventions were implemented.

Concluding Comments

Suicide can be a common topic during intake interviews and ongoing therapy. Even beginning therapists shouldn't sit down in a room with a client unless they understand how to competently conduct a suicide assessment. Dealing with suicidal clients without adequate preparation isn't only anxiety provoking, it's also risky and unprofessional.

There's no replacement for direct practice in conducting suicide assessment interviews. Repeated practice increases your chances of conducting suicide assessment interviews competently and without excessive anxiety.

We encourage you to quiz yourself regarding risk factors and other interview information covered in this chapter. If someone asks you to assess a potentially suicidal client, you should immediately think: risk factors, depression, thoughts, plan, control, intent, collaborative safety plan, consultation, and documentation. Checklists are included in this chapter to assist you in remembering key suicide assessment interviewing ingredients. Proceeding with knowledge and caution, obtaining supervision, developing a norm of consulting with colleagues, and documenting factors contributing to your clinical decision are the basic rules for handling this area of mental health care.

SUMMARY

Suicide is a significant social problem, a preventable cause of death, and a highly stressful issue to face when providing assessment or therapy services. Suicide rates in the United States generally hover around 12 per 100,000 people. This makes suicide a rare and difficult-to-predict phenomenon.

Many different risk factors are associated with suicidal behavior, including, but not limited to: (a) mental disorders and discharge from psychiatric hospitals; (b) social isolation, (c) physical illness, (d) previous attempts, (e) unemployment, and (f) struggles with sexuality. A comprehensive 20-item risk-factor checklist is included in this chapter.

Conducting a suicide risk assessment involves the following steps:

- Gathering information about suicide risk factors.
- Asking directly about suicidal thoughts and plans.
- Gathering information about suicide intent and client self-control.
- Consultation with one or more professionals.
- Implementation of one or more suicide interventions.
- Collaboratively developing a safety plan
- Provision of safety resources (e.g., telephone numbers) to clients.
- Documentation of your assessment and decision-making process.

Traditional medical-diagnostic-psychological approaches to suicide assessment have emphasized the therapist's responsibility for examining client suicidality and making appropriate decisions. More recently, there has been a strong emphasis on collaborative suicide-assessment procedures. These procedures depathologize suicidal impulses and view them as an important personal communication to be explored and understood.

Research on differential activation theory suggests that traditional evaluation approaches can activate depressive processes within clients who have a history of depression. Consequently, to maintain balance, therapists should ask both positive and negative questions when evaluating for suicide potential.

When working with suicidal clients, it's important to establish rapport and a therapeutic relationship through effective listening strategies. Supportive empathy is crucial. Suicidal clients may not have previously informed anyone of their suicidal thoughts and wishes. Let them know you hear their pain and misery, but at the same time, help them begin to see that there are good reasons to be hopeful; most clients who are depressed and suicidal improve and begin to feel life is worth living again.

Deciding whether a client's suicidal impulses warrant immediate hospitalization is difficult. A client's suicide risk can be rated to help facilitate decision making, but there's no foolproof formula available to help therapists decide how to most effectively manage each suicidal case. Ratings of suicidality range from nonexistent, mild, moderate, severe, to extreme. Clients who are mildly or moderately suicidal can normally be managed in an outpatient setting. Clients who experience severe and extreme suicide ideation often require hospitalization.

Therapists should know and adhere to professional standards when working with suicidal clients. When possible, therapists should consult with other professionals about suicidal clients. Clearly document all professional decisions. In the unfortunate event of a client committing suicide, therapists are advised to follow several key steps.

SUGGESTED READINGS AND RESOURCES

Professional Books and Articles

Campbell, F. R. (2006). *Aftermath of suicide: The clinician's role*. Washington, DC: American Psychiatric Publishing.

This book focuses on how to be of help to individuals who survive a suicide. In particular, the author discusses the outreach role for clinicians and how to approach the initial period following loss.

Healy, D. (2000). Antidepressant induced suicidality. *Primary Care in Psychiatry*, 6, 23–28.

This article describes ways in which serotonin-specific reuptake inhibitors may, in some cases, increase client suicidality.

Jobes, D. A. (2006). *Managing suicidal risk: A collaborative approach*. New York, NY: Guilford Press.

Jobes's text is an excellent resource for individuals who will be working with suicidal clients. As discussed in this chapter, it emphasizes empathic collaboration as the cornerstone of suicide assessment and intervention.

Joiner, T. (2005). *Why people die by suicide*. Cambridge, MA: Harvard University Press.

This book describes Joiner's interpersonal theory of suicide.

Jordan, J. R. & McIntosh, J. L. (2011) *Grief after suicide: Understanding the consequences and caring for the survivors*. New York, NY: Routledge.

A landmark publication in the suicide bereavement literature, this book contains information on supporting those bereaved by suicide as well as information on promising national and international programs for suicide bereavement.

Meichenbaum, D. (2006). *Trauma and suicide: A constructive narrative perspective*. Washington, DC: American Psychological Association.

Written by one of the premier psychologists of our time, this book emphasizes an important link between trauma and suicide.

Shea, S. C. (2011). *The practical art of suicide assessment: A guide for mental health professionals and substance abuse counselors* (2nd ed.). New York, NY: Wiley.

This entire book focuses primarily on interview methods for uncovering suicide ideation and intent in clients.

Shneidman, E. S. (1996). *The suicidal mind*. New York, NY: Oxford University Press.

In this powerful book, the most renowned suicidologist in the world reviews three cases that illustrate the psychological pain associated with suicidal impulses.

Stanley, B. & Brown, G. K. (2012). Safety planning intervention: A brief intervention to mitigate suicide risk. *Cognitive and Behavioral Practice*, 19(2), 256–264.

This article describes a brief intervention for suicidal client, the Safety Planning Intervention (SPI), which has been identified as a best practice by the Suicide Prevention Resource Center/American Foundation for Suicide Prevention Best Practices Registry for Suicide Prevention.

Szasz, T. S. (1986). The case against suicide prevention. *American Psychologist*, 41, 806–812.

In this article, Szasz outlines his provocative belief that coercive suicide-prevention efforts violate individual human rights.

Wendler, S., & Matthews, D. (2006). Cultural competence in suicide risk assessment. In R. I. Simon & R. E. Hales (Eds.), *The American Psychiatric Publishing textbook of suicide assessment and management*. Washington, DC: American Psychiatric Publishing.

This chapter examines culture, immigration, acculturation, and other factors as they relate to suicide and suicide risk.

Suicide Support Organizations and Websites

American Foundation for Suicide Prevention, 120 Wall Street, 22nd Floor, New York, NY 10005. Phone: 888-333-AFSP or 212-363-3500. www.afsp.org

American Association of Suicidology, Alan L. Berman, PhD, executive director, 4201 Connecticut Avenue, NW, Suite 310, Washington, DC 20008. Phone: 202-237-2280. www.suicidology.org

National Organization for People of Color Against Suicide, P.O. Box 75571, Washington, DC 20013 202-549-6039. E-mail: info@nopcas.org

http://www.cdc.gov/violenceprevention/suicide/

http://www.save.org

http://www.sprc.org/

http://www.suicidepreventionlifeline.org/

Suicide Prevention Resource Center (SPRC), Education Development Center, Inc., 43 Foundry Avenue, Waltham, MA 02453, 1 877-GET-SPRC (877-438-7772), www.sprc.org

Suicide Prevent Triangle: http://SuicidePreventTriangle.org lists support groups, suicide self-assessment procedures, software, and educational/resource information on suicide.

Diagnosis and Treatment Planning

CHAPTER OBJECTIVES

From the perspective of the medical model, the primary—and sometimes only—purpose of a clinical interview is to identify an appropriate diagnosis and treatment plan. In this chapter, we look at philosophical and practical aspects of diagnosis; we also review several approaches for developing treatment plans for counseling or psychotherapy clients.

After reading this chapter, you will understand:

- Basic principles of psychiatric diagnosis, including the definition of mental disorders according to the *Diagnostic and Statistical Manual of Mental Disorders*, 5th Edition (*DSM-5*; American Psychiatric Association, 2013).
- Common problems associated with assessment and diagnosis.
- Methods and procedures for diagnostic assessment.
- A balanced approach for conducting diagnostic clinical interviews.
- An integrated or biopsychosocial approach to treatment planning.
- How to identify client problems, associated goals, and establish a treatment plan to guide the therapy process.
- The importance of matching client resources with specific approaches to clinical treatment.

PRINCIPLES OF PSYCHIATRIC DIAGNOSIS

In 1993, Frank and Frank wrote: "We propose to group those who receive psychotherapy into five rough categories: the psychotic, the neurotic or persistently disturbed, the shaken, the misbehaving, and the discontented" (p. 11). This is an example of one of many formal and informal diagnostic systems that exist for grouping individuals with mental health problems. These systems may be as simple and intuitive as Frank and Frank's (1991) or as complex as the fifth edition of the *Diagnostic and Statistical Manual of Mental Disorders (DSM-5)* The *DSM-5* now includes nearly 300 mental disorders in its 947 pages (American Psychiatric Association, 2013).

The revision process for the *DSM-5* has been nothing short of amazing. We mean this in at least two ways; the effort has been amazing: " . . . hundreds of people working toward a common goal over a 12-year process" (American Psychiatric Association, 2013, p. 5). And the politics have been amazing. Originally planned for publication in May, 2011 after significant delays related to many factors, including conflicts of interest among work group members, it was finally released at the American Psychiatric Association annual meeting in San Francisco on May 18, 2013. Along the way, there were strong letters of protest from many constituents, much gnashing of teeth, and wailing of the sort that can only happen on the Internet. To help capture the controversy, here's a short excerpt from a *Psychology Today* article written by Allen Frances, MD, former chair of the *DSM-IV* Task Force and professor emeritus at Duke University.

> This is the saddest moment in my 45 year career. . . . The . . . American Psychiatric Association has . . . [approved] . . . a deeply flawed *DSM-5* containing many changes that seem clearly unsafe and scientifically unsound.

Despite criticisms the *DSM* has been and will likely continue to be the authoritative diagnostic guide for North American mental health professionals. The first edition was published in 1952; the second, in 1968; the third, in 1980; a revision of the third edition, in 1987; the fourth edition in 1994; and in 2000, a text revision of *DSM-IV (DSM-IV-TR)*. Even with so many editions and extensive review, psychiatric diagnosis remains controversial. As Widiger and Clark (2000) claimed of the *DSM-IV*: "There might not in fact be one sentence within *DSM-IV* for which well-meaning clinicians, theorists, and researchers could not find some basis for fault" (p. 946). But, of course, the *DSM-5* has outdone the *DSM-IV* both in terms of complexity and controversy. This controversy has already led to extensive discussion, debate, and publication within the mental health professions. For example, as of February 1, 2013, there were over 300 professional publications listed on PsycINFO with the word "*DSM-5*" in the title . . . despite the fact that the 5th edition of the *DSM* wouldn't be published for another 3 months.

Disputes surrounding psychiatric diagnosis and the concept of mental disorders run so deep that the *DSM-IV-TR* and *ICD-10* both include explanations or disclaimers for why the term "mental disorder" is used. The *DSM-IV-TR* contained a brief but articulate section titled "Definition of Mental Disorder." In this section, the *DSM* authors admitted they have produced a manual for diagnosing a concept that lacks an adequate operational definition:

> . . . although this manual provides a classification of mental disorders, it must be admitted that no definition adequately specifies precise boundaries for the concept of "mental disorder." The concept of mental disorder, like many other concepts in medicine and science, lacks a consistent operational definition that covers all situations. (American Psychiatric Association, 2000, p. xxx)

Interestingly, although the *DSM-5* continues to use the term mental disorder (and not mental illness), this time around the authors refrained from commenting on the reasoning behind this choice.

As we discuss diagnostic interviewing strategies in the following pages, be forewarned that you are venturing into only partially charted waters. Nonetheless, as scientists and professionals, we believe it's a fascinating journey, filled with adventure, intrigue, and more than an occasional unresolved dispute.

Defining Mental Disorders

From your own experiences you probably recognize that it's often difficult to draw a clear line between mental disorders and physical illness. When you become physically ill, sometimes it's obvious that your stress level, lack of sleep, or mental state has contributed to your illness. Other times, when you're distressed psychologically, your physical condition can contribute to a disturbed emotional state and thinking processes (Jakovljevic, 2006; Witvliet et al., 2008). The difficulty distinguishing between mental and physical problems was acknowledged in the *DSM-IV-TR*:

> A compelling literature documents that there is much "physical" in "mental" disorders and much "mental" in "physical" disorders. The problem raised by the term "mental" disorders has been much clearer than its solution, and, unfortunately, the term persists in the title of *DSM-IV* because we have not found an appropriate substitute. (American Psychiatric Association, 2000, p. xxx)

Despite ongoing quandaries over what to call mental disorders, and whether mind or body is the primary contributor to such disorders, it's safe to say that the *DSM-5* contributors have identified numerous important cognitive, emotional, and behavioral problems or deviances that exist in many people throughout the world. These mental conditions or mental disorders produce immense suffering, conflict, and distress in the lives of millions. Without a doubt, and no matter what we call them, mental disorders are frequently identifiable and have clear and adverse effects on individuals, couples, families, and communities.

The *DSM-5* remains a primarily descriptive and categorical system. This means it provides descriptions of symptom sets associated with specific diagnoses and that individuals are classified as having or as not having psychiatric diagnoses. Although the *DSM-5* has been reorganized to reflect developmental and dimensional issues in psychopathology it has not moved significantly away from a categorical approach: "Despite the problem posed by categorical diagnoses the *DSM-5* Task Force recognized that it is premature scientifically to propose alternative definitons for most disorders" (p. 13).

In its introduction, the *DSM-5* offers a general definition of *mental disorder*:

> A mental disorder is a syndrome characterized by clinically significant disturbance in an individual's cognition, emotion regulation, or behavior that reflects a dysfunction in the psychological, biological, or developmental processes underlying mental functioning. Mental disorders are usually associated with significant distress or disability in social, occupational, or other important activities. (American Psychiatric Association, 2013, p. 20)

The *DSM-5* also includes information about what is not a mental disorder:

An expectable or culturally approved response to a common stressor or loss, such as the death of a loved one, is not a mental disorder. Socially deviant behavior (e.g., political, religious, or sexual) and conflicts that are primarily between the individual and society are not mental disorders unless the deviance or conflict results from a dysfunction in the individual, as described above. (p. 20)

Not surprisingly, significant vagueness in the *DSM-5* definition of *mental disorder* remains. If you go back and read through the *DSM-5* definition of mental disorder several times, you'll find substantial lack of clarity. For example, there's plenty of room for debate regarding what constitutes "a clinically significant disturbance." Additionally, how can it be determined if human behavior "reflects a dysfunction in the psychological, biological, or developmental processes underlying mental functioning" (p. 20)? Further, the manual recognizes that "an expected or culturally approved" behavioral response is not a mental disorder, but doesn't provide any guidelines for making this judgment (this is an example of a universal exclusion criterion, as discussed in Chapter 6).

Over the years the *DSM* system has received much criticism for being vague, subjective, and political (Eriksen & Kress, 2005; Horwitz, 2002; Horwitz & Wakefield, 2007). As a historical example, Szasz (1970) wrote:

Which kinds of social deviance are regarded as mental illnesses? The answer is, those that entail personal conduct not conforming to psychiatrically defined and enforced rules of mental health. If narcotics-avoidance is a rule of mental health, narcotics ingestion will be a sign of mental illness; if even-temperedness is a rule of mental health, depression and elation will be signs of mental illness; and so forth. (p. xxvi)

Szasz's point is well taken. After all is said and done, *DSM*'s general definition of *mental disorder* and the criteria for each individual mental disorder consist of carefully studied, meticulously outlined, and politically influenced subjective judgments. This is an important perspective to keep in mind as we continue down the road toward clinical interviewing as a means for psychiatric diagnosis and treatment planning.

Why Diagnose?

Like Szasz (1970), many of our students want to reject the entire concept of diagnosis. They're critical of and cynical about the *DSM*, or they believe that applying diagnoses dehumanizes clients by affixing a label to them and then ignoring their individual qualities, what Morrison (2007) has referred to as *pigeonholing*. Whatever their arguments, our position regarding diagnosis remains consistent. We empathize with our students' complaints, commiserate about problems associated with diagnosing unique individuals, criticize the many examples of inappropriate diagnostic proliferation (e.g., bipolar disorder in youth), but we continue to value the teaching and learning of diagnostic assessment strategies and procedures, justifying ourselves with both philosophical and practical arguments.

Philosophical Support

No matter what we call them, mental disorders exist. As far as we know, emotional distress, mental suffering, character pathology, and suicidal behavior have existed from day one. Psychiatric diagnosis is designed to classify or categorize mental disorders based on specific defining characteristics. Knowledge about mental disorders, their similarities, differences, usual course and prognosis, and prevalence helps mental health professionals provide more appropriate and more effective treatments. Such knowledge is reassuring and empowering to therapists who want to help clients. Additionally, this knowledge base guides research on preventing mental disorders.

Practical Support

There are a number of positive practical outcomes of accurate diagnosis. A *diagnosis* is a consolidated, organized description of client symptoms. Arriving at this shorthand description requires careful observation and inquiry. After the best diagnosis is obtained, clinicians can communicate with other professionals, insurance or managed care companies, and other interested parties.

At best, a diagnosis is a working hypothesis. It forces clinicians to bring together disparate pieces of the puzzle and tentatively name a cluster of symptoms. It then suggests a general course of action that, if pursued, should yield somewhat predictable responses. It lays the groundwork for planned interventions and informed use of theory and technique.

In addition to enabling professional communication and hypothesis testing, a final positive and practical aspect of diagnosing is this: Sometimes, a label is a huge relief for clients. Clients come for help with a confusing and frightening symptom set. They may feel alone and uniquely troubled. They may feel no one else in the world has ever been so dysfunctional, odd, or anxious. It can be a big relief to be *diagnosed*, to have your problems named, categorized, and defined. It can be comforting to realize that others—many others—have reacted to trauma in similar ways, experienced depression in similar ways, or even developed similar maladaptive coping strategies (such as irrational thoughts or damaging compulsions). The wise clinician realizes that diagnosis can imply and instill hope (Frank & Frank, 1991; Pierce, 2004; Mulligan, MacCulloch, Good, & Nicholas, 2012).

Specific Diagnostic Criteria

In contrast to establishing a satisfactory general definition for mental disorders, identifying a *DSM* diagnosis for a particular client may seem, on the surface, rather straightforward. After all, psychiatric diagnosis is based on a process where clinicians determine the presence or absence of various symptom clusters (i.e., syndromes). In most cases, the *DSM-5* provides specific, more or less measurable criteria for its diagnoses. Typically, *DSM* diagnoses are characterized by a symptom list for defining the condition. For example, to qualify for generalized anxiety disorder, individuals must meet the criteria in Table 10.1.

The diagnostic criteria for generalized anxiety disorder illustrate challenging tasks associated with accurate diagnosis. First, based on criterion A, diagnostic interviewers must establish whether a given client is experiencing "excessive"

Table 10.1 Diagnostic Criteria for Generalized Anxiety Disorder (*DSM-5*: 300.02)

This table is a summary and adaptation of the *DSM-5* diagnostic criteria for generalized anxiety disorder. For the actual criteria, you should consult the *DSM-5* (American Psychiatric Association, 2013, p. 222).

A. The client has "excessive anxiety and worry" that occurs "more days than not for at least 6 months" and pertains to "a number of events or activities."

B. The client has difficulty controlling the anxiety or worry.

C. Three or more of the specific symptoms listed below are present and linked to the anxiety/worry

   A. feeling restlessness or "keyed up or on edge"
   B. feelings of fatigue that come on easily
   C. blank mind or problems with concentration
   D. "irritability"
   E. "muscle tension"
   F. problems sleeping

D. The preceding symptoms "cause clinically significant distress or impairment in social, occupational, or other important areas of functioning."

E. The symptoms aren't caused by a substance or a medical condition.

F. The symptoms aren't "better explained by another mental disorder."

---

anxiety and worry, how frequently the anxiety is occurring, how long the anxiety has been occurring, and how many events or activities the individual is anxious or worried about. This information relies on the interviewer's ability to gather appropriate symptom-related information *and* the client's ability to articulately report symptom-related information. In addition, obtaining information required by criterion A involves interviewer and client subjectivity (i.e., the determination of what constitutes "excessive").

Second, under criterion B, interviewers must assess how difficult clients find it to control their worry. This information requires an evaluation of client coping skills and efforts, which essentially involves asking questions about what clients have tried to do to quell their anxiety and how well these coping efforts have worked in the past.

Third, and perhaps the most straightforward diagnostic task, interviewers must identify whether clients are experiencing specific anxiety-related symptoms (see Table 10.1). Unfortunately, even this apparently simple task is fraught with complications, especially in cases where clients are motivated to either overreport or underreport symptoms. For example, clients seeking disability status for an anxiety disorder may be motivated to exaggerate their symptoms, and clients who desperately want to remain in the workplace may minimize symptoms. Consequently, along with questioning about these specific anxiety symptoms, the interviewer must stay alert to the validity and reliability of the client's self-reported symptoms (Feinn, Gelernter, Cubells, Farrer, & Kranzler, 2009; Gilboa & Verfaellie, 2010; J. Sommers-Flanagan & Sommers-Flanagan, 1998).

Fourth, to label an individual as having *generalized anxiety disorder* (GAD), interviewers need considerable knowledge of other *DSM* diagnostic criteria. Eleven other diagnoses that may need to be ruled out are listed in GAD criterion F.

An interviewer needs to have working knowledge of many other diagnostic criteria to assign or rule out a GAD diagnosis. Obviously, this is no small task; it requires lengthy education, training, and supervision.

Fifth, criterion D requires interviewers to determine whether reported anxiety symptoms cause "clinically significant distress or impairment in social, occupational, or other important areas of functioning." Criterion D is the distress and impairment criterion. Although this criterion is essential for diagnosis, it is also inherently subjective. Nowhere in *DSM-5* is a clinically significant impairment defined.

Sixth, based on criterion E, before establishing a definitive diagnosis, interviewers need to determine whether the anxiety symptoms are caused by exposure to or intake of a substance, or a general medical condition. Substances and medical conditions need to be ruled out as causal factors in virtually every *DSM-5* diagnostic category.

Overall, the GAD example illustrates a range of tasks and issues with which diagnostic interviewers must grapple. The reality is that, based on the *DSM*'s diagnostic paradigm, a psychiatric diagnosis is seated within the context of a unique individual. Indeed, if it were not for unique individuals and their confusing variability in reporting their personal experiences and their confounding and confusing motivational and interpersonal dynamics, psychiatric diagnosis would be a simpler process.

Assessment and Diagnosis Problems

To determine if a client meets the diagnostic criteria for GAD, interviewers must determine whether the client has three of six symptoms from criterion C. Given this fact, it may be sufficient (and justifiable) to directly ask the client a series of specific *DSM-5*–generated questions pertaining to generalized anxiety disorder. For example, the following questions could be asked:

1. Over the past 6 months or more, have you felt restless, keyed up, or on edge for more days than not?
2. Over the past 6 months, have you felt easily fatigued more often than not?
3. Over the past 6 months, have you noticed, on most days, that you have difficulty concentrating or that your mind keeps going blank?
4. Over the past 6 months, have you felt irritable at some point on most days?
5. Over the past 6 months, have you found yourself troubled by muscle tension more often than not?
6. Over the past 6 months, have you had difficulty falling asleep, or have you found that you regularly experience restless or unsatisfying sleep?

Using this simple and straightforward diagnostic approach may, in some circumstances, produce an accurate diagnosis. However, in reality, accurate diagnostic assessment is considerably more complex. As suggested from constructive critiques of psychiatric diagnosis and differential activation theory, the preceding practice of asking six consecutive negatively worded questions focusing on anxiety may adversely affect the patient, the patient's mood, the working alliance, and consequently diagnostic reliability and validity (Eriksen & Kress, 2005; Lau, Segal, & Williams, 2004).

Further, in *DSM-5*'s introductory section, it is emphasized that diagnostic criteria should not be applied in a check-list manner:

> The case formulation for any given patient must involve a careful clinical history and concise summary of the social, psychological, and biological factors that may have contributed to developing a given mental disorder. Hence, it is not sufficient to simply check off the symptoms in the diagnostic criteria to make a mental disorder diagnosis. (American Psychiatric Association, 2013, p. 19)

Before moving on to a detailed description of diagnostic assessment strategies and procedures, we identify several specific problems associated with establishing an accurate diagnostic label for individual clients:

Client deceit or misinformation: Clients may not be straightforward or honest in their symptom descriptions (Feinn et al., 2009; Jaghab, Skodnek, & Padder, 2006). Even in cases when they are honest, they may have difficulty accurately describing their symptoms in ways that match *DSM* criteria. In addition, if you gather information from individuals other than clients (e.g., from teachers, parents, romantic partners), you may obtain invalid information for many different reasons. In fact, research indicates that when children, parents, teachers, and others rate the same individual, their interrater agreement is generally low (Rothen et al., 2009). Despite this fact, obtaining diagnostic-related information from parents and other available informants remains essential.

Interviewer countertransference: When using a diagnostic interview, you may lose your objectivity and/or distort client information. This may occur partly because of countertransference (Aboraya, 2007). For example, if a client triggers a negative reaction in you, you may feel an impulse to "punish" the client by giving a more severe diagnostic label. Similarly, you may minimize psychopathology and associated diagnoses if you like your client.

Diagnostic comorbidity: In many cases, clients qualify for more than one *DSM* diagnosis. In fact, with regard to children, diagnostic comorbidity occurs more often than not (Samet & Hasin, 2008; Watson, Swan, & Nathan, 2011). This comorbidity problem makes sorting out appropriate diagnostic labels even more difficult.

Differential diagnosis: Although some clients report symptoms consistent with more than one diagnostic entity and are appropriately assigned two or more diagnostic labels, other clients report confusing symptom clusters requiring extensive questioning for diagnostic clarity. For example, it's notoriously difficult, albeit important, to discriminate some diagnoses from others (e.g., mood disorder with psychotic features versus schizoaffective disorder versus schizophrenia versus delusional disorder). Despite difficulties sorting out these various disorders, diagnostic specificity is important because of treatment implications (i.e., medication type, treatment approach, hospitalization, prognosis).

Confounding cultural or situational factors: in the *DSM-5* it is acknowledged that culture and context will influence diagnosis: " . . . The boundaries between normality and pathology vary across cultures for specific types of behaviors." (p. 14). Consequently, your diagnostic task includes a consideration of your clients' individual social, cultural, and situational contexts when providing diagnoses, which is not always an easy task (Hays, 2008).

Given these problems, many therapists and researchers advise using what has been referred to as "multimethod, multirater, multisetting assessment procedures" (J. Sommers-Flanagan & Sommers-Flanagan, 1998, p. 191). This means that, under ideal circumstances, diagnosticians gather a broad spectrum of diagnostic-related information from (a) various assessment methods (e.g., clinical interview, behavior rating scales, projective assessments); (b) various raters (e.g., parents, teachers, clinicians, and/or romantic partners); and (c) various settings (e.g., school, home, clinician's office, work).

DIAGNOSTIC ASSESSMENT: METHODS AND PROCEDURES

After this brief taste of diagnostic interviewing problems and tasks, you may feel overwhelmed. Learning diagnostic interviewing assessment procedures is a formidable challenge. However, amazingly, many mental health professionals have learned to use the *DSM system* with sensitivity, precision, and grace. Doing so requires tenacity, rote learning, patience, and balance.

A number of methods are available for gathering diagnostic-relevant information, including diagnostic interviewing, social/developmental history, questionnaires and rating scales, physical examinations, behavioral observations, projective techniques, and performance-based testing. Because this book is on interviewing-based approaches, our discussion focuses on diagnostic interviewing.

Diagnostic Interviewing

There are two basic forms of diagnostic interviews: semistructured and structured. They're defined as:

> [A] semistructured interview typically includes a predetermined set of questions followed by either unplanned questioning or a free response or exploration period. (Sommers-Flanagan et al., 2014, in press)
> [A] structured clinical interview is a tightly managed protocol or process wherein clinicians ask a systematic series of predetermined questions, including follow-up questions. In this approach there is little or no opportunity for unplanned or spontaneous questioning by clinicians and little or no spontaneous exploration of diverse topics by patients. (Sommers-Flanagan et al., 2014, in press)

Many published diagnostic interviewing procedures exist, most of which are based on the *DSM-III-R* or *DSM-IV* diagnostic criteria. Determining an appropriate diagnostic label is the primary or exclusive goal of these procedures. Diagnostic interviews can be administered by counselors, social workers, psychologists, physicians, or technicians with specific training in administering a particular diagnostic interview (Segal & Hersen, 2010). In some cases, the training required for an individual to administer a particular diagnostic interview is extensive.

Adult Diagnostic Interviewing

Numerous adult diagnostic interviewing schedules exist. Some schedules are broad spectrum; they assess for a wide range of *DSM* disorders (First, Spitzer, Gibbon, & Williams, 1995; Lobbestael, Leurgans, & Arntz, 2011; Spitzer, Williams, Gibbon, & First, 1992). Other schedules are more specific and circumscribed; for example, some structured and semistructured interview schedules such as the Alcohol Use Disorder and Associated Disabilities Interview Schedule-IV (AUDADIS-IV) or the Anxiety Disorders Interview Schedule for *DSM-IV* (ADIS-IV) evaluate only for the presence or absence of specific conditions (Grisham, Brown, & Campbell, 2004; Ruan et al., 2008).

Child Diagnostic Interviewing

There are also numerous child-diagnostic interviewing schedules. Again, these can be classified as either broad spectrum (e.g., The Child Assessment Schedule; Hodges, 1985) or circumscribed (e.g., Anxiety Disorders Interview Schedule for Children; Silverman, 1987).

Advantages Associated With Structured Diagnostic Interviewing

Advantages associated with structured diagnostic interviewing include:

1. Structured diagnostic interview schedules are standardized and straightforward to administer. Therapists can ask clients specific diagnostic-relevant questions.
2. Diagnostic interview schedules generally produce a *DSM* diagnosis, consequently relieving clinicians of subjectively weighing many alternative diagnoses.
3. Diagnostic interview schedules generally exhibit greater interrater reliability than therapists functioning without such schedules.
4. Diagnostic interviews are well suited for scientific research. It's imperative that researchers obtain valid and reliable diagnoses to effectively study the nature, course, prognosis, and treatment responsiveness of particular disorders.

Disadvantages Associated With Diagnostic Interviewing

There are also numerous disadvantages associated with diagnostic interviewing:

1. Many diagnostic interviews require considerable time for administration. For example, the Schedule for Affective Disorders and Schizophrenia for School-Age Children (Puig-Antich, Chambers, & Tabrizi, 1983) may take 1 to 4 hours to administer, depending on whether both parent and child are interviewed.
2. Diagnostic interviews don't allow experienced diagnosticians to take shortcuts. This is cumbersome because experts in psychiatric diagnosis might require less information to accurately diagnose clients than beginning therapists.

3. Some clinicians complain that diagnostic interviews are too structured and rigid, de-emphasizing rapport-building and basic interpersonal communication between client and therapist. Extensive structure may not be acceptable for practitioners who prefer using intuition and who emphasize relationship development.

4. Although structured diagnostic interviews have demonstrated reliability, some clinicians question their validity. All diagnostic interviews are limited and leave out important information about client personal history, personality style, and more. Critics contend that two different therapists may administer the same interview schedule and consistently come up with the same incorrect diagnosis.

Given their time-intensive requirements in combination with mental health provider needs for time-efficient evaluation and treatment, it's not surprising that diagnostic interviewing procedures are underutilized and sometimes unutilized in clinical practice. In fact, critics contend that even the diagnostic criteria themselves are more oriented toward researchers than clinicians (Phillips et al., 2012):

> It is difficult to avoid the conclusion that the diagnostic criteria are mainly useful for researchers, who are obligated to insure a uniform research population. (p. 2)

The reality is that researchers and academics are—far and away—the primary users of structured diagnostic interviewing procedures.

THE SCIENCE OF CLINICAL INTERVIEWING: DIAGNOSTIC RELIABILITY AND VALIDITY

The clinical interview is the cornerstone of diagnostic assessment (Sommers-Flanagan et al., 2014, in press). No self-respecting (or ethical) mental health professional would consider diagnosing a client without conducting a clinical interview. Nevertheless, the scientific question remains: Do diagnostic interviews provide reliable and valid diagnostic data and thereby conclusions?

Reliability refers to replicability and stability. If a procedure, such as a diagnostic interview, is reliable, it consistently produces the same result; two therapists, interviewing the same client, would come up with the same diagnosis. Statistically speaking, it's a commonly agreed on fact that an instrument or procedure must be reliable (it must produce consistent results) to be valid (producing a correct or truthful result). However, it's also possible for an interview procedure to be highly reliable but invalid—when two or more interviewers consistently agree on diagnoses, but the diagnoses are incorrect.

In 1980, along with the publication of the *DSM-III*, many mental health professionals, especially psychiatrists, breathed a collective sigh of relief. Finally, after nearly 30 years of rampant diagnostic subjectivity, there was a comprehensive and atheoretical system for objectively determining whether an individual suffered from a mental disorder. More importantly, there was now a system, complete with measurable diagnostic criteria, for determining identifying specific mental disorders. The *DSM-III* was showered with praise. The reliability problem (the problem articulated by the fact that two different psychiatrists, seeing the same patient in a brief period of time, often disagreed about the proper diagnosis) was finally addressed; in the minds of some mental health professionals, the reliability problem was solved (Sommers-Flanagan et al., 2014, in press).

However, other professionals believed that *DSM*'s diagnostic reliability problem was far from solved. In their scathing critique of contemporary diagnosis, Kutchins and Kirk (1997) wrote:

> Twenty years after the reliability problem became the central scientific focus of *DSM*, there is still not a single major study showing that *DSM* (any version) is routinely used with high reliability by regular mental health clinicians. Nor is there any credible evidence that any version of the manual has greatly increased its reliability beyond the previous version. The *DSM* revolution in reliability has been a revolution in rhetoric, not in reality. (p. 53)

Although Kutchins and Kirk's (1997) position is sometimes considered radical, mainstream and conservative researchers also consistently question the *DSM* system's reliability and validity (Craig, 2005; Hersen & Turner, 2003). For example, in a study of how clinicians make judgments about mental disorders in youth, it was determined that diagnostic decisions vary—perhaps appropriately—based on social context and race. However, perhaps less appropriately, clinician theoretical orientation, age, and occupation were also significantly associated with final diagnostic decisions (Pottick, Kirk, Hsieh, & Tian, 2007).

A summary of diagnostic interviewing reliability published in the *Encyclopedia of Clinical Psychology* described the reliability and validity problem this way:

> The scientific consensus is that psychiatric diagnostic reliability greatly improved with the 1980 publication of *DSM-III* and subsequent development of structured or semi-structured clinical interviewing protocols like the SCID-I. Despite this progress, problems with inter-rater reliability and questions about validity persist. Typically researchers have reported kappa coefficients (a measure of reliability) for the SCID-I ranging from −0.03 to 1.00 (with a recent study using *DSM-IV* criteria ranging from 0.61 to 0.83; Lobbestael, Leurgans, and Arntz 2011). For the SCID-II kappa coefficients have ranged from 0.43 to 1.00 (and 0.77 to 0.94 in a more recent study using *DSM-IV*; Lobbestael et al., 2011). It should be noted that these research studies have used highly trained interviewers and that there is little scientific evidence demonstrating that independent clinicians would obtain similar reliability using the SCID or other structured diagnostic assessment interviews. (Sommers-Flanagan et al., 2014, in press)

As it turns out, obtaining diagnostic validity for specific cultural and age-based subgroups is an additional diagnostic challenge. For example, in a study of adolescent alcohol users, the researchers were surprised to discover that youth participants didn't drink in ways that matched the diagnostic criteria. Specifically, the youths puzzled over the diagnostic criterion "drinking more or longer than intended" because their behavioral goal had been to drink until intoxication; they hadn't considered setting pre-drinking limits on consumption (Chung & Martin, 2005). Consequently, that diagnostic criterion made little sense to them.

Although controversy over the reliability and validity of the *DSM* system still persists, a number of scientifically supported conclusions can be drawn from the literature on clinical interviewing for psychiatric diagnoses thus far:

- Generally, the diagnostic criteria for *DSM-IV* had more potential and, in many cases, higher reliability than previous diagnostic nomenclatures; it remains unclear whether the *DSM-5* will further improve reliability.
- The more closely you stick to the *DSM* diagnostic criteria, the more likely you can produce reliable diagnoses. Even so, reliability among clinical practitioners is likely to be only moderate at best.
- The more formal training you receive in a diagnostic interviewing procedure, the more likely you are to produce reliable diagnoses.
- More structured interviewing procedures that de-emphasize contextual factors are more likely to produce reliable diagnoses; however, de-emphasizing contextual factors de-emphasizes individual uniqueness, which can result in cookbook approaches to diagnostic assessment.

Some diagnostic criteria aren't a good fit for culturally diverse clients, youth, the elderly, and others; consequently, although emphasizing individual uniqueness complicates the diagnostic process, it's often essential.

A BALANCED APPROACH TO CONDUCTING DIAGNOSTIC CLINICAL INTERVIEWS

We advocate a middle ground position on diagnostic interviewing. We recognize that some clinicians prefer to ignore or minimize diagnostic interviewing, whereas others promote it as essential (Horwitz & Wakefield, 2007). Although developing diagnostic skills is standard for many counselors, social workers, psychologists, and psychiatrists, if too much attention is paid to diagnosis, clients' unique, human qualities can be overlooked. Consequently, consistent with professional ethical codes and principles, we believe a diagnostic interview is a collaborative process between therapist and client that leads logically to a theoretically or empirically supported treatment plan (see Chapter 5). As such, a diagnostic interview should, at a minimum, contain the following components:

1. An introduction characterized by culturally sensitive warmth, role induction, and active listening. During this introduction, culturally appropriate standardized questionnaires and intake/referral information may be used.
2. An extensive review of client problems, associated goals, and a detailed analysis of the client's primary problem and goal. This should include questions about the client's symptoms using the *DSM-5* as a guide—but not as a cookbook.
3. A brief discussion of experiences (personal history) relevant to the client's primary problem. This should include a history of the presenting problem if such a history hasn't already been conducted.
4. A brief mental status examination.
5. A review of the client's current situation, including his or her social support network, coping skills, physical health, and personal strengths.

Introduction and Role Induction

All clients should be greeted with warmth and compassion. The goal of developing a diagnosis and treatment plan shouldn't change the therapist's interest in the client as a unique individual.

After reviewing confidentiality limits, skillful clinicians introduce diagnostic interviews to clients using a statement similar to the following:

> Today, we'll be working together to try to understand what has been troubling you. This means I want you to talk freely with me, but also, I'll be asking lots of questions to clarify as precisely as possible what you've been experiencing. The better we can identify your main concerns, the better we'll be able to come up with a plan for resolving them. Does that sound okay to you?

This statement emphasizes collaboration and deemphasizes pathology. The language "try to understand" and "main concerns" are client-friendly ways of talking about diagnostic issues. This statement is a role induction designed to educate clients about the interview process. When clients understand what to expect, they'll be more responsive to questions. Additionally, clients usually become engaged in the interview when asked "Does that sound okay to you?" Rarely do clients respond to this collaborative invitation with "No! It's not okay!" If they do, you've instantly obtained important diagnostic information.

Throughout the interview, don't forget to use active listening skills. Beginning therapists often become too structured, excluding client spontaneity, or too unstructured, allowing clients to ramble. Remember to integrate active listening and diagnostic questioning throughout your diagnostic interview.

Reviewing Client Problems

Although we covered client problem conceptualization systems in Chapter 7, we'd like to reiterate a few basic issues in the diagnostic interviewing context. At a minimum, a diagnostic interview should include an extensive review of client problems (and questioning about symptoms based on *DSM* diagnostic criteria), associated goals, and a detailed analysis of the client's primary problem and goal. While reviewing these areas, consider the following issues.

Respect Your Client's Perspective, but Don't Automatically Accept Your Client's Self-Diagnosis as Valid

Diagnostic information is available to the general public. Consequently, many clients will begin diagnostic interviews with professional diagnostic language. For example:

- Over the past 3 months, I've been so depressed. It's really getting to me.
- I think my child has ADHD.
- I've figured out that I'm bipolar.
- I just get these compulsive behaviors that I can't stop. I have no control over them.
- My main problem is panic. Whenever I'm out in public, I just freeze.

Some diagnostic terminology has been so popularized that its specificity has been lost. This is especially true with the term *depression*. Many people now use the word depression to describe feelings of sadness. The astute diagnostician recognizes that depression is a syndrome and not a mood state. In the first example on the preceding list, further questioning about sleep dysfunction, appetite or weight changes, and concentration problems are necessary before concluding that clinical depression is present. Research has shown that using the single question "Are you depressed?" isn't an adequate substitute for an appropriate diagnostic interview (Kawase et al., 2006; Vahter, Kreegipuu, Talvik, & Gross-Paju, 2007).

Similarly, the lay public overuses the terms *compulsive*, *panic*, *hyperactive*, and *bipolar*. In diagnostic circles, compulsive behavior generally alerts the clinician to symptoms associated with either obsessive-compulsive disorder or obsessive-compulsive personality disorder. In contrast, many individuals with eating disorders and substance abuse disorders refer to their behaviors as *compulsive*. Similarly, panic disorder is a very specific syndrome in *DSM-5*. However, many individuals with social phobias, agoraphobia, or public speaking anxiety talk about panic. Therefore, when clients describe themselves as having *panic*, additional information is needed before assigning a panic disorder diagnosis. Finally, diagnostic rates of bipolar disorder in both youth and adults have skyrocketed (Blader & Carlson, 2007; Moreno et al., 2007). As a result, the public (and, unfortunately some mental health professionals), are inclined to quickly attribute irritability or mood swings to *bipolar disorder*. In contrast, we still recommend using established diagnostic criteria and hope that *DSM-5* will help resolve this problem.

Keep Diagnostic Checklists Available

When questioning clients about problems, it's crucial to keep *DSM-5* diagnostic criteria in mind, but few of us have perfect memories for the *DSM* diagnostic conditions. To cope with this challenge, we recommend using checklists to aid in recalling specific *DSM-5* diagnostic criteria. Homemade diagnostic checklists can help you become familiar with key diagnostic criteria, without necessarily committing them to memory.

Accept the Fact That You May Not Be Able to Accurately Diagnose After a Single Interview

It's good to have high expectations and lofty goals. However, as cognitive theory and therapy has shown, unreasonably high expectations can set us up for frustration and disappointment (Leahy, 2004). It's important to recognize that, in many cases, you won't be able to assign an accurate diagnosis to a client after a single interview. In fact, you may leave the first interview more confused than when you began. Fear not. The *DSM-5* provides practitioners with procedures for handling diagnostic uncertainty (see American Psychiatric Association, 2013). These procedures include:

> *V codes: DSM-5* includes V codes for indicating that treatment is focusing on a problem that doesn't meet diagnostic criteria for a mental disorder. Examples include V61.20 (parent-child relational problem) and V62.82 (bereavement).

Code 300.9: This code refers to *Unspecified Mental Disorder*. It's used when the clinician determines symptoms are present, but full criteria for a specific mental disorder are not met. Also, the clinician doesn't specify why the criteria aren't met.

Provisional diagnosis: When a specific diagnosis is followed by the word *provisional* in parentheses, it communicates a degree of uncertainty. A provisional diagnosis is a working diagnosis, indicating that additional information may modify the diagnosis.

Client Personal History

Even when time is very limited, a minimal social or developmental history helps ensure accurate diagnosis. For example, *DSM-5* lists numerous disorders that have depressive symptoms as one of their primary features, including (a) persistent depressive disorder, (b) major depressive disorder, (c) adjustment disorder with mixed anxiety and depressed mood, (d) adjustment disorder with depressed mood, (e) bipolar I disorder, (f) bipolar II disorder, and (g) cyclothymic disorder. Additionally, many other disorders include depressive-like symptoms or symptoms that are commonly comorbid with one of the previously listed depressive disorders. These include, but are not limited to: (a) posttraumatic stress disorder, (b) generalized anxiety disorder, (c) anorexia nervosa, (d) bulimia nervosa, and (e) conduct disorder. The question is not necessarily whether depressive symptoms exist in a particular client, but rather, which depressive symptoms exist, in what context, and for how long? Without adequate historical information, you can't discriminate between various depressive disorders and comorbid conditions.

In some cases, accurate diagnosis is directly linked to client history. For example, a panic disorder diagnosis requires information about previous panic attacks (Sanfelippo, 2006). Similarly, post-traumatic stress disorder, by default, requires a trauma history, and AD/HD can't be diagnosed unless there was evidence that symptoms existed prior to age 12. With regard to conduct disorder, if the youth is or has been living in a neighborhood with a strong culture of violence, drug use, and theft, it may be an inappropriate diagnosis.

Mental Status Examination

As emphasized in Chapter 8, mental status examinations aren't the same as diagnostic interviews and shouldn't be considered diagnostic procedures. However, current mental state is often linked to diagnostic conditions. In particular, mental status information can help determine whether substance use is an immediate factor affecting client consciousness and functioning. Mental status examinations also inform you of client thinking and perceptual processes that may be associated with particular diagnostic conditions.

Current Situation

Obtaining information about a client's current functioning is a standard part of the intake interview. With regard to diagnostic interviewing, a few significant issues should be reviewed and emphasized.

A detailed review of your client's current situation includes an evaluation of his or her typical day, social support network, coping skills, physical health (if this area hasn't been covered during a medical history), and personal strengths. Each of these areas can provide information crucial to the diagnostic process.

The Usual or Typical Day

Yalom (2002) has written that he believes an inquiry in to the "patient's daily schedule" is especially revealing. He wrote:

> . . . in recent initial interviews this inquiry allowed me to learn of activities I might not otherwise have known for months: two hours a day of computer solitaire; three hours a night in Internet sex chat rooms under a different identity; massive procrastination at work and ensuing shame; a daily schedule so demanding that I was exhausted listening to it; a middle-aged woman's extended daily (sometimes hourly) phone calls with her father; a gay woman's long daily phone conversations with an ex-lover whom she disliked but from whom she felt unable to separate. (pp. 208–209)

Asking about the client's typical day can seem boring and tedious, but can open up a cache of diagnostically rich data that moves you toward identifying appropriate treatment goals and an associated treatment plan.

Client Social Support Network

Sometimes, it's critical to obtain diagnostic information from people other than the client, especially when interviewing children and adolescents. In such cases, parents are often interviewed as part of the diagnostic work-up (see Chapter 13 for more detailed information on strategies for interviewing young clients and their parents). However, even when interviewing adults, outside information may be necessary. To rely exclusively on a single clinical interview to establish a diagnosis may be inappropriate and unprofessional. As Morrison (2007) wrote:

> Adults can also be unaware of their family histories or details about their own development. Patients with psychosis or personality disorder may not have enough perspective to judge accurately many of their own symptoms. In any of these situations, the history you obtain from people who know your patient well may strongly influence your diagnosis. (p. 203)

People other than your client who provide you with information are often referred to as *collateral informants*. To collect information from collateral informants you'll need to have your client sign the requisite releases.

Client Coping Skills Assessment

Client coping skills may be related to diagnosis and can facilitate treatment planning. For example, clients with anxiety disorders frequently use avoidance strategies to reduce anxiety (e.g., agoraphobics don't leave their homes; individuals with claustrophobia stay away from stuffy rooms or enclosed spaces). It's important to examine whether clients are coping with their problems and moving toward mastery or simply reacting to problems and thereby exacerbating symptoms and/or restricting themselves from social or vocational activities.

Coping skills also may be assessed by using projective techniques or behavior observation. Projective techniques include having clients imagine a particular stressful scenario (sometimes referred to as a simulation), and behavioral observations may be collected either in an office or in outside setting (e.g., school, home, workplace). As noted previously, collateral informants may provide information regarding how clients cope when outside your office.

Physical Examination

Often, a conclusive psychiatric diagnosis can't be achieved without at least a cursory medical examination. Therapists should inquire about most recent physical examination results when interviewing new clients. Some therapists ask for this information on their intake form and discuss it with clients.

As noted at the beginning of this chapter, physical and mental states can have powerful and reciprocal influences on each other. For instance, a long-term illness or serious injury can contribute to anxiety and depression. Consider the following options when completing a diagnostic assessment:

1. Gather information about physical examination results.
2. Consult with the client's primary care physician.
3. Refer clients for a physical examination.

It's a professional obligation to make sure potential medical or physical causes or contributors to mental disorders are considered and noted.

Client Strengths

Clients who come for professional assistance may have lost sight of their personal strengths and positive qualities. Further, after experiencing an hour-long diagnostic interview, clients may feel even more sad or demoralized. As we've mentioned before—especially within the context of suicide assessment interviewing—it's important to ask clients to identify and elaborate on positive personal qualities throughout the interview, but especially toward the end of an assessment/ diagnostic process. For example:

> I appreciate you telling me about your problems and symptoms. But I'd also like to hear more about your positive qualities. Like, how you've managed to be a single parent and go to school and fight off those depressive feelings you've been talking about?

Exploring client strengths provides important diagnostic information. Clients who are more depressed and demoralized have trouble with these questions and may not be able to identify strengths. Nonetheless, be sure to provide support, reassurance, and positive feedback. In addition, as solution-oriented theorists emphasize, don't forget that diagnosis and assessment procedures can—and should—include a consistent orientation toward the positive. For example, Bertolino and O'Hanlon (2002) stated:

> Formal assessment procedures are often viewed solely as a means of uncovering and discovering deficiencies and deviances with clients and their lives. However, as we've learned, they can assist with learning about clients' abilities, strength, and resources, and in searching for exceptions and differences. (p. 79)

Effective diagnostic interviewing isn't an exclusively fact-finding, impersonal process. Throughout the interview, skilled diagnosticians express compassion and support for a fellow human being in distress (Jobes, 2006; O'Donohue, Cummings, & Cummings, 2006). The purpose of diagnostic interviewing goes beyond establishing a diagnosis or "pigeonhole" for clients. Instead, it's an initial step in developing an individualized treatment plan.

TREATMENT PLANNING

The initial clinical interview is designed to obtain assessment information. In turn, this information is used to aid in the diagnostic process and diagnosis broadly informs treatment. However, more specifically, clients and therapists collaborate to identify specific client problems and these specific problems are much more helpful for treatment planning than psychiatric diagnosis. Even further, case formulation (aka case conceptualization) is the bridge between client diagnosis or problem and specific treatments to be implemented. Before exploring these issues in greater depth, consider the following questions:

- What assessment procedures will I use with clients to identify problems and monitor progress?
- What problems have the client and I identified as the focus of our work together?
- How do these problems translate into mutual therapy goals?
- What means or methods (theoretically based or empirically supported) will the client and I use as we work toward achieving these goals?
- How will we measure progress toward our goals?
- How will we know if and when it's time to refer the client for an alternative or adjunctive treatment?
- How will we know when it's time for therapy to end?

Your answers to these questions will depend on many factors, including, but not limited to, (a) your treatment setting, (b) your theoretical orientation, (c) client preference, (d) client resources, (e) third-party payer requirements and limits.

Many different treatment-planning models exist. A sampling of eclectic or atheoretical models include the BASIC ID (Lazarus, 2006), DO A CLIENT MAP (Seligman & Reichenberg, 2012), and the "treatment planners" (Jongsma et al., 2006). A great many theoretically based conceptual systems are also available (Greenberg, 2002; Luborsky & Crits-Christoph, 1998; Shapiro, 2002; Woody, Detweiler-Bedell, Teachman, & O'Hearn, 2003).

Choosing Effective Treatments

There are entire books that focus on selecting effective treatments (Seligman & Reichenberg, 2012). We begin our brief coverage of this growing area with an overview of two general models.

The Psychosocial Treatment Planning Model

The psychosocial model focuses on psychological and social/cultural experiences as causing and contributing to the maintenance of emotional and behavioral problems. This model identifies psychological and social/cultural interventions as ideal approaches to treatment. To develop a psychosocial treatment plan, therapists conduct an initial intake interview as described in Chapter 7, wherein client and therapist collaboratively explore (a) what brings the client to therapy (presenting problem and initial goals), (b) the client's personality style and personal history (the person), and (c) the client's current life circumstances (the situation). After exploring these fundamental issues, goals are established interactively with the client and a plan for goal attainment is developed. Based on this model, the case formulation and proposed interventions emphasize psychological, social, cultural, and behavioral components (Bisson et al., 2010; Miklowitz, Goodwin, Bauer, & Geddes, 2008). Additionally, this approach involves an emphasis on collaborative client problem identification and a lesser emphasis on establishing a definitive psychiatric diagnosis. This treatment planning model can include a focus on problems and/or a focus on solutions and goals (see *Putting It in Practice* 10.1 for as assessment approach based on one theoretically based psychosocial model).

PUTTING IT IN PRACTICE 10.1

Gathering Family History Information for Assessment and Treatment Planning

It may not always be easy to get clients to talk about their family and or family background. One strategy for facilitating an open and balanced discussion about family factors in any area (including suicide, family history of mental disorder, etc.) is the genogram or Adlerian family constellation interview. This strategy or approach has been described elsewhere by many authors and is briefly reviewed here (Carlson et al., 2006; Mosak & Maniacci, 1999; J. Sommers-Flanagan & Sommers-Flanagan, 2012).

Draw a Genogram or Family Tree

As appropriate, early in a clinical interview, we typically initiate a family constellation interview by saying something like, "Of course, we've just met and I don't know you very well, and so one of the ways I have of getting to know you better is to draw a family tree. Is that okay?" In nearly every case, perhaps due to natural curiosity, clients agree to help draw a family tree.

We then proceed to draw a genogram, starting with the client himself/herself and extending back in time to his/her grandparents (Shellenberger, 2007). Usually, because of time constraints, we focus primarily on the client's siblings, parents, and grandparents—although a brief discussion of prominent aunts, uncles, cousins may emerge. With some culturally diverse clients who have collectivist ways of being, this process can become even more inclusive. In some cases, the focus is less on biological parents and more on kinship relations, foster parents, or adoptive parents.

Convey Interest and Curiosity About the Family of Origin

Every family is unique; the genogram or family tree provides a structure for exploring that uniqueness. The genogram provides a visual method for identifying not only family structure, but also chronology. Along with the genogram, a timeline can be drawn to identify when significant events occurred (parental divorce, remarriage, moving from one residence to another, school problems or successes, etc.).

Ask a Balance of Positive and Negative Questions

The Adlerian family constellation interview includes specific questions about how the client viewed or views different family members and family relationships (Sweeney, 2009). One of the great things about the family constellation interview is that it focuses on the client's perceptions or descriptions of his/her family—which is not inherently positive or negative. Potential questions or prompts include:

- Give me three words to describe your mother (father, sister, brother, etc.).
- Who did (do) you feel closest to in your family?
- Who did (do) you fight the most with?
- Who was (is) your mom's favorite?
- Who was (is) your dad's favorite?
- Who was (is) the best musician (athlete, artist, student, etc.)?
- Who was (is) the goody-goody kid?
- Who got in the most trouble?
- Who can you talk with when you need to talk?
- Who is impossible to talk with?

Other questions that can be integrated into a family constellation interview have been described elsewhere (Mosak and Maniacci, 1999; Sweeney, 2009).

Use the Family Constellation Interview to Gather Family History Data

In addition to information about divorce, remarriage, step-parents and other family history data, the family constellation interview provides an excellent structure for inquiring about the family's mental health history.

(continued)

(continued)

Specifically, to assess for relevant suicide risk factors, you might ask the following:

- Has anyone in your family had mental health troubles like depression, schizophrenia, or bipolar disorder?
- Does anyone in your family have any special positive qualities or a positive legacy (like being a great musician, athlete, business person)?
- Has anyone in your family ever committed suicide? If so, what do you know about that situation?
- Has anyone in your family ever attempted suicide, but then decided to live? If so, what do you know about that situation?
- Has anyone in your family been arrested or convicted of a crime or had big troubles with drugs or alcohol?
- Out of everyone in your family, who do you feel closest to (or who do you think is your best role model)?

As you can see, the family constellation model is a flexible tool for evaluating many family history dynamics in an interesting and engaging format. We especially like to use it for getting to know adolescents early in therapy (J. Sommers-Flanagan & Sommers-Flanagan, 2007b).

The Biomedical Treatment Planning Model

The biomedical or psychiatric approach to conceptualizing client problems and identifying client treatments is a powerfully compelling paradigm that continues to increase in popularity and dominance (Overholser, 2006; J. Sommers-Flanagan & Campbell, 2009). Using this approach, therapists formulate client problems as illness based and perform diagnostic assessments to identify biomedical treatments. If you review the psychiatric literature, you'll see many statements articulating the biomedical perspective using disease and illness language. For example, "Depressive disorders are often familial recurrent illnesses associated with increased psychosocial morbidity and mortality" (Birmaher et al., 2007, p. 1503).

The biomedical approach views therapists as experts who know *DSM-5* diagnostic criteria and related efficacy research and apply this expertise accordingly. This approach emphasizes accurate diagnostic labeling, a primary purpose of which is to assist in identification of appropriate medication treatment.

In practice, most therapists recognize that integrating psychosocial and biological treatment-planning approaches is useful and do so to some extent. This is referred to as the biopsychosocial model (Engel, 1980; Engel, 1997). However, when biomedical and psychosocial treatments are combined, the biomedical approach (also known as the medical model) tends to dominate case formulation and treatment planning (Sommers-Flanagan & Campbell, 2009; see *Multicultural Highlight* 10.1 for a different perspective on the biopsychosocial model).

Factors to Consider

In addition to considering the preceding general models, identifying appropriate treatments requires that therapists consider the following information:

Client Diagnosis/Problem and Empirically Supported Treatments

Although exceptions exist, evidence-based treatment guidelines or approaches exist for many psychiatric diagnoses (e.g., major depression, obsessive compulsive disorder, post-traumatic stress disorder). This is one reason why it's crucial for providers to have well-developed diagnostic skills. However, there are also many cases in which it's more difficult to select an evidence-based treatment (Eells, 2009). Examples include:

- Your client's diagnosis is unclear.
- There are comorbid (more than one diagnosis) conditions that complicate treatment selection.
- Your client is opposed to using an evidence-based strategy.
- You're not trained in a specific evidence-based strategy.
- Your client has problems-in-living that don't qualify for a psychiatric diagnosis.

The past 10–15 years has seen a strong movement toward evidence-based treatment planning. This approach is derived from the medical model, but emphasizes reliance on research data and often integrates psychosocial interventions. Most evidence-based treatments are cognitive-behavioral, oriented toward psychiatric diagnosis, and relatively time limited (Dickerson & Lehman, 2011; Drisko & Grady, 2012; Kosciulek, 2010).

Interestingly, although third-party payers require medical diagnosis for reimbursement, they often prefer treatment plans that emphasize behavioral problem indices over diagnoses (Jongsma, Peterson, & Bruce, 2006). Similarly, although they sometimes push practitioners toward using evidence-based treatments, they also prefer briefer treatments, such as solution-focused brief therapy, despite the minimal empirical evidence attesting to the efficacy of such therapies (Corcoran & Pillai, 2009; Gingerich & Eisengart, 2000; Kim, Smock, Trepper, McCollum, & Franklin, 2010). Overall, when working with third-party payers, it's important to speak the language of psychiatric diagnosis, but also to be able to link client symptoms or problems directly to specific evidence-based, theoretically supported, and solution-focused interventions.

There are a number of websites you can use to identify evidence-based or empirically supported treatments. To explore these therapies and the process by which they have achieved empirically supported status, see the website for Division 12 of the American Psychological Association (http://www.apa.org/divisions/div12/cppi.html).

MULTICULTURAL HIGHLIGHT 10.1

Listening to the Dalai Lama: A Social-Psycho-Bio Model

At a conference at Emory University, Charles Nemeroff, MD, presented a paper to His Holiness the Dalai Lama (Nemeroff, 2007). In his presentation, Nemeroff noted with authority that one-third of all depressive disorders are genetic and two-thirds are environmentally based. Nemeroff then discussed the trajectory of "depressive illness," presenting findings from animal and human studies of trauma and depression. Nemeroff concluded that trauma seems to initiate a biologically based depressive tendency in the brains of some individuals (and mice) but not others. At one point during the presentation there was a flurry of interactions between the Dalai Lama, his interpreter, and Dr. Nemeroff. Finally, the interpreter posed a question to Dr. Nemeroff, saying something like: "His Holiness is wondering, if two-thirds of depression is caused by human experience and one-third is caused by genetics, but humans who are genetically predisposed to depression must have a trauma to trigger a depressive condition, then wouldn't it be true to say that all depression is caused by human experience?" After a brief silence, Nemeroff conceded, "Yes. That would be true."

Such admissions, as well as our own observations, have led us to believe that the ordering of the terms in the biopsychosocial model may be misleading. It may be more accurate to say *social-psycho-bio*, because early *social* interactions or relationships create *psychological* or *cognitive* patterns that eventually contribute to particular *biological* states.

Evidence-Based Relationships

As discussed in Chapter 5, relationship factors are significantly associated with positive treatment outcomes (Norcross, 2011). As a consequence, to develop an empirically informed treatment plan, relationship factors should be incorporated into treatment planning. For example, specific interactions such as collaborative goal setting and progress monitoring are relationship based and also constitute technical strategies (Norcross, 2011). Furthermore, making sure you attend to the development and maintenance of a strong working alliance is essential to positive outcomes. This is true despite the fact that the manner in which you develop and maintain a working alliance will vary from client to client; alliance building should be integrated into your treatment plan.

Therapist Skill or Expertise

Therapist competence is always an ethical and practical consideration in treatment planning (S. K. Anderson & Handelsman, 2013). Specifically, as you design a treatment plan, you must have expertise in whatever approaches you're incorporating into the plan. For example, if you have no training or experience in a particular treatment technique (e.g., hypnosis or eye-movement desensitization reprocessing), that technique shouldn't be employed—or if it is employed, it should be done under close supervision.

Therapist Preference

Therapist preference matters. Mental health professionals vary in their preferred theoretical orientation. Some adhere to psychoanalytic treatment formulations; others are behavioral in their approach to treatment. As long as an informed consent is provided that explains your theoretically or empirically supported treatment and possible treatment alternatives, it's perfectly appropriate for clinicians to offer clients their preferred form of treatment (J. Sommers-Flanagan & Sommers-Flanagan, 2012).

Client Preference

Client preference also matters. Given the choice, clients may prefer one form of treatment over another. For example, some clients struggling with maladaptive habits prefer short-term, specific behavioral therapy to successfully change the habit. Others prefer depth work, seeking to understand the role or purpose of the habit in their lives. Still others prefer medication treatment. Client treatment preference can strongly influence treatment compliance.

Client Resources

Professional counseling and psychotherapy is expensive. Some clients have coverage from insurance companies or other third-party payers. Each health care program has specific benefits and limits for mental health-care coverage. The client's health-care coverage and the resources available after the coverage runs out are important practical and ethical considerations in charting a treatment plan.

Unfortunately, considering available resources doesn't mean simply picking a problem that fits into the number of paid sessions available or the number of sessions a client can budget from private funds. Certainly, it's important to clarify primary and secondary problems and to recognize that problems can't always be addressed in a given course of treatment. Ethically, therapists are required to choose among theoretically or empirically based treatments and to see the client through to some kind of responsible closure or offer reasonable alternatives, such as a transfer to another counselor or service (S. K. Anderson & Handelsman, 2010). Therefore, in agreeing to a course of treatment, you must assess your own resources as well, including availability, willingness to reduce fees, adequate referral network, appropriate supervision, and access to collateral professionals (attorneys, medical personnel, etc.).

Besides resources represented in finances and insurance benefits, and the resources represented in the person and practice of the professional, there are other resources to be considered in treatment planning. These include client motivation, ego strength, and psychological mindedness of the client. It's your duty to assess, formally or informally, each client's capacity to engage in treatment.

Treatment Matching

Treatment matching can occur along a number of dimensions. As noted previously, specific treatments are commonly matched with specific psychiatric disorders or symptoms. However, in recent years, an alternative perspective that emphasizes therapy principles instead of diagnosis has gained increased scientific recognition.

Beutler (2011) has developed a treatment matching approach referred to as *systematic treatment selection*. This model uses empirically driven principles to help clinicians select specific treatment approaches. Some of Beutler's main principles include:

- Clients who have greater functional impairments are more likely to respond to medication approaches.
- Clients with more aggressive symptoms or externalizing styles tend to respond more favorably to symptom-focused approaches.
- Conversely, clients who are more inhibited or have more internalizing symptoms tend to respond more favorably to insight-oriented approaches.
- When client resistance to treatment is high, less directive therapies are more effective.
- When clients are engaged in treatment, more directive therapies are successful (Beutler, 2011; Beutler, Forrester, Gallagher-Thompson, Thompson, & Tomlins, 2012).

Although empirically driven guidelines are useful, like any approach, there are limitations. For example, the following two cases illustrate exceptions to treatment matching based on client preference and client history.

CASE EXAMPLE—RESPECTING CLIENT PREFERENCES

Opal, a 63-year-old Caucasian woman, was referred for counseling by her personal physician. She was referred because of repeated panic attacks. Her life history was rich and varied in many fascinating respects. The biggest trauma or loss she disclosed was the death of her oldest daughter to breast cancer 2 years earlier. This daughter, Emily, had been a strong, feminist woman with a successful career who had often chided her mother for her "old-fashioned, subservient ways." Opal was married to her third husband, a farmer named Jeff. Jeff was wealthy and traditional in his views of marriage. Opal's job was to keep the house clean, prepare meals that met with Jeff's approval, and "keep herself presentable." Her panic attacks began about six months before the referral and, at first, happened exclusively outside grocery stores as Opal was preparing to buy the week's groceries. Opal was forced to seek a neighbor's assistance in obtaining groceries because Jeff refused to be seen in a grocery store.

After three sessions devoted primarily to assessment, collaborative goal setting, psychoeducation, and alliance building, the counselor developed enough of a relationship with Opal to suspect that she would not do well with depth work regarding her grief, her conflicts over her marital role, and other related issues. However, it seemed important to involve Opal in this treatment decision. The counselor explained two treatment options: (1) continue training to manage panic attacks with behavioral strategies, imagery, and medication or (2) begin to explore the meaning of the panic attacks, their possible linkage to role conflicts, and perhaps even looking at Opal's deep and mostly buried grief and anger over losing her daughter. Without hesitation, Opal indicated she had no interest in any depth work unless it was absolutely necessary.

The treatment plan continued along cognitive-behavioral lines. After eight more sessions, Opal resumed grocery shopping on her own. She left therapy feeling a sense of accomplishment and closure. She assured the counselor she would be back if "things didn't hang together in her head."

As this case illustrates, client problems can be multilayered and complex. Although Beutler's system might suggest that an insight-oriented treatment plan would be a good match for Opal's internalizing symptoms, her life situation and related treatment preference made insight-oriented approaches a poor fit.

CASE EXAMPLE—MATCHING TREATMENT APPROACH WITH CLIENT HISTORY

Jane came to see a counselor because she was worrying excessively about her 3-year-old daughter, Kate. Jane had picked Kate up from day care approximately a month earlier, and Kate had said, "Mommy, I hate it when they stick yucky things in my mouth." Jane experienced a rush of fear and carefully questioned Kate, afraid that someone at the day care had abused or violated Kate. Kate, clearly alarmed by her mother's reaction, refused to talk about day care. This interaction unleashed all sorts of worries for Jane. She found that she could no longer leave Kate at day care and was paying for an in-home nanny. Finances were strained. In addition, Jane would no longer allow Kate to play with her boy cousins or her older half-brother. This was causing marital strain. Finally, Jane was having trouble allowing Kate out of her sight, which was, as Jane said, "making everyone totally crazy."

Directly addressing Jane's behavior by pointing out the irrational nature of her fears and urging her to create a chart and reward herself for leaving Kate for longer and longer periods were treatment options in this case. In addition, these options might stand a good chance of success. However, as many astute readers might have guessed, Jane's sudden overfocus and self-proclaimed overreaction to her daughter's situation were clues to an unaddressed life experience of Jane's. Jane had been sexually molested by her uncle at age 4. She remembered the uncle kissing and fondling her, often forcing his tongue down her throat, but she had never told anyone about her experiences.

As a part of treatment, Jane was able to access community support groups for adults who had experienced child sexual abuse. She used her

(continued)

(*continued*)
therapy time carefully, exploring her pattern of ignoring her own pain and refusing to talk about her emotions. Although it may have helped in the short run, a behavioral approach to Jane's anxiety wouldn't have addressed Jane's underlying needs.

Jane's anxiety is another example of an internalizing symptom. In this case, Beutler's model correctly matches Jane with a more insight-oriented treatment approach. These two case studies illustrate the importance of using an eyes-wide-open approach when selecting treatment plans. The unique individual and situational factors linked to a client may be far more important than empirical data suggesting a particular treatment approach is best for a particular client problem.

Case Formulation and Treatment Planning: A Cognitive-Behavioral Example

As mentioned previously, whether you're using a psychosocial (problem focused) or biomedical (diagnostic) model, case formulation is the bridge between clinical assessment and treatment planning. Persons (2008) identified four case formulation steps from the cognitive-behavioral (CBT) perspective:

1. Create a problem list.
2. Identify possible mechanisms causing the problems.
3. Identify precipitants (triggers) that currently activate the problem.
4. Consider historical origins of the client's problem.

Using a case adapted from Ledley et al. (2010), the steps of CBT case formulation will be described and then linked to a specific treatment plan.

The Problem List

Michael, a 40-year-old White male, referred himself for therapy due to being socially anxious "for as long as he could remember" (Ledley et al., p. 59). Based on an initial assessment, including reflections on his *DSM* diagnosis, the following problem list was collaboratively generated:

- Social anxiety.
- Confusion about career choices.
- Family conflict.

The initial and primary problem focus was social anxiety.

Underlying Mechanisms

Persons (2008) described three steps for determining mechanisms underlying specific problems. Her steps include: (1) select a symptom or symptoms on which to focus; (2) select a theory or theories to explain the symptom(s); and (3) use your theory to extrapolate to the individual case.

For Michael, the presenting problem of social anxiety had several component symptoms, including fear/anxiety, flushing/sweating, and avoidance behaviors. Beck's (2011) cognitive theory was used to help Michael understand his symptoms. The symptoms—and their cognitive explanations included:

Automatic thoughts occurring before and during social contact
- I always look anxious.
- They will think I'm an idiot.
- They will think I'm incompetent.

Intermediate (distorted) thoughts
- People who make mistakes are rejected.
- I make more mistakes than other people.
- It's terrible to make mistakes.
- I must "get it right" all the time.

A core schemata or belief
- If I am not perfect, I will be rejected.

(All of the above are adapted from: Ledley et al., 2010, p. 70.)

Current Precipitants (Triggers)

During his initial interview, two situational triggers for Michael's social anxiety were identified. These included: (1) casual social encounters; and (2) public speaking. Michael also reported specific automatic thoughts that occurred in anticipation of and during these social contacts.

Problem Origins

Cognitive-behavioral therapy (CBT) is a form of therapy that focuses primarily on the present. Nevertheless, there are good reasons why CBT includes exploration of the origins of clients' problems. Ledley et al. (2010) explain the rationale for this:

> . . . spending some time exploring early experiences during the process of assessment can reveal some valuable clues to the clinician as to how problem behaviors developed in the first place and why maladaptive thoughts and behaviors are maintained in the present. Furthermore, sharing his or her personal history makes a client feel more understood which can serve to strengthen the therapeutic relationship. (p. 71)

Michael's Treatment Plan

Recall that case formulation is the bridge from the client's presenting problem to the treatment plan. Using Persons' (2008) model, there will be a focus on cognitive mechanisms that create and sustain Michael's symptoms. Treatment will include specific components that directly address the cognitive mechanisms underlying Michael's symptoms. In this case, the treatment plan included use of an evidence-based treatment manual for social anxiety.

The following treatment plan is adapted from Ledley et al. (2010):

Session 1

Problem: Michael's distorted, maladaptive beliefs.
Intervention: Provide educational material on social anxiety.
Goals: Normalize the phenomenon of social anxiety; introduce Michael to the CBT model.

Session 2

Problem: Michael's distorted, maladaptive beliefs.
Intervention: Design hierarchy of feared situations.
Goals: Identify feared social situations; plan for how to proceed with exposure.

Session 3

Problem: Michael's distorted, maladaptive beliefs.
Intervention: Begin cognitive restructuring.
Goals: Teach Michael to identify, question, and reframe his maladaptive thoughts.

Session 4

Problem: Michael's distorted, maladaptive beliefs.
Intervention: Continue cognitive restructuring; plan initial exposure experience.
Goals: Continued skill building for identifying, questioning, and reframing his maladaptive thoughts; teach Michael how to initiate behavioral exposure.

Session 5

Problem: Michael's beliefs AND his physiological response to social contact AND his behavioral pattern of avoidance.
Intervention: First exposure session.
Goals: Demonstration and experiential learning about how exposure can challenge maladaptive beliefs.

Sessions 6–18

Problem: Michael's beliefs AND his physiological response to social contact AND his behavioral pattern of avoidance AND his core beliefs about himself.
Intervention: Continued exposure; continued cognitive restructuring
Goals: Minimize physiological responses to social contact; internalize new beliefs about social anxiety, avoidance, and modify core beliefs about the self.

Sessions 19 and 20

Problem: Michael's beliefs AND his physiological response to social contact AND his behavioral pattern of avoidance AND his core beliefs about himself.

Intervention: Relapse prevention, goal setting, termination
Goals: Prepare and plan for termination, including future expectations and
goals.

The preceding evidence-based CBT treatment plan is, in many ways, the
state-of-the-science in treatment planning. Following Persons' (2008) approach
to case formulation allows clinicians to individualize treatment, thus expanding
the potential of evidence-based approaches. However, it should be noted that
this approach also has many limitations. For example, third party payers may not
be inclined to commit to a 20-session treatment protocol. Additionally, although
evidence suggests this is an appropriate treatment for White clients from the
dominant culture, there's no compelling evidence that this approach is either
appropriate of effective for diverse or minority clients.

Multicultural Adaptations

As noted intermittently in this text, contemporary clinicians must address multicultural complexities during clinical assessment and treatment (Gray & Rose,
2012; Shea et al., 2012). One way this plays out for treatment planning is that
clinicians should engage in mutual exploration to enhance the working alliance
before launching into specific interventions. This chapter closes with *Multicultural
Highlight* 10.2, where a case is used to illustrate a more tentative approach where
mutual exploration is the primary intervention—rather than a specific empirically
supported intervention or procedure.

MULTICULTURAL HIGHLIGHT 10.2

Cultural Issues in Treatment Planning: A Case Example

Often, client cultural issues take center stage in treatment planning.
The following very brief example is adapted and summarized from "The
Case of Dolores" (Sommers-Flanagan, 2001, in Paniagua, 2001).

Dolores, a 43-year-old American Indian woman, came to counseling because she was suffering from sadness, difficulty concentrating,
insomnia, and anhedonia. These depressive symptoms were associated
with two major concerns. First, Dolores was upset because her husband
of 23 years, Gabe, was suffering from a serious gambling addiction but
refusing to go to treatment. Second, Dolores was worried that, because
of her diminished functioning and her husband's gambling, she might
lose custody of her adopted daughter, Sage.

Even with the minimal information provided in this example, several
cultural issues rise to the fore. Specifically, because Dolores's major
concerns center around family issues, it's important to explore the onset
and duration of her concerns in the context of familism—as Dolores's
symptoms might be more directly associated with her family identity
than with her "self." Additionally, it could be that the decision to come
to counseling was producing nearly as much stress as her family situation

(*continued*)

(*continued*)

because some American Indian tribes consider it disloyal to say negative things about other family members. Consequently, Dolores's feelings about counseling and what it says about her Indian identity (or about her losing her Indian identity) may be a focus of treatment—especially if she's seeing a counselor from the dominant culture.

Dolores's fears of losing her adopted daughter also bring up cultural issues. In this case, the adoption was an informal tribal arrangement; she may need to consult with legal professionals and her tribe to determine if the adoption is binding. It's likely the U.S. government would support the adoption placement under the Indian Child Welfare Act (O'Brien, 1989); therefore, communication with her tribe is more important than exposing Dolores to the U.S. legal system. Finally, although to some counselors it may seem that Dolores's anxiety about losing her child is overblown, historically, American Indians have experienced intergenerational trauma when children are taken from families. Hence, Dolores's feelings about those historical facts (and personal experiences) should be evaluated before pathologizing her anxiety.

In summary, for American Indian and other multicultural clients, treatment planning should be culture specific and culture sensitive. For example, the following treatment planning interventions might be used:

- Explore Dolores's feelings about pursuing counseling.
- Explore what Dolores is thinking and feeling when she makes negative statements about her family members.
- Educate Dolores regarding the Indian Child Welfare Act.
- Encourage Dolores to discuss custody fears with tribal members and possibly a tribal lawyer.
- Discuss Dolores's fears of losing her daughter in the context of multigenerational trauma.

SUMMARY

This chapter addresses basic principles and processes of diagnosis and treatment planning. Controversies about psychiatric diagnosis abound, but there are important reasons for all mental health professionals to develop diagnostic skills. A diagnosis can serve an organizing function and thereby facilitate treatment planning and treatment process. It can be seen as a working hypothesis and can offer clients relief by assuring them that others suffer with similar reactions, struggles, and complaints. The most commonly used diagnostic manual in North America is the *DSM-5* (*Diagnostic and Statistical Manual of Mental Disorders*); the fifth edition was published in May, 2013. Because diagnosis always involves some subjectivity, practitioners are encouraged to be careful and tentative when assigning specific diagnoses.

Therapists should use a balanced approach to conducting diagnostic interviews, including (a) a warm introduction to diagnostic assessment with an explanation of what the client should expect; (b) an extensive review of client problems and associated goals; (c) a brief review of client personal history, especially those historical experiences closely associated with the client's primary problem; (d) a brief mental status examination; and (e) a review of the client's current situation, including social supports, coping skills, physical health, and personal strengths. In the diagnostic interviewing context, no one can be expected to keep all diagnostic parameters in mind. Therapists are encouraged to purchase or develop their own abbreviated diagnostic checklists so they can adequately address the specific domains in question for a certain diagnostic inquiry.

Treatment planning flows directly from diagnosis or problem analysis. Professionals can use psychosocial approaches to treatment planning, wherein the problem complex is the guide for treatment goals and objectives; or they can use the medical or biological approach, wherein symptoms are categorized into a diagnosis, which then dictates treatment choice. It's also possible to combine these two and use a biopsychosocial approach, which includes diagnosis but also addresses specific symptoms and problems interactively with clients.

There are many factors to consider when developing treatment plans. These include (a) client diagnosis/problem(s); (b) evidence-based relationship factors; (c) therapist skill or areas of expertise; (d) therapist preferences; (e) client preferences; (f) client resources; and (g) treatment matching variables.

Case formulation is the bridge between client diagnosis/problem and treatment planning. A sample case formulation and treatment plan from the cognitive-behavioral perspective is described.

Multicultural adaptations to treatment planning should be considered on a case-by-case basis. This many involve clinicians engaging in more extensive mutual exploration to enhance the working alliance before launching into the application of specific interventions. A case example involving multicultural adaptation is provided.

SUGGESTED READINGS AND RESOURCES

Numerous publications focus on training practitioners to use *DSM-IV* (but not *DSM-5*, yet) as a diagnostic guide and as a guide to psychological treatment. There are also many publications available on treatment planning. The following list is limited in scope but provides some ideas for further reading and study.

American Psychiatric Association. (2013). *Diagnostic and statistical manual of mental disorders* (5th ed.). Washington, DC: Author.
      This is the citation for the *DSM-5*.
Bryceland, C., & Stam, H. J. (2005). Empirical validation and professional codes of ethics: Description or prescription? *Journal of Constructivist Psychology, 18*(2), 131–155.
      This article discusses and critiques a new trend in ethics codes mandating that therapists use empirically or theoretically supported treatments.
Jongsma, A. E., Peterson, L. M., & Bruce, T. J. (2006). *The complete adult psychotherapy treatment planner* (4th ed.). New York, NY: Wiley.
      This book is the latest adult version of Jongsma and Peterson's series of psychotherapy treatment planners. Their series of publications in this area is voluminous and often used by practicing clinicians to help with treatment planning formulation.
Kutchins, H., & Kirk, S.A. (1997). *Making us crazy: DSM: The psychiatric bible and the creation of mental disorders*. New York, NY: Free Press.

In this book, the authors provide a strong critique of the development and promotion of the *DSM* system as a method of categorizing mental disorders. In particular, the chapters on homosexuality and racism are enlightening reading.

Lazarus, A. A. (2006). *Brief but comprehensive psychotherapy: The multimodal way*. New York, NY: Springer.

This publication will orient you to how to effectively use Lazarus's BASIC ID treatment model.

Norcross, J. C., Beutler, L. E., & Levant, R. F. (Eds.). (2006). *Evidence-based practices in mental health: Debate and dialogue on the fundamental questions*. Washington, DC: American Psychological Association.

This edited volume covers a wide range of pertinent questions related to evidence-based practice.

Seligman, L., & Reichenberg, L. W. (2012). *Selecting effective treatments: A comprehensive, systematic guide to treating mental disorders* (4th ed.). Hoboken, NJ: Wiley.

This is the 4th edition of Seligman's very practical and accessible text on diagnosis and treatment planning.

Woody, S. R., Detweiler-Bedell, J., Teachman, B. A., & O'Hearn, T. (2003). *Treatment planning in psychotherapy: Taking the guesswork out of clinical care*. New York, NY: Guilford Press.

Woody and colleagues provide a clear and straightforward approach to treatment planning.

PART FOUR

Interviewing Special Populations

Interviewing in a Diverse and Multicultural World

CHAPTER OBJECTIVES

We live in a colorful and diverse world, filled with people who are radically different than ourselves. No matter what our own ethnocultural background may be, it's certain that some of our clients will not share much common ground with us. This makes it crucial for us to broaden our perspectives and increase our cultural sensitivities.

After reading this chapter, you will understand:

- The reasons mental health professionals need to embrace cultural diversity.
- The imperative of cultural competence and the importance of understanding your cultural biases and cultural self.
- Basic issues in interviewing clients from First Nations, African American, Hispanic/Latina/o American, and Asian American ethnocultural backgrounds.
- Basic issues to address when interviewing gay, lesbian, transgender, disabled, or religiously committed clients.
- A system for recognizing and dealing with the multiple cultural and individual factors affecting client identity.
- Specific ethnic- and culture-bound syndromes.
- Professional etiquette to consider when interviewing minority clients.

Along with most mental health professionals, multicultural researchers and writers recognize the centrality of the therapeutic relationship in effective multicultural counseling (Hays, 2008; Ho, Rasheed, & Rasheed, 2004; S. Sue, 2006). But what components of such a relationship are essential? How can we avoid cultural arrogance when working with diverse clients? This chapter provides food for thought and pieces of the puzzle, but obtaining answers to these profound questions is a lifelong endeavor. In 1974, Thomas Merton wrote:

> Let me be quite succinct: the greatest sin of the European-Russian-American complex which we call the West (and this sin has spread its own way to China) is not only greed and cruelty, not only moral dishonesty and infidelity to the truth, but above all *its unmitigated arrogance toward the rest of the human race*. (p. 380, italics in original)

This quote articulates the deep awareness and humility necessary to overcome past arrogance and wrongdoings. Although humility won't solve problems of oppression and racism, it's a necessary ingredient.

Facing a Multicultural World

The United States continues to grow more diverse. As noted in Chapter 1, in the last census about 28% of U.S. residents identified themselves as other than White (U.S. Census Bureau, 2011). Increasingly, (and thankfully) graduate programs have students from a wide variety of cultural and racial backgrounds. This requires dedication to multicultural education and training that goes beyond the occasional nod to people-other-than-White-people (Chao, 2012).

As President Barack Obama was sworn in for his second term, his inaugural speech on January 21, 2013 (Martin Luther King Day) included this excerpt:

> We recall that what binds this nation together is not the colors of our skin or the tenets of our faith or the origins of our names. What makes us exceptional—what makes us American—is our allegiance to an idea, articulated in a declaration made more than two centuries ago:
>
> "We hold these truths to be self-evident, that all men are created equal, that they are endowed by their Creator with certain unalienable rights, that among these are Life, Liberty, and the pursuit of Happiness."
>
> Today we continue a never-ending journey, to bridge the meaning of those words with the realities of our time. For history tells us that while these truths may be self-evident, they have never been self-executing. (Obama, 2013)

These comments are directly relevant to this chapter. The belief that we should treating each other as equals is not "self-executing." It doesn't happen without effort and education. It takes a deep and persistent commitment to embrace all people as equal.

The increase in cultural diversity provides an exciting and daunting possibility for mental health professionals; exciting for the richness that a diverse population extends to communities, and for the professional and personal growth that accompanies cross-cultural interactions; daunting because of increased responsibility for learning culturally relevant approaches. In the late 1990s, Christine C. Iijima Hall (1997) made a case for the idea of "cultural malpractice" for those who practice with inadequate knowledge of cultural dynamics and warned that without significantly changing how cultural issues are addressed, psychology will become obsolete. Ten years later, similar concerns were expressed by Fouad and Arredondo (2007b). Although psychology hasn't become obsolete, much work remains in training programs to prepare mental health professionals to become competent to serve the mental health needs of diverse populations.

Therapist, Know Thyself

Many multicultural theorists and experts believe that increasing cultural self-awareness is a precondition for moving from an ethnocentric, culturally encapsulated perspective to a truly multicultural perspective. The ability to understand how your own thoughts and feelings are influenced by your cultural heritage helps you understand how culture has influenced others. Hopefully, understanding other perspectives will help you avoid imposing your cultural values on your clients.

In the next section of this chapter, we provide basic, information about specific groups of people identified by race and/or cultural background. In addition, we've included brief sections addressing persons with different sexual orientations, persons with disabilities, and persons with religious convictions. An argument could be made for including women, the elderly, and other groups who experience oppression or don't fit the mold of young, White, and male (Hays, 2008). There are many ways people find themselves grouped together and many ways these groupings affect identity formation, functioning in the world, and quality of life in the dominant culture. As Sue, Ivey, and Pedersen (1996) stated:

> Each client (individual, family, group, organization) has multiple cultural identities which most likely do not progress or expand at the same rate. For example, a man may be quite aware of his identity as a Navajo but less aware of himself as a heterosexual or Vietnam veteran. As such, comprehensive multicultural therapy may focus on helping him and others like him become ever more aware of the impact of cultural issues on their being. (p. 17)

As you read on, tune into the thoughts, feelings and impulses you experience that might be related to your cultural identity. The goal of this "tuning in" is to increase your developing cultural self-awareness. While you're at it, keep in mind that, although awareness is a prerequisite for many things, it's also a naturally empowering experience (Brown, 2010).

FOUR LARGE WORLDVIEWS

In the introduction to *Growing Up Latino* (Augenbraum & Stavans, 1993), Ilan Stavans wrote:

> Today, at the center of the conflict is the Hispanic, the man, woman, or child who speaks Castilian Spanish as his or her mother tongue, or whose ancestors did so. We in the United States often perceive Hispanics as a monolithic or amorphous group. They have divided loyalties, we say, and live between two cultures and two languages. But this is a narrow definition, a figment that Americans have created to fill our need to make these diverse peoples into a single one that we can then understand. (p. xvi)

Stavans was writing about Hispanics, but he could have inserted any of the larger or smaller minority groups in the United States and been equally accurate. Ethnic groupings tend to be huge, with an astonishing amount of diversity within each. The same can be said for White culture, or the dominant culture. We would be hard pressed to define *White*. Would we include Italian Americans? Would we include Jewish Americans? Does the word *Anglo* communicate more accurately than *White?* Even if we said "persons of Western European descent," it wouldn't be clear as to who's in and who is out. First Nations peoples have been forced to ask: What blood quantum is necessary to be defined as a member of the tribe? With apologies for these obvious gross generalizations, we make divisions to compare and contrast very broad differences between cultures. Many more distinctions could and should be made (Chang & O'Hara, 2013; Gallardo, Yeh, Trimble, & Parham, 2011; McGoldrick, Giordano, & Garcia-Preto, 2005).

The following information is barely enough to whet the appetite and acknowledge basic potential cultural differences among clients. The old adage "The map is not the territory" is especially pertinent here, because these descriptions are meant to simply orient you toward experiencing the territory. The actual cultural landscape will be unique to the individual and likely look different from the following map.

First Nation Peoples Cultures

According to the 2010 census, there are 564 federally recognized tribal groups represented in the United States. Not surprisingly, each tribe has distinct values, customs, and histories. Berkhoffer (1978) noted that more than 2,000 cultures were represented on the North American continent when Europeans first arrived in the late 15th century. These cultures had diverse languages, practices, and friendly or warlike interrelationships. They didn't think of themselves as a single people and remained remarkably diverse, even after centuries of pressures to acculturate.

There are many terms used to refer to these minority groups: Indian, American Indian, Native American, and Alaskan Native are all common. Yellow Bird (2001) wrote, "Indians, American Indians, and Native Americans are 'colonized' and 'inaccurate' names that oppress the identities of First Nation Peoples." (p. 61).

In contrast, Dean (2003) wrote, with some authority:

> In the United States, the most correct term for referring to indigenous people is Native American. In Canada, indigenous people are often referred to as aboriginal or First Nations people. (p. 62)

As implied previously, diversity is the rule even within small cultural minority groups. Consequently, it's important to note that First Nations peoples have grown up with these labels and will have an opinion on the matter. We've had the good fortune to have students and colleagues who are members of the Blackfeet, Crow, Salish, Kootenai, Northern Cheyenne, Navaho, Blood, Assiniboine (Nakota), Chippewa-Cree, Gros Ventre, and Ogalala Sioux Nations. Often, these people have different preferences for referencing their culture(s). Therefore, it's wise to ask before assuming someone's preference in this domain. Interestingly, as we've asked our Native students and clients over the years what they'd like to be called, many of them—in contradiction to the perspectives of Yellow Bird and Dean—say, "Indian." After some discussion, our students will often tell us something like, "You know, as long as you say it respectfully, it doesn't matter whether you refer to us as Indians or Native Americans or First Nations peoples."

In this chapter we use the terms *Natives, Native Americans*, as well as *First Nation peoples*, knowing that preferences for these terms vary among the peoples they represent. We also will do our best to use these terms in ways that convey respect to First Nation peoples.

It's a mistake to assume more commonality among First Nation peoples than exists. On the other hand, there are aspects of past and current native life that allow people from different tribal backgrounds to find common ground. Unfortunately, some of the common ground has to do with genocidal practices that these First Nation peoples experienced at the hands of European settlers for more than two centuries. The trauma, intergenerational grief, and despair associated with these experiences are still powerful forces in most tribal cultures. Although these individuals come to counseling for all the reasons anyone in the dominant culture might come to counseling, we must remember that historically, their cultures were systematically decimated. Consider Chief Sitting Bull's response to the American policy of assimilation in the late 19th and early 20th centuries:

> I am a red man. If the Great Spirit had desired me to be a white man, he would have made me so in the first place. He put in your heart certain wishes and plans, in my heart he put other and different desires. Each man is good in His sight. It is not necessary for eagles to be crows. (Deloria, 1994, p. 198)

Cultural decimation and assimilation still have direct counseling ramifications, especially if the counselor represents White European culture. Although genocidal policies in the United States are now mainly historical, contemporary struggles regarding land use and tribal sovereignty continue. The recent heroic struggle by the late Elouise Cobell, member of the Blackfeet Nation, is illustrative. Ms. Cobell recognized that the federal government had badly mismanaged funds associated with First Nation lands—to the tune of billions of dollars. Her class action suit, on behalf of 280,000 Native people, slowly made its way to the U.S Supreme Court and attracted considerable media attention. In 2010 Congress settled with Cobell for $3.4 billion. In 2011, notices went out to hundreds of thousands Native Americans who were to receive compensation of about $1,800 each. Elouise Cobell died on October 16, 2011. After a series of appeals prolonged the process, distribution of compensation checks began on December 17, 2012.

The Cobell story illustrates how past events continue to affect minority groups in the present and into the future. Of course, most White European counselors bear little direct responsibility for past events. However, they can still be *perceived* as representative of a dominant culture that has and continues to encroach on the rights of Native peoples. From a relationship-building perspective, establishing trust may require extra time and sensitivity (Goodkind et al., 2011).

The danger of overgeneralization notwithstanding, a few specific cultural variables that can be used to help orient a therapist working with Native clients follow.

Tribal Identity

Asking Native American clients about tribal membership or identification can be an important component of an initial interview. Clients may choose not to tell you much, but nearly all identify themselves as belonging to a tribe, band, or clan (Sutton & Broken Nose, 2005). Although it may reveal your unfamiliarity with the tribe named, therapists should not be shy about asking for the correct pronunciation and spelling. Even Native counselors don't know the names and practices of every existing tribe (although most are far ahead of non-Native American counselors). No matter how much or how little tribal identity exists in given individuals, it's an important component of their cultures (Wetsit, personal communication, July 11, 1998). Asking about tribal affiliation and identity begins an important process between the counselor and the client. After clients identify their tribes, an easy follow-up question is:

Tell me the things you value most about being Assiniboine.

When non-Native therapists pretend to know too much about reservation life or tribal issues, they risk damaging rapport with Native clients. Respectful questioning about tribal affiliation is more appropriate and less presumptive.

The Role of Family

Across most or all tribes, extended family is deeply important to Native peoples. Kinship systems vary, but the roles of adopted and biological grandparents, aunts, uncles, cousins, and siblings are central and important. Funerals, weddings, births, and community and family celebrations are occasions of great import and often supersede other obligations. Sometimes, the family considers tribal elders and medicine people as family members; under some circumstances, these members may be appropriate to include in family-based interventions or interviews.

Tribal customs for family roles vary, as do parenting practices. Given the importance of these areas, asking about differences can provide helpful information if your clients come from families with mixed tribal backgrounds (Ho et al., 2004; Sutton & Broken Nose, 2005).

The Role of Humor

In Montana, Native Americans are the largest minority group, comprising about 6.4% of the population. We've had the good fortune of working with a number of Native American students. One theme they often tell us about is the prominence of Native humor.

Over the years our Native American students have told us many jokes and humorous stories. One of our favorites combines the valuing of family with the valuing of humor. It goes like this: "Hey. Do you know the three methods of communication up on the Rez?" [No.] "Yeah. Well. There's telephone, telegraph, and tell-a-cousin."

Using humor with any client or minority group can be risky; however, when working with Native American clients, it's good to remember the potential positive role of humor. You must make sure that your efforts at humor are well-timed and respectful, but if the opportunity arises, laughing together can help deepen your therapeutic connection.

The Role of Spirituality

Though every First Nation person is not spiritually oriented, for many Natives, the spirit world is significant. There are sacred connections among tribal members, living, dead, and those yet to be born, between nature and humans, and between Creator and created. These connections affect the way life is lived in the present and the way family and tribal society is viewed. It is a wholistic, nonlinear view that includes a belief that the Creator speaks in visions and dreams (Ho et al., 2004). In gatherings such as honoring ceremonies or powwows, a prayer (or song) is usually offered.

Garrett et al. (2005) also wrote about the spiritual role of humor in Native culture.

> Native humor as a spiritual tradition often goes unnoticed by people from the mainstream culture as a powerful healing force in the lives of Native people, as it has been for ages. The fact that so many Native nations have survived the horror of countless acts of cultural genocide committed by people from mainstream America in the name of civilization serves as a testament, in part, to the resilience of Native humor, having stood the test of time. (p. 195)

Respect and honor are additional key values among Native people. When working with this minority group, it's especially important to show that you respect and honor their spirituality. This respect for the Native perspective is basic to establishing a positive therapeutic relationship.

Sharing and Material Goods

Among First Nations peoples, sharing and gifting is a more common practice than in the dominant culture. Gifting is an act of honoring and is considered an integral part of the culture (Sutton & Broken Nose 2005). This nonmaterialistic emphasis on generosity and the common good stand in stark contrast to the far more capitalistic dominant culture, in which giving often takes a backseat to acquisition. These differences can create a clash of values for young Native people as they try to maintain cultural identity and lead successful lives as measured by dominant cultural standards. It's not uncommon for Native American clients to give their therapists gifts to demonstrate appreciation. In general, ethical codes discourage accepting gifts, but in this situation, cultural sensitivity and respect suggests that you should accept the gift graciously (R. Sommers-Flanagan & Sommers-Flanagan, 2007).

Time

Many cultures view the passage of time in a more relaxed, circular fashion than dominant European and U.S. cultures. Arriving at an agreed-on time for an appointment is standard for most persons of European descent. However, arriving on time is not always related to the clock for people of other cultures. "On time" can mean arriving at the time that things worked out to arrive. A corollary to this, often experienced by our interns who work at tribal college counseling services, is reluctance on the part of some Native people to schedule weekly meetings. Although no-showing for scheduled appointments is common, the walk-in center receives brisk business. Many Native Americans are more oriented to the here-and-now and less oriented to the future (Sutton & Broken Nose, 2005). When there's a felt need for counseling experienced in the present, it is sought. However, agreeing to an arrangement in the future may or may not work out, depending on what's happening when the future becomes the present.

Communication Styles

Many Native people believe silence is a sign of respect. Listening carefully to another is a great compliment, and not listening is seen as very disrespectful. However, there are culturally appropriate ways to demonstrate attentive listening that are different from common White listening habits. The liberal use of questions is not seen as sign of listening; in fact, asking too many questions may be viewed as rude. Therefore, during an interview you should keep questions brief and limited. In addition, you shouldn't expect many questions from Native clients. Strive for clarity and pause liberally when you ask if clients have questions for you. Clients may want time to formulate one well-worded question rather than asking many.

Eye contact norms vary across cultures. Respect might be communicated to others by listening quietly and avoiding direct eye contact. This is especially true when a First Nations person is wishing to communicate respect to an elder or someone of perceived higher status. Arranging seating so less direct eye contact is easy and natural may facilitate comfort and conversation.

For some Native clients, note taking during an initial interview may not be experienced as a listening behavior. It's wise to watch for nonverbal signals that taking notes is seen as rude, and to stop taking notes if possible (Paniagua, 1998). If you must take notes, explain the function of your notes and try to compensate for the distraction they represent.

A case example of an initial interview and case formulation with a member of the Navajo Nation is provided in *Putting It in Practice* 11.1.

PUTTING IT IN PRACTICE 11.1

An Initial Interview With a Navajo Client

Willard is a 26-year-old, single Navajo male who grew up on the Navajo reservation in rural New Mexico. He served 4 years in the Navy immediately after high school and is now a junior in college majoring in mathematics and education. College administration required Willard to seek counseling after he was arrested for assault during a fight in the dorm; his status in school was contingent on completing five sessions. The incident report noted that he and two other students became involved in an altercation after one of the other students made inappropriate gestures toward Willard's girlfriend.

During his first session, it was noted that he was a large, well-muscled young man with long hair freely falling around his shoulders. He did not smile upon introduction. However, he did make direct eye contact. He indicated that he was aware of the conditions placed on his continued enrollment, but he was not enthusiastic about participating in counseling.

Working in small groups or dyads, consider how you might proceed with an initial interview with Willard. Begin by creating a list of items that need to be considered given the circumstances of his referral. (For example, what is the impact of being mandated to counseling?) Which of the items on your list have cultural implications? Next, consider the issues that are relevant to establishing a therapy relationship with Willard. How would you begin the interview? (Practice this with your small group or dyad.) Finally, what information would you want to know about Willard that would influence your work with him in the future? Do you hold any stereotypes or assumptions about Native Americans? (For example, one might be curious if any of the participants in the fight were under the influence of alcohol.) Discuss these with your group.

Black or African American Cultures

Similar to First Nation peoples, the relationship between African (Black) Americans and European settlers didn't begin as a mutual, voluntary relationship. Both of these now-minority cultures experienced decimation of family structure, severe illness, loss of property and custom, and loss of liberty due to involuntary contact with Whites. Between 1518 and 1870, approximately 15 million Africans were forcibly brought to serve as slaves in the New World (Black & Jackson, 2005). The resulting intergenerational trauma, role confusion, grief, and loss reverberate in the African American culture. There are spectacular success stories and examples of healing, depth, and wisdom throughout African American culture, but intergenerational trauma is still evident.

Also similar to First Nation peoples, there is much diversity within the Black American population. This diversity is often ignored in research and clinical practice (Bryant, Taylor, Lincoln, Chatters, & Jackson, 2008). For example, Teah Moore (personal communication, August 11, 2012) wrote:

> It's never stated in books, but it's offensive to compare African-Americans with other people of African-descent. We are so different. We experience a different type of racism. There is much diversity. Even Southern blacks and Northern blacks have different racial experiences.

We refer to African Americans or Black Americans, recognizing there's clearly much more nuance and diversity among and within this population than we're able to capture and articulate in this short section.

The Role of Family

People of African descent generally place great importance on nuclear family and extended kinship systems. This pattern of family relationship was true in Africa before they came to North America, and for those who came as slaves, the extreme conditions families faced further reinforced this. Every family member, no matter how remotely related biologically, is highly valued.

When interviewing individuals, couples, or families of African descent, you should be sensitive to family roles. The family head may be the father, the mother, or older siblings. In addition, unrelated community members (godparents, pastors, and close friends) may serve important familial roles. Although a genogram can help with assessment or treatment, African American kinship systems may contain information not openly acknowledged. Hines and Boyd-Franklin (2005) pointed out that secrets such as births to unwed mothers, parental marital status, family members with legal troubles, or deaths due to AIDS, violence, or substance abuse may be facts not known to every member of a family system, and might be information that key members are hesitant to discuss with a stranger. Obviously, trust should be established before you can expect open sharing of personal family information. Therapists should carefully respect family privacy, even when the context of an interview setting implies openness. If you hold expectations for complete transparency in intercultural interactions you'll likely be frustrated. It's important to maintain realistic expectations, and not interpret caution as defensiveness or as a personal affront.

Religion and Spirituality

Many, but certainly not all African Americans are reluctant to seek professional help and instead turn to their communities or clergy for support (Aten, Topping, Denney, & Hosey, 2011; Bell-Tolliver & Wilkerson, 2011). On the other hand, some research suggests that a significant portion of African Americans are disillusioned with church-related resources and instead will turn to secular support services (Hardy, 2012). This suggests that although it's important to be sensitive to religion and spirituality issues during interviews, it's equally important not to stereotype and assume all African Americans are religiously oriented.

For cases in which African American clients are connected to religious or faith communities, their involvement with that community and with pastors or other religious leaders might be as influential and central as family (Hardy, 2012). Other community resources in African American communities, such as salons and barber shops also are places where disclosures, consultation, and guidance are sought (Teah Moore, personal communication, August 11, 2012). Consequently, asking Black clients who they confide in and where they get their support may produce useful information. Additionally, if your client seems inclined, you may want to explore the possibility of inviting church members or church leaders to the assessment or therapy process. If outside community or church members are integrated into assessment or therapy processes, it's essential to be very clear about confidentiality procedures because maintaining trust is especially helpful to intercultural relationships with service providers (Mattis & Grayman-Simpson, 2013; O'Malley, Sheppard, Schwartz, & Mandelblatt, 2004).

Couple and Gender Roles

Black males within the dominant American culture have reported feeling marginalized. Franklin (2007) coined the term *invisibility syndrome*, referring to White culture's fear-based tendencies to treat Black males as if they were invisible. It's possible that the invisibility syndrome could creep into the clinical interview, either in the form of stereotyped assumptions about the male who is present in the family system, or about the absence of a male in the family system. It should also be noted that African American males have a lower life expectancy than White males or females of either race primarily because of murder, incarceration, mental and physical disabilities, drug and alcohol abuse, and dangerous employment situations (Franklin, Boyd-Franklin, & Kelly, 2006). Professionals should be sensitive to potential health and safety issues within the Black American male population.

Historically, African American family roles have tended to be more egalitarian than those in the White patriarchy, where women's roles were limited to child-bearing and homemaking. However, there are many exceptions to this general rule and both geography and subculture appear to contribute to these exceptions. For example, Jamaican couples who migrated to the United States reported greater egalitarianism and higher marital satisfaction than Jamaican couples living in Jamaica (Foner, 2005). Generally, however, Black American women occupy strong family roles; they may be family providers, function in an equal or dominant parenting role, and wield substantial power in family decision-making—including the decision of whether to seek professional assistance.

As with all couples, relationship dynamics among Black Americans tend to be complex and variable. That said, most research indicates that Black American women are less satisfied in marriage than Black American males—although Black Caribbean men and women report approximately equal relationship satisfaction (Bryant et al., 2008). Despite lower satisfaction, African American women have been noted to stay in dysfunctional relationships because of a reluctance to add further distress to the burdened lives of African American men (Hines & Boyd-Franklin, 2005). This is certainly not unique to African American couples. In any couples' therapy, it can be difficult to work with the dynamic of partners who are making significant or self-limiting sacrifices for the other partner. Bryant et al (2008) reported on the structural constraints existing within some Black American communities that can contribute to relationship frustrations that Black women sometimes report:

> Research suggests that Black women face significant structural constraints in the likelihood of marriage. Two constraints, the small pool of eligible Black men and economic barriers to marriage, are commonly discussed in the literature with regard to Black marriage rates and the overall quality of marital relationships. These two factors are also related in that the shortage of Black men is thought to negatively impact relationship quality; when men are in short supply, they tend to be less committed to any given relationship. (p. 241)

Historic trauma can reverberate in cultures for generations. The wise mental health professional is careful not to judge, but rather seeks to facilitate growth and healing, with the pace and direction set collaboratively with clients.

Issues of Assumptions

There are approximately 38.9 million Americans of African descent (U.S. Census Bureau, 2011). At 12.6% of the total population, they make up the largest non-White cultural group in the United States.

Statistically, African Americans are poorer, have less education, suffer from more unemployment, and have more teen pregnancies as compared to White Americans. There are currently substantial regional differences in attitudes toward African Americans. In some settings positive relationships between African Americans and Whites seem easy and natural, whereas, in other settings, deep-seated conflicts remain. It's essential to remember that a little knowledge based on a little experience can be a dangerous thing. It's tempting to believe that because we once had an African American friend, roommate, girlfriend, or boss, we somehow know how to work with all Black Americans. Such assumptions are hazardous with regard to any person from another culture, but seem especially likely to be problematic between Whites and African Americans. To help improve sensitivity and effectiveness when working with African American clients, we recommend a local community immersion experience similar to the Multicultural Action Project (Hipolito-Delgado, Cook, Avrus, & Bonham, 2011) that we discuss toward the end of this chapter.

An example of an initial interview with an African American client is included in *Putting It in Practice* 11.2.

PUTTING IT IN PRACTICE 11.2

Working With an African American Client

Marvin was a 36-year-old African American male who had been married for 12 years and had two children, ages 6 and 8. He referred himself for counseling a short time after receiving a substantial promotion at the accounting firm where he had worked for the past 5 years. He indicated a preference for working with an African American counselor; however, he didn't feel he could wait for the next opening (estimated to be 3 months). He, therefore, reluctantly agreed to meet with a White male counselor who was about his age.

Marvin appeared uneasy on meeting his counselor. He shook hands, made brief eye contact, and offered a pensive smile. He reported feeling an enormous amount of stress a few months before his promotion. Fulfilling his role as a husband and father was nearly impossible while meeting the demands of his work. Then he said, "but you being White probably don't understand." He continued angrily, "There's NO WAY you can know what it's like to be a Black man in a White man's business—hell, in a White man's WORLD!"

Take a few minutes to contemplate this scenario. What stereotypes of Black men might emerge in your mind after this interaction? How would you deal with them? What would you feel?

How would you respond to Marvin? One option would be to say something like this, "You're right, there's no way I can truly understand what it's like for you, but I'd like to try. Can you tell me more about being Black in your place of work?"

What would a question like this accomplish? What other responses might you try?

Take this example into discussion with your peers or professor. The question of how to make intercultural connections can't be answered simply or briefly. Really, it's a process because if you work with different minority groups you may find some clients lead with anger (like Marvin), whereas others will appear more withdraw, depressed, distracted, or anxious. And, underneath their emotional presentation there will be many more layers of diversity.

Hispanic/Latina/o American Cultures

For the purposes of this chapter, we take our meaning for the term *Hispanic* from Marin and Marin (1991), who indicate that Hispanic people are "individuals who reside in the United States and who were born in or trace the background of their families to one of the Spanish-speaking Latin American nations or Spain" (p. 1). This term is not perfect and Gallardo (2013) prefers using "...the term Latina/o...as a culturally consistent term..." (p. 44). Consistent with Gallardo's perspective, some Mexican Americans prefer the term Latino because it does not harken back to the conqueror, Spain (Dana, 1993).

Therapists should be aware that personal, national, and ethnic identity is affected by this terminology issue (Norris, 2007). In an effort to be inclusive, some researchers and writers have begun using both terms: *Hispanic and Latino/a*. We will follow this trend, noting that the people thus grouped together represent many different countries, cultures, sociopolitical histories, and reasons for being in the United States. Therefore, an important place to begin a clinical interview is to ask about the client's country of origin.

> Proclaiming their nationality is very important to Latinos: it provides a sense of pride and identity that is reflected in the stories they tell, their music, and their poetry. Longing for their homeland is more pronounced when they are unable to return to their home either because they are here as political exiles, or as illegal aliens, or because they are unable to afford the cost of travel. In therapy, asking the question, "What is your country of origin?" and listening to the client's stories of immigration helps to engage the therapist and gives the therapist an opportunity to learn about the country the client left behind, the culture, and the reasons for leaving. (Garcia-Preto, 1996, p. 142)

Religion and Related Belief Systems

The Catholic Church is very influential in many Hispanic/Latina/o cultures. The priest, therefore, is often central in helping solve individual and family problems. Mental health problems are sometimes seen as being caused by evil spirits, and, therefore, the church is the logical place to seek assistance (Cuellar & Paniagua, 2000). As a result, mental health professionals may be contacted only after all other avenues in the church and community have been accessed.

Some people in the Hispanic/Latino culture believe that individuals bring on their own mental and/or physical problems by engaging in certain forms of behavior, and that others can be inflicted with such problems by *mal de ojo* (the evil eye) directed at them (Cuéllar & Paniagua, 2000). Such beliefs are related to a fatalism that some have identified as common to many Hispanic/Latino cultures (Ho et al., 2004). *Fatalism* is a belief that a person cannot do much about his or her fate—adversity and good fortune are out of the control of the individual. In counseling, this belief can be counterproductive when the therapist is trying to encourage an internal locus of control. On the other hand, it can absolve individuals of blame for traumatic life circumstances that are indeed out of their control. It is ill-advised to strongly confront Hispanic/Latinos regarding their fatalistic or external locus of control orientation.

Personalismo, Respeto, and Charlar

Qualitative and quantitative research supports the use of personalismo, respeto, and charlar with Hispanic/Latino clients (Gallardo, 2013). Personalismo refers to a personable and friendly demeanor; respeto refers to the expression of respect in relationships; charlar refers to small talk.

Members of the broad Hispanic/Latino/a cultural group are known for placing great emphasis on interpersonal relationships and valuing warmth, closeness, and honest self-disclosure. These values may dictate the choice of counselor more than credentials per se (Comas-Diaz, 2006). As a professional, you might be surprised by the level of inquiry and interest in your personal life and tastes, but the intention is not invasiveness, it's about connection. However, it's advisable to integrate respeto into your friendly small talk. This suggests also maintaining formality at first, to signal professional relationship boundaries. Using last names and acting with deliberate respect during the first interview can help this process.

In addition, this personal orientation finds expression in the giving of gifts to the counselor during therapy. Paniagua (1996) noted:

> Therapists working with Hispanic/Latino clients need to recognize and acknowledge the conditions under which it is culturally appropriate to accept such gifts (e.g., during Christmas, the therapist may receive from a Mexican American client a wooden cup made in Mexico) and those conditions under which it may be clinically appropriate to reject the gift (e.g., receiving the cup as a form of payment for therapy). (pp. 42–43)

The Role of Family

Similar to other cultures discussed in this chapter, family is extremely important to Hispanic/Latino people and is more broadly defined than traditional White American nuclear families. Family members have most likely been consulted before an individual comes for counseling; and in many cases, involving the family directly is helpful. There is a strong emphasis on the family's needs over individual needs.

However, in contrast to other nondominant cultures in the United States and in contrast to White culture, role flexibility in the family is less common in Hispanic/Latino communities. Generally, in traditional families, the father is head of the household and is to be respected as such. The mother is the homemaker and cares for the children. The sense of family obligation, honor, and responsibility runs deep for most traditional Hispanic/Latino families (Gibbs & Huang, 2004; Losada et al., 2006).

Gender Roles

Machismo and *marianismo* are central notions that influence interpersonal relationships, especially between the sexes. *Machismo* denotes masculinity as evidenced in physical prowess, aggression, attractiveness to women, protector of the family, and sometimes consumption of large quantities of alcohol, thereby commanding respect from others. This respect has many important dimensions in Hispanic/Latino culture. A person who shows appropriate *respeto* for the right people is seen as someone who has been well-educated or well-reared (Guilamo-Ramos et al., 2007).

Marianismo, or traditional Hispanic/Latino womanhood, is based on the Catholic worship of the Virgin Mary. It connotes obedience, timidity, sexual abstinence until marriage, emotionality, and gentleness. According to Comas-Díaz (1994), the concept of *marianismo* includes a belief in the spiritual superiority of women, who endure all the suffering produced by men. This cultural value has meaning and power in the psychological and physical well-being of Latina women (Moreno, 2007; Vazquez & Clauss-Ehlers, 2005).

Needless to say, machismo and marianismo are not always socially acceptable gender-role guidelines in the dominant culture in the United States. Traditional Hispanic/Latino families who have immigrated may experience conflicts as younger generations acculturate and refuse to conform to these traditional roles and expectations.

A case example of working with a Hispanic/Latino client is provided in *Putting It in Practice* 11.3.

PUTTING IT IN PRACTICE 11.3

Working With a Hispanic/Latino Client

Rosa is a 19-year-old single female whose family (mother, father, and five siblings) moved from Mexico to Michigan 15 years ago. She has two sisters, ages 16 and 21, and three brothers, ages 14, 17, and 22. She and her family live in a primarily Mexican American community where Catholicism is a significant part of people's lives. Rosa is living at home while she studies journalism at a local college, where she has consistently been named to the Dean's list for academic excellence.

Rosa came to counseling because she had been feeling depressed over the last two months. She noted that she's not sleeping or eating well, and is "having a hard time just getting through each day." She stated that it was difficult to come to counseling because her family would not approve of her discussing personal things with an outsider, but she came anyway because friends at her college strongly encouraged her.

When asked about her life, she burst into tears. She was thoroughly enjoying college until she noticed that her family was treating her differently. Looking back, she thought it started as soon as she began college, but the novelty of the experience had distracted her. Rosa said her brothers, especially, were keeping their distance from her and when they spoke to her, they treated her like an outsider. Once she overheard her older brother accuse her of trying to be better than them. She also noticed that she couldn't relate as well to her old friends. When they met, they often ran out of things to say after a few awkward minutes. She finally said, "It's just not worth it to me—I'm going to quit college. I just don't know who I am anymore!"

- How would you explore the importance of familia with Rosa?
- What else would you need to know about her? Her friends?

(continued)

> (*continued*)
> - Would you consider incorporating other helping sources in your work with Rosa?
> - What values might you hold that would come into conflict with honoring Rosa's possible choices and options?
>
> Discuss these questions and others that come to mind with a partner.

Asian American Cultures

Once again, the idea that a prototypical Asian American client exists and will walk into your office for a clinical interview is naïve and potentially harmful. Chang and O'Hara (2013) briefly described the range of people who are classified as Asian:

> Both the 2000 and 2010 U.S. census included several Asian-related categories...(a) Asian Indian, (b) Chinese, (c) Filipino, (d) Japanese, (e) Korean, (f) Vietnamese, or (g) Other Asian write-in category. Pacific Islander categories included (a) Native Hawaiian, (b) Guamanian or Chamorro, (c) Samoan, (d) or Other Pacific Islander write-in category. An additional challenge is that not all individuals from the Asian continent identify as Asian. For example, persons of Iranian, Indian, or Russian heritage may prefer to identify by region (e.g., South Asian, Middle Eastern) or country of origin. These examples underscore the fact that racial categories are fluid and that Asian Americans are heterogeneous both between and within subgroups.

Overall, more than 40 disparate cultural groups are represented under the term Asian Americans. The term *Asian* obviously represents vast numbers of peoples and cultures.

The Role of Family

Asian cultures are typically more collectivist than most White cultures, with stronger, more inclusive and defined family roles and obligations. For example, the strong achievement orientation often reported within Asian families is not exclusively for the self, but also gives honor and prestige to the family (Chang & O'Hara, 2013). In this regard, Asians are referred to as both individualistic and relational (Khanna, McDowell, Perumbilly, & Titus, 2009).

Despite traces of individualism with respect to achievement, decisions affecting the family (which include most or all decisions) generally should be decided by the family. The family also should be strong enough, wise enough, and have enough resources to handle problems encountered by the individual. If circumstances are such that it is necessary to seek outside counseling help, some Asian families may experience a sense of shame, and a loss of face. Therefore, when conducting a first session with an Asian client or family you should consider that a great deal of stress may have prompted the client(s) to seek help (Chang & O'Hara, 2013).

Similar to Hispanic/Latino family structure, there can be strong hierarchical relationships inside and outside families, often based on sex/gender. The father is considered the head of the household and holds the dominant role. Mothers and women are viewed as more passive and subservient. Children are taught to value family harmony and respect authority (Chang & O'Hara, 2013). At the same time, parents may see themselves as valuing their children over themselves and practicing a sacrificial love (Wong, Wong, & Obeng, 2012). This potentially conflicting family style can lead to mixed feelings about whether to allow or limit children's integration into the dominant culture (Khanna et al., 2009).

Many Asian families living in the United States are in an acculturation process. The children often become bilingual, thereby assuming a power in the family that upsets traditional roles. Further, some families have members living in the home country and some members living here, which adds more relational and role strain (Khanna et al., 2009).

Orientation Toward Authority

As noted, Asian cultures are more rigidly hierarchical (Matsumoto & Yoo, 2005; Negy, 2004) than some cultures. This is directly related to the concept mentioned earlier called *filial piety*, which refers to the honor, reverence, obedience, and loyalty owed to those hierarchically above you (Cheung, Kwan, & Ng, 2006). Deference toward authority manifests in a number of ways. Asian American clients expect a counselor to be an expert and to act with authority.

In the same vein, verbal communication with a mental health professional may not be direct and certainly is not confrontational. For example, Khanna et al. (2009) reported from a Delphi study wherein Asian Indians were described as:

> . . . more inclined to engage in high context, non-verbal communication—that is, they often value indirect communication and base decisions on non-verbal cues. (p. 57)

This style combined with the high value placed on harmonious relationships makes it likely that an Asian American client, when faced with conflict or uncertainty in your office, will offer the most polite, affirmative response available. Emotional restraint and self-control are highly esteemed interpersonal skills. Among Asians, as among many First Nation tribes, silence is a sign of respect. Patterns of socially appropriate eye contact are also similar. Direct eye contact is invasive and disrespectful, especially when interacting with persons of higher status or authority (Fouad & Arredondo, 2007a).

It is important to be respectful to all clients, but Asian American clients may respond especially well to being treated with formal respect. Using Mr., Mrs., and Ms. and a last name is a signal of respect and should not be discontinued until the client directly invites a first-name address. However, be aware that traditionally, in most Asian countries, women keep their own family surnames and may wish to be called by that surname even if, because of customs in the United States, she has begun to use her husband's surname. A simple inquiry along these lines indicates respect.

Even during a first interview, many Asian American clients will expect concrete and tangible advice. This runs contrary to most training models; therefore, you may need to consider several options: (a) explain to clients that your approach doesn't involve giving direct advice; (b) explain to clients that you will offer advice, but not until you've completed an assessment process; or (c) prepare yourself to be more directive and offer research-based advice that you believe can be helpful (Carolyn Berger, personal communication, August 13, 2012).

Spiritual and Religious Matters

A common practice among many Asian cultures has been the keeping of an ancestor altar. A reverence toward ancestors and various beliefs regarding ancestral spirits, wishes, or presence in family matters can be central to individual and family functioning and decision making. Religious orientations are as varied as the countries from which Asian Americans have come, including such diverse belief systems as Buddhism, Islam, Hinduism, Christianity, Jainism, and many branches in each.

Much has been written about the Western mind or worldview and the Eastern mind or worldview in religious and philosophical literature. Although the following quote may not help the therapist with any particular Asian American client, it may serve as a guide in our quest to be more authentically multicultural:

> A Cup of Tea
>
> Nan-in, a Japanese master during the Meiji era (1868–1912), received a university professor who came to inquire about Zen. Nan-in served tea. He poured his visitor's cup full, and then kept on pouring.
>
> The professor watched the overflow until he no longer could restrain himself. "It is overfull. No more will go in!"
>
> "Like this cup," Nan-in said, "you are full of your own opinions and speculations. How can I show you Zen unless you first empty your cup?" (Senzaki & Reps, 1939)

A case example of working with an Asian American client is provided in *Putting It in Practice* 11.4.

PUTTING IT IN PRACTICE 11.4

Working With an Asian American Client

In the journal *Psychotherapy*, John Chambers Christopher, a colleague of ours, reported on the following case:

Simon, an East Asian international student, referred himself to the university counseling center after about one year of studying in the United States. Simon reported low self-esteem, difficulty concentrating, and problems with socializing. His stated goal for therapy was to become "more assertive in his interactions with others" (Christopher, 2001 p. 124). In particular, Simon expressed a desire to become more similar to his American roommates and less like other international students from his homeland.

Presented by a different therapist and/or a different client, this case might simply be cast into the rather straightforward mold of assertiveness training. However, as described by Christopher (2001) Simon's presenting problem stimulated deeper personal reflection:

> I confess that initially this case placed me in a difficult position with respect to my own values. Having spent a number of years critiquing Western culture and learning about the moral visions of non-Western traditions, my tendency was to focus on the limitations of assertiveness and the individualism it manifests and supports. Moreover, I was troubled to see someone from a cultural tradition as rich as Simon's almost eager to forsake this heritage to become Western. I felt a sense of reservation about helping Simon with his stated goals. (p. 125)

This case illustrates an interesting potential contextual dilemma associated with cross-cultural counseling. That is, how does the therapist handle a situation in which he or she values a client's culture to a greater degree than the client?

Take some time to reflect on John Christopher's dilemma. How would you be affected by a similar situation? Are there any particular ethnocultural perspectives, philosophies, or behavior patterns that you find more desirable than those of your own culture's?

OTHER DIVERSE CLIENT POPULATIONS

The groups with which we identify—the ones we claim and the ones that claim us—are profoundly influential. Our families of origin; our ethnic, cultural, and/or racial identities; our age, socioeconomic background, and our sexual identities, affect our lives continuously, both consciously and unconsciously. Further, our chosen beliefs and the experiences life brings shape our identities and the quality of our lives. In this sense, all counseling is multicultural counseling (D. W. Sue & Sue, 2013). No two human beings have exactly the same life experience. However, certain life experiences or genetic or biological circumstances of birth exert significant and sometimes profound force on our lives. The following groups of individuals are included as illustrations, but this is not an exclusive list (see *Putting It in Practice 11.5* for specific information on interviewing immigrants).

PUTTING IT IN PRACTICE 11.5

Considerations When Interviewing Immigrants

Globalization has led to increased immigration around the world. Currently 12 percent of the U.S. population is made up of immigrants and over 10 million of the school-aged U.S. children are children of
(continued)

(*continued*)

immigrants (Camarota, 2005). Migrating to another country often leads to increased levels of stress, depression, and anxiety (Oh, Koeske, & Sales, 2002; Portes & Rumbaut, 2006; Van Oudenhoven, Ward, & Masgoret, 2006). Considering the number of immigrants and the mental health difficulties these immigrants experience as a result of migration, the possibility of working with an immigrant at some point in your career is very high.

Immigrants might be classified as voluntary and involuntary (Ogbu, 1992). Voluntary immigrants choose to leave their country, whereas the involuntary ones are forced to leave their home country due to safety reasons (Ward, Bochner, & Furnham, 2001). Both groups go through an acculturation and adjustment process. Berry (2006) defines acculturation as "a process of cultural and psychological change that results from the continuing contact between people of different cultural backgrounds" (p. 27). Sometimes the concept of acculturation is confused with assimilation. Assimilation results from immigrants wanting to adapt to the new culture as their own, opting not to maintain their cultural identity (Berry, 2006). Some immigrants may choose to assimilate, while others may want to become bicultural, keeping their own ethnic identity and culture while also acquiring the culture of the new country. Either choice should be respected. There is evidence that immigrants' ethnic identity correlates with positive mental health outcomes, such as a higher self-esteem (Phinney & Chavira, 1992).

Immigrants experience challenges as they adjust to their new home (e.g., Van Oudenhoven et al., 2006), including language proficiency, loss and lack of social support system, and cultural differences. Children of immigrants face an additional set of challenges. While trying to adjust and acculturate, these children may be expected to take on adult roles by serving as a translator for their parents and helping them with immigration-related paperwork (Trickett & Jones, 2007). Overall, immigrants tend to have an easier adjustment process if their own culture and the culture in the new country are similar (Ward et al., 2001). It is important for mental health practitioners to understand the daily struggles of immigrants to be able to provide effective services. Gentle inquiry is in order with questions such as: How are you adjusting to your life here? How is your family adjusting? What are some challenges you're facing? How are you handling these challenges?

Compared to legal immigrants, illegal immigrants might be at a higher risk for poor mental health due to being under the stress of being caught and deported. Many adults with illegal immigration status are afraid to seek mental health services (Cabassa, 2007). They are concerned that they might be discovered and deported. Regardless of these concerns, however, sometimes immigrants have no choice but to seek help (e.g., family counseling to deal with a child who has behavioral problems). Sensitive therapists should avoid questions about immigrant's legal status in order to gain trust. In addition, if the illegal status of the family is mentioned, a reminder that this information will stay strictly confidential may help build trust and reduce anxiety.

Media portrayals of immigrant groups can be quite influential and damaging. For example, following the September 11th attacks in the United States, media in many parts of the world have portrayed Arabs as terrorists, Muslims, and enemies of the Western countries. However, many Arab groups are friends of the Western world, and some of these groups belong to the Christian or Jewish faith. This negative portrayal of Arabs has contributed to increased prejudice and bias toward Arabs (Abu-Ras, 2007). It is important for therapists to be aware of potential biases toward immigrants and to make sure that these biases do not come across in the interview as an untrusting, closed-off, or fearful attitude.

Another errant assumption therapists could make relates to a client's English proficiency. A few immigrants may speak English without an accent (e.g., the ones who were schooled in English-speaking international schools), but many immigrants have an accent or use broken English. Therapists need to guard against the assumption that an accent or broken English is a sign that the person is uneducated. Many immigrants hold professional degrees and might have had professional careers in their home countries. Ask immigrants about their education and employment history in their country of origin: "I would like to hear a little about your life back home. It might help me understand more about some of the positive and not so positive things you left behind." Of course, not every client who speaks English with an accent is an immigrant. The client may have been born in a neighborhood where his or her exposure to English was limited.

When working with immigrants, it is important to stay away from slang, idioms, or cultural sayings, as it may be harder for an immigrant to understand what the therapist means. For example, "killing two birds with one stone" and "feeling between a rock and a hard place" are expressions that an immigrant client may not understand. This can be further illustrated by the following example:

Client: When I came here to join my husband, I thought everything was going to be nice. But, I miss my family a lot. I wake up in the mornings, I don't want to do anything, I don't get out of bed . . .

Counselor: You feel down in the dumps.

Instead of using a slang expression, a statement similar to "you are feeling lonely and sad." will be easier for the client to understand.

Another issue the counselor may face is related to children being used as translators in sessions. Children frequently help their immigrant parents communicate with their new world by translating for them in various domains (Orellana, Reynolds, Dorner, & Meza, 2003). Parents may bring children to translate when they seek counseling. Benefits

(continued)

(continued)
and disadvantages of this method should be carefully considered. Parents may not feel comfortable when the subject matter is sensitive. If possible, arrange for an adult to provide the translation or ask that clients bring an adult around whom they would feel comfortable discussing psychological experiences and sensitive issues.

Contributed by Senel Poyrazli, PhD

Gay, Lesbian, Bisexual, and Transgender People

To understate the obvious, sexual orientation is occasionally controversial (Morrow & Messinger, 2006). Many dominant world religions declare homosexual sex to be sinful, although there are certainly substantial numbers of religions, and denominations within the religions, that don't take this stand. For many years, homosexuality was considered a mental disorder, and to this day, controversial treatments designed to "cure" homosexuals exist (Borowich, 2008; Ford, 2001). However, this is an affront to most of the GLBT community.

As Lyla White wrote in the Foreword of her former husband's book:

> Mel had no choice about being a homosexual. Believe me, if he had a choice, I know he would have chosen his marriage, his family, and his unique ministry; for Mel's values, like most gays and lesbians I know, are the same as mine and my heterosexual friends: love, respect, commitment, nurture, responsibility, honesty, and integrity. We are all on this journey together and we must ensure that the road is safe for everyone, including our homosexual brothers and sisters who for far too long have been unfairly condemned and rejected. Isn't it past time that we opened our hearts and our arms to welcome them home instead of seeing them as strangers still waiting at the gate?
>
> *—Lyla White, former wife of gay pastor*
> *Mel White, author of* Stranger at the Gate *(1994)*

Sexual identity and sexual orientation are intensely personal and central matters to most people. Sexual attraction is a powerful motivator of human behavior and is foundational to a sense of self. The longing for a soul mate is probably as old as life itself. To date, there has been no definitive explanation for the fact that across time and culture, a consistent minority of humans are attracted to members of the same sex. Many theories have been offered, but at present, it seems best to consider homosexuality, like left- or right-handedness, as simply a fact of nature. Some people are attracted to opposite-sex partners for sexual intimacy, some people are attracted to same sex partners, and some are attracted to both.

Many homosexual people report knowing they were homosexual even before kindergarten, and others report becoming aware much later in life (White, 1994; Worthington, Navarro, Savoy, & Hampton, 2008). Because of stigma and lack of cultural role models, many homosexual people have, at times, struggled with their sexual orientation and tried to ignore or change it.

People with gender identity or sexual orientations other than heterosexual go to counselors for all the reasons heterosexual people go, and they don't necessarily identify their sexual orientation as part of the problem(s). However, many have endured verbal abuse, violence, vicious labeling, loneliness, and harsh judgments; for some clients these experiences occurred during childhood or adolescence (Jeltova & Fish, 2005), while others report these experiences are more recent or current. These cruelties can exact a great developmental and psychological price. As Judy Grahn (1990) wrote, discovering connections with others with diverse sexual orientations can be a great relief.

> The day I saw a poster declaring the existence of an organization of Gay American Indians, I put my face into my hands and sobbed with relief. What Americans call Gayness not only has distinct cultural characteristics, its participants have long held positions of social power in history and ritual among people all over the globe. (p. 105)

Given the oppression that many Gay, Lesbian, Bisexual, and Transgender (GLBT) individuals have experienced, providing affirmative psychotherapy to GLBT clients has become a major movement within counseling and psychotherapy (Heck, Flentje, & Cochran, 2013). *Affirmative psychotherapy* emphasizes that LGBT clients need a corrective emotional experience that affirms and validates their sexual identity (Alexander & French, 1946). Because heterosexism and homophobia can contribute to psychopathology, affirmative therapy can help compensate for the experiences they face challenges from living in an invalidating environment (Heck et al., 2013).

Many people who are homosexual, bisexual, or transgender won't share that information during an initial interview; they may share their sexuality with very few people. Therapists should listen for themes suggesting struggles with sexual identity, dating, and attraction. Because many nonheterosexual people anticipate harsh judgment and rejection, some gay-friendly therapists suggest leaving homosexual-friendly pamphlets or literature in the waiting room to communicate an open attitude toward these issues (Amadio & Pérez, 2008; Kort, 2008). It's also important that care is taken to avoid using gender-specific words indicating the assumption of heterosexuality. For example, when inquiring about intimate relationships, the term *romantic partner* rather than *boyfriend* or *girlfriend* should be used. This allows clients to reveal the partner's gender when ready. For younger clients, or clients who are dating, it's helpful to ask general questions about romantic relationships or romance in general.

Therapists need to be sensitive to relationship and family issues among homosexual, bisexual, and transgender clients. Never make assumptions about whether clients are out to their family. Instead of assumptions, gentle exploration without judgment is in order. It's not the therapist's job to push clients toward coming out. Again, sensitivity to where clients are in their process is best.

Gay and lesbian couples come with all the varieties of needs and problems that trouble heterosexual couples, but sometimes, with more complicating factors. In particular, they're often without societal and familial supports and sanctions that help and nurture heterosexual couples. In times of illness or loss, a gay or lesbian life partner may not be recognized or accorded the same privileges of a heterosexual partner. Additionally, many such individuals experienced harsh rejection from one or more family members. These experiences may lead them to be reluctant to admit their sexual orientation (Heck et al., 2013).

Persons With Disabilities

An extensive literature exists for therapists wishing to work with clients who have physical, developmental, or emotional disabilities (Dell Orto & Power, 2007). Graduate level training programs in special education, rehabilitation counseling, and rehabilitation psychology are available. Having an open and accepting attitude is an essential prerequisite to working with people with disabilities. However, there are many technical aspects to specific medical conditions and disabilities and so your compassionate attitude needs to be combined with competence (Falvo, 2011). The information here is provided only to inform you that individuals with disabilities constitute a special population subject to discrimination and oppression; to work specifically with individuals with disabilities, substantial training and supervision are required.

Sometimes, when interviewing a person with an obvious disability, professionals assume it's more polite to ignore crutches, missing limbs, wheelchairs, or even canes indicating blindness. However, as stated earlier with regard to race and culture, asking directly, with an open, curious, but noninvasive attitude, about the difference is usually welcomed. Such questions as "Have you used a wheelchair all your life, or is this a more recent addition?" can open the door to a candid discussion of the disability. With other physical disfigurements it's appropriate to treat the person with the affirming style you would toward all clients and then explore the individual's disability very soon in the session if it's directly related to the referral question and later in the session if the issue is less related to the referral question.

Facing and managing a disability can affect all areas of an individual's life. However, too often, mental health professionals without rehabilitation training don't know how to contextualize a disability. The disability is either treated as the defining feature of the individual, overshadowing all else, or it is ignored; ignoring a disability implies that it should have no impact on an individual's emotional and interpersonal functioning.

Culture interacts with disability in significant ways. Able-bodiedness has gendered values, and culture plays a central role in defining masculinity and femininity. Cultures vary widely in their acceptance of disability, provisions for access, and general expectations for the individual with a disability. Because of the stereotypic independence linked to masculinity, men with disabilities have to reconsider maleness and create new values and ways of being. This can take a great deal of time and psychological work (Marini, 2007).

The Religiously Committed

For certain religious clients, seeking help from a secular mental health professional may feel like a contradiction of faith—or at least a very risky thing to do. Therefore, you should be particularly sensitive to behaviors suggesting a challenge to religious authority. Mental health issues and problems are obviously very connected to religious concerns. Finding a comfortable middle ground that denies neither perspective can be challenging. As Samuel M. Natale (1985) wrote in *Psychotherapy and the Religiously Committed Patient*:

> There are few problems more demanding in psychotherapy than dealing with a client's religious beliefs. This is so for a number of reasons, which include not only a lack of sensitivity and understanding on the part of the therapist but also a hesitation, avoidance, and even downright fear on the part of the therapist to explore distinctly religious values with a client. (p. 107)

There's a growing openness in counseling and psychology to integrate spiritual dimensions into therapy (Johnson, 2013; Pargament & Saunders, 2007). Although this may be true with regard to more liberal-thinking religious clients, fundamentalists and deeply committed people from most organized religions generally prefer not to seek secular help (Stern, 1985). Therefore, for some deeply religious persons, the first visit may be because of a family or personal crisis. Their entry into the professional mental health world generally isn't a casual inquiry into the potential use of psychotherapy to expand and grow. More likely, it's an expression of desperation. Personal or family conflicts have become too great, and the answers, cures, or solutions within their religious framework have failed to address the problems sufficiently.

Because religion represents both culture and personal choice, differences between counselor and client, though not visible, can be pronounced and unsettling, requiring awareness and specific clinical skills in this area (Onedera, 2008). You might be directly asked about your religious beliefs in an initial interview. We recommend a balanced response:

- First, as a professional, it's your job to explore both the cause for concern and the concerns themselves as they relate to the client's problems and needs.
- Second, have a truthful and carefully considered answer ready. Refusing to share a summary of your spirituality will adversely affect the therapy alliance (Johnson, 2013). After your summary, return the topic to how it feels for the client to work with you. Don't debate matters of faith.

One of our colleagues, a psychologist who is also an ordained minister, often provides religious clients with a commentary similar to the following:

> I understand it can be hard for a person with strong religious beliefs to consult a professional about personal problems. One way I look at it is like this: I know some people who are doing very well psychologically and very poorly in their spiritual life. On the other hand, I know some people who are doing fine with their religious life, but they have some psychological or emotional work to do. Although many times religious and psychological well-being are highly connected, being well in one area doesn't *necessarily* mean you are feeling well in the other. If you want to, I think we can work on the emotional and psychological concerns here, without violating issues of faith.

Some mental health professionals identify their religious affiliations or beliefs in their advertising, on their cards, or in their informed consent paperwork.

Others develop specific specialties in areas dealing with religious concerns. Also, treatment planning may certainly include consultation with religious leaders or authorities, including mental health professionals who practice within a particular religious identity (Reber, 2006).

CULTURAL COMPLEXITIES AND IDENTITIES

What's your personal identity? Do you more readily describe yourself as Black or female? As Navajo or as a graduate student? As a Muslim, a feminist, an environmentalist, or a conservative? Assuming you can name a few identifications, which are you willing to describe? Which are most dominant in making you who you are? Which cause you the most difficulties? Even more complicated, what if you are biracial, a nontraditionally-aged grad student, and the grandmother of a child with severe disabilities? Many groups want to claim your allegiance and will influence the ways you see the world (Hall, 2004; Kallivayalil, 2007).

Pamela Hays (2008), author of *Addressing Cultural Complexities in Practice* noted that many people tend to think of themselves as complex and multidimensional, while usually considering others as more one dimensional. In her book, Hays described a framework to help mental health professionals recognize the many dynamics that contribute to cultural differences among us. She uses the acronym "ADDRESSING," which stands for Age, Developmental and acquired Disabilities, Religion, Ethnicity, Socioeconomic status, Sexual orientation, Indigenous heritage, Native origin, and Gender (Hays, 2008).

This acronym offers therapists a succinct guide for observing and inquiring about the many dimensions in working with people different than ourselves. An example might be helpful. Imagine you're an intern in a medical center dedicated to serving low-income clients. The administrative aide tells you that your next appointment is with a woman who "looks Asian" but the aide can tell you little else because the woman was difficult to understand.

You bring the client, Mrs. Cho, back to your office. She's animated and eager to talk, but her accent is strong, and you have some difficulty following her. After going over the informed consent and intake forms, you invite her to tell you why she's seeking counseling. You listen carefully, sometimes apologizing that you didn't understand something, and asking her to repeat it. In your mind, you begin observing and listening for the ADDRESSING areas.

> **Age:** How old is Mrs. Cho? You check the form, and see that she has left this blank. Her gray hair suggests late midlife. What might this mean in her life and culture? Why is the age left blank? Is this significant?
>
> **Developmental Disabilities:** You see no evidence of any developmental disabilities, but you realize that with Mrs. Cho's heavy accent, she might be seen as lacking in intelligence or communication abilities. She may have even been treated this way. And of course, you don't know her well enough yet to make any assumptions about intellectual or developmental disabilities or abilities.
>
> **Disabilities Acquired Later in Life:** You noticed that when she came in, Mrs. Cho walked with a slight limp and wears thick eyeglasses. You don't know the extent of life impact of either of these, but you're alert to the possibilities of these factors, and other potential disabilities contributing to understanding Mrs. Cho's story and needs.

Religion: Mrs. Cho mentioned that she's Vietnamese. You've been reading a book by a Vietnamese Buddhist named Ticht Nach Hahn. In your mind, you wonder if Mrs. Cho has heard of him. You wonder if she was raised with a spiritual or religious background that now informs her life. Then she shares with you that one of the reasons she is seeking counseling is that a member of her church, the First United Methodist Church, suggested that she might need to get counseling. Mrs. Cho tells you that after praying about it, she decided to follow this advice. [So much for the Buddhism theory.]

Ethnic/Racial Identity: Mrs. Cho's accent suggests her first language wasn't English. She stated that she's Vietnamese, but when you ask her to repeat something you didn't understand, she asked if you speak French, because that would be easier. You don't know what being Vietnamese or what speaking French means to her. You suspect both are important. You wonder if you'll need an interpreter who speaks French.

Socioeconomic Status: Mrs. Cho has come to a low-income clinic. She is modestly dressed. You might assume she's living in poverty. You could be correct, or you could be mistaken. She could be of comfortable means, but have no health insurance. Listening for clues will help you know about this dimension of her life. Even when you feel reasonably clear about her current conditions, there's more to consider. Was she raised in a very poor family? What's her current neighborhood like?

Sexual Orientation: Therapists shouldn't assume someone is heterosexual because of marriage. Also, Mrs. Cho may have children or others in her life for whom sexual orientation is an important issue.

Indigenous Heritage: Mrs. Cho doesn't have any readily apparent connections to indigenous peoples, but you maintain an awareness of this factor.

National Identity: We don't know how Mrs. Cho sees herself in terms of citizenship or national identity. She mentions she has a son living in Canada and wishes she could move there. She hasn't mentioned Vietnam, other than saying that she's Vietnamese. You hold several hypotheses about national identity and its role in Mrs. Cho's life.

Gender-Related Information: Mrs. Cho mentioned that her second husband, Albert, would be very angry if he knew she was seeking counseling. You wonder about gender roles and expectations present in Mrs. Cho's life and how her upbringing might have affected these.

This example helps underline the many facets of individual identity that make humans multidimensional and complex. Using the ADDRESSING acronym can help expand your understanding of diversity.

ASSESSMENT AND CULTURE-BOUND SYNDROMES

In many cultures, consulting with a mental health professional from the dominant culture comes as a last resort. Seeing an outsider for personal problems might go against traditional problem-solving strategies. Clients from another culture may experience enormous stress or anxiety because of counseling—in addition to the stress that brought them in. Moreover, they could have expectations for counseling that may or may not match the therapist's approach. Therefore, extra care should be taken to ensure that clients feel welcome, to establish credibility, and to build trust. Even the establishment of trust requires a sensitivity to how trustworthiness is assessed in a given culture (Branzei, Vertinsky, & Camp, 2007). A key goal is to ensure that clients believe their problems can be addressed without negating their worldview.

Using standardized assessment instruments with diverse clients may produce anxiety, confusion, or anger. Standardized assessment procedures may or may not be appropriate, partly because historically, diagnostic testing procedures have been misused with diverse clients (Paniagua, 2010). Although efforts have been made to address bias in assessment instruments, cultural bias still exists.

Additional guidelines for interviewing culturally diverse clients are provided in Table 11.1.

Culture-Bound Syndromes

Because theories of human functioning are based in our cultural views and experiences, our current diagnostic system for mental health problems is heavily culturally influenced (Paniagua, 2010). In addition, the manifestation of mental angst and distress occurs through different culturally specific symptom complexes that change over time. For example, in contrast to Freud's era (Jones, 1955), not many women in the United States currently have vapors or fainting spells; however, eating disorders, while common today, were almost unheard of a hundred years ago. Posttraumatic stress symptoms reflect common human responses to trauma across cultures, but the name of the disorder has varied over many centuries. In addition, what's considered traumatic and what to do about it is culturally specific (Malgady, 2010).

The terms used to refer to culturally related syndromes or distress have changed over the years and concerns have been raised about the simplicity and assumptions of various terms (Ranganathan & Bhattacharya, 2007; Tseng, 2006). Summarizing the work of Griffith and Baker (1993); Rubel, O'Nell, and Collado-Ardon (1984); and Simons and Hughes (1993), Paniagua (1998) compiled a list of common syndromes from various cultures. This illustrative but noncomprehensive list is provided in Table 11.2.

A colleague of ours offered this case example. A young Puerto Rican man was living with his mother in the United States. He was dating a girl and planned to get married. He started having hallucinations that a very large white ghost would visit him while he was sleeping or lying in bed with his girlfriend. The ghost would sit on his chest and prevent him from breathing. Many Western-trained psychologists might begin wondering about the onset of a psychotic disorder.

When the young man began counseling, he was able to talk about the fact that he wasn't attracted to his girlfriend, and instead, was attracted to men. A part of him was telling him that he was gay, but another part was telling him to fight that image—because being gay wasn't culturally acceptable. He believed that his mother would die if he came out gay. It was interesting that the ghost would visit him whenever he was in bed with his girlfriend. Clearly the conflict was playing out. Then, the counselor found out that the phenomenon of ghost-visiting was common in this young man's home culture, especially when people were experiencing internal conflict. The ghost represented a cultural manifestation of the conflict; it was not a hallucination. As for the treatment plan, perhaps

Table 11.1 Dos and Don'ts of Initial Interviews With Multicultural Clients

The following are suggestions for therapists working with clients who come from cultural, racial, ethnic, religious, or life experience backgrounds different from themselves. The applicability and relevance of each suggestion must be evaluated with the particular clinical situation at hand. Our intention is to provide a thought-provoking checklist.

Open Inquiry

1. Do ask about tribal, ethnic, or background differences that are obvious or are made obvious by information provided by the client.
2. Don't insist on a more thorough exploration of these differences than is offered.
3. Do realize that acculturation and cultural identity are fluid and developmental.
4. Don't assume all members of a given family group or couple have the same levels of cultural identity or the same experiences interfacing with the dominant culture.

Family

1. Do recognize that for many or most nondominant cultures in the United States, the role of family is central. The concept of family is often broader, more inclusive, and more definitive in a given individual's sense of identity. Therefore, be attuned to matters of family with heightened awareness and sensitivity, whether you are a member of the dominant culture, or from a minority culture.
2. Don't impose either your own definition of family or the definition of family you've read about with regard to the client's culture. Simply be open to the client's sense of family.
3. Do graciously allow family members to attend some part of an initial interview if they request to do so.
4. Don't define family strictly along biological lines.

Communication Styles

1. Do remember that patterns of eye contact, direct verbalization of problem areas, storytelling, and note taking all have culturally determined norms that vary widely.
2. Don't assume a chatty or overly familiar style, even if that is your predominant style. Strive to demonstrate respect.
3. Do ask for clarification if something is not clear.
4. Don't ask for clarification in a manner that suggests your lack of clarity is the client's problem.

(continued)

Table 11.1 *(continued)*

Religious and Spiritual Matters

1. Do accept the client's beliefs regarding the sources of distress: ancestral disapproval, the evil eye, God's wrath, or trouble because of misbehavior in another life. A strong relationship of trust must be established before one can determine the adaptive and maladaptive aspects of such beliefs and thereby work within the frame toward healing or growth.
2. Don't assume you are being told the whole story regarding faith or belief systems early on. Most are powerful and quite private and will not be easily or fully shared.
3. Do take advantage of any possible link to meaningful spiritual or religious beliefs or connections that may help address the current distress.
4. Don't hesitate to allow input into the problem from religious or spiritual persons respected by the client.

Table 11.2   Culturally Specific Mental, Emotional, and Behavioral Disorders

Name of Disorder	Cultural Origins	Symptoms	Cause
Ataque de nervios	Hispanic/Latino	Out-of-consciousness state	Evil spirits
Falling-out	African American	Seizure-like symptoms	Traumatic events such as robbery
Ghost sickness	First Nations	Weakness, dizziness	Action of witches, evil forces
Hwa-byung	Asian communities	Pain in upper abdomen, fear of death, tiredness	Imbalance between reality and anger
Koro	Asian men	Desire to grab penis	Belief that it will retract into body and cause death
Mal puesto, hex, rootwork, voodoo death	African American and Hispanic/Latino	Unnatural disease or death	Power of people who use evil spirits
Susto, eapanto pasmo, miedo	Hispanic/Latino	Tiredness, weakness	Frightening or startling experiences
Wackinko	First Nations	Anger, withdrawal, mutism, suicide	Disappointment, interpersonal problems
Wind/cold illness	Hispanic/Latino and Asian	Fear of cold wind, feeling weak and susceptible to illness	Belief that natural and supernatural elements are not balanced

some mental health professionals would have referred him to a psychiatrist for medications. However, in this case the counselor helped him arrange a visit to his home country and was able to help him find gay-friendly clergy to speak with. The client eventually broke up with his girlfriend, and the ghost visits stopped.

The information in Table 11.2 reveals many things about the broad field of mental health diagnostic systems. First, *symptoms* may be similar across cultures, but the causes may be viewed very differently. (Psychotic thinking, anxiety, or depressive symptoms may be consistently described across cultures but viewed as caused by satanic influence, bad behavior, brain disease, trauma, family patterns, learning, etc.) Second, *causes* of human distress (brain disease, trauma, exposure, grief, attachment loss, or disturbance) may be identified similarly across cultures, but the disturbance or distress may show itself in vastly different symptoms. For a general discussion regarding issues in diagnosis, refer to Chapter 10; however, from a multicultural viewpoint, remember that much of our understanding of human distress is culture bound; there are many things to learn from other cultural perspectives.

PROFESSIONAL CONSIDERATIONS

When working with clients who are racially, culturally, or socioeconomically different than yourself, it helps to follow some basic rules of multicultural etiquette and to take the time necessary to get complete and accurate information. The pressure to be culturally aware and sensitive can sometimes cause professionals to seek quick or easy answers to complex questions. Unfortunately, there are few valid shortcuts, and nothing can substitute for cultural humility and empathic sensitivity to differences.

Use Multiple Sources for Cultural Consultation and Education

Consulting with members of a given cultural group can be enlightening. However, no single source of information can capture the vast texture and fabric of any complex cultural group. Many informational sources may have a sociopolitical agenda and shouldn't be considered the sole spokesperson for an entire cultural or social group. No single veteran of the global war on terror can speak for all veterans; no African American for all African Americans; no woman for all women. Therefore, be wary of those who would purport to speak for an entire population. To become acquainted with another culture or set of life experiences requires much multifaceted exposure, reading, discussing, experiencing, thinking, and rethinking. No one really gets a terminal degree or is declared culturally competent. There is always more to know—even about your own culture.

Also, be sensitive to the notion that you should not expect one single colleague to be your cultural educator. It is up to you to find multiple sources of input as you work to understand the clients you serve from different cultural backgrounds.

Considerations in Small Communities

Effective interviewing across cultures often requires asking about very personal and culturally specific matters in the client's life. Small communities of humans are notorious for breaks in confidentiality among insiders and for providing inaccurate or simply no information to outsiders. When clients provide you with information about their culture, someone clearly outside the community, they might feel they're violating a cultural trust, even if it is in the context of trying to work out their own problems. If clients are members of a culture embedded in a different, dominant culture, this almost guarantees that they're members of a small community, even if they live in a large urban area. Examples of such communities abound, from gay and lesbian communities to religious communities to "Indian Country," where, as mentioned previously, the joke is that there are three ways to spread information: telephone, telegraph, and tell-a-cousin. Preserving confidentiality within small communities is hard.

Many cultural groups have had the experience of being asked about their culture by persons who misunderstood or abused the information. Some cultural truths are considered sacred and not to be shared with outsiders. Outsiders may not recognize the importance of the information, and unfortunately, sometimes information is sought for less than charitable reasons.

With all this in mind, it makes perfect sense that sharing intimate information with a stranger has added complexity and stress for people from small cultural communities. You are an outsider, at least by virtue of your profession. If you live in the community or are a member of the culture, you might be a blend of insider-outsider. If you work at an agency, relatives and friends of the client may work there or have been there as clients. Assumptions about who knows what and who will share what are not the same assumptions urban people from the dominant culture make. It may take patience, extra education, careful, repeated explanation, and a great deal of time to build the trust that allows the deep sharing necessary for a therapeutic relationship to develop (R. Sommers-Flanagan & Sommers-Flanagan, 2007).

Culture is often very local. That makes it difficult to experience and learn about someone's culture from a distance. If you intend to work closely with a particular cultural group we recommend you pursue what's been termed a "Cultural immersion" (CIM) project. CIMs are based on the idea that significant, deliberate, and direct contact between different social groups over time can reduce tensions and misunderstandings (DeRicco & Sciarra, 2005). An appropriate CIM might require a 3–6 month commitment to work within a local community. Students who engage in these activities should have close multicultural supervision to guide them as they reflect on immersion experiences before, during, and after their experience (Hipolito-Delgado et al., 2011).

Considerations for Professionals From Other Cultural Backgrounds

Graduate students from nondominant cultures are often both highly valued for the diversity and insight they bring to their training programs and burdened by repeatedly being asked to be intercultural ambassadors. They also experience subtle and not-so-subtle discriminations that continue to plague the human community. As professionals, they may feel pressure to subvert their cultural identities in favor of identifying with their credentials. This is as limited as asking clients to subvert their culture and identify as someone in need. In *Voices of Color: First-Person Accounts of Ethnic Minority Therapists* (Rastoqi & Wieling, 2004), Monika Sharma wrote, "I no longer strive to blend in and be invisible.

Instead, I now stand up and want people to see me for the multifaceted Asian Indian American woman that I am" (p. 20).

For therapists who are also members of different cultures, challenges of multicultural sensitivity are exceptionally complex. If their client appears to be from the dominant culture, therapists may have to be on guard for countertransference stemming from their own experiences of oppression while working to create a therapeutic alliance with a person from the culture that oppressed them. If the client appears to be from another minority culture, there may be other assumptions or stereotypes to overcome. And finally, if the client appears to be from the same cultural or racial background as the therapist, given the vast diversity of experiences, the assumptions of similarity may or may not be accurate or helpful.

SUMMARY

Changing demographics in the United States require counselors and psychotherapists to integrate cultural and diversity competencies into their work. Recent census data and other factors support this position. This chapter focuses on therapist self-awareness and various minority populations who are likely to seek professional help.

General information associated with the four most populous minority cultures in the United States—First Nations peoples, African Americans, Hispanic/Latina/os, and Asian Americans—are reviewed in this chapter. Each of these broad cultural groupings represent many distinct cultures and subcultures, and any attempts at overall generalizations fall far short of the specificity necessary to offer effective, culturally appropriate mental health assistance. Information provided in this chapter is merely a beginning.

This chapter also discussed basic guidelines for working with GLBT people, persons with disabilities, and persons who have strong religious worldviews. Each of these minority groups has a unique history and requires increased awareness and therapist sensitivity.

Culturally different clients must be understood, not only from their cultural perspective, but also from an individually unique contextual perspective. This chapter explores dimensions of diversity using Pamela Hays' acronym, ADDRESSING (2008). Additionally, the clinical interview and assessment procedures were briefly examined as contextual variables that might affect culturally different clients. A sampling of culture-bound syndromes and matters of professional etiquette pertaining to multicultural counseling and psychotherapy are also reviewed, along with recommendations for cultural immersion experiences and a discussion of issues facing minority group therapists of color.

SUGGESTED READINGS AND RESOURCES

Dell Orto, A. E., & Power, P. W. (2007). *The psychological and social impact of illness and disability* (5th ed.). New York, NY: Springer.

This book is a good initial orientation for students who would like to work with individuals who have disabilities.

Gibbs, J. T., & Huang, L. N. (Eds.). (2004). *Children of color: Psychological interventions with culturally diverse youth* (2nd ed.). Hoboken, NJ: Wiley.

This book presents information on culturally sensitive assessment and treatment approaches for African American, Asian American, Central American, Latinos, Native American, biracial-bicultural, and other so-called minority youth.

Johnson, R. (2013). Spirituality in counseling and psychotherapy. Hoboken, NJ: Wiley.

Johnson provides a balanced and practical perspective on integrating religion and spirituality into therapy.

McGoldrick, M., Giordano, J., & Garcia-Preto, N. (2005). *Ethnicity and family therapy* (3rd ed.). New York, NY: Guilford Press.

This book discusses methods for working with ethnicity in family therapy. It addresses a much broader range of cultures (e.g., Indonesian, Dutch, German, Jewish, and Iranian) than many other texts.

Ponterotto, J. G., Casas, J. M., Suzuki, L. A., & Alexander, C. M. (Eds.). (2010). *Handbook of multicultural counseling* (3rd ed.). Thousand Oaks, CA: Sage.

With 57 chapters and over 800 pages, this handbook will give you plenty of interesting multicultural information with which to grapple.

Portes, A., & Rumbaut, R. G. (2006). *Immigrant America: A portrait*. Berkeley: University of California Press.

This book provides us all with a much needed glimpse at immigrant life in America.

Rastoqi, M., & Wieling, E. (Eds.). (2004). *Voices of color: First person accounts of ethnic minority therapists*. New York, NY: Sage.

In this edited volume, therapists of color discuss cases, experiences, and challenges they face as minority therapists working with individuals, couples, and families from both dominant and other minority cultural groups.

Challenging Clients and Demanding Situations

CHAPTER OBJECTIVES

Initially, most therapists prefer working with cooperative clients in comfortable, safe, and secure settings. It seems less stressful and more gratifying to work with clients who are motivated, eager to learn, and with whom rapport and a working alliance develop smoothly.

But eventually many mental health professionals, including ourselves, have learned to love working with clients who challenge us or in situations that offer more chaos than comfort.

One problem associated with these two interviewing situations is we often don't know in advance when they will emerge. This chapter offers an introduction to—but not extensive preparation for—working with challenging clients and demanding situations.

After reading this chapter, you will understand:

- Why resistance is a naturally occurring phenomenon in therapy along with general strategies for understanding and addressing resistance.
- Specific techniques for working effectively with different types of resistance.
- Motivational interviewing strategies and techniques for working with clients who have substance-related problems.
- Methods for the assessment and prediction of clients who may be violent and/or dangerous.
- The psychological first aid model for assisting with humanitarian and crisis situations.
- Professional responsibilities and interviewing strategies for working with trauma survivors.

CHALLENGING CLIENTS

Although some clients will eagerly arrive for counseling with positive expectations, not all clients are equally cooperative. Here are a few opening lines we've heard over the years:

- How long have you been doing this?
- Do I have to be here?
- Nothing against you, but I hate counselors.
- I will never talk to you about anything important.
- This is a shitty little office; you must be a shitty little therapist.
- How long will this take?
- Do you actually get paid for doing this?
- You look like you've got too many problems of your own to help me (Neil Duchac, personal communication, August 27, 2012).
- What do you know about my problems? (Jonathan Lent, personal communication, August 28, 2012)

In our work with adolescents and young adults, we've had the pleasure (or pain) of many meetings with people who want little to do with therapy and nothing to do with us. We've had clients refuse to be alone in the room with us, others who refused to speak, a few who insisted on standing, and many who told us with great disdain (and sometimes with exuberant profanity) that they *don't believe in counseling*. At such moments, it's good to seek a bit of internal comic relief—such as imagining a sudden "poof" wherein we disappear, thus proving that, in fact, the client was right, and counseling doesn't exist after all . . . and neither do counselors!

Part one of this chapter is about therapy with clients who generally oppose the helping process. It's also about the great joy of working with clients who slowly or suddenly shift their attitude toward therapy. When these clients eventually enter the room, begin speaking, stop swearing, agree to sit, and begin believing in counseling (and counselors!), it can be a deeply rewarding experience.

Defining and Exploring Resistance

Traditionally, Freud viewed resistance as inevitable and ubiquitous. Following Freud's lead, therapists sometimes have labeled all client behaviors that oppose their ideas as resistance. Traditional signs of client resistance can include:

- Talking too much.
- Talking too little.
- Arriving late.
- Arriving early.
- Being unprepared for psychotherapy.
- Being overprepared for psychotherapy.
- Too much emotional control during therapy.
- Too little emotional control during therapy.

Similar to clients who don't believe in counseling, some writers and practitioners don't believe in resistance. In 1984, writing from a solution-focused perspective, Steven de Shazer pronounced the *Death of Resistance* and buried it in his backyard (de Shazer, 1984); other constructive theorists have followed his lead in claiming that resistance doesn't exist (Engle & Arkowitz, 2006; McCormack, 2002). These writers believe resistance is an unhelpful linguistic creation that developed because sometimes clients don't want to do what their "bossy-pants" therapist wants them to do. In other words, resistance isn't a problem centered within the client's psyche; it's a problem created by therapists who want their clients to always follow their sage advice.

De Shazer and other solution-focused therapists have an excellent point about resistance. Therapists can behave in ways that create more resistance than cooperation. A focus on confronting or interpreting resistance, rather than on the client's positive potential for change, can derail the change process. This is especially the case with teenage clients or clients from diverse cultures and backgrounds— when therapist insensitivity can easily offend and alienate. However, we also believe that sometimes resistance is real and palpable and originates from clients' beliefs, attitudes, ambivalence, or opposition to therapy.

We don't see resistance as inevitable or ubiquitous (like Freud), but we also don't see it as dead or as something a bossy and controlling therapist independently creates (like de Shazer). Instead, research and clinical observation points to the fact that resistance is multi-determined: Sometimes therapists contribute to resistance; sometimes clients bring the resistance; and most of the time, resistance is partly due to the therapist, the client, and the situation (Beutler, Harwood, Michelson, Song, & Holman, 2011; McKelley, 2007).

Resistance as a Function of the Situation

It's neither useful nor therapeutic to blame clients for opposing authority figures or for being reluctant to disclose personally shameful information to strangers. Often, resistance to a clinical interview isn't the client's fault, but instead a product of a difficult and uncomfortable situation. Additionally, it's a situation into which some clients enter into with very negative expectations. Even more importantly, negative expectations that mandated clients have for therapy is legitimate and rational. Individuals who are forced to come to therapy may previously have received poor or abusive treatment from adult authority figures. For most mandated clients and for many ambivalent clients, resistance to therapy should be framed for the most part as a natural behavior, given the situation (J. Sommers-Flanagan, Richardson, & Sommers-Flanagan, 2011).

This doesn't mean that aggressively provocative and oppositional behavior displayed by some mandated or ambivalent clients is easy to handle or helpful in therapy. For example, when a client states, "You have a shitty little office, so you must be a shitty little therapist;" or offers a vicious glare; or refuses to speak; or speaks only with profanity, or aggressively attacks our intelligence, credentials, or appearance, it may be appropriate to acknowledge that the client's behavior, although explainable and perhaps justifiable, is an excellent example of resistance (J. Sommers-Flanagan et al., 2011; J. Sommers-Flanagan & Sommers-Flanagan, 2004).

Overall, it's unrealistic to expect all clients—especially adolescents or mandated adults—to immediately speak openly and honestly and work productively with an unfamiliar adult authority figure. It's also unrealistic to expect clients to whom therapy is a new and uncomfortable experience, to immediately begin sharing their innermost thoughts. Similarly, it's unrealistic to pretend resistance doesn't exist and describe obnoxiously challenging and provocative behaviors as normal or adaptive. Consequently, we prefer the term "natural resistance," which offers both empathy for the client's entry into an uncomfortable situation and acknowledges the need to construct effective strategies and techniques for dealing with challenging client behaviors. The question to be addressed is: What therapist behaviors can reduce natural client resistance and defensiveness?

Recognizing and Managing Resistance

In their groundbreaking text, *Motivational Interviewing*, Miller and Rollnick (1991; 2002; 2013) described a practical approach to recognizing and managing client resistance. They emphasized that most humans are ambivalent about making personal changes due to competing motivations. For example, a client may simultaneously have a rationally based motivation to quit smoking cigarettes (smoking is expensive and unhealthy) and a rationally based motivation to continue smoking cigarettes (smoking is pleasurable and provides a sense of emotional control).

Imagine yourself in an interview situation. You recognize your client is engaging in a self-destructive behavior (e.g., smoking, cutting, punching walls). In response, you might have an impulse to educate your client. You might even try making a case for giving up the self-destructive behavior. Miller and Rollnick (2002) described this scenario from a motivational interviewing perspective:

> [The therapist] then proceeds to advise, teach, persuade, counsel or argue for this particular resolution to [the client's] ambivalence. One does not need a doctorate in psychology to anticipate what [the client's] response is likely to be in this situation. By virtue of ambivalence, [the client] is apt to argue the opposite, or at least point out problems and shortcomings of the proposed solution. It is natural for [the client] to do so, because [he or she] feels at least two ways about this or almost any prescribed solution. It is the very nature of ambivalence. (pp. 20–21)

Based on the motivational interviewing model, resistance occurs when clients are siding with the less healthy, more destructive, or more fearful side of their ambivalence. The solution to resistance is straightforward. As Miller and Rollnick (2002) elegantly stated, "All of this points toward a fundamental dynamic in the resolution of ambivalence: It is the client who should be voicing the arguments for change" (p. 22). To summarize, Miller and Rollnick's guidance is: Listen for ambivalence. Then help the clients themselves to begin articulating the healthier side of their ambivalence.

Opening Questions and Goal-Setting Strategies

When working with reluctant, ambivalent, resistant, or hostile clients, you have a better chance for a good meeting if you begin the interview in a positive, strength-focused, empathic, and nonblaming manner. Solution-focused and narrative therapists often lead with goal-oriented questions:

- What would make this a helpful visit?
- If we have a great meeting today, what will happen?
- What would need to happen for this to be productive?

To get a better sense of how a solution-focused counselor might work with a resistant client to establish positive goals, consider the following example (Cheng, 2007). This example was based in an emergency room setting:

Clinician: What would make today's . . . visit helpful? *(Clinician asks for goals.)*

Patient: I want to kill myself, just let me die . . . . *(Patient states unhealthy goal/task).*

Clinician: I'm sure you must have your reasons for feeling that way. . . . What makes you want to hurt yourself? *(Clinician searches for underlying healthy goal.)*

Patient: I just can't stand the depression anymore and all the fighting at home. I just can't take it. *(The underlying healthy goal/task may be trying to cope with depression and fighting.)*

Clinician: . . . So we need to find a way to help you cope with the depression and the fighting. You told me yourself that there used to be less fighting at home. What would it be like if we found a way to reduce the fighting, have people getting along more?

Patient: A lot better, I guess. But it's probably not going to happen.

Clinician: Okay, I can see why you're frustrated and . . . that probably the depression makes it hard to see hope. But I believe that there is a part of you that is stronger and more hopeful, because otherwise you wouldn't be here talking with me. *(Clinician externalizes unhealthy thoughts or behaviors as being part of the depression and tries to help the patient ally against the depression.)* That hopeful part of you said that your mood used to be happy. What would it be like if we could get your mood happy again?

Patient: A lot better I guess.

Clinician: Just to help me make sure I'm getting this right then, what would you like to see different with your mood? *(The clinician reinforces the client's goals by having the client articulate them.)*

Patient: I want to be happy again.

Clinician: And at home, what would you like to see with how people get along?

Patient: I want us to get along better.

Clinician: Let's agree then that we will work together on finding a way to help people get along, as well as help your mood get better. How does that sound? *(Clinician paraphrases patient's healthy goals.)*

Patient: Sounds good . . . . *(Patient agrees with goals.)* (p. 163)

In the preceding example, Cheng (2007) illustrated how the interviewer (in this case a physician) was able to help the patient articulate his goals and acknowledge the potential benefits of positive change. Although the physician initiated the interaction with a negatively worded question—"What makes you want to hurt yourself?"—he was listening for the positive, health-oriented goals lying underneath the patient's suicidal motivations. This is an important principle: Even when exploring the client's emotional pain, you can be listening for the unfulfilled positive goals contributing to that pain.

Using Reflection

Throughout this text we've described and emphasized nondirective interviewing skills—paraphrasing, reflection of feeling, and summarization. Research on motivational interviewing with resistant substance-using clients affirms this emphasis, showing that these reflective techniques are powerful tools for managing and eliminating resistance. Miller and Rollnick (2002, 2013) provided several examples of simple reflection responses that can reduce resistance:

Client: I'm trying! If my probation officer would just get off my back, I could focus on getting my life in order.

Therapist: You're working hard on the changes you need to make.

or

Therapist: It's frustrating to have a probation officer looking over your shoulder.

Client: Who are you to be giving me advice? What do you know about drugs? You've probably never even smoked a joint!

Therapist: It's hard to imagine how I could possibly understand.

Client: I couldn't keep the weight off even if I lost it.

Therapist: You can't see any way that would work for you.

or

Therapist: You're rather discouraged about trying again. (pp. 100–101)

In the preceding examples, when therapists accurately reflect their clients' efforts, frustration, hostility, and discouragement, the need for clients to further describe and defend their positions is lessened.

For similar reasons, reflections can elicit a positive and constructive clarification from clients. Recently, in hundreds of brief interviews conducted by graduate students in psychology and counseling with client-volunteers from introductory psychology courses, consistent with Miller and Rollnick's (1991, 2002, 2013) motivational interviewing work, we found that clients have a strong need for their therapists to accurately hear what they're saying. When their therapist made an inaccurate reflection, the client felt compelled to clarify their feelings and beliefs—often in ways that rebalanced their ambivalence. For example, when a therapist "went too far" with a reflection, the following exchange was typical:

Client: I'm pissed at my roommate. She won't pick up her clothes or do the dishes or anything.

Therapist: You'd sort of like to fire her as a roommate.

Client: No. Not exactly. There are lots of things I like about her, but her messiness really annoys me.

This phenomenon suggests that therapists could intentionally overstate their clients' perspective in an effort to get clients to come back around to clarify or articulate the more positive side of an issue. In fact, this is a particular motivational interviewing technique referred to as *amplified reflection*.

When used intentionally, amplified reflection can seem manipulative—which is why amplified reflection is used along with genuine empathy. Instead of being a manipulative response it can also be viewed as an effort on the therapist's part to more deeply empathize with the client's frustration, anger, and discouragement. Examples of this technique include:

Client: My child has a serious disability and so I have to be home for him.
Therapist: You really need to be home 24–7 and really need to turn off any needs you have to get out and take a break.
Client: Actually, that's not totally true. Sometimes, I think I need to take some breaks so I can do a better job when I am home.

Client: When my grandmother died last semester I had to miss classes and it was a total hassle.
Therapist: You don't have much of an emotional response to your grandmother's death—other than it really inconveniencing you.
Client: Well, it's not like I don't miss her, too.

Again, we should emphasize that amplified reflection is an empathic effort to get completely in touch with or resonate with one side of the client's ambivalence.

Using Emotional Validation, Radical Acceptance, Reframing, and Genuine Feedback

Clients sometimes begin interviews with expressions of hostility, anger, or resentment. If this is handled well, these clients may eventually open up and cooperate. The key is to refrain from lecturing, scolding, or retaliating when clients express hostility. Speaking from the consultation-liaison psychiatry perspective, Knesper (2007) noted: "Chastising and blaming the difficult patient for misbehavior seems only to make matters worse" (p. 246).

Instead, empathy, emotional validation, and concession are more effective responses. We often coach graduate students on how to use concession when power struggles emerge, especially when they're working with adolescent clients (J. Sommers-Flanagan & Sommers-Flanagan, 2007b). For example, if a young client opens a session with, "I'm not talking and you can't make me," we recommend responding with complete concession of power and control: "You're absolutely right. I can't make you talk, and I definitely can't make you talk about anything you don't want to talk about." This statement validates the client's need for power and control and concedes an initial victory in what the client might be viewing as a struggle for power.

Empathic, emotionally validating statements are also important. If clients express anger at meeting with you, a reflection of feeling and/or feeling validation response can let them know you hear their emotional message loud and clear. In some cases, as in the following example, therapists might go beyond empathy and emotional validation and actually join clients with a parallel emotional response:

- Of course you feel angry about being here.
- I don't blame you for feeling pissed about having to see me.
- I hear you saying you don't trust me, which is totally normal. After all, I'm a stranger, and you shouldn't trust me until you get to know me.
- It pretty much sucks to have a judge require you to meet with me.
- I know we're being forced to meet, but we're not being forced to have a bad time together.

Radical acceptance is a dialectical behavior therapy principle and technique based on person-centered theory (Linehan, 1993). It involves consciously accepting and actively welcoming any and all client comments—even odd, disturbing, or blatantly provocative comments (J. Sommers-Flanagan & Sommers-Flanagan, 2007a). For example, we've had experiences where clients begin their sessions with angry statements about the evils of psychology or counseling:

Opening Client Volley: I don't need no stupid-ass counseling. I'm only here because my wife is forcing me. This counseling shit is worthless. It's for pansy-ass wimps like you who need to sit around and talk rather than doing any real work.

Radical Acceptance Return: Wow. Thanks for being so honest about what you're thinking. Lots of people really hate psychologists but they just sit here and pretend to cooperate. So I really appreciate you telling me exactly what you're thinking.

Radical acceptance can be combined with reframing to communicate a deeper understanding about why clients have come for therapy. Our favorite version of this is the "Love reframe" (J. Sommers-Flanagan & Barr, 2005).

Client: This is total bullshit. I don't need counseling. The judge required this. Otherwise, I can't see my daughter for unsupervised visitation. So let's just get this over with.

Therapist: I hear you saying this is bullshit. You must really love your daughter...to come here even when you think it's a worthless waste of your time.

Client: (Softening) Yeah. I do love my daughter.

The magic of the love reframe is that clients nearly always agree with the positive observation about loving someone, which turns the interview toward a more pleasant focus.

Often, when working with angry or hostile clients, there's no better approach than reflecting and validating feelings...pausing...and then following with honest feedback and a solution-focused question.

I hear you saying you hate the idea of talking with me, and I don't blame you for that. I'd hate to be forced to talk to a stranger about my personal life too. But can I be honest with you for a minute? *[Client nods in assent]*. You know, you're in legal trouble. I'd like to try to be helpful—even just a little. We're stuck meeting together. We can either sit and stare at each other and have a miserable hour or we can talk about how you might dig yourself out of this legal hole you're in. I can go either way. What do you think...if we had a good meeting today, what would we accomplish?

Coming Alongside (Using Paradox)

Based on Miller and Rollnick's (2013) formulation of client ambivalence, it makes sense that when working with clients who are immediately resistant to counseling, a paradoxical, but compassionate statement may help. For example, a therapist might mention that it's common for people to feel frightened or reluctant about discussing personal topics and, therefore, it's not necessary to take such a risk right away. This approach might stimulate ambivalent clients to prove you wrong, and they may begin sharing more openly. At the same time, if clients realize that you understand how hard it is for them, they may begin seeing their reluctant feelings as normal. This belief, in turn, may reduce anxiety and reduce resistance. A word of caution: Paradoxical techniques are risky and require specific training, careful consideration, and supervision.

Miller and Rollnick (2002, 2013) refer to paradox as *coming alongside*. Similar to amplified reflection, this technique must be used with empathy and respect. Examples include:

Client: I don't think this is going to work for me, either. I feel pretty hopeless.

Therapist: It's certainly possible that after giving it another try, you still won't be any better off, and so it might be better not to try at all. What's your inclination?

Client: That's about it, really. I probably drink too much sometimes, and I don't like the hangovers, but I don't think it's that much of a concern, really.

Therapist: It may just be worth it to you to keep on drinking as you have, even though it causes some problems. It's worth the cost.

The key to using this technique is to feel, from the client's perspective, the motivation associated with the less healthy side of the ambivalence. This requires deep empathy for the motivation to continue with a negative behavior pattern.

Miller and Rollnick (2002) commented on the difference between using coming alongside as compared to more traditional paradoxical strategies:

> ...we confess some serious discomfort with the ways in which therapeutic paradox has sometimes been described. There is often the sense of paradox being a clever way of duping people into doing things for their own good. In some writings on paradox, one senses almost a glee in finding innovative ways to trick people without their realizing what is happening. Such cleverness lacks the respectful and collaborative tone that we understand to be fundamental to the dialectical process of motivational interviewing. (p. 107)

Using paradox or coming alongside with clients raises ethical issues. Our position is similar to Miller and Rollnick. Paradoxical techniques shouldn't be used as a clever means to outwit and influence clients. These techniques shouldn't be divorced from the basic person-centered core attitudes of congruence, unconditional positive regard, and empathic understanding. See *Putting It in Practice* 12.1 for a discussion of these attitudes.

PUTTING IT IN PRACTICE 12.1

The Core Attitudes

Many writers have tried to operationalize Carl Rogers's core conditions. Unfortunately, in many ways, efforts to transform person-centered therapy core conditions into specific skills or behaviors will always fall short. As Natalie Rogers (J. Sommers-Flanagan, 2007) emphasized, translating the core conditions (or attitudes) of person-centered therapy into concrete behaviors is a sign that the writer or therapist simply doesn't understand person-centered principles.

The core Rogerian attitudes are attitudes, not behaviors. This is a basic conceptual principle that has been difficult to understand—especially for behaviorists. The point Rogers was making then, and that still holds today, is that therapists should enter the consulting room with (a) deep belief in the potential of the client; (b) sincere desire to be open, honest, and authentic; (c) palpable respect for the individual self of the client; and (d) a gentle focus on the client's inner thoughts, feelings, and perceptions. Further complicating this process is the fact that the therapist must rely primarily on indirectly communicating these attitudes because efforts to directly communicate trust, congruence, unconditional positive regard, and empathic understanding is nearly always contradictory to each of the attitudes.

With regard to the effort to communicate understanding, Kurt Kraus noted:

> When a supervisee errantly says, "I know how you feel" in response to a client's disclosure, I twitch and contort. I believe that one of the great gifts of multicultural awareness is for me accepting the limitations to the felt-experience of empathy. I can only imagine how another feels, and sometimes the reach of my experience is so short as to only approximate what another feels. This is a good thing to learn. I'll upright myself in my chair and say, "I used to think that I knew how others felt too. May I teach you a lesson that has served me well?" (J. Sommers-Flanagan & Sommers-Flanagan, 2012, p. 146)

Kraus's lesson is an excellent one for all of us to remember.

Dealing With Resistant Clients Who May Be Lying or Delusional

Many clients will tell stories during a clinical interview that may or may not be true. In particular, when meeting separately with a therapist, young clients may minimize or exaggerate their problems or perspective (Sommers-Flanagan & Bequette, 2013).

Having a general policy of including family members or parents or caregivers for some or all of an initial interview can help in discerning a more accurate picture of what the client is experiencing. A more specific policy of contacting significant others when your clinical judgment leads you to question your client's reliability is another reasonable option. If you decide to use these policies, they should be written into your informed consent.

Sometimes clients who are prone to lying or who are delusional will directly ask the therapist, "Do you believe me?" This question can be problematic because it puts you on the spot; it places you in an either-or situation. If you say, "Yes, I believe you," you may have indicated to a client with antisocial traits that you believe his lies (or you may be telling a delusional client that you believe she is being harassed by the FBI). Alternatively, if you say you don't believe the client, the alliance will likely be damaged. To address this challenging situation, Robinson (2007) offered the following ideas—with the goal of stimulating further client disclosure:

Client: Do you believe me?
Interviewer: I'm keeping an open mind.
or

Interviewer: I can't decide without more information.
or

Interviewer: My job is to understand what your views are.
or

Interviewer: [Your] story is an unusual one, so I really want to hear more before making a decision; tell me [more] about . . . (refer patient back into an affectively charged detail from the story). (p. 241)

Our usual response in this situation is similar to Robinson's:

That's a good question. My job isn't to judge whether you're telling the truth. Only you know if what you say is true. I don't want to be an investigator or cop. My job is to listen to you and my goal is to be helpful. And usually, it's way more likely that I'll be able to be helpful if you're honest with me. But that's up to you.

There are many reasons why clients lie, most involving some form of self-protection or the belief that they profit from lying. As a general rule (with exceptions), people tend to lie more if they feel the need to lie and tend to lie less when they experience trust. As a consequence, your goal is to build an alliance that includes enough trust to facilitate honesty. Confrontation of obvious or subtle lying behavior may be less productive than waiting for rapport and trust to build and for honest disclosure to flow more naturally. This perspective or stance can be a relief; when in the role of therapist (and not judge) facts are usually less important than feelings. To summarize, resistance, or whatever we choose to call it, is a natural part of the change process. In fact, research suggests that client resistance is an opportunity for deeper work. When resistance is worked through, the likelihood for positive outcomes is increased (Mahalik, 2002).

In the end, it's helpful to remember that resistance emanates from the very center of a person and is part of the force that gives people stability and predictability in their interactions with others. Resistance exists because change and pain are often frightening and more difficult to face than retaining the old ways of being, even when the old ways are maladaptive. Finally, with culturally or developmentally different clients, resistance may actually be caused when the therapist refuses or fails to make culturally or developmentally sensitive modifications in his or her approach (J. Sommers-Flanagan & Sommers-Flanagan, 2007b). Table 12.1 includes a summary of strategies and techniques for managing resistance.

Table 12.1 Summary Checklist of Strategies and Techniques for Managing Resistance

☐ 1. Adopt an attitude of acceptance and understanding because developing a therapeutic alliance is almost always a higher priority than confrontation.

☐ 2. Recognize that clients will feel some ambivalence about working toward and achieving positive change.

☐ 3. Resist your impulses to teach, preach, and persuade clients to make healthy decisions.

☐ 4. In the beginning and throughout the session, ask open-ended questions that are linked to potential positive goals.

☐ 5. Look for positive goals that are underlying your clients emotional pain and discouragement—and then help your client be the one who articulates those goals.

☐ 6. Use simple reflection to reduce clients' needs to exhibit resistance.

☐ 7. Use concession "You're right. I can't make you talk with me" to affirm to clients that they're in control of what they say to you.

☐ 8. Use amplified reflection to encourage clients to discuss the healthier side of their ambivalence.

☐ 9. Use emotional validation when clients are angry or hostile.

☐ 10. Use radical acceptance to compliment clients for their openness—even though the openness may be aggressive or disturbing.

☐ 11. Reframe client hostility and negativity into more positive impulses whenever possible.

☐ 12. Provide genuine feedback related to your concerns to your clients.

☐ 13. Use paradox carefully to respectfully come up alongside clients' resistance.

☐ 14. If you're concerned about truthfulness, interview a significant other to help you get an accurate story.

☐ 15. When clients ask "Do you believe me?" use a response that will encourage more disclosure, like, "I'm not here to judge the truth, but just to listen and try to be of help."

☐ 16. Remember (and be glad) that you're a mental health professional and not a judge.

Interviewing Clients With Substance Issues or Problems

Interviewing clients with substance abuse or substance dependence problems requires specialized training and experience. This brief section is designed to whet your appetite for further training in working with this interesting and challenging population.

Some professionals who work with alcohol- and substance-abusing clients have a personal history of substance abuse or dependence. Research and clinical observation suggests that having your own substance-abuse history can be a benefit or a liability (Curtis & Eby, 2010; Gallagher, 2010). If you've experienced substance problems, you're more likely to know the big issues from the inside out, and this can give you greater empathy for and knowledge about client dynamics. Alternatively, having had your own personal substance-abuse problems makes it more possible for you to project your issues and your own idiosyncratic solutions onto clients (see *Putting It in Practice* 12.2).

Gathering Information

Gathering valid information from substance-abusing clients can be challenging (Knight et al., 2007; Laforge, Borsari, & Baer, 2005). To aid with the process, researchers and clinicians have developed numerous brief interview approaches to gathering diagnostic information about substance use. These approaches are especially important in settings in which obtaining diagnostic information quickly and efficiently is a high priority.

PUTTING IT IN PRACTICE 12.2

Exploring Your Personal Attitudes Toward Substances

Reflecting on your present attitude toward alcohol and drug use is worthwhile. Whether you grew up in a family with strong prohibitions against drinking alcohol or a family with members suffering from some sort of addiction, your family experiences shaped how you think about people who use (or don't use) alcohol and other drugs. To become more effective in working with substance-abusing clients, it helps to reflect on your personal alcohol and drug history, your current attitude toward substances, and your family's alcohol and drug history.

As you continue reading this chapter, be sure to keep reflecting on your attitudes toward alcohol and drugs. Also, as you study different approaches for assessing and working with substance-abusing clients, imagine yourself in both the therapist's and the client's shoes. Ask yourself some of the following questions:

- Do I have any assumptions about how therapists should act when interviewing substance-abusing clients?
- Is it necessary to be strongly confrontational—to get clients to "fess up" about their substance use? Or, will confrontational techniques increase client defensiveness and reduce honesty?

(continued)

(*continued*)
- If I stay nonconfrontational with clients who are addicted to substances, will they just avoid admitting they have any problems?
- What do I think about the CAGE assessment questions (see text)? How about the NIAAA criteria (see text) for alcohol consumption? How would I answer the questions? Do I, or have I ever had a problem with alcohol or other drugs?

Regardless of your specific answers to the preceding questions, be sure to talk with someone, privately or in a setting with people you trust, about your attitudes toward and experiences with alcohol and other drugs. Becoming aware of and working through your issues is part of your continuing development as a professional therapist.

Determining whether an individual is suffering from a substance use disorder is a specific diagnostic procedure. When faced with this task, some therapists simply pull out their latest edition of the *DSM* (or *ICD*) and ask clients questions based on the manual's diagnostic criteria. In contrast, alcohol and drug researchers are likely to use a more detailed and lengthy diagnostic interview schedule as their "gold standard" for determining whether a substance-related disorder exists (Grant et al., 2003; Ruan et al., 2008).

The question of "How much is too much?" substance use is often not answerable. However, several useful methods, aside from current *DSM-5* criteria and extensive structured interviews, have been developed. A commonly used brief interview for identifying alcohol problems is the CAGE questionnaire (Dervaux et al., 2006; do Amaral & Malbergier, 2008). The letters C-A-G-E form an acronym to help you remember four important questions to ask clients about their alcohol use. The questions are:

C: Have you ever felt that you should CUT DOWN on your drinking?
A: Have people ANNOYED you by criticizing your drinking?
G: Have you ever felt GUILTY about your drinking?
E: Have you ever had an EARLY morning (eye opener) drink first thing in the morning to steady your nerves or to get rid of a hangover?

Although diagnosis of an alcohol disorder should never be based on a single, brief interview procedure such as the CAGE questionnaire, many therapists, as well as the National Institute on Alcoholism and Alcohol Abuse (NIAAA), consider a "yes" to any one of the CAGE questions to be possible evidence of an alcohol problem—although often the criterion of two "yes" answers is reported as a more valid cut-off (do Amaral & Malbergier, 2008).

Additionally, the NIAAA has established use criteria; for men, in excess of 14 drinks a week or 4 drinks per occasion is considered a sign of alcohol abuse or alcoholism. For women, more than 7 drinks per week or 3 drinks per occasion is considered problematic (Friedmann, Saitz, Gogineni, Zhang, & Stein, 2001).

Facilitating Change: The Traditional Substance Abuse Interviewing Approach

In the not-so-distant past, it was generally assumed that interviewing substance-abusing clients required directive and confrontational interviewing techniques (Miller & Rollnick, 2013). It was thought that because individuals who abuse alcohol and other drugs are defensive—they deny or minimize their substance problems—direct confrontation was needed to break down or break through the client's defenses. For example, a traditional interview with an alcoholic might look like this:

Client: Really, Doc, I'm just a social drinker; I don't have a problem.

Interviewer: You've got a choice. You can face your problem with booze or go on jeopardizing your health, your safety, and your family. If you do choose to face your problem, then you'll need to do as I say and follow our treatment program. If you don't, you'll probably end up in a gutter somewhere, lying in your own vomit. Or maybe you'll end up in jail. The fact is you've got a problem, and you'll be better off admitting it right now.

As you can see, this approach to interviewing clients is very forceful. It involves presenting clients with evidence about their problem; this evidence is supposed to help clients accept their problem or diagnosis and embrace treatment. However, based on his research in the late 1970s and early 1980s, William R. Miller came to two dramatic conclusions: (1) ratings of therapist empathy were the best predictors of positive treatment outcomes with "problem drinkers" and (2) when therapists used confrontation and educational approaches, clients often became more resistant (W. R. Miller, 1978, 1983). These conclusions led to the development of motivational interviewing as a distinct approach to working with clients who have addictions problems.

Facilitating Change: Using Motivational Interviewing Strategies and Techniques

Miller and his colleague Stephen Rollnick originally published *Motivational interviewing* (MI) in 1991. In 1995, concerned that the concept had broadened and become diluted and confusing in the literature, Rollnick and Miller (1995) offered the following definition: "Motivational interviewing is a directive, client-centered counseling style for eliciting behavior change by helping clients to explore and resolve ambivalence" (p. 326). Motivational interviewing is nonconfrontational and based explicitly on person-centered principles. The MI process involves using nondirective and questioning strategies to help clients explore their substance use patterns. Through this process clients may become more aligned with their personal motivations for change.

The last two decades have seen a remarkable growth in MI for various client and problem types. A recent PsycINFO search for publications with "motivational interviewing" in the title produced 683 hits. These publications include MI for addictions, changing HIV risk behaviors, smoking, diet/exercise, domestic violence, criminal justice, and juvenile justice (Barnett, Sussman, Smith,

Rohrbach, & Spruijt-Metz, 2012; Ceperich & Ingersoll, 2011). A video training series and intensive workshop trainings are both available if you'd like to add this approach to your skill and knowledge base (see Suggested Readings and Resources).

Motivational Interviewing With Substance-Using Clients: Procedures and Techniques

Although MI procedures are largely nondirective, conducting a substance-related interview requires structuring the interview around a number of substance use and abuse questions and issues. Rollnick and Bell (1991) recommended covering 10 different content areas.

1. *Bring up the subject of substance use.* Do this gently and openly. For example, following about 5 to 10 minutes of building rapport, transition to the substance issue by using a summary statement and swing question:

> We've been talking a while in general about how your life is going.
> It sounds like you've had a bit of stress lately. Would you mind if
> I asked you now about your use of alcohol?

In most cases, clients cooperate with this gentle offer to explore their drinking patterns. This approach is tentative, gives clients control, and engages clients in a conversation about substance use.

2. *Ask about substance use or abuse in detail.* Rollnick and Bell (1991) suggested questions such as "What kind of a drinker are you?" or "Tell me about your use of marijuana; what effect does it tend to have on you?" (p. 206). The purpose of these questions is to let clients talk about how they view their drinking. These questions can be followed up with more specific queries: "You said you like to have a few beers with your friends after work. What's a 'few beers' for you?"

3. *Ask about a typical day/session.* When clients are habitual users, they often use in consistent patterns. For example, if you prompt clients with, "Tell me about your drinking patterns on a typical day," you're likely to hear about usual or regular use, which is helpful assessment information. Additionally, you can follow these more general queries with specifics, "About how much does it take for you to get high?" or "When you're at your favorite bar, what's your favorite drink, who's your best buddy, and how many do you have?"

4. *Ask about lifestyle and stress.* From both conceptual and practical perspectives, it's important not to become preoccupied with asking about substances during a clinical interview. Consequently, by moving away from talking about substances—to talking about life stress—and then back again, you help clients know you're interested in more than just gathering information about substance use. This often has the effect of opening clients up to talking more about the substances, rather than less. For example, if a client talks about using substances for coping with stress, you can expand the discussion towards life stressors:

Client: It's nice just to have a drink/smoke and relax (Rollnick & Bell, 1991, p. 207)

> **Interviewer:** It sounds like kicking back and relaxing is important to you. What kinds of things are happening in your life that are so nice to get away from when you kick back and smoke?

5. *Ask about health, then substance use.* If your client has health issues related to substance use, it's helpful to focus first on the health issues and then to gently explore the relationship between health and substance use. For example, after discussing asthma symptoms, you might ask, "How does your marijuana use work with the asthma problems we've been talking about?"

6. *Ask about the good things and the less good things.* The point of this strategy is to get clients to openly discuss what they like about their substance use (what is good) as well as some of the less good things about their substance use. Eventually, the goal is to get clients to expand on what's less good (from their perspective) to the point that, if appropriate, they can be conceptualized as "concerns." For example, a client may love the feeling of getting high and identify it as a good thing, but also identify the "munchies," the expense, and negative feedback from his girlfriend as less good. Also, Rollnick and Bell (1991) suggested that it's better to explore what is good/less good about "having a drink" rather than "your drinking" (p. 207).

7. *Ask about substance use in the past and now.* In many cases, client substance use patterns shift over the years. By asking, "How have your drinking patterns changed over the years?" therapists can open up the discussion to a variety of issues such as blackouts, tolerance, reverse tolerance, eye openers, and so on.

8. *Provide information and ask, "What do you think?"* When therapists assume an expert role and begin explaining about addiction concepts and problems to clients, they risk increasing client defensiveness. Therefore, if you provide addiction information or addiction education, do so in an open and collaborative manner. For example, you might say:

> I recently came across some interesting information on marijuana potency now, as compared to the 1970s. Would you mind if I shared some of this information with you? *(Then, after sharing the information, you should follow up with a question like, "What do you think about all this?")*

9. *Ask about concerns directly.* At some point in a substance use interview, directly inquire about clients' concerns about use patterns. Rollnick and Bell (1991) suggested using an open question such as "What concerns do you have about your alcohol use?" rather than a closed question such as "Are you concerned about your use of alcohol?" (p. 208).

10. *Ask about the next step.* After clients identify concerns about using a particular substance, you can broach the issue of what actions might be taken to address the stated concerns. Once again, Rollnick and Bell (1991) provided an example. They use a paraphrase, followed by an indirect question, to inquire about the next step: "It sounds like you are concerned about your use of marijuana. I wonder, what's the next step?"

Motivational interviewing is an evidence-based approach for working with clients who are using substances.

Assessment and Prediction of Violence and Dangerousness

During an assessment interview, John had the following exchange with a 16-year-old client.

John: I hear you've been pretty mad at your shop teacher.

Client: I totally hate Mr. Smith. He's a jerk. He puts us down just to make us feel bad. He deserves to be punished.

John: You sound a little pissed off at him.

Client: We get along fine some days.

John: What do you mean when you say he "deserves to be punished"?

Client: I believe in revenge. Really, I feel sorry for him. But if I kill him, I'll be doing him a favor. It would end his miserable life and stop him from making other people feel like shit.

John: So you've thought about killing him?

Client: I've thought about walking up behind him and slitting his throat.

John: How often have you thought about that?

Client: Just about every day. Whenever he talks shit in class.

John: And exactly what images go through your mind?

Client: I just slip up behind him while he's talking with Cassie [fellow student] and then slit his throat with a welding rod. Then I see blood gushing out of his neck and Cassie starts screaming. But the world will be a better place without his sorry ass tormenting everybody.

John: Then what happens?

Client: Then I guess they'll just take me away, but things will be better.

John: Where will they take you?

Client: To jail. But I'll get sympathy because everyone knows what a dick he is.

During an initial interview or ongoing therapy, many clients describe aggressive thoughts and images. Some clients, as in the preceding example, will be clear and concise about their thoughts, feelings, and images. Others will be less clear. Still others will be evasive and will avoid telling you anything about their violent thoughts or intentions.

Assessing for violence potential is similar to assessing for suicide potential; it involves a huge and stressful responsibility and is difficult. Also, similar to suicide assessment, we have a legal and ethical responsibility to conduct a violence or dangerousness assessment that meets professional standards.

Over the years, there have been arguments about how to most accurately predict violence (Hilton, Harris, & Rice, 2006). Essentially, there are three perspectives.

1. Some researchers contend that actuarial prediction based on specific, predetermined statistical risk factors is consistently the most accurate procedure (Quinsey, Harris, Rice, & Cormier, 2006).
2. Some clinicians believe that because actuarial variables are dimensional and interactive with individual and situational characteristics, prediction based on the clinician's experience and intuition is most accurate (Cooke, 2012).
3. Others take a moderate position, believing that combining actuarial and clinical approaches is best (Campbell, French, & Gendreau, 2009).

Despite the existence of these three perspectives, the research literature consistently shows that actuarial approaches to violence prediction are more accurate than clinical judgment (Monahan, 2013). However, actuarial violence prediction is not without its flaws (Szmukler, 2012; Tardiff & Hughes, 2011).

Narrowing in on Particular Violent Behaviors

Researchers who investigate actuarial assessment protocols have reported that different violent behavior patterns require an assessment of different predictor variables. Below, we provide three examples of violence predictors for specific violent behaviors or populations—with the goal of sensitizing you to different violent behavior patterns.

Fire setting. Fire setting is a particular dangerous behavior that may or may not be associated with interpersonal violence. Nonetheless, depending on your work setting and the clinical population you serve, you may find yourself in a situation in which you need to decide whether to warn a family or potential victim about potential for fire-setting behavior.

Mackay and colleagues (2006) reported on specific behaviors included on a fire-setting prediction assessment. Specifically, they noted that the following behaviors—in decreasing order—are predictive of fire setting:

- Younger age at the time of the first fire-setting behavior.
- A higher total number of fire-setting offenses.
- Lower IQ.
- Additional criminal activities associated with the index (initial) fire.
- An offender acting alone in setting the initial fire.
- A lower offender's aggression score. (Interestingly, offenders with higher aggression scores were more likely to be violent, but less likely to set fires.)

We focus on fire setting here for two main reasons. First, examining the variables that predict fire setting is inherently interesting. Second, fire-setting predictors illustrate a general violence-prediction principle. That is, it's not simply that past violent behavior predicts future violent behavior in general; instead, as you can see from the predictor variables listed, the principle is that specific past violent behavior predicts specific future violent behavior (e.g., fire-setting potential is best predicted by past fire-setting behavior). Similarly, physical aggression is best predicted by past physical aggression. But a history of physical aggression is not a good predictor of fire setting.

Homicide Among Young Men. Loeber and associates (2005) conducted a large-scale landmark study of homicide among young men living in Pittsburgh. This study is notable because it was both prospective and comprehensive; the authors tracked 63 risk factor (predictor) variables in 1,517 inner-city youth. Obviously, even this large-scale study is quite limited in scope, and technically the results cannot be generalized much beyond inner-city Pittsburgh youth. Nevertheless, the outcome data are interesting and lend insight into risk factors that might contribute to homicidal violence in other populations.

Results from the study indicated that violent offenders scored significantly higher than nonviolent offenders on 49 of 63 risk factors across domains associated with child, family, school, and demographic risk factors. The range and nature of these predictors were daunting. The authors reported:

> . . . predictors included factors evident early in life, such as the mother's cigarette or alcohol use during pregnancy, onset of delinquency prior to 10 years of age, physical aggression, cruelty, and callous/unemotional behavior. In addition, cognitive factors, such as having low expectations of being caught, predicted violence. Poor and unstable child-rearing factors contributed to the prediction of violence, including two or more caretaker changes prior to 10 years of age, physical punishment, poor supervision, and poor communication. Undesirable or delinquent peer behavior, based either on parent report or self-report, predicted violence. Poor school performance and truancy were also among the predictors of violence. Finally, demographic factors indicative of family disadvantage (low family SES, welfare, teenage motherhood) and residence in a disadvantaged neighborhood also predicted violence. Among the proximal correlates associated with violence were weapon carrying, weapon use, gang membership, drug selling, and persistent drug use. (p. 1084)

Homicidal violence was best predicted by a subset of general violence predictor variables. Specifically, homicide was predicted by "the presence or absence of nine significant risk factors . . . (i.e., screening risk score, positive attitude to substance use, conduct disorder, carrying a weapon, gang fight, selling hard drugs, peer delinquency, being held back in school, and family on welfare)" (p. 1086). In particular, boys who had at least four of these nine risk factors were 14 times more likely to have a future homicide conviction than violent offenders with a risk score less than four.

Violence and schizophrenia. In and of itself, a diagnosis of schizophrenia doesn't confer increased violence risk. Instead, research indicates there are specific symptoms—when seen among individuals diagnosed with schizophrenia—that are associated with increased risk. These specific symptoms include severe manifestations of:

- Hallucinations.
- Delusions.
- Excitement.
- Thinking disturbances. (Fresán, Apiquian, & Nicolini, 2006)

This research suggests that clinicians should be especially concerned about violence when clients diagnosed with schizophrenia have acute increases in the intensity of their psychotic symptoms.

Research Versus Practice

You may conclude from this short research review that therapists who hope to conduct accurate violence assessments should know actuarial violence prediction risk factors. However, as is often the case, scientific research doesn't always parallel real-life situations. For example, although much of the actuarial violence research has been conducted on forensic or prison populations—with the designated outcome measure being violent recidivism—therapists typically face situations in schools, residential treatment centers, and private practice (Juhnke et al., 2011). Consequently, although actuarial violence-prediction risk factors may be helpful, they probably don't generalize well to situations in which a counselor is making a judgment about whether there's duty to protect (and, therefore, warn) a shop teacher about a boy (who has never been incarcerated) who reports vivid images of slitting his shop teacher's throat.

Given these limits, it's better for us to refer to clinical interview-based assessments in school and agency settings as violence assessment, rather than violence prediction. This distinction helps clarify the fact that what most clinicians do in general practice settings, including public and private schools, falls far short of scientific, actuarial-based violence prediction.

A Reasonable Approach to Violence Risk Assessment

Predicting violence is a challenging proposition. There are many shifting variables that change based on the specifics of any given situation. There is also a very low base rate of violence, which makes predicting violent behavior especially difficult. Despite these challenges, this section provides general guidelines that may be helpful should you find yourself in a situation in which violence assessment is necessary. Of course, in addition to this guide, you should always pursue consultation and supervision support when working with potentially violent clients.

Table 12.2 includes a general guide to violence assessment. However, it doesn't include actuarial risk factors from two common instruments, the Violent Rate Appraisal Guide (VRAG; Harris, Rice, & Quinsey, 1993) or the Psychopathy Checklist-Revised (PCL-R; Hare et al., 1990; Harpur, Hakstian, & Hare, 1988). If you find yourself intrigued with violence risk assessment you may want to learn more about the VRAG and PCL-R and explore a potential career in forensic psychology.

DEMANDING SITUATIONS: CRISIS AND TRAUMA

This section provides guidance for demanding interviewing situations. These situations might include emergency settings, disaster relief, or interviews following personal or community-wide traumatic events. Therapists might find themselves trying to cope with substantial cultural differences, limited resources, restricted settings, and psychological distress. Physical injury, loss of home, loved ones, or a sense of identity may further complicate these situations. Information about interviewing trauma survivors and potential interventions currently used in the aftermath of trauma are provided.

Interviewing in Difficult Situations

No one needs to be reminded that many human-caused and natural disasters deeply and irrevocably affect the survivors. With the Internet providing instant information, and transportation readily available, the world continues to shrink. We can now hear about and travel very quickly to the sites of emergencies, disasters, and tragedies all over the globe. This easy accessibility belies the complexities of the skills and knowledge needed, should one choose to

Table 12.2   A General Guide to Violence Assessment

The following checklist is offered as a general guide to conducting violence assessment. It should not be used as a substitute for actuarial prediction.

☐ 1. Ask direct and indirect questions about violent behavior history. Be especially alert to physical aggression and cruelty. If the violent behavior that's being threatened is similar to a past violent behavior, the risk of violence may be higher.

☐ 2. Because potentially violent individuals aren't always honest about their violence history, you may need to ask collateral informants—someone other than the client—about the client's history of violent behavior (assuming you have a release of information signed or have determined you have an ethical-legal responsibility to protect someone from harm).

☐ 3. You should listen for details that might help you identify potential victims. If the details are not forthcoming, you may need to ask specific questions in an effort to obtain those details. Identification of a specific victim increases violence risk (and provides you with information about whom you should warn).

☐ 4. As clients talk about violent urges, you should listen for specifics about the plan. As needed, you may, through curious and indirect questioning, make efforts to further assess the specificity of the client's violence plan. More specific plans are associated with increased violence risk.

☐ 5. If clients don't tell you about his or her access to a weapon or means for committing his or her planned violent act, you should ask. Similar to suicidal situations, access to lethal means increases violence risk.

☐ 6. Historical information is doubly important. Generally speaking, the sooner violent behavior patterns began, the more likely they are to continue, and clients raised in chaotic and violent environments (including gang involvement) are at higher risk for violence.

☐ 7. Diagnostic information may be helpful. When looking at *DSM* diagnoses, the best violence predictors include items from list A of the *DSM-5's* antisocial personality diagnostic criteria (American Psychiatric Association, p. 659).

☐ 8. Evaluate current cognitions. If clients have low expectations of being caught or of having consequences, risk may be higher.

☐ 9. Consider substance use. Positive attitudes toward substance use and substance use when carrying weapons confer greater risk.

☐ 10. Notice your intuition. Intuition isn't a great predictor of anything, but if you have images of violence linked to a particular client, it's reasonable to err on the conservative side and begin the process of warning potential victims.

volunteer to be of assistance in such situations (Benyakar & Collazo, 2005). In addition to skills and knowledge, therapists need to attend to ethical considerations in crisis and humanitarian mental health interviewing (R. Sommers-Flanagan, 2007).

Many avenues are available to mental health professionals who wish for involvement in humanitarian or crisis intervention work. At the national and international level, there are volunteer organizations, such as the Red Cross and Red Crescent. There are churches and government programs that help organize and place volunteers. Longer-term placements are also possible through entities such as the United Nations or Peace Corps. At the local and state level, sometimes agencies not primarily dedicated to disaster interventions respond to disasters or tragedies within communities. These wide-ranging opportunities come with their own expectations, guidelines, and trainings or preparations. Some provide serious and comprehensive training, including language immersion, cultural knowledge, and experiential components. Others are less able to provide volunteers with these foundational necessities.

In 1991, the American Psychological Association (APA) launched the Disaster Response Network. The APA website includes a statement about the limited role of psychologists in disaster relief situations.

> On disaster relief operations, these psychologists do not provide therapy. Instead, they use their training and professional judgment to help people employ their own coping skills and resources to deal with extremely stressful and often tragic circumstances. Psychologists help people to problem-solve, make referrals to community resources, advocate for workers' and survivors' needs, provide information and listen. (retrieved February 3, 2013 from the American Psychological Association; http://www.apa.org/practice/programs/drn/)

Organizations related to the APA have also formed and are dedicated to responsible, culturally sensitive training and service provision. Similarly, the American Counseling Association (ACA) has developed emergency response opportunities, as has the National Association of Social Workers. Such developments speak to the need for skilled and immediate psychological assistance across cultures in the event of natural or human-caused disasters. If you desire training to provide disaster-relief services, you will be well served to work through your particular professional organization.

It's beyond the scope of this text to prepare you fully for conducting skilled and ethical mental health interviews across cultures, in the aftermath, or during ongoing struggles associated with acute disasters or humanitarian crises. However, we provide basic guidelines for two reasons. First, we intend these guidelines to raise awareness that volunteering to conduct mental health interviews in disaster and crisis situations requires specialized training. Without adequate preparation, you may do more harm than good (Collins & Collins, 2005; Smith, 2006). Second, you may find yourself in demanding situations for which you are unprepared. Disaster can strike any community at any time, and although you may not be specifically prepared, you may be asked to provide assistance.

Disaster Intervention Guidelines: Psychological First Aid

The initial publication on psychological first aid (PFA) appeared in 1945. This article focused on (a) preventing victim maladjustment, and (b) helping individuals deal with tensions and personal problems arising from specific incidents (Blain, Hoch, & Ryan, 1945). Subsequently, there was little discussion of PFA in the literature until the early 21st century. Subsequently, PFA has become the recommended approach for helping individuals who have experienced disasters (Ruzek et al., 2007; Vernberg et al., 2008).

Ruzek and colleagues described the origins and purpose of PFA:

> PFA is aimed at reducing initial post-trauma distress and supporting short- and long-term adaptive functioning. It is designed for delivery anywhere that trauma survivors can be found. Following a disaster, it can be offered in shelters, schools, hospitals, homes, staging areas, feeding locations, family assistance centers, and other community settings. The principles can also be applied immediately following traumatization in many non-disaster settings, including hospital trauma centers, rape crisis centers, and warzones. PFA is designed for simple and practical administration in field settings. (p. 18)

PFA was designed to address a practical need. In some ways it was developed specifically as an alternative to critical incident stress debriefing (CISD). Research on CISD had shown mixed results and there was discontent regarding possible adverse reactions with some clients (Campfield & Hills, 2001; Everly Jr. & Boyle, 1999). Interestingly, although there's a logical rationale for replacing CISD with PFA, there's only very minimal empirical evidence to support using PFA. Consequently, PFA shouldn't be considered an evidence-based approach—despite the fact that it's generally regarded as a best practice. Additional research is sorely needed.

The guidelines that follow are organized around the eight core actions in the psychological first aid model (Everly, Phillips, Kane, & Feldman, 2006; Ruzek et al., 2007).

Contact and Engagement

It's recommended that mental health service providers enter disaster situation under the auspices of "an authorized helping organization with a structured Incident Command System" (p. 24). There's little room or tolerance for lone rangers with disaster settings.

Mental health providers should approach disaster situations with calmness and self-control. This is because survivors often look to follow the lead of helping personnel. Calmness and control among mental health providers can elicit more calmness from disaster survivors.

The goal of contact and engagement is to respond to affected individuals who approach you and to initiate helping contacts in a compassionate and non-intrusive manner. If initiating contact, providers should seek permission. In either case, service providers should offer information about themselves and their role in the situation.

Safety and Comfort

In many crisis situations, the environment is chaotic. We have colleagues who have conducted interviews sitting on fallen trees, standing in the backyard of what was once a house, or searching through tornado ruins for a lost but precious item with their stricken client. Counseling work might happen in the back of a gym, on a neighbor's front porch, in a warehouse, or a vacated business. No matter what, you're a visitor to the scene and may or may not have much control over arranging your interviewing environment. Nonetheless, you can try to create some sense of privacy and comfort.

Ruzek et al. (2007) recommended:

Because disasters or terrorist incidents are often unexpected, shocking, and confusing, sense of safety and control can sometimes be strengthened by providing the survivor with accurate information, about what to do next, what is being done to assist them, what is currently known about the unfolding event, available services, and self and family care. But as with other elements of PFA, helpers should use judgment as to whether and when to present information. Does the individual appear able to comprehend what is being said, is he or she ready to hear the content of the messages, and are other things more important right now? (p. 27)

Moving to a place of safety and security, observing survivor functioning, and obtaining medical intervention as needed, are crucial components prior to stabilization.

Stabilization

Strong emotions following crisis and trauma are normal. However, in some cases, if individuals are so powerfully affected they cannot comprehend the situation and respond to assistance, stabilization may be necessary. Potentially helpful interventions include (adapted from Ruzek et al., 2007):

- Seeking aid from family members or friends.
- Taking the affected person to a quiet place.
- Talking quietly with the person with friends and family close by.
- Trying to address the individual's primary concern.
- Providing a few minutes alone.
- Using grounding procedures (e.g., asking them to report what they can see in the here and now).

Providing stabilization is crucial to moving to the next PFA step.

Information Gathering: Current Needs and Concerns

The goal of information gathering is to identify immediate survivor concerns and needs. This allows for tailoring of subsequent PFA interventions.

One challenge of the information gathering PFA activity is determining the extent to which survivors can respond to questioning. In many ways, information gathering takes a back seat to stabilization, but information gathering can also contribute to stabilization. Important information may include:

- The nature of any ongoing threat.
- Location and safety of loved ones.
- Physical health status and whether medications are needed.
- Whether an immediate referral is needed.
- The survivor's preexisting support network.
- Previous, current, and future possible substance use and prior mental health treatment.

PFA providers must use clinical judgment in determining how much to probe and how much to support when gathering information.

Practical Assistance

Practical assistance involves helping survivors address immediate concerns and needs. This stage of PFA usually includes more detailed or in-depth discussions about the survivor's primary problems and what might help with that problem. In cases where survivors are able to articulate their needs, every effort should be made to make an active response. This might involve assisting with paperwork, setting up an appointment of some sort, and other concrete and practical ways of being helpful.

Connection With Social Supports

Re-establishing social-support connections is essential for most individuals during a crisis or disaster situation. These connections may involve family, friends, and community support personnel who have been helpful in the past. In this step, PFA providers work to establish connection and communication. This may be via telephone, e-mail, Internet chat, Skype, or any form of communication available.

Information on Coping Support

The primary educational action or function during PFA is providing information on coping support. This includes information that may help in the here-and-now and into the future.

Some survivors may be alarmed not only by the situation, but also by their response to the situation. They may engage in powerful negative self-talk or self-evaluation, referring to themselves as weak, defective, or inadequate. In such cases, providing information that helps normalize crisis and trauma responses is recommended. It's especially important to avoid diagnosing, pathologizing, or negatively labeling any survivor symptoms. It's also important, depending on survivor receptivity, to gently discuss differences between positive and negative coping responses.

Linkage With Collaborative Services

Some survivors will want supportive services in the future, whereas others are more reluctant (possibly due to beliefs that needing continued support is a sign of weakness). Again, linking survivors with helpful services requires sensitivity and clinical judgment. However, in many cases walking survivors to services or connecting them with agencies via telephone is exactly the type of concrete assistance that's needed. Having handouts with referral information may also be helpful. If you do hand out referral information, it's important to make sure the survivor has a place to keep such material.

Professional Responsibilities

Beyond basic PFA, mental health personnel working with crisis and disaster may have additional professional responsibilities. These include the usual and customary ethical responsibilities associated with being a professional. The following information may overlap with and need to be integrated into a PFA approach.

Informed Consent and Record-Keeping

Depending on the nature of your contact with crisis and trauma survivors, there may be more or less need for an informed consent process. The more your contact involves PFA and is under the umbrella of a crisis services agency, the more likely you are to function in the moment as a part of a crisis team. In such cases you will defer to your agency in terms of the most appropriate informed consent and record-keeping procedures.

You may also serve as a referral source for crisis or disaster survivors. It's good to remember that individuals who have survived a disaster or been traumatized have experienced a devastating loss of control. They need to gain control, and at the same time, may need more structure and direction than is provided in a usual psychotherapy interview.

Within the context of your contact with survivors an informed consent process is unlikely to involve the usual paperwork, insurance forms, and so on. It will more likely be an interactive verbal process—and a brief one, at that. It should include the basic parameters of what you can offer, who you are, why you are there, how long you can talk with the client, how many times you can meet together, what limits there might be to keeping your conversation confidential, what the client can expect to gain from talking with you, and an explanation of any techniques you might use. If you have the option of making referrals, your client should be aware of this. If you'll be keeping case notes, let the client know why, where they might be stored, and for how long. If your organization requires some kind of information on the clients you interview, be sure to let clients know this as well. The point of all this is to provide survivors with basic, but not overwhelming information about you and your role is a way that gives them a sense of control. Given the immediate swirl of chaos inherent in the situation, it's easy to forget about informed consent . . . so be sure to remember not to forget.

Assessment Decisions

Depending on your assigned duties, it may be necessary to engage in screening activities using formal or informal assessment strategies. Assessment can help determine your client's basic human needs, emotional condition, and psychological disturbance. You may be responsible to monitor for signs of shock, dissociation, and/or suicidal impulses. Other relevant assessment areas might include medical/physical needs, availability of social support systems, and ability to communicate. Most likely, you will be monitoring for current functioning (think mental status examination) and the ability to identify, access, and effectively use whatever resources are available (Myer, 2001).

Human responses to trauma and crisis vary across at least three domains: (1) the nature of the crisis; (2) coping skills, ego strength, and resources available to individual survivors; and (3) cultural beliefs and practices associated with trauma (Chiang, Lu, & Wear, 2005). This wide range in how individuals respond to trauma implies that therapists should proceed with caution regarding diagnostic labeling in trauma-related circumstances. Smith (2006) noted that a frequent error in clinical judgment of a practitioner who is poorly trained in this area is to pathologize victims based on reactions that are normal reactions to abnormal and extremely stressful situations. Survivors of disaster don't need the added stigma from diagnostic labels that seem to insinuate their responses are indicative of some kind of personal weakness or mental illness (Yehuda & Bierer, 2005). However, accurate diagnosis can contribute to understanding the magnitude of the impact and can play a role in the availability of aftercare and resources for recovery. Walking the line between accurate diagnosis and inappropriate labeling during a time of crisis is a major challenge.

To address differences between a natural trauma reaction and a diagnosable condition, the *DSM-5* diagnostic criteria for acute stress disorder include the presence of at least nine trauma-related symptoms for a minimum of three days. A post-traumatic stress disorder diagnosis includes the presence of at least six trauma-related symptoms for longer than one month (APA, 2013).

Confidentiality

Confidentiality is often limited during crisis. It may not seem as important as it might in other settings, but it remains a central feature in professional crisis work (it's much less important in unprofessional crisis work—which we hope to help you avoid). You might be in a setting where people can see and hear as you work with a survivor. It's up to you to assess the safety of the content and, on occasion, to calibrate the emotional level of the conversation. If clients are sharing deep and very personal information, you may relocate if possible, or search for other ways to protect them from inadvertently revealing more than they wish. Within a crisis context, your client may temporarily experience impaired judgment and not be able to make decisions about his or her own privacy. Therefore, assuring confidentiality, or at least a shred of confidentiality, becomes a greater responsibility for the therapist.

Unless you have obtained specific permission to recount your interviewees' stories, you aren't free to do so. This is true even when you return to your home community or to your everyday practice. Recounting these stories will be tempting because of the compelling and dramatic nature of the circumstances and due to your own personal need to talk about vicarious trauma. Depending on many factors, you may be able to discuss the general parameters of your experience and the more generic aspects of what people experienced during the crisis and in the aftermath. Before doing so, it's wise to seek professional consultation. It's highly unethical to reveal the specifics of the suffering of others and to potentially expose or re-expose them to public scrutiny. If you're feeling a strong internal pressure to disclose stories about horrific traumas you witnessed or had described to you, make an appointment to obtain your own personal therapy so you can speak freely and confidentially with a professional.

Techniques and Resistance

As noted earlier in this chapter, resistance includes a protective set of interpersonal behaviors that come into play when there is a perception of threat. Trauma destroys the sense of invulnerability we all cling to in order to trust and make sense of our day-to-day world (Herman, 1992; Janoff-Bulman, 2004). Some of our friends who have been exposed to war describe trauma as a betrayal experience—an experience in which everything they knew about the world and depended upon was ripped away. Knowing that trauma experiences are deeply intertwined with trust may help you better understand why some survivors become strongly resistant to humanitarian and well-meaning interventions.

The truth is that many survivors might be ambivalent about trusting again—including trusting anyone purporting to offer help. This fact produces an understandable and predictable variability in the presentation of crisis survivors. Some may present as extremely upset, needy, and dependent, almost begging to be told what to do, how to feel better, and how to make sense of their terrifying experiences. Others may present as guarded, suspicious, and resistant to exploring emotions or cognitions related to their experiences. Still others may present with a perplexing combination of neediness and suspicion.

Secondary or Vicarious Trauma

We have long known that helpers exposed to other's trauma can be deeply, powerfully, and adversely affected. Early writers framed these effects as contributing to burnout and/or as causing significant countertransference difficulties (Figley, 1995). However, in 1990, McCann and Pearlman noted that the term *vicarious trauma* was a more comprehensive and accurate description of this common and concerning phenomenon. Of course, trauma and/or crisis work does contribute to burnout and trauma work is an excellent trigger for countertransference (McCann & Pearlman, 1990). However, reactions to working with trauma victims extend beyond these two concepts. Caring professionals who work directly with humans who are horribly wounded, bereaved, and/or psychologically devastated, cannot and should not expect to be unscathed by their exposure (Pearlman & Mac Ian, 1995). For example, after you listen to gripping stories with horrific images of physical and emotional suffering, it will be natural for you to have difficulty removing these images and stories from your mind. You may even begin to experience *flashbacks* or nightmares related to scenes and situations that you never directly experienced. These post-traumatic stress symptoms may require that you enter personal counseling or psychotherapy.

Trippany, Kress, and Wilcoxon (2004) wrote that counselors working with trauma survivors are likely to experience a range of difficult reactions. They identified five needs common to all healthy humans that trauma work can affect. These include

1. Safety needs
2. Trust needs
3. Esteem needs
4. Intimacy needs
5. Needs for control

As you work with trauma survivors, if you don't attend to your basic personal needs, you may end up a wounded healer—which means you'll be less helpful to trauma victims. Consequently, we strongly recommend that you take specific actions to lessen the vicariously traumatic experiences associated with crisis work. These include (a) seeking adequate supervision (Pearlman & Mac Ian, 1995), (b) keeping your caseload within reason, (c) seeking adequate education and training (Trippany et al., 2004), and (d) engaging in adequate professional and personal self-care. When managed well, there's evidence that vicarious trauma can stimulate personal growth and development (Brockhouse, Msetfi, Cohen, & Joseph, 2011; Cohen & Collens, 2012).

Cultural Differences

As in all interviewing situations, cultural background plays a large role in establishing healthy working relationships. In crisis and disaster work, there's little time to prepare, or to seek adequate cultural knowledge, even though it can play an extremely important role in therapeutic efficacy (Eagle, 2005; Shinfuku, 2005). Further, in more ordinary interviewing contexts, there's time to allow or encourage the client to educate the therapist about relevant cultural practices and beliefs, at least to some extent. This is far less true in crisis work. Therefore, therapists who wish to do effective humanitarian crisis work must add specific cultural knowledge to their training list—hopefully before you arrive on the scene. The U.S. Department of Health and Human Services (DHHS) provides a free online resource titled "Developing Cultural Competence in Disaster Mental Health Programs" (USDHHS, 2003). It's useful for both volunteer professionals and those assembling the necessary services in a given locale.

Boundary Concerns

Therapists who work in crisis situations are likely to find certain boundary challenges to be quite salient. When you're affected emotionally by the same devastation that your client is struggling with, it's difficult to maintain a proper therapeutic distance (Benyakar & Collazo, 2005). Your goal is be open and empathic, but not emotionally immersed in the tragedy to the point that you have nothing but shared misery to offer. Obviously, if crisis survivors begin consoling their therapists, appropriate boundaries and roles have not been maintained.

Disaster circumstances are extremely compelling. This may cause both clients and therapists to have stronger and wider emotional reactions than usual. The combined emotional intensities can activate very strong transference and countertransference reactions (Weaver, 1995). For example, your kind and balanced involvement might ignite a positive romantic transference reaction in a bereft or traumatized client. Needless to say, this trauma bonding or heightened attraction is neither a wise nor ethical basis for a personal relationship.

Another boundary issue to consider is self-referral. The APA Disaster Response Network concurs with the American Red Cross's stance that all mental health professionals who work with clients in disaster contexts may not make self-referrals unless there is absolutely no other option in the region. Even then, the referral must be approved by the national office (American Psychological Association, 2008).

Although complicated and professionally challenging, volunteering to offer clinical interviews and crisis counseling in crisis or humanitarian situations can be rewarding and personally transforming. At the end of this chapter, we provide a short list of websites and contact information for organizations that offer training and support for mental health professionals who would like to embark on the gratifying path of humanitarian volunteer work.

Interviewing Trauma Survivors

This section continues with material related to trauma, but it assumes that the interview is taking place within usual clinical practice contexts. Many clients come to therapy because they're struggling with a trauma experience. When individuals are exposed to traumatic events, such as natural disasters, school or workplace shootings, sexual assault, or war-related violence, they often experience immediate and longer-term emotional and psychological symptoms. In this section, we briefly review issues associated with interviewing trauma survivors.

Defining Trauma

In 1980, when post-traumatic stress disorder was first included in the *DSM*, *trauma* was defined as an event "outside the range of usual human experience" (p. 236). As Judith Herman (1992) wrote in her powerful book, *Trauma and Recovery*, "Sadly this definition has proved to be inaccurate" (p. 33). The sad part of this inaccuracy is the fact that many individuals, particularly women, experience sexual abuse, rape, and/or physical battering as a part of their usual human experience (Herman, 1992). Additionally, soldiers, police officers, and emergency personnel experience trauma as a part of their occupational roles.

A newer definition for trauma, recently updated in *DSM-5*, includes a general statement about trauma, followed by four specific ways in which trauma exposure may have occurred: The individual must have experienced "Exposure to actual or threatened death, serious injury, or sexual violence in one (or more) of the following ways" (p. 271)

1. Direct experiencing of the trauma.
2. Witnessing of the event as it "occurred to others" (p. 271).
3. "Learning that the traumatic event(s) occurred to a close family member or close friend" (p. 271).
4. "Experiencing repeated or extreme exposure to aversive details of the traumatic event(s)" (p. 271). This specifically includes first responders and police officers and implies that other professionals who experience repeated exposure may qualify for a post-traumatic stress disorder diagnosis.

As you reflect on these diagnostic criteria, you can probably see why individuals who experience trauma bring unique issues with them to a clinical interview.

Interviewing Clients Who Have Experienced Trauma: Issues and Challenges

The benefits of talking about trauma are virtually indisputable (Cochran, Pruitt, Fukuda, Zoellner, & Feeny, 2008; Pennebaker, Zech, & Rimé, 2001). Nearly everyone who experiences trauma should talk about it—sometime, somehow, some way. However, despite the clear benefits of talking, traumatized people are often reluctant to talk about their horrific thoughts and feelings for at least three reasons: (1) thinking about and talking about trauma brings up extremely uncomfortable feelings; (2) trauma often involves a violation of trust or betrayal (e.g., sexual assault), making it difficult for trauma victims to trust anyone, and especially difficult to trust and confide in a virtual stranger (a mental health provider); and (3) trauma survivors frequently feel guilty about surviving and sometimes ashamed that the traumatic event happened to them (Foa & Riggs, 1994). As an example of this, the *DSM-5* includes the following statements about features commonly associated with acute stress disorder.

Individuals with acute stress disorder commonly engage in catastrophic or extremely negative thoughts about their role in the traumatic event, their response to the traumatic experience, or the likelihood of future harm. [They] may feel excessively guilty about not having prevented the traumatic event or about not adapting to the experience more successfully. (American Psychiatric Association, p. 283)

These barriers to talking about trauma must be delicately managed using specific therapy skills and approaches (Steenkamp et al., 2011). Therefore, when working with traumatized clients, rapport and trust building is a central emphasis; otherwise, clients may be unwilling to share their stories or, if they do, they may feel re-traumatized by your questioning.

Another factor that makes working with trauma survivors problematic is the fact that traumatized clients often benefit from talking about their experiences very soon, usually within 48 hours, after the traumatic event (Campfield & Hills, 2001; G. Miller, 2012). Consequently, for therapists, there's a major conflict between trying to establish trust, which often takes time, and encouraging the client to begin talking about traumatic experiences right away.

Keep in mind that when a client discloses a trauma you have a heightened professional responsibility to make sure the sharing of the trauma doesn't adversely affect the client. A calm and caring demeanor is essential. A good sense of time boundaries is important as well. It's irresponsible to allow someone to go too far into the deep emotions surrounding a trauma and conclude the session without adequate time for emotional regrouping. Moving gently away from the trauma itself to problem solving about therapeutic coping strategies can be helpful if a client discloses a painful trauma during a first session. In addition, getting a clear picture of trauma symptoms—rather than emphasizing a direct discussion of the trauma itself—is more appropriate.

Collins and Collins (2005) wrote that helping trauma survivors can be challenging because often the presenting problems have arisen due to adaptations and coping strategies that came into being as a way to deal with the trauma. Because these coping efforts have felt protective, it's hard to consider giving them up. Survivors are also ambivalent about delving into events and trauma sequelae, and they may harbor shame or fears that they were somehow at fault in the event or trauma.

Interviewing people who have been traumatized requires skilled supervision and postgraduate training, regardless of whether the interview takes place directly in the aftermath of the trauma or later in the context of more general mental health services. Given the compelling and tragic psychological devastation associated with trauma, it is an advanced set of skills well worth acquiring.

SUMMARY

This chapter reviews strategies for working with specific populations who present particular challenges. Resistance has historically been framed as an obstacle to effective interviewing and intervention. However, current theorists and clinicians regard it as a natural part of the human change process. Resistance is partly associated with the client, partly with the therapist and partly with the situation.

There are several general strategies and specific techniques that can help therapists effectively manage resistance. These include the transtheoretical model, motivational interviewing, solution-focused openings, amplified reflections, emotional validation, radical acceptance, reframing, genuine feedback, and coming alongside. Using these strategies and techniques can give therapists a better chance of working effectively with mandated or unmotivated clients.

Similar to suicide assessment, assessing dangerousness and violence potential may become necessary in the course of a typical day for professional therapists. Although research suggests that actuarial systems are more accurate in predicting violence, unfortunately, most real-life interviewing situations don't closely parallel research violence-prediction scenarios. Consequently, clinicians are forced to use research-based knowledge in combination with clinical intuition and sensitivity to make decisions about potentially violent or dangerous clients. A checklist to assist in this process is included in this chapter.

Clinical interviewing in crisis or humanitarian disasters requires advanced skills and awareness of concerns related to this important but difficult professional activity. The current standard of care is called psychological first aid (PFA). PFA includes eight primary components: (1) contact and engagement, (2) safety and comfort, (3) stabilization, (4) information gathering, (5) practical assistance, (6) connection with social supports, (7) information on coping support, and (8) linkage with collaborative services.

Addressing the mental health needs of those traumatized by human or natural disaster not only demands knowledge and skill, it also requires a solid theoretical orientation, familiarity with techniques, and an awareness of the unique ethical constraints presented in this work.

SUGGESTED READINGS AND RESOURCES

There are many readings and resources for addressing resistance and working with crisis and trauma. This short list is only a small taste of what's available.

Readings

de Shazer, S. (1984). The death of resistance. *Family Process*, 23, 79–93.
   This is de Shazer's original article in which he holds a funeral for resistance and symbolically buries it in his backyard.
Horner, A. J. (2005). *Dealing with resistance in psychotherapy*. Lanham, MD: Jason Aronson.
   Horner focuses on resistance from the psychoanalytic perspective.
James, R. K., & Gilliland, B. E. (2012). *Crisis intervention strategies* (7th ed). Pacific Grove, CA: Brooks/Cole.
   This is a good general resource for learning about crisis intervention strategies.
Miller, G. (2011). *Fundamentals of crisis counseling*. Hoboken, NJ: Wiley.
   This book includes theory as well as hands-on techniques to assist clients in recovery from crisis.
Sommers-Flanagan, J., & Sommers-Flanagan, R. (2004). *The challenge of counseling teens: Counselor behaviors that reduce resistance and facilitate connection*. North Amherst, MA: Microtraining Associates.
   In this training video we provide examples of how to work effectively with youth who display resistant behaviors. However, we must admit the students we recruited to participate were far more cooperative than we expected.

Webber, J., Bass, D., & Yep, R. (2005). *Terror, trauma, and tragedies: A counselor's guide to preparing and responding*. Alexandria, VA: American Counseling Association.
    This edited volume provides a wide variety of stimulating material for counselors who want to work within humanitarian crisis settings.

Websites

The web address for professionals wishing to connect with Substance Abuse and Mental Health Services Administration is http://www.samhsa.gov/Disaster/professional _disaster.aspx.
    The website is filled with connections and information related to volunteering in the context of a national disaster.

The web address for Salus World, whose mission statement is "Promoting psychological wellbeing across the globe" is http://www.salusworld.org.
    This organization was created by members of Division 39 of the American Psychological Association. It offers training, placement, and post-volunteer support.

The web address for the Disaster Response Network of the American Psychological Association is: http://www.apa.org/practice/programs/drn/index.aspx.
    This network provides members who wish to volunteer for disaster and crisis intervention work with placement, training, and support.

For school-related resources go to:

http://www.nasponline.org/resources/crisis_safety/, sponsored by the National Association of School Psychologists.

http://www.schoolcounselor.org/content.asp?contentid=672, sponsored by the American School Counseling Association, specifically offering guidance for the aftermath of school shootings.

Interviewing and Working With Young Clients

CHAPTER OBJECTIVES

As our young clients often remind us, interacting with children and teens can be strikingly different from interacting with adults. In this chapter, we provide practical recommendations for interviewing young clients.

After reading this chapter, you will understand:

- Major considerations for working with children and adolescents.
- How to adjust your approach so you can speak and understand the language of children and adolescents and work more effectively with this special population.
- What the interviewing stages of introduction, opening, body, closing, and termination might look when working with young clients.
- How you can modify your interactions—and even your clothing—to make a good first impression with young clients.
- How to discuss confidentiality, informed consent, referral information, and assessment and therapy with youth.
- A specific technique for talking with young clients about therapy goals.
- Youth-friendly assessment and information-gathering strategies.
- Methods for reassuring, supporting, and empowering youth.
- Important termination issues to address with young clients.

To this point, our primary focus has been on interviewing, assessment, and treatment planning with individual adult clients. Unfortunately, "adult interviewing skills" often won't directly translate into child and adolescent interviewing skills (J. Sommers-Flanagan & Bequette, 2013). As you may already know, young clients think, act, and interact much differently than adult clients.

> Mr. Quimby wiped a plate and stacked it in the cupboard. "I'm taking an art course, because I want to teach art. And I'll study child development—"

Ramona interrupted. "What's child development?"

"How kids grow," answered her father.

Why does anyone have to go to school to study a thing like that? wondered Ramona. All her life she had been told that the way to grow was to eat good food, usually food she didn't like, and get plenty of sleep, usually when she had more interesting things to do than go to bed.

—Beverly Cleary, *Ramona Quimby, Age 8* (2009)

In the preceding excerpt, it's clear that Ramona Quimby thinks differently from how her father thinks. This chapter explores the exciting world of interviewing and working with young clients.

CONSIDERATIONS IN WORKING WITH CHILDREN

When working with children, it can be hard to stay balanced and objective. For example, some adults will come to view each individual child as either a good or bad kid. If you give in to this tendency, it can result in dreading or celebrating your clients' arrival, which can further lead to a self-fulfilling prophecy wherein your outcomes are more negative with some children than others (Guyll, Madon, Prieto, & Scherr, 2010; Stinson, Logel, Shepherd, & Zanna, 2011).

Therapists, teachers, and other adults may overidentify or underidentify with children. Adults suffering from overidentification may project their own childhood conflicts onto children, fail to set appropriate boundaries, or be unable to appreciate unique aspects of children with whom they work. Adults who underidentify with children may experience children as alien beings—puzzling creatures who need to be controlled or managed. Not being able to identify with children may also reduce counselor empathy; reduced empathy can contribute to increased child abuse or mistreatment (Moor & Silvern, 2006).

Children are *not* just like us, nor are they like we were when we were younger. Though different, they're not unfathomable creatures either. Instead, children are somewhere in the middle—rapidly developing, fully human, deserving of respect and age-appropriate communication and information.

There are educational requirements needed to work effectively with young clients (Mellin & Pertuit, 2009). In some ways, interviewing children is a form of cross-cultural counseling (J. Sommers-Flanagan & Sommers-Flanagan, 2007b). You need to be familiar with basic cognitive and social/emotional developmental theory and have direct experience with children (i.e., you should have spent some time with children in either a caretaking or emotionally connected manner).

You also need to be aware of your own reactions toward children. For example, if you feel frightened, intimidated, or irritated about the idea of providing counseling to children, adolescents, or parents, it's important to explore and work through these reactions. You may or may not be well suited to working with young clients. Professional preparation, self-reflection, supervision, consultation, or perhaps personal counseling might be in order.

Another danger sign is a tendency to repeatedly get overly involved in children's lives. Signs of overinvolvement include fantasies about adopting or rescuing children in difficult circumstances or breaking traditional boundaries and doing things for children outside professional relationship parameters. Overinvolvers need to reach a greater understanding of themselves and find other ways to meet their needs before working therapeutically with children.

A healthy professional and psychological balance is especially necessary when working with children. Children are uniquely able to push our buttons, throw us off balance, and trigger emotional reactions. Making this balance even more essential is the fact that children constitute a very vulnerable population. Adult clients possess greater maturity, more education and life experience, and have a more fully developed sense of self. They're usually more able to advocate for themselves. They have more resources and are more autonomous. Most adults can extricate themselves from manipulative or unhelpful relationships with mental health providers, but most children cannot. Most adults can express their disappointments and needs in ways that make sense to the counselor; often, children cannot or will not communicate directly. For all these reasons, we must be especially attuned to the skills, education, and attitudes necessary to work effectively with children.

The remainder of this chapter is organized around Shea's (1998) interviewing stages. However, when it comes to interviewing young clients, this chapter merely scratches the surface. If you want to work with young clients you need much more education, training, and supervision. Additional readings and professional resources are listed at the conclusion of this chapter.

THE INTRODUCTION

As you may recall from Chapter 6, the introduction stage of the interview involves first contact and initiation of the helping or assessment relationship. It also includes planning—and when it comes to working with young clients, organization and planning is essential.

Preparation and Planning

Usually, young people don't seek mental health services willingly (Richardson, 2001; J. Sommers-Flanagan, Richardson, & Sommers-Flanagan, 2011). Children are referred to professionals by parents, guardians, caretakers, or school personnel (Dugger & Carlson, 2007). Young clients may not have prior knowledge about who they'll meet with and/or the meeting's purpose. In some cases, they may not think there's anything wrong in their world; they may not even have been informed in advance that they have a counseling appointment. In other cases, they may be very clear regarding their distress or the distress others are experiencing because of them.

With minors, the role of the caretaker (e.g., parent, grandparent, stepparent, foster parent, older sibling, group home manager) in the interview is central and requires conscious attention. Some caretakers presume they'll be present during the entire interview; others follow the "I'm just dropping my child off for you to fix" philosophy. In most cases, the nature of caretaker involvement will be determined by your assessment of what would be best given the presenting problem, child's age, and relevant agency policies, and should be established up front. Some therapists may spend time with the child and caretakers together first and move forward from there; but others prefer meeting first with parents or caretakers to establish goals and begin developing a treatment plan. There are pitfalls linked to both approaches:

- If you meet with parents alone, the child (especially teens) will wonder if you're working as an agent for the parents or see you as an untrusted authority figure; this makes establishing trust more challenging.

- If you meet with the whole family first, parents (or children/adolescents) may quickly engage in conflict or blaming that, unless you've got skills for managing conflict, can damage everyone's perception of the therapy process; also parents may share information about themselves or the situation that's inappropriate for the child to hear.
- It may be preferable to meet with angry, hostile, or stressed parents alone, rather than risk subjecting the child to a barrage of negativity.

Because interviewing children usually involves caretaker(s), time management can be very difficult. You may need to schedule an extended initial interview session so the child has adequate time for self-expression and the caretakers also feel their concerns are sufficiently addressed.

First Contact

First contact with young clients and caretakers can be both stimulating and overwhelming. There are many management issues to be addressed. In particular, a written informed consent is crucial and should be followed by an oral description of your informed consent and confidentiality policies. For example, if you meet with parents first, but the child is your primary client, the child deserves to know at least generally what has been said about him or her. Letting caretakers know that you'll be summarizing and sharing information you feel is important with the child will help set a meaningful semipermeable boundary (more on this in the informed consent section).

In the following example, the counselor is clear in advance about her plan and sets limits with a dominant parent figure. Without a clear plan and assertive behavior, you run the risk of having a strong family member control the interview and treatment plan.

CASE EXAMPLE

Sandy Smith, a 12-year-old child of mixed racial descent, was adopted by a mixed-race couple who later divorced. She was a gifted violinist and athlete but had begun "hanging with the wrong crowd." Her father and stepmother insisted on counseling for Sandy. Her mother and stepfather were less eager, but felt something must be done about her increasing defiant behavior. As planned via an initial telephone conversation, all four parent figures plus Sandy's 3-year-old half-brother arrived at the counseling office. However, Sandy's father was paying for the counseling and clearly planned to talk with the counselor alone before anyone else was interviewed.

The counselor gave Sandy's father a warm smile, but oriented to Sandy in the waiting room, saying, "Hi. You must be Sandy. Looks like you've a pretty big fan club along with you today."

Sandy shrugged and mumbled, "Hi."

The counselor then said, "How about if everyone comes back for a few minutes so I can meet everyone together?"

Sandy's father asked pointedly, "Can I just see you first for a couple minutes?"

The counselor again smiled warmly and said, "To start, I'd like everyone to come in and hear about how I work with young people (significant smile is sent in Sandy's direction). If we haven't gotten to some of your concerns, Mr. Smith, we may need to set up a separate time to meet. Will that work for you?"

Mr. Smith nodded and the whole group proceeded to the counselor's office.

Children's guardians have many legal rights, but if you plan to do individual therapy with a child, it's essential that the child realize that your primary allegiance is to him or her (Stone, 2005). This realization can be seriously hampered by too much attention to the caretakers' desires and concerns and not enough attention to the child. Early on, preferably even while appointments are being made, it's good to be clear about caretaker roles in assessment and therapy. A telephone conversation with a mother of a 15-year-old boy might proceed like this:

Counselor: Hello, my name is Maxine Brown. I'm returning your call to the Riverside Counseling Center.

Mom: Oh yeah, I called yesterday because I want an appointment for my 15-year-old son. I'm a single parent and I can't seem to get through to him. He's been angry and impossible to deal with. When can I get him in?

Counselor: I have open times next Monday at 1 P.M. and 3 P.M.

Mom: Great. I'll take 3 P.M.

Counselor: Sounds good. (Therapist explains fee arrangement, office forms to be completed, and directions to the counseling center.) Also, at the beginning of the session, I'll meet with you and your son together. During that time, I'll talk with both of you about how I work with young people and we'll establish goals for the counseling. Does that sound okay to you?

Mom: So you want me to actually come in, too? I thought I could just drop him off and run back to work.

Counselor: Yes, it's important for me to meet with both of you to start. That should take about 20 minutes. Then I'll meet with your son alone so I can get to know him and we can begin working together. Altogether, I meet with him, I'd like you to stick around* and complete some paperwork in the waiting room. Okay?

Mom: All right. I guess I'll have to make some arrangements for this at work.

Counselor: That would be great. I'll look forward to meeting with both of you on Monday.

*Note: Experienced child therapists have noted that some parents want to run errands or leave the premises while you meet with their child. This may or may not be acceptable—depending on the policies of your particular agency (Carolyn Berger, personal communication, August 10, 2012).

Whether directly on the telephone (as in the preceding example) or at the outset of the interview (as in the first example), it's essential to manage caretaker involvement in therapy. Each situation is different, but articulating your general policies and guidelines early clears up potential confusion and allows you to develop a working alliance with the child (and parent or caretaker).

PUTTING IT IN PRACTICE 13.1

A Checklist to Prepare for First Contact

☐ 1. Consider the pros and cons of meeting with the whole family, parents only, or child only; be clear who to include in the first interview and for how long.

☐ 2. Develop an informed consent form that describes your approach and that lets adults and young clients know how you'll handle confidentiality. This should include information on whether it's acceptable for parents to leave the premises while you're counseling their child.

☐ 3. Consider scheduling a longer-than-typical initial session so all parties (adults and children) have an opportunity to express themselves and feel heard.

☐ 4. Get ready to manage caretakers, children, and potential conflicts. It's not unusual for therapists to have to do a little limit-setting during initial sessions.

☐ 5. Keep reading this and other materials on counseling children, adolescents, and families; this will help you know what to expect and will help you identify strategies for dealing with the unexpected.

THE OPENING

The reason that all the children in our town like Mrs. Piggle-Wiggle is because Mrs. Piggle-Wiggle likes them. Mrs. Piggle-Wiggle likes children, she enjoys talking to them and best of all they don't irritate her.

—B. MacDonald, *Mrs. Piggle-Wiggle*

This section describes effective strategies for getting acquainted with young clients. Child/adolescent interviews include two general goals: (1) to learn as much as possible about the client and (2) to establish a warm and respectful relationship. Relationship building can present a special challenge because children and adolescents are likely to be unfamiliar with interviewing and counseling procedures and may be shy, reluctant, or resistant (Sommers-Flanagan & Bequette, 2103). Therapists can manage this challenge more easily if they follow Mrs. Piggle-Wiggle's lead: Young people quickly perceive whether mental health professionals like them and enjoy spending time with them. They also readily notice if professionals are threatened or irritated by child/adolescent attitudes and behaviors. Perhaps another reason Mrs. Piggle-Wiggle did so well with children is that she joyfully accepted them as children and spoke to them in their developmental language, rather than prematurely trying to drag them into an adult world. If young clients don't believe they're liked or respected as children or teens, there's much less chance that they'll listen, open up, or, if they have a choice in the matter, continue therapy (Oetzel & Scherer, 2003; J. Sommers-Flanagan & Sommers-Flanagan, 2007b).

First Impressions

Although it may be tempting to immediately engage in adult talk with parents in the waiting room, doing so can make rapport building with young clients more difficult. It's helpful to try connecting with young clients when initially meeting them. A wave, fist-bump, or a handshake and a friendly "Hi, you must be Whitney" is a good start, followed by more quick exchanges, such as "It's very nice to meet you" or "Great biking weather out there, huh?" or "That's a great looking batman shirt." Many child counselors make it a habit to try to get down to the child's height level (Eric Davis, personal communication, September 30, 2012). Your goal is to send the message that you've been looking forward to meeting the young person and are eager to engage with him or her. A little adult chatter is fine, too, as long as you don't forget to connect with the child.

Children should often be considered involuntary clients. As with any involuntary client, the therapist is wise to seek assent and introduce a few creative choices within the interview frame. For instance, you might say something like:

- Hi, Felix. Your mom and stepdad are going to fill out some boring old paperwork while you and I talk together. I have some toys in this closet. You can pick two to bring with us to my office.
- Well, Hallie, I need to explain three important things to you. One is about how we will spend our time together today. One is about a word called *confidentiality*. And one is about why my office is so messy. Which one would you like me to talk about first?

Another way to empower and connect with young people is to offer food or drink. The options, depending on your values, budget, guardians' consent, and setting, might include milk, hot chocolate, juice, or sports drinks. Although you should watch out for food allergies, snacks might be pretzels, chips, granola bars, fresh fruit, crackers, candy, or yogurt. To feed or not to feed is a professional question we don't discuss at length in this book. Suffice it to say, feeding young people builds relationship (J. Sommers-Flanagan & Sommers-Flanagan, 2007b). Hungry people tend to think about being hungry. Lest you think we're deviating too much from being a neutral professional, even Freud was known to have fed clients when they were hungry (J. Sommers-Flanagan & Sommers-Flanagan, 2012). Food may be an especially important therapy tool when young children are meeting with you immediately after school. Although we try to avoid beverages with caffeine and highly sugary foods, other therapists we know use such items after obtaining parent or guardian permission.

Office Management and Personal Attire

Professional offices are not necessarily youth-friendly. It can help to place a few "cool" items in clear view. Items such as popular sports cards, fantasy books, playing cards, drawing pads, clay, and hats may be appropriate. Trendy toys are always the mark of a cool counselor, but you have to make a commitment to being up on the trends. Hardly any of John's young clients show much interest in playing with his Freud action figure. We would suggest items, but by the time you read this book, they might be uncool. We leave you to your own devices to discover what's cool, what's not, and what toys you can tolerate having in your office. It's also possible to try too hard. Striking a balance so that you're child-friendly but authentic should be your goal. More generically, soothing play-therapy objects, such as puppets and stuffed animals, can increase clients' comfort level. Sometimes, teenagers may comment negatively about such items because they're normally associated with younger children, but the comments are probably just a cover for their comfort and dependency needs (Behr, 2003). Overall, the office should be interesting and welcoming to young people to whatever extent possible.

Although you may offer particular toys or objects for children to play with or hold, it's probably better to let clients notice particular items on their own. Their natural exploratory behavior can help them become comfortable in a new setting. In addition, their reaction to office items is valuable assessment information. Some children will orient to the sports cards and begin estimating their resale value; others cuddle up with pillows and stuffed animals; still others ignore everything, appear overtly sullen, and roll their eyes if you ask questions. Some clients aren't able to keep their hands off certain items. Some materials may need to be placed in drawers or boxes if they become too distracting; others, such as clay or a doodle pad, can give the client something to "mess around with" while talking with the therapist. Having something to hold or squeeze or draw with can reduce client anxiety (Hanna, Hanna, & Keys, 1999).

Adolescents will sometimes take note of your clothing choices. This doesn't mean you have to shop at American Eagle or Abercrombie & Fitch (or even cooler places that old people like us don't know about). Nonetheless, we recognize that one of the most successful female therapists we've ever known attracts difficult adolescent girls, in part, because she dresses "way cool." If you're wondering how we know this, it's because teens seen in therapy often compare notes; they talk with each other about their respective "shrinks" and offer progress reports about their friends who are seeing other therapists. Listening to these assessments can be informative.

In contrast, some clothing choices may be off-putting. Traditional, conservative attire (suit jacket, shirt, and tie) may be viewed by adolescents, especially those with oppositional and misconduct behaviors, as signs of a rigid authority figure. Many adolescents have strong transference reactions to authority figures, and such reactions can impair or inhibit initial rapport (J. Sommers-Flanagan & Sommers-Flanagan, 2007b).

You may decide to have youth-oriented interviews that move away from traditional seating or settings. This might involve being on the floor, going outside, or using child sized tables/chairs. If so, you'll likely want clothing that allows for bending, squatting, or crawling comfortably.

Generally, more casual attire is recommended when interviewing young clients. This doesn't mean clients can't overcome reactions to more formal clothing choices. However, when working with youth, it's useful to eliminate even superficial obstacles to rapport. Although therapists need to present themselves and their work in a way that feels personally and professionally authentic, keeping an eye to youth-friendly accessories can be helpful.

Discussing Confidentiality and Informed Consent

Many young people (especially teens) are sensitive to personal privacy, and so you should discuss confidentiality at the very *beginning* of the first session. It's also advisable to review confidentiality with children and adolescents occasionally to ensure the concept is fully understood and to allow for questions that may arise. In addition, teenagers sometimes believe therapists are working undercover for their parents; they may fear that what they say in private will be reported back to caretakers or authority figures. Written parent informed consent forms and child assent forms should be read and signed before the initial session begins (Alkhatib, Regan, & Jackson, 2008). When working with teens or preteens and their parents, we recommend an approach similar to the following:

- Todd, you and your mom both may have read about confidentiality on the registration forms, or you may have heard the word before, but I want to talk about it for a minute. Confidentiality is like privacy. That means what you say in here stays in here; it's private and personal. Of course, I have a supervisor and I keep files, but my supervisor will keep information private, and my files are locked up.
- I won't talk about what you say to me outside of here, except for a couple different situations. For example, if either you or your mom is dangerous to yourself or to anyone else, I won't keep that private. Also, if I find out about child abuse that has happened or is happening, I won't keep that information private either. That doesn't mean I think any of those things are happening; I'm just required to tell you about the limits of your privacy before we get started. Do either of you have any questions about confidentiality (privacy) here? [Respond directly to whatever questions come up.]
- Now (while looking at Todd), one of the trickiest situations is whether I should tell your mom about what we talk about in here. Let me tell you how I like to work and see if it's okay with you. (Look at Mom.) I believe Todd needs to trust me. So, I would like you to agree that information I give to you about my private conversations with him be limited to general progress reports. Aside from general progress reports, I won't tell you what he tells me. Of course, there are some exceptions to this, such as if he is planning to do something that might be harmful to himself or others. In those cases, I'll tell Todd (turn to Todd) that we need to have everyone (turn back to Mom) come in for an appointment so we can all talk directly about whatever dangerous thing has come up. Is this arrangement okay with both of you?

(For a sample adolescent informed consent form, go to The Center for Ethical Practice website at: http://www.centerforethicalpractice.org/Form-Adolescent Consent.)

Teenagers need to hear how their privacy will be maintained and protected. Also, most parents appreciate their children's need to talk privately with someone outside the family. In cases where diagnostic interviewing results are shared with a referral source or child study team, the child should be made aware of this. If parents insist on being in the room continuously or constantly apprised of therapeutic details, a family systems interview/ intervention is more appropriate.

Confidentiality laws related to minors vary from state to state. All mental health professionals and trainees should review paperwork and practices with regard to regulations in each particular setting and state. In addition, specific school counseling settings and agency settings may have idiosyncratic limits on confidentiality. For example, it's not unusual for schools to have a policy that requires all staff to report students who are in possession of drugs or weapons within a school. All limits to confidentiality should be fully explained to young clients both in writing and in person.

Teenagers may respond better to a modified version of the previous confidentiality disclosure. Sometimes humorous examples are appropriate. For example, when turning to the teenager, the following statement may be made:

So, if you're planning to do something dangerous or destructive, such as holding the mailman hostage, we'll need to have a meeting with your parents to talk that over, and I'd need to warn your mailman. But the usual stuff that you're trying to sort out, stuff that's bugging you, even if it's stuff *about* your parents or teachers or whoever—we can keep that private.

Work to develop your own way of talking with young people and their parents about counseling and confidentiality. Confidentiality is a unique and powerful aspect of therapeutic relationship development. Leve (1995) wrote:

Children are almost never told that what they say to an adult will be held in strict confidence and never be told to another adult. This indicates that the therapist respects the child in a way they have never before experienced, and it is a signal that the child's thoughts and actions are important, probably in a way they never dreamed possible. As a result, children sense that therapy is an experience very different from other adult relationships and that it will have an unusual importance in their life. (p. 245)

Rehearsing different approaches to talking with clients about this important issue can help (see *Multicultural Highlight* 13.1).

MULTICULTURAL HIGHLIGHT 13.1

Individualizing Introductory Statements With Young Clients

This chapter includes sample statements for introducing yourself and interviewing and counseling to young clients. These statements are a good start, but you can come up with better opening statements for yourself. Whatever you say in the first few minutes should fit your personality. If you're using a standard opening, but the opening is uncomfortable for you, children will sense that there's something weird or phony going on. This activity involves formulating opening statements to use with young clients that fit with your personality. These statements focus on:

1. Introducing yourself to the child and family.
2. Describing confidentiality and its limits to the child and family.
3. Describing other interviewing/counseling features (e.g., psychological assessment).

Take a few minutes to think about the words you want to use when discussing these issues with children. Now, shift your focus and imagine how you might change your introductory comments in situations with ethnically diverse clients. How would your introductory comments change if you were working with an American Indian, African American, Asian American, or Hispanic child and family? Would you alter your statements when working with populations from different economic classes or geographic regions? What issues would rise to the surface and require a comment from you? If you have an ethnically diverse background, imagine the differences that might arise if you were working with a White child versus someone from your own background. Discuss these issues with your class or classmates.

Another variation you may face involves interviewing immigrant children—because one in five children in the United States is a child of an immigrant (U.S. Government Printing Office, 2012). The stresses of fitting in are sometimes magnified by having parents or caretakers who speak a different language and have customs different from those of people at school and in the neighborhood. Clinicians shouldn't make assumptions about immigrant families or young people. It can be harmful to ignore intergenerational stress that may exist in immigrant families. It can also be harmful to assume that an immigrant family is suffering because of the bicultural demands it faces. The challenges might make family life interesting, or they may be daunting and painful. Review the guidance offered in Chapter 11 by Senel Poyrazi. You might make observations and ask opening questions such as:

> I notice your mom is wearing a traditional H'mong skirt, Tu. But you've got on jeans and a T-shirt. Do you dress traditional sometimes?

> or

> Your parents have a cool accent. What languages do you speak at home?

Making a few observations that are neutral or slightly positive and following that with a question about the young person's cultural involvement communicates that you're interested in the struggles and points of pride involved in being a family spanning two or more cultures.

Handling Referral and Background Information

Teachers, family members, or others concerned about children's behavior frequently refer youth for therapy or evaluation. In most cases, therapists should tell young clients exactly why they were referred. We refer to this as "acknowledging reality" and consider it an essential part of rapport-building (J. Sommers-Flanagan & Sommers-Flanagan, 2007b). That doesn't mean you tell clients every detail of what you've heard; but you should be sure to say something about what you know. For example, a concerned teacher who, undetected, observed a student throwing up in the bathroom after lunch may contact a school counselor. At the teacher's request, the counselor may invite the student for a meeting. We believe it would be a mistake to fail to mention the reason for concern. Of course, you must make these policies very clear to referral sources. The information source may or may not need to remain anonymous, but the information itself, in most situations, should be tactfully, compassionately, and honestly conveyed. Here's a possible scenario from our *Tough Kids, Cool Counseling* text (J. Sommers-Flanagan & Sommers-Flanagan, 2007b):

> Immediately after introducing herself and offering a summary of the limits of confidentiality, [the therapist] states, "I'm sure you know I talked with your parents and your probation officer before this meeting. So, instead of keeping you in the dark about what they said about you, I'd like to just go ahead and tell you about what I've been told. This sheet of paper has a summary of all that (counselor holds up sheet of paper). Is it okay if I just share all this with you?"
>
> After receiving the client's assent, the [therapist] moves her chair alongside the client, taking care to respect client boundaries while symbolically moving to a position where they can read the referral information together. She then reviews the information, which includes both positive information (the client is reportedly likeable, intelligent, and has many friends) and information about the legal and behavioral problems the adolescent has recently experienced. After sharing each bit of information, she checks in with the client by saying, "It says here that you've been caught shoplifting three times, is that correct?" or "Do you want to add anything to what your mom said about how you will all of a sudden get really, really angry?" When positive information is covered, the [therapist] says thing like, "So it looks like your teachers think you're very intelligent and say that you're well-liked at school . . . do you think that's true . . . are you intelligent and well-liked?" (p. 32)

If the information you have from teachers, parents, or probation officers is especially negative, be sure to screen and reframe the information so it isn't overwhelming or offputting to young clients. Also, if you're planning to share referral information with clients, you should warn and prepare referral sources; if not, the referral sources may feel betrayed. Also, when sharing negative information, it's important to show empathy and side with the client's feelings, while not endorsing the negative behaviors. For example, "I can see you're really mad about your mom telling me all this stuff about you. I don't blame you for being mad. It's hard to have people talking about you, even if they have good intentions."

Keeping secrets about why the youth was sent to therapy can harm the relationship. Remember, the referral source, no matter how distraught, isn't the primary client.

After discussing confidentiality and informed consent, it's time to get an idea of the reasons the client has come for therapy. Common reasons for bringing preschool- to latency-age (4- to 12-year-olds) children for an interview include:

- Moodiness, irritability, or aggressive behavior patterns.
- Behaviors that caretakers believe to be abnormal or especially irritating.
- Unusual fears or tendencies to avoid age-appropriate play activities.
- Unusual sexual behaviors.
- Exposure to trauma or difficult life circumstances, such as divorce, death, or abuse.
- Hyperactivity or problems with inattentiveness.
- Enuresis or encopresis.
- Custody battles between parents.
- School issues related to academics and/or bullying.

This list is neither exhaustive nor comprehensive; it's intended to help you glimpse a typical young child referral. Like younger children, older children and adolescents usually don't request therapy themselves. Common reasons for adolescent therapy referrals include:

- Depressive symptoms (usually recognized by a caretaker or teacher).
- Oppositional/defiant behaviors (usually experienced by authority figures).
- Anger management.
- Eating disorders or weight problems.
- Traumatic experiences (rape, sexual abuse, divorce, death in the family).
- Suicide ideation, gestures, or attempts or non-suicidal cutting.
- A court order or juvenile probation mandate.
- Substance abuse problems (usually identified by having been caught using or driving under the influence).

Although it's important to have a general understanding of childhood psychopathology and typical complaints, each situation is unique and needs to be addressed with individualized concern. Every child who comes to therapy should be asked about his or her understanding of the visit's purpose. However, it's not unusual for young clients to give vague or surprising responses:

- My mom wants to talk with you because I've been bad.
- I don't know . . . I didn't even know we were coming here today.
- Because I hate my teacher and won't do my homework.
- My mom offered to buy me a new computer game if I came to see you.
- Because my parents are stupid and *they* think I have a problem.

Some young clients will remain quiet when asked about reasons for counseling; it may be they're (a) unable to understand the question, (b) unable to formulate or articulate a response, (c) unwilling or afraid to talk about their true thoughts and feelings with their parents in the room, (d) unwilling or afraid to talk openly about their true thoughts and feelings with a stranger, or (e) unaware of, or strongly resistant to, admitting personal problems.

Resistant or nonresponsive children present therapists with a practical challenge. How can you obtain information and begin a working alliance if the client won't speak? A focus on wishes and goals, described next, can facilitate engagement and bypass resistance. Some children and teens may have a difficult time putting their distress into words. Nonverbal strategies may be helpful and are discussed later in this chapter.

Wishes and Goals

The following statement/question is designed for use with children over six years old when caretakers are present. For younger children, it's often best to meet with parents separately to focus on parenting strategies (J. Sommers-Flanagan & Sommers-Flanagan, 2011):

> I'm interested in why you're all here and so I want to ask about your goals for counseling. Usually, even though parents (look at parents) have goals in mind for counseling, I'd like to start by asking the youngest person in the room. So, Remy (look at child), you're the youngest, so you get to go first. If you came to counseling a while and, for whatever reason, your life got better, what would change? What would you like to get better in your life?

Some children/adolescents understand this question and respond directly. However, several potential problems and dynamics may occur. First, the child may not understand the question. Second, the child may be resistant, or family dynamics may cause the child to be reluctant to respond to the question. Third, the child may refocus the discussion onto the parents' problems. Fourth, the parents may begin making encouraging comments to their child, some of which may even include tips on how to respond to the counselor's question. Whatever the case, two rules follow: (1) If the child/adolescent doesn't answer the question satisfactorily, the question should be clarified in terms of wishes (see the following), and (2) for assessment purposes, you should make mental notes regarding family dynamics.

Introducing the Wish

Using wishes as an approach to assessing problem areas and obtaining treatment goals from young clients is useful because it involves using a language young people are more likely to accept (J. Sommers-Flanagan & Sommers-Flanagan, 1995). The following wish-based question is similar to the solution-focused miracle question (de Shazer et al., 2007):

> Let me put the question another way. If you had three wishes, or if you had a magic lamp, like in the movie *Aladdin*, and you could wish to change something about yourself, your parents, or your school, what would you wish for?

This question structures goal setting into three categories—self-change, family change, and school change. The child/adolescent has a chance to identify personal goals (and implied problems) in any or all of these categories. Depending on the child (and the parents' influence), there may still be resistance to identifying a wish in one or more of these areas. If there's resistance, the question can be amplified:

> You don't have any wishes to make your life better? Wow! Maybe I should wish to change places with you. How about your parents? Isn't there one little thing you might change about them if you could? (Pause for answers.) How about yourself? Isn't there anything, even something small, that you might change about yourself? (Pause again.) Now, I know there must be something about your school or your teachers or your principal you'd like to have change . . . they can't all be perfect.

Nervous, shy, or shut-down children/adolescents may continue to resist this questioning process. If so, allow them to pass:

> Would you like to pass on this question for now? I'll ask your parents next, but if you come up with wishes of your own, you can bring them up any time you want.

The purpose of this questioning procedure is to get young clients, in a somewhat playful way, to share their hopes for positive change. The interaction can provide diagnostic-related information as well. Usually, clients with disruptive behavior disorders (e.g., attention-deficit/hyperactivity disorder, oppositional defiant disorder, or conduct disorder) will report that the school and parents have problems but admit few, if any, personal problems. In contrast, clients with internalizing disorders (e.g., anxiety and depression) identify their own personal shortcomings and goals (e.g., "I'd like to be happier.").

It's not uncommon for some children to jump right into negative and accusatory statements about their parents. If this happens, stay calm and take advantage of the opportunity to model active listening skills, acceptance, and reframing. Experienced child and family therapists remind us that it may also be necessary to assist parents in responding in a healthy and receptive manner to their child (Jennifer Pereira, personal communication, August 12, 2012).

Obtaining Parental or Caretaker Goals

After young clients identify at least one way their life isn't perfect, or after they pass on the question, shift the focus to the parents. Direct interaction and attention to parent concerns is crucial to getting the full picture and to treatment compliance (e.g., if parents don't perceive their concerns as addressed they won't support therapy).

During joint meetings with parents and children, actively work to limit the number of negative comments parents make about their children. Usually, three problem statements are enough. Setting this limit protects young clients from feeling devastated or overwhelmed by their parents' criticism. If parents have additional concerns, you can invite them to write down the concerns for you to review later. Another strategy is to shift the conversation by asking parents to name a few of their child's strengths, or reframe their concerns using positive language. For instance, if a parent says "Anya is irresponsible and rude," you might say, "You are hopeful that Anya can become more responsible and kind."

In some cases, after rapport is established between therapist and child, a separate meeting with parents can be conducted (with the young client's permission) to address parent concerns more completely. You can ask young clients "Is it okay for your mom and dad to make me a list of their concerns?" If everyone has been informed of how important it is to have this information, and if an initial trusting relationship has been established, resistance to these information-gathering strategies can be minimized.

Managing Tension

During the wish-making procedure, tension may rise, especially if young clients are asked to make wishes about how their parents might change. Despite this tension, child/adolescent wishes about parents are a crucial part of the assessment process. It's reassuring to most young clients to hear the therapist say things like "I guess your parents aren't perfect either." Focusing on parental behaviors at the outset of therapy may provide a foundation for working with parents to change their behaviors during counseling. Finally, as suggested previously, parent-child interactions during this goal-setting procedure can reveal interesting family dynamics. We've observed children who seem afraid to comment on their parents' behavior (and their parents don't reassure them), and we've seen children who are vicious in their wishes for parental change. After help, encouragement, and humor, and after passing on their initial opportunity to wish for life change, if the young client is still unable or unwilling to identify a personal therapeutic goal, the therapy prognosis may not be promising.

Assessing Parents or Caretakers

Sometimes caretakers who bring children for an interview have more problems than the children. This can be a delicate situation for clinicians of all ages and experience levels.

If parents present with extreme psychological problems or display disturbing interactions with their children, you may be professionally obligated to take action. These actions can range from mild to extreme, depending on your perception of the severity of the parent-child problem. For example:

- You may be able to ignore the unhealthy patterns during the first session and wait until rapport has been established before providing feedback.
- You may need to provide some gentle feedback immediately.
- You may need to gather further assessment information to determine if the child is in immediate danger.
- You may need to inform the parent of your obligation to report child abuse and proceed to do so.

In most cases, if possible, it's best to wait for additional sessions and a stronger therapeutic relationship to give feedback and suggestions to parents. This is because parents are often naturally vulnerable and defensive (J. Sommers-Flanagan & Sommers-Flanagan, 2011). However, if unhealthy behaviors are mild and the parent seems open to feedback, you may be able to provide feedback during an initial session. Also, you may be able to assign some therapeutic homework for addressing the problematic behavior.

Based on Diana Baumrind's original work (1975, 1991), research has generally focused on four common parenting styles: authoritative parents, autocratic parents, permissive parents, and unengaged parents (Gfroerer, Kern, Curlette, White, & Jonyniene, 2011; Salem-Pickartz & Donnelly, 2007). *Authoritative* parents, referred to by Coloroso (1995) as *backbone* parents, are highly demanding and highly responsive to their children and typically raise children with healthier lifestyles, self-esteem, and self-control. Authoritative parents tend to set reasonable rules, parent democratically, and listen to their children's ideas, while maintaining final authority. In contrast, *autocratic* parents (also known as *brickwall* parents) make rules etched in stone and govern the home with a dictatorial "my way or the highway" style. *Permissive* parents (also known as *jellyfish* parents) have difficulty setting and enforcing family rules and values. Children of jellyfish parents tend to rule the house. Some parents are more *unengaged* in the parenting process, leaving their children to raise themselves. To facilitate treatment planning, it can be useful to informally assess whether a young client's parent is authoritative, autocratic, permissive, or unengaged (see J. Sommers-Flanagan & Sommers-Flanagan, 2011, for information on working directly with parents).

In addition to parenting styles, family status and the child's living situation are important factors to evaluate and address sensitively. Many children who come to therapy have lived through or are currently living through divorce, remarriage, and stepfamily life. Other children reside in group homes, residential living centers, foster/kinship care, and other alternative settings. These unique situations and settings present significant challenges to children in their day-to-day lives. These challenges must be part of your consideration as a professional in the child's life. Supervision and further reading to help you develop greater understanding for children who experience these demanding situations is essential (see Suggested Readings and Resources).

Discussing Assessment and Therapy Procedures

After initial concerns and goals have been identified, a brief review or explanation of the next steps in your time together is appropriate. Depending on the situation, you may ask parents to return to the waiting room with an assignment or questionnaire (e.g., developmental history questionnaire or problem behavior checklist). If you need to interview the parents alone, young clients can be given drawing assignments or questionnaires to complete in the waiting room. With adolescent clients it can be useful to have individual time and then have parents return for 5 to 10 minutes at the session's end to review therapy or follow-up procedures (e.g., appointment frequency, who will be attending, or a description of specific treatment approaches such as anger management or cognitive-behavioral treatment of depression).

THE BODY OF THE INTERVIEW

After obtaining child and parent perspectives on the presenting problems and therapy goals, it's time to shift to the body of the interview.

Meeting Separately With Parents or Caretakers

Parenting in the 21st century is difficult and sometimes confusing. Parents have many sources of information and may be exceptionally sophisticated, misinformed, or uninformed when it comes to obtaining professional services. Consequently, although to this point we've emphasized meeting individually with children or jointly with parents and children, for many reasons, it may be best for you to initially meet with parents separately to identify the most appropriate treatment plan.

Using Radical Acceptance

For many reasons, interviewing parents can be even more challenging than interviewing children or adolescents. Consequently, we strongly recommend using radical acceptance as a core attitude and strategy when working with parents (see also, Chapter 12).

Radical acceptance is a concept derived from person-centered theory and therapy (Rogers, 1980). It involves graciously and actively welcoming even the most absurd or offensive client statements. A generic response that embodies radical acceptance consists of something like, "I'm very glad you brought that up."

Radical acceptance is especially warranted when parents say something you personally or philosophically oppose (J. Sommers-Flanagan & Sommers-Flanagan, 2007a). These statements may be unusual, disagreeable, racist, sexist, or insensitive. Two examples of aversive parent statements and radical acceptance follow:

Parent: I believe in discipline. Parents need to be the authority in the home. And yes, that means I believe in giving my kid a swat or two if he (she) gets out of line.

Clinician: I'm very glad you brought up the topic of spanking.

Parent: I can't accept homosexuality. My son has to resist it and I won't endorse his behavior. He has to turn away from sin or leave my house.

Clinician: Many parents have views like yours but won't say them in here, and so I especially appreciate you sharing your beliefs so openly.

Radical acceptance involves actively welcoming any and all client comments (Theriault, 2012). To use this technique, you must move beyond feeling threatened, angry, or judgmental about what parents say and do and embrace whatever comes up while maintaining balance or objectivity.

Radical acceptance, as illustrated in the preceding examples, is more active, directive, and value-laden than traditional person-centered therapy approaches. The goal is to communicate commitment to openness during the assessment and treatment process. If you don't value and welcome openness, parents may hold underlying beliefs that are never spoken. Parents are unlikely to experience insight or be motivated to modify their beliefs or behaviors unless they are able to expose those beliefs to the light of personal and professional inspection.

Radical acceptance involves letting go of the need to immediately correct, counter, or teach parents a new way (J. Sommers-Flanagan & Sommers-Flanagan, 2011). Instead, the therapist invests in a process that allows unhealthy beliefs to be accepted and consequently shrink, melt, crumble, or deconstruct. For example, parents who use corporal punishment may feel a strong need to articulate their position at the outset of therapy. After proclaiming their position and having their rights to have that position affirmed, they may be able to also admit they don't enjoy spanking, and they may consider alternatives to punishment. Similarly, parents who won't accept their teenager's homosexuality may need to have painful feelings affirmed in order to move beyond those feelings and recover other (more constructive) feelings of love and affection.

Linehan (2000) and Hayes (2002) have articulated this paradox and integrated it into their specific therapeutic approaches (i.e., dialectal behavior therapy and acceptance and commitment therapy). These approaches emphasize that patient change or progress is stimulated when the patient's emotional condition is completely embraced or accepted. In essence, the therapist is saying (and believing), "I accept you as you are, and I am helping you to change."

Assessing Family Contingencies

Many parents inadvertently pay excessive attention to their children's negative or undesirable behaviors and far too little attention to positive or desirable behaviors. For example, many caretakers scold or yell at their children immediately following misbehavior and ignore positive behaviors. From a behavioral perspective, this pattern generally constitutes positive reinforcement of negative behaviors and extinction of positive behaviors (Kazdin, 2008).

Regardless of theoretical orientation, all clinicians working with children and families should assess family contingency patterns. There are two straightforward ways to obtain this contingency-related assessment data. Specifically, you can (a) observe for positive and/or dysfunctional reinforcement patterns during the caretaker-child session and/or (b) separate caretaker and child and then inquire directly about "what happens next" during family conflicts.

Some parents will hold negative views about positive reinforcement, equating it to bribery. If parents object to positive reinforcement (or perhaps before they object), it can be explained that *bribery* is defined as "paying someone in advance to do something illegal" and that research shows positive reinforcement to be a more efficient behavior modifier than punishment (McCart, Priester, Davies, & Azen, 2006); this can be emphasized by inquiring about positive reinforcements parents receive in their daily lives. In addition, encouraging parents to spend time with their children (instead of material items) can help parents use one of the most powerful positive reinforcements of all.

User-Friendly Assessment and Information-Gathering Strategies

Formal assessment or evaluation procedures are used to obtain information about client functioning to help with diagnosis and treatment planning (Weisz, 2004). Formal assessment approaches include behavioral checklists, intellectual assessment, and personality inventories (e.g., the Child Behavior Checklist; Wechsler intelligence scales; Minnesota Multiphasic Personality Inventory). While many mental health professionals use these traditional assessment procedures, many don't. Those who don't use traditional assessments may view it as invalid or as unhelpful in the therapy process (Schneider & Krug, 2010).

Young clients often express criticism and/or sarcasm when asked to participate in traditional assessment (e.g., "This test totally sucks."). They may resist completing the instruments fully and thoughtfully. Fortunately, there are alternatives to using formal assessment procedures for obtaining information. The following procedures, sometimes referred to as qualitative or informal assessments, can help therapists gather information, while at the same time, capturing client interest and cooperation. Because these techniques can facilitate rapport and trust, they usually have a positive effect on cooperation with and validity of more standardized assessments (Oetzel & Scherer, 2003). These assessment procedures aren't a replacement for formal assessments, rather they're viewed as complementary or as appropriate in situations in which formal assessment isn't necessary.

What's Good (Bad) About You?

A relationship-building assessment procedure that provides a rich interpersonal interaction between young clients and counselors is the "What's good about you?" question-and-answer game (J. Sommers-Flanagan & Sommers-Flanagan, 2007b). The procedure provides useful information regarding child/adolescent self-esteem. Initially, it's introduced as a game with specific rules:

> I want to play a game with you. Here's how it goes. I'm going to ask you the same question 10 times. The only rule is that you can't use the same answer twice. So, I'll ask you the same question 10 times, but you have to give me 10 different answers.

Clinicians then ask, "What's good about you?" (while writing a list of the client's responses). Each client answer is responded to with "Thank you" and a smile. If the client responds with "I don't know," the response is simply written down the first time it's used; if "I don't know" (or any response) is used a second time, the therapist gently provides a reminder that answers can be used only one time.

The "What's good about you?" game provides insights into client self-perceptions and self-esteem. Some youth have difficulty stating a talent, skill, or positive attribute. They may identify possessions, such as "I have a nice bike" or "I have some good friends" instead of taking personal ownership of an attribute: "I am a good bike rider" or "My friendly personality helps me make friends." They also may describe a role (e.g., "I'm a good son.") rather than specific behaviors that make them good at the particular role (e.g., "I'm thoughtful with my parents and so I'm a good son."). The ability to articulate positive personal attributes implies healthy self-esteem.

Interpersonal assessment data also can be obtained through the "What's good about you?" procedure. We've had assertive or aggressive children request or insist that they be allowed to ask us the "What's good about you?" questions. We always comply with these requests as it provides a modeling opportunity and the clients with an empowerment experience. Additionally, the manner in which young clients respond to this interpersonal request can be revealing. Some youth will ridicule or mock the procedure; most other children and adolescents cooperate and seem to enjoy the process.

An optional follow-up to the "What's good about you?" procedure is the "What's bad about you?" query. You could also use "What do you not like so well about yourself?" or "What are some challenging things about you?" Young clients frequently are quicker at coming up with negative attributes than they are at coming up with positive attributes. In addition, sometimes they identify as negative some of the same traits that were included on their positive attribute list. Usually we ask negative questions only five times.

When using "What's good about you?" and "What would you change about you?" it can be useful to observe how clients describe positive and negative traits.

For example, adolescents frequently use qualifiers when describing their positive traits (e.g., "I'm a good basketball player, sometimes."). When describing negative traits, adolescents may quote someone else (e.g., an adult authority figure), and they may make an excessively strong statement (e.g., "My teachers say that I'm *never* able to pay attention in school.").

Using Projective Drawings

Projective assessment techniques, including the Draw-A-Person, Kinetic Family Drawing, House-Tree-Person and other creative drawing techniques, can be excellent strategies for simultaneously obtaining information and building rapport. Projective assessments are justifiably criticized as unreliable and not good behavioral predictors (Wood, Nezworski, Lilienfeld, & Garbm, 2008); however, their utility in helping young clients open up and express themselves is high.

Projective drawings are fun, interesting, and because of how they bubble right out of a child's consciousness they can be so compelling that therapists can jump to inappropriate conclusions about the meaning of children's drawings. For example, when a child introduces sexuality into a drawing, it's all too easy for therapists to quickly and sometimes inappropriately conclude that sexual abuse has occurred. Instead, projective drawings should be used to motivate conversation, generate hypotheses, and build rapport. Although drawings can be used to initiate a conversation about sex and sexuality, they shouldn't be used to conclude that child sexual abuse has occurred.

Projective drawings may help initiate conversations about cultural issues. Children will often include objects with personal and cultural meaning in their drawings.

General Considerations for the Body of the Interview

Limit setting can be a challenge for many clinicians—especially clinicians who naturally interact playfully with children. For one of us, getting poked in the eye during an initial interview with a rather active 10-year-old boy, served as inspiration for learning to gently, firmly, and empathically set limits with children. We encourage you to think in advance about the boundaries or limits you want in your work with children. Similarly, you should think ahead about the positive and acceptable behaviors that children are permitted to engage in while in your office. The following guidelines may help you develop comfortable rules and freedoms when working with children:

- Plan ahead by thinking through what behaviors are acceptable and unacceptable in your office.
- Have simple basic ground rules you state in advance (e.g., "During our play time you can play with any of these toys, but my two main rules are 'No breaking toys' and 'No throwing toys'"). For every "no," be sure to have something positive to offer.
- Fewer rules will likely encourage free expression.
- Be prepared for a variety of limit-testing; we've had young clients (a) leave the room, (b) climb out a window, (c) grab items off a desk, (d) call and text on their cell phone, (e) spit, (f) fall asleep, (g) swear for 30 minutes, (h) quickly light a cigarette and blow smoke.

Rather than having a multitude of stated rules covering every possibility (which would be impossible), it's better to prepare yourself to set firm limits as needed. Some theoretical orientations prefer to leave all rules unstated; others suggest the statement of one or two basic rules (Behr, 2003). For example:

Carlos, you're welcome to play with toys in my office (or things from the toy closet). We don't have too many rules about playing here, but it's important that you know my basic rules: It's not okay to break things or hurt yourself or anyone else with the toys or art supplies.

Cleaning up and putting things away also provides assessment information. Depending on your theoretical orientation, it may be important to keep time boundaries that include cleanup time before closing the interview. Doing so provides information about how the child interacts when play is ending. An abrupt shift in attitude toward the toys or game may occur. Emotions directed toward you or the toys may be an important signal about how the child handles transitions. Does the child ignore you or refuse to cooperate? Does he or she scurry around, cleaning frantically to impress you? Those few cleanup minutes at the session's end can be very revealing. To give young clients the best possible chance to handle clean up and the ending of the session, you should make your expectations clear and provide periodic "alerts" about when the session will be ending:

Hey Jameel, we've got 10 minutes left today and so in 5 minutes we'll start cleaning up together.

The following section describes supplies helpful in working with children; *Putting It in Practice* 13.2 lists these supplies and suggests a group art assignment.

PUTTING IT IN PRACTICE 13.2

Art Activities: Supplies and Practice

Art therapy is a specialized profession in which practitioners obtain master's- level training. However, using art in working with young people doesn't require a degree in art therapy and can be rewarding for both you and your client. Most materials are simple and inexpensive. Before integrating advanced materials into your work (e.g., acrylic paints) you should be familiar and comfortable with their use. If you're interested in using art to stimulate conversation and explore young clients' issues, consider the following items and see if you can convince your graduate faculty or fellow graduate students to pool resources and go shopping.

Drawing pencils (or charcoal pencils)
Colored pencils
Fat or skinny (and washable) markers and crayons
Colored plasticine clay
A big stack of nice white paper or colored construction paper
A roll of newsprint paper

A big box of old magazines
A few aprons
Colored chalk
Oil pastels
Watercolor paint sets
A few basic color tubes of acrylic paint
Some bottles of tempera paint
Egg cartons for paint mixing
Paintbrushes
Good-quality paper towels
Rags
Chocolate (optional)

Right before finals is an excellent time for an experiential art party. Get a group together and engage in expressive art. Pair up and reflect on the process. Remember: be open, nondirective, and nonjudgmental—with yourself and with your partners. Ask indirect or open questions like "Tell me about your work" or "How did it feel to do this?" or "What do you notice about your work?"

Treat each art piece respectfully. Notice the medium you chose. Finger-painting is the "loosest"; colored pencils are one of the more controlled choices. In suggesting art as a modality to your client, you'll be more effective, insightful, relaxed, and convincing if you've recently used art yourself.

Arts and Crafts

Drawing is a favorite activity of many children and some adults (especially in the form of doodling through long boring meetings). All that's necessary are a few sharp pencils with good erasers, paper, and a nice flat surface. Crayons, washable markers, and pastels can bring out color. In addition to the structured projective drawing procedures discussed previously, abstract and spontaneous assignments, such as "Draw me a quick sketch of how you feel about math" can be informative.

You might wonder what you should do while your client is drawing. The goal is to give your client appropriate amounts of time, space, and tracking—and to do so intentionally. Several reasonable options may work for you:

- Doodle in a way that's neither attention seeking or distracting.
- Sit patiently, unobtrusively glancing at the child on occasion and commenting in ways consistent with your purpose (e.g., encouragement—"I can see you're working hard at that drawing" or exploration—"I wonder what you're drawing now?").
- Draw something yourself (but if you choose this option you should do so with purpose and try not to move the focus from the child to yourself; sometimes John likes to draw a picture of the child drawing the picture and then share what he observed while the child was drawing).
- Avoid hovering too much (this depends on the child and his/her comfort with you and the task).

Although children and adolescents sometimes will spontaneously explain their drawing choices, gentle curious questioning can help (e.g., "What's that on the person's head?" or "Tell me about your picture.").

Play-Doh is a familiar commodity in child therapist offices. It provides a tactile, expressive modality and is comfortable for most children. Having a cleanable surface is essential. If your office is carpeted, a plastic tablecloth can solve mess-management problems. Play-Doh accoutrements include all molds and machines, but we prefer the projective process of letting children create things freeform.

Clay (plasticine) is similar to Play-Doh but dries out less quickly and requires more working before becoming malleable. Clays that require firing are more difficult to use in controlled, meaningful ways unless the professional is familiar with this medium.

Painting is a common expressive modality used in art therapy (Moon, 2010). Although messier and harder to control than drawing, paints can elicit more emotion. Given the opportunity to work with tempera or watercolor paints, some children shift from nonresponsive and uninvolved to happy, verbal, and very connected to the process.

Collage building (using pictures or words) has become a favorite therapeutic use for old or unwanted magazines. Glue (or tape), scissors, magazines or picture calendars, and posterboard are the essential ingredients. You can ask clients to select pictures or phrases that illustrate different issues or emotions: life events, internal states, family troubles, school worries, and so on. Clients can attach their selections in any way they wish, sometimes creating an expression that would have been impossible to achieve with words.

CASE EXAMPLE

Cary was a 12-year-old intellectually gifted boy struggling with a father who believed deeply in control and a mother with depressive symptoms. Cary's mother was 55 and his father was 61. His elderly grandparents on his mother's side lived in the family home. Both grandparents were frail and needed extra care, which was provided by Cary's mother. Cary was referred for therapy by his school counselor because his grades had slipped significantly, he refused to engage in his usual social activities, and he made self-destructive comments in class. The therapist invited Cary to build a collage about his family life. Until that point, Cary had, with his large, impressive vocabulary, indicated acceptance of his grandparents' needs and pride in his mother for caring for them. However, the collage was filled with pictures of young parents with little children and peppered with happy, upbeat words from advertisements. As the therapist commented on the contents, Cary burst into tears and shared his longing for a "normal" family with young parents and happy, healthy grandparents. Although the therapist couldn't change Cary's family situation, the collage project provided assessment information that helped formulate a treatment plan to help Cary articulate his grief and move forward with his personal development.

Generally, wetter art modalities will produce more emotionality and can stimulate a loss of self-control in some children. An art therapist colleague warns that finger-painting may produce emotional looseness in young clients—a looseness that can result in an in-session loss of bowel or bladder control! (Kim Brown Campbell, personal communication, November 3, 2007).

Nondirective, Interactive, and Directive Play Options

For children, play is the means through which they work out pain, achieve mastery, explore new terrain, and take new risks. It's also a means through which they can distance themselves from things too difficult to deal with directly.

Therapists vary greatly in their use of play in working with children. Some model themselves after Virginia Axline, who advocated a nondirective, minimally interactive play therapy format, beautifully described in the book *Dibs: In Search of Self* (Axline, 1964). Others use play and storytelling to enhance the therapeutic relationship and explore children's issues (J. Sommers-Flanagan & Sommers-Flanagan, 2007b). Still others find more direct ways to use play and playful interactions to teach empathy and adaptive behaviors (Kottman, 2011).

Not all therapists have access to a full set of play items. Given this limitation, it's helpful to know that play therapy experts select toys to represent the following categories:

- Family/nurturing
- Scary
- Aggressive
- Expressive
- Real life
- Pretend/fantasy (Ray, 2011)

The following toy and supply list of items commonly used in child interviewing and therapy can be used to facilitate playful child-therapist interactions.

Action figures, dolls, and puppets are fabulous instruments for encouraging and enhancing personal expression. There are many media- and culturally based action figures and dolls. Ken and Barbie, Sesame Street characters, and generic puppets can stimulate rich interactions. Superhero figures can lead to conversations about fears, strengths, and longed-for superpowers. Given the strong presence and influence of military within American culture, regardless of your political leanings, it's useful to have a collection of a few "gray and green figures" to stimulate interactions and emotions that may be associated with war, conflict, or parental military involvement.

Sand trays come in all sizes and shapes. Working with a sand tray is a specialized skill that can become a central treatment modality (Russo, Vernam, & Wolbert, 2006). However, it can also be used simply for play or "fiddling around" while talking. Sand is a tantalizingly movable medium that many children can't resist. A good, sturdy lid and adequate floor covering is essential. You can collect items to play with, such as tractors, trucks, action figures, stones, and so on.

Stuffed animals offer a comforting presence in a clinical office. Sometimes, child-oriented mental health professionals collect a set of stuffed animals for display and potential interaction. Children may create relationships among the animals. Having a family of stuffed animals can help young clients to act out family dynamics.

Dress-up clothes are less common than most categories in this list, but are easy to obtain. A small suitcase of dress-up clothes can facilitate a breakthrough with an otherwise unresponsive child. Outfits that express themes such as cowpoke, firefighter, artist, plumber, and ballerina can be easily assembled. The suitcase itself can also elicit play themes. Young children can be powerfully drawn toward dress-up activities.

Construction sets vary in size, numbers of parts, and age-appropriateness. Legos, Lincoln Logs, and Tinker Toys are all helpful in engaging young clients in therapeutic activities. They shouldn't be used with small children and you might want to hide them if you're working with children who have impulse control problems or violence histories. They can easily be used as real or imagined weapons.

Special props can be especially useful with adolescent clients. For example, Rubix cubes, magic 8 balls, puzzles, stress balls or anything they can manipulate while talking is fair game.

Aggression items should be carefully considered. Your own values, professional training, agency policies, and general background will dictate your comfort level with toy guns, knives, swords, and other play weapons. They allow for expression of aggressive urges. Some therapists worry that they're too provocative and promote violent expression; others worry that having them in an office suggests an approval of violence. These are issues for discussion in classes and with supervisors and colleagues as you determine which play items you're comfortable having in your office. The question is: "How can these items be used for assessment or therapeutically?"

Dollhouses or other homelike environments are classic props for allowing children to reenact life dramas and traumas. The dollhouse is a time-honored play therapy tool. Many toy companies produce schoolhouses, gas stations, playgrounds, city blocks, and other plastic-molded environments complete with figures, vehicles, pets, furnishings, miniature toys, and so on. Children can use these props and settings to build communities of friends, enemies, and families. Themes emerging in play can provide you with insights about challenges and situations your client is facing in various environments outside counseling.

Anatomically correct dolls are both common and can be controversial. For a short time, child abuse investigators were urged to use anatomically accurate dolls with young children. If children had the dolls interact sexually, this was interpreted to indicate likely sexual exposure. Controversy quickly arose regarding the accuracy of such interpretations (Dickinson, Poole, & Bruck, 2005; Faller, 2005; Hungerford, 2005). Although anatomically accurate dolls still serve useful functions, it's *essential* that users seek adequate training and supervision before using them (see also, *Putting it in Practice* 13.3).

Reviewing this information about investigational interviews with children (*Putting it in Practice* 13.3) reminds us of how important it is to remain sensitive and knowledgeable about the particular developmental abilities and limitations associated with interviewing children. It also reminds us of how competence in this specific area is impossible without advanced training.

PUTTING IT IN PRACTICE 13.3

Questions and Investigative Interviews With Children

It should come as no surprise to find that children, even as young as 3 years old, can be reliable and valid reporters of their own personal experiences. However, there are a number of challenges and strategies that should be considered when interviewing children about personal—and sometimes traumatic—experiences.

Obtaining reliable and valid information from children via a clinical investigative interview is a particular professional activity that requires substantial advanced education, training, and supervision. Given that caveat, we provide the following information as a general guide to gathering information from children and as a means of facilitating your interest in obtaining advanced training in this fascinating area. The following points provide a few highlights of professional investigative interviewing practice and research.

A colleague of ours has elegantly articulated the main challenge of gathering information from children. He said, "The door to children's feelings and memories locks from the inside. All we can do, as parents or professionals, is to knock gently and respectfully and hope children trust us enough to unlock their emotional doors and allow us access."

Children have developmental limitations in terms of how they respond to direct questioning during clinical or investigative interviews. For example, they tend to respond very briefly to open-ended questions.

Young children up to about age 9 will comply with adults and provide a response to a query, even when they have virtually no understanding of the question asked of them. Unless precautions are taken, an interviewer may inadvertently coerce young clients into responding to questions that they don't even understand.

As Salmon (2006) noted, "[P]arents tend to underestimate their child's distress about painful or traumatic experiences, particularly when they have participated in the episodes that caused the child's distress" (p. 54). This suggests that parents may not be valid reporters about the intensity of their children's distress.

Toys and dolls may be especially helpful in putting children at ease in a clinical interview. Toys and dolls also may help children re-enact specific traumatic events. However, whether toys and dolls are helpful or distracting in facilitating accurate disclosures depends on whether the individual interviewer uses these items in an evidence-based manner (Chang, Ritter, & Hays, 2005; Salmon, 2006; Vig, 2007).

Open-ended prompts ("tell me about") and cued invitations ("You said he hurt you; tell me about the hurting") tend to be the most effective approaches to gathering accurate information from children. Additionally, Salmon noted: "[P]osing these kinds of questions in relation to neutral events (e.g., a school activity) at the beginning of the interview can facilitate rapport while providing the child with practice in retrieving and reporting her or his experiences and shaping accurate expectations of what is to come" (p. 55).

A final comment about collecting your toys: Be aware that you can inadvertently collect toys that are culturally or socioeconomically narrow. A good general guideline is to collect toys and dolls that aren't overly expensive, that have different racial features, and are sturdy and inviting.

Fantasy and Games

This therapeutic category includes activities that include verbal interaction. They can be used in the body of an interview for both assessment and therapeutic purposes.

Storytelling procedures have captivated and influenced children for centuries. Inviting a client to listen to a story, to make one up, or to share the process back and forth can be entertaining and revealing (Gardner, 1993). There are many ways to use stories and storytelling activities (BigFoot & Dunlap, 2006; Cook, Taylor, & Silverman, 2004). Very few materials are needed, but an active imagination helps. It also may help to have a few memorized favorite stories (see *Putting It in Practice* 13.4).

Acting or miming can be a highly projective activity. Often, children love to make up a play and assign the acting parts. This activity can uncover important themes in children's lives. Having the child write a script and act it out can be revealing to both therapist and child—especially as the child assumes the roles of the various characters in the play.

PUTTING IT IN PRACTICE 13.4

Storytelling

Some people believe that good storytellers are born, not made. We beg to differ. For this activity, you need one or more partners and access to the creative side of your personality.

Sit with a fellow student or more and start telling a story. You can tell any story you want. The only rules are that the story should have a beginning, middle, and ending. It also helps if the story includes characters (e.g., people, Martians, ants) that can have thoughts and feelings. The story can be about you, about animals, about spaceships, about anything. Simply start telling the story. Then stop telling it, while it's still incomplete, after about 30 to 60 seconds. At that point, another person takes over telling the same story, taking it in any direction desired. After about 30 to 60 seconds, switch storytelling authors again. The goals are to generate a story together with your partner or partners and further develop your storytelling skills and talents. At the end of the story, you may provide one another with gentle interpretive statements (e.g., "I noticed Howard always brought conflict or tension back into the story, but Joyce seemed to always get everything resolved so that all the characters were feeling good again."). However, be sure to request permission before interpreting the meaning of anyone else's storyline.

This activity will help prepare you for creative storytelling activities with young clients. You may also want to look at various storytelling resources (i.e., Gardner's, 1971, *Mutual Storytelling Technique*; Chapter 5 of our *Tough Kids, Cool Counseling*; see Suggested Readings and Resources).

Familiar child games such as Jenga, Connect Four, and Candy Land, or card games such as Crazy Eights and Uno, can help break the ice and establish relationships with children. For adolescents, games like checkers, chess, and backgammon can be either used therapeutically, or used for something to do together while talking about therapy issues. With all these games, assessment and therapy should be the focus (e.g., observing the young client's handling of setup, turn-taking, rule obedience, disappointing events, strategy, and winning or losing).

Therapeutic games are available through a number of companies that serve mental health professionals' needs. They vary in format, themes covered, appeal, and sophistication (Bellinson, 2002). It's worth obtaining a catalogue and checking your options, depending on the type of interviewing work you intend to do (see Suggested Readings and Resources).

Sometimes, children spontaneously generate an idea for a game. The level at which you choose to participate (if you participate at all) is a decision worth forethought. For example, one 7-year-old girl, referred because of social-skill problems, decided it would be fun to play a form of hide and seek with a stuffed animal, a very fuzzy raccoon. Her inexperienced therapist agreed and closed his eyes. The child climbed up the back of the couch and placed the animal directly on the filament of a halogen lamp. The odor of burning polyester provided an excellent clue for helping the student therapist locate the singed raccoon.

Creative ways and means to work effectively with children are abundant in the treatment literature (Hurn, 2006; Springer & Misurell, 2012). It's important to assess the needs, skills, and developmental level of the given child, the ramifications of the identified problem areas, your setting and its limitations, and your own exposure and comfort levels with the various tools and strategies listed in this section.

THE CLOSING

Children experience time differently than adults. In fact, even the linear, non-reversible quality of time isn't fully grasped by young children (Henderson & Thompson, 2011). Therefore, telling a child there are 10 minutes left during a session may be less helpful than saying something more concrete, such as:

> We just have a few more minutes left together today. Probably enough time to read one more page (color one more picture, tell one more short story), and then I'll summarize what we've talked about and see if I remember everything. Then we'll make a plan for next week, okay?

As with adult interviews, you'll probably always wish you could gather more information than you were able to get in 50 minutes. Unfortunately, you need to stop playing or gathering information and begin to wind down activities to ensure a smooth, unhurried closing with your child client.

Reassuring and Supporting Young Clients

Young people need support in their efforts to relate to you, so be sure to offer support throughout the interview. Especially during the closing, provide reassuring, supportive feedback. Make comments such as:

- You did some neat things with that Lego set.
- I know you told me this is your first time in counseling, but you know what? You're pretty good at it.
- I appreciate all that you told me about your family and your teachers and you.
- Thanks for being so open and sharing so much with me.

Because most child clients don't come to therapy on their own, it's all the more important to let them know you appreciate the risks they've taken. Some young clients, especially challenging adolescents, may have behaved rudely or defensively. You might experience countertransference impulses such as urges to withdraw, reprimand, or even punish the child (Willock, 1986; 1987). It's helpful to note the difficulty of being "dragged off to counseling" in an empathic comment and notice the client seemed reluctant about being open. However, as with adults, expressing disappointment toward young clients who are resistant, defensive, or quiet is inappropriate; such reactions make it less likely they'll seek professional help again in the future. Instead, if your client is defensive, try to remain optimistic:

> I know it wasn't your idea to come in and talk with me today, and I don't blame you for being upset about it and not wanting to talk with me. We might be able to find some ways to make this less of a pain. In fact, I might even know some ways that would make this whole thing go by pretty fast and then you'd be all done with counseling.

(For more information on termination strategies with difficult young clients, see "Termination as Motivation," in J. Sommers-Flanagan & Sommers-Flanagan, 2007b.)

Summarizing, Clarifying, and Engaging

The most important closing tasks with young people are: (a) clearly summarizing your understanding of the problem areas; (b) making connections between the problems and possible counseling interventions (assuming you see such connections); (c) reminding the client about ways caretakers will or will not be involved; and (d) as possible, seeking some kind of positive involvement or engagement with the child. Two case examples follow. The first is an example of a 7-year-old struggling with nightmares. The second is an adolescent who repeatedly was caught stealing from classmates.

CASE EXAMPLE 1: CLOSING

Beth, our time is almost up. You've helped me understand what it's like for you trying to sleep at night. You get pretty frightened. Then everybody gets mad at you for not staying in bed. I think there are some things we can do to help you, but it'll mean coming back to talk some more...I hope that's okay with you. It also might mean having your mom and dad and big brother come in so we can all talk about ways to help. But you'll be here with me when I do that, and you and I will make a plan first. I think it would be good for us to meet again next week. Is that okay with you? We might draw some more pictures, and I have a story I want to read to you. Do you have any questions before you go?

CASE EXAMPLE 2: CLOSING

Tommy, we've got a few minutes left together. I know this hasn't exactly been fun, but hey, at least it was something different. People are pretty upset with you for taking stuff—and even though you say you're just borrowing stuff, it's getting you in more trouble than it might be worth. I really appreciate the time you've taken to tell me what you think about all this and to answer my questions. I think we could work together to get things to chill out a little in your life. It wouldn't take too long because you're pretty smart, but at least a few more sessions to work together. I doubt if we need to involve your mom much, unless you get in more trouble. It can be just some planning and thinking between the two of us. I bet we could come up with some ideas that will help. But it will mean you and me talking. Do you think you can stand coming back and talking with me a few more times?

Empowering Young Clients and Soliciting Feedback

Because young people don't have final authority over many aspects of their lives, they usually respond well to being given choices and opportunities to ask questions. Therefore, be sure to leave time to shift the focus and allow time for questions and for reflecting on the process of being together with you:

- You know, I've asked lots of questions. Do you have any questions?
- Has our time together been like you thought it would be?
- Is there anything about this meeting we've had that's bothering you?
- Is there anything you want to say that I should have asked about?
- I wonder if you felt there was anything I could have done in this interview that would have helped you feel more comfortable (or helped you talk more freely)?

These queries help give the young client a sense of power and control and, as with adult interviews, asking for feedback is a collaborative and evidence-based strategy (Lambert & Shimokawa, 2011). Although, it's important to maintain control toward the end of an interview, it's also important to (carefully) share a small portion of that control with the child.

Tying Up Loose Ends

With young people, reconnecting with parent or guardian is an essential piece of closure. Children aren't able to arrange the details necessary to get themselves back to another session or independently follow through on recommendations resulting from the interview. Therefore, therapists must clear these things with the caretaker, preferably with the child present. Other related matters, such as fee payment and scheduling, can be addressed as well.

TERMINATION

The same general principles are true for children as for adults regarding termination. It may be helpful for you to review the termination section in Chapter 6 as you prepare for a child interview. The main differences to anticipate are a matter of degree rather than substance. Children can be more overt and extreme in their termination-related behaviors. An adult may *wish* to hug you but refrain, whereas a child may snuggle right up for a hug. An adult may fantasize telling you to "F—off" toward the end of the interview, but an adolescent might just say it. Adults may feel a bit sad; children may burst into tears. Adults may express disappointment; children may give you an ugly look and complain loudly that their time is up or they may rush out early. You need to stay in your role of observer, empathizer, and gentle limit-setter. Sometimes, children feel things, reflect things, and enact things quite acutely and dramatically. It can become part of the goodbye process.

SUMMARY

In many ways, interviewing children is qualitatively different from interviewing adults. This chapter identifies basic differences between children and adults and discusses ways to professionally address these differences. In the introduction phase of the interview, the role of the child's caretaker must be considered and clarified. However, it's imperative for the therapist to pay attention to children, address them directly, and help them to understand the upcoming interview.

Some situations will call for you to interview parents or caretakers separately before or after meeting with a child. This practice is fine as long as the therapist organizes the manner in which the interview will proceed and communicates this effectively. This requires a clear and comprehensive written informed consent form. With young clients, there are special issues in confidentiality that must be addressed. The child is a legal minor, and therefore, parents and guardians have certain rights to therapy information.

During the opening phase, if young clients are unable or unwilling to identify personal goals for therapy, we advocate using a procedure called *wishes and goals* to establish a positive tone, allow the child to engage in the process, and give parents a sense of being heard as well.

Using nonverbal and verbal interaction strategies can help with the process of obtaining assessment information during the body of a child interview. These may include arts and crafts, nondirective or directive play, and fantasy or games. In addition, specific user-friendly assessment and information-gathering strategies should be used to simultaneously obtain information and develop rapport. When formal assessment instruments are used with young clients, their use should be explained to the client and assessment feedback should be provided.

Closing and termination procedures with children are similar to processes with adults, but they become more complicated for several reasons: There are more players to consider, more time demands to balance, and children may express their reactions to their interview experiences more overtly or bluntly than adults.

SUGGESTED READINGS AND RESOURCES

Castro-Blanco, D., & Karver, M. S. (2010). *Elusive alliance: Treatment engagement strategies with high-risk adolescents*. Washington, DC: American Psychological Association.

This book includes many ideas for how to connect and work effectively with teenagers who can be very difficult.

Dugger, S. M., & Carlson, L. (Eds.). (2007). *Critical incidents in counseling children*. Alexandria, VA: American Counseling Association.

This book offers clinical commentary on dozens of mental health and school-based child counseling scenarios.

Hersen, M., & Thomas, J. C. (2007). *Handbook of clinical interviewing with children*. Thousand Oaks, CA: Sage.

This thorough handbook includes a wide range of topics associated with interviewing children, including diverse topics such as mental status examinations and fire setting.

Kottman, T. (2011). *Play therapy: Basics and beyond*. Alexandria, VA: American Counseling Association.

Kottman describes how counselors can use toys, art supplies, games, and other play media to communicate with children on their developmental level. She also focuses on the power of play to address issues from communication to catharsis and the skills clinicians need to use play effectively.

Murphy, J. (2008). *Solution-focused counseling with middle and high school students* (2nd ed.). Alexandria, VA: American Counseling Association.

There are many solution-focused books on counseling youth, and we believe this one is far and away the best. Murphy explains the principles of solution-focused counseling with youth very well, but what makes his book stand out is that he clearly understands young people and is able to describe ways of being empathic with them that are consistent with solution-focused principles. Too many other solution-focused books are, more or less, disrespectful of real youth issues. Not so with Murphy's excellent work.

Richardson, B. (2001). *Working with challenging youth: Lessons learned along the way*. Philadelphia, PA: Brunner-Routledge.

Richardson offers more than 50 lessons he has learned about providing counseling to difficult or challenging youth. Not only does it offer numerous practical ideas about counseling youth, but also this book is well organized and written in a style that makes for pleasant reading. Richardson is also an excellent storyteller who "gets" youth and their family systems.

Sommers-Flanagan, R., Elander, C. D., & Sommers-Flanagan, J. (2000). *Don't divorce us!: Kids' advice to divorcing parents*. Alexandria, VA: American Counseling Association.

This book is based on interviews and surveys of individuals, both children and adults, who have experienced divorce firsthand. The book emphasizes the children's perspective and covers issues ranging from predivorce, parent-parent conflict during and after divorce, and new families.

Sommers-Flanagan, J., & Sommers-Flanagan, R. (2007). *Tough kids, cool counseling: User-friendly approaches with challenging youth* (2nd ed.). Alexandria, VA: American Counseling Association.

This book's positive qualities include the fact that it's an easy read and has a distinctly applied focus. It includes many techniques and strategies, all of which are seen as having a goal of establishing and deepening the therapy relationship. The chapters on suicide and medication issues are especially practical and relevant.

Sommers-Flanagan, J., & Sommers-Flanagan, R. (2011). *How to listen so parents will talk and talk so parents will listen*. Hoboken, NJ: Wiley.

In this book, we focus on professional knowledge and skills needed to work effectively with parents. Because parents are a special population, we recommend ongoing education, supervision, and training for clinicians who want to develop skills to work with this challenging and rewarding population.

Principles and Tips for Interviewing Couples and Families

CHAPTER OBJECTIVES

Working with couples and families is one of the most exciting and intimidating situations a mental health professional can face. It isn't something everyone wants to do, but it can be very rewarding work. Although reading this brief chapter doesn't provide you with adequate information and training for working competently with couples and families, it provides an important overview.

After reading this chapter, you will understand:

- Some ironies of working with couples and families, including that clinicians have less time to work with more clients.
- How the terms *couple* and *family* are typically defined.
- How to apply the interviewing stages and tasks to interviewing couples and families.
- Practical issues in identifying, managing, and modifying conflict (and setting limits) in couple and family interviews.
- When (and if) shifting from individual to couple or family therapy is appropriate or ethical.
- Basic family therapy concepts, such as identification, projection, joining, and avoiding.

At this point in this text we should all be in agreement: Clinical interviewing with one individual is a challenging task. Now, imagine interviewing two or more clients—at the same time!

Instead of assessing and addressing one client's problem areas, motivations, and expectations, when interviewing couples, you have two people *and* their relationship in the room with you. All the diverse problems, motivations, and expectations of two different individuals attempting to maintain a relationship and to love each other must be addressed. In addition, when working with families, clinicians dive into the sometimes-stormy seas of family motivations, expectations, and relationships. Generally, as the number of clients increase, so does the complexity of therapeutic assessment and treatment.

Although this chapter reviews basic principles and provides practical tips for interviewing couples and families, our coverage merely scratches the surface and reflects our own biases and orientations. Couples and families are powerful systems with both explicit and hidden emotional coalitions and conflicts. As professionals, we must respect these systems and their power. Sometimes, when we teach about couple and family therapy, we tell our students to *be afraid, be very afraid*. We say this not to scare students away from the incredibly gratifying profession of couple and family counseling, but to help them understand that this isn't simple work. Couples and families can overwhelm an inadequately trained clinician. Consequently, consider this chapter, more than any other, a small sampling of an exciting feast—one that requires additional education, training, and supervision for proper consumption.

> All happy families resemble one another; every unhappy family is unhappy in its own-way.
>
> —Leo Tolstoy, *Anna Karenina* (2003)

> The fact that something is difficult must be one more reason to do it. To love is also good, for love is difficult. For one human being to love another is perhaps the most difficult task of all, the epitome, the ultimate test. It is that striving for which all other striving is merely preparation.
>
> —Rainer Maria Rilke, *Letters to a Young Poet* (1992)

SOME IRONIES OF INTERVIEWING COUPLES AND FAMILIES

Working with couples and families involves several ironic truths.

More Clients, Less Time

Despite the fact that interviewing couples and families is more complex than interviewing individuals, most therapists must work faster with couples and families than they do with individuals. This is because, on average, couples and families don't stay in counseling as long as individuals (Russell Crane & Payne, 2011). There are several possible reasons for this shorter length of treatment.

- Couples and families usually come to counseling with different motivation levels, expectations, and agendas among the members. Some family members, or half the couple, may be reluctant to step into a professional's office. This motivational variability may lead to premature termination (Gold & Morris, 2003; Schwartz, 2011).
- Insurance companies and managed-care organizations don't always reimburse for couple or family therapy (Coffey, Olson, & Sessions, 2001). This reduces the time period families or couples can afford therapy.

- There may be cultural barriers to seeking couple or family therapy. For example, LGBTQ couples and families will be reluctant to enter or stay in therapy unless it is clear that the professional is practicing from a multiculturally sensitive and/or gay-friendly perspective.
- The therapist must connect and develop therapeutic relationships with more than one person; "[A]ny one person's strong negative feelings can lead to premature termination for the entire family [or couple]" (Friedlander, Escudero, Heatherington, & Diamond, 2011, p. 101).
- Logistically, it's hard for busy couples or families to find a time when everyone can consistently attend therapy. Difficulty scheduling may reduce the time couples and families spend in counseling.

Defining the Word "Couple"

Another irony about working with couples or families is that before you begin, you must define the terms you use to describe your client; this is because there's disagreement in the professional and general population regarding how to define a *couple* (Greenan & Tunnell, 2006; Swainson & Tasker, 2006). Some professionals advertise marriage or marital therapy; others use the term *couple counseling* or *couple therapy*.

Our position on the couple versus marital therapy issues is based on inclusion. Throughout this chapter, we refer to interviewing and counseling techniques that include two people who are in a romantic relationship as *couple counseling*. Couple counseling may involve work with unmarried gay and lesbian couples, unmarried heterosexual couples (who never plan to marry), unmarried couples (who are pursuing premarital counseling), couples who have made a life commitment they regard as marriage, even though not legally recognized, and legally married couples. It also includes couples who are divorced and reconciling. In contrast, *marital therapy* refers specifically to therapeutic efforts occurring between two people committed to each other through the bonds of matrimony, as defined by the laws of the state.

Couple counseling also has been referred to as *relationship therapy* or *relationship enhancement*. However, unless you're using the specific approach entitled *relationship enhancement therapy* (Guerney, 2001; Scuka, 2005), we recommend avoiding this term because it doesn't distinguish among couple therapy, family therapy, mediation, and so on. Also, two family members (e.g., mother and daughter, father and son) may pursue therapy together to improve their relationship. This is most aptly referred to as *family therapy* because it includes two members of one family who aren't romantically involved.

Defining Families

The definition of family has, unfortunately, become a politically loaded topic. We believe families come in all shapes and sizes. Family theorists and therapists differ with regard to whether they will treat subsets of family members when conducting family therapy (Goldenberg & Goldenberg, 2012). In our transient, mobile society, at any given time, the family may be defined and configured differently than it was a week ago or than it will be next week.

Children in co-parenting situations often see themselves as having two or more families. Children raised in extended kinship systems, as reflected in many

American Indian and other cultures, may live for periods with grandparents, aunts, uncles, or older siblings (Ho, Rasheed, & Rasheed, 2004). Furthermore, families may include foster children, elderly relatives, and part-time members. As another example, African American lesbian couples and families may define family as blood relatives, extended kinship networks, lifelong friends who are experienced as siblings, LGBTQ youth, other LGBTQ minority persons, religious leaders, and community members (Kimberly Johnson, personal communication, August 9, 2012). Also, sometimes, people who consider themselves family do not reside together, either by choice or by law; it's not uncommon to do therapy with a family in which one member is living in a juvenile detention facility or group home.

Family-oriented clinicians must find both a comfortable working definition of family and a theoretical basis for determining appropriate treatment modalities. Theoretical approaches to interviewing families and conducting family therapy are diverse and sometimes contentious (Murray, Sommers-Flanagan, & Sommers-Flanagan, 2012). This theoretical and practical diversity, along with the complexities noted previously, requires that beginning clinicians *not* conduct family interviews or family therapy without close supervision. Our preference is for beginning clinicians to obtain training experiences by conducting family interviews in conjunction with immediate supervisors or with a *reflecting team* of colleagues/supervisors outside a one-way mirror so immediate feedback is available (Selicoff, 2006; Shurts et al., 2006).

The Generic Interview

This chapter includes a generic or atheoretical approach to interviewing couples and families. However, when it comes to interviewing couples or families, practitioners from various theoretical approaches strongly disagree about how to conduct a clinical interview. Some practitioners might even argue that there's no such thing as a generic approach to interviewing families or couples because the clinician's theoretical and treatment orientation is always present. We believe, however, that there are basic elements in family interviews common to most accepted family treatment theories and, at the risk of offending everyone, focus on these elements in this chapter.

INTERVIEWING STAGES AND TASKS

Similar to work with individuals and children or adolescents, clinical interviewing with couples and families can be viewed in Shea's (1998) five stages.

The Introduction

The introduction stage includes preparation and planning, first contact or scheduling, initial meeting and greeting, and client education.

Preparation and Planning

In all clinical work, our own beliefs and values will influence the way we work. This is especially true when working with families and couples. Although you may already appreciate how important it is to develop awareness of your own issues, sometimes family-related biases or unresolved issues have a special way of surprising us! (K. Fuenfhausen, personal communication, September 12, 2012). In particular, your frame of reference for how things worked in your family (for better or worse) will deeply influence what you consider normal and abnormal in the families with whom you work. This can make it difficult to understand and empathize with families who may operate very differently (different rules, roles, rituals, values, etc.). This can affect the interviewing process in important ways. For example:

- Clinicians may not ask important questions because they assume they know the answer.
- Clinicians may get flustered when they observe behaviors or get verbal responses that are far outside their expectations of "normal" family functioning.
- Clinicians may project their own unresolved couple and family issues onto clients, which can interfere with effective counseling.

Before working directly with couples and families, K. Fuenfhausen (personal communication, September 12, 2012) encourages you to (a) consider your ideas about what normal families look like; (b) question whether the concept of normal families/couples exists; and (c) thoroughly explore and reflect on your own family history, patterns, and experiences.

First Contact: Scheduling With Couples

When couples refer themselves for professional assistance, one partner is usually more eager than the other to engage in counseling. Ordinarily, the person who makes the initial telephone call is more motivated for treatment than the other party. However, this isn't always the case. On occasion, one party will call at the insistence of the other:

Client: Hello, my name is Bert Smith. I'm calling to schedule an appointment for marriage counseling.

Clinician: Okay, before we schedule the appointment, let me give you some information about our services and ask you a few questions. (*The clinician informs the client about the agency's fee structure, asks about insurance, asks about best appointment times, etc.*)

Client: Yeah, well, we can come in on Friday afternoons. You know, my wife told me to make this call or I could just forget about our marriage. She thinks we need counseling. So I'd like to get this appointment scheduled right away.

For cases in which one party has made an ultimatum, the less motivated party sometimes calls. The less motivated party may make his or her attitude known early on. This can also be true when the more motivated person calls:

I'm calling to make an appointment for marriage counseling. Our marriage is falling apart. I've been trying to get my husband to come for counseling for years. Now, I'm just making an appointment. Either he'll come with me or I'll come by myself.

Couples are notorious for engaging in what therapists commonly refer to as *triangulation* and *coalition building*. Definitions of these two terms vary depending on theoretical orientation, but triangulation occurs when one or both members of a relationship turn to a third party to focus on instead of the couple conflict. When this third party is also overtly asked to take sides in the conflict, the triangulation has the added dimension of coalition building.

It's not unusual for the person who makes the phone call for couple counseling to immediately begin actively soliciting sympathy from the clinician; this is an effort at coalition building. Coalition building is common, but generally viewed as a less-than-optimal (sometimes pathological) strategy for obtaining greater power (Weeks, Odell, & Methven, 2005). We should note, however, that the desire to build coalitions and find someone who is sympathetic or supportive of your position outside the romantic relationship is very natural.

Often, the clinician's gender or sexual orientation is an important variable when couples call for an appointment; each partner may have strong beliefs that one gender or the other will understand his or her problems better. In training clinics, sometimes an opposite-sex co-therapy team can work with couples and families. Although doing co-therapy adds therapist communication challenges to the already complicated mix, it's usually seen as advantageous, especially in training clinics. Less-experienced therapists gladly look to each other for support and direction when they're unclear about how to proceed. In contrast, more advanced therapists may regard a co-therapist as a burden; they can find comments from a co-therapist detract from an efficient therapy process. However, if co-therapists are compatible and communicate well with each other, having two perspectives usually offers couples and families a more comprehensive service.

Unfortunately for clients, clinicians rarely practice co-therapy in clinic or independent practice settings. There are exceptions, and some theoretical orientations consider a two-therapist team as fundamental (Young-Eisendrath, 1993). Generally, however, having two professionals work jointly with a couple or family is too costly. In some training clinics, the option for either a male or female therapist is presented when couples counseling has been requested:

Clinician: Sometimes, people coming for couples counseling prefer to see a male or a female therapist. Do you have a preference?

Client: Hmm. Actually, she never said whether she wants to work with a lady or a man. I guess she'd rather work with a lady counselor, but I'd rather talk to another man about this. Yeah, you better schedule us with a man.

This client's choice may represent an initial hope for a coalition; the husband is hoping that a male clinician might see things more from his perspective. As usual, we recommend that clinicians make mental notes of first impressions from the outset of their telephone contact, including whether the client who telephoned was trying hard to gain sympathy or support from the clinician. It's not always possible to provide couples with their preferences, but it's always important to note them.

Gay or lesbian couples may also ask about the therapist's skills and/or attitudes in working with homosexual couples. Skilled and ethical therapists will answer such questions honestly. However, you shouldn't feel pressured to answer personal questions about your sexual orientation, religious beliefs, numbers of children, and/or other personal matters unless it's your practice to do so.

Meeting and Greeting Couples

Clinicians should be careful to greet couples with relatively equal warmth and mild enthusiasm. Couples may be watching for subtle signs that the clinician favors one client over the other. Whenever possible, avoid even the appearance of a coalition; equal treatment is the order of the day.

Potential triangulation makes chitchatting with couples in the waiting room a delicate task, requiring thought and observation. If you talk about the weather, the woman may take offense because she's already angry with her husband, who she believes talks about the weather too often (instead of "more important" issues). If you talk about how it was to locate the office, they may plunge quickly into a conflict regarding who "took the wrong turn" when navigating to your office. When meeting and greeting couples in conflict, virtually anything you say can and will be used against you.

Despite prospective dangers, friendly waiting room small talk is still helpful. Stick with relatively neutral trivia, knowing that even such trivia may have baggage. If you shake hands, do so with both parties, and generally avoid comments that might be interpreted as too personal or as evidence that you identify more with one client than the other.

Telephone Contact or Scheduling With Families

Much of the previous advice can be applied to initial family therapy telephone contacts. The primary difference is that unless you work in a *family therapy clinic* it's unusual for a family member to call with a clear request for family counseling. The request for help usually centers on a description of certain troubling behavior patterns in one or more family member(s). Theoretical orientation, research evidence, and clinical judgment will help you determine whether family or individual therapy is the treatment of choice. For example, empirical research suggests:

- Multisystemic family therapy for adolescent drug abuse is a highly efficacious evidence-based approach (Henderson, Dakof, Greenbaum, & Liddle, 2010; Liddle, Dakof, Turner, Henderson, & Greenbaum, 2008; Liddle, Rowe, Dakof, Henderson, & Greenbaum, 2009).
- Family therapies are helpful for improving schizophrenia treatment outcomes (Barbato & D'Avanzo, 2000; Bressi, Manenti, Frongia, Porcellana, & Invernizzi, 2007).
- Functional family therapy appears to reduce repeat offending among initial criminal offenders (Gordon, Graves, & Arbuthnot, 1995; Sexton & Turner, 2010).
- Family therapy appears promising for families with children who have health problems (Ng et al., 2008; Young, Northern, Lister, Drummond, & O'Brien, 2007).

When someone calls to request help with a situation that might best be handled by family therapy, it's advisable to arrange a time when all family members can attend an initial interview. All members may not attend all sessions, but meeting with everyone who lives in the family home is standard procedure when initiating family therapy (Goldenberg & Goldenberg, 2012). Further, some family therapists welcome or encourage initial participation by extended family members. An example of a telephone conversation follows:

Clinician:	Ms. Fallon-Tracy? This is Carry Bolton. I'm a counseling trainee at the University Counseling Center, returning your call.
Ms. F-T:	Yes, I'd like to make an appointment to talk with someone about my husband and daughter. Well, actually, my husband said he might be willing to come too, but I just wasn't sure what would be best. Do you have any openings? Dr. Green said your center would be good because we don't have insurance right now and you have a sliding fee.
Clinician:	Yes, we have openings. I have several late-afternoon openings right now. It sounds like you want some help with family relationships. Is that right?
Ms. F-T:	Well, I don't know. My husband, Bill, is just so upset these days with our daughter, Kim. She's 15, and she's got a mouth on her, if you know what I mean. And she's been pushing him. He's a quiet guy most of the time. Our son, Wally, is just kind of lost in the fighting. Maybe I should just bring Kim in, but she says it isn't her fault. She says she won't come if her dad doesn't come too.
Clinician:	Kids growing up can be hard on everyone. One of the ways I've been trained to help people is through family therapy. It's best if all of you could come in for at least the first few times. Do you have others living at home besides your husband, son, and daughter?
Ms. F-T:	No. That's it. Sometimes, that feels like a few too many.
Clinician:	So, do you think everyone could come in for an hour-and-a-half next Thursday at 4?

There are an infinite number of variations on the themes in this phone call. Parents who call for counseling may not even be aware that family therapy is available and can be confused about what might help with some of the struggles they face. Initial phone calls require clinical judgment and education to set up a family therapy intake interview.

Meeting and Greeting Families

As with couples, small talk with families requires consideration. Generally, it's better to find global comments that pertain to the whole family than to single out individuals. Some theorists emphasize orienting to the youngest family members first, even in the waiting room (Whitaker & Burnberry, 1988). If physical surroundings are reasonably private, it's best to greet each family member by name before going to the counseling room.

Couple and Family Education

As with individuals, couples and families must be educated regarding counseling procedures and the plan for the interview. It's important to have a well-written informed consent form, and to cover confidentiality very carefully, going over the legally mandated reasons you might break confidentiality. Because the potential for needing to report child abuse is higher in couples or family work, you need to make a special point of carefully informing your clients about the laws and ethical practices in your state, your agency, and your profession. You'll also need to explain your policy with regard to (a) meeting separately with each member of the couple or family, (b) whether you'll take phone calls from one member of the couple or family that might involve discussing couple or family issues, and (c) whether you'll agree to keep secrets, temporarily or on an ongoing basis. A common scenario follows:

> Jill, a psychology intern, meets with Betty and Barney for the first time. Initially, Betty bursts into tears and says she's sure Barney doesn't love her anymore. Barney gets defensive, and verbally dominates the meeting. Betty cries throughout. Jill does her best to get both involved in helping her understand their background and needs as a couple. The session ends with Jill feeling she needs two or three more hours with them before she can establish treatment goals. She sends them home with a marital satisfaction inventory to complete. The next day, Barney calls, and before Jill can get a word in, he explains that he's having an affair, but that he won't tell Betty. He wants to stay with Betty until their youngest child graduates next year, which is why he agreed to come to counseling. He claims Jill can't tell Betty anything unless he gives her permission to do so.

Clarity about secrets is essential in couple and family therapy. According to the IAMFC (International Association for Marriage and Family Counseling, 2005) ethics code, if Jill hasn't stated otherwise, Barney's assumption is correct:

> Unless alternate arrangements have been agreed upon by all participants, statements by a family member to the counselor during an individual counseling or consultation contact are not disclosed to other family members without the individual's permission. (p. 75)

Other areas of confidentiality also require special attention in couple and family work. Concerns about child physical or sexual abuse might arise, as well as concerns about custodial rights should the relationship end in divorce. It's important to explain these possible eventualities carefully and to be very clear about both the law and your office policies (see *Putting It in Practice* 14.1).

Always inform the couple and/or the family about what will be expected of them during the interview and what behaviors are unacceptable. Mental health professionals who work with couples or families range in their willingness to tolerate open conflict, destructive interactions, profanity, raised voices, and so on. Novices are advised to maintain control through guidelines that prohibit destructive conflict. We cover this area more extensively later in this chapter.

An example of setting up rules to limit conflict for a couple follows:

> Betty, Barney, I want to let you know a little bit about how we'll work together. We may be talking about some difficult, emotional things and

I'm going to reserve the right to interrupt if either of you gets too far off track or too wound up. Sometimes, counselors let couples actually get into a big argument to see how that goes, but that doesn't fit with how I work. It will be hard sometimes, but we're going to work together on positive ways to solve the problems you face.

Sometimes, indirect methods work as well. One student who was working with a family that included a very vocal, controlling, middle-aged man made the following observation:

Mr. Smith, I should tell you this room is only partially soundproofed. So, when you raise your voice that much, the secretary and the people upstairs can hear you.

From that point on, Mr. Smith did a much better job of keeping his voice within reasonable limits.

Besides dealing with shouting and other forms of conflict, clinicians need to consider their own activity level and style. Most couple and family counselors are more active and directive than individual counselors. They redirect client statements, rephrase, check in, have people change seats, and stand in for family members during role-plays. They give assignments, homework, and minilectures on communication, coupling, family needs, and their theoretical perspective. Clients deserve fair warning about these activities and interventions.

Couples and families also learn about interview process and ground rules by observing clinician behavior. From the beginning, clinicians should make sure everyone is aware of general information obtained while setting up the appointment. This involves restating information obtained over the telephone. By restating this information, a no-secrets approach to counseling is modeled:

Clinician: It's nice to meet both of you. Sandy, you made the call and set up the appointment, so I just want to let Miguel know what we talked about. Miguel, when Sandy called she said you had both agreed to try counseling, but that it was more her idea. If I remember right, she said you'd had a trial separation last year, but it upset the kids so much you moved back together. Did I get all of our conversation, Sandy?

Sandy: Yeah, that's about it. But there's a lot more to why we're here. Miguel has been pretty mean to me.

Clinician: (Interrupting) Thanks, Sandy. First I just want to make sure Miguel knows what we talked about so we're all on equal footing. We'll get into what brought you here in a couple of minutes. Miguel, does that fit with what you knew?

Miguel: I knew she called and that's right . . . I'm not too jacked about being here. But I guess we have to do something.

Clinician: Thanks, Miguel. It's important that both of you know what I know. There are always at least two sides to relationship problems. Like it says in the consent form you both read, it's my policy, when working with couples, not to keep secrets about what either person says to me. Now, after I talk about how I work with couples and give you some information, I'll ask each of you about the problem areas, okay?

This quick but important check-in provides a natural link to the topic of secret-keeping and individual contacts between one member of the couple and the therapist. Policies and orientations vary, so try to establish your own stance (based on theory, supervision, and agency policy; see *Putting It in Practice* 14.1 for a discussion of keeping secrets with couples).

PUTTING IT IN PRACTICE 14.1

To Keep Secrets or to Not Keep Secrets?

Think about all the possible information you might hear in that first phone call:

Imagine a couple named Raphael and Trina. When Trina calls for the appointment, she tells you that Raphael has been very depressed and lethargic. She tells you he shows no sexual interest in her anymore, and she thinks it's related to the biology of depression. She also mentions that Raphael's father committed suicide last year. How much of this information do you repeat during the initial session?

When she calls for the appointment, Trina tells you she had an affair last year, but she ended it recently. She also says she hasn't told her partner about the affair and that she's not sure she needs to. What do you tell her about your policy on keeping secrets in couple therapy?

Let's say Raphael calls you for the appointment and tells you that he's lost sexual interest in Trina because she's gained 30 pounds over the past 2 years. He also tells you he's developed a pornography addiction and he's spending lots of time on the Internet, rather than interacting with his wife. When they come in for their first session, do you share this information openly? What if Trina had called for the appointment and had described the same situation (that she had gained 30 pounds and suspected her husband was addicted to pornography)? Would you be more or less inclined to share the information during the first session?

As you can see from these scenarios, deciding confidentiality boundaries with couples is challenging. Should you have a policy that you always repeat everything the caller tells you to the other party? (If so, you must make this policy clear *before* the caller starts telling you about their relationship problems.) Alternatively, do you *selectively remember* what the first caller said...do you bring it all up later...and if you don't bring it up, what message does that send to the first caller about secret-keeping and a possible coalition?

Before you take couple therapy calls, get clear on your policy. We know therapists in our community who not only refuse to keep secrets but who also directly ask the caller if there is an affair happening. If the caller indicates there's an affair, these therapists refuse to conduct an initial interview until the "love triangle" has been discussed and terminated.

Consider your position. Will you keep secrets between romantic partners? Will you work with partners if one or both are having active affairs? How will you decide your position on these issues?

(continued)

(*continued*)

To deal with these issues up front, Laura Brown, PhD, a psychologist in Seattle, includes the following statement on her informed consent form:

> The next is not a legal exception to your confidentiality. However, it is a policy you should be aware of if you are in *couples therapy* with me.
>
> If you and your partner decide to have some individual sessions as part of the couples therapy, what you say in those individual sessions will be considered to be a part of the couples therapy, and can and probably will be discussed in our joint sessions. *Do not tell me anything you wish kept secret from your partner.* I will remind you of this policy before beginning such individual sessions (from: http://www.drlaurabrown.com/media/PsychotherapyConsentForm.pdf).

The Opening

The opening in a family or couple interview varies depending on theoretical orientation. One important component of the opening for couples, no matter what comes next, is to obtain information from each person about why they've come for counseling. A simple, balanced statement can help begin this portion of the interview. It may be unrealistic to expect everyone to participate equally, but it's important to hear from each member during the opening phase.

The Clinician's Opening Statement in Couple Counseling

After asking for any final procedural questions they might have, the interview opening begins with a statement:

> I want to hear about what each of you believe brought you here and what you want to work on as a couple. It doesn't matter who starts, but I want to hear from each of you. I know you might disagree on some things, so you can check in with each other along the way and I will, too.

It's informative to monitor how the decision is made about who goes first. Couples express their feelings toward each other and about counseling via voice tone. In many cases, these feeling expressions are less than subtle.

Bornstein and Bornstein (1986) provide an alternative example of an opening statement:

> My plan for today's session is as follows. First, I'd like to get to know you folks a little. Second, I'll need some information about what brings you in. Third, while I want to hear from you, I will be asking a considerable number of questions today. Finally, by the time we are finished, I'd like to be able to give you some initial feedback and let you know if I think I can be of service to you. (p. 54)

Note that in this sample opening statement, the clinician provides the couple with greater structure and direction. The Bornsteins' opening statement is dictated, to some degree, by their behavioral orientation. They seek more control over the direction and course of couple interviews.

Maintaining Balance

Simultaneously attending to both parties is important. If you observe nonverbal signs of anger, pain, or disagreement, you can model a balanced approach:

> Just a minute, Betty. Barney looks like he needs to say something. I know you aren't done, but let's check in with him for a moment.

> *(Turning to Barney)* Barney, I noticed you winced and looked away when Betty spoke about the Internet. Betty isn't quite done explaining her perceptions. Would it be all right with you to have her finish and then come back to this area, or do you need to check in with her?

Even though you've just begun getting the reasons for their visit, by actively structuring initial communications, you model your style and orientation. Allowing one member of the couple to ignore distress displayed by the other is poor modeling; further, balance and fairness are essential components of good couples work. Therefore, if Barney indicates he needs to correct Betty's rendition of the Internet issue, allow him time, summarize his concerns, and get back to Betty:

> Thanks, Barney. It's helpful to know you have some differences. I bet we'll discover quite a few areas where you two don't see eye to eye. We'll work on that. Let's let Betty continue now.

Although orienting toward nonverbal signs of client distress is important, it's equally important to recognize that some clients will continually interrupt their partners through intrusive nonverbal behaviors. If nonverbal interruptions become problematic, clinicians should begin acknowledging, but minimizing, nonverbal reactions:

> Hang on a moment. I can see that Barney is having strong reactions to what you're saying, Betty. Barney, I can see you're upset, but I want you to hold onto your reactions and keep trying to listen and understand Betty's version of what brings you both here for counseling. You'll get your chance to give your perspective soon.

Maintaining a balance of power in couple and family therapy is very challenging. This is partly because couples frequently come into counseling with a power imbalance and the partner who has greater power tends not to be motivated to support a power shift (Ward & Knudson-Martin, 2012). When addressing power imbalances it's best to proceed delicately; it can be helpful to encourage the partner with power to pursue a more relational perspective. One of our couple therapist friends sometimes captures power dynamics with married couples by stating: "You can be right or you can be married; you get to decide which."

Evaluating Couple Interactions and Behavior

As couples discuss their reasons for counseling, you should observe their interactions along several dimensions. Couples often differ in their intimacy and autonomy needs. One partner may push for more time together, whereas the other expresses (either directly or indirectly) an interest in being alone or away from the relationship. It's not unusual for intimacy and autonomy differences to manifest themselves during an initial interview. Sometimes, this has the feel of a chase scene or drama occurring in the relationship: One partner is chasing while the other is running for cover.

Intimacy and autonomy issues are sometimes attributed to general sex differences (Land, Rochlen, & Vaughn, 2011). In this framework, men are viewed as cooler, more distant, and more autonomous; women are viewed as warmer, closer, and more intimate. Although viewing couple conflicts as stemming primarily from male-female differences may be helpful at times, sex-typed behavior models tend to be overused and abused (J. Gray, 2004; Tannen, 1990). Indeed, you may find men more often seek autonomy and women more often seek intimacy in the work you do with couples; however, such an observation shouldn't lead you to assume that an autonomous style in males and an intimate style in females is either normal or desirable. Holding rigid assumptions about what's normal and desirable also should be avoided when working with same sex couples. GLBTQ couples struggle from some of the same and some different intimacy and autonomy dynamics (Frost, 2011). Instead of operating on assumptions, watch for partner preferences and tendencies so you can more deeply understand couple dynamics and thereby assist the couple in attaining what's likely to be more adaptive or healthy dynamics for them.

Couple-relationship researcher, John Gottman, has focused on the importance of "emotional bids" (J. M. Gottman & DeClaire, 2001). He emphasizes that loving partners offer up emotional bids to each other and, if the relationship is healthy, they receive and respond empathically to each other's emotional needs. For example, continuing with the scenario, Betty might claim:

> I spent all day Saturday cleaning the garage while he was on the Internet. And then, when I came in and told him I was finished, instead of supporting me, he just said, "Boy, you sure took a long time cleaning up our tiny garage."

In this situation Betty offered a bid for emotional support and connection that Barney completely missed. Watching for these missed opportunities can help clinicians gain insight into negative communication patterns.

The Family Clinician's Opening Statement

Referral needs and theoretical orientation will dictate tone and content of your opening statements as a family clinician. When tension is high, mild humor might be helpful:

- I suppose you're all wondering why I called you together.
- What does a nice family like you do together when you're not hanging out in a counseling center?

We hasten to add that such humor can be a very bad idea. It requires clinical judgment and a high level of clinician comfort and confidence. After getting everyone settled, consider a statement similar to the following:

> We're going to spend the next hour together, getting acquainted. I'll do some talking and I hope each of you will talk too. It's important that I get an idea of what's been going on and what brought you here.

Family therapy openings are wide-ranging, depending on the clinician's theoretical orientation. A classic approach was described by Satir (1967):

> In the first interview, the therapist starts out by asking questions to establish what the family wants and expects from treatment. He [or she] asks each person present, though not necessarily in these words:
> "How did you happen to come here?"
> "What do you expect will happen?"
> "What do you hope to accomplish here?" (p. 109)

Maintaining Balance With Families

A common situation in family work is the *identified-patient* phenomenon (Goldenberg & Goldenberg, 2012). The identified patient is the family member who is *the one with the problem*. However, family-systems theory suggests that dynamics within the family system are creating problems within the identified patient and allowing everyone else to avoid personal responsibility for his or her own dysfunctional behaviors. Even in the opening minutes of an initial interview, your job is to make sure one person isn't attacked or scapegoated. It's also your task to determine how and when you begin to alter the system. Theory, supervision, and experience are essential components of developing this important skill.

CASE EXAMPLE

The Ragsdale-Hagan family came in for therapy because their 14-year-old, Theo, was extremely aggressive toward his 9-year-old sister, Sira. The parents, Thomas and LaChelle, disagreed on how to handle it, but agreed that Theo was way out of line. After hearing basic confidentiality information and the counselor's opening statement, Thomas took the floor and complained bitterly that his son seemed bent on killing his sister. "I ought to pound that boy once a day. Maybe more. But his mother won't hear of it." LaChelle put her hand on Thomas's arm and said, "Now, Baby. You know he'll be bigger than you before you know it. He's not going to change 'cause you pound him, are you, Theo?" Theo said to the counselor, "He's not my real dad. He's been with my momma a long time, but he's not my dad. He's her dad, though (Theo glares at Sira)."

The parents started into why the biology didn't matter. Theo was obviously directing the interactions. Sira was silent. To achieve balance, the clinician needed to intervene and redirect the conversation to involve Sira.

Evaluating Family Interactions and Behavior

From the opening to termination, your powers of observation must be on high alert. The family is your client. It's a complex organism, always communicating simultaneously with you and among its members. The potential number of communiqués at any given moment are staggering to consider and daunting to observe, let alone manage. However, communication observation and management is the heart of most family-therapy approaches. Both verbal and nonverbal communication patterns should be observed.

CASE EXAMPLE

The mother of two daughters called to make a counseling appointment for their younger daughter, Alissa, (age 14). She said Alissa had bizarre behaviors and ideas that were making her husband and her wonder if Alissa was crazy. She reported that Alissa was afraid of crowds, heard voices as she fell asleep at night, was overly attached to her boyfriend, and was skipping school and underachieving, even though she was very smart. The older daughter no longer lived in the home. The counselor asked both parents to attend the initial interview with their daughter to determine whether family or individual therapy would be a better fit and the mother agreed.

When they came in, the parents talked openly about their professional lives, their religious convictions, and their pride in their daughters. Alissa was verbally active and had a quick sense of humor, which she interjected frequently. The parents weren't overly blaming of their daughter and expressed concern for her well-being. The counselor was impressed with the sophisticated vocabulary and open communications and had begun wondering what could be troubling this nice, normal family. Then, out of the corner of her eye, she noticed the daughter had slipped off her shoe and was stroking the top of her father's shoe, under his chair, with her bare foot. The father was completely ignoring this action, and the daughter did nothing to call attention to it either.

This isn't ordinary father-daughter behavior in an initial counseling session. It alerted the counselor that there was more going on here than was apparent on the surface. Although it would have been a mistake to draw attention to the foot stroking until more of a relationship was established and she knew more about the family dynamics, her observations led her to investigate a number of boundary issues more thoroughly. She also determined that she needed to meet with members individually and perhaps in dyads to fully understand the family coalitions.

The Body

Assuming you've juggled the many tasks and challenges associated with the introduction and opening, you then proceed to the body of the interview. The body flows from the opening and is where deeper and lengthier assessment and interventions occur. Like the opening, the body of the family or couple interview is strongly influenced by your theoretical orientation or specific approach.

Theoretical Orientations With Couples

There are many approaches to working with couples. Some are based in traditional counseling and psychotherapy theories, others in research, and still others are more skill- or value-based, such as therapies specifically oriented toward improved sexual functioning (Jones, Meneses da Silva, & Soloski, 2011; Rutter, 2012). Some examples follow.

Behaviorally oriented professionals systematically inquire about desirable and undesirable behaviors that occur within the couple context. They emphasize that couples who rate their relationships as satisfying usually report a higher frequency of mutually pleasing or mutually enjoyable interactions (Gaspar, 2006). However, when evaluating what each partner desires from the other, behaviorists proceed carefully. Imagine the following scenario:

Counselor: I'd like each of you to tell the other what he or she could do to make the relationship more positive for you.

Yoko: I would like him to work harder to hold down a job, stay home more often, and stop criticizing me.

Brandon: Are you kidding? This is the same stuff she tells me every day. I don't need to come to therapy to hear this!

From the behavioral perspective, this interaction carries the same old mutually punishing quality that already exists in Yoko and Brandon's relationship (Christensen, McGinn, & Williams, 2009). Instead of asking each partner what the *other* person could do to make the relationship better, the clinician should ask each partner what he or she is willing to do to make the relationship more enjoyable:

Counselor: Brandon, would you begin first by saying what you're willing to do to improve your relationship with Yoko. Just say what you're willing to do that might help. Don't say anything about what you want from Yoko.

Brandon: Okay. I'm willing to spend more time with her if she would just get off my case about my job.

Counselor: Oops. Hang on a minute. Remember Brandon, right now, just focus on what you're willing to do—completely on your own—regardless of whether she gets on your case about anything. We'll get to that soon. But for now, just focus on what you're willing to do—no matter what she does.

Brandon: Yeah. Right. Well, I'm willing to go out more with her and to plan a weekend away from the kids.

You can see from this example how tempting it is for couples to comment on their partner's aversive behaviors. Of course, commenting on a partner's aversive behavior is just another form of aversive behavior. What the behavioral clinician is trying to do is to help both parties identify and increase positive behaviors before shifting to a focus on reducing mutually negative or punishing behaviors.

From a cognitive perspective, much of what occurs in the body of a couple interview involves active assessment of and education about the role of cognitions in causing and shaping couple conflict (Dattilio, 2010). In the preceding example of Yoko and Brandon, the clinician would likely try to help them reframe their perceptions and change their attributions of one another's behavior. For example, Brandon's negative reaction to Yoko's comments about his employment problems might be based on his underlying belief that she sees him as incompetent. Instead, her comments might be more associated with her financial anxiety. As the clinician helps each party understand their own assumptions about each other, the couple can clarify their comments and reframe them as more positive.

Communication is central for most couples. Consequently, regardless of theoretical orientation, communication within the session provides an assessment and educational opportunity. Initially, couples may discuss their problems and conflicts directly with the clinician, sometimes in a way suggesting the other person isn't even present in the room. Clinicians who emphasize communication-skills training often tell the clients something similar to the following:

> Sara and Linda, this may seem strange, but most of the time when the two of you are talking about your issues and conflicts in here, I want you to talk to each other. Instead of directing comments and questions to me, I want you to direct your comments toward each other. When speaking about anything that has to do with the two of you, you should look at and talk to each other. Sometimes I'll interrupt and help you change your communication patterns, but I can do that best if I watch you communicate with each other.

Even after this instruction, couples will often keep turning to you, making statements such as:

> I just don't know how to tell if she is interested in talking with me. I come home and she says hello, but she doesn't initiate conversation, and I just feel so alone.

In a communications model, your intervention would consist of saying in kind voice:

> Okay, Linda, I'd like you to turn to Sara and restate what you said, only this time, please talk to her directly.

An underlying assumption of this model is that it's more important for Sara and Linda to learn to communicate effectively with each other than it is for them to learn to communicate effectively with you.

The preceding descriptions and examples represent common couple counseling approaches. However, other specific forms of couple therapy are available in the research and popular literature. A small sampling includes:

- Emotion-focused therapy for couples: Originally developed by Leslie Greenberg and Susan Johnson, this approach emphasizes emotional expression and attachment patterns. Johnson's recent work currently may be the most popular therapy approach for working with couples (Greenberg & Goldman, 2008).

- Research-based approaches, such as the Gottman approach, which is based on his extensive research on couples in his research lab (J. M. Gottman, 2011).
- Therapy approaches for specific populations, such as religious groups (Mormons, Catholics, Muslims, etc.), the military, gay, lesbian, and bisexual couples (O'Brien, 2012; Rutter, 2012).
- Sexuality therapy that may or may not include sexual surrogates for exploring bisexuality, homosexuality, and heterosexuality (Iantaffi, 2010; Poelzl, 2011).
- Relationship-enhancement couple work: this approach draws heavily from Carl Rogers's person-centered theory and involves teaching couples skills for listening to each other (Guerney, 1977).
- Jungian approaches applied to couples, including imago relationship therapy (Hendrix, 2007) and dialogue therapy (Young-Eisendrath, 1993).

Theoretical Orientations With Families

Most family therapy theorists and modalities come from a systems (Murray, Sommers-Flanagan, & Sommers-Flanagan, 2012) or ecological (Bronfenbrenner, 2005) perspective. Such perspectives, though similar to each other, are a radical departure from seeing counseling as a process that cures or eliminates the pathologies of an individual or family. From these perspectives, the context for the dysfunction may be more important than the dysfunction itself. Individual troubles are often seen to be a signal about things going wrong in the family environment. From Whitaker's symbolic-experiential family therapy to Bowenian theory and therapy with its concepts of differentiation and multigenerational transmission, writers and therapists with a family orientation attend to a broader domain than those focusing on individuals.

The theoretical terrain for working with families is complex and we cannot do it justice here. Please see the Suggested Readings and Resources section at the end of this chapter to pursue additional knowledge.

Common Areas to Address

Regardless of theoretical orientation in working with couples or families, certain assessment domains should be considered and possibly explored during the body of an initial interview. These domains are described next. The first three assessment domains—sex, money, and commitment—are specific to couples.

Sex

When working with romantic partners, satisfaction with sexual intimacy is a central assessment area. It can be difficult for students to ask questions about sexual functioning, so you should practice asking unusual or difficult questions. One of our favorite homework assignments is: "During the next week, spend several hours loudly discussing the details of your sex life with your partner (or friend) while out at a crowded local restaurant."

After giving this assignment (and watching for the looks of horror on the faces of our students), we follow it with: "Okay, if you don't want to complete the original assignment, then just go somewhere and have conversations about sex quietly, in a private and confidential setting." The point is that students, mental health professionals, and couples benefit from becoming comfortable talking about sex and sexuality (see *Multicultural Highlight* 14.1).

MULTICULTURAL HIGHLIGHT 14.1

What's Normal and What's Not?: Expanding Your Comfort Zone With Diverse Sexual Values and Behaviors

The purpose of this activity isn't to change your sexual values or behaviors, but to help you expand your comfort zone so you can work effectively with clients who have different sexual values and behaviors than you. To engage in this activity, all you need to do is read the following examples and reflect on your personal reactions or discuss your reactions with classmates. Of the following three examples, two are excerpts from professional journal articles and the third is a vignette from one of our supervision experiences.

This first example is a technical description of an issue that can and sometimes should be explored when interviewing gay males who are experiencing sexual dysfunction. This is an excerpt from the journal *Sexual and Relationship Therapy* (Rutter, 2012):

> An important set of questions to include in clinical sexology intake interviews and assessments would be potential use of recreational or illicit psychoactive substances. [In a study]... of gay men who were seropositive [there was] a high comorbidity with erectile dysfunction, ejaculatory incompetence and potential desire decline.... The confusing element here is that MDMA use, in the moment, can actually cause sexual stimulation and feelings of attractiveness. It is the actual "mechanics" that suffer once physically engaged with a partner, i.e., erection may be partial or absent, ejaculate minimal or absent.... (Rutter, 2012, p. 37)

One, among many, questions for you to think about in response to the preceding excerpt is: "How would you feel about asking gay males about the quality of their erections?"

This next excerpt is from the *Journal of Bisexuality*. It focuses on the use of sexual surrogates to explore and develop comfort with individual sexuality. An experienced sexual surrogate authored the article (Poelzl, 2011):

> When Sally began working with me, she was desperate to clarify her sexual identity and find a way to meet and relate to women who would return her feelings fully. She had mixed feelings all the way around. She was attracted to men, but not her husband, and it was clear that they needed to divorce. She knew she was attracted to women emotionally and sexually, and she often lubricated profusely when she spent time with Alice: There was often affectionate touch involved, primarily hugging and holding hands during their intimate emotional exchanges. She

tended to prefer more feminine women ("soccer moms," she called them, who were often straight) and had avoided venturing into the lesbian community because she was terrified of butch, "manly" women. She also never thought about women's genitals as particularly sexually interesting. It was the face-to-face and eye contact that she craved. (p. 386)

What kinds of questions might you have if Sally were your client? Is bisexuality more confusing to consider than either hetero- or homosexuality?

One final scenario:

Not long ago, an openly Christian, conservative colleague (we'll call him Sam) who works at an inpatient youth training facility asked us to consult on a case of a young male who was exploring bisexuality and his desire to be a *furry*. A furry is a label that describes people who derive sexual satisfaction through role playing with other people—all of whom simultaneously play various animal roles. We imagined that Sam might be uncomfortable working with this young man, but instead, Sam was curious, open, and deeply invested in being an effective counselor and advocate for his client. There was no proselytizing and not a shred of evidence that Sam was judging the young man in any negative way. This example illustrates that professionals with very traditional and conservative value systems can work with clients using core attitudes of acceptance and empowerment. We encourage you to stretch yourselves in ways that allow you to work effectively with a broad range of clients—in ways similar to Sam.

What kinds of reactions might you have to young clients with provocative or unusual sexual aspirations? How might this affect your work with a couple struggling with different sexual desires or practices?

You may be relieved to know that many couples may have a more difficult time answering your questions about their sex life than you have asking, but of course, this makes your comfort with this aspect of couple functioning all the more important. In a first interview, you may or may not get a chance to ask about sex, and when you do ask, you may get a quick "Oh, fine. We're just fine in that area." Later, after more trust has been established, different answers to questions about sexual functioning may surface. What matters is that you ask about sexual functioning, compatibility, and satisfaction in a natural, caring way, and be as ready as possible to accept whatever you hear.

Money

Money is often a difficult issue for couples. Questions about monetary practices include who pays the bills, whether checking accounts are joint or separate, if there's agreement with regard to saving and spending, and so on. By evaluating how couples manage money in their relationship, clinicians may also glimpse how power is managed (or abused) in the relationship. Interestingly, asking about money can be as difficult as ask about sex in our culture. Economic status and spending practices can be a taboo subject.

Relationship Commitment

When it comes to relationship commitment, couples probably arrive at counseling for one of four reasons:

1. To improve an already solid and satisfying relationship: These couples arrive excited and interested to explore ways to increase their relationship satisfaction and are fully committed to continuing the relationship.
2. To repair or work on certain troublesome areas in their relationship: These couples haven't seriously considered ending the relationship. They're committed, but are experiencing significant distress.
3. Because of a marked imbalance in their commitment, with one questioning whether to stay in the relationship and the other desperately committed to keeping things together.
4. As a last resort: Neither party is exceptionally committed to continuing the relationship.

Directly or indirectly, it's important to obtain information about where couples fall along this commitment continuum. The *Stuart Couples' Precounseling Inventory* (Stuart & Stuart, 1975) provides each client with questions that clinicians can use to assess commitment without asking about it directly in front of the other partner during an interview. Additional couple relationship measures range from the 280-item Marital Satisfaction Scale (Snyder, 1979) to the 32-item Dyadic Adjustment Scale (Graham, Liu, & Jeziorski, 2006).

Family of Origin

Despite our belief that unresolved family-of-origin issues can influence couple interactions, we advise against family-of-origin-based couple-conflict interpretations during initial interviews. Premature interpretation in the couple context is generally inappropriate and can turn couples off to counseling. Instead, make a mental or written note indicating that family-of-origin issues may be fueling couple conflict. Additionally, it may be appropriate to acknowledge this likelihood, but not describe the dynamics in an initial session:

> As you both probably know, your childhood experiences, your relationships with your mother and father or brothers and sisters can shape the way you relate to each other. I'm not sure if this is the case with the two of you, but as we work together, it may be useful for us to occasionally discuss how your family of origin may contribute to your current conflicts and the ways you try to resolve these conflicts. But, because this is our first session, I won't even venture any guesses about how your childhood experiences might be influencing your relationship.

Family-of-origin dynamics may be deeply influential, but they may also be outside client awareness (Gurman, 2008; Odell & Campbell, 1998). Consequently, as in the case of psychoanalytic interpretations (discussed in Chapter 5), family-of-origin interpretations must wait for sufficient rapport and supporting information (or data) before they can be used effectively. As a family-therapy technique, interpreting intergenerational family themes is probably less threatening, but should still be approached carefully.

Genograms

Couple and family clinicians often use genograms as tools for understanding multigenerational family dynamics. There are slight variations in the construction guidelines, but knowing how to do a basic genogram is essential (McGoldrick, Gerson, & Petry, 2008; Shellenberger, 2007). The counselor may not actually do a genogram with the family present but may accumulate the data necessary to complete one. Numerous books are available for teaching clinicians how to complete genograms (McGoldrick et al., 2008; Shellenberger, 2007). From an Adlerian perspective, genograms are referred to as family constellations and can be used to explore family history, legacies, birth order, and other family-of-origin dynamics that may influence the current couple relationship (Englar-Carlson & Carlson, 2012; Robey & Carlson, 2011).

Gathering Family Therapy Goals

When gathering information, many family therapists maintain balance by systematically orienting toward each family member. For example, Lankton, Lankton, and Matthews (1991) stated: "We always ask each member what he or she would like to have changed in the family and how, and even if members contradict each other, each input becomes the basis of a goal" (p. 241). In order to avoid blame and scapegoating, it may be wise to remind everyone that it's great to have goals for family change, but we can never have a goal that requires someone else to change—we can change ourselves, and we can change situations, but we can't force someone else to change.

A key to gathering goals in family therapy is to emphasize inclusion and minimize scapegoating or constant references to the identified patient. It's crucial to explore the range and quality of strengths and deficits of all family members and to begin determining how they are influencing the identified patient (Thomas, 2005; Werner-Wilson, Zimmerman, & Price, 1999).

Willingness to Make Changes

A close corollary to relationship commitment in couple interviewing is each person's willingness to do homework, try new things, experiment with change, and try out new perspectives. Besides asking directly, a good way to assess this area is to have each member try a new behavior or listening skill during the interview. This can be as simple as saying:

- Fred, I wonder if you could take Wilma's hand for a minute and just let her cry.
- Mom, it seems like you and Karen are sitting closer together than anyone else. I wonder if you could have Karen sit by her brother for a few minutes while Dad moves over here and we talk a bit further.

If the couple or family agrees to homework or to setting aside talking time, clinicians should inquire as to when and where these new behaviors will occur.

Kids, Parents, Neighbors, Friends

Often, couples and/or families are the core of a circle of wider relationships, all of which contribute to one another's well-being or struggles. Getting an idea of the interpersonal and role demands operating on the couple or family system is important. Grandparents, children and their friends, stepchildren, in-laws, close friends, and other associates can play influential roles in the happiness or unhappiness of a couple or family and can contribute to, or use up, many relationship resources. Considering the rich and interactive ways in which many outside factors influence couples and families is a core concept of the ecological approach to therapy (Bronfenbrenner, 1976, 1986, 2005).

Sexual minorities (i.e., LGBTQ individuals and couples) are especially vulnerable to cultural stressors. Herek et al. (2007) used the term *sexual stigma* to describe how dominant cultural beliefs belittle, discredit, and invalidate LGBTQ identities as deviant from heterosexuality. This stigma can also be institutionalized; for example, some public, private, and governmental institutions directly and indirectly stigmatize and marginalize LGBTQ people. Not surprisingly, research by Hatzenbuehler and colleagues (2009) indicated that:

> [L]esbian, gay, and bisexual people living in states that enacted laws preventing same-sex partnerships from receiving the same legal benefits as heterosexual couples experience higher rates of mood disorders, anxiety disorders, alcohol use disorders, and psychiatric comorbidity than those living in states without such legislation. (see Heck et al., 2013, p. 24)

As a consequence, clinicians who work with sexual minority couples should be aware of how parents, neighbors, friends, and the dominant culture can increase their clients' distress and dysfunction. In many cases, moving sexual minority couples into settings that are not only tolerant but also affirming can decrease stress and improve functioning.

Drugs, Alcohol, and Physical Violence

Gathering information about drugs, alcohol, and violence is essential. For some clients it may be easier to check an item on your intake form about drugs/alcohol/violence than it is to bring it up in a session; this is one reason why practitioners may use an intake form that includes these. Similar to talking about sex, asking clients questions about drugs, alcohol, and violence may stimulate an "Everything's fine" answer, at least until trust has been established. However, asking about these issues, either in writing or verbally, communicates to clients that you're interested in hearing about trouble in these areas.

When questionnaires or intake forms are used to inquire about sensitive issues, clinicians should review the forms thoroughly and discuss significant issues with the couple or family. Depending on your perspective, it should be made clear to couples and families that any issues mentioned on questionnaires or intake forms are *not confidential* in the family or couple system and, therefore, may be discussed during the interview.

The Closing

Watching the clock closely is essential when interviewing families and couples because time often will pass very quickly. There are more clients to manage and central issues may be raised with just moments left in a session. When new issues are raised at the session's end, it's appropriate, unless the issue represents a true crisis, to close the session by saying something like:

> Rosa, I'm glad you brought up the fact that you want to change your curfew. Unfortunately, we're out of time for today. So, next time, if you'll remind us about the curfew issue we can discuss it earlier in the session, when we have enough time to talk it through.

Family or couple sessions may last 1.5 or 2 hours. Allowing plenty of time to "put things back together" is essential because the session may involve intense emotional material. You can't be responsible for making each person feel better about the situation, nor is it ethical to minimize the problems so everyone leaves feeling artificially hopeful. On the other hand, it is in your power to support and compliment everyone's efforts in coming for help. It's also in your power to provide structure that enables each person to regain composure and to offer direction and hope to the family.

As with all closings, summarization is important. Couples or families who come and share their problems and fears need to know they've been heard. They also need help finding closure and preparing to leave. A thorough, sensitive summary helps facilitate these goals:

> We certainly covered lots of important material today. Your family has been through a lot and you have ideas about things that you'd like to work on. Grandma's death seemed like it would be much easier than it has been, given she had been ill for so long. Her death, along with Peter's recent legal trouble and Ginny's decision to move in with her boyfriend next month, has seemed like too much, and your old comfortable ways of talking with each other have disappeared. Dad, you're often angry. Mom, you feel torn 50 different ways. Ginny, you feel nobody pays much attention to you, and Peter, everyone pays *too* much attention to you. Now, I may not have repeated everything, but I think that catches some of the main areas. Did I miss any big ones?

Homework assignments are another common closing tool. This might involve communication time, journaling, charting behaviors, going on dates, reading, listening to instructional recordings, or other activities. Your opening explanation of how you work should alert the couple or family to the idea that you'll be asking them to do something between sessions.

Finally, in closing with multiple people, it can be helpful to acknowledge how their lives will continue in new and interesting ways after the session. You may want to devise a short statement, the essence of which communicates, "This will be different at home." Here's an example:

> Being in counseling together, with me here to guide, ask questions, and even boss people around, is different from when you're together at home. We've talked about areas that are troubling. I'm sure you'll continue

talking about them at home, but I hope you remember the guidelines we've used today. If you try to talk things through at home and get stuck, remember, we'll have more time to work together next week. It's okay if everything doesn't get solved at once.

Termination

As noted earlier, working with couples and families is complex simply because of the number of people involved. Even scheduling the next meeting can be difficult, so allow time for this. It's awkward and unprofessional to run out of time and leave people unsure about the details of the next meeting.

Concluding comments should be brief, reassuring, and upbeat. Expressing respect for their choice to come in, your appreciation for their work, or noting events upcoming in the week (birthdays, travel plans) can be good transitional termination talk.

SPECIAL CONSIDERATIONS

The following discussion focuses on situations and issues that clinicians who plan to work with couples and families should consider. These situations and issues are unique to working with couples and families.

Identifying, Managing, and Modifying Conflict

Couples or families who come for help are frequently experiencing serious conflicts in their relationship(s) and often lack conflict management skills. Counselors must identify, manage, and sometimes modify how couples and families are addressing conflict. Some couples and families will be conflict avoidant and others will fight with each other with dizzying speed and intensity.

Conflict Process Versus Conflict Content

Common areas of conflict reported by couples are money, sex, and in-laws. Of course, there are many other potential couple conflict areas, including division of labor, child rearing, and recreational and religious pursuits/preferences (Sperry, Carlson, & Peluso, 2006). Families, too, arrive in counseling with a variety of conflict areas. Shared duties, chores, children's individuation needs, and fairness in family resource allocation are common family issues presented in counseling.

Some have noted that when working with minority couples and families, conflicts often involve child rearing, co-parenting/parental rights, competition for attention between biological child and partner, relationship invisibility, religious beliefs, coming out, role identification, and how to handle stress and stigma (Kimberly Johnson, personal communication, August 10, 2012). Although it's good to be aware of conflict-laden areas for specific cultural groups, it's also important to recognize that there will be similarities and unique differences in what specific couples and families argue about.

Conflict content refers to *what* is argued about. In contrast, *conflict process* refers to *how* everyone argues. This is an important distinction; during the first session clinicians help couples and families identify both *what* they are arguing about as well as *how* they are arguing with one another.

It's likely that many couples and families who come to therapy have significant skill deficits in communication and conflict management. They're having problems with the *how* of conflict. This is natural, as most humans aren't built to communicate and handle conflict well (Wilmot & Hocker, 2010).

Conflict content and process are always present during initial family or couple interviews. Both are important. Further, it's likely that you may have personal reactions to *what* families and couples argue about and *how* they argue.

How Do You Feel About Conflict?

Not everyone enjoys open conflict. Some people are conflict avoiders and others conflict seekers (Wilmot & Hocker, 2010). This is true about counselors as well as clients. If you find yourself having strong conflict avoidance qualities, you may not be well suited to being a couple or family counselor. Generally, before entering the couple/family counseling field, it's advisable to explore how you respond to interpersonal conflict and what conflict issues push your buttons (see *Putting It in Practice* 14.2).

PUTTING IT IN PRACTICE 14.2

Exploring Your Conflict Buttons

To explore how you might respond to various couple and family conflict scenarios, reflect on some of the following questions:

1. Do you have specific conflict topics that push your emotional buttons? For example, some clinicians bring so much personal baggage about in-laws into the session they can't help but reveal biases when couples discuss their in-laws.

2. Do you have any biases about how couples should behave in their marriage or partnership, or ways parents, children, and other family members must behave to be a "healthy" family? Some counselors may have idealistic visions of couple or family relationships. Having an overly idealistic attitude toward relationships may cause you to rigidly promote a particular ideal for couples or families, and this ideal may not fit for the clients in your office.

3. Do you carry conflict home with you? Working with families and couples can be emotionally charged. The conflicts you witness, help manage, and sometimes become a part of, can be very draining.

4. When you were growing up, what conflict issues and process styles were characteristic of your family? Did your mother and father avoid conflict, did they engage in scary and threatening conflicts, or did they handle conflict gracefully? There could be unresolved conflicts in your own family or romantic relationship that could get activated if clients discuss similar conflicts—clinicians should seek personal therapy for this.

How Much Should You Let People Argue and Fight During Sessions?

As you might guess from material covered in this chapter, our answer to this question is: Not much. Usually families and couples come to counseling partly because their joint conflict management skills are poor or dysfunctional. Therefore, if you allow them to engage in open conflict without intervening and changing the process, they recapitulate their dysfunctional conflict patterns. It's your responsibility, among other things, to disrupt these patterns and help people establish new, different, and more adaptive conflict management patterns.

The only reasonable rationale for allowing couples or families to engage in their usual dysfunctional conflict patterns is to gather assessment information. It can be useful to glimpse how people usually argue and fight with one another. However, this observation period should be brief, followed by discussion and guidance toward improved communication and conflict management. To help couples or families transition from deep emotional conflict to a more intellectual analysis of their conflict patterns, make a statement similar to the following:

> Okay, I'd like you two (or in the case of families, everyone) to stop your argument now.

Depending on the intensity of the conflict, this statement may need to be stated in a strong, authoritative manner—and then repeated.

> You've given me a glimpse into how you handle conflict. Let me tell you what I saw. First, Ari, I saw you express criticism toward Raul about his lack of involvement in housecleaning. Then, Raul, I saw you defend yourself by complaining that Ari's housecleaning standards are too high. Then, Ari countered Raul's statement by suggesting that his housecleaning standards are abysmally low. And then, Raul, you started talking about how, usually, men and women have different cleanliness standards and that Ari needs to loosen up and be different from her mother. Finally, the reason I interrupted is that you both seemed to be getting increasingly frustrated because you weren't making progress. Is that right?

As you can see from this relatively tame example, conflict interactions accumulate rapidly. Many things happen simultaneously. It can be daunting to track and summarize conflict process. This task is not simple. It requires exceptional listening skills, concise communication, and sensitivity. Couples will be wary about whether you're siding more with one partner than the other. Aligning with a certain family member in family work is a potent intervention and should be done intentionally (Murray et al., 2012). Managing conflict requires tact and timing because clinicians must determine when and how to interrupt couple conflict.

Some theoretical orientations emphasize that couple conflict process is guided and sometimes determined by unresolved family of origin issues (Luquet, 2006). While managing conflict, it's also wise to note both content and process with this intergenerational view in mind. *Putting It in Practice* 14.3 provides a sample couple conflict scenario.

PUTTING IT IN PRACTICE 14.3

Couple Conflict Intervention

Imagine you're the clinician for the following scenario. As you read the example, evaluate how comfortable you'd feel during the session. Write, word-for-word, an intervention you might try after the couple returned to your office. Compare and contrast your answers with those of others.

Darren is a 58-year-old American Indian. He is married to Anita, a 45-year-old Caucasian. It's Darren's third marriage and Anita's second marriage. During the first few minutes of their initial session, Anita erupts in anger toward Darren. She accuses him of physical abuse, tells him she now understands why he's been divorced twice before, and marches out of your office. Darren jumps up and runs after her. They both return about one minute later. Anita continues to look angry, and Darren is pleading with her to stay in the session and try to work things out. Anita turns to you and says that she refuses to speak to Darren for the remainder of the session, but she will stay if you will try to "talk some sense into his head."

Reflect, either on your own or with a partner, how you might handle this counseling situation.

Conflict can escalate quickly. This is especially true in cases of physically or emotionally abusive couples or families. Abusive or highly conflicted couples and families often have so much emotional energy and baggage that their conflicts erupt in powerful outbursts (Horwitz, Santiago, Pearson, & LaRussa-Trott, 2009). We've had clients refuse to speak for the remainder of a session, try to hit or kick each other in the counseling office, and abruptly leave sessions amidst a flurry of profanity. The potential emotional explosiveness of couple and family interviews requires that clinicians maintain control throughout the session. With more disturbed couples or family systems, greater structure and control is needed. In extreme cases, you may act as an intermediary, paraphrasing almost everything that is said and sometimes not allowing the conflicting parties to speak directly to each other.

In summary, allowing families or couples to act out their emotionally based, destructive conflict processes during counseling is ill-advised. Clients shouldn't be allowed to repeatedly yell at one another, raise abusive accusations, or repeatedly use ineffective communication skills. Instead, clinicians structure the session and become more active, especially when working with high-conflict families and couples (Gurman, 2008).

Limit Setting in the Service of Therapy

Couples and families sometimes have impulsive and destructive styles and aren't able to effectively set limits themselves. Setting limits on couples and families can be therapeutic for several reasons: (a) the limit prevents the couple or family from further damaging behavior in session; (b) applying reasoned and thoughtful limits provides clients with role modeling for how to stop destructive exchanges; (c) there's a chance that gentle and well-reasoned external limits can be internalized;

and (d) heightened conflict can distract clients and keep them from focusing productively on underlying issues and so limits help refocus the therapy (see *Putting It in Practice* 14.4 to explore your ability to set limits with couples and families).

PUTTING IT IN PRACTICE 14.4

Limit Setting With Couples and Families

Imagine the following scenarios:

Scenario 1: Antonio and Lucy have been married 4 years and are struggling as a couple. They have an 8-month-old baby girl. Unfortunately, they were unable to obtain a babysitter and, therefore, they arrive at their intake interview session, much to your surprise, with their little girl in tow. Although she's quiet during the session's initial 10 minutes, she progressively becomes more distressed and begins wailing and screeching in a way that makes it impossible to continue the interview. Discuss the following questions with your class, discussion group, or supervisor:

1. Can you end the session politely and reschedule another appointment?
2. Would you be able to gently ask the parents to leave their child with a babysitter during the next appointment time?
3. How would you respond if, despite your gentle reminder, the parents showed up at the next appointment with their daughter and stated, "We really tried to get a babysitter, but still couldn't come up with one."
4. If the parents insist on meeting with you while their daughter is present, can you imagine any circumstances under which you would agree to meet with the parents even though they brought their fussy 8-month-old child?

Scenario 2: The Johnsons have been referred by youth court for family therapy. The family includes Margie Johnson, mother of twins Rick and Roy Johnson, and Calvin, Margie's live-in boyfriend. Margie is 37 and the twins are 15. Calvin has lived with Margie and the twins for the past 3 years. His daughter, Mollie, visits on weekends. The boys' father is currently in prison for forgery and hasn't seen the boys since they were infants. During the initial visit, Margie, Roy, Rick, and Calvin are all present. The twins begin having a burping contest and Margie gets the giggles. Calvin does nothing. The counselor waits until things settle down and then asks another question. Roy and Rick both burp in response. Margie begins laughing again. No one responds to the question. Discuss the following questions.

1. What's your initial response to the scene? Do you wish you could call youth court and send back the referral? Do you imagine laughing along with Margie or sitting stone silent,

like Calvin? Do you imagine feeling intimidated or disgusted or hopeless?
2. Can you think of ways to get some cooperative interactions going?
3. What are your reactions to the idea of burping along with the boys?
4. For whom do you have the deepest empathy? How could you use this empathy in the service of therapy?

Diversity Issues

Working with gay and lesbian couples or couples and families from different cultural backgrounds can present clinicians with unique challenges (Bigner & Wetchler, 2004). As discussed in Chapter 11, when a clinician and client have clear and unmistakable differences, the client may initially scrutinize the clinician more closely than if the client and clinician are culturally similar or of the same sexual orientation. These circumstances call for sensitivity, tact, and a discussion of the obvious. Imagine the following scenario:

You're a White, heterosexual, Christian male. You have a new appointment at 3 P.M. with Sandy Davis and Latisha Johnson for couple counseling. When you get to the waiting room, you see two African American females sitting side by side. You introduce yourself and on the short walk back to your office you mentally process the situation and come to several conclusions: (a) You're about to meet with an African American lesbian couple; (b) you've never done therapy with this particular cultural minority group; (c) you're aware of your uncertainty and your concerns about your lack of knowledge makes you feel uncomfortable, but you also recognize that you want the couple to be comfortable with you and realize they may be feeling similar discomfort about your cultural differences; (d) you are clear that it's your ethical mandate to provide services to the best of your ability; and (e) although you don't feel competent to work with this couple, this is a low-income clinic and so the couple may not have many alternatives. How do you proceed?

Below is a brief list of how a clinician might specifically handle this situation. After this list, we provide a description of the underlying principles:

- Welcome the couple to your office with the warmth and engagement you offer to all clients (e.g., "I'm glad you could come to the clinic today for your appointment and am happy to meet you. . . . ").
- Explain confidentiality and the limits of confidentiality. Also, review relevant agency policies that you routinely review with new clients.
- If you know the purpose of their visit (e.g., couple counseling) because of the registration form, explain how you usually work with couples.
- Let the couple know you'd like them to ask any questions of you they may have . . . but before they ask the questions, explain:

My usual approach with couples is primarily based on work with heterosexual couples. I don't have experience working with African American lesbian couples. I'd like to work with you as long as you're comfortable working with me and it seems like the work is helpful. I know there aren't lots of couple's counseling options available. What I propose—if it's okay with the two of you—is that we start working together today. Today I'll be asking you directly about your goals for counseling, but also about your interests, values, spirituality and other things that will help me know you better as individuals and as a couple. And toward the end of our session I'll ask you for feedback about how you think our work together is going and I'll try to honor that feedback and make adjustments so we can work well together. If, for whatever reason, it looks like we can't work together effectively, I'll do my best to find you a good referral to another therapist. What do you think of that plan?

As described in Chapter 11, the general multicultural competencies include: (a) awareness (e.g., knowing your biases and limitations); (b) knowledge (e.g., gathering information pertaining to specific cultural groups); and (c) skills (e.g., applying culturally specific interventions in a culturally sensitive manner). In addition to these competencies, the preceding case illustrates the need for clinicians to explicitly address cultural differences using the following strategies:

- Cultural universality (treating culturally different clients with same respect you offer to culturally similar clients).
- Collaboration (working with the clients to understand the particulars of their culture and situation).
- Feedback (soliciting ongoing feedback about client perceptions of how the interview is proceeding and make adjustments based on that feedback).

No clinician can be expected to have awareness, knowledge, and skills for working with every possible diverse client. That being the case, if you also rely on cultural universality, collaboration, and feedback to help strengthen the therapeutic alliance, you'll have a better chance for therapy to proceed in an ethically and professionally acceptable manner.

Shifting From Individual to Couple or Family Therapy

Throughout this chapter we've emphasized that clinicians should treat all couple and family members equally and that relationship partners and family members may try to build coalitions with clinicians to attain greater power or control. For these reasons, we recommend that you avoid the ubiquitous temptation to shift from individual to couple or family therapy with people from the same family system. We also advise against simultaneous individual and couple or family work by the same counselor. Our rules are:

- Once an individual client, always an individual client. Generally, we will not do individual counseling with someone and then initiate couple or family work that involves that person. Instead, we refer those involved to a competent colleague.
- Following completion of couple or family counseling, on rare occasions, we might consider working in individual therapy with one family member. However, when doing so, we always make it clear: Once we start individual therapy, we won't return to couple or family therapy.

For a number of reasons, many therapists don't abide by these suggestions; consider the following scenarios:

- An individual client says something to the therapist such as, "Because we've already been working together, I trust you. I don't want to start all over and go see someone else for marriage therapy. My husband says he doesn't mind."
- A teenage boy and his therapist mutually conclude that family therapy is needed. The boy states, "I absolutely refuse to go to therapy with anyone else but you! There's no way I'm going to see a different shrink!"
- Therapists may want to prolong therapy with a person because they enjoy working with that client or because they need to maintain their caseload for financial reasons.
- Clients may believe that a particular therapist is the best choice because he or she is already well versed in the couple's or family's therapy issues. It feels safe to stay with the same professional.

You may have noticed that we referred to the potential shift from individual to couple or family therapy as the "ubiquitous temptation." From a therapist's perspective, it's nearly always tempting to continue counseling when there has been some success with a client, or when a client expresses a strong preference to continue counseling with you, or when there is potential financial gain from continuing counseling. This is also a temptation because shifting from individual to couple or family therapy includes many potential problems that are easy to overlook. As you read about and reflect on our views regarding this issue, keep in mind that we're expressing our professional opinion and bias—therapists and counselors may disagree with this cautious perspective (Hecker, 2010).

Conflicts of Loyalty

Perhaps the greatest reason to avoid shifting from individual to couple or family therapy is that conflicts of loyalty inevitably ensue. Unless you make great efforts to build trust and rapport with the original client's romantic partner or family, the new parties are likely to believe you hold a deeper loyalty to the original client. Additionally, if you, for any reason, side with the new client against the original client, the original client may feel betrayed and abandoned. This could leave you stuck in a no-win therapy bind: both or all clients quickly suspect you've already "sided" with the original client, or have switched allegiances. Such dynamics add unnecessarily to an already difficult task.

You Are (Almost Always) Not the Only (Competent) Therapist in Town

An excuse often offered for simultaneously doing individual, couple, and family work with the same people is that the people involved insist on it. Underlying their preference is their belief that you've done excellent work. This is flattering, but choosing to cross boundaries can undo the good work you did in the first place. Avoiding dual or multiple roles, an ethical guideline present in all mental health professional ethics codes, includes avoiding being someone's family therapist and individual therapist if being in both roles compromises your objectivity (R. Sommers-Flanagan, 2012).

Catering to the clients' ideas that you're the best or only option isn't necessarily healthy. Helping clients attain a more flexible manner of functioning in the world and increasing their capacities for relationships are goals that undergird most therapies. Encouraging an individual to try a different therapist can be an important vote of confidence in the client. It communicates that you believe the client can connect with another professional and can use that therapeutic relationship to grow and change. It's rarely justified to allow or encourage client dependence on you. Obviously, in some rural settings, managing (or juggling) multiple therapy relationships in one family may be unavoidable. In fact, you may not be the *only competent* therapist in town, you may be the *only* therapist in town.

Identification, Projection, Joining, and Avoiding

As you work with couples and families, you may find it challenging to keep your *own* early learning, beliefs, and attachment issues from affecting your work. The common term for this reaction is *countertransference* (see Chapter 5). Couples and families can elicit significant countertransference reactions. Your reactions can involve overidentification with certain conflicts, projection of your own emotions or issues onto family members, and unconscious avoidance of material you don't want to think or talk about.

Adding to the complexity is the fact that effective assessment and therapy is enhanced by clinicians' life experiences. Even if it were possible to exclude your own personal family and relationship issues from your work (including your unconscious processes and conflicts), it would be inadvisable. Common experiences form part of the foundation of any relationship and assist us in understanding other peoples' experiences. *Multicultural Highlight* 14.2 describes a technique to help you explore your own relationship and family issues.

MULTICULTURAL HIGHLIGHT 14.2

Family Choreography

Family choreography is a technique developed by Peggy Papp (1976) and used in many treatment programs. To explore some family-of-origin material, choose members of the class to represent the salient members of your family of origin and position them physically according to the roles they played in your family. Then position yourself in your own role. You can hold a particular arrangement for a minute or two and feel the power of the rigid positions or direct movement and interactions that represent your family dynamics. Then have someone stand in for you and walk around the creation you've fashioned, observing the stand-in family members. Finally, change the action or structure in some way that would have been positive for you. Move positions, change interrelationships, remove members. Do whatever you like and view what you've done.

After everyone sits down, share your feelings about the experience. Also, invite those who were involved to share whatever reactions they had.

As you explore your unique, personal family dynamics within a group setting, it's especially revealing to examine issues associated with culture and ethnicity (Ho et al., 2004). In the context of your class, you may have individuals who are male, female, disabled, gay, lesbian, straight, Asian, African American, American Indian, Hispanic, older, younger, liberal, conservative, and so on. If your class is up to the task, discuss the major differences in family style between these unique individuals.

Working with couples and families usually involves a joining that's more intense than in individual work. It's analogous to empathy but perhaps more inclusive. This joining involves coming not only into the worldview of each individual, but also into the worldview of the relationship(s). In the process, you bring your own points of view. Your presence in the system, of course, alters the system. In addition, your views are altered by having joined the system. Keeping a professional perspective in the midst of all this exposure isn't easy. Sometimes, counselors "overjoin" and lose perspective completely. Other times, they avoid joining at all, staying aloof and clinically removed. This is safer, but less informative and probably less therapeutic.

Minuchin and Fishman (1981) discussed the concept of *joining*:

> Joining is more an attitude than a technique, and it is the umbrella under which all therapeutic transactions occur. Joining is letting the family know that the therapist understands them and is working with and for them. Only under this protection can the family have the security to explore alternatives, try the unusual, and change. Joining is the glue that holds the therapeutic system together. (pp. 31–32)

Joining with a couple or family increases the likelihood of tripping on our own unresolved family or relationship issues. A big problem with unconscious unresolved issues that might affect our work is—they're unconscious! The following list may help you glimpse areas that may be active conflicts for you.

- Do you have topics you'd rather not talk about? Not only can it be difficult to bring up sexual matters in counseling, but other topics like mothers-in-law, miscarriage, belts for punishment, the denial of pets, forced consumption of food. All of these can push our buttons.
- Do you have any biases about clients from diverse cultural or ethnic backgrounds? For example, some counselors have difficulty accepting patriarchal or macho styles associated with some Hispanic, Middle Eastern, or religious couples.
- Does your cultural orientation inhibit your ability to work with some family dynamics? For example, Crow and Navajo cultures often teach that the son-in-law and mother-in-law shouldn't speak. Other cultures may be uncomfortable with men who directly express their sadness or grief through tears. Can you work with families in a way that accepts their cultural ways?
- Do you have biases against gay or lesbian people? Further, do you have beliefs about the appropriateness of lifetime exclusive romantic commitments between people of the same sex (i.e., gay and lesbian marriages)?

- Do you find you cannot get certain conflicts or client problems out of your mind? This may manifest by finding yourself thinking about a family or couple excessively, or dreaming about them, or barely resisting talking about them with family or friends.
- Are certain conflict areas guaranteed to cause you to condemn one person or be overly sympathetic to the other?

This is, of necessity, not an exhaustive list. It's important to track your reactions and ways of being on an ongoing basis and to seek professional supervision and collegial support when you suspect your own background, values, beliefs, or conflicts are getting in the way of your work with couples or families. If necessary, we hope you will have the courage and energy to seek personal therapy to explore your own unresolved issues.

SUMMARY

Working with couples and families presents a number of unique challenges and ironies. These include: (a) the need to work with more people with less time; and (b) controversies in defining couples and families.

Although theoretical orientation is a strong determinant of therapist activities that occur during each stage of couple and family interviews, some tasks are dealt with more generically. During the introduction phase of the clinical interview with couples and families therapists must clarify confidentiality, identify who will attend sessions, and provide a detailed informed consent process. The therapist's opening statement helps further orient clients and establishes norms about the inclusion of everyone's voice. Maintaining balance is of particular importance during the opening stage.

The interview body is most influenced by theoretical orientation and presenting problem. There are both traditional and popular approaches to to working with couples and families. Currently, emotion-focused therapy, Gottman's research-based model, and cognitive and behavioral approaches are common. Additionally, specific approaches for particular treatment populations are very important. These include feminist therapies and affirmative therapies for sexual minority clients.

The closing is a challenge to manage, both informationally and emotionally; it usually requires significantly more time than closing with an individual. Maintaining balance, looking toward the future, and homework assignments are important tasks associated with both the closing and termination interview stages.

A number of formal assessments can be used effectively with couples and families. Special considerations for couple and family clinicians include: (a) managing interpersonal conflict, (b) setting limits, (c) seeing an individual in the family system for individual therapy, and (d) working with gay or lesbian couples and families.

Finally, we describe ways that countertransference plays an unavoidable role in couple and family work. Suggestions for recognition and management of clinician countertransference were offered.

SUGGESTED READINGS AND RESOURCES

American Association for Marriage and Family Therapy. (2012). *AAMFT code of ethics*. Washington, DC: Author.

This is the code of ethics for members of the American Association of Marriage and Family Therapy. Go to: http://www.aamft.org/imis15/content/legal_ethics/code_of_ethics.aspx.

Bigner, J., & Wetchler, J. L. (2004). *Relationship therapy with same-sex couples*. New York, NY: Haworth.

This is an edited work simultaneously published in the *Journal of Couple and Relationship Therapy*. Given the paucity of published material on working with same-sex couples, this book is especially useful for increasing your sensitivity to the salient issues and providing you with a foundation from which you can seek additional information.

Gottman, J. M., & DeClaire, J. (2001). *The relationship cure: A five-step guide for building better connections with family, friends, and lovers*. New York, NY: Crown.

Gottman is the premier marriage researcher and writer in the United States. His books are based on his vast research and knowledge of marriage and family functioning.

Gurman, A. S. (2008). *Clinical handbook of couple therapy* (4th ed.). New York, NY: Guilford.

This text offers broad coverage of many couple therapy interventions and theoretical perspectives. It also includes material on divorce, multicultural couple therapy, and how to work with couples who struggle with various medical or psychiatric problems.

Hecker, L. (Ed.) (2010). *Ethical issues in couple and family therapy*. New York, NY: Routledge.

This book offers an excellent overview of the many sticky ethical issues that can arise in couple and family therapy.

Helm, K. M., & Carlson, J. (2013). *Love, intimacy, and the African American couple*. New York, NY: Routledge.

This edited volume provides specific information about African American norms and values within couple relationships and is essential reading for practitioners who consistently work with African American couples.

Ho, M. K., Rasheed, J. M., & Rasheed, M. N. (2004). *Family therapy with ethnic minorities* (2nd ed.). Thousand Oaks, CA: Sage.

This text offers guidance for how to provide family therapy services to major ethic minority groups—including First Nations Peoples, Latinos, Asian Americans, and African Americans.

Johnson, S. (2008) *Hold me tight: Seven conversations for a lifetime of love*. New York, NY: Little, Brown.

In this very popular book about the emotion-focused model, Sue Johnson writes directly to couples to guide them through conversations that will help them maintain their loving relationships into the future.

Johnson, S. M. (2004). *The practice of emotionally focused couple therapy*. New York, NY: Brunner-Routledge.

This book describes emotion-focused couple therapy, an empirically supported approach to working with couples. It combines research evidence with practical advice on how to apply this approach to couples work.

Minuchin, S., & Fishman, H. C. (1981). *Family therapy techniques*. Cambridge, MA: Harvard University Press.

This is a classic family therapy text and good basic reading for anyone who wants to do family therapy.

Odell, M., & Campbell, C. E. (1998). *The practical practice of marriage and family therapy: Things my training supervisor never told me*. New York, NY: Haworth.

In contrast to more theoretical and sterile approaches to writing about and teaching marriage and family therapy, this book has a strong practical and clinical focus. For example, chapters include: "It Ain't Like the University Clinic," and "So What Do I Do After the Intake?" This practical approach is usually appreciated by beginning students who've had enough of reading and discussing theory.

Interviewing in Online and Other Non– Face-to-Face (Non-FtF) Environments

CHAPTER OBJECTIVES

Chances are that as a graduate student in this cyber-infused century, you've had significant opportunities to learn, teach, play, shop, and maybe even date online. In fact, many of you may have started and/or ended all sorts of relationships online. The online community is active, vibrant, and extremely large. By the time you read this, over one billion people will have Facebook pages, including over 50% of the North American population (http://www.internetworldstats.com/facebook.htm).

After reading this chapter, you will understand:

- How technology has become an extension of the self.
- Ways in which face-to-face (FtF) clinical interviewing is the same as or different from non-FtF clinical interviewing.
- How to use basic clinical interviewing skills in text-only or online formats.
- Distinct non-FtF communication modalities.
- What the research says about telephone and online therapeutic process and outcomes.
- Ethical and practical problems and solutions.
- How to prepare for non-FtF interviews.
- The challenge and importance of retaining multicultural sensitivity when working in non-FtF domains.

The time spent texting and talking on cell phones continues to increase every year and is a central aspect of many personal and professional relationships. For many people in the electronic age, face-to-face (FtF) contact has been replaced by non-FtF contact. This shift to non-FtF contact is not only the norm for many, but also a preference (Havas, de Nooijer, Crutzen, & Feron, 2011; Sánchez-Ortiz et al., 2011). All this less direct human contact is causing rumblings within the traditional counseling and psychotherapy world. Publications focusing on electronic and social media are growing as our profession struggles to leap across the digital divide in responsive and ethical ways (Graff & Hecker, 2010; Yuen, Goetter, Herbert, & Forman, 2012). The question of how to appropriately integrate this rapidly developing dimension of the human community into professional practice is on the minds of many helping professionals.

In this chapter, we provide background, examples, and suggestions for interviewing assessment and building a therapeutic alliance in situations when the client is not sitting in the room with you. These situations begin with asynchronous written correspondence (e.g., letter writing), but also include telephone interviews, videoconferencing, text-only synchronous messaging, and Second Life and similar Web-based virtual environments that are designed to allow social and professional interactions using avatars. The permutations are endless, but we hope to provide you with basics that apply across these exciting but still-developing domains.

This chapter focuses primarily on two dimensions of the online and non-FtF clinical interactions:

1. Clinical interviewing as an assessment procedure.
2. Clinical interviewing as a procedure for developing a therapeutic alliance and initiating counseling or psychotherapy.

TECHNOLOGY AS AN EXTENSION OF THE SELF

As online instruction began gaining traction and expanding, teachers venturing into this new educational realm had to learn a whole new set of skills to effectively deliver the same content they had successfully taught in person for years. The chalkboard wasn't enough anymore. Similarly, as online or telephone clinical mental health work has become available as an alternative or adjunct to FtF work, professionals have needed to make similar adjustments (Epstein & Klinkenberg, 2001; Yoshino et al., 2001). We've had to learn new technical skills, consider new ethical concerns, and adjust our clinical skills to be effective. It seems almost unnecessary to say this, but human communication cannot be separated from the constraints and benefits of the method or means of expression, connection, delivery, and reception. Information arriving through words on a screen is experienced differently than words spoken on a cell phone or during video-chat, and, of course, all are different from information shared in person. However, each of these communication methods adheres to many of the same human communication rules and dimensions as the FtF modality.

What's the Same and What's Different?

Recently I decided to include a special social media policy in my professional informed consent paperwork. I did this because after I established Facebook and LinkedIn accounts, I began fielding requests to become "friends" and connections with former and current clients. At first, without reflection, I said yes, but then quickly retreated after discovering a range of problems with having social-media contact with clients. As the ethics codes imply, it's not that having multiple relationships with clients is always inappropriate or harmful; it's just complicated, sometimes it's confusing, and as professionals we should avoid these multiple relationships unless they clearly benefit clients. My discovery is that boundaries are boundaries, whether digital or flesh and blood. (Paraphrased comment by a Clinical Interviewing workshop participant, April 2011)

At the heart of ethical and effective clinical interviewing is a professional relationship built on interpersonal communication. The various technological options now available for communicating are simply fancy tools we use to reach and serve more people in more ways. It's still a professional human being on one end, and a person or set of people in need of services and expertise on the other.

The basic attending, listening, and action skills outlined and described in Chapters 3 and 4 still form the foundation of understanding interviewer behavior—regardless of whether interviewer responses are delivered via voice or text. Another way of saying this is that a paraphrase is a paraphrase is a paraphrase. The purpose and function of a paraphrase, a nondirective reflection of feeling, or other interviewer responses remain consistent across various human communication delivery systems.

This is true even though the method or manner in which a nondirective reflection of feeling is expressed may be different; with text-based mediums, emoticons are a handy method of reflecting feelings.

When I read your words on the screen it seems you're expressing sadness at the loss of your romantic relationship☺.

Of course, many ways of responding to client feelings or emotions can be expressed without sound and without visual contact. This means that when it comes to addressing client emotions, a competent online clinical interviewer will be able to appropriately use a range of different responses, such as:

- U seem angry. (nondirective reflection of feeling)
- Your words have anger in them. (nondirective reflection of feeling)
- Tho I'm not totally sure, there seems to be anger or resentment under what ur saying. (interpretive feeling reflection)
- Ur words say one thing☹, but I can't help but think there's something else going on for u too☺. (interpretive feeling reflection)
- When I imagine myself in your shoes, I feel angry. (feeling validation)
- :((an emoticon all by itself might have a feeling reflection purpose and function, but it also might convey a message of feeling validation)
- When I read ur words, I feel sad. (this is a self-disclosure with an interpretive reflection of feeling quality designed to lead the client to get more in touch with sad feelings that haven't yet been acknowledged)

With the exception of video-based communication (e.g., Skype), a major difference with non-FtF contact is that interviewers don't have visual or audio access to nonverbal feedback. This can be problematic on many levels. As discussed in Chapter 3 (see Birdwhistell, 1970; Hall, 1966), much of human communication is nonverbal. The inability to use nonverbal communication to express empathy, for example, places a greater burden on interviewers to do so using text.

When it comes to basic attending and listening skills, the absence of nonverbal cues can affect both interviewer and client. As you recall, basic attending skills include: (a) eye contact, (b) body language, (c) vocal qualities, and (d) verbal tracking (Ivey & Ivey, 1999). Traditionally, demonstrating that you're listening has been viewed as essential in the counseling relationship, and not demonstrating adequate or culturally appropriate listening skills can adversely affect the process and outcome (Ivey & Ivey, 1999). However, in the text-only interviewing and counseling domain, eye contact, body language, and vocal qualities now have zero impact on the clinical encounter.

The elimination of nonverbal/visual contact between interviewer and client places far more emphasis on language. An interesting consequence of this venue is the fact that many recipients of online interviewing and counseling services feel increased relief, comfort, and control as a result of not having face-to-face visual and verbal contact. Just as the businessperson who stays at home and participates in a voice-only conference call can choose to remain in pajamas all day, the client engaging in online counseling has the luxury of avoiding in-person human contact and all the tedious social requirements associated with such contact. For some, avoiding direct human contact while having an alternative form of human contact feels quite good and alleviates significant interpersonal anxiety. However, in spite of our pajama comment, it should also be emphasized that many online counselors make a point of dressing professionally for appointments as a way of shifting into a more professional persona (Kristopher Goodrich, personal communication, September 15, 2012).

Silence is another traditional interviewer response that's handled differently in the absence of visual contact. Without accompanying nonverbal signals and cues, silence can be misinterpreted. Anyone who has experienced dead sound during a telephone conversation can testify to the capacity for humans to project thoughts, feelings, and behaviors onto a blank screen. Similarly, when silence or a lapse in communication occurs online, it could be that the client has decided to take a bathroom break or is sipping coffee and thoughtfully reflecting on what to say next, or has gotten angry and turned off the computer. Because it's natural and human to wonder what might really be going on when the other party goes quiet, if interviewers plan to wait for further input, or not respond, it should be done explicitly. For example, typing a message like the following can be helpful:

> I'm just waiting and looking forward to hearing what you have to say next. No pressure, though.

This leads us to another difference between FtF and online communication. In FtF interviewing, time is set aside for the contact, and measured in minutes. In the cyberworld, time is stretched and distorted. Of course, most people multitask when talking on their phones or e-mailing. Text and Facebook messages can be posted anytime, and can be as short or as long as the sender might like. It may be common for online counseling clients to expect to hear back via text, instant messaging (IM), or e-mail quickly. This may be due to exposure to Internet social media platforms in which the news-feed process is continuous. Therefore, if commentary isn't made within a few minutes or an hour of posting, the post moves into the past and is unlikely to garner much attention. Although this phenomenon might seem akin to a Gestalt therapy "Be here now" process, it also seems to translate into both (a) an increased pressure for immediate responsiveness and (b) a diminished likelihood to focus on a slower, less immediately gratifying response process. One way we think of this is that although electronic messages and messaging may never die, they do quickly fall out of focus within the user's Gestalt figure/ground formation process (J. Sommers-Flanagan & Sommers-Flanagan, 2012).

To adapt to immediacy expectations and volume issues, online or text-only interviewers need to explicitly communicate their policy and typical response time to prospective clients. It may be important to frame interviewer responses as coming at a distinct pace and volume so users can anticipate and perhaps add significance and meaning to interviewer/counselor communication. Professional online interviewers and counselors can benefit from framing their communications to foster positive anticipation.

Definition of Terms and Communication Modalities

There are many non-FtF clinical interviewing strategies and venues. In this section we define key terms that are crucial to our later discussion of how traditional clinical interviewing responses and strategies can be employed in non-FtF venues.

Text-Only Asynchronous Communication

This communication modality involves nonconcurrent written communication. A key factor in asynchronous communication is that participants send or post messages at different times; immediacy is lacking. Examples include letter writing, e-mail, and listserv communications. Like all asynchronous communication, text-based communications may be either unidirectional (one person writes and the other reads) or interactive.

Therapeutic letter writing has likely been an informal treatment modality since the development of written language. Most of us intuitively understand the therapeutic potential associated with receiving a handwritten letter. Words placed on paper and intentionally sent to another person carry with them substantial interpersonal significance and can create strong intellectual and emotional responses. Many people save letters for decades and even centuries.

In terms of modern psychotherapy and historical precedence, Sigmund Freud used letter writing as his main therapy strategy in the famous case of Little Hans (Freud, 1909). He communicated asynchronously with Little Hans's father while delivering his case formulation and treatment. More recently, narrative therapists have advocated therapeutic letter writing. Specifically, White (1995) speculated that one letter may be the equivalent of four or five face-to-face therapy sessions. We've used a trimmed-down version of this approach (i.e., note passing) in FtF work with children and adolescents (J. Sommers-Flanagan & Sommers-Flanagan, 2007b).

Voice-Only Asynchronous Communication

This communication modality involves vocal recordings passed back and forth from one party to another. Again, this doesn't allow for spontaneous or immediate interaction. Examples include audio-recorded self-help recordings, CDs, and podcasts. These communications also may be either unidirectional (one person listens) or interactive.

Interviewers might choose to use a voice-only asynchronous communication to initiate an assessment or intervention process. For example, instructions for completing an assessment or implementing a cognitive self-monitoring procedure can be delivered via audio recording or podcasting. As an intervention, an interviewer might offer an audio recording of a relaxation or meditation procedure. Typically, these assessment and intervention strategies have a more educational or cognitive and behavioral theoretical foundation.

Voice-Only Synchronous Distance Communication

Synchronous voice-only communications allow for more spontaneous verbal interaction, but of course, are limited to audio only. There are many examples of audio-only or telephonic clinical assessments and interventions. Examples include telephone assessments and crisis counseling hotlines.

Kramer et al. (2009) described advantages and potential limits of using telephonic assessment procedures:

> [T]he telephone facilitates access to [clients] who prefer this option, live far from the research center, reside in unsafe environments, or are not available during workday hours. These logistic advantages, however, must be balanced against the possibility that information gathered by telephone may not be comparable to information collected in person. (p. 623)

Because telephone assessment and intervention provide increased anonymity and social distance, clients may feel inclined toward more openness and honesty. Alternatively, FtF contact can facilitate deeper trust, which could translate into greater client honesty. These potential pros and cons have been discussed for at least seven decades (Wallin, 1949).

Text-Only Synchronous Communication

In this highly popular communication modality, interviewer and client exclusively use text (no audio or visual contact), and although there may be an asynchronous delay, responses may also be immediate and continuous. Examples include instant messaging (IM), online chatting (OC), and live or synchronous text messaging using smart phones.

The text message phenomenon seems especially popular among young technology users (Plester, Wood, & Bell, 2008). For example, in high school, college, and university settings students often maintain more or less continuous text contact with friends, family, and others. Texting often happens during class, during FtF counseling or psychotherapy sessions, and (unfortunately) while driving. This form of communication has rather quickly become the norm in many social groups. Because texting feels natural to young clients, it holds significant potential as a method for reaching this age group for assessment and intervention purposes (Windham, 2012).

There are also opportunities for text-only communications to expand into the 3-D virtual world through programs such as Second Life, or other programs using avatars and created environments. The choices of avatar, setting, and such move this modality slightly beyond text-based, but since the "contact" and visual input is not actually the counselor or the client, it might fit best, for now, in the text-based category.

Video-Link Synchronous Distance Communication

This communication modality involves interactions using both audio and visual representations of interviewer and client in real time. At present, these formats are the closest technological approximations to FtF interviewing assessment and intervention, but they still aren't the same as FtF. There are a number of important distinctions.

Full audio/video synchronous communication allows interviewers to send and receive nonverbal messages, including eye contact, body posture, vocal quality, and verbal tracking. However, even though the interviewer and client can see and hear each other in more or less real time, there are still significant problems with client identity misrepresentation, confidentiality, and emergency responsiveness (Rummell & Joyce, 2010). These issues will be discussed in greater detail later in this chapter.

Each of the preceding non-FtF communication formats has a history and a smaller or larger body of medical/psychological, mental health, and counseling literature (Epstein & Klinkenberg, 2001; Graff & Hecker, 2010; McCoyd & Kerson, 2006; Mitchell, Chen, & Medlin, 2010). They also are referred to by various terms. Rummell and Joyce (2010) discussed the proliferation of terminology used to reference these divergent approaches:

> There are many different terms that have been used in the literature to describe the specific type of computer-mediated communication that is used in online counseling, for example, e-mail therapy, telepsychiatry, Internet psychotherapy, cyberpsychology, cybertherapy, webcounseling, and computer-mediated psychotherapy. (p. 483)

Additional terms include but are not limited to the following:

- Online counseling (Mallen, Vogel, Rochlen, & Day, 2005)
- Internet-based therapy (Lampe, 2011)
- E-therapy (Graff & Hecker, 2010)
- Online therapy (Hanley, 2009)
- Videoconferencing or tele-assessment (Bernard et al., 2009)
- Telepsychiatry or Internet-mediated telemental health (Yoshino et al., 2001; Yuen et al., 2012)

Many of these terms are very specific, whereas others are more general. Interestingly, in some cases, the terms are more specific than their accompanying definitions. For example, Mallen et al. (2005) use *online counseling* and, although that term implies use of the Internet, they defined it as

> [A]ny delivery of mental and behavioral health services, including but not limited to therapy, consultation and psychoeducation, by a licensed practitioner to a client in a non–face-to-face setting through distance communication technologies such as the telephone, asynchronous e-mail, synchronous chat, and videoconferencing. (p. 764)

For our purposes, we lean toward using terminology to fit the specific modality, such as non-FtF assessment and intervention, or telephone assessment, or online counseling/Internet-based therapy. Perhaps eventually, leaders in the field will come to a clearer consensus about a single preferred terminology. Until then, we're choosing some degree of specificity over generality.

NON-FTF ASSESSMENT AND INTERVENTION RESEARCH

> I have connected deeply with you psychologically and emotionally on my computer, yet still remain isolated from you in every physical sense (no vision, no sound, no touch). It is very personal and not personal at all. (Lago, 1996, p. 288)

Non-FtF technology has changed the terrain of what constitutes intimacy. As Hanley (2009) stated, on one hand: "Critics challenge online practice because they believe relationships cannot reach sufficient levels of intimacy" (p. 5). On the other hand, it's perfectly clear that for some individuals Internet relationships are substantially gratifying and sometimes preferred. In the following sections we explore research on non-FtF clinical assessments, intervention processes, and outcomes.

The Therapeutic Alliance (Relationship)

> People meet and fall in love on the Internet. Why would a therapeutic relationship not also be possible? (Alleman, 2002, p. 201)

The therapeutic alliance is considered the strongest predictor of positive counseling and psychotherapy outcomes over which interviewers or therapists can exert direct control (Norcross & Lambert, 2011; Schneider & Krug, 2010). The alliance is viewed as facilitating not only psychotherapeutic treatment, but also the validity and reliability of interview-based assessments. Given the foundational role of the therapy alliance, it makes sense to examine what the research says about therapy alliances in non-FtF formats.

There is a small but growing research literature evaluating the therapeutic alliance in non-FtF assessment and therapy. In a summary article, Hanley and Reynolds (2009) stated:

> Each of the [five] studies [overall $n = 161$] ... supports the notion that good therapeutic alliances can be developed online. ... [C]lients perceived the alliance between them and the counsellor to be moderate or strong in nature. ... [W]ithin three out of the four studies that made comparisons to face-to-face equivalents, the online alliance proved higher than the comparison group. Such findings provide persuasive evidence supporting online therapy and challenge theoretical assumptions that relationships of sufficient quality to create therapeutic change cannot be developed online. (p. 8)

They further suggested that "a high percentage of the 161 total participants felt the quality of the relationship to be of a sufficient quality to create therapeutic change" (p. 9).

In a recent editorial focusing specifically on Internet-based therapy with trauma patients, Jain (2011) summarized research by Knaevelsrud and Maercker (2006, 2007), stating:

> Overall, they found evidence to suggest that a stable and positive online therapeutic relationship can be established via the Internet. Eighty-six percent of the sample described their Internet clinician experience as being personal and 60% reported that they did not miss face-to-face communication. However, this sample consisted largely of young, well-educated women with a range of PTSD symptoms, which limits the generalizability of these results. (p. 544)

There are also studies suggesting limits in the nature and quality of non-FtF therapeutic alliances. Specifically, Hufford, Glueckauf, and Webb (1999) reported on a study examining the working alliance using a videoconferencing format. Overall, the videoconferencing group had a weaker working alliance than a face-to-face control group.

Similarly, King, Bambling, Reid, and Thomas (2006) published a naturalistic study comparing an online working alliance with a working alliance associated with telephone counseling. Although working alliances were significantly more positive in the telephone counseling condition, both groups reported positive experiences and positive outcomes.

The British online counseling researcher T. Hanley (2009) also conducted a mixed-methods study focusing on the development and maintenance of a therapeutic alliance with youth. He reported that 76% of his sample rated their working alliance as either medium or high. Additionally, his summary of qualitative dimensions of his study illuminated issues that likely contribute to an online working alliance.

> The findings from the qualitative interviews aid our understanding of what elements of the meetings help the working alliance to develop or break down in this setting.... These range from practical necessities such as a room where the client will not be fearful of being interrupted, through the quality of the interactions during the sessions, to the trust the individual has in the counsellor/service.... [C]onsiderations such as the potential lack of privacy and the altering power differentials due to the increased control of the adolescent client are specifically highlighted. (p. 266)

Treatment Outcomes

Treatment-outcomes research for non-FtF assessment and interventions is limited but growing. Much of the research isn't well controlled, involves small sample sizes, and doesn't include random assignment to treatment and control conditions (Yuen et al., 2012). We feel certain this will be an area that will receive increased examination in the future.

Telephone Assessment

Historically the telephone has been the primary medium through which assessment and treatment have been provided from a distance. Telephone assessment procedures have been used for many years and, therefore, have the most established research base. Additionally, the fact that approximately 85% of U.S. adults own a cell phone speaks to the potential accessibility to clients that can be established through this communication modality (Zickuhr, 2011).

For the most part, research suggests that telephone assessment procedures are equivalent or nearly equivalent to FtF procedures. In particular, cognitive assessment of adults via telephone, especially older adults, is a widely accepted practice (Martin-Khan, Wootton, & Gray, 2010; van Uffelen, Chin A Paw, Klein, van Mechelen, & Hopman-Rock, 2007; Wilson & Bennett, 2005; Wilson et al., 2010). These assessments include a wide range of approaches to evaluating cognitive functioning or mental status, including both self-report and performance-based testing. Wilson and Bennett (2005) and Wilson et al. (2010) have concluded that administering cognitive test batteries by telephone is both valid and cost-effective for assessing cognitive functioning. As another example, Martin-Khan et al. (2010) showed that the 22-item Mini-Mental Status Examination (MMSE) was simple to administer by phone and correlated well with the face-to-face administration of the MMSE (see the Appendix for an extended mental status examination protocol that can be administered FtF, by phone, or online).

Telephonic diagnostic interviewing also has been shown to have adequate reliability and validity (Senior et al., 2007). Administration of many different diagnostic scales over the telephone has been reported (Maust et al., 2011). For example, in a study of in-person versus telephone diagnosis of social anxiety disorder, (SAD) "very high" agreement between the two assessment modalities was reported (Crippa et al., 2008). Crippa et al. (2008) concluded that "in-person and telephone SAD diagnoses obtained with the [Structured Clinical Interview for *DSM–IV*] SCID are comparable" (p. 244). This is a good example of the utility of non-FtF interviewing for clients whose anxiety might make them unlikely to visit a professional interviewer in person.

Telephone Interventions

There is a significant body of research focusing on the utility and effectiveness of telephone therapy for a variety of client problems and situations. Research has been conducted in at least the following areas:

- Treatment of tobacco and nicotine dependence (Swartz, Cowan, Klayman, Welton, & Leonard, 2005)
- Therapy for obsessive-compulsive disorder (Lovell et al., 2006; Turner, Heyman, Futh, & Lovell, 2009)
- Trauma treatment (Hirai & Clum, 2005; Lange et al., 2003)
- Therapy for clinical depression (Mohr et al., 2005; Ransom et al., 2008)
- Interventions for insomnia (Bastien, Morin, Ouellet, Blais, & Bouchard, 2004)
- Interventions for obesity (Befort, Donnelly, Sullivan, Ellerbeck, & Perri, 2010; Sherwood et al., 2006)

In most cases the effectiveness of these mental health and behavioral interventions via telephone is approximately equivalent to FtF therapy (Senior et al., 2007).

Online Counseling/Psychotherapy Outcomes

Barak, Hen, Boniel-Nissim, and Shapira (2008) published one of the earliest comprehensive reviews of Internet-based psychotherapy outcomes. They evaluated 92 studies that included 9,764 clients who received a wide range of Internet-based counseling and psychotherapy. Overall, based on Cohen's (1977) guidelines for effect size, they concluded that online work is moderately effective. They reported an overall mean-weighted effect size of $d = 0.53$. This effect size is slightly lower but within the same general range of effect sizes as for FtF counseling and psychotherapy.

In a subsequent review and reanalysis of Barak et al.'s (2008) data, Hanley and Reynolds (2009) focused more specifically on text-only, one-on-one online counseling and psychotherapy. They excluded research focusing on chat rooms and research including more sensory modalities (e.g., audio or video components). They concluded:

> Excluding these findings leaves a total of 16 relevant studies for this review and cumulatively involve 614 clients. More specifically, they reflect effect sizes for text-based interventions using e-mail (Effect size $= 0.51$) and chat (Effect size $= 0.53$). (p. 7)

More recent research is consistent with previous reviews. For example, in a randomized controlled study comparing the efficacy of FtF versus Internet-based therapy in 75 clients diagnosed with social phobia, both groups reported significant gains in terms of symptom reduction and disability measures (Andrews, Davies, & Titov, 2011). Further, there were no significant differences between FtF and Internet-delivered therapy efficacy. Similarly, in another randomized control trial ($n = 205$), it was reported that Internet-based interventions were efficacious for clients with alcohol use problems (Blankers, Koeter, & Schippers, 2011). Blankers et al. (2011) summarized their findings, stating:

> Results support the effectiveness of cognitive-behavioral therapy/ motivational interviewing Internet-based therapy and Internet-based self-help for problematic alcohol users. At 6 months postrandomization, Internet-based therapy led to better results than Internet-based self-help. (p. 330)

It should be noted that the preceding results are just a small sampling of recent and emerging research in the increasingly popular area of Internet-based psychological and behavioral interventions.

Overall, it's safe to say that whether conducted via telephone, via videoconference, or in text-only formats, non-FtF approaches to clinical assessment and intervention hold promise and potential. The data suggest that a positive therapy alliance can be established and that these procedures are reasonably efficacious and effective. These findings have especially important implications for clients who, due to distance, disability, preference, or other factors, might not otherwise seek professional assessment or treatment.

ETHICAL AND PRACTICAL ISSUES: PROBLEMS AND SOLUTIONS

There are many emerging ethical and practical issues facing practitioners who deliver non-FtF services. In this section, we review common online or Internet interviewing problems and offer ideas for potentially addressing or resolving these problems.

The Interviewer Doesn't Have Access to Nonverbal Cues

Most mental health professionals are well trained in behavioral observation skills and strategies. However, non-FtF interviewing and counseling modalities eliminate nonverbal communication cues. Rummell and Joyce (2010) discussed this dilemma:

> [C]ommunicating purely in a text-based or even telephone domain lacks some ingredients that have always been considered important or possibly even essential for doing good psychotherapy. Without the visual cues required to identify nonverbal behaviors, the psychotherapist misses out on another dimension of important information about the client. In a text-based format . . . [w]hatever the client does not provide in the conversation text, the psychotherapist does not know about. (p. 487)

Non-FtF interviewers must rely on alternative observational or assessment strategies. Even though it might be tempting to lament the lack of direct auditory or visual observational data, longing for what's missing in this new format can get in the way of taking full advantage of the information and data at your disposal. We take comfort in the fact that history has shown that emotional attachments and meaningful relationships can be established as well as maintained through letter writing (Moules, 2003; White & Epston, 1990). Furthermore, although speculative, experienced online clinical interviewers can most certainly read between the lines in text-only formats and make interpretive statements similar to what they might do while observing nonverbal behaviors. It's both reasonable and sometimes recommended that telephone or online interviewers directly ask clients to describe their nonverbal experiences:

- If I could see your face right now, what would it tell me?
- Describe what your body might say about what you're feeling about your work with me.

There's Increased Potential for Clients to Misrepresent Themselves

The ability to recognize clients and know who's on the other end of your clinical interview is difficult or impossible when contact is restricted to Internet chat, e-mail, or text-only messaging. You may or may not know if you're communicating with your client; with his or her spouse, parent, or child; or even with a stranger.

To address this issue, Rummell and Joyce (2010) suggested formulating a *challenge question* with clients during an initial session. This question (and answer) can be used at the beginning of subsequent sessions to verify client identity. They stated: "If the client does not give the decided-upon answer, the therapist can then be alerted to a possible confidentiality breach" (p. 492).

Mental Health Provider Credentials May Be Absent

Just as it's difficult to ascertain the true identity of a client via the Internet, it can be equally challenging to determine whether an alleged mental health provider is, in fact, a credentialed professional. Unfortunately, many online counseling service providers don't appear to have a professional license or professional training. This is a disturbing reality. Although there's no national policy or enforcement of nonlicensed providers offering services, it's incumbent upon licensed providers to make verification of their license status available. Rummell and Joyce (2010) recommended providing a website link to enable prospective and ongoing clients to check on licensure status.

Practitioners also should be aware that crossing state lines to offer services to clients (even virtual state lines) can result in legal problems (see Rummell & Joyce, 2010, for an excellent review on the ethics of online service provision, and *Putting It in Practice* 15.1 for a summary of our online search for Internet clinical services).

Increased Potential for Immediate and Explicit Disclosure

Online communication sometimes diminishes inhibition. This is a polite way of saying that e-mail or online exchanges can quickly become ugly. J. Suler (2004) used the term *toxic disinhibition* to describe online acting out (also sometimes called flaming). Flaming typically includes insults, profanity, and other behaviors that can be damaging to both the writer and the target (Lapidot-Lefler & Barak, 2012; Suler, 2004, 2010). Text-based flaming behaviors can involve direct and indirect threats to self and others, such as

- Somebody should make sure that person dies a quick death.
- Maybe I should just kill myself and put myself out of my misery.

PUTTING IT IN PRACTICE 15.1

Online Counseling: Ethics and Reality

As a part of reviewing information for this chapter, we perused Internet therapy options available to potential consumers. Previous publications suggested a possible plethora of Internet counseling and psychotherapy providers with questionable professional credentials (Heinlen, Welfel, Richmond, & O'Donnell, 2003; Shaw & Shaw, 2006). Although we

(continued)

(continued)

hoped that Internet-service-provision standards had improved, we weren't overly impressed with our results. Generally, we found that most providers may have more expertise in business and marketing than they do in professional clinical work. Affixed on this foundation of business and marketing, we found two distinct approaches: the more ethical and the less ethical.

The Less Ethical Approach

Many providers offer online services but don't acknowledge having specific credentials (e.g., a license) typically associated with clinical expertise. For example, practitioners with bachelor's degrees (or less) made statements similar to the following:

> I am a counselor, yoga instructor, and spiritual guide with over 23 years of rich experience. I have studied the fields of education, counseling, psychology, personal growth, relationships, communications, business, computer programming and technology, languages, and spirituality!! In addition to my diverse training, my 18-year relationship with my partner has deepened my capacity to help others with relationship issues.

This sort of enthusiastic introduction was typically followed by an equally enthusiastic statement about the breadth of services offered:

> My online counseling services specialties include, but are not limited to: problems with guilt, trust issues, anxiety/panic, self-esteem, couples counseling, relationship advice, life and career coaching, emotional intelligence, personal growth, affairs, work and career, abuse/boundary problems, communication skills, conflict resolution and mediation, grief, emotional numbness, spiritual development, stress management, blame, court-ordered counseling, codependency, problem resolution, jealousy, attachment, anger problems, depression, food and body, and developing tranquility in life.

Curiously, we found that the broad range of claims on websites such as these did not move us toward developing tranquility—at least professionally.

The More Ethical Approach

There were also websites that included professional, licensed providers. For example, one website listed and described eight *licensed* practitioners with backgrounds in professional counseling, social work, and psychology. These professionals offered webcam therapy, text therapy, e-mail therapy, and telephone therapy.

Prices included:

- E-mail therapy: $25 per online counselor reply
- Unlimited e-mail therapy: $200 per month
- Chat therapy: $45 per 50-minute session
- Telephone therapy: $80 per 50-minute session
- Webcam therapy: $80 per 50-minute session

The more ethical professional Internet services also tended to include information related to theoretical orientation. For example, a "postmodern" approach was described as involving: "Staying positive . . . focused on the here and now . . . offering solutions that meet your needs . . . a collaborative and respectful environment . . . quick results . . . "

How to Choose an Internet Services Provider

The National Directory of Online Counselors now exists to help consumers choose an online provider. They state:

We have personally verified the credentials and the websites of each therapist listed in the National Directory of Online Counselors. Feel assured that the therapists listed are state board licensed, have a Master's Degree or Doctoral Degree in a mental health discipline, and have online counseling experience.
The listed therapists and websites are set up and ready to handle secure communication, and offer various services such as eMail Sessions, Chat Sessions, and Telephone Sessions. All work conducted by the professional licensed therapists meet[s] strict confidentiality standards overseen by their professional state board (http://www.etherapyweb.com/, retrieved March 6, 2012).

Both of these distinct approaches to online therapy emphasize that help is only a mouse click away.

In nearly every case, these written messages can and should be quickly countered with a clarification response (see Chapter 3). Responses such as the following can be helpful:

- When you say that person should die a quick death, it tells me you're angry, but it's also the kind of statement that I take very seriously. Are you saying you're planning to hurt this person?
- You wrote that maybe you should just kill yourself. And so now I really need to hear if you're seriously thinking about suicide. Are you saying that you want to or plan to kill yourself?

The preceding clarifications are a best first response because their seriousness and boundary-setting nature can help clients retract their disinhibited homicidal or suicidal statements. When this happens, a focus on affect behind the threat is important:

> Okay. I'm relieved to hear you're not homicidal (or suicidal). But your statement tells me you're feeling lots of anger (or sadness/hopelessness, etc.) about this that we should explore.

Although seeking clarification through direct questioning can pull clients back from their verbal edge, sometimes it doesn't—at which point you're then dealing with an emergency situation from a distance, and that introduces an additional online ethical and practical conundrum.

Emergency Response Procedures From a Distance Are Complex and Anxiety-Provoking

Working FtF with clients who are suicidal or homicidal is already one of the most stressful situations a clinical interviewer can experience (Kleespies & Richmond, 2009). Part of this stress is caused by feelings of not being in control over the client's suicidal or homicidal impulses. However, when you're facing this situation and working from a distance, you may feel greater stress and angst because you have less direct control and influence. Rummell and Joyce (2010) offer sage advice for proactively dealing with this type of situation:

> [T]he client should be aware what behaviors will be construed by the clinician as an emergency (e.g., the client abruptly terminating the chat session, allusions to suicide, or direct threats) and what action will then be taken in the event that any of these behaviors occur. Similarly, clinicians should collect identifying client information, as well as the client's location and contact information, so that they are able to alert an emergency management team or Child Protective Services, if necessary, and direct them to the right place. One could make this a mandatory requirement for engaging in online psychotherapy. (p. 491)

Rummell and Joyce (2010) also recommend that online providers be aware of resources in the client's local community. Although this may be challenging, it reminds us of the inherent two-way risks associated with client emergency situations. Although immediate client risk is always the number-one priority, there's a simultaneous legal and ethical risk to clinical interviewers that further raises anxiety and doubt in these provocative situations. As noted in previous chapters on emergency situations, there's no substitute for having colleagues and supervisors available for both proactive and responsive consultation.

New and Significant Limitations on Confidentiality

Confidentiality is always limited in videoconferencing, telephone, or online assessment and intervention venues. When it comes to electronic or Internet confidentiality, most professionals immediately think about Internet security, records storage, passwords, firewalls, sockets, and other technological methods for data security. Although these are critical issues, there are also practical and imminent confidentiality threats to online or telephonic service provision.

Perhaps the biggest threat to client confidentiality is the potential presence of another person in the room or identity theft of a client by a close (and curious) family member or friend. Imagine the following scenario:

> Margaret is getting online therapy for depression. As therapy progresses, it becomes clear that her depressive symptoms are related to a dissatisfying relationship with her romantic partner, Ruben. Not surprisingly, Ruben assumes that he's a common topic during Margaret's online therapy sessions. He can't resist the temptation and eventually contacts the therapist from Margaret's laptop, trying to initiate a discussion about what he (as Margaret) really thinks of Ruben. Perhaps even worse, if Ruben is a controlling sort, he might insist on being present in the room observing (and reading over Margaret's shoulder) the next time she logs on for her online counseling session.

This scenario illustrates the necessity of dealing with confidentiality or data security on two levels. The first level—whether the client is actually present and in an adequately private setting—can be dealt with using a prearranged challenge question as proposed by Rummell and Joyce (2010). If this is the procedure you plan to use, you should spell it out in your informed consent agreement and in your initial online session. You can also cope with this by always assuming that someone is looking over your client's shoulder as you type.

Of course, with Skype or Face Time, the counselor can see the client's face, and whatever else the client might wish to show the counselor. This visual access is limited, and does not guarantee that there are not others present in the room or within earshot. It does substantially reduce the chances of any kind of identity theft or intrusion.

The second level—data security—requires a technological rather than interpersonal solution. Unless you have terrific technology skills yourself, you should strongly consider hiring a consultant to walk you (and your computer or electronic hardware and software) through a security detail. Establishing data encryption, use of secure socket layer (SSL) encryption, and/or firewalls requires significant technological expertise (we know this partly because one of our experiences with encryption resulted in us not being able to access our own computer!).

Parental Consent to Work Directly With Minor Clients Can Be Problematic

Confidentiality and parental consent are challenging issues for clinical interviewers who work with minors. The nature of privilege and confidentiality for minors varies from state to state, and individual parents will alternate from wanting complete access to their minor child's records to showing little or no interest in events that occur during the clinical hour. If you plan to work with minors online or from a distance, you should include descriptions of your specific privacy, confidentiality, and reporting policies. You may also need to hold a telephone or videoconference with parents to assure that the major players are all on the same page.

The General Solution: Informed Consent

Most of the complex and thorny issues associated with providing professional mental health services online can and should be dealt with using a clear, complete, and collaborative informed consent process (Rummell & Joyce, 2010). To help consumers understand this process, the National Directory of Online Counselors includes a statement pertaining to informed consent.

> The therapist is obligated to provide information about treatment protocol, often called "informed consent" which is informative literature on the process of therapy, costs, confidentiality policies, security measures on the Internet, and termination policies. It includes information about what can and cannot be disclosed from the records created and kept by the therapist. It can also include treatment approaches used, and other important rules for the operation of the therapeutic alliance. (from http://www.etherapyweb.com/problems.html, retrieved March 6, 2012)

One problem with using a detailed informed-consent process is that the excess detail may adversely affect client views of online therapy. This conundrum makes it important for ethical online interviewers and counselors to strike a balance between an overwhelming and exhaustive informed consent and a cursory one. A potential solution to this is to provide some of the informed consent procedures up front with an informed consent form and then additional bits and pieces during an initial synchronous Internet contact.

The process can be collaborative as well. Clients can make choices about the level of security and confidentiality they are comfortable with, and can provide the counselor with important information, such as emergency services available in the client's community.

CONDUCTING ONLINE OR NON-FTF INTERVIEWS

> The five general counseling labs [in Second Life] each contained two couches, a coffee table, a side table, and an interactive box of Kleenex. Each counseling lab had different decorations for the walls and tables. One of the counseling labs emulated a school counselor's office. (Walker, 2009, p. 37)

Preparation

Before entering into a non-FtF professional relationship, it's imperative that clinical interviewers conduct a personal and professional competency check. Because explicit professional standards for online counseling don't yet exist, it's up to individual practitioners to self-monitor their preparation and competence in this area.

Conducting a Professional Competency Check

This competency check should be based partly on early research on Internet therapy and partly on common sense or logic. The main competencies necessary for effective online or Internet clinical assessment or intervention include the following:

- Typing speed and accuracy (or an alternative voice-activated system that's both efficient and accurate).
- Computer literacy.
- An understanding of data security and other methods for protecting confidentiality (this may require consultation with an expert in technology).
- Knowledge and skills for using common text-based expressions (e.g., abbreviations and emoticons).
- Confidence and experience communicating in whatever venue you're operating from (e.g., videoconferencing, telephonic assessment and intervention, as well as various text-only communication modalities).
- An informed-consent form and process that is both accessible and thorough (as noted previously, this will likely involve presenting key informed-consent topics in chunks so as not to overwhelm prospective online clients).

Traditionally, the three foundational pieces that support clinical practice within any domain are education, training, and supervision. For our purposes, this translates into a minimal competency level that includes:

- Reading professional journal articles and books about online service provision.
- Attending professional workshops on non-FtF assessment and treatment.
- Obtaining individual or group supervision and/or consultation in the practice of online counseling.
- Obtaining technical instruction and support as needed.

In recent years there also has been growing emphasis on using client feedback systems to monitor clinical practice (Lambert & Shimokawa, 2011). Although complicated, we encourage online practitioners to integrate both direct and anonymous feedback systems into their online counseling system.

Determining the Purpose of the Online or Non-FtF Interview

As with FtF clinical contact, the non-FtF interview process and outcomes are driven primarily by the interview's purpose. If we boil down the purpose of clinical interviewing to its minimal essentials, two components rise to the surface: assessment (or evaluation) and treatment (or intervention).

Similarly, although the nature of clinical interviewing can shift in many subtle ways, the specifics of what you offer to distance or online clients are primarily driven by two main factors:

1. What the client wants.
2. What you're competent to offer.

Although this sounds simple, it's always good to remember how easy it is to imagine that we're more broadly competent than we are in reality (see *Putting It in Practice* 15.1 for a warning about this tendency).

Preparing the Room

It may seem odd to talk about preparing the room for online clinical interviewing. However, in some ways room preparation is even more important when interviewing from a distance. This is especially possible when using Web-based virtual worlds like Second Life, with avatars used for conducting therapy in virtual counseling rooms (Walker, 2009). However, even with text-only online assessment and counseling, there can be an inherent lack of control over your personal space or your client's personal space. Further, losing control of either your space or the client's space can detract from the reliability and validity of an online assessment process or interfere with the efficacy of online therapy interventions.

Essentially, the online room is prepared using two strategies. First, a detailed (but not overwhelming) informed consent document is created. Using simple and straightforward language, this document should walk prospective clients and clients through the importance of privacy for optimal online therapeutic work. It should detail the risks inherent any therapy conducted in a non-FtF manner. Second, some sort of challenge question or method for checking with the client regarding personal privacy is necessary. Straightforward but discreet questions such as: "Are you ready for your session today?" or "Is now a comfortable time for us to begin?" may be all that's needed, although the answer the client provides needs to be agreed upon in advance if it is to be used to ascertain that it really is your client. The answer should not be one that anyone would easily offer to such a query. Something as simple as having the initial answer include two pound-signs could provide counselors with some level of assurance that it really is their client typing to them.

Multicultural Issues

Just as online communication processes can reduce inhibition of self-expression, they also may allow clients who are culturally limited or repressed to express themselves in ways that don't fit with their cultural norms. This can be a liberating experience. Slama (2010) described an online chatting phenomenon among Indonesian youth:

> Due to the particular misogyny inherent in Indonesian gender ideologies, women, especially married and elderly women, are more easily excused when not conforming to the refined (male) standards of self-control, as they just fulfill the cliché of the spiritual inferiority of women. In this article I have investigated how such normally devalued behavior was positively appropriated online to become part of a youth culture that enabled also young, unmarried women, who are otherwise expected to be shy and to retreat, to actually speak out and to articulate feelings. (p. 316)

The Internet offers unparalleled intercultural opportunity and contact. As a consequence, there is the danger of overwhelming individual cultural norms with online norms and values of free expression. This can lull online practitioners into assuming that cultural universality reigns supreme in the cyberworld. Nevertheless, all professional interviewers must still work toward deepening self-awareness, gathering multicultural knowledge, and developing specific culturally sensitive and appropriate assessment and intervention techniques.

The following is a small sampling of multicultural communication standards and sensitivities to be integrated into non-FtF interviewing:

- *Charlar* (small talk) and *personalismo* (friendliness): Some cultural groups (and individuals) will want and need friendly chatter prior to more serious self-disclosures.
- *Familia* (focusing on family relations): Many Latino and Asian individuals and families expect formal inquiry about the health and wellness of immediate family members.
- *Filial piety*: Honoring and caring for one's parents and ancestors may be a prominent dimension for Asian youth and adults.
- *Tribal identity*: It may be appropriate both to disclose your knowledge of particular Native American tribes and to inquire about your client's tribal affiliation.
- *Spirituality*: Spiritual and religious dimensions of life can be central for most clients, but especially for clients outside the dominant U.S. culture.

Although it's true that all clients using computerized interviewing and counseling services are inserting themselves into modern online culture, this can't and shouldn't serve as an excuse to ignore diverse cultural perspectives (Wood & Smith, 2005). Continually remembering and refocusing on cultural awareness, cultural knowledge, and specific skills for working with cultural issues form a central component of interviewer competence (D. W. Sue & Sue, 2013).

SUMMARY

In this chapter, beginning with the concept of technology as an extension of the self, we have provided an overview of issues salient to offering non-FtF clinical services. The 21st century has seen substantial increases in the numbers of Internet and smart phone users as well as counseling and psychotherapy services offered online.

Conducting non-FtF clinical interviews is both similar to and different from FtF interviewing procedures. Although methods for using specific interviewer responses shift due to missing nonverbal client data (e.g., silence), interviewers must still use the same range of skills necessary in FtF interviewing formats.

There are several distinct non-FtF communication modalities available to interviewers and counselors. These include: (a) text-only asynchronous, (b) voice-only asynchronous, (c) voice-only synchronous, (d) text-only synchronous, (e) video-link synchronous, and (f) virtual counseling settings set up through programs such as Second Life

Although current research on non-FtF and online counseling is limited, studies have focused both on the development of therapeutic relationships, telephone assessment procedures, and online therapy treatment outcomes. For the most part, initial research is promising in that it appears therapeutic alliances can be established, telephone assessments are roughly equivalent to in-person assessments, and treatment outcomes are moderately positive for a range of different telephone and online interventions.

There are numerous ethical and practical problems facing practitioners who conduct assessment and therapy interviews online or over the telephone. These include: (a) no access to client nonverbal behavior, (b) increased potential for clients to misrepresent themselves or to have others act as if they are your client, (c) mental-health-provider credentials may be absent, (d) increased potential for disinhibited and disturbing disclosures, (e) complex and anxiety-provoking emergency procedures, (f) new and significant limits on confidentiality, and (g) challenges in obtaining parental consent.

The chapter closed with important information on how to prepare for non-FtF interviews and with a reminder of the importance of maintaining multicultural sensitivity within the context of a universal online culture.

SUGGESTED ONLINE TRAINING RESOURCES

In addition to the resources cited in this chapter, there are various organizations that are working to offer credentialing and training experiences to providers interested in online counseling. The following is a short list, and we suspect resources in this area will fluctuate considerably.

All CEUs offers e-therapy certification training at: http://www.allceus.com/e-therapy -certification/

The American Distance Counseling Association offers membership, resources, and is working toward a credentialing system at: http://www.adca-online.org/about.htm

The Online Therapy Institute offers training, certification, and specialist certificates at: http://onlinetherapyinstitute.com/

Both the American Counseling Association and American Psychological Association occasionally post articles on their websites regarding online counseling and psychotherapy. Go to www.counseling.org or www.apa.org

Extended Mental Status Examination— Interview Protocol

This appendix provides a structured protocol for conducting a face-to-face (FtF), telephone, or videoconferencing mental status examination (MSE) interview. Some of the material is modified from the Mini-Mental State Examination (MMSE; Folstein, Folstein, & McHugh, 1975). We encourage you to further modify the content or process in ways that work well within your particular setting.

The protocol includes space for writing notes and scoring client responses to some questions. However, this procedure is not standardized and has no normative sample. Gathering information using this protocol will allow you to write a clear and concise MSE report. It also may support a much more extensive psychological or evaluation report. For a standardized process complete with norms, an alternative approach should be used (e.g., see the *Mini-Mental State Exam*, 2nd edition [MMSE-2]).

This protocol generates qualitative assessment data. Using your clinical judgment, you can choose to organize the data into three broad evaluation categories:

1. No concerns
2. Mild concerns
3. Significant concerns

A mental status examination is primarily based on interviewer observation. Although there are traditional and specific methods for obtaining MSE data, an MSE interview doesn't always involve the same procedures; an MSE is also not necessarily highly structured. The process involves an interviewer interacting with a client in such a way as to glean data about client functioning that can be organized into the nine categories typically included in a mental status examination report. Detailed information about MSE process and content is in Chapter 8 of this book. Reviewing Chapter 8 can help provide a foundation for conducting this interview more thoroughly and skillfully.

PREPARATION

In some cases, the structured nature of this interview assessment protocol (and all structured interviews) may facilitate relationship development and interviewer/counselor credibility. In other cases, if the interview isn't well framed or used in a manner consistent with your personal and professional style, it can adversely affect rapport and credibility. We generally recommend using the protocol flexibly while emphasizing the development and maintenance of a collaborative relationship.

Materials Needed

Mental status examiners should have a private setting and materials available for note taking.

The Importance of Small Talk

When using this or any structured interview protocol, it's important to engage in friendly small talk before formally initiating the interview. After informed consent is obtained, if you're interviewing from a distance, you might ask about the local weather, what room the client is in, and whether he or she is comfortable and ready to begin. To prepare for small talk, you can go online and skim through local newspapers to check on recent news events. For example, when interviewing clients from remote areas it can enhance rapport if you can comment on and ask about popular local news items (e.g., a moose wandering into a small town, performance of local sports teams, etc.).

Introducing the Assessment Protocol

After a bit of small talk, it's time to transition to the formal assessment process. As you gain confidence and experience, you'll find your own way to introduce this interview. In the meantime, you can use the following script to guide what you say.

> In just a few minutes I'll start a more formal method of getting to know you that involves asking you lots of questions. It will include easier and harder questions, some questions that might seem different or odd, and even a little mental math. This interview is just a standard process to help me to get to know you better and for me to understand a little more about how your brain works. As we go through this interview you can ask me questions at any time and I'll try my best to answer them. Do you have any questions before we start? *[Answer directly and honestly whatever questions are asked; after the client's questions are answered, proceed with the formal assessment process.]*
> Are you ready? *[Hopefully you'll get an affirmative answer here. If not, keep answering questions and chatting or conversing about the process and anything else that seems necessary.]*

MSE CATEGORIES

You can use the following outline to guide your interview process. You may want to write down client responses in the spaces provided.

Orientation and Consciousness

This is the technical opening of the MSE interview. Say something like: "We'll start with some easier things and then get to some harder things."

Then ask: "What is your full name?"

_____

Ask: "What is today's date?"

_____

Ask: "What day of the week is it today?"

_____

Ask: "What season of the year is it?"

_____

Ask: "What's the name of the town or city where you're living now?"

_____

Say, "Now, this might be a hard one." Then ask: "Who is the governor of your state?"

_____

Evaluation of consciousness is conducted by observation. After the examination is over, you should identify and circle which of the following words is the best descriptor of your client's level of consciousness:

Alert, Confused, Clouded, Stuporous, Unconscious/Comatose

Immediate Memory

Ask: "Is it okay if I do a little test of your memory?"
Then say, "I'm going to say three items and then I'll stop and have you say them back to me. Ready? Cup, newspaper, banana. Okay, now repeat those back to me."
Write down how many items the client immediately recalls.

_____

If the client can't recall all three items, go ahead and repeat them back. Continue repeating them and having the client try again until it's clear the client will likely not get them. Up to six trials are recommended in the Mini-Mental State Examination, but depending on frustration level and persistence you can stop sooner or later.

Attention and Calculation

Depending on how your client did with the first memory task, you might say something like: "Now I've got a harder one for you" or "How do you feel about numbers?" Then say: "I'd like you to start with the number 100 and then count backward by 7s. It's like 100, minus 7, and so on."

Many clients will work hard at this (or not). Either way, you can stop after five subtractions (93, 86, 79, 72, 65). You can think about the client's response categorically from no errors to one error to two errors to three errors to being unable to complete the task. You can also watch for the client's self-talk and strategies for dealing with a cognitive challenge.

If the client has difficulty with the task, be sure to express empathy or validation: "That's a hard one. Many college students struggle with subtracting 7s."

The attention and calculation category is useful for observing the client's level of consciousness, memory, mathematical ability (and mathematical confidence or self-efficacy), and/or ability to concentrate and calculate.

Intermediate or Remote Memory

Ask the client: "Who is currently president of the United States?"
Follow that question with: "Who was president before him?"

Continue asking about presidents. The correct order going back in time is: Obama, Bush, Clinton, Bush, Reagan, Carter, Ford, Nixon, Johnson, Kennedy. You can stop when the client gets stuck or when he or she makes it to Reagan. If the client is from a different cultural or an international setting, ask about recent and present political leaders there. Although this task technically involves memory assessment, it's also a reasonable gauge of fund of knowledge or exposure to news and information.

Mood and Affect

After making a transition statement like, "Now I have some different questions for you," ask the client: "How do you feel right now?"

_____

(This question is a direct assessment of mood, which is the client's self-report of his or her prevailing emotional state.)
Ask: "Rate your mood right now, with 0 being the worst possible mood you could have—0 would mean you're totally depressed and you're just going to kill yourself. A rating of 10 is the best possible mood. It would mean that you're totally happy and maybe up on the roof dancing. What rating would you give your mood right now?"

_____

Ask: "Now, what's the worst or lowest mood rating you've ever had?"

_____

Ask: "What was going on then to make you feel so down?"

_____

Ask: "Now, what would be a normal mood rating for you on a normal day?"

_____

Ask: "Now tell me, what's the best mood rating you think you've ever had?"

_____

Ask: "What was going on then to help you have such a high mood rating?"

_____

Affect is the client's observable moment-to-moment emotional tone. Affect is observed and measured in terms of:

Affect content (circle one): Angry, Anxious, Ashamed, Euphoric, Fearful, Guilty, Happy, Irritable, Joyful, Sad, Surprised, Other

_____

Affect range (circle one): Blunted, Constricted, Expansive, Flat, Labile, Other

_____

_____

Affect appropriateness (circle one): Appropriate or Inappropriate Observations:

_____

_____

Affect depth or intensity (circle one): Shallow, Normal, Intense

Intermediate Memory Recall

Tell the client: "Now I've got a tricky question. Ready?"
Say: "Remember a while ago I asked you to remember three items. Can you remember those three items now?"
Circle the items recalled: Cup, Newspaper, Banana
Total number recalled without prompts:

_____

For this item, be sure to wait for the client to make a sincere effort. After 15 to 20 seconds, you can test to see (for each item) if the client can use a cue to recapture a trace memory (the purpose of this is to see if a prompt can help with memory retrieval, which is of less concern than complete absence of recall).

For cup, you can say: "It's something you might drink from."
For newspaper, you can say: "It's something you read."

For banana, you can say: "It's a type of fruit."
Total number recalled with prompts:

Speech and Thought

Say: "Now I'm going to ask you a few questions about your thoughts and thinking. Are you ready?"

Ask: "Do you ever have particular thoughts that get stuck in your head that you think over and over?" (This focuses on obsessional thoughts.)

If the client says yes, ask: "What's an example of a type of thought that might get stuck in your head?"

If warranted, ask: "How do you finally manage to get that thought back out of your head?" (If the client's response suggests obsessive thinking, you should explore this with a few follow-up questions exploring frequency, intensity, duration, and so on.)

Ask: "Do you have any beliefs that some people consider unusual or odd? If so, what are they?" (Again, explore these beliefs as appropriate.)

Ask the client to repeat the phrase: "No ifs, ands, or buts."

Observe the client's speech throughout the MSE.

Note whether the client's speech is: Loud, Normal, or Soft; Fast (pressured), Normal, or Slow (poverty of speech).
Also rate the speech as: Spontaneous, Labored, Blocked.
Note the presence of: Stuttering, Cluttering, Dysarthria, Dysprosody (see the MSE chapter for more information on this.)

Be sure to track your client's thinking process. Circle one or more of the following terms:

Circumstantiality, Clang associations, Flight of ideas, Mutism, Neologisms, Perseveration, Tangentiality, Word salad

Perceptual Disturbances

Ask: "Do you ever see or hear things that other people don't see or hear?"

If the answer is yes, gently explore the client's experience with questions like:

"What do you see/hear that others don't?"

_____

"Can you give me an example?"

_____

"How do you know others can't also hear/see this?"

_____

Ask: "Do you ever think the radio or television is speaking directly about you or directly to you?"

_____

If yes, ask: "Can you think of an example of that?"

_____

Ask: "Has anyone ever tried to steal your thoughts or read your mind?"

_____

If yes, ask: "Can you think of an example of that?"

_____

Cognitive Skills (Intelligence), Abstract Thinking, and Social Judgment

Ask the following questions:

"Can you name six large U.S. cities?"

_____

_____

"What poisonous chemical is in automobile exhaust?"

_____

"In what way are a pencil and computer alike?"

_____

"What would you do if you found a gun hidden in the bushes near your home?"

_____

_____

"If you won a million dollars, what would you do?"

_____

_____

"What would you do if a person who was much smaller than you tried to pick a fight with you?"

"What would you do if a person who was much bigger than you tried to pick a fight with you?"

"What would you do if you had a close friend who obviously had a drug or alcohol problem?"

Insight and Reliability

Insight and reliability are difficult to measure directly. You may be able to infer them from the preceding questions and activities. Reliability is especially difficult because it's hard to tell if someone is being honest or dishonest. Do your best to rate both insight and reliability.

Insight: Absent, Poor, Partial, Good
Reliability: Unreliable, Questionable, Reliable and honest

End the interview with thanks and by asking the interviewee if he or she has any questions for you. Answer whatever questions the interviewee may have as directly, honestly, and gently as you can. For example, if a client had difficulty with a portion of the assessment, you could say: "It seemed like there were parts of the interview that were harder for you. You had trouble with subtracting 7s and remembering presidents, but you did better with some of the other questions."

Appearance

Client appearance cannot be evaluated unless you're conducting an assessment face-to-face or via video link. If you were able to observe your client's appearance, consider which of the following adjectives best describes his or her appearance.

Well-groomed, Disheveled
Note anything unusual about the appearance of the client's eyes, facial expression, posture, clothing, makeup, and other observables. Also note whether the client looks older, younger, or about his or her actual age.

Behavior or Psychomotor Activity

Client behavior or psychomotor activity cannot be evaluated unless you conducted an assessment face-to-face or via video link. If you were able to observe your client's behavior, write down anything unusual or distinctive about his or her physical movements, gestures, repeated behaviors, and so on.

_____

_____

Attitude Toward the Examiner (and Examination)

Clients will have different responses to participating in an MSE. When determining a client's attitude toward the examiner, you're relying on observational data. No direct questions are asked about this. After completing the assessment, come back to this section and circle the words that best describe your observations of the client's attitude.

> Cooperative, Resistant, Hostile, Indifferent, Ingratiating, Seductive, Suspicious, Impatient, Pleasant, Open, Curious

Evaluating and Communicating Results

As noted previously, this protocol is not standardized and therefore can only yield qualitative information about your client. When you initially begin using the protocol you may feel odd or awkward or unsure how to use the data effectively. Keep in mind that experience helps, as does discussion and exploration of the specific items with classmates and with your instructor. It's an excellent idea to dissect the questions and tasks in small groups. For example, consider different possible responses to the "Million Dollar" question. Typical responses include ideas about: (a) saving money, (b) spending money, and (c) giving away money. Analyzing client responses can give you a sense of their values and judgment. Obviously there are no correct or incorrect answers, but the client who tells you, "Hell, I'd just book a trip to Hawaii, buy a bunch of pot, and smoke it all up" conveys something distinctly different than the client who says, "I'd invest half of it in something safe, buy a decent house, and then give 10% away to charity."

The goal of a mental status examination is to evaluate client mental state as well as other client dimensions. This makes the process inherently judgmental. It also makes it all the more important for you to be tentative in your conclusions and, whenever possible, to stick with a reporting of your observations instead of making strong inferences about your observations. For guidance in writing up a mental status examination report, you should review Chapter 8 in this book.

References

Aboraya, A. (2007). Clinicians' opinions on the reliability of psychiatric diagnoses in clinical settings. *Psychiatry, 4*(11), 31–33.

Abu-Ras, W. (2007). Cultural beliefs and service utilization by battered Arab immigrant women. *Violence Against Women, 13*(10), 1002–1028. doi: 10.1177/1077801207306019

Achebe, C. (1994). *Things fall apart.* New York, NY: Doubleday.

Ackerman, S. J., Benjamin, L. S., Beutler, L. E., Gelso, C. J., Goldfried, M. R., Hill, C., ... Rainer, J. (2001). Empirically supported therapy relationships: Conclusions and recommendations of the division 29 task force. *Psychotherapy: Theory, Research, Practice, Training, 38*(4), 495–497.

Ackerman, S. J., & Hilsenroth, M. J. (2003). A review of therapist characteristics and techniques positively impacting the therapeutic alliance. *Clinical Psychology Review, 23*(1), 1–33.

Adler, A. (1930). *Individual psychology.* Oxford, England: Clark University Press.

Akhtar, S. (Ed.). (2007). *Listening to others: Developmental and clinical aspects of empathy and attunement* Lanham, MD: Jason Aronson.

Alexander, F., & French, T. M. (1946). *Psychoanalytic psychotherapy.* New York, NY: Ronald.

Alkhatib, A., Regan, J., & Jackson, J. (2008). Informed assent and informed consent in the child and adolescent. *Psychiatric Annals, 38*(5), 337–339. doi: http://dx.doi.org/10.3928/00485713-20080501-01

Alleman, J. R. (2002). Online counseling: The Internet and mental health treatment. *Psychotherapy: Theory, Research, Practice, Training, 39*(2), 199–209.

Amadio, D. M., & Pérez, R. M. (2008). *Affirmative counseling and psychotherapy with lesbian, gay, bisexual, and transgender clients.* Reno, NV: Bent Tree Press.

American Counseling Association. (2005). *The American Counseling Association code of ethics.* Alexandria, VA: Author.

American Psychiatric Association. (2000). *Diagnostic and statistical manual of mental disorders* (4th ed., text rev.). Washington, DC: Author.

American Psychiatric Association. (2013). *Diagnostic and statistical manual of mental disorders* (5th ed.). Washington, DC: Author.

American Psychological Association. (2013). Disaster Response Network. Retrieved from http://www.apa.org/practice/programs/drn/

American Psychological Association. (2008). *Disaster response network member guidelines.* Retrieved from http://www.apa.org/practice/drnguide.html#standards

American Psychological Association. (2010). *Ethical principles for psychologists and code of conduct.* Washington, DC: Author.

American Psychological Association. (2010). *Publication manual of the American Psychological Association* (6th ed.). Washington, DC: Author.

Anderson, R. N. (2001). Deaths: Leading causes for 1999. *National Vital Statistics Reports, 49*(11), 1–87.

Anderson, R. N., Kochanek, K. D., & Murphy, S. L. (1997). *Report of final mortality statistics, 1995.* (Monthly Vital Statistics Report No. 45). Hyattsville, MD: National Center for Health Statistics.

Anderson, S. K., & Handelsman, M. M. (2010). *Ethics for psychotherapists and counselors: A proactive approach*. London, England: Wiley-Blackwell.

Anderson, S. K., & Handelsman, M. M. (2013). A positive and proactive approach to the ethics of the first interview. *Journal of Contemporary Psychotherapy, 43*(1), 3–11.

Andover, M. S., Morris, B. W., Wren, A., & Bruzzese, M. E. (2012). The co-occurrence of non-suicidal self-injury and attempted suicide among adolescents: Distinguishing risk factors and psychosocial correlates. *Child and Adolescent Psychiatry and Mental Health, 6*(11). doi: http://dx.doi.org/10.1186/1753-2000-6-11

Andrews, G., Davies, M., & Titov, N. (2011). Effectiveness randomized controlled trial of face to face versus Internet cognitive behaviour therapy for social phobia. *Australian and New Zealand Journal of Psychiatry, 45*(4), 337–340. doi: 10.3109/00048674.2010.538840

Aten, J. D., Topping, S., Denney, R. M., & Hosey, J. M. (2011). Helping African American clergy and churches address minority disaster mental health disparities: Training needs, model, and example. *Psychology of Religion and Spirituality, 3*(1), 15–23. doi: http://dx.doi.org/10.1037/a0020497

Augenbraum, H., & Stavans, I. (1993). *Growing up Latino*. Boston, MA: Houghton Mifflin.

Axline, V. M. (1964). *Dibs in search of self*. New York, NY: Ballantine Books.

Ayón, C., & Aisenberg, E. (2010). Negotiating cultural values and expectations within the public child welfare system: A look at familismo and personalismo. *Child & Family Social Work, 15*(3), 335–344. doi: 10.1111/j.1365-2206.2010.00682.x

Azorin, J., Kaladjian, A., Adida, M., Hantouche, E., Hameg, A., Lancrenon, S., & Akiskal, H. S. (2009). Risk factors associated with lifetime suicide attempts in bipolar I patients: Findings from a French national cohort. *Comprehensive Psychiatry, 50*(2), 115–120. doi: http://dx.doi.org/10.1016/j.comppsych.2008.07.004

Baker, T. B., McFall, R. M., & Shoham, V. (2008). Current status and future prospects of clinical psychology: Toward a scientifically principled approach to mental and behavioral health care. *Psychological Science in the Public Interest, 9*(2), 67–103. doi: 10.1111/j.1539-6053.2009.01036.x

Baldwin, S. A., Wampold, B. E., & Imel, Z. E. (2007). Untangling the alliance-outcome correlation: Exploring the relative importance of therapist and patient variability in the alliance. *Journal of Consulting and Clinical Psychology, 75*(6), 842–852. doi: 10.1037/0022-006X.75.6.842

Banaka, W. H. (1971). *Training in depth interviewing*. New York, NY: Harper & Row.

Bandler, R. (2008). *Get the life you want: The secrets to quick and lasting life change with neuro-linguistic programming*. Deerfield Beach, FL: Health Communications.

Bandler, R., & Grinder, J. (1975). *The structure of magic. I: A book about language and therapy*. Palo Alto, CA: Science and Behavior Books.

Barak, A., Hen, L., Boniel-Nissim, M., & Shapira, N. (2008). A comprehensive review and a meta-analysis of the effectiveness of Internet-based psychotherapeutic interventions. *Journal of Technology in Human Services, 26*(2–4), 109–160. doi: 10.1080/15228830802094429

Barbato, A., & D'Avanzo, B. (2000). Family interventions in schizophrenia and related disorders: A critical review of clinical trials. *Acta Psychiatrica Scandinavica, 102*(2), 81–97. doi: 10.1034/j.1600-0447.2000.102002081.x

Barnett, E., Sussman, S., Smith, C., Rohrbach, L. A., & Spruijt-Metz, D. (2012). Motivational interviewing for adolescent substance use: A review of the literature. *Addictive Behaviors, 37*(12), 1325–1334. doi: http://dx.doi.org/10.1016/j.addbeh.2012.07.001

Barnett, J. E. (2011). Psychotherapist self-disclosure: Ethical and clinical considerations. *Psychotherapy, 48*(4), 315–321. doi: http://dx.doi.org/10.1037/a0026056

Barone, D. F., Hutchings, P. S., Kimmel, H. J., Traub, H. L., Cooper, J. T., & Marshall, C. M. (2005). Increasing empathic accuracy through practice and feedback in a clinical interviewing course. *Journal of Social & Clinical Psychology, 24*(2), 156–171. doi: 10.1521/jscp.24.2.156.62275

Bastien, C. H., Morin, C. M., Ouellet, M., Blais, F. C., & Bouchard, S. (2004). Cognitive-behavioral therapy for insomnia: Comparison of individual therapy, group therapy, and telephone consultations. *Journal of Consulting and Clinical Psychology, 72*(4), 653–659. doi: 10.1037/0022-006X.72.4.653

Batson, C. D. (2009). These things called empathy: Eight related but distinct phenomena. In C. D. Batson, *The social neuroscience of empathy* (pp. 3–15). Cambridge, MA: MIT Press.

Baumrind, D. (1975). The contributions of the family to the development of competence in children. *Schizophrenia Bulletin, 14*, 12–37.

Baumrind, D. (1991). The influence of parenting style on adolescent competence and substance use. *Journal of Early Adolescence. Special Issue: The Work of John P. Hill: I. Theoretical, Instructional, and Policy Contributions, 11*(1), 56–95. doi: 10.1177/0272431691111004

Beck, A. T. (1976). *Cognitive therapy and the emotional disorders.* New York, NY: New American Library.

Beck, J. S. (2011). *Cognitive behavioral therapy: Basics and beyond* (2nd ed.). New York, NY: Guilford Press.

Befort, C. A., Donnelly, J. E., Sullivan, D. K., Ellerbeck, E. F., & Perri, M. G. (2010). Group versus individual phone-based obesity treatment for rural women. *Eating Behaviors, 11*(1), 11–17. doi: 10.1016/j.eatbeh.2009.08.002

Beghi, M., & Rosenbaum, J. F. (2010). Risk factors for fatal and nonfatal repetition of suicide attempt: A critical appraisal. *Current Opinion in Psychiatry, 23*(4), 349–355. doi: http://dx.doi.org/10.1097/YCO.0b013e32833ad783

Behr, M. (2003). Interactive resonance in work with children and adolescents: A theory-based concept of interpersonal relationship through play and the use of toys. *Person-Centered and Experiential Psychotherapies, 2*(2), 89–103.

Beitman, B. D. (1983). Categories of countertransference. *Journal of Operational Psychiatry, 14*(2), 82–90.

Bellinson, J. (2002). *Children's use of board games in psychotherapy.* Lanham, MD: Jason Aronson.

Bell-Tolliver, L., & Wilkerson, P. (2011). The use of spirituality and kinship as contributors to successful therapy outcomes with African American families. *Journal of Religion & Spirituality in Social Work: Social Thought, 30*(1), 48–70.

Bem, D. J., & Allen, A. (1974). On predicting some of the people some of the time: The search for cross-situational consistencies in behavior. *Psychological Review, 81*(6), 506–520. doi: 10.1037/h0037130

Benjamin, A. (1987). *The helping interview with case illustrations.* Boston, MA: Houghton Mifflin.

Bennett, C. C. (1984). "Know thyself." *Professional Psychology: Research and Practice, 15*(2), 271–283. doi: 10.1037/0735-7028.15.2.271

Benyakar, M., & Collazo, C. (2005). Psychological interventions for people exposed to disasters. In J. J. Lopez-Ibor, G. Christodoulou, M. Maj, N. Sartorius & A. Okasha (Eds.), *Disasters and mental health* (pp. 81–97). Hoboken, NJ: Wiley.

Berg, I. K., & Dolan, Y. (2001). *Tales of solutions: A collection of hope-inspiring stories.* New York, NY: Norton.

Berg, I. K., & Shafer, K. C. (2004). *Working with mandated substance abusers: The language of solutions.* New York, NY: Guilford Press.

Berg, I. K., & DeJong, P. (2005). Engagement through complimenting. *Journal of Family Psychotherapy, 16*(1–2), 51–56.

Berg, R. C., Landreth, G. L., & Fall, K. A. (2006). *Group counseling: Concepts and procedures* (4th ed.). New York, NY: Routledge Taylor & Francis.

Berkhoffer, R. F. J. (1978). *The white man's Indian: Images of the American Indian from Columbus to the present.* New York, NY: Vintage Press.

Bernard, M., Janson, F., Flora, P. K., Faulkner, G. E. J., Meunier-Norman, L., & Fruhwirth, M. (2009). Videoconference-based physiotherapy and tele-assessment for homebound older adults: A pilot study. *Activities, Adaptation & Aging, 33*(1), 39–48. doi: 10.1080/01924780902718608

Berry, J. W. (2006). *Contexts of acculturation.* New York, NY: Cambridge University Press.

Bertolino, B. (1999). *Therapy with troubled teenagers: Rewriting young lives in progress.* New York, NY: Wiley.

Bertolino, B., & O'Hanlon, B. (2002). *Collaborative, competency-based counseling and psychotherapy.* Needham Heights, MA: Allyn & Bacon.

Betan, E., Heim, A. K., Conklin, C. Z., & Westen, D. (2005). Countertransference phenomena and personality pathology in clinical practice: An empirical investigation. *American Journal of Psychiatry, 162*(5), 890–898. doi: 10.1176/appi.ajp.162.5.890

Beutler, L. E. (2011). Prescriptive matching and systematic treatment selection. *History of psychotherapy: Continuity and change* (2nd ed., pp. 402–407). Washington, DC: American Psychological Association. doi: http://dx.doi.org/10.1037/12353-019

Beutler, L. E., Forrester, B., Gallagher-Thompson, D., Thompson, L., & Tomlins, J. B. (2012). Common, specific, and treatment fit variables in psychotherapy outcome. *Journal of Psychotherapy Integration, 22*(3), 255–281. doi: http://dx.doi.org/10.1037/a0029695

Beutler, L. E., Harwood, T. M., Michelson, A., Song, X., & Holman, J. (2011). Resistance/reactance level. *Journal of Clinical Psychology, 67*(2), 133–142. doi: http://dx.doi.org/10.1002/jclp.20753

Bickford, J. O. (2004). Preferences of individuals with visual impairments for the use of person-first language. *RE:View, 36*(3), 120–126.

BigFoot, D. S., & Dunlap, M. (2006). Storytelling as a healing tool for American Indians. In T. M. Witko (Ed.), *Mental health care for urban Indians: Clinical insights from native practitioners* (pp. 133–153). Washington, DC: American Psychological Association. doi: 10.1037/11422-007

Bigner, J., & Wetchler, J. L. (Eds.). (2004). *Relationship therapy with same-sex couples.* New York, NY: Haworth.

Bike, D. H., Norcross, J. C., & Schatz, D. M. (2009). Processes and outcomes of psychotherapists' personal therapy: Replication and extension 20 years later. *Psychotherapy: Theory, Research, Practice, Training, 46*(1), 19–31. doi: 10.1037/a0015139

Birdwhistell, R. L. (1970). *Kinesics and context: Essays on body motion communication.* Philadelphia, PA: University of Pennsylvania Press.

Birmaher, B., Brent, D., Bernet, W., Bukstein, O., Walter, H., Benson, R. S., et al. (2007). Practice parameter for the assessment and treatment of children and adolescents with depressive disorders. *Journal of the American Academy of Child & Adolescent Psychiatry, 46*(11), 1503–1526.

Bisson, J. I., Tavakoly, B., Witteveen, A. B., Ajdukovic, D., Jehel, L., Johansen, V. J., ... Olff, M. (2010). TENT guidelines: Development of post-disaster psychosocial care guidelines through a delphi process. *The British Journal of Psychiatry, 196*(1), 69–74. doi: http://dx.doi.org/10.1192/bjp.bp.109.066266

Black, L. & Jackson, V. (2005). *Families of African origin: An overview.* New York, NY: Guilford Press.

Black, S. A., Gallaway, M. S., Bell, M. R., & Ritchie, E. C. (2011). Prevalence and risk factors associated with suicides of army soldiers 2001–2009. *Military Psychology, 23*(4), 433–451.

Blader, J. C., & Carlson, G. A. (2007). Increased rates of bipolar disorder diagnoses among U.S. child, adolescent, and adult inpatients, 1996–2004. *Biological Psychiatry, 62*(2), 107–114.

Blain, D., Hoch, P., & Ryan, V. G. (1945). A course in psychological first aid and prevention. *American Journal of Psychiatry, 101,* 629–634.

Blankers, M., Koeter, M. W. J., & Schippers, G. M. (2011). Internet therapy versus Internet self-help versus no treatment for problematic alcohol use: A randomized controlled trial. *Journal of Consulting and Clinical Psychology, 79*(3), 330–341. doi: 10.1037/a0023498

Bloomgarden, A., & Mennuti, R. B. (Eds.). (2009). *Psychotherapist revealed: Therapists speak about self-disclosure in psychotherapy.* New York, NY: Routledge.

Bolton, J. M., Pagura, J., Enns, M. W., Grant, B., & Sareen, J. (2010). A population-based longitudinal study of risk factors for suicide attempts in major depressive disorder. *Journal of Psychiatric Research, 44*(13), 817–826. doi: http://dx.doi.org/10.1016/j.jpsychires.2010.01.003

Bordin, E. S. (1979). The generalizability of the psychoanalytic concept of the working alliance. *Psychotherapy: Theory, Research & Practice, 16*(3), 252–260. doi: 10.1037/h0085885

Bordin, E. S. (1994). Theory and research on the therapeutic working alliance: New directions. In A. O. Horvath & L. S. Greenberg (Eds.), *The working alliance: Theory, research, and practice* (pp. 13–37). Oxford, England: Wiley.

Bornstein, P. H., & Bornstein, M. T. (1986). *Marital therapy: A behavioral-communications approach*. New York, NY: Pergamon Press.

Borowich, A. E. (2008). Failed reparative therapy of orthodox Jewish homosexuals. *Journal of Gay & Lesbian Mental Health, 12*(3), 167–177. doi: http://dx.doi.org/10.1080/19359700802111072

Boyer, D. (ed.). (1988). *In and out of street life: Readings on interventions with street youth*. Portland, OR: Tri-county Youth Consortium.

Brammer, L. M. (1979). *The helping relationship*. Englewood Cliffs, NJ: Prentice Hall.

Branzei, O., Vertinsky, I., & Camp, R. D., II. (2007). Culture-contingent signs of trust in emergent relationships. *Organizational Behavior and Human Decision Processes, 104*(1), 61–82. doi: 10.1016/j.obhdp.2006.11.002

Breggin, P. R. (2010). Antidepressant-induced suicide, violence, and mania: Risks for military personnel. *Ethical Human Psychology and Psychiatry: An International Journal of Critical Inquiry, 12*(2), 111–121. doi: http://dx.doi.org/10.1891/1559-4343.12.2.111

Bressi, C., Manenti, S., Frongia, P., Porcellana, M., & Invernizzi, G. (2007). Systemic family therapy in schizophrenia: A randomized clinical trial of effectiveness. *Psychotherapy and Psychosomatics, 77*(1), 43–49. doi: 10.1159/000110059

Brockhouse, R., Msetfi, R. M., Cohen, K., & Joseph, S. (2011). Vicarious exposure to trauma and growth in therapists: The moderating effects of sense of coherence, organizational support, and empathy. *Journal of Traumatic Stress, 24*(6), 735–742. doi: http://dx.doi.org/10.1002/jts.20704

Brody, C. M. (Ed.). (1984). *Women therapists working with women: New theory and process of feminist therapy*. New York, NY: Springer.

Bronfenbrenner, U. (1976). The ecology of human development: History and perspectives. *Psychologia Wychowawcza, 19*(5), 537–549.

Bronfenbrenner, U. (1986). Ecology of the family as a context for human development: Research perspectives. *Developmental Psychology, 22*(6), 723–742. doi: 10.1037/0012-1649.22.6.723

Bronfenbrenner, U. (Ed.). (2005). *Making human beings human: Bioecological perspectives on human development* Thousand Oaks, CA: Sage.

Brown, G. K., Have, T. T., Henriques, G. R., Xie, S. X., Hollander, J. E., & Beck, A. T. (2005). Cognitive therapy for the prevention of suicide attempts: A randomized controlled trial. *JAMA, 294*(5), 563–570. doi: 10.1001/jama.294.5.563

Brown, L. S. (2010). *Feminist therapy*. Washington, DC: American Psychological Association.

Bryant, C. M., Taylor, R. J., Lincoln, K. D., Chatters, L. M., & Jackson, J. S. (2008). Marital satisfaction among African Americans and Black Caribbeans: Findings from the national survey of American life. *Family Relations: An Interdisciplinary Journal of Applied Family Studies, 57*(2), 239–253. doi: http://dx.doi.org/10.1111/j.1741-3729.2008.00497.x

Bryceland, C., & Stam, H. J. (2005). Empirical validation and professional codes of ethics: Description or prescription? *Journal of Constructivist Psychology, 18*(2), 131–155.

Busch, K. A., & Fawcett, J. (2004). A fine-grained study of inpatients who commit suicide. *Psychiatric Annals, 34*(5), 357–364.

Buyukdura, J. S., McClintock, S. M., & Croarkin, P. E. (2011). Psychomotor retardation in depression: Biological underpinnings, measurement, and treatment. *Progress in Neuro-Psychopharmacology & Biological Psychiatry, 35*(2), 395–409. doi: http://dx.doi.org/10.1016/j.pnpbp.2010.10.019

Cabaniss, D. L., Cherry, S., Douglas, C. J., & Schwartz, A. R. (2011). *Psychodynamic psychotherapy: A clinical manual*. London, England: Wiley-Blackwell.

Cabassa, L. J. (2007). Latino immigrant men's perceptions of depression and attitudes toward help seeking. *Hispanic Journal of Behavioral Sciences*, *29*(4), 492–509. doi: 10 .1177/0739986307307157

Camarota, S. A. (2005). *Immigrants at mid-decade: A snapshot of America's foreign-born population in 2005*. Washington, DC: Center for Immigration Studies Washington.

Campbell, M. A., French, S., & Gendreau, P. (2009). The prediction of violence in adult offenders: A meta-analytic comparison of instruments and methods of assessment. *Criminal Justice and Behavior*, *36*(6), 567–590. doi: http://dx.doi.org/10.1177/ 0093854809333610

Campfield, K. M., & Hills, A. M. (2001). Effect of timing of critical incident stress debriefing (CISD) on posttraumatic symptoms. *Journal of Traumatic Stress*, *14*(2), 327–340. doi: 10.1023/A:1011117018705

Cannon, W. B. (1939). *The wisdom of the body* (Revised ed.). New York, NY: Norton.

Capra, F. (1975). *The tao of physics*. New York, NY: Random House.

Carkhuff, R. R. (1987). *The art of helping* (6th ed.). Amherst, MA: Human Resource Development Press.

Carlson, J., Watts, R. E., & Maniacci, M. (2006). *Adlerian therapy: Theory and practice*. Washington, DC: American Psychological Association. doi: 10.1037/11363-000

Cassidy, F. (2011). Risk factors of attempted suicide in bipolar disorder. *Suicide and Life-Threatening Behavior*, *41*(1), 6–11. doi: http://dx.doi.org/10.1111/j.1943-278X .2010.00007.x

Castonguay, L. G., Boswell, J. F., Constantino, M. J., Goldfried, M. R., & Hill, C. E. (2010). Training implications of harmful effects of psychological treatments. *American Psychologist*, *65*(1), 34–49. doi: 10.1037/a0017330

Castro-Blanco, D. E., & Karver, M. S. (2010). *Elusive alliance: Treatment engagement strategies with high-risk adolescents*. Washington, DC: American Psychological Association.

Centers for Disease Control and Prevention, & National Center for Injury Prevention and Control. (2012). *Injury prevention & control: Data and statistics (WISQARS)*. Retrieved from http://www.cdc.gov/injury/wisqars/index.html

Ceperich, S. D., & Ingersoll, K. S. (2011). Motivational interviewing + feedback intervention to reduce alcohol-exposed pregnancy risk among college binge drinkers: Determinants and patterns of response. *Journal of Behavioral Medicine*, *34*(5), 381–395. doi: http://dx.doi.org/10.1007/s10865-010-9308-2

Chambless, D. L., Crits-Christoph, P., Wampold, B. E., Norcross, J. C., Lambert, M. J., Bohart, A. C., . . . Johannsen, B. E. (2006). *What should be validated?* Washington, DC: American Psychological Association. doi: 10.1037/11265-005

Chang, C. Y., & O'Hara, C. (2013). The initial interview with Asian American clients. *Journal of Contemporary Psychology*, *43*(1), 33–42.

Chang, C. Y., Ritter, K. B., & Hays, D. G. (2005). Multicultural trends and toys in play therapy. *International Journal of Play Therapy*, *14*(2), 69–85.

Chao, R. C. (2012). Racial/ethnic identity, gender-role attitudes, and multicultural counseling competence: The role of multicultural counseling training. *Journal of Counseling & Development*, *90*(1), 35–44.

Chao, C. M. (1992). The inner heart: Therapy with Southeast Asian families. In L. A. Vargas & J. D. Koss-Chioino (Eds.), *Working with culture: Psychotherapeutic interventions with ethnic minority children and adolescents* (pp. 157–181). San Francisco, CA: Jossey-Bass.

Cheng, A. T. A., Hawton, K., Chen, T. H. H., Yen, A. M. F., Chang, J., Chong, M., . . . Chen, L. (2007). The influence of media reporting of a celebrity suicide on suicidal behavior in patients with a history of depressive disorder. *Journal of Affective Disorders*, *103*(1–3), 69–75. doi: 10.1016/j.jad.2007.01.021

Cheng, M. K. S. (2007). New approaches for creating the therapeutic alliance: Solution-focused interviewing, motivational interviewing, and the medication interest model. *Psychiatric Clinics of North America*, *30*(2), 157–166. doi: 10.1016/j.psc.2007.01.003

Cheung, C., Kwan, A. Y., & Ng, S. H. (2006). Impacts of filial piety on preference for kinship versus public care. *Journal of Community Psychology, 34*(5), 617–634. doi: 10.1002/jcop.20118

Cheyne, J. A., & Girard, T. A. (2007). Paranoid delusions and threatening hallucinations: A prospective study of sleep paralysis experiences. *Consciousness and Cognition: An International Journal, 16*(4), 959–974. doi: 10.1016/j.concog.2007.01.002

Chiang, H., Lu, Z., & Wear, S. E. (2005). To have or to be: Ways of caregiving identified during recovery from the earthquake disaster in Taiwan. *Journal of Medical Ethics, 31,* 154–158.

Christensen, A., McGinn, M., & Williams, K. J. (2009). *Behavioral couples therapy.* Arlington, VA: American Psychiatric Publishing.

Christopher, J. C. (2001). Culture and psychotherapy: Toward a hermeneutic approach. *Psychotherapy: Theory, Research, Practice, Training, 38*(2), 115–128.

Christopher, J. C., & Bickhard, M. H. (2007). Culture, self and identity: Interactivist contributions to a metatheory for cultural psychology. *Culture & Psychology, 13*(3), 259–295. doi: 10.1177/1354067X07079881

Chung, T., Maisto, S. A., Mihalo, A., Martin, C. S., Cornelius, J. R., & Clark, D. B. (2011). Brief assessment of readiness to change tobacco use in treated youth. *Journal of Substance Abuse Treatment, 41*(2), 137–147. doi: 10.1016/j.jsat.2011.02.010

Chung, T., & Martin, C. S. (2005). What were they thinking? Adolescents' interpretations of DSM-IV alcohol dependence symptom queries and implications for diagnostic validity. *Drug and Alcohol Dependence, 80*(2), 191–200. doi: 10.1016/j.drugalcdep .2005.03.023

Clark, A. J. (2002). *Early recollections: Theory and practice in counseling and psychotherapy.* New York, NY: Brunner-Routledge.

Clark, A. J. (2010). Empathy: An integral model in the counseling process. *Journal of Counseling & Development, 88,* 348–356.

Clark, D. C. (1998). *The evaluation and management of the suicidal patient.* New York, NY: Guilford Press.

Cleary, B. (2009). *Ramona Quimby, age 8.* New York: NY: HarperCollins.

Cochran, B. N., Pruitt, L., Fukuda, S., Zoellner, L. A., & Feeny, N. C. (2008). Reasons underlying treatment preference: An exploratory study. *Journal of Interpersonal Violence, 23*(2), 276–291. doi: 10.1177/0886260507309836

Coffey, E. P., Olson, M. E., & Sessions, P. (2001). The heart of the matter: An essay about the effects of managed care on family therapy with children. *Family Process, 40*(4), 385–399. doi: http://dx.doi.org/10.1111/j.1545-5300.2001.4040100385.x

Cohen, K., & Collens, P. (2012). The impact of trauma work on trauma workers: A metasynthesis on vicarious trauma and vicarious posttraumatic growth. *Psychological Trauma: Theory, Research, Practice, and Policy.* doi:

Cohen, J. (1977). *Statistical power analysis for the behavioral sciences* (rev. ed.). Hillsdale, NJ: Erlbaum.

Collins, B. G., & Collins, T. M. (2005). *Crisis and trauma: Developmental-ecological intervention.* Boston, MA: Lahaska Press.

Colorosso, B. (1995). *Kids are worth it.* New York, NY: Avon Books.

Comas-Díaz, L. (Director). (1994). *Ethnocultural psychotherapy* [Video/DVD]. Washington, DC: American Psychological Association.

Comas-Díaz, L. (2006). Latino healing: The integration of ethnic psychology into psychotherapy. *Psychotherapy: Theory, Research, 43*(4), 436–453. doi: 10.1037/0033-3204 .43.4.436

Comas-Díaz, L. (2011). Multicultural approaches to psychotherapy. In J. C. Norcross, G. R. VandenBos, & D. K. Freedheim (Eds.), *History of psychotherapy: Continuity and change* (2nd ed., pp. 243–267). Washington, DC: American Psychological Association. doi: 10.1037/12353-008

Constantine, M. G., Fuertes, J. N., Roysircar, G., & Kindaichi, M. M. (2008). (2008). Multicultural competence: Clinical practice, training and supervision, and research.

In W. B. Walsh (Ed.), *Biennial review of counseling psychology: Volume 1* (pp. 97–127). New York, NY: Routledge/Taylor & Francis.

Constantino, M. J., Castonguay, L. G., & Schut, A. J. (2002). The working alliance: A flagship for the "scientist-practitioner" model in psychotherapy. In G. S. Tryon (Ed.), *Counseling based on process research: Applying what we know* (pp. 81–131). Boston, MA: Allyn & Bacon.

Cook, J. W., Taylor, L. A., & Silverman, P. (2004). The application of therapeutic storytelling techniques with preadolescent children: A clinical description with illustrative case study. *Cognitive and Behavioral Practice, 11*(2), 243–248. doi: 10.1016/S1077-7229(04)80035-X

Cooke, D. J. (2012). Violence risk assessment: Things that I have learned so far. *Antisocial behavior and crime: Contributions of developmental and evaluation research to prevention and intervention* (pp. 221–237). Cambridge, MA: Hogrefe Publishing.

Coppen, A. (1994). Depression as a lethal disease: Prevention strategies. *Journal of Clinical Psychiatry, 55*(4, Suppl), 37–45.

Corcoran, J. (2005). *Building strengths and skills: A collaborative approach to working with clients.* New York, NY: Oxford University Press.

Corcoran, J., & Pillai, V. (2009). A review of the research on solution-focused therapy. *British Journal of Social Work, 39*(2), 234–242. doi: 10.1093/bjsw/bcm098

Cormier, L. S., Nurius, P. S., & Osborn, C. J. (2012). *Interviewing and change strategies for helpers: Fundamental skills and cognitive-behavioral interventions* (7th ed.). Belmont, CA: Brooks/Cole.

Council for Accreditation of Counseling and Related Educational Programs. (2009). *2009 standards for accreditation.* Alexandria, VA: Author.

Cox, D. W., Ghahramanlou-Holloway, M., Greene, F. N., Bakalar, J. L., Schendel, C. L., Nademin, M. E., . . . Kindt, M. (2011). Suicide in the United States Air Force: Risk factors communicated before and at death. *Journal of Affective Disorders, 133*(3), 398–405. doi: http://dx.doi.org/10.1016/j.jad.2011.05.011

Craig, R. J. (Ed.). (2005). *Clinical and diagnostic interviewing* (2nd ed.). Lanham, MD: Jason Aronson.

Crippa, J. A. S., de Lima Osório, F., Del-Ben, C. M., Filho, A. S., da Silva Freitas, M. C., & Loureiro, S. R. (2008). Comparability between telephone and face-to-face structured clinical interview for DSM-IV in assessing social anxiety disorder. *Perspectives in Psychiatric Care, 44*(4), 241–247. doi: 10.1111/j.1744-6163.2008.00183.x

Cuellar, I., & Paniagua, F. A. (Eds.). (2000). *Handbook of multicultural mental health: Assessment and treatment of diverse populations.* New York, NY: Academic Press.

Curtis, S. L., & Eby, L. T. (2010). Recovery at work: The relationship between social identity and commitment among substance abuse counselors. *Journal of Substance Abuse Treatment, 39*(3), 248–254. doi: http://dx.doi.org/10.1016/j.jsat.2010.06.006

Dana, R. H. (1993). *Multicultural assessment perspectives for professional psychology.* Boston, MA: Allyn & Bacon.

Daniel, M., & Gurczynski, J. (2010). Mental status examination. In D. L. Segal & M. Hersen (Eds.), *Diagnostic interviewing* (pp. 61–88). New York, NY: Springer. doi: 10.1007/978-1-4419-1320-3_4

Dasgupta, N., & Asgari, S. (2004). Seeing is believing: Exposure to counterstereotypic women leaders and its effect on the malleability of automatic gender stereotyping. *Journal of Experimental Social Psychology, 40*(5), 642–658. doi: 10.1016/j.jesp.2004.02.003

Dattilio, F. M. (2010). *Cognitive-behavioral therapy with couples and families: A comprehensive guide for clinicians.* New York, NY: Guilford Press.

D'augelli, A. R., Grossman, A. H., Salter, N. P., Vasey, J. J., Starks, M. T., & Sinclair, K. O. (2005). Predicting the suicide attempts of lesbian, gay, and bisexual youth. *Suicide and Life-Threatening Behavior, 35*(6), 646–660. doi: 10.1521/suli.2005.35.6.646

Davidson, C. L., & Wingate, L. R. (2011). Racial disparities in risk and protective factors for suicide. *Journal of Black Psychology, 37*(4), 499–516. doi: http://dx.doi.org/10.1177/0095798410397543

Davidson, M. W., Wagner, W. G., & Range, L. M. (1995). Clinicians' attitudes toward no-suicide agreements. *Suicide and Life-Threatening Behavior, 25*(3), 410–414.

de Jong, P., & Berg, I. K. (2008). *Interviewing for solutions* (2nd ed.). Belmont, CA: Thomson.

de Shazer, S. (1984). The death of resistance. *Family Process, 23,* 79–93.

de Shazer, S. (1985). *Keys to solution in brief therapy.* New York, NY: Norton.

de Shazer, S. (1988). *Clues: Investigating solutions in brief therapy.* New York: Norton.

de Shazer, S., Dolan, Y., Korman, H., McCollum, E., Trepper, T., & Berg, I. K. (2007). *More than miracles: The state of the art of solution-focused brief therapy.* New York, NY: Haworth Press.

de Vega, M. H., & Beyebach, M. (2004). Between-session change in solution-focused therapy: A replication. *Journal of Systemic Therapies, 23*(2), 18–26. doi: 10.1521/jsyt.23.2.18.36644

Dean, R. A. (2003). Native American humor: Implications for transcultural care. *Journal of Transcultural Nursing, 14*(1), 62–65. doi: http://dx.doi.org/10.1177/1043659602238352

Dell Orto, A. E., & Power, P. W. (Eds.). (2007). *The psychological and social impact of illness and disability* (5th ed.) New York, NY: Springer.

Deloria, V. (1994). *God is red.* Golden, CO: Fulcrum.

DeRicco, J. N., & Sciarra, D. T. (2005). The immersion experience in multicultural counselor training: Confronting covert racism. *Journal of Multicultural Counseling and Development, 33*(1), 2–16. doi: http://dx.doi.org/10.1002/j.2161-1912.2005.tb00001.x

Dervaux, A., Baylé, F. J., Laqueille, X., Bourdel, M., Leborgne, M., Olié, J., & Krebs, M. (2006). Validity of the CAGE questionnaire in schizophrenic patients with alcohol abuse and dependence. *Schizophrenia Research, 81*(2-3), 151–155. doi: http://dx.doi.org/10.1016/j.schres.2005.09.012

Descant, J. J., & Range, L. M. (1997). No-suicide agreements: College students' perceptions. *College Student Journal, 31*(2), 238–242.

Diamant, A. (1997). *The red tent.* New York, NY: St. Martin's Press.

Dickerson, F. B., & Lehman, A. F. (2011). Evidence-based psychotherapy for schizophrenia. *Journal of Nervous and Mental Disease, 199*(8), 520–526. doi: http://dx.doi.org/10.1097/NMD.0b013e318225ee78

Dickinson, J. J., Poole, D. A., & Bruck, M. (2005). Back to the future: A comment on the use of anatomical dolls in forensic interviews. *Journal of Forensic Psychology Practice, 5*(1), 63–74. doi: 10.1300/J158v05n01_04

DiLillo, D., DeGue, S., Kras, A., Di Loreto-Colgan, A. R., & Nash, C. (2006). Participant responses to retrospective surveys of child maltreatment: Does mode of assessment matter? *Violence and Victims, 21*(4), 410–424.

do Amaral, R. A., & Malbergier, A. (2008). Effectiveness of the CAGE questionnaire, gamma-glutamyltransferase and mean corpuscular volume of red blood cells as markers for alcohol-related problems in the workplace. *Addictive Behaviors, 33*(6), 772–781. doi: http://dx.doi.org/10.1016/j.addbeh.2007.12.006

Driessen, E., Cuijpers, P., de Maat, S. C. M., Abbass, A. A., de Jonghe, F., & Dekker, J. J. M. (2010). The efficacy of short-term psychodynamic psychotherapy for depression: A meta-analysis. *Clinical Psychology Review, 30*(1), 25–36. doi: 10.1016/j.cpr.2009.08.010

Drisko, J. W., & Grady, M. D. (2012). *Evidence-based practice in clinical social work.* New York, NY: Springer Science + Business Media. doi: http://dx.doi.org/10.1007/978-1-4614-3470-2

Drye, R. C., Goulding, R. L., & Goulding, M. E. (1973). No-suicide decisions: Patient monitoring of suicidal risk. *American Journal of Psychiatry, 130*(2), 171–174.

Duan, C., Rose, T. B., & Kraatz, R. A. (2002). Empathy. In G. S. Tryon (Ed.), *Counseling based on process research: Applying what we know* (pp. 197–231). Boston, MA: Allyn & Bacon.

Dugger, S. M., & Carlson, L. (Eds.). (2007). *Critical incidents in counseling children* Alexandria, VA: American Counseling Association.

Duncan, B. L., Miller, S. D., Wampold, B. E., & Hubble, M. A. (Eds.). (2010). *The heart and soul of change: Delivering what works in therapy* (2nd ed.). Washington, DC: American Psychological Association. doi: 10.1037/12075-000

Dunner, D. L. (2005). Depression, dementia, or pseudodementia? *CNS Spectrums, 10*(11), 862.

Duval, S., & Wicklund, R. A. (1972). *A theory of objective self awareness.* Oxford, England: Academic Press.

D'Zurilla, T. J., & Nezu, A. M. (2010). *Problem-solving therapy.* New York, NY: Guilford Press.

Eagle, G. (2005). Therapy at the cultural interface: Implications of African cosmology for traumatic stress intervention. *Journal of Contemporary Psychotherapy, 35*(2), 199–209.

Edlund, A., Lundström, M., Karlsson, S., Brännström, B., Bucht, G., & Gustafson, Y. (2006). Delirium in older patients admitted to general internal medicine. *Journal of Geriatric Psychiatry and Neurology, 19*(2), 83–90. doi: 10.1177/0891988706286509

Edwards, R. (2003). Counselling youth: Foucault, power, and the ethics of subjectivity. *British Journal of Guidance & Counselling, 31*(2), 251–252. doi: http://dx.doi.org/10.1080/0306988031000114295

Edwards, S. J., & Sachmann, M. D. (2010). No-suicide contracts, no-suicide agreements, and no-suicide assurances: A study of their nature, utilization, perceived effectiveness, and potential to cause harm. *Crisis: The Journal of Crisis Intervention and Suicide Prevention, 31*(6), 290–302. doi: http://dx.doi.org/10.1027/0227-5910/a000048

Eells, T. D. (2009). Review of the case formulation approach to cognitive-behavior therapy. *Psychotherapy: Theory, Research, Practice, Training, 46*(3), 400–401. doi: http://dx.doi.org/10.1037/a0017014

Ekman, P. (2001). *Telling lies: Clues to deceit in the marketplace, politics, and marriage.* New York, NY: Norton.

Elliott, R., Bohart, A. C., Watson, J. C., & Greenberg, L. S. (2011). Empathy. *Psychotherapy, 48*(1), 43–49. doi: 10.1037/a0022187

Ellis, T. E. (Ed.). (2006). *Cognition and suicide: Theory, research, and therapy* Washington, DC: American Psychological Association. doi: 10.1037/11377-000

Engel, G. L. (1980). The clinical application of the biopsychosocial model. *American Journal of Psychiatry, 137*(5), 535–544.

Engel, G. L. (1997). From biomedical to biopsychosocial: I. Being scientific in the human domain. *Psychotherapy and Psychosomatics, 66*(2), 57–62.

Englar-Carlson, M., & Carlson, J. (2012). Adlerian couples therapy: The case of the boxer's daughter and the momma's boy. *Engaging men in couples therapy* (pp. 81–103). New York, NY: Routledge/Taylor & Francis.

Engle, D. E., & Arkowitz, H. (2006). *Ambivalence in psychotherapy: Facilitating readiness to change.* New York, NY: Guilford Press.

Epp, A. M., & Dobson, K. S. (2010). *The evidence base for cognitive-behavioral therapy.* New York, NY: Guilford Press.

Epstein, J., & Klinkenberg, W. D. (2001). From Eliza to Internet: A brief history of computerized assessment. *Computers in Human Behavior, 17*(3), 295–314. doi: 10.1016/S0747-5632(01)00004-8

Erickson, M. H., Rossi, E. L., & Rossi, S. (1976). *Hypnotic realities.* New York, NY: Irvington.

Eriksen, K., & Kress, V. E. (2005). *Beyond the DSM story: Ethical quandaries, challenges, and best practices.* Thousand Oaks, CA: Sage.

Everly Jr., G. S., & Boyle, S. H. (1999). Critical incident stress debriefing (CISD): A meta-analysis. *International Journal of Emergency Mental Health, 1*(3), 165–168.

Everly, G. S., Phillips, S. B., Kane, D., & Feldman, D. (2006). Introduction to and overview of group psychological first aid. *Brief Treatment and Crisis Intervention, 6*(2), 130–136. doi: http://dx.doi.org/10.1093/brief-treatment/mhj009

Fairbairn, W. R. D. (1952). *Psychoanalytic studies of the personality.* London, England: Tavistock Publications and Kegan Paul, Trench, & Trubner.

Faller, K. C. (2005). Anatomical dolls: Their use in assessment of children who may have been sexually abused. *Journal of Child Sexual Abuse, 14*(3), 1–21.

Falvo, D. (2011). *Medical and psychosocial aspects of chronic illness and chronic disability* (4th ed.). Sudbury, MA: Jones and Bartlett Learning.

Farber, B. A. (2006). *Self-disclosure in psychotherapy.* New York, NY: Guilford Press.

Farber, B. A., & Doolin, E. M. (2011). Positive regard and affirmation. *Psychotherapy relationships that work: Evidence-based responsiveness* (2nd ed., pp. 168–186). New York, NY: Oxford University Press.

Fawcett, J., Clark, D. C., & Busch, K. A. (1993). Assessing and treating the patient at risk for suicide. *Psychiatric Annals, 23*(5), 244–255.

Feinn, R., Gelernter, J., Cubells, J. F., Farrer, L., & Kranzler, H. R. (2009). Sources of unreliability in the diagnosis of substance dependence. *Journal of Studies on Alcohol and Drugs, 70*(3), 475–481.

Fenichel, O. (1945). *The psychoanalytic theory of neurosis.* New York, NY: Norton.

Figley, C. R. (1995). Compassion fatigue: Toward a new understanding of the costs of caring. In B. H. Stamm (Ed.), *Secondary traumatic stress: Self-care issues for clinicians, researchers, and educators* (pp. 3–28). Lutherville, MD: Sidran.

First, M. B., Spitzer, R. L., Gibbon, M., & Williams, J. B. W. (1995). The structured clinical interview for DSM-III-R personality disorders (SCID-II): I. description. *Journal of Personality Disorders, 9*(2), 83–91.

Foa, E. B., & Riggs, D. S. (1994). *Posttraumatic stress disorder and rape.* Baltimore, MD: Sidran Press.

Foley, R., & Sharf, B. F. (1981). The five interviewing techniques most frequently overlooked by primary care physicians. *Behavioral Medicine, 8,* 26–31.

Folstein, M. F., Folstein, S. E., & McHugh, P. R. (1975). Mini-mental state: A practical method for grading the cognitive state of patients for the clinician. *Journal of Psychiatric Research, 12*(3), 189–198. doi: 10.1016/0022-3956(75)90026-6

Foner, N. (2005). Strangers at the gates: New immigrants in urban America. *Contemporary Sociology: A Journal of Reviews, 34*(3), 295–296.

Fong, M. L., & Cox, B. G. (1983). Trust as an underlying dynamic in the counseling process: How clients test trust. *Personnel & Guidance Journal, 62*(3), 163–166.

Fontes, L. A. (2008). *Interviewing clients across cultures: A practitioner's guide.* New York, NY: Guilford Press.

Ford, J. G. (2001). Healing homosexuals: A psychologist's journey through the ex-gay movement and the pseudo-science of reparative therapy. *Journal of Gay & Lesbian Psychotherapy, 5*(3–4), 69–86. doi: http://dx.doi.org/10.1300/J236v05n03_06

Forester, C. (2007). Your own body of wisdom: Recognizing and working with somatic countertransference with dissociative and traumatized patients. *Body, Movement and Dance in Psychotherapy, 2*(2), 123–133. doi: 10.1080/17432970701374510

Forsyth, D. R., O'Boyle, E. H., & McDaniel, M. A. (2008). East meets west: A meta-analytic investigation of cultural variations in idealism and relativism. *Journal of Business Ethics, 83*(4), 813–833. doi: 10.1007/s10551-008-9667-6

Fouad, N. A., & Arredondo, P. (2007a). *Becoming culturally oriented: Practical advice for psychologists and educators.* Washington, DC: American Psychological Association. doi: 10.1037/11483-000

Fouad, N. A., & Arredondo, P. (2007b). *Introduction to multicultural-centered practices.* Washington, DC: American Psychological Association. doi: 10.1037/11483-001

Fowler, J. C. (2012). Suicide risk assessment in clinical practice: Pragmatic guidelines for imperfect assessments. *Psychotherapy, 49*(1), 81–90. doi: http://dx.doi.org/10.1037/a0026148

Fox, R. E. (1995). The rape of psychotherapy. *Professional Psychology: Research and Practice, 26*(2), 147–155. doi: http://dx.doi.org/10.1037/0735-7028.26.2.147

Frances, A. J., & Widiger, T. (2012). Psychiatric diagnosis: Lessons from the DSM-IV past and cautions for the DSM-5 future. *Annual Review of Clinical Psychology, 8,* 109–130. doi: http://dx.doi.org/10.1146/annurev-clinpsy-032511-143102

Frank, J. D. (1961). *Persuasion and healing.* Baltimore, MD: Johns Hopkins University Press.

Frank, J. D., & Frank, J. B. (1991). *Persuasion and healing: A comparative study of psychotherapy* (3rd ed.). Baltimore, MD: Johns Hopkins University Press.

Franklin, A. J. (2004). *From brotherhood to manhood: How Black men rescue their relationships and dreams from the invisibility syndrome.* Hoboken, NJ: Wiley.

Franklin, A. J. (2007). *Gender, race, and invisibility in psychotherapy with African American men.* Washington, DC: American Psychological Association. doi: 10.1037/11500-013

Franklin, A. J., Boyd-Franklin, N., & Kelly, S. (2006). *Racism and invisibility: Race-related stress, emotional abuse and psychological trauma for people of color.* Binghamton, NY: Haworth Maltreatment and Trauma Press/ Haworth Press.

Fresán, A., Apiquian, R., & Nicolini, H. (2006). Psychotic symptoms and the prediction of violence in schizophrenic patients. *Schizophrenic psychology: New research* (pp. 239–254). Hauppauge, NY: Nova Science.

Freud, S. (1909). Analysis of a phobia in a five-year-old boy. In J. Strachey (Ed.), *Standard edition of the complete psychological works of Sigmund Freud* (pp. 3–149). London, England: Hogarth Press.

Freud, S. (1910/1957). The future prospects of psycho-analytic therapy. In J. Strachey (Ed.), *The standard edition of the complete works of Sigmund Freud* (J. Strachey, Trans.) (pp. 139–151). London: Hogarth Press.

Freud, S. (1912/1958). On the beginning of treatment: Further recommendations on the technique of psychoanalysis. In J. Strachey (Ed.), *Standard edition of the complete psychological works of Sigmund Freud.* (J. Strachey, Trans.) (pp. 122–144). London, England: Hogarth Press.

Freud, S. (1949). *An outline of psychoanalysis.* New York, NY: Norton.

Freud, S. (1963). *Introductory lectures on psycho-analysis.* (J. Strachey Trans.). London: Hogarth Press.

Friedlander, M. L., Escudero, V., Heatherington, L., & Diamond, G. M. (2011). Alliance in couple and family therapy. *Psychotherapy relationships that work: Evidence-based responsiveness* (2nd ed., pp. 92–109). New York, NY: Oxford University Press.

Friedmann, P. D., Saitz, R., Gogineni, A., Zhang, J. X., & Stein, M. D. (2001). Validation of the screening strategy in the NIAAA "physicians" guide to helping patients with alcohol problems. *Journal of Studies on Alcohol, 62*(2), 234–238.

Frost, D. M. (2011). Similarities and differences in the pursuit of intimacy among sexual minority and heterosexual individuals: A personal projects analysis. *Journal of Social Issues, 67*(2), 282–301. doi: http://dx.doi.org/10.1111/j.1540-4560.2011.01698.x

Gallagher, J. R. (2010). Licensed chemical dependency counselors views of professional and ethical standards: A focus group analysis. *Alcoholism Treatment Quarterly, 28*(2), 184–197. doi: http://dx.doi.org/10.1080/07347321003648695

Gallardo, M. E. (2013). Context and culture: The initial clinical interview with the Latina/o client. *Journal of Contemporary Psychotherapy, 43*(1), 43–52.

Gallardo, M. E., Yeh, C. J., Trimble, J. E., & Parham, T. A. (Eds.). (2011). *Culturally adaptive counseling skills: Demonstrations of evidence-based practices.* New York, NY: Sage.

Garb, H. N. (2007). Computer-administered interviews and rating scales. *Psychological Assessment, 19*(1), 4–13. doi: 10.1037/1040-3590.19.1.4

Garcia-Preto, N. (1996). Latino families: An overview. In M. McGoldrick, J. Giordano & J. K. Pearce (Eds.), *Ethnicity and family therapy* (2nd ed., pp. 141–154). New York, NY: Guilford Press.

Gardner, H. (1983). *Frames of mind: The theory of multiple intelligences.* New York, NY: Basic Books.

Gardner, H. (1999). *Intelligence reframed: Multiple intelligences for the 21st century.* New York, NY: Basic Books.

Gardner, R. A. (1971). Mutual storytelling: A technique in child psychotherapy. *Acta Paedopsychiatrica, 38*(9), 253.

Gardner, R. A. (1993). *Storytelling in psychotherapy with children.* Lanham, MD: Jason Aronson.

Garrett, M. T., Garrett, J. T., Torres-Rivera, E., Wilbur, M., & Roberts-Wilbur, J. (2005). Laughing it up: Native American humor as spiritual tradition. *Journal of Multicultural*

Counseling and Development, 33(4), 194–204. doi: http://dx.doi.org/10.1002/j.2161-1912.2005.tb00016.x

Gaspar, R. M. (2006). Terapia integral de pareja. / Integrative behavioral couple therapy. *EduPsykhé: Revista De Psicologia y Psicopedagogia, 5*(2), 273–286.

Gazda, G. M., Asbury, F. S., Balzer, F. J., Childers, W. C., & Walters, R. P. (1984). *Human relations development: A manual for educators* (3rd ed.). Boston, MA: Allyn & Bacon.

Gelso, C. J., & Hayes, J. A. (1998). *The psychotherapy relationship: Theory, research, and practice.* New York, NY: Wiley.

Gelso, C. J., & Hayes, J. A. (2007). *Countertransference and the inner world of the psychotherapist: Perils and possibilities.* Mahwah, NJ: Erlbaum.

Gergen, K. J. (2009). *An invitation to social construction* (2nd ed.). Thousand Oaks, CA: Sage.

Gershoff, E. T. (2002). Corporal punishment, physical abuse, and the burden of proof: Reply to Baumrind, Larzelere, and Cowan (2002), Holden (2002), and Parke (2002). *Psychological Bulletin, 128*(4), 602–611.

Gershoff, E. T., & Bitensky, S. H. (2007). The case against corporal punishment of children: Converging evidence from social science research and international human rights law and implications for U.S. public policy. *Psychology, Public Policy, and Law, 13*(4), 231–272. doi: 10.1037/1076-8971.13.4.231

Gershoff, E. T., Lansford, J. E., Sexton, H. R., Davis-Kean, P., & Sameroff, A. J. (2012). Longitudinal links between spanking and children's externalizing behaviors in a national sample of White, Black, Hispanic, and Asian American families. *Child Development, 83*(3), 838–843. doi: 10.1111/j.1467-8624.2011.01732.x

Gfroerer, K. P., Kern, R. M., Curlette, W. L., White, J., & Jonyniene, J. (2011). Parenting style and personality: Perceptions of mothers, fathers, and adolescents. *The Journal of Individual Psychology, 67*(1), 57–73.

Gibbs, M. A. (1984). The therapist as imposter. In C. M. Brody (Ed.), *Women therapists working with women: New theory and process of feminist therapy* (pp. 21–33). New York, NY: Springer.

Gibbs, J. T., & Huang, L. N. (Eds.). (2004). *Children of color: Psychological interventions with culturally diverse youth.* San Francisco, CA: Jossey-Bass.

Gilbert, J. (2009). Power and ethics in psychosocial counselling: Reflections on the experience of an international NGO providing services for Iraqi refugees in Jordan. *Intervention: International Journal of Mental Health, Psychosocial Work & Counselling in Areas of Armed Conflict, 7*(1), 50–60. doi: http://dx.doi.org/10.1097/WTF.0b013e32832ad355

Gilboa, A., & Verfaellie, M. (2010). Telling it like it isn't: The cognitive neuroscience of confabulation. *Journal of the International Neuropsychological Society, 16*(6), 961–966. doi: http://dx.doi.org/10.1017/S135561771000113X

Gingerich, W. J., & Eisengart, S. (2000). Solution-focused brief therapy: A review of the outcome research. *Family Process, 39*(4), 477–498. doi: 10.1111/j.1545-5300.2000.39408.x

Gladwell, M. (2005). *Blink: The power of thinking without thinking.* New York, NY: Little, Brown.

Glasser, W. (1998). *Choice theory: A new psychology of personal freedom.* New York, NY: HarperCollins.

Glasser, W. (2000). *Reality therapy in action.* New York, NY: HarperCollins.

Glasser, W. (2003). *Warning: Psychiatry can be hazardous to your health.* New York, NY: HarperCollins.

Gluck, M., Mercado, E., & Myers, C. (2013). *Learning and memory: From brain to behavior* (2nd ed.). New York, NY: Worth.

Goates-Jones, M., & Hill, C. E. (2008). Treatment preference, treatment-preference match, and psychotherapist credibility: Influence on session outcome and preference shift. *Psychotherapy: Theory, Research, Practice, Training, 45*(1), 61–74. doi: http://dx.doi.org/10.1037/0033-3204.45.1.61

Gold, J. M., & Morris, G. M. (2003). Family resistance to counseling: The initial agenda for intergenerational and narrative approaches. *The Family Journal, 11*(4), 374–379. doi: http://dx.doi.org/10.1177/1066480703255619

Gold, S. H., & Hilsenroth, M. J. (2009). Effects of graduate clinicians' personal therapy on therapeutic alliance. *Clinical Psychology & Psychotherapy, 16*(3), 159–171. doi: 10.1002/cpp.612

Goldenberg, H., & Goldenberg, I. (2012). *Family therapy: An overview*. Pacific Grove, CA: Brooks/Cole.

Goldfried, M. R. (2001). Conclusion: A perspective on how therapists change. *How therapists change: Personal and professional reflections* (pp. 315–330). Washington, DC: American Psychological Association. doi: http://dx.doi.org/10.1037/10392-017

Goldfried, M. R., & Davison, G. C. (1976). *Clinical behavior therapy*. New York, NY: Holt, Rinehart & Winston.

Goldfried, M. R., & Davison, G. C. (1994). *Clinical behavior therapy* (2nd ed.). Oxford, England: Wiley.

Goldfried, M. R. (2007). What has psychotherapy inherited from Carl Rogers? *Psychotherapy: Theory, Research, Practice, Training, 44*(3), 249–252. doi: 10.1037/0033-3204.44.3.249

Goldfried, M. R., Greenberg, L. S., & Marmar, C. (1990). Individual psychotherapy: Process and outcome. *Annual Review of Psychology, 41*, 659–688. doi: 10.1146/annurev.ps.41.020190.003303

Gonçalves, M. M., Matos, M., & Santos, A. (2009). Narrative therapy and the nature of "innovative moments" in the construction of change. *Journal of Constructivist Psychology, 22*(1), 1–23. doi: 10.1080/10720530802500748

Goodkind, J. R., Ross-Toledo, K., John, S., Hall, J. L., Ross, L., Freeland, L., . . . Lee, C. (2011). Rebuilding trust: A community, multiagency, state, and university partnership to improve behavioral health care for American Indian youth, their families, and communities. *Journal of Community Psychology, 39*(4), 452–477. doi: http://dx.doi.org/10.1002/jcop.20446

Goodman, L. A., & Epstein, D. (2008). *Listening to battered women: A survivor-centered approach to advocacy, mental health, and justice*. Washington, DC: American Psychological Association.

Gordon, D. A., Graves, K., & Arbuthnot, J. (1995). The effect of functional family therapy for delinquents on adult criminal behavior. *Criminal Justice and Behavior, 22*(1), 60–73. doi: 10.1177/0093854895022001005

Gottman, J. M. (2011). *The science of trust: Emotional attunement for couples*. New York, NY: Norton.

Gottman, J. M., & DeClaire, J. (2001). *The relationship cure: A five-step guide for building better connections with family, friends, and lovers*. New York, NY: Crown.

Gould, M., Jamieson, P., & Romer, D. (2003). Media contagion and suicide among the young. *American Behavioral Scientist. Special Issue: Suicide in Youth, 46*(9), 1269–1284. doi: 10.1177/0002764202250670

Graff, C. A., & Hecker, L. L. (2010). E-therapy: Developing an ethical online practice. In L. Hecker (Ed.), *Ethics and professional issues in couple and family therapy* (pp. 243–255). New York, NY: Routledge/Taylor & Francis.

Graham, J. M., Liu, Y. J., & Jeziorski, J. L. (2006). The dyadic adjustment scale: A reliability generalization meta-analysis. *Journal of Marriage and Family, 68*(3), 701–717. doi: 10.1111/j.1741-3737.2006.00284.x

Grahn, J. (1990). *Another mother tongue*. Boston, MA: Beacon Press.

Grant, B. F., Dawson, D. A., Stinson, F. S., Chou, P. S., Kay, W., & Pickering, R. (2003). The alcohol use disorder and associated disabilities interview schedule-IV (AUDADIS-IV): Reliability of alcohol consumption, tobacco use, family history of depression and psychiatric diagnostic modules in a general population sample. *Drug and Alcohol Dependence, 71*(1), 7–16. doi: http://dx.doi.org/10.1016/S0376-8716(03)00070-X

Gray, J. (2004). *Men are from Mars, women are from Venus: The classic guide to understanding the opposite sex*. New York, NY: HarperCollins.

Gray, J. S., & Rose, W. J. (2012). Cultural adaptation for therapy with American Indians and Alaska Natives. *Journal of Multicultural Counseling and Development, 40*(2), 82–92. doi: http://dx.doi.org/10.1002/j.2161-1912.2012.00008.x

Greenan, D. E., & Tunnell, G. (2006). *Sex, drugs, rock 'n' roll . . . and children: Redefining male couples in the twenty-first century*. New York, NY: Haworth Press.

Greenberg, L. S. (2002). *Emotion-focused therapy: Coaching clients to work through their feelings*. Washington, DC: American Psychological Association.

Greenberg, L. S., & Goldman, R. N. (2008). *Emotion-focused couples therapy: The dynamics of emotion, love, and power*. United States: American Psychological Association. doi: http://dx.doi.org/10.1037/11750-000

Greenberg, L. S., Watson, J. C., Elliott, R., & Bohart, A. C. (2001). Empathy. *Psychotherapy: Theory, Research, Practice, Training, 38*(4), 380–384.

Greenberg, L. S., Watson, J. C., & Lietaer, G. (1998). *Handbook of experiential psychotherapy*. New York, NY: Guilford Press.

Greenson, R. R. (1965). The working alliance and the transference neurosis. *Psychoanalytic Quarterly, 34*(2), 155–179.

Greenson, R. R. (1967). *The technique and practice of psychoanalysis*. New York, NY: International University Press.

Griffith, E. E. H., & Baker, F. M. (1993). Psychiatric care of African Americans. In A. C. Gaw (Ed.), *Culture, ethnicity, and mental illness* (pp. 147–173). Washington, DC: American Psychiatric Press.

Grinder, J., & Bandler, R. (1976). *The structure of magic: II*. Oxford, England: Science & Behavior.

Griner, D., & Smith, T. B. (2006). Culturally adapted mental health intervention: A meta-analytic review. *Psychotherapy: Theory, Research, 43*(4), 531–548. doi: 10.1037/0033-3204.43.4.531

Grisham, J. R., Brown, T. A., & Campbell, L. A. (2004). *The anxiety disorders interview schedule for DSM-IV (ADIS-IV)*. Hoboken, NJ: Wiley.

Groth-Marnat, G. (2009). *Handbook of psychological assessment* (5th ed.). Hoboken, NJ: Wiley.

Guerney, B. (1977). *Relationship enhancement therapy*. San Francisco: Jossey-Bass.

Guerney, L. (2001). Child-centered play therapy. *International Journal of Play Therapy, 10*(2), 13–31.

Guilamo-Ramos, V., Dittus, P., Jaccard, J., Johansson, M., Bouris, A., & Acosta, N. (2007). Parenting practices among Dominican and Puerto Rican mothers. *Social Work, 52*(1), 17–30.

Gurman, A. S. (2008). *Clinical handbook of couple therapy* (4th ed.). New York, NY: Guilford Press.

Guterman, J. T. (2006). *Mastering the art of solution-focused counseling*. Alexandria, VA: American Counseling Association.

Guyll, M., Madon, S., Prieto, L., & Scherr, K. C. (2010). The potential roles of self-fulfilling prophecies, stigma consciousness, and stereotype threat in linking Latino and ethnicity and educational outcomes. *Journal of Social Issues, 66*(1), 113–130. doi: http://dx.doi.org/10.1111/j.1540-4560.2009.01636.x

Haas, A. P., Eliason, M., Mays, V. M., Mathy, R. M., Cochran, S. D., D'Augelli, A. R., . . . Clayton, P. J. (2011). Suicide and suicide risk in lesbian, gay, bisexual, and transgender populations: Review and recommendations. *Journal of Homosexuality, 58*(1), 10–51. doi: http://dx.doi.org/10.1080/00918369.2011.534038

Hacker, K., Collins, J., Gross-Young, L., Almeida, S., & Burke, N. (2008). Coping with youth suicide and overdose: One community's efforts to investigate, intervene, and prevent suicide contagion. *Crisis: The Journal of Crisis Intervention and Suicide Prevention, 29*(2), 86–95. doi: http://dx.doi.org/10.1027/0227-5910.29.2.86

Hadland, S. E., Marshall, B. D. L., Kerr, T., Qi, J., Montaner, J. S., & Wood, E. (2012). Suicide and history of childhood trauma among street youth. *Journal of Affective Disorders, 136*(3), 377–380. doi: http://dx.doi.org/10.1016/j.jad.2011.11.019

Hadley, S. W., & Strupp, H. H. (1976). Contemporary views of negative effects in psychotherapy: An integrated account. *Archives of General Psychiatry, 33*(11), 1291–1302.

Hagedorn, W. B. (2005). *Counselor self-awareness and self-exploration of religious and spiritual beliefs: Know thyself*. Alexandria, VA: American Counseling Association.

Hahn, W. K., & Marks, L. I. (1996). Client receptiveness to the routine assessment of past suicide attempts. *Professionsl Psychology: Research and Practice, 27*, 592–594.

Haley, J. (1976). *Problem solving therapy*. San Francisco, CA: Jossey-Bass.

Hall, C. C. I. (1997). Cultural malpractice: The growing obsolescence of psychology with the changing U.S. population. *American Psychologist, 52*(6), 642–651. doi: 10.1037/0003-066X.52.6.642

Hall, C. C. I. (2004). Mixed-race women: One more mountain to climb. *Women & Therapy, 27*(1-2), 237–246. doi: 10.1300/J015v27n01_16

Hall, E. T. (1966). *The hidden dimension*. New York, NY: Doubleday.

Hall, R. C. W., Platt, D. E., & Hall, R. C. W. (1999). Suicide risk assessment: A review of risk factors for suicide in 100 patients who made severe suicide attempts: Evaluation of suicide risk in a time of managed care. *Psychosomatics: Journal of Consultation Liaison Psychiatry, 40*(1), 18–27.

Hammer, A. L. (1983). Matching perceptual predicates: Effect on perceived empathy in a counseling analogue. *Journal of Counseling Psychology, 30*(2), 172–179. doi: 10.1037/0022-0167.30.2.172

Hanley, T. (2009). The working alliance in online therapy with young people: Preliminary findings. *British Journal of Guidance & Counselling, 37*(3), 257–269. doi: 10.1080/03069880902956991

Hanley, T., & Reynolds, D. J. (2009). Counselling Psychology and the internet: A review of the quantitative research into online outcomes and alliances within text-based therapy. *Counselling Psychology Review, 24*(2), 4–13.

Hanna, F. J., Hanna, C. A., & Keys, S. G. (1999). Fifty strategies for counseling defiant, aggressive adolescents: Reaching, accepting, and relating. *Journal of Counseling & Development, 77*(4), 395–404.

Hardy, K. M. (2012). Perceptions of African American Christians' attitudes toward religious help-seeking: Results of an exploratory study. *Journal of Religion & Spirituality in Social Work: Social Thought, 31*(3), 209–225. doi: http://dx.doi.org/10.1080/15426432.2012.679838

Hardy, G., Cahill, J., & Barkham, M. (2007). *Active ingredients of the therapeutic relationship that promote client change: A research perspective*. New York, NY: Routledge/Taylor & Francis.

Hare, R. D., Harpur, T. J., Hakstian, A. R., Forth, A. E., Hart, S. D., & Newman, J. P. (1990). The revised psychopathy checklist: Reliability and factor structure. *Psychological Assessment: A Journal of Consulting and Clinical Psychology, 2*(3), 338–341. doi: 10.1037/1040-3590.2.3.338

Harpur, T. J., Hakstian, A. R., & Hare, R. D. (1988). Factor structure of the psychopathy checklist. *Journal of Consulting and Clinical Psychology, 56*(5), 741–747. doi: 10.1037/0022-006X.56.5.741

Harris, G. T., Rice, M. E., & Quinsey, V. L. (1993). Violent recidivism of mentally disordered offenders: The development of a statistical prediction instrument. *Criminal Justice and Behavior, 20*(4), 315–335. doi: 10.1177/0093854893020004001

Hartley, J. (2002). Notetaking in non-academic settings: A review. *Applied Cognitive Psychology, 16*(5), 559–574. doi: 10.1002/acp.814

Hasley, J. P., Ghosh, B., Huggins, J., Bell, M. R., Adler, L. E., & Shroyer, A. L. W. (2008). A review of "suicidal intent" within the existing suicide literature. *Suicide and Life-Threatening Behavior, 38*(5), 576–591. doi: http://dx.doi.org/10.1521/suli.2008.38.5.576

Hatzenbuehler, M. L. (2009). How does sexual minority stigma "get under the skin"? A psychological mediation framework. *Psychological Bulletin; Psychological Bulletin, 135*(5), 707.

Havas, J., de Nooijer, J., Crutzen, R., & Feron, F. (2011). Adolescents' views about an Internet platform for adolescents with mental health problems. *Health Education, 111*(3), 164–176. doi: 10.1108/09654281111123466

Hawton, K. (2007). Restricting access to methods of suicide: Rationale and evaluation of this approach to suicide prevention. *Crisis: The Journal of Crisis Intervention and Suicide Prevention, 28*(Suppl 1), 4–9. doi: 10.1027/0227-5910.28.S1.4

Hayes, J. A., Gelso, C. J., & Hummel, A. M. (2011). Managing countertransference. *Psychotherapy relationships that work: Evidence-based responsiveness* (2nd ed., pp. 239–258). New York, NY: Oxford University Press.

Hayes, S. C. (2002). Buddhism and acceptance and commitment therapy. *Cognitive & Behavioral Practice, 9*(1), 58–66.

Hayes, S. C. (2004). Acceptance and commitment therapy, relational frame theory, and the third wave of behavioral and cognitive therapies. *Behavior Therapy, 35*(4), 639–665. doi: 10.1016/S0005-7894(04)80013-3

Hays, P. A. (2008). *Addressing cultural complexities in practice: Assessment, diagnosis, and therapy* (2nd ed.). Washington, DC: American Psychological Association, Washington, DC. doi: http://dx.doi.org/10.1037/11650-000

Hays, P. A. (2013). *Connecting across cultures: The helper's toolkit.* Thousand Oaks, CA: Sage.

Heck, N. C., Flentje, A., & Cochran, B. N. (2013). Intake interviewing with lesbian, gay, transgender, and bisexual clients: Starting from a place of affirmation. *Journal of Contemporary Psychotherapy, 43*(1), 23–32.

Hecker, L. (Ed.). (2010). *Ethics and professional issues in couple and family therapy.* New York, NY: Routledge.

Hegarty, E. L. H., Catalano, G., & Catalano, M. C. (2007). New onset delusions in the aftermath of the September 11th terrorist attacks. *Journal of Psychiatric Practice, 13*(6), 405–410.

Heine, S. J., Takemoto, T., Moskalenko, S., Lasaleta, J., & Henrich, J. (2008). Mirrors in the head: Cultural variation in objective self-awareness. *Personality and Social Psychology Bulletin, 34*(7), 879–887. doi: 10.1177/0146167208316921

Heinlen, K. T., Welfel, E. R., Richmond, E. N., & O'Donnell, M. S. (2003). The nature, scope, and ethics of psychologists' e-therapy web sites: What consumers find when surfing the web. *Psychotherapy: Theory, Research, Practice, Training, 40*(1-2), 112–124. doi: 10.1037/0033-3204.40.1-2.112

Helm, K. M., & Carlson, J. (Eds.). (2013). *Love, intimacy, and the African American couple.* New York, NY: Routledge.

Henderson, C. E., Dakof, G. A., Greenbaum, P. E., & Liddle, H. A. (2010). Effectiveness of multidimensional family therapy with higher severity substance-abusing adolescents: Report from two randomized controlled trials. *Journal of Consulting and Clinical Psychology, 78*(6), 885–897. doi: 10.1037/a0020620

Henderson, D. A., & Thompson, C. L. (2011). *Counseling children* (8th ed.). Belmont, CA: Brooks/Cole.

Hendrix, H. (2007). *Getting the love you want: A guide for couples.* New York, NY: Holt.

Herek, G. M. (2007). Confronting sexual stigma and prejudice: Theory and practice. *Journal of Social Issues, 63*(4), 905–925.

Herman, J. L. (1992). *Trauma and recovery: The aftermath of violence—from domestic abuse to political terror.* New York, NY: Basic Books.

Hermann, M. A., & Herlihy, B. R. (2006). Legal and ethical implications of refusing to counsel homosexual clients. *Journal of Counseling & Development, 84*(4), 414–418.

Heron, M. (2007). *Deaths: Leading causes for 2004* (No. 56). Hyattsville, MD: National Center for Health Statistics.

Hersen, M., & Thomas, J. C. (2007). *Handbook of clinical interviewing with children.* Thousand Oaks, CA: Sage.

Hersen, M., & Turner, S. M. (2003). *Diagnostic interviewing* (3rd ed.). New York, NY: Kluwer Academic/Plenum Publishers.

Hill, C. E. (2008). Rejoinder: The what, when, and how of immediacy. *Psychotherapy: Theory, Research, Practice, Training, 45*(3), 324–328. doi: http://dx.doi.org/10.1037/a0013308

Hill, C. E. (2009). *Helping skills: Facilitating, exploration, insight, and action* (3rd ed.). Washington, DC: American Psychological Association.

Hill, C. E., Stahl, J., & Roffman, M. (2007). Training novice psychotherapists: Helping skills and beyond. *Psychotherapy: Theory, Research, Practice, Training, 44*(4), 364–370. doi: 10.1037/0033-3204.44.4.364

Hilton, N. Z., Harris, G. T., & Rice, M. E. (2006). Sixty-six years of research on the clinical versus actuarial prediction of violence. *Counseling Psychologist, 34*(3), 400–409. doi: 10.1177/0011000005285877

Hines, P. M., & Boyd-Franklin, N. (2005). *African American families*. New York, NY: Guilford Press.

Hipolito-Delgado, C. P., Cook, J. M., Avrus, E. M., & Bonham, E. J. (2011). Developing counseling students' multicultural competence through the multicultural action project. *Counselor Education and Supervision, 50*(6), 402–421. doi: http://dx.doi.org/10.1002/j.1556-6978.2011.tb01924.x

Hirai, M., & Clum, G. A. (2005). An Internet-based self-change program for traumatic event related fear, distress, and maladaptive coping. *Journal of Traumatic Stress, 18*(6), 631–636. doi: 10.1002/jts.20071

Ho, M. K., Rasheed, J. M., & Rasheed, M. N. (2004). *Family therapy with ethnic minorities* (2nd ed.). Thousand Oaks, CA: Sage.

Hodges, K. (1985). *Manual for the child assessment schedule*. Unpublished manuscript.

Holikatti, P., & Grover, S. (2010). Risk factors for suicide. *The British Journal of Psychiatry, 196*(5), 415. doi: http://dx.doi.org/10.1192/bjp.196.5.415

Hor, K., & Taylor, M. (2010). Suicide and schizophrenia: A systematic review of rates and risk factors. *Journal of Psychopharmacology, 24*(11, Suppl 4), 81–90. doi: http://dx.doi.org/10.1177/1359786810385490

Horesh, N., Levi, Y., & Apter, A. (2012). Medically serious versus non-serious suicide attempts: Relationships of lethality and intent to clinical and interpersonal characteristics. *Journal of Affective Disorders, 136*(3), 286–293. doi: http://dx.doi.org/10.1016/j.jad.2011.11.035

Horvath, A. O., & Bedi, R. P. (2002). The alliance. *Psychotherapy relationships that work: Therapist contributions and responsiveness to patients* (pp. 37–69). New York, NY: Oxford University Press.

Horvath, A. O., Re, A. C. D., Flückiger, C., & Symonds, D. (2011). Alliance in individual psychotherapy. In J. C. Norcross (Ed.), *Psychotherapy relationships that work: Evidence-based responsiveness* (2nd ed., pp. 25–69). New York, NY: Oxford University Press.

Horwitz, A. V. (2002). *Creating mental illness*. Chicago, IL: University of Chicago Press.

Horwitz, A. V., & Wakefield, J. C. (2007). *The loss of sadness: How psychiatry transformed normal sorrow into depressive disorder*. New York, NY: Oxford University Press.

Horwitz, S. H., Santiago, L., Pearson, J., & LaRussa-Trott, M. (2009). Relational tools for working with mild-to-moderate couple violence: Patterns of unresolved conflict and pathways to resolution. *Professional Psychology: Research and Practice, 40*(3), 249–256. doi: http://dx.doi.org/10.1037/a0012992

Hoyt, M. F. E. (Ed.). (1996). *Constructive therapies* (Vol. 2). New York, NY: Guilford Press.

Hufford, B. J., Glueckauf, R. L., & Webb, P. M. (1999). Home-based, interactive videoconferencing for adolescents with epilepsy and their families. *Rehabilitation Psychology, 44*(2), 176–193. doi: 10.1037/0090-5550.44.2.176

Hughes, C. C. (1993). Culture in clinical psychiatry. In A. C. Gaw (Ed.), *Culture, ethnicity, and mental illness* (pp. 3–41). Washington, DC: American Psychiatric Association.

Human, L. J., & Biesanz, J. C. (2011). Through the looking glass clearly: Accuracy and assumed similarity in well-adjusted individuals' first impressions. *Journal of Personality and Social Psychology, 100*(2), 349–364. doi: 10.1037/a0021850

Human, L. J., & Biesanz, J. C. (2012). Accuracy and assumed similarity in first impressions of personality: Differing associations at different levels of analysis. *Journal of Research in Personality, 46*(1), 106–110. doi: 10.1016/j.jrp.2011.10.002

Hung, E. K., Binder, R. L., Fordwood, S. R., Hall, S. E., Cramer, R. J., & McNiel, D. E. (2012). A method for evaluating competency in assessment and management of suicide risk. *Academic Psychiatry, 36*(1), 23–28. doi: http://dx.doi.org/10.1176/appi.ap.10110160

Hungerford, A. (2005). The use of anatomically detailed dolls in forensic investigations: Developmental considerations. *Journal of Forensic Psychology Practice, 5*(1), 75–87. doi: 10.1300/J158v05n01_05

Hurn, R. (2006). Snakes and solutions: An example of using a traditional board game to exemplify the techniques of solution-focused therapy. *Counselling Psychology Review, 21*(2), 12–18.

Iantaffi, A. (2010). A personal reflection on the next 25 years of sex and relationship therapy, research and theory. *Sexual and Relationship Therapy, 25*(4), 369–371. doi: http://dx.doi.org/10.1080/14681994.2010.521315

International Association for Marriage and Family Counseling. (2005). Ethical code for the International Association for Marriage and Family Counseling. *The Family Journal, 14*(1) 92–98.

Iverson, G. L. (2004). Objective assessment of psychomotor retardation in primary care patients with depression. *Journal of Behavioral Medicine, 27*(1), 31–37. doi: 10.1023/B:JOBM.0000013642.43978.f9

Ivey, A., Ivey, M., Zalaquett, C. P., & Quirk, K. (2012). *Essentials of intentional interviewing: Counseling in a multicultural world* (2nd ed.). Pacific Grove, CA: Brooks/Cole.

Ivey, A. E. (1971). *Microcounseling: Innovations in interviewing training*. Oxford, England: Charles C. Thomas.

Ivey, A. E., & Ivey, M. B. (1999). Toward a developmental diagnostic and statistical manual: The vitality of a contextual framework. *Journal of Counseling & Development, 77*(4), 484–490.

Ivey, A. E., Ivey, M. B., & Zalaquett, C. P. (2010). *Intentional interviewing and counseling: Facilitating client development in a multicultural society* (7th ed.). Belmont, CA: Brooks/Cole.

Ivey, A. E., Ivey, M. B., & Zalaquett, C. P. (2011). *Essentials of intentional interviewing: Counseling in a multicultural world* (2nd ed.). Belmont, CA: Brooks/Cole.

Ivey, A. E., Normington, C. J., Miller, C. D., Morrill, W. H., & Haase, R. F. (1968). Microcounseling and attending behavior: An approach to prepracticum counselor training. *Journal of Counseling Psychology, 15*(5, Pt.2), 1–12. doi: http://dx.doi.org/10.1037/h0026129

Izard, C. E. (1977). *Human emotions*. New York, NY: Plenum Press.

Izard, C. E. (1982). *Measuring emotions in infants and children*. New York, NY: Cambridge University Press.

Jacobs, M. (2011). The aims of personal therapy in training. *Psychodynamic Practice: Individuals, Groups and Organisations, 17*(4), 427–439. doi: 10.1080/14753634.2011.613258

Jaghab, K., Skodnek, K. B., & Padder, T. A. (2006). Munchausen's syndrome and other factitious disorders in children—case series and literature review. *Psychiatry, 3*(3), 46–55.

Jain, S. (2011). Treating posttraumatic stress disorder via the Internet does therapeutic alliance matter? *JAMA: Journal of the American Medical Association, 306*(5), 543–544. doi: 10.1001/jama.2011.1097

Jakovljevic, M. (2006). The modern psychopharmacotherapy, mind-body medicine and science of well-being. body, brain, mind & spirit: All for one, and one for all. *Psychiatria Danubina, 18*(3–4), 148–149.

Janoff-Bulman, R. (2004). Posttraumatic growth: Three explanatory models. *Psychological Inquiry, 15*, 30–34.

Jarry, J. L. (2010). Core conflictual relationship theme-guided psychotherapy: Initial effectiveness study of a 16-session manualized approach in a sample of six patients. *Psychology and Psychotherapy: Theory, Research and Practice, 83*(4), 385–394. doi: http://dx.doi.org/10.1348/147608310X486093

Jefferis, J. M., Mosimann, U. P., Taylor, J., & Clarke, M. P. (2011). "Do your eyes play tricks on you?" Asking older people about visual hallucinations in a general eye clinic. *International Psychogeriatrics, 23*(6), 1014–1015. doi: http://dx.doi.org/10.1017/S104161021100072X

Jeltova, I., & Fish, M. C. (2005). Creating school environments responsive to gay, lesbian, bisexual, and transgender families: Traditional and systemic approaches for consultation. *Journal of Educational & Psychological Consultation. Special Issue: Helping Nonmainstream Families Achieve Equity within the Context of School-Based Consulting, 16*(1–2), 17–33. doi: 10.1207/s1532768xjepc161&2_2

Jobes, D. A. (2006). *Managing suicidal risk: A collaborative approach.* New York, NY: Guilford Press.

Jobes, D. A., Moore, M. M., & O'Connor, S. S. (2007). Working with suicidal clients using the collaborative assessment and management of suicidality (CAMS). *Journal of Mental Health Counseling, 29*(4), 283–300.

Jobes, D. A., Nelson, K. N., Peterson, E. M., Pentiuc, D., Downing, V., Francini, K., et al. (2004). Describing suicidality: An investigation of qualitative SSF responses. *Suicide and Life-Threatening Behavior, 34*(2), 99–112.

Jobes, D. A., & O'Connor, S. S. (2009). The duty to protect suicidal clients: Ethical, legal, and professional considerations. In J. L. Werth, Jr., E. R. Welfel, & G. A. H. Benjamin (Eds.), *The duty to protect: Ethical, legal, and professional considerations for mental health professionals* (pp. 163–180). Washington, DC: American Psychological Association. doi: http://dx.doi.org/10.1037/11866-011

Jobes, D. A., Rudd, M. D., Overholser, J. C., & Joiner, T. E. (2008). Ethical and competent care of suicidal patients: Contemporary challenges, New developments, and considerations for clinical practice. *Professional Psychology: Research and Practice, 39*(4), 405–413. doi: http://dx.doi.org/10.1037/a0012896

Jobes, D. A., Wong, S. A., Conrad, A. K., Drozd, J. F., & Neal-Walden, T. (2005). The collaborative assessment and management of suicidality versus treatment as usual: A retrospective study with suicidal outpatients. *Suicide and Life-Threatening Behavior, 35*(5), 483–497.

Johnson, R. (2013). *Spirituality in counseling and psychotherapy: An integrative approach that empowers clients.* Hoboken, NJ: Wiley.

Johnson, S. (2008). *Hold me tight: Seven conversations for a lifetime of love.* New York, NY: Little, Brown.

Johnson, S. S., Paiva, A. L., Cummins, C. O., Johnson, J. L., Dyment, S. J., Wright, J. A., . . . Sherman, K. (2008). Transtheoretical model-based multiple behavior intervention for weight management: Effectiveness on a population basis. *Preventive Medicine: An International Journal Devoted to Practice and Theory, 46*(3), 238–246. doi: 10.1016/j.ypmed.2007.09.010

Johnson, S., & Bradley, B. (2009). *Emotionally focused couple therapy: Creating loving relationships* London, England: Wiley-Blackwell. doi: 10.1002/9781444310238.ch27

Joiner, T. (2005). *Why people die by suicide.* Cambridge, MA: Harvard University Press.

Joiner, T. E., & Silva, C. (2012). Why people die by suicide: Further development and tests of the interpersonal-psychological theory of suicidal behavior. In P. R. Shaver & M. Mikulincer (Eds.), *Meaning, mortality, and choice: The social psychology of existential concerns* (pp. 325–336). Washington, DC: American Psychological Association, Washington, DC. doi: http://dx.doi.org/10.1037/13748-018

Jones, E. (1955). *The life and work of Sigmund Freud* (Vol II). New York, NY: Basic Books.

Jones, K. D. (2010). The unstructured clinical interview. *Journal of Counseling & Development, 88*(2), 220–226. doi: 10.1002/j.1556-6678.2010.tb00013.x

Jones, K. E., Meneses da Silva, A. M., & Soloski, K. L. (2011). Sexological systems theory: An ecological model and assessment approach for sex therapy. *Sexual and Relationship Therapy, 26*(2), 127–144. doi: http://dx.doi.org/10.1080/14681994.2011.574688

Jongsma, A. E., Peterson, L. M., & Bruce, T. J. (2006). *The complete adult psychotherapy treatment planner* (4th ed.). Hoboken, NJ: Wiley.

Jordan, J. V. (2010). *Relational–cultural therapy*. Washington, DC: American Psychological Association.

Jost, J. T., & Kay, A. C. (2005). Exposure to benevolent sexism and complementary gender stereotypes: Consequences for specific and diffuse forms of system justification. *Journal of Personality and Social Psychology, 88*(3), 498–509. doi: 10.1037/0022-3514.88 .3.498

Juhnke, G. A., Granello, D. H., & Granello, P. F. (2011). *Suicide, self-injury, and violence in the schools: Assessment, prevention, and intervention strategies*. Hoboken, NJ: Wiley.

Kabat-Zinn, J. (1995). *Wherever you go, there you are: Mindfulness meditation in everyday life*. New York, NY: Hyperion.

Kabat-Zinn, J. (2005). *Full catastrophe living: Using the wisdom of your body and mind to face stress, pain, and illness (15th anniversary ed.)*. New York, NY: Delta Trade Paperback/ Bantam Dell.

Kallivayalil, D. (2007). Feminist therapy: Its use and implications for south Asian immigrant survivors of domestic violence. *Women & Therapy, 30*(3–4), 109–127.

Kamens, S. R. (2011). On the proposed sexual and gender identity diagnoses for DSM-5: History and controversies. *The Humanistic Psychologist, 39*(1), 37–59. doi: 10.1080/ 08873267.2011.539935

Kanjee, R., Watter, S., Sévigny, A., & Humphreys, K. (2010). A case of foreign accent syndrome: Acoustic analyses and an empirical test of accent perception. *Journal of Neurolinguistics, 23*(6), 580–598. doi: http://dx.doi.org/10.1016/j.jneuroling.2010 .05.003

Katz, E. C., Brown, B. S., Schwartz, R. P., O'Grady, K. E., King, S. D., & Gandhi, D. (2011). Transitioning opioid-dependent patients from detoxification to long-term treatment: Efficacy of intensive role induction. *Drug and Alcohol Dependence, 117*(1), 24–30. doi: http://dx.doi.org/10.1016/j.drugalcdep.2010.12.024

Kawase, E., Karasawa, K., Shimotsu, S., Imasato, S., Ito, K., Matsuki, H., . . . Horikawa, N. (2006). Evaluation of a one-question interview for depression in a radiation oncology department in Japan. *General Hospital Psychiatry, 28*(4), 321–322. doi: 10.1016/ j.genhosppsych.2006.02.003

Kazdin, A. E. (2008). *The Kazdin method for parenting the defiant child: With no pills, no therapy, no contest of wills*. Boston, MA: Houghton Mifflin Company.

Keats, D. M. (2000). *Interviewing: A practical guide for students and professionals*. Buckingham, England: Open University Press.

Kelly, G. A. (1955). *The psychology of personal constructs*. New York, NY: Norton.

Kendall, P. C., & Bemis, K. M. (1983). Thought and action in psychotherapy: The cognitive-behavioral approaches. In M. Hersen, A. E. Kazdin & A. S. Bellack (Eds.), *The clinical psychology handbook* (pp. 565–592). New York, NY: Pergamon Press.

Khanna, A., McDowell, T., Perumbilly, S., & Titus, G. (2009). Working with Asian Indian American families: A Delphi study. *Journal of Systemic Therapies, 28*(1), 52–71. doi: http://dx.doi.org/10.1521/jsyt.2009.28.1.52

Kielbasa, A. M., Pomerantz, A. M., Krohn, E. J., & Sullivan, B. F. (2004). How does clients' method of payment influence psychologists' diagnostic decisions? *Ethics & Behavior.Special Issue: Ethics and Behavior, 14*(2), 187–195. doi: 10.1207/s15327019eb1402_6

Kim, J. S., Smock, S., Trepper, T. S., McCollum, E. E., & Franklin, C. (2010). Is solution-focused brief therapy evidence-based? *Families in Society, 91*(3), 300–306.

King, R., Bambling, M., Reid, W., & Thomas, I. (2006). Telephone and online counselling for young people: A naturalistic comparison of session outcome, session impact and therapeutic alliance. *Counselling & Psychotherapy Research, 6*(3), 175–181. doi: 10.1080/ 14733140600874084

Kivlighan, D. M., Jr. (2002). Transference, interpretation, and insight: A research-practice model. In G. S. Tryon (Ed.), *Counseling based on process research: Applying what we know.* (pp. 166–196). Boston, MA: Allyn & Bacon.

Kleespies, P. M., & Richmond, J. S. (2009). Evaluating behavioral emergencies: The clinical interview. In P. M. Kleespies (Ed.), *Behavioral emergencies: An evidence-based resource for evaluating and managing risk of suicide, violence, and victimization* (pp. 33–55). Washington, DC: American Psychological Association. doi: 10.1037/11865-002

Knaevelsrud, C., & Maercker, A. (2006). Does the quality of the working alliance predict treatment outcome in online psychotherapy for traumatized patients? *Journal of Medical Internet Research, 8*(4) doi: 10.2196/jmir.8.4.e31

Knaevelsrud, C., & Maercker, A. (2007). Internet-based treatment for PTSD reduces distress and facilitates the development of a strong therapeutic alliance: A randomized controlled clinical trial. *BMC Psychiatry, 7* doi: 10.1186/1471-244X-7-13

Knapp, M. L., Hall, J. A., & Horgan, T. G. (2013). *Non-verbal communication in human interaction* (8th ed.). Boston, MA: Wadsworth.

Knesper, D. J. (2007). My favorite tips for engaging the difficult patient on consultation-liaison psychiatry services. *Psychiatric Clinics of North America, 30*(2), 245–252. doi: 10.1016/j.psc.2007.01.009

Knight, J. R., Harris, S. K., Sherritt, L., Van Hook, S., Lawrence, N., Brooks, T., . . . Kulig, J. (2007). Adolescents' preference for substance abuse screening in primary care practice. *Substance Abuse, 28*(4), 107–117. doi: http://dx.doi.org/10.1300/J465v28n04_03

Kohut, H. H. (1984). *How does analysis cure?* Chicago: University of Chicago Press.

Kolden, G. G., Klein, M. H., Wang, C., & Austin, S. B. (2011). Congruence/genuineness. *Psychotherapy relationships that work: Evidence-based responsiveness* (2nd ed.) (pp. 187–202). New York, NY: Oxford University Press.

Korchin, S. J. (1976). *Modern clinical psychology: Principles of intervention in the clinic and community*. New York, NY: Basic Books.

Kort, J. (2008). *Gay affirmative therapy for the straight clinician: The essential guide*. New York, NY: Norton.

Kosciulek, J. F. (2010). Evidence-based rehabilitation counseling practice: A pedagogical imperative. *Rehabilitation Education, 24*(3–4), 205–212.

Kotbi, N., & Mahgoub, N. (2009). Somatic delusions and treatment challenges. *Psychiatric Annals, 39*(6), 320–320, 324. doi: http://dx.doi.org/10.3928/00485713-20090529-01

Kottler, J. A. (2010). *On being a therapist* (4th ed., rev. and updated). San Francisco, CA: Jossey-Bass.

Kottman, T. (2011). *Play therapy: Basics and beyond* (2nd ed.). Alexandria, VA: American Counseling Association, Alexandria, VA.

Kramer, J. R., Chan, G., Kuperman, S., Bucholz, K. K., Edenberg, H. J., Schuckit, M. A., . . . Bierut, L. J. (2009). A comparison of diagnoses obtained from in-person and telephone interviewsing the semi-structured assessment for the genetics of alcoholism (SSAGA). *Journal of Studies on Alcohol and Drugs, 70*(4), 623–627.

Kroes, M. C. W., Whalley, M. G., Rugg, M. D., & Brewin, C. R. (2011). Association between flashbacks and structural brain abnormalities in posttraumatic stress disorder. *European Psychiatry, 26*(8), 525–531. doi: http://dx.doi.org/10.1016/j.eurpsy.2011.03.002

Kuba, T., Yakushi, T., Fukuhara, H., Nakamoto, Y., Singeo, S. T., Tanaka, O., & Kondo, T. (2011). Suicide-related events among child and adolescent patients during short-term antidepressant therapy. *Psychiatry and Clinical Neurosciences, 65*(3), 239–245. doi: http://dx.doi.org/10.1111/j.1440-1819.2011.02204.x

Kurt, P., Yener, G., & Oguz, M. (2011). Impaired digit span can predict further cognitive decline in older people with subjective memory complaint: A preliminary result. *Aging & Mental Health, 15*(3), 364–369. doi: http://dx.doi.org/10.1080/13607863.2010.536133

Kutchins, H., & Kirk, S. A. (1997). *Making us crazy*. New York, NY: Free Press.

Laforge, R. G., Borsari, B., & Baer, J. S. (2005). The utility of collateral informant assessment in college alcohol research: Results from a longitudinal prevention trial. *Journal of Studies on Alcohol, 66*(4), 479–487.

Lago, C. (1996). Computer therapeutics. *The Journal of the British Association for Counselling*, 7(4), 287–289.

Lambert, M. (2007). Presidential address: What we have learned from a decade of research aimed at improving psychotherapy outcome in routine care. *Psychotherapy Research*, 17(1), 1–14. doi: 10.1080/10503300601032506

Lambert, M. J. (2010). *Prevention of treatment failure: The use of measuring, monitoring, and feedback in clinical practice*. Washington, DC: American Psychological Association, Washington, DC. doi: http://dx.doi.org/10.1037/12141-000

Lambert, M. J., & Shimokawa, K. (2011). Collecting client feedback. In J.C. Norcross, *Psychotherapy relationships that work: Evidence-based responsiveness* (2nd ed.) (pp. 203–223). New York, NY: Oxford University Press.

Lambert, M. J., & Shimokawa, K. (2011). Collecting client feedback. *Psychotherapy*, 48(1), 72–79. doi: 10.1037/a0022238

Lampe, L. A. (2011). Internet-based therapy: Too good to be true? *Australian and New Zealand Journal of Psychiatry*, 45(4), 342–343. doi: 10.3109/00048674.2011.560138

Land, L. N., Rochlen, A. B., & Vaughn, B. K. (2011). Correlates of adult attachment avoidance: Men's avoidance of intimacy in romantic relationships. *Psychology of Men & Masculinity*, 12(1), 64–76. doi: http://dx.doi.org/10.1037/a0019928

Lange, A., Rietdijk, D., Hudcovicova, M., van de Ven, J., Schrieken, B., & Emmelkamp, P. M. G. (2003). Interapy: A controlled randomized trial of the standarized treatment of posttraumatic stress through the Internet. *Journal of Consulting and Clinical Psychology*, 71(5), 901–909. doi: 10.1037/0022-006X.71.5.901

Lankton, S. R., Lankton, C. H., & Matthews, W. J. (1991). *Ericksonian family therapy*. Philadelphia, PA: Brunner/Mazel.

Lapidot-Lefler, N., & Barak, A. (2012). Effects of anonymity, invisibility, and lack of eye-contact on toxic online disinhibition. *Computers in Human Behavior*, 28(2), 434–443. doi: 10.1016/j.chb.2011.10.014

Large, M., Sharma, S., Cannon, E., Ryan, C., & Nielssen, O. (2011). Risk factors for suicide within a year of discharge from psychiatric hospital: A systematic meta-analysis. *Australian and New Zealand Journal of Psychiatry*, 45(8), 619–628. doi: http://dx.doi.org/10.3109/00048674.2011.590465

Latham, G. P., & Locke, E. A. (2006). Enhancing the benefits and overcoming the pitfalls of goal setting. *Organizational Dynamics*, 35(4), 332–340. doi: 10.1016/j.orgdyn.2006.08.008

Latham, G. P., & Locke, E. A. (2007). New developments in and directions for goal-setting research. *European Psychologist*, 12(4), 290–300. doi: 10.1027/1016-9040.12.4.290

Lau, M. A., Segal, Z. V., & Williams, J. M. G. (2004). Teasdale's differential activation hypothesis: Implications for mechanisms of depressive relapse and suicidal behaviour. *Behaviour Research and Therapy. Special Issue: Festschrift Special Issue for John Teasdale*, 42(9), 1001–1017. doi: 10.1016/j.brat.2004.03.003

Lazarus, A. A. (1976). *Multimodal behavior therapy*. New York, NY: Springer.

Lazarus, A. A. (1994). How certain boundaries and ethics diminish therapeutic effectiveness. *Ethics & Behavior*, 4(3), 255–261.

Lazarus, A. A. (1996). Some reflections after 40 years of trying to be an effective psychotherapist. *Psychotherapy: Theory, Research, Practice, Training*, 33(1), 142–145.

Lazarus, A. A. (2006). *Brief but comprehensive psychotherapy: The multimodal way*. New York, NY: Springer.

Leahy, R. L. (Ed.). (2004). *Contemporary cognitive therapy: Theory, research, and practice* New York, NY: Guilford Press.

Ledley, D. R., Marx, B. P., & Heimberg, R. G. (2010). *Making cognitive-behavioral therapy work: Clinical process for new practitioners* (2nd ed.). New York, NY: Guilford Press.

Leenaars, A. (1999). *Lives and deaths: Selections from the works of Edwin S. Shneidman* Routledge.

Leenaars, A. A. (2010). Edwin S. Shneidman on suicide. *Suicidology Online*, 1, 5–18.

Leon, A. C., Solomon, D. A., Li, C., Fiedorowicz, J. G., Coryell, W. H., Endicott, J., & Keller, M. B. (2011). Antidepressants and risks of suicide and suicide attempts a 27-year observational study. *Journal of Clinical Psychiatry*, *72*(5), 580–586. doi: http://dx.doi.org/10.4088/JCP.10m06552

Lester, D., McSwain, S., & Gunn, J. F. (2011). A test of the validity of the IS PATH WARM warning signs for suicide. *Psychological Reports*, *108*(2), 402–404. doi: http://dx.doi.org/10.2466/09.12.13.PR0.108.2.402-404

Leve, R. M. (1995). *Child and adolescent psychotherapy: Process and integration*. Needham Heights, MA: Allyn & Bacon.

Levenson, H. (2010). *Brief dynamic psychotherapy*. Washington, DC: American Psychological Association.

Liddle, H. A., Dakof, G. A., Turner, R. M., Henderson, C. E., & Greenbaum, P. E. (2008). Treating adolescent drug abuse: A randomized trial comparing multidimensional family therapy and cognitive behavior therapy. *Addiction*, *103*(10), 1660–1670. doi: 10.1111/j.1360-0443.2008.02274.x

Liddle, H. A., Rowe, C. L., Dakof, G. A., Henderson, C. E., & Greenbaum, P. E. (2009). Multidimensional family therapy for young adolescent substance abuse: Twelve-month outcomes of a randomized controlled trial. *Journal of Consulting and Clinical Psychology*, *77*(1), 12–25. doi: 10.1037/a0014160

Lin, H., Wu, C., & Lee, H. (2009). Risk factors for suicide following hospital discharge among cancer patients. *Psycho-Oncology*, *18*(10), 1038–1044. doi: http://dx.doi.org/10.1002/pon.1483

Linehan, M. (1993). *Cognitive behavioral therapy of borderline personality disorder*. New York, NY: Guilford Press.

Linehan, M. M. (2000). Commentary on innovations in dialectal behavior therapy. *Cognitive & Behavioral Practice*, *7*(4), 478–481.

Links, P., Nisenbaum, R., Ambreen, M., Balderson, K., Bergmans, Y., Eynan, R., . . . Cutcliffe, J. (2012). Prospective study of risk factors for increased suicide ideation and behavior following recent discharge. *General Hospital Psychiatry*, *34*(1), 88–97. doi: http://dx.doi.org/10.1016/j.genhosppsych.2011.08.016

Linton, S. J., Boersma, K., Jansson, M., Overmeer, T., Lindblom, K., & Vlaeyen, J. W. S. (2008). A randomized controlled trial of exposure in vivo for patients with spinal pain reporting fear of work-related activities. *European Journal of Pain*, *12*(6), 722–730. doi: 10.1016/j.ejpain.2007.11.001

Litman, R. E. (1995). Suicide prevention in a treatment setting. *Suicide and Life-Threatening Behavior.Special Issue: Suicide Prevention: Toward the Year 2000*, *25*(1), 134–142.

Lobbestael, J., Leurgans, M., & Arntz, A. (2011). Inter-rater reliability of the structured clinical interview for DSM IV axis I disorders (SCID I) and axis II disorders (SCID II). *Clinical Psychology & Psychotherapy*, *18*(1), 75–79. doi: 10.1002/cpp.693

Loeber, R., Pardini, D., Homish, D. L., Wei, E. H., Crawford, A. M., Farrington, D. P., . . . Rosenfeld, R. (2005). The prediction of violence and homicide in young men. *Journal of Consulting and Clinical Psychology*, *73*(6), 1074–1088. doi: 10.1037/0022-006X.73.6.1074

Losada, A., Shurgot, G. R., Knight, B. G., Márquez, M., Montorio, I., Izal, M., & Ruiz, M. A. (2006). Cross-cultural study comparing the association of familism with burden and depressive symptoms in two samples of Hispanic dementia caregivers. *Aging & Mental Health*, *10*(1), 69–76. doi: 10.1080/13607860500307647

Lovell, K., Cox, D., Haddock, G., Jones, C., Raines, D., Garvey, R., . . . Hadley, S. (2006). Telephone administered cognitive behaviour therapy for treatment of obsessive compulsive disorder: Randomised controlled non-inferiority trial. *BMJ: British Medical Journal*, *333*(7574), 883–883. doi: 10.1136/bmj.38940.355602.80

Luborsky, L. (1984). *Principles of psychoanalytic psychotherapy: A manual for supportive-expressive treatment*. New York, NY: Basic Books.

Luborsky, L., & Barrett, M. S. (2006). The history and empirical status of key psychoanalytic concepts. *Annual Review of Clinical Psychology, 2,* 1–19. doi: 10.1146/annurev.clinpsy .2.022305.095328

Luborsky, L., & Crits-Christoph, P. (1998). *Understanding transference: The core conflictual relationship theme method* (2nd ed.). Washington, DC: American Psychological Association. doi: 10.1037/10250-000

Luborsky, L., Singer, B., & Luborsky, L. (1975). Comparative studies of psychotherapies: Is it true that "everyone has won and all must have prizes"? *Archives of General Psychiatry, 32,* 995–1008.

Luquet, W. (2006). *Short-term couples therapy: The imago model in action* (2nd ed.). New York, NY: Brunner/Mazel.

Lushington, K., & Luscri, G. (2001). Are counseling students stressed? A cross-cultural comparison of burnout in Australian, Singaporean and Hong Kong counseling students. *Asian Journal of Counselling, 8*(2), 209–232.

MacKay, S., Henderson, J., Del Bove, G., Marton, P., Warling, D., & Root, C. (2006). Fire interest and antisociality as risk factors in the severity and persistence of juvenile firesetting. *Journal of the American Academy of Child & Adolescent Psychiatry, 45*(9), 1077–1084.

Mackintosh, N. J. (2011). *History of theories and measurement of intelligence.* New York, NY: Cambridge University Press. doi: http://dx.doi.org/10.1017/CBO9780511977244 .002

Mackrill, T. (2010). Goal consensus and collaboration in psychotherapy: An existential rationale. *Journal of Humanistic Psychology, 50*(1), 96–107. doi: 10.1177/0022167 809341997

Madigan, S. (2011). *Narrative therapy.* Washington, DC: American Psychological Association.

Mahalik, J. R. (2002). Understanding client resistance in therapy: Implications from research on the counseling process. In G. S. Tryon (Ed.), *Counseling based on process research: Applying what we know* (pp. 66–80). Boston, MA: Allyn & Bacon.

Maj, M. (2008). Delusions in major depressive disorder: Recommendations for the DSM-V. *Psychopathology, 41*(1), 1–3. doi: 10.1159/000109948

Malchiodi, C. A. (Ed.). (2005). *Expressive therapies* New York, NY: Guilford Press.

Malgady, R. G. (2010). Treating Hispanic children and adolescents using narrative therapy. In J. R. Weisz, & A. E. Kazdin (Eds.), *Evidence-based psychotherapies for children and adolescents* (2nd ed., pp. 391–400). New York, NY: Guilford Press.

Mallen, M. J., Vogel, D. L., Rochlen, A. B., & Day, S. X. (2005). Online counseling: Reviewing the literature from a counseling psychology framework. *The Counseling Psychologist, 33*(6), 819–871. doi: 10.1177/0011000005278624

Manthei, R. J. (2007). Research digest. *Counselling Psychology Quarterly, 20*(1), 115–118. doi: 10.1080/09515070701239735

Marangell, L. B., Bauer, M. S., Dennehy, E. B., Wisniewski, S. R., Allen, M. H., & Miklowitz, D. J. (2006). Prospective predictors of suicide and suicide attempts in 1,556 patients with bipolar disorders followed for up to 2 years. *Bipolar Disorders, 8*(5, pt 2), 566–575.

Marin, G., & Marin, B. V. (1991). *Research with Hispanic populations.* Newbury Park, CA: Sage.

Marini, I. (2007). *Cross-cultural counseling issues of males who sustain a disability.* New York, NY: Springer.

Martin, D. J., Garske, J. P., & Davis, M. K. (2000). Relation of the therapeutic alliance with outcome and other variables: A meta-analytic review. *Journal of Consulting and Clinical Psychology, 68*(3), 438–450. doi: http://dx.doi.org/10.1037/0022-006X.68.3.438

Martin-Khan, M., Wootton, R., & Gray, L. (2010). A systematic review of the reliability of screening for cognitive impairment in older adults by use of standardised assessment tools administered via the telephone. *Journal of Telemedicine and Telecare, 16*(8), 422–428. doi: 10.1258/jtt.2010.100209

Martiny, C., de Oliveira e Silva, Adriana Cardoso, Neto, J. P. S., & Nardi, A. E. (2011). Factors associated with risk of suicide in patients with hemodialysis. *Comprehensive Psychiatry*, *52*(5), 465–468. doi: http://dx.doi.org/10.1016/j.comppsych.2010.10.009

Maslow, A. (1968). *Toward a psychology of being* (2nd ed.). New York, NY: Harper & Row.

Maslow, A. (1970). *Motivation and personality* (2nd ed.). New York, NY: Harper & Row.

Matsumoto, D. (2007). Culture, context, and behavior. *Journal of Personality*, *75*(6), 1285–1320. doi: 10.1111/j.1467-6494.2007.00476.x

Matsumoto, D., & Yoo, S. H. (2005). *Culture and applied nonverbal communication*. Mahwah, NJ: Erlbaum.

Mattis, J. S., & Grayman-Simpson, N. A. (2013). *Faith and the sacred in African American life*. Washington, DC: American Psychological Association. doi: http://dx.doi.org/10.1037/14045-030

Maurer, R. E., & Tindall, J. H. (1983). Effect of postural congruence on client's perception of counselor empathy. *Journal of Counseling Psychology*, *30*(2), 158–163. doi: 10.1037/0022-0167.30.2.158

Maust, D. T., Mavandadi, S., Eakin, A., Streim, J. E., DiFillipo, S., Snedden, T., & Oslin, D. W. (2011). Telephone-based behavioral health assessment for older adults starting a New psychiatric medication. *The American Journal of Geriatric Psychiatry*, *19*(10), 851–858. doi: 10.1097/JGP.0b013e318202c1dc

Mayotte-Blum, J., Slavin-Mulford, J., Lehmann, M., Pesale, F., Becker-Matero, N., & Hilsenroth, M. (2012). Therapeutic immediacy across long-term psychodynamic psychotherapy: An evidence-based case study. *Journal of Counseling Psychology*, *59*(1), 27–40. doi: http://dx.doi.org/10.1037/a0026087

McAuliffe, G. J., & Milliken, T. F. (2009). Promoting cultural relativism in counselors through the cultural de-centering model. *International Journal for the Advancement of Counselling*, *31*(2), 118–129. doi: 10.1007/s10447-009-9072-6

McCall, W. V. (2011). Insomnia is a risk factor for suicide—What are the next steps? *Sleep: Journal of Sleep and Sleep Disorders Research*, *34*(9), 1149–1150.

McCann, I. L., & Pearlman, L. A. (1990). Vicarious traumatization: A framework for understanding the psychological effects of working with victims. *Journal of Traumatic Stress*, *3*(1), 131–149. doi: 10.1007/BF00975140

McCart, M. R., Priester, P. E., Davies, W. H., & Azen, R. (2006). Differential effectiveness of behavioral parent-training and cognitive-behavioral therapy for antisocial youth: A meta-analysis. *Journal of Abnormal Child Psychology*, *34*(4), 527–543. doi: http://dx.doi.org/10.1007/s10802-006-9031-1

McCormack, J. R. (2002). There is no such thing as resistant client. *Marriage & Family: A Christian Journal*, *5*(1), 39–45.

McCoyd, J. L. M., & Kerson, T. S. (2006). Conducting intensive interviews using email: A serendipitous comparative opportunity. *Qualitative Social Work: Research and Practice*, *5*(3), 389–406. doi: 10.1177/1473325006067367

McGlothlin, J. M. (2008). *Developing clinical skills in suicide assessment, prevention, and treatment*. Alexandria, VA: American Counseling Association.

McGoldrick, M., Gerson, R., & Petry, S. (2008). *Gengrams: Assessment and intervention* (3rd ed.). New York, NY: Norton.

McGoldrick, M., Giordano, J., & Garcia-Preto, N. (2005). *Ethncity and family therapy* (3rd ed.). New York, NY: Guilford Press.

McIntosh, P. (1998). White privilege: Unpacking the invisible knapsack. In M. McGoldrick (Ed.), *Re-visioning family therapy: Race, gender and culture in clinical practice* (pp. 147–152). New York, NY: Guilford Press.

McKelley, R. A. (2007). Men's resistance to seeking help: Using individual psychology to understand counseling-reluctant men. *Journal of Individual Psychology*, *63*(1), 48–58.

McKenzie, I., & Wurr, C. (2001). Early suicide following discharge from a psychiatric hospital. *Suicide and Life-Threatening Behavior*, *31*(3), 358–363.

McNiel, D. E., Fordwood, S. R., Weaver, C. M., Chamberlain, J. R., Hall, S. E., & Binder, R. L. (2008). Effects of training on suicide risk assessment. *Psychiatric Services*, *59*(12), 1462–1465. doi: http://dx.doi.org/10.1176/appi.ps.59.12.1462

Meador, B., & Rogers, C. R. (1984). Person-centered therapy. In R. Corsini (Ed.), *Current psychotherapy* (pp. 142–195). Itasca, IL: Peacock.

Meichenbaum, D. (2006). *Trauma and suicide: A constructive narrative perspective*. Washington, DC: American Psychological Association.

Meier, S. T., & Davis, S. R. (2011). *The elements of counseling* (7th ed.). Belmont, CA: Thomson Brooks/Cole Publishing Co.

Meissner, W. W. (2007). Therapeutic alliance: Theme and variations. *Psychoanalytic Psychology, 24*(2), 231–254. doi: 10.1037/0736-9735.24.2.231

Mellin, E. A., & Pertuit, T. L. (2009). Research priorities for mental health counseling with youth: Implications for counselor preparation, professional development, and research. *Counselor Education and Supervision, 49*(2), 137–155. doi: http://dx.doi.org/10.1002/j.1556-6978.2009.tb00093.x

Merton, T. (1974). *A Thomas Merton reader*. New York, NY: Doubleday.

Messer, S. B., & McWilliams, N. (2007). *Insight in psychodynamic therapy: Theory and assessment*. Washington, DC: American Psychological Association. doi: 10.1037/11532-001

Metcalf, K., Langdon, R., & Coltheart, M. (2007). Models of confabulation: A critical review and a New framework. *Cognitive Neuropsychology, 24*(1), 23–47.

Meuret, A. E., White, K. S., Ritz, T., Roth, W. T., Hofmann, S. G., & Brown, T. A. (2006). Panic attack symptom dimensions and their relationship to illness characteristics in panic disorder. *Journal of Psychiatric Research, 40*(6), 520–527. doi: 10.1016/j.jpsychires.2005.09.006

Miklowitz, D. J., Goodwin, G. M., Bauer, M. S., & Geddes, J. R. (2008). Common and specific elements of psychosocial treatments for bipolar disorder: A survey of clinicians participating in randomized trials. *Journal of Psychiatric Practice, 14*(2), 77–85. doi: http://dx.doi.org/10.1097/01.pra.0000314314.94791.c9

Miller, G. (2012). *Fundamentals of crisis counseling*. Hoboken, NJ: Wiley.

Miller, J. B. (1986). *Toward a New psychology of women* (2nd ed.). Boston, MA: Beacon Press.

Miller, M. (1985). *Information center: Training workshop manual*. San Diego, CA: The Information Center.

Miller, S. D., & Donahey, K. M. (2012). Feedback-informed treatment (FIT): Improving the outcome of sex therapy one person at a time. *New directions in sex therapy: Innovations and alternatives* (2nd ed., pp. 195–211). New York, NY: Routledge/Taylor & Francis.

Miller, W. R. (1978). Behavioral treatment of problem drinkers: A comparative outcome study of three controlled drinking therapies. *Journal of Consulting & Clinical Psychology, 46*(1), 74–86.

Miller, W. R. (1983). Motivational interviewing with problem drinkers. *Behavioural Psychotherapy, 11*(2), 147–172.

Miller, W. R., & Rollnick, S. (1991). *Motivational interviewing: Preparing people to change addictive behavior*. New York, NY: Guilford Press.

Miller, W. R., & Rollnick, S. (2002). *Motivational interviewing: Preparing people for change* (2nd ed.). New York, NY: Guilford Press.

Miller, W. R., & Rollnick, S. (2013). *Motivational interviewing: Preparing people for change* (3rd ed.). New York, NY: Guilford Press.

Minuchin, S., Rosman, B. L., & Baker, L. (1978). *Psychosomatic families: Anorexia nervosa in context*. Oxford: Harvard University Press.

Minuchin, S., & Fishman, H. C. (1981). *Family therapy techniques*. Cambridge, MA: Harvard University Press.

Miret, M., Nuevo, R., & Ayuso-Mateos, J. L. (2009). Documentation of suicide risk assessment in clinical records. *Psychiatric Services, 60*(7), 994. doi: http://dx.doi.org/10.1176/appi.ps.60.7.994

Mischel, W. (1968). *Personality and assessment*. New York, NY: Wiley.

Mitchell, A., Chen, C., & Medlin, B. D. (2010). Teaching and learning with Skype. In C. Wankel (Ed.), *The 16th Americas conference on information systems* (pp. 36–56). Greenwich, CT: IAP Information Age Publishing.

Mohr, D. C., Hart, S. L., Julian, L., Catledge, C., Honos-Webb, L., Vella, L., & Tasch, E. T. (2005). Telephone-administered psychotherapy for depression. *Archives of General Psychiatry, 62*, 1007–1014.

Mohr, J. J., Gelso, C. J., & Hill, C. E. (2005). Client and counselor trainee attachment as predictors of session evaluation and countertransference behavior in first counseling sessions. *Journal of Counseling Psychology, 52*(3), 298–309.

Molnar, B. E., Berkman, L. F., & Buka, S. L. (2001). Psychopathology, childhood sexual abuse and other childhood adversities: Relative links to subsequent suicidal behaviour in the US. *Psychological Medicine, 31*(6), 965–977. doi: 10.1017/S0033291701004329

Monahan, J. (2013). *Violence risk assessment*. Hoboken, NJ: Wiley.

Moon, C. H. (Ed.). (2010). *Materials and media in art therapy*. New York, NY: Routledge.

Moor, A., & Silvern, L. (2006). Identifying pathways linking child abuse to psychological outcome: The mediating role of perceived parental failure of empathy. *Journal of Emotional Abuse, 6*(4), 91–114. doi: http://dx.doi.org/10.1300/J135v06n04_05

Moraga, A. V., & Rodriguez-Pascual, C. (2007). Acurate diagnosis of delirium in elderly patients. *Current Opinion in Psychiatry, 20*(3), 262–267.

Moreno, C. L. (2007). The relationship between culture, gender, structural factors, abuse, trauma, and HIV/AIDS for latinas. *Qualitative Health Research, 17*(3), 340–352. doi: 10.1177/1049732306297387

Moreno, C., Laje, G., Blanco, C., Jiang, H., Schmidt, A. B., & Olfson, M. (2007). National trends in the outpatient diagnosis and treatment of bipolar disorder in youth. *Archives of General Psychiatry, 64*(9), 1032–1039.

Morrison, J. (2007). *The first interview* (3rd ed.). New York, NY: Guilford Press.

Morrow, D. F., & Messinger, L. (Eds.). (2006). *Sexual orientation & gender expression in social work practice: Working with gay, lesbian, bisexual, & transgender people* New York, NY: Columbia University Press.

Mosak, H. H. (1985). Interrupting a depression: The pushbutton technique. *Individual Psychology, 41*, 210–214.

Mosak, H. H. (1989). Adlerian psychotherapy. In R. J. Corsini & D. Wedding (Eds.), *Current psychotherapies*. (4th ed., pp. 65–116). Itasca, IL: F. E. Peacock.

Mosak, H. H., and Maniacci, M.P. (1999). *A primer of Adlerian psychology: The analytic-behavioral-cognitive psychology of Alfred Adler*. Philadelphia, PA: Taylor & Francis.

Moules, N. J. (2003). Therapy on paper: Therapeutic letters and the tone of relationship. *Journal of Systemic Therapies, 22*(1), 33–49. doi: 10.1521/jsyt.22.1.33.24091

Muhtz, C., Daneshi, J., Braun, M., & Kellner, M. (2010). Carbon-dioxide-induced flashback in a healthy man with a history of near-drowning. *Psychotherapy and Psychosomatics, 80*(1), 55–56. doi: http://dx.doi.org/10.1159/000316798

Mulligan, J., MacCulloch, R., Good, B., & Nicholas, D. B. (2012). Transparency, hope, and empowerment: A model for partnering with parents of a child with autism spectrum disorder at diagnosis and beyond. *Social Work in Mental Health, 10*(4), 311–330. doi: http://dx.doi.org/10.1080/15332985.2012.664487

Murphy, B. C., & Dillon, C. (2011). *Interviewing in action in a multicultural world* (2nd ed.). Belmont, CA: Thomson Brooks/Cole.

Murphy, J. J. (2008). *Solution-focused counseling in middle and high schools*. Alexandria, VA: American Counseling Association.

Murray, K. W., Sommers-Flanagan, J., & Sommers-Flanagan, R. (2012). Family systems theory and therapy. In J. Sommers-Flanagan, & R. Sommers-Flanagan (Eds.), *Counseling and psychotherapy theories in context and practice: Skills, strategies, and techniques* (2nd ed.), (pp. 405–438). Hoboken, NJ: Wiley.

Myer, R. A. (2001). *Assessment for crisis intervention: An assessment triage model*. Belmont, CA: Wadsworth.

Natale, S. M. (1985). Confrontation and the religious beliefs of a client. In E. M. Stern (Ed.), *Psychotherapy and the religiously committed patient* (pp. 107–116). New York, NY: Haworth Press.

Nayak, N., Powers, M. B., & Foa, E. B. (2012). In Beck J. G., Sloan D. M. (Eds.), *Empirically supported psychological treatments: Prolonged exposure*. New York, NY: Oxford University Press.

Neff, K. D., & Harter, S. (2003). Relationship styles of self-focused autonomy, other-focused connectedness, and mutuality across multiple relationship contexts. *Journal of Social and Personal Relationships, 20*(1), 81–99. doi: http://dx.doi.org/10.1177/0265407503020001189

Negy, C. (2004). *Cross-cultural psychotherapy: Toward a critical understanding of diverse clients*. Reno, NV: Bent Tree Press.

Neimeyer, R. A., Fortner, B., & Melby, D. (2001). Personal and professional factors and suicide intervention skills. *Suicide and Life-Threatening Behavior, 31*(1), 71–82. doi: 10.1521/suli.31.1.71.21307

Nemeroff, C. B. (2007). Early life factors in depression. *Investigating the Mind: Mindfulness, Compassion, and the Treatment of Depression*. Paper presented at the Emory University Mind and Life Institute. Atlanta, GA.

Ng, S. M., Li, A. M., Lou, V. W. Q., Tso, I. F., Wan, P. Y. P., & Chan, D. F. Y. (2008). Incorporating family therapy into asthma group intervention: A randomized waitlist-controlled trial. *Family Process. Special Issue on Families and Asthma, 47*(1), 115–130. doi: 10.1111/j.1545-5300.2008.00242.x

Norcross, J. C. (2000). Psychotherapist self-care: Practitioner-tested, research-informed strategies. *Professional Psychology: Research and Practice, 31*(6), 710–713. doi: 10.1037/0735-7028.31.6.710

Norcross, J. C. (Ed.). (2011). Evidence-based therapy relationships. *Psychotherapy relationships that work: Evidence-based responsiveness* (2nd ed.). New York, NY: Oxford University Press.

Norcross, J. C., & Guy, J. D. (2007). *Leaving it at the office: A guide to psychotherapist self-care*. New York, NY: Guilford Press.

Norcross, J. C., & Lambert, M. J. (2011). Psychotherapy relationships that work II. *Psychotherapy, 48*(1), 4–8. doi: 10.1037/a0022180

Norris, S. (2007). The micropolitics of personal national and ethnicity identity. *Discourse & Society, 18*(5), 653–674. doi: 10.1177/0957926507079633

Nosek, B. A., Greenwald, A. G., & Banaji, M. R. (2005). Understanding and using the implicit association test: II. method variables and construct validity. *Personality and Social Psychology Bulletin, 31*(2), 166–180. doi: 10.1177/0146167204271418

Nyklíček, I., Vingerhoets, A., & Denollet, J. (2002). Emotional (non-)expression and health: Data, questions, and challenges. *Psychology & Health, 17*(5), 517–528. doi: http://dx.doi.org/10.1080/08870440290025740

Obama, B. H. (2013). 2013 Inaugural Address. Retrieved from http://www.whitehouse.gov/the-press-office/2013/01/21/inaugural-address-president-barack-obama

O'Brien, R. P. (2012). *Cognitive-behavioral therapy with military couples*. New York, NY: Routledge/Taylor & Francis Group.

O'Connor, M. F. (1992). Psychotherapy with gay and lesbian adolescents. In S. H. Dworkin, & F. J. Gutierrez (Eds.), *Counseling gay men and lesbians: Journey to the end of the rainbow* (pp. 3–22). Alexandria, VA: American Association for Counseling and Development.

Odell, M., & Campbell, C. E. (1998). *The practical practice of marriage and family therapy: Things my training supervisor never told me*. New York, NY: Hawthorne Press.

O'Donohue, W. T., & Cucciare, M. A. (Eds.). (2008). *Termination: A clinician's guide*. New York, NY: Routledge.

O'Donohue, W., Cummings, N. A., & Cummings, J. L. (Eds.). (2006). *Clinical strategies for becoming a master psychotherapist* Amsterdam, Netherlands: Elsevier.

Oetzel, K. B., & Scherer, D. G. (2003). Therapeutic engagement with adolescents in psychotherapy. *Psychotherapy: Theory, Research, Practice, Training, 40*(3), 215–225.

Ogbu, J. U. (1992). Understanding cultural diversity and learning. *Educational Researcher, 21*, 5–14.

Oh, Y., Koeske, G. F., & Sales, E. (2002). Acculturation, stress and depressive symptoms among Korean immigrants in the United States. *Journal of Social Psychology, 142*(4), 511–526.

O'Hanlon, W. H. (1998). Possibility therapy: An inclusive, collaborative, solution-based model of psychotherapy. In M. F. Hoyt (Ed.), *The handbook of constructive therapies* (pp. 137–158). San Francisco, CA: Jossey-Bass.

Olatunji, B. O., Cisler, J. M., & Deacon, B. J. (2010). Efficacy of cognitive behavioral therapy for anxiety disorders: A review of meta-analytic findings. *Psychiatric Clinics of North America, 33*(3), 557–577. doi: 10.1016/j.psc.2010.04.002

O'Malley, A. S., Sheppard, V. B., Schwartz, M., & Mandelblatt, J. (2004). The role of trust in use of preventive services among low-income African-American women. *Preventive Medicine: An International Journal Devoted to Practice and Theory, 38*(6), 777–785. doi: http://dx.doi.org/10.1016/j.ypmed.2004.01.018

Onedera, J. D. (Ed.). (2008). *The role of religion in marriage and family counseling* New York, NY: Routledge/Taylor & Francis.

Orellana, M. F., Reynolds, J., Dorner, L., & Meza, M. (2003). In other words: Translating or "paraphrasing" as a family literacy practice in immigrant households. *Reading Research Quarterly, 38*(1), 12–34. doi: 10.1598/RRQ.38.1.2

Ortiz, S. O., & Ochoa, S. H. (2005). *Advances in cognitive assessment of culturally and linguistically diverse individuals: A nondiscriminatory interpretive approach.* New York, NY: Guilford Press.

Ostrosky-Solís, F., & Lozano, A. (2006). Digit span: Effect of education and culture. *International Journal of Psychology, 41*(5), 333–341. doi: 10.1080/00207590500345724

Othmer, E., & Othmer, S. C. (2002). *The clinical interview using DSM-IV-TR: Vol 1: Fundamentals.* Washington, DC: American Psychiatric Publishing.

Overholser, J. C. (2006). Panacea or placebo: The historical quest for medications to treat depression. *Journal of Contemporary Psychotherapy, 36*(4), 183–190. doi: 10.1007/s10879-006-9023-z

Pabian, Y. L., Welfel, E., & Beebe, R. S. (2009). Psychologists' knowledge of their states' laws pertaining to Tarasoff-type situations. *Professional Psychology: Research and Practice, 40*(1), 8–14. doi: http://dx.doi.org/10.1037/a0014784

Packman, W. L., Marlitt, R. E., Bongar, B., & Pennuto, T. O. (2004). A comprehensive and concise assessment of suicide risk. *Behavioral Sciences & the Law, 22*(5), 667–680. doi: 10.1002/bsl.610

Paniagua, F. A. (1996). Cross-cultural guidelines in family therapy practice. *The Family Journal, 4*(2), 127–138. doi: 10.1177/1066480796042005

Paniagua, F. A. (1998). *Assessing and treating culturally diverse clients: A practical guide* (2nd ed.). London, England: Sage.

Paniagua, F. A. (2001). *Diagnosis in a multicultural context.* Thousand Oaks, CA: Sage.

Paniagua, F. A. (2010). Assessment and diagnosis in a cultural context. In M. M. Leach, & J. D. Aten (Eds.), *Culture and the therapeutic process* (pp. 65–98). New York, NY: Routledge/Taylor & Francis.

Papp, P. (1976). Family choreography. In P. J. Guerin, Jr. (Ed.), *Family therapy: Theory and practice* (pp. 276–299). New York, NY: Gardner Press.

Parens, E., & Johnston, J. (2010). Controversies concerning the diagnosis and treatment of bipolar disorder in children. *Child and Adolescent Psychiatry and Mental Health, 4*(9). doi: 10.1186/1753-2000-4-9

Pargament, K. I., & Saunders, S. M. (2007). Introduction to the special issue on spirituality and psychotherapy. *Journal of Clinical Psychology. Special Issue: Spirituality and Psychotherapy, 63*(10), 903–907. doi: 10.1002/jclp.20405

Patrick, S., & Connolly, C. M. (2009). The token activity: Generating awareness of power in counseling relationships. *Journal of Multicultural Counseling and Development, 37*(2), 117–128. doi: http://dx.doi.org/10.1002/j.2161-1912.2009.tb00096.x

Patterson, C. H., & Watkins, C. E., Jr. (1996). *Theories of psychotherapy* (5th ed.). New York, NY: HarperCollins College.

Pearlman, L. A., & Mac Ian, P. S. (1995). Vicarious traumatization: An empirical study of the effects of trauma work on trauma therapists. *Professional Psychology: Research and Practice, 26*(6), 558–565. doi: 10.1037/0735-7028.26.6.558

Pennebaker, J. W., Zech, E., & Rimé, B. (2001). *Disclosing and sharing emotion: Psychological, social, and health consequences.* Washington, DC: American Psychological Association. doi: 10.1037/10436-022

Persons, J. B. (2008). *The case formulation approach to cognitive-behavior therapy.* New York, NY: Guilford Press.

Peterson, J. F., Pun, B. T., Dittus, R. S., Thomason, J. W. W., Jackson, J. C., Shintani, A. K., & Ely, E. W. (2006). Delirium and its motoric subtypes: A study of 614 critically ill patients. *Journal of the American Geriatrics Society, 54*(3), 479–484. doi: 10.1111/j.1532-5415.2005.00621.x

Phillips, J., Frances, A., Cerullo, M. A., Chardavoyne, J., Decker, H. S., First, M. B., ...Zachar, P. (2012). The six most essential questions in psychiatric diagnosis: A pluralogue part 3: Issues of utility and alternative approaches in psychiatric diagnosis. *Philosophy, Ethics, and Humanities in Medicine, 7* doi: http://dx.doi.org/10.1186/1747-5341-7-9

Phinney, J. S., & Chavira, V. (1992). Ethnic identity and self-esteem: An exploratory longitudinal study. *Journal of Adolescence, 15*(3), 271–281. doi: 10.1016/0140-1971(92)90030-9

Pierce, R. D. (2004). A narrative of hope. *Psychiatric Rehabilitation Journal, 27*(4), 403–409. doi: 10.2975/27.2004.403.409

Pipes, R. B., & Davenport, D. S. (1999). *Introduction to psychotherapy: Common clinical wisdom.* Englewood Cliffs, NJ: Prentice Hall.

Plester, B., Wood, C., & Bell, V. (2008). Txt msg n school literacy: Does texting and knowledge of text abbreviations adversely affect children's literacy attainment? *Literacy, 42*(3), 137–144.

Poe, E. A. (1985). *Works of Edgar Allan Poe.* New York, NY: Avenel.

Poelzl, L. (2011). Reflective paper: Bisexual issues in sex therapy: A bisexual surrogate partner relates her experiences from the field. *Journal of Bisexuality, 11*(4), 385–388. doi: http://dx.doi.org/10.1080/15299716.2011.620454

Polanski, P. J., & Hinkle, J. S. (2000). The mental status examination: Its use by professional counselors. *Journal of Counseling & Development, 78*(3), 357–364.

Pomerantz, A. M. (2011). *Clinical psychology: Science, practice, and culture* (2nd ed.). Thousand Oaks, CA: Sage.

Pomerantz, A., & Handelsman, M. (2004). Informed consent revisited: An updated written question format. *Professional Psychology: Research & Practice, 35*(2), 201–205.

Ponterotto, J. G., Casas, J. M., Suzuki, L. A., & Alexander, C. M. (Eds.). (2010). *Handbook of multicultural counseling* (3rd ed.). Thousand Oaks, CA: Sage.

Pope, K. S. (1990). Therapist-patient sex as sex abuse: Six scientific, professional and practical dilemmas in addressing victimization and rehabilitation. *Professional Psychology: Research & Practice, 21*, 227–239.

Portes, A., & Rumbaut, R. G. (2006). *Immigrant America: A portrait.* Berkeley: University of California Press.

Pottick, K. J., Kirk, S. A., Hsieh, D. K., & Tian, X. (2007). Judging mental disorder in youths: Effects of client, clinician, and contextual differences. *Journal of Consulting and Clinical Psychology, 75*(1), 1–8. doi: 10.1037/0022-006X.75.1.1

Pouliot, L., & De Leo, D. (2006). Critical issues in psychological autopsy studies. *Suicide and Life-Threatening Behavior, 36*(5), 491–510. doi: 10.1521/suli.2006.36.5.491

Prochaska, J. O. (1979). *Systems of psychotherapy: A transtheoretical analysis.* Chicago, IL: Dorsey.

Prochaska, J. O., & DiClemente, C. C. (2005). *The transtheoretical approach.* New York, NY: Oxford University Press.

Prochaska, J. O., Norcross, J. C., & DiClemente, C. C. (1994). *Changing for good.* New York, NY: William Morrow.

Pseekos, A. C., & Lyddon, W. J. (2009). The use of metaphor to address gender and sexual orientation stereotypes in counseling: A feminist perspective. *Women & Therapy*, *32*(4), 393–405. doi: 10.1080/02703140903153286

Puig-Antich, J., Chambers, W., & Tabrizi, M. A. (1983). The clinical assessment of current depressive episodes in children and adolescents: Interviews with parents and children. In D. Cantweel, & G. Carlson (Eds.), *Childhood depression* (pp. 157–179). New York, NY: Spectrum.

Quinsey, V. L., Harris, G. T., Rice, M. E., & Cormier, C. A. (2006). *Actuarial prediction of violence*. Washington, DC: American Psychological Association. doi: 10.1037/11367-008

Rand, M. L. (2006). Postural mirroring: Conscious and unconscious. *Annals of the American Psychotherapy Association*, *9*(3), 38.

Ranganathan, S., & Bhattacharya, T. (2007). Culture-bound syndromes: A problematic category. *Psychological Studies*, *52*(2), 153–157.

Ransom, D., Heckman, T. G., Anderson, T., Garske, J., Holroyd, K., & Basta, T. (2008). Telephone-delivered, interpersonal psychotherapy for HIV-infected rural persons with depression: A pilot trial. *Psychiatric Services*, *59*(8), 871–877. doi: 10.1176/appi.ps.59.8.871

Rassin, E., Cougle, J. R., & Muris, P. (2007). Content difference between normal and abnormal obsessions. *Behaviour Research and Therapy*, *45*(11), 2800–2803. doi: 10.1016/j.brat.2007.07.006

Rassin, E., & Muris, P. (2007). Abnormal and normal obsessions: A reconsideration. *Behaviour Research and Therapy*, *45*(5), 1065–1070. doi: 10.1016/j.brat.2006.05.005

Rastoqi, M., & Wieling, E. (Eds.). (2004). *Voices of color: First person accounts of ethnic minority therapists*. New York: NY: Sage.

Ray, D. C. (2011). *Advanced play therapy: Essential conditions, knowledge, and skills for child practice*. New York, NY: Routledge.

Read, J., Agar, K., Barker-Collo, S., Davies, E., & Moskowitz, A. (2001). Assessing suicidality in adults: Integrating childhood trauma as a major risk factor. *Professional Psychology: Research and Practice*, *32*(4), 367–372. doi: 10.1037/0735-7028.32.4.367

Reber, J. S. (2006). Secular psychology: What's the problem? *Journal of Psychology & Theology*, *34*(3), 193–204.

Reiter, M. D. (2010). Hope and expectancy in solution-focused brief therapy. *Journal of Family Psychotherapy*, *21*(2), 132–148. doi: 10.1080/08975353.2010.483653

Richardson, B. G. (2001). *Working with challenging youth: Lessons learned along the way*. Philadelphia, PA: Brunner-Routledge.

Rilke, R. M. (1992). *Letters to a young poet* (J. Burnham, trans.). San Rafael, CA: New World Library.

Roberts, A. R., Monferrari, I., & Yeager, K. R. (2008). Avoiding malpractice lawsuits by following risk assessment and suicide prevention guidelines. *Brief Treatment and Crisis Intervention*, *8*(1), 5–14. doi: http://dx.doi.org/10.1093/brief-treatment/mhm029

Robey, P. A., & Carlson, J. (2011). Adlerian therapy with couples. *Case studies in couples therapy: Theory-based approaches* (pp. 41–51). New York, NY: Routledge/Taylor & Francis.

Robinson, D. J. (2007). My favorite tips for exploring difficult topics such as delusions and substance abuse. *Psychiatric Clinics of North America*, *30*(2), 239–244. doi: 10.1016/j.psc.2007.01.008

Robinson, F. (1950). *Principles and procedures in student counseling*. New York, NY: Harper & Row.

Rogers, C. R. (1942). *Counseling and psychotherapy*. Boston, MA: Houghton Mifflin.

Rogers, C. R. (1951). *Client-centered therapy*. Boston, MA: Houghton Mifflin.

Rogers, C. R. (1957). The necessary and sufficient conditions of therapeutic personality change. *Journal of Consulting Psychology*, *21*, 95–103.

Rogers, C. R. (1958). The characteristics of a helping relationship. *Personnel and Guidance Journal*, *37*, 6–16.

Rogers, C. R. (1961). *On becoming a person*. Boston, MA: Houghton Mifflin.

Rogers, C. R. (1980). *A way of being*. Boston, MA: Houghton Mifflin.

Rolling, E. S., & Brosi, M. W. (2010). A multi-leveled and integrated approach to assessment and intervention of intimate partner violence. *Journal of Family Violence, 25*(3), 229–236. doi: 10.1007/s10896-009-9286-8

Rollnick, S., & Bell, A. (1991). Brief motivational interviewing for use by the nonspecialist. *Motivational interviewing* (pp. 203–213). New York, NY: Guilford Press.

Rollnick, S., & Miller, W. R. (1995). What is motivational interviewing? *Behavioural & Cognitive Psychotherapy, 23*(4), 325–334.

Roosevelt, E. (1937/1992). *The autobiography of Eleanor Roosevelt*. New York, NY: Da Capo Press.

Rosenberg, J. I. (1999). Suicide prevention: An integrated training model using affective and action-based interventions. *Professional Psychology: Research and Practice, 30*(1), 83–87. doi: 10.1037/0735-7028.30.1.83

Rosenberg, J. I. (2000). The complexities of suicide prevention and intervention training: A response to Sommers-Flanagan, Rothman, and Schwenkler (2000). *Professional Psychology: Research and Practice, 31*(1), 100–101. doi: 10.1037/0735-7028.31.1.100

Rosengren, D. B. (2009). *Building motivational interviewing skills: A practitioner workbook*. New York, NY: Guilford Press.

Rothen, S., Vandeleur, C. L., Lustenberger, Y., Jeanprêtre, N., Ayer, E., Gamma, F., . . . Preisig, M. (2009). Parent-child agreement and prevalence estimates of diagnoses in childhood: Direct interview versus family history method. *International Journal of Methods in Psychiatric Research, 18*(2), 96–109. doi: http://dx.doi.org/10.1002/mpr.281

Ruan, W. J., Goldstein, R. B., Chou, S. P., Smith, S. M., Saha, T. D., Pickering, R. P., . . . Grant, B. F. (2008). The alcohol use disorder and associated disabilities interview schedule-IV (AUDADIS-IV): Reliability of new psychiatric diagnostic modules and risk factors in a general population sample. *Drug and Alcohol Dependence, 92*(1–3), 27–36. doi: http://dx.doi.org/10.1016/j.drugalcdep.2007.06.001

Rubel, A. I., O'Nell, C. W., & Collado-Ardon, R. (1984). *Susto: A folk illness*. Berkeley: University of California Press.

Rudd, M. D., Mandrusiak, M., & Joiner, T. E. (2006). The case against no-suicide contracts: The commitment to treatment statement as a practice alternative. *Journal of Clinical Psychology, 62*(2), 243–251. doi: http://dx.doi.org/10.1002/jclp.20227

Rummell, C. M., & Joyce, N. R. (2010). "So wat do u want to wrk on 2day?": The ethical implications of online counseling. *Ethics & Behavior, 20*(6), 482–496. doi: 10.1080/10508422.2010.521450

Russell Crane, D., & Payne, S. H. (2011). Individual versus family psychotherapy in managed care: Comparing the costs of treatment by the mental health professions. *Journal of Marital and Family Therapy, 37*(3), 273–289. doi: http://dx.doi.org/10.1111/j.1752-0606.2009.00170.x

Russo, M. F., Vernam, J., & Wolbert, A. (2006). Sandplay and storytelling: Social constructivism and cognitive development in child counseling. *The Arts in Psychotherapy, 33*(3), 229–237. doi: 10.1016/j.aip.2006.02.005

Rutter, P. A. (2012). Sex therapy with gay male couples using affirmative therapy. *Sexual and Relationship Therapy, 27*(1), 35–45. doi: http://dx.doi.org/10.1080/14681994.2011.633078

Ruzek, J. I., Brymer, M. J., Jacobs, A. K., Layne, C. M., Vernberg, E. M., & Watson, P. J. (2007). Psychological first aid. *Journal of Mental Health Counseling, 29*(1), 17–49.

Sáez-Fonseca, L. L., & Walker, Z. (2007). Long-term outcome of depressive pseudodementia in the elderly. *Journal of Affective Disorders, 101*(1–3), 123–129. doi: http://dx.doi.org/10.1016/j.jad.2006.11.004

Safran, J. D., Muran, J. C., & Eubanks-Carter, C. (2011). Repairing alliance ruptures. In J. C. Norcross (Ed.). *Psychotherapy relationships that work: Evidence-based responsiveness* (2nd ed.) (pp. 224–238). New York, NY: Oxford University Press.

Safran, J. D., Muran, J. C., & Rothman, M. (2006). *The therapeutic alliance: Cultivating and negotiating the therapeutic relationship*. Amsterdam, Netherlands: Elsevier.

Saint-Exupéry, A. d. (1971). *The little prince*. New York, NY: Harcourt Brace Jovanovich.

Salem-Pickartz, J., & Donnelly, J. (2007). *The family as a source of strength and life skill: The role of authoritative parenting in building resilience*. Westport, CT: Praeger Publishers/Greenwood Publishing Group.

Salmela, S., Poskiparta, M., Kasila, K., Vähäsarja, K., & Vanhala, M. (2009). Transtheoretical model-based dietary interventions in primary care: A review of the evidence in diabetes. *Health Education Research, 24*(2), 237–252. doi: 10.1093/her/cyn015

Salmon, K. (2006). Toys in clinical interviews with children: Review and implications for practice. *Clinical Psychologist, 10*(2), 54–59. doi: 10.1080/13284200600681601

Samet, S., & Hasin, D. (2008). Clinical implications of epidemiologic data for diagnosis and treatment of psychiatric comorbidity. *Psychiatric Annals, 38*(11), 709–715. doi: http://dx.doi.org/10.3928/00485713-20081101-10

Sánchez-Ortiz, V. C., House, J., Munro, C., Treasure, J., Startup, H., Williams, C., & Schmidt, U. (2011). "A computer isn't gonna judge you": A qualitative study of users' views of an internet-based cognitive behavioural guided self-care treatment package for bulimia nervosa and related disorders. *Eating and Weight Disorders, 16*(2), e93–e101.

Sanfelippo, A. J. (Ed.). (2006). *Panic disorders: New research*. Hauppauge, NY: Nova Biomedical Books.

Satir, V. M. (1967). *Conjoint family therapy* (Revised ed.). Palo Alto, CA: Science and Behavior Books.

Schneider, B. (2012). Suicide: Risk factors and prevention. *Advances in psychology research* (Vol. 89, pp. 185–189). Hauppauge, NY: Nova Science.

Schneider, K. J., & Krug, O. T. (2010). *Existential–humanistic therapy*. Washington, DC: American Psychological Association.

Schoenholtz, J. C. (2012). *The managed healthcare industry: A market failure* (2nd ed.). North Charleston, SC: CreateSpace.

Schwartz, A. (2011). *Working with family resistance to treatment*. New York, NY: Norton.

Schwartz, J. (2008). *The mind-body fertility connection*. Woodbury, MN: Llewellyn Publications.

Schwartz, R. C., & Wendling, H. M. (2003). Countertransference reactions toward specific client populations: A review of empirical literature. *Psychological Reports, 92*(2), 651–654. doi: 10.2466/PR0.92.2.651-654

Scuka, R. F. (2005). *Relationship enhancement therapy: Healing through deep empathy and intimate dialogue*. Oxford, England: Routledge.

Segal, D. L., & Hersen, M. (Eds.). (2010). *Diagnostic interviewing* (4th ed.). New York, NY: Springer.

Seim, R. W., Willerick, M. S., Gaynor, S. T., & Spates, C. R. (2008). Circumventing the vasovagal fainting response: A novel method of in vivo exposure for injection phobia. *Clinical Case Studies, 7*(5), 409–422. doi: 10.1177/1534650108316932

Selicoff, H. (2006). Looking for good supervision: A fit between collaborative and hierarchical methods. *Journal of Systemic Therapies, 25*(1), 37–51. doi: 10.1521/jsyt.2006.25.1.37

Seligman, L., & Reichenberg, L. W. (2012). *Selecting effective treatments: A comprehensive, systematic guide to treating mental disorders* (4th ed.). Hoboken, NJ: Wiley.

Senior, A. C., Kunik, M. E., Rhoades, H. M., Novy, D. M., Wilson, N. L., & Stanley, M. A. (2007). Utility of telephone assessments in an older adult population. *Psychology and Aging, 22*(2), 392–397. doi: 10.1037/0882-7974.22.2.392

Senzaki, N., & Reps, P. (1939). *101 zen stories*. Philadelphia, PA: David McKay.

Serby, M. (2003). Psychiatric resident conceptualizations of mood and affect within the mental status examination. *American Journal of Psychiatry, 160*(8), 1527–1529. doi: 10 .1176/appi.ajp.160.8.1527

Sexton, T., & Turner, C. W. (2010). The effectiveness of functional family therapy for youth with behavioral problems in a community practice setting. *Journal of Family Psychology, 24*(3), 339–348. doi: 10.1037/a0019406

Shapiro, F. (2002). *EMDR as an integrative psychotherapy approach: Experts of diverse orientations explore the paradigm prism.* Washington, DC: American Psychological Association.

Sharpley, C. F. (1984). Predicate matching in NLP: A review of research on the preferred representational system. *Journal of Counseling Psychology, 31*(2), 238–248. doi: 10.1037/0022-0167.31.2.238

Shaw, H. E., & Shaw, S. F. (2006). Critical ethical issues in online counseling: Assessing current practices with an ethical intent checklist. *Journal of Counseling & Development, 84*(1), 41–53. doi: 10.1002/j.1556-6678.2006.tb00378.x

Shea, M., Cachelin, F., Uribe, L., Striegel, R. H., Thompson, D., & Wilson, G. T. (2012). Cultural adaptation of a cognitive behavior therapy guided self-help program for Mexican American women with binge eating disorders. *Journal of Counseling & Development, 90*(3), 308–318. doi: http://dx.doi.org/10.1002/j.1556-6676.2012.00039.x

Shea, S. C. (1998). *Psychiatric interviewing: The art of understanding* (2nd ed.). Philadelphia, PA: Saunders.

Shedler, J. (2010). The efficacy of psychodynamic psychotherapy. *American Psychologist, 65*(2), 98–109. doi: 10.1037/a0018378

Shellenberger, S. (2007). *Use of the genogram with families for assessment and treatment.* Hoboken, NJ: Wiley.

Sher, L. (2006). Alcoholism and suicidal behavior: A clinical overview. *Acta Psychiatrica Scandinavica, 113*(1), 13–22.

Sherwood, N. E., Jeffery, R. W., Pronk, N. P., Boucher, J. L., Hanson, A., Boyle, R., ...Chen, V. (2006). Mail and phone interventions for weight loss in a managed-care setting: Weigh-to-be 2-year outcomes. *International Journal of Obesity, 30*(10), 1565–1573. doi: 10.1038/sj.ijo.0803295

Shinfuku, N. (2005). The experience of the Kobe earthquake. In J. J. Lopez-Ibor, G. Christodoulou, M. Maj, N. Sartorius & A. Okasha (Eds.), *Disasters and mental health* (pp. 127–136). Hoboken, NJ: Wiley.

Shneidman, E. S. (1980). Psychotherapy with suicidal patients. In T. B. Karasu, & A. S. Bellack (Eds.), *Specialized techniques in individual psychotherapy.* (pp. 306–328). New York, NY: Brunner/Mazel.

Shneidman, E. S. (1984). Aphorisms of suicide and some implications for psychotherapy. *American Journal of Psychotherapy, 38*(3), 319–328.

Shneidman, E. S. (1996). *The suicidal mind.* New York, NY: Oxford University Press.

Shneidman, E. S. (2004). *Autopsy of a suicidal mind.* New York, NY: Oxford University Press.

Shurts, W. M., Cashwell, C. S., Spurgeon, S. L., Degges-White, S., Barrio, C. A., & Kardatzke, K. N. (2006). Preparing counselors-in-training to work with couples: Using role-plays and reflecting teams. *The Family Journal, 14*(2), 151–157. doi: 10.1177/ 1066480705285731

Siassi, I. (1984). Psychiatrtic interview and mental status examination. In G. Goldstein, & M. Hersen (Eds.), *Handbook of psychological assessment* (pp. 259–275). New York, NY: Pergamon Press.

Silverman, W. (1987). *Anxiety disorders interview schedule for children (ADIS).* Albany, New York, NY: Graywind.

Simha-Alpern, A. (2007). "I finally have words!" integrating a psychodynamic psychotherapeutic approach with principles of emotional intelligence training in treating trauma survivors. *Journal of Psychotherapy Integration, 17*(4), 293–313. doi: 10.1037/1053-0479 .17.4.293

Simons, R. C., & Hughes, C. C. (1993). Cultural-bound syndromes. In A. C. Gaw (Ed.), *Culture, ethnicity, and mental illness* (pp. 75–93). Washington, DC: American Psychiatric Press.

Sklare, G. B. (2005). *Brief counseling that works: A solution-focused approach for school counselors and administrators* (2nd ed.). Thousand Oaks, CA: Corwin Press.

Skovholt, T. M., & Trotter-Mathison, M. (2011). *The resilient practitioner: Burnout prevention and self-care strategies for counselors, therapists, teachers, and health professionals* (2nd ed.). New York, NY: Routledge/Taylor & Francis.

Skovholt, T. M., & Jennings, L. (2004). *Master therapist: Exploring expertise in therapy and counseling*. Needham Heights, MA: Allyn & Bacon.

Slama, M. (2010). The agency of the heart: Internet chatting as youth culture in Indonesia. *Social Anthropology/Anthropologie Sociale, 18*(3), 316–330. doi: 10.1111/j.1469-8676 .2010.00110.x

Smith, H. F. I. (2011). *The mental status examination and brief social history in clinical psychology*. lulu.com: Author.

Smith, H. B. (2006). Providing mental health services to clients in crisis or disaster situations. *VISTAS Online, Article 3*, February 17, 2008.

Smith, L., Constantine, M. G., Graham, S. V., & Dize, C. B. (2008). The territory ahead for multicultural competence: The "spinning" of racism. *Professional Psychology: Research and Practice, 39*(3), 337–345. doi: 10.1037/0735-7028.39.3.337

Smith, M. L., & Glass, G. V. (1977). Meta-analysis of psychotherapy outcome. *American Psychologist, 32*, 752–760.

Smith, M. L., Glass, G. V., & Miller, T. I. (1980). *The benefits of psychotherapy*. Baltimore, MD: Johns Hopkins University Press.

Smith-Hanen, S. S. (1977). Effects of nonverbal behaviors on judged levels of counselor warmth and empathy. *Journal of Counseling Psychology, 24*(2), 87–91. doi: 10.1037/ 0022-0167.24.2.87

Snarr, J. D., Heyman, R. E., & Slep, A. M. S. (2010). Recent suicidal ideation and suicide attempts in a large-scale survey of the U.S. Air Force: Prevalences and demographic risk factors. *Suicide and Life-Threatening Behavior, 40*(6), 544–552. doi: http:// dx.doi.org/10.1521/suli.2010.40.6.544

Snyder, D. K. (1979). Multidimensional assessment of marital satisfaction. *Journal of Marriage & the Family, 41*(4), 813–823. doi: 10.2307/351481

Snyder, M. (1974). Self-monitoring of expressive behavior. *Journal of Personality and Social Psychology, 30*(4), 526–537. doi: 10.1037/h0037039

Sommers-Flanagan, J. (2007). The development and evolution of person-centered expressive art therapy: A conversation with Natalie Rogers. *Journal of Counseling & Development, 85*(1), 120–125.

Sommers-Flanagan, J., & Barr, L. (2005). Three constructive interventions for divorced, divorcing, or never-married parents. *The Family Journal, 13*(4), 482–486. doi: 10.1177/ 1066480705278725

Sommers-Flanagan, J., & Bequette, T. (2013). The initial psychotherapy interview with adolescent clients. *Journal of Contemporary Psychotherapy, 43*(1), 13–22.

Sommers-Flanagan, J., & Campbell, D. (2009). Psychotherapy and (or) medications for depression in youth? An evidence-based review with recommendations for treatment. *Journal of Contemporary Psychotherapy, 39*(2), 111–120.

Sommers-Flanagan, J., & Heck, N. (2012). Counseling skills: Building the pillars of professional counseling. In K. MacCluskie, & D. Perera (Eds.), *The counselor educator's survival guide* (pp. 149–166). New York, NY: Routledge.

Sommers-Flanagan, J., & Means, J. R. (1987). Thou shalt not ask questions: An approach to teaching interviewing skills. *Teaching of Psychology, 14*(3), 164–166.

Sommers-Flanagan, J., Richardson, B. G., & Sommers-Flanagan, R. (2011). A multi-theoretical, evidence-based approach for understanding and managing adolescent resistance to psychotherapy. *Journal of Contemporary Psychotherapy, 41*(2), 69–80. doi: 10.1007/s10879-010-9164-y

Sommers-Flanagan, J., & Sommers-Flanagan, R. (1989). A categorization of pitfalls common to beginning interviewers. *Journal of Training & Practice in Professional Psychology*, *3*(1), 58–71.

Sommers-Flanagan, J., & Sommers-Flanagan, R. (1995a). Intake interviewing with suicidal patients: A systematic approach. *Professional Psychology: Research & Practice*, *26*(1), 41–47.

Sommers-Flanagan, J., & Sommers-Flanagan, R. (1995b). Psychotherapeutic techniques with treatment-resistant adolescents. *Psychotherapy: Theory, Research, Practice, Training. Special Issue: Adolescent Treatment: New Frontiers and New Dimensions*, *32*(1), 131–140. doi: 10.1037/0033-3204.32.1.131

Sommers-Flanagan, J., & Sommers-Flanagan, R. (1998). Assessment and diagnosis of conduct disorder. *Journal of Counseling & Development*, *76*(2), 189–197.

Sommers-Flanagan, J. and Sommers-Flanagan, R. (Directors). (2004). *The challenge of counseling teens: Counselor behaviors that reduce resistance and facilitate connection.* [Video/DVD] North Amherst, MA: Microtraining Associates.

Sommers-Flanagan, J., & Sommers-Flanagan, R. (2007a). Our favorite tips for interviewing couples and families. *Psychiatric Clinics of North America*, *30*(2), 275–281. doi: 10.1016/j.psc.2007.02.003

Sommers-Flanagan, J., & Sommers-Flanagan, R. (2007b). *Tough kids, cool counseling: User-friendly approaches with challenging youth* (2nd ed.). Alexandria, VA: American Counseling Association.

Sommers-Flanagan, J., & Sommers-Flanagan, R. (2011). *How to listen so parents will talk and talk so parents will listen.* Hoboken, NJ: Wiley.

Sommers-Flanagan, J., & Sommers-Flanagan, R. (2012). *Counseling and psychotherapy theories in context and practice: Skills, strategies, and techniques* (2nd ed.). Hoboken, NJ: Wiley.

Sommers-Flanagan, J., Zeleke, W., & Hood, M. E. (in press). The clinical interview. In R. Cautin and S. Lilienfeld (Eds). *The encyclopedia of clinical psychology* (page numbers unknown). London: Wiley-Blackwell.

Sommers-Flanagan, R. (2001). The case of Dolores. In F. A. Paniagua, (ed.). *Diagnosis in a multicultural context* (pp. 119–122). Thousand Oaks, CA: Sage.

Sommers-Flanagan, R. (2007). Ethical considerations in crisis and humanitarian interventions. *Ethics & Behavior*, *17*(2), 187–202.

Sommers-Flanagan, R. (2012). *Boundaries, multiple roles, and the professional relationship.* Washington, DC: American Psychological Association. doi: 10.1037/13271-009

Sommers-Flanagan, R., Elander, C., & Sommers-Flanagan, J. (2000). *Don't divorce us!: Kids' advice to divorcing parents.* Alexandria, VA: American Counseling Association.

Sommers-Flanagan, R., Elliott, D., & Sommers-Flanagan, J. (1998). Exploring the edges: Boundaries and breaks. *Ethics & Behavior*, *8*(1), 37–48. doi: 10.1207/s15327019eb0801_3

Sommers-Flanagan, R., & Sommers-Flanagan, J. (2007). *Becoming an ethical helping professional: Cultural and philosophical foundations.* Hoboken, NJ: Wiley.

Sonne, J. L., & Pope, K. S. (1991). Treating victims of therapist-patient sexual involvement. *Psychotherapy: Theory, Research, Practice, Training. Special Issue: Psychotherapy with Victims*, *28*(1), 174–187. doi: 10.1037/0033-3204.28.1.174

Sperry, L., Carlson, J., & Peluso, P. R. (2006). *Couples therapy: Integrating theory and technique* (2nd ed.). Denver, CO: Love Publishing Company.

Spiegler, M. D., & Guevremont, D. C. (2010). *Contemporary behavior therapy* (5th ed.). Belmont, CA: Wadsworth/Cengage Learning.

Spitzer, R. L., Williams, J. B., Gibbon, M., & First, M. B. (1992). The structured clinical interview for DSM-III—R (SCID): I. history, rationale, and description. *Archives of General Psychiatry*, *49*(8), 624–629. doi: 10.1001/archpsyc.1992.01820080032005

Spokas, M., Wenzel, A., Stirman, S. W., Brown, G. K., & Beck, A. T. (2009). Suicide risk factors and mediators between childhood sexual abuse and suicide ideation among male and female suicide attempters. *Journal of Traumatic Stress*, *22*(5), 467–470. doi: http://dx.doi.org/10.1002/jts.20438

Springer, C., & Misurell, J. R. (2012). Game-based cognitive-behavioral therapy individual model for child sexual abuse. *International Journal of Play Therapy, 21*(4), 188–201. doi: http://dx.doi.org/10.1037/a0030197

Stahl, J. V., & Hill, C. E. (2008). A comparison of four methods for assessing natural helping ability. *Journal of Community Psychology, 36*(3), 289–298. doi: 10.1002/jcop.20195

Stanley, B., & Brown, G. K. (2012). Safety planning intervention: A brief intervention to mitigate suicide risk. *Cognitive and Behavioral Practice, 19*(2), 256–264. doi: http://dx.doi.org/10.1016/j.cbpra.2011.01.001

Steenkamp, M. M., Litz, B. T., Gray, M. J., Lebowitz, L., Nash, W., Conoscenti, L., . . . Lang, A. (2011). A brief exposure-based intervention for service members with PTSD. *Cognitive and Behavioral Practice, 18*(1), 98–107. doi: http://dx.doi.org/10.1016/j.cbpra.2009.08.006

Stefansson, J., Nordström, P., & Jokinen, J. (2012). Suicide intent scale in the prediction of suicide. *Journal of Affective Disorders, 136*(1-2), 167–171. doi: http://dx.doi.org/10.1016/j.jad.2010.11.016

Stern, E. M. (1985). *Psychotherapy and the religiously committed patient.* New York, NY: Haworth Press.

Sternberg, R. J. (1985). *Beyond IQ: A triarchic theory of human intelligence.* New York, NY: Cambridge University Press.

Sternberg, R. J. (2005). *The triarchic theory of successful intelligence.* New York, NY: Guilford Press.

Sternberg, R. J., & Wagner, R. K. (1986). *Practical intelligence: Origins of competence in the everyday world.* New York, NY: Cambridge University Press.

Stinson, D. A., Logel, C., Shepherd, S., & Zanna, M. P. (2011). Rewriting the self-fulfilling prophecy of social rejection: Self-affirmation improves relational security and social behavior up to 2 months later. *Psychological Science, 22*(9), 1145–1149. doi: http://dx.doi.org/10.1177/0956797611417725

Stocks, E. L., Lishner, D. A., Waits, B. L., & Downum, E. M. (2011). I'm embarrassed for you: The effect of valuing and perspective taking on empathic embarrassment and empathic concern. *Journal of Applied Social Psychology, 41*(1), 1–26. doi: http://dx.doi.org/10.1111/j.1559-1816.2010.00699.x

Stolle, D., Hutz, A., & Sommers-Flanagan, J. (2005). The impracticalities of R. B. Stuart's practical multicultural competencies. *Professional Psychology: Research and Practice, 36*(5), 574–576. doi: 10.1037/0735-7028.36.5.574

Stolzenberg, S., & Pezdek, K. (2013). Interviewing child witnesses: The effect of forced confabulation on event memory. *Journal of Experimental Child Psychology, 114*(1), 77–88. doi: http://dx.doi.org/10.1016/j.jecp.2012.09.006

Stone, C. B. (2005). *School counseling principles: Ethics and law.* Alexandria, VA: American School Counselor Association.

Stone, J., Smyth, R., Carson, A., Warlow, C., & Sharpe, M. (2006). La belle indifférence in conversion symptoms and hysteria: Systematic review. *British Journal of Psychiatry, 188*(3), 204–209. doi: 10.1192/bjp.188.3.204

Stover, C. S., McMahon, T. J., & Easton, C. (2011). The impact of fatherhood on treatment response for men with co-occurring alcohol dependence and intimate partner violence. *The American Journal of Drug and Alcohol Abuse, 37*(1), 74–78. doi: 10.3109/00952990.2010.535585

Strong, S. R. (1968). Counseling: An interpersonal influence process. *Journal of Counseling Psychology, 15*(3), 215–224.

Strub, R. L., & Black, F. W. (1977). *The mental status exam in neurology.* Philadelphia, PA: Davis.

Strupp, H. H. (1983). Psychoanalytic psychotherapy. In M. Hersen, A. E. Kazdin, & A.S. Bellack (Eds.), *The clinical psychology handbook* (471–488). New York, NY: Pergamon Press.

Strupp, H. H., & Binder, J. L. (1984). *Psychotherapy in a new key.* New York, NY: Basic Books.

Stuart, R. B., & Stuart, F. (1975). *Premarital counseling inventory manual*. Ann Arbor, MI: Compuscore.

Sue, D. W., Arredondo, P., & McDavis, R. J. (1992). Multicultural counseling competencies and standards: A call to the profession. *Journal of Counseling & Development*, 70(4), 477–486.

Sue, D. W., Ivey, A. E., & Pedersen, P. B. (1996). *A theory of multicultural counseling and therapy*. Belmont, CA: Thomson Brooks/Cole.

Sue, D. W., & Sue, D. (2013). *Counseling the culturally diverse: Theory and practice* (6th ed.). Hoboken, NJ: Wiley.

Sue, S. (1977). Community mental health services to minority groups: Some optimism, some pessimism. *American Psychologist*, 32, 616–624.

Sue, S. (1998). In search of cultural competence in psychotherapy and counseling. *American Psychologist*, 53, 440–448.

Sue, S. (2006). Cultural competency: From philosophy to research and practice. *Journal of Community Psychology. Special Issue: Addressing Mental Health Disparities through Culturally Competent Research and Community-Based Practice*, 34(2), 237–245. doi: 10.1002/jcop.20095

Sue, S., & Zane, N. (2009). The role of culture and cultural techniques in psychotherapy: A critique and reformulation. *Asian American Journal of Psychology*, S(1), 3–14.

Suler, J. (2004). The online disinhibition effect. *CyberPsychology & Behavior*, 7(3), 321–326. doi: 10.1089/1094931041291295

Suler, J. (2010). Interpersonal guidelines for texting. *International Journal of Applied Psychoanalytic Studies*, 7(4), 358–361. doi: 10.1002/aps.268

Sutton, C. T., & Broken Nose, M. A. (2005). *American Indian families: An overview*. New York, NY: Guilford Press.

Swainson, M., & Tasker, F. (2006). Genograms redrawn: Lesbian couples define their families. *An introduction to GLBT family studies* (pp. 89–115). New York, NY: Haworth Press.

Swartz, S. H., Cowan, T. M., Klayman, J. E., Welton, M. T., & Leonard, B. A. (2005). Use and effectiveness of tobacco telephone counseling and nicotine therapy in Maine. *American Journal of Preventive Medicine*, 29(4), 288–294. doi: 10.1016/j.amepre.2005.06.015

Sweeney, T. J. (2009). *Adlerian counseling and psychotherapy: A practitioner's approach* (5th ed.). New York, NY: Routledge/Taylor & Francis.

Szasz, T. S. (1970). *The manufacture of madness*. New York, NY: McGraw-Hill.

Szasz, T. (1986). The case against suicide prevention. *American Psychologist*, 41(7), 806–812.

Szmukler, G. (2012). Risk assessment for suicide and violence is of extremely limited value in general psychiatric practice. *Australian and New Zealand Journal of Psychiatry*, 46(2), 173–174. doi: http://dx.doi.org/10.1177/0004867411432214

Talley, B. J., & Littlefield, J. (2009). Efficiently teaching mental status examination to medical students. *Medical Education*, 43, 1200–1202. doi: 10.1111/j.1365-2923.2009.03494.x

Tannen, D. (1990). *You just don't understand me: Women and men in conversation*. New York, NY: Ballantine Books.

Tardiff, K., & Hughes, D. M. (2011). *Structural and clinical assessment of risk of violence*. Hoboken, NJ: Wiley. doi: http://dx.doi.org/10.1002/9781118093399.ch15

Taylor, L. (2005). A thumbnail map for solution-focused brief therapy. *Journal of Family Psychotherapy*, 16(1–2), 27–33. doi: 10.1300/J085v15n04_03

Teasdale, J. D., & Dent, J. (1987). Cognitive vulnerability to depression: An investigation of two hypotheses. *British Journal of Clinical Psychology*, 26(2), 113–126.

Teyber, E., & McClure, F. (2011). *Interpersonal process in therapy: An integrative model* (6th ed.). Belmont, CA: Brooks/Cole.

Theriault, B. (2012). Radical acceptance: A nondual psychology approach to grief and loss. *International Journal of Mental Health and Addiction*, 10(3), 354–367. doi: http://dx.doi.org/10.1007/s11469-011-9359-9

Thomas, L. (1974). *The lives of a cell*. New York, NY: Bantam Books.

Thomas, V. (2005). *Initial interview with a family*. Ashland, OH: Hogrefe & Huber.

Thompson, M. P., & Light, L. S. (2011). Examining gender differences in risk factors for suicide attempts made 1 and 7 years later in a nationally representative sample. *Journal of Adolescent Health, 48*(4), 391–397. doi: http://dx.doi.org/10.1016/j.jadohealth.2010.07.018

Thoresen, C. E., & Mahoney, M. J. (1974). *Behavioral self-control*. New York, NY: Holt, Rinehart & Winston.

Tohn, S. L., & Oshlag, J. A. (1996). Solution-focused therapy with mandated clients: Cooperating with the uncooperative. In M. F. Hoyt (Ed.), *Handbook of solution-focused brief therapy*. (pp. 152–183). San Francisco, CA: Jossey-Bass.

Tolstoy, L. (2003). *Anna Karenina*. New York, NY: Penguin.

Tombini, M., Pellegrino, G., Zappasodi, F., Quattrocchi, C. C., Assenza, G., Melgari, J. M., …Rossini, P. M. (2012). Complex visual hallucinations after occipital extrastriate ischemic stroke. *Cortex: A Journal Devoted to the Study of the Nervous System and Behavior, 48*(6), 774–777. doi: http://dx.doi.org/10.1016/j.cortex.2011.04.027

Trickett, E. J., & Jones, C. J. (2007). Adolescent culture brokering and family functioning: A study of families from vietnam. *Cultural Diversity and Ethnic Minority Psychology, 13*(2), 143–150. doi: 10.1037/1099-9809.13.2.143

Trimble, J. E. (2010). Bear spends time in our dreams now: Magical thinking and cultural empathy in multicultural counselling theory and practice. *Counselling Psychology Quarterly. Special Issue: Integrating Traditional Healing Practices into Counselling and Psychotherapy, 23*(3), 241–253. doi: 10.1080/09515070.2010.505735

Trippany, R. L., Kress, V. E. W., & Wilcoxon, S. A. (2004). Preventing vicarious trauma: What counselors should know when working with trauma survivors. *Journal of Counseling & Development, 82*(1), 31–37.

Trull, T. J., & Prinstein, M. (2013). *Clinical psychology* (8th ed.). Belmont, CA: Wadsworth.

Tryon, G. S., & Winograd, G. (2011). Goal consensus and collaboration. *Psychotherapy relationships that work: Evidence-based responsiveness* (2nd ed., pp. 153–167). New York, NY: Oxford University Press.

Tseng, W. (2006). From peculiar psychiatric disorders through culture-bound syndromes to culture-related specific syndromes. *Transcultural Psychiatry, 43*(4), 554–576. doi: 10.1177/1363461506070781

Tsuchida, T. (2007). The relationship between emotional expression and illness: A dressing to the effects of emotional repression on self-efficacy regarding health behavior. *Japanese Journal of Counseling Science, 40*(1), 51–58.

Tummala-Narra, P. (2007). Skin color and the therapeutic relationship. *Psychoanalytic Psychology, 24*(2), 255–270. doi: 10.1037/0736-9735.24.2.255

Turner, C., Heyman, I., Futh, A., & Lovell, K. (2009). A pilot study of telephone cognitive-behavioural therapy for obsessive-compulsive disorder in young people. *Behavioural and Cognitive Psychotherapy, 37*(4), 469–474. doi: 10.1017/S1352465809990178

Turner, E. H., Matthews, A. M., Linardatos, E., Tell, R. A., & Rosenthal, R. (2008). Selective publication of antidepressant trials and its influence on apparent efficacy. *New England Journal of Medicine, 358*(3), 252–260. doi: 10.1056/NEJMsa065779

U.S. Census Bureau. (2011). *2010 census of the population*. Washington, DC: U.S. Government Printing Office.

U.S. Government Printing Office. (2012). *America's children in brief: Key national indicators of well-being*. Washington, DC: Federal Interagency Forum on Child and Family Statistics.

Ullman, L. P., & Krasner, L. (1969). *A psychological approach to abnormal behavior*. Oxford, England: Prentice-Hall.

United States Department of Health and Human Services (2003). Developing cultural competence in disaster mental health programs. Retrieved from http://store.samhsa.gov/product/Developing-Cultural-Competence-in-Disaster-Mental-Health-Programs/SMA03-3828.

United States Food and Drug Administration. (2007). *FDA proposes new warnings about suicidal thinking, behavior in young adults who take antidepressant medications.* Retrieved from http://www.fda.gov/bbs/topics/NEWS/2007/NEW01624.html

Vahter, L., Kreegipuu, M., Talvik, T., & Gross-Paju, K. (2007). One question as a screening instrument for depression in people with multiple sclerosis. *Clinical Rehabilitation, 21*(5), 460–464. doi: 10.1177/0269215507074056

Valenstein, M., Kim, H. M., Ganoczy, D., Eisenberg, D., Pfeiffer, P. N., Downing, K., . . . McCarthy, J. F. (2012). Antidepressant agents and suicide death among US Department of Veterans Affairs patients in depression treatment. *Journal of Clinical Psychopharmacology, 32*(3), 346–353. doi: http://dx.doi.org/10.1097/JCP.0b013e3182539f11

Van Orden, K. A., Witte, T. K., Cukrowicz, K. C., Braithwaite, S. R., Selby, E. A., & Joiner, T. E. (2010). The interpersonal theory of suicide. *Psychological Review, 117*(2), 575–600. doi: http://dx.doi.org/10.1037/a0018697

Van Orden, K. A., Witte, T. K., Gordon, K. H., Bender, T. W., Joiner, T. Jr., (2008). Suicidal desire and the capability for suicide: Tests of the interpersonal-psychological theory of suicidal behavior among adults. *Journal of Consulting and Clinical Psychology, 76*(1), 72–83,

Van Oudenhoven, J. P., Ward, C., & Masgoret, A. (2006). Patterns of relations between immigrants and host societies. *International Journal of Intercultural Relations, 30*(6), 637–651. doi: 10.1016/j.ijintrel.2006.09.001

van Uffelen, Jannique G. Z., Chin A Paw, Marijke J. M., Klein, M., van Mechelen, W., & Hopman-Rock, M. (2007). Detection of memory impairment in the general population: Screening by questionnaire and telephone compared to subsequent face-to-face assessment. *International Journal of Geriatric Psychiatry, 22*(3), 203–210. doi: 10.1002/gps.1661

Vargas, L. (2012). Reflections of a process-oriented contextualist. In J. Sommers-Flanagan & R. Sommers-Flanagan, *Counseling and psychotherapy theories in context and practice* (2nd ed., pp. 20–21). Hoboken, NJ: Wiley.

Vazquez, C. I., & Clauss-Ehlers, C. S. (2005). Group psychotherapy with Latinas: A cross-cultural and interactional approach. *NYS Psychologist, 17*(3), 10–13.

Vernberg, E. M., Steinberg, A. M., Jacobs, A. K., Brymer, M. J., Watson, P. J., Osofsky, J. D., . . . Ruzek, J. I. (2008). Innovations in disaster mental health: Psychological first aid. *Professional Psychology: Research and Practice, 39*(4), 381–388. doi: http://dx.doi.org/10.1037/a0012663

Vig, S. (2007). Young children's object play: A window on development category. *Journal of Developmental and Physical Disabilities, 19*(3), 201–215. doi: 10.1007/s10882-007-9048-6

Wagner, L., Davis, S., & Handelsman, M. M. (1998). In search of the abominable consent form: The impact of readability and personalization. *Journal of Clinical Psychology, 54*(1), 115–120. doi: 10.1002/(SICI)1097-4679(199801)54:1<115::AID-JCLP13>3.0.CO;2-N

Walitzer, K. S., Dermen, K. H., & Conners, G. J. (1999). Strategies for preparing clients for treatment: A review. *Behavior Modification, 23*(1), 129–151. doi: 10.1177/0145445599231006

Walker, V. L. (2009). *Using three-dimensional virtual environments in counselor education for mental health interviewing and diagnosis: Student perceived learning benefits. Dissertation Abstracts International Section A: Humanities and Social Sciences.* (MSTAR_622196210; 2010-99031-352).

Wallin, P. (1949). An appraisal of some methodological aspects of the Kinsey report. *American Sociological Review, 14*(0003-1224, 0003-1224), 197–210. doi: 10.2307/2086853

Walters, R. P. (1980). *Amity: Friendship in action. Part I: Basic friendship skills.* Boulder, CO: Christian Helpers.

Wampold, B. E. (2001). *The great psychotherapy debate: Models, methods, and findings.* Mahwah, NJ: Erlbaum.

Ward, A., & Knudson-Martin, C. (2012). The impact of therapist actions on the balance of power within the couple system: A qualitative analysis of therapy sessions. *Journal of Couple & Relationship Therapy, 11*(3), 221–237. doi: http://dx.doi.org/10.1080/15332691.2012.692943

Ward, C., Bochner, S., & Furnham, A. (2001). *The psychology of culture shock* (2nd ed.). New York, NY: Routledge.

Waterhouse, L. (2006). Inadequate evidence for multiple intelligences, Mozart effect, and emotional intelligence theories. *Educational Psychologist, 41*(4), 247–255.

Watkins, J. G., & Watkins, H. H. (1997). *Ego states: Theory and therapy.* New York, NY: Norton.

Watson, H. J., Swan, A., & Nathan, P. R. (2011). Psychiatric diagnosis and quality of life: The additional burden of psychiatric comorbidity. *Comprehensive Psychiatry, 52*(3), 265–272. doi: http://dx.doi.org/10.1016/j.comppsych.2010.07.006

Watts, R. E., & Eckstein, D. (2009). Individual psychology. In American Counseling Association (Ed.), *The ACA encyclopedia of counseling* (pp. 281–283). Alexandria, VA: American Counseling Association.

Watzlawick, P., Weakland, J. H., & Fisch, R. (1974). *Change: Principles of problem formation and problem resolution.* Oxford, England: Norton.

Weakland, J. H. (1993). Conversation-but what kind? In S. G. Gilligan & R. Price (Eds.), *Therapeutic conversations* (pp. 136–145). New York, NY: Norton.

Weaver, J. (1995). *Disasters: Mental health interventions.* Saraota, FL: Professional Resource Press.

Wechsler, D. (1958). *The measurement and appraisal of adult intelligence* (4th ed.). Baltimore: Williams & Wilkins.

Weeks, G. R., Odell, M., & Methven, S. (2005). *If only I had known: Avoiding common mistakes in couples therapy.* New York, NY: Norton.

Weiner, I. B. (1998). *Principles of psychotherapy* (2nd ed.). New York, NY: Wiley.

Weiner-Davis, M. (1993). Pro-constructed realities. In S. G. Gilligan & R. Price (Eds.), *Therapeutic conversations* (pp. 149–157). New York, NY: Norton.

Weiss, A. (2001). The no-suicide contract: Possibilities and pitfalls. *American Journal of Psychotherapy, 55*(3), 414–419.

Weisz, J. R. (2004). *Psychotherapy for children and adolescents: Evidence-based treatments and case examples.* New York, NY: Cambridge University Press.

Welfel, E. R. (2013). *Ethics in counseling and psychotherapy: Standards, research, and emerging issues* (5th ed.). Belmont, CA: Brooks/Cole.

Werner-Wilson, R. J., Zimmerman, T. S., & Price, S. J. (1999). Are goals and topics influenced by gender and modality in the initial marriage and family therapy session? *Journal of Marital and Family Therapy, 25*(2), 253–262. doi: http://dx.doi.org/10.1111/j.1752-0606.1999.tb01126.x

Westefeld, J. S., & Furr, S. R. (1987). Suicide and depression among college students. *Professional Psychology: Research and Practice, 18*(2), 119–123.

Whitaker, C. A., & Burnberry, W. M. (1988). *Dancing with the family: A symbolic experiential approach.* New York, NY: Brunner/Mazel.

White, L. (1994). *Stranger at the gate.* New York, NY: Simon & Schuster.

White, M. (1988). The process of questioning: A therapy of literary merit? *Dulwich Centre Newsletter,* 8–14.

White, M. (1995). *Re-authoring lives: Interviews and essays.* Adelaide, South Australia: Dulwich Centre Publications.

White, M., & Epston, D. (1990). *Narrative means to therapeutic ends.* New York, NY: Norton.

Widiger, T. A., & Clark, L. A. (2000). Toward *DSM-V* and the classification of psychopathology. *Psychological Bulletin. Special Issue: Psychology in the 21st Century, 126*(6), 946–963. doi: 10.1037/0033-2909.126.6.946

Wilcox, H. C., & Fawcett, J. (2012). Stress, trauma, and risk for attempted and completed suicide. *Psychiatric Annals, 42*(3), 85–87. doi: http://dx.doi.org/10.3928/00485713-20120217-04

Williams, J. M. G., Van der Does, A. J. W., Barnhofer, T., Crane, C., & Segal, Z. S. (2008). Cognitive reactivity, suicidal ideation and future fluency: Preliminary investigation of a differential activation theory of hopelessness/suicidality. *Cognitive Therapy and Research, 32*(1), 83–104. doi: http://dx.doi.org/10.1007/s10608-006-9105-y

Williams, M., Teasdale, J., Segal, Z., & Kabat-Zinn, J. (2007). *The mindful way through depression: Freeing yourself from chronic unhappiness.* New York, NY: Guilford Press.

Williams, T. T. (1991). *Refuge: An unnatural history of family and place.* New York, NY: Vintage Books.

Willock, B. (1986). Narcissistic vulnerability in the hyper-aggressive child: The disregarded (unloved, uncared-for) self. *Psychoanalytic Psychology, 3,* 59–80.

Willock, B. (1987). The devalued (unloved, repugnant) self: A second facet of narcissistic vulnerability in the aggressive, conduct-disordered child. *Psychoanalytic Psychology, 4,* 219–240.

Wilmot, W. W., & Hocker, J. L. (2010). *Interpersonal conflict* (7th ed.). New York, NY: McGraw-Hill.

Wilson, R. S., & Bennett, D. A. (2005). Assessment of cognitive decline in old age with brief tests amenable to telephone administration. *Neuroepidemiology, 25*(1), 19–25. doi: 10.1159/000085309

Wilson, R. S., Leurgans, S. E., Foroud, T. M., Sweet, R. A., Graff-Radford, N., Mayeux, R., & Bennett, D. A. (2010). Telephone assessment of cognitive function in the late-onset Alzheimer's disease family study. *Archives of Neurology, 67*(7), 855–861. doi: 10.1001/archneurol.2010.129

Winslade, J. M., & Monk, G. D. (2007). *Narrative counseling in schools: Powerful & brief* (2nd ed.). Thousand Oaks, CA: Corwin Press.

Witvliet, C. V. O., Worthington, E. L., Root, L. M., Sato, A. F., Ludwig, T. E., & Exline, J. J. (2008). Retributive justice, restorative justice, and forgiveness: An experimental psychophysiology analysis. *Journal of Experimental Social Psychology, 44*(1), 10–25. doi: 10.1016/j.jesp.2007.01.009

Wolberg, L. R. (1995). *The technique of psychotherapy.* (4th rev. ed.). New York, NY: Grune & Stratton.

Wollersheim, J. P. (1974). The assessment of suicide potential via interview methods. *Psychotherapy: Theory, Research & Practice, 11*(3), 222–225.

Wong, A., Wong, Y. J., & Obeng, C. S. (2012). An untold story: A qualitative study of Asian American family strengths. *Asian American Journal of Psychology, 3*(4), 286–298. doi: http://dx.doi.org/10.1037/a0025553

Wood, A. F., & Smith, M. J. (2005). *Online communication: Linking technology, identity, and culture* (2nd ed.). Mahwah, NJ: Erlbaum.

Wood, J. M., Nezworski, M. T., Lilienfeld, S. O., & Garbm, H. N. (2008). *The Rorschach inkblot test, fortune tellers, and cold reading.* Amherst, NY: Prometheus Books.

Woods, D. L., Kishiyama, M. M., Yund, E. W., Herron, T. J., Edwards, B., Poliva, O., ... Reed, B. (2011). Improving digit span assessment of short-term verbal memory. *Journal of Clinical and Experimental Neuropsychology, 33*(1), 101–111. doi: http://dx.doi.org/10.1080/13803395.2010.493149

Woodside, M., Oberman, A. H., Cole, K. G., & Carruth, E. K. (2007). Learning to be a counselor: A prepracticum point of view. *Counselor Education and Supervision, 47*(1), 14–28.

Woody, S. R., Detweiler-Bedell, J., Teachman, B. A., & O'Hearn, T. (2003). *Treatment planning in psychotherapy: Taking the guesswork out of clinical care.* New York, NY: Guilford Press.

Worell, J., & Remer, P. (2003). *Feminist perspectives in therapy: Empowering diverse women* (2nd ed.). Hoboken, NJ: Wiley.

World Health Organization. (2004). *ICD 10: International statistical classification of diseases and health-related problems* (2nd ed.). London, England: Cambridge University Press.

Worthington, R. L., Navarro, R. L., Savoy, H. B., & Hampton, D. (2008). Development, reliability, and validity of the measure of sexual identity exploration and commitment (MOSIEC). *Developmental Psychology, 44*(1), 22–33. doi: 10.1037/0012-1649.44.1.22

Wright, J. H., & Davis, D. (1994). The therapeutic relationship in cognitive-behavioral therapy: Patient perceptions and therapist responses. *Cognitive and Behavioral Practice, 1*(1), 25–45. doi: 10.1016/S1077-7229(05)80085-9

Wubbolding, R. E. (2011). *Reality therapy*. Washington, DC: American Psychological Association.

Wubbolding, R. E., Brickell, J., Imhof, L., Kim, R. I., Lojk, L., & Al-Rashidi, B. (2004). Reality therapy: A global perspective. *International Journal for the Advancement of Counselling, 26*(3), 219–228. doi: 10.1023/B:ADCO.0000035526.02422.0d

Yalom, I. D. (1989). *Love's executioner*. New York, NY: Basic Books.

Yalom, I. D. (2002). *The gift of therapy*. New York, NY: HarperCollins.

Yalom, I. D., & Leszcz, M. (2005). *The theory and practice of group psychotherapy* (5th ed.). New York, NY: Basic Books.

Yehuda, R., & Bierer, L. M. (2005). Re-evaluating the link between disasters and psychopathology. In J. J. Lopez-Ibor, G. Christodoulou, M. Maj, N. Sartorius, & A. Okasha (Eds.), *Disasters and mental health* (pp. 65–80). Hoboken, NJ: Wiley.

Yellow Bird, M. (2001). Critical values and First Nations peoples. In R. Fong, & S. M. Fulero (Eds.), *Culturally competent practice: Skills, interventions, and evaluations* (pp. 61–74). Needham Heights, MA: Allyn & Bacon.

Yoshino, A., Shigemura, J., Kobayashi, Y., Nomura, S., Shishikura, K., Den, R.,... Ashida, H. (2001). Telepsychiatry: Assessment of televideo psychiatric interview reliability with present- and next-generation internet infrastructures. *Acta Psychiatrica Scandinavica, 104*(3), 223–226. doi: 10.1034/j.1600-0447.2001.00236.x

Young, K. M., Northern, J. J., Lister, K. M., Drummond, J. A., & O'Brien, W. H. (2007). A meta-analysis of family-behavioral weight-loss treatments for children. *Clinical Psychology Review, 27*(2), 240–249. doi: 10.1016/j.cpr.2006.08.003

Young-Eisendrath, P. (1993). *You're not what I expected: Breaking the "he said-she said" cycle*. New York, NY: Touchstone.

Yuar, S., & Chen, C. (2011). Relationship among client's counseling expectations, perceptions of the counselor credibility and the initial working alliance. *Chinese Journal of Guidance and Counseling, 30*, 1–29.

Yuen, E. K., Goetter, E. M., Herbert, J. D., & Forman, E. M. (2012). Challenges and opportunities in internet-mediated telemental health. *Professional Psychology: Research and Practice, 43*(1), 1–8. doi: 10.1037/a0025524

Zahl, D. L., & Hawton, K. (2004). Repetition of deliberate self-harm and subsequent suicide risk: Long-term follow-up study of 11 583 patients. *British Journal of Psychiatry, 185*(1), 70–75. doi: 10.1192/bjp.185.1.70

Zeer, D., & Klein, M. (2000). *Office yoga: Simple stretches for busy people*. San Francisco, CA: Chronicle Books.

Zetzel, E. R. (1956). Current concepts of transference. *International Journal of Psychoanalysis, 37*, 369–376.

Zickuhr, K. (2011). Generations and their gadgets. Pew Internet & American Life Project. Retrieved from http://pewinternet.org/Reports/2011/Generations-and-gadgets.aspx gadgets.

Zuckerman, E. L. (2010). *The clinician's thesaurus: The guide to conducting interviews and writing psychological reports* (7th ed.). New York, NY: Guilford Press.

Zuckerman, M. (1990). Some dubious premises in research and theory on racial differences: Scientific, social, and ethical issues. *American Psychologist, 45*(12), 1297–1303. doi: 10.1037/0003-066X.45.12.1297

Zuckerman, M. (2000). *Vulnerability to psychopathology: A biosocial model*. Washington, DC: American Psychological Association.

Zur, O. (2007). *Boundaries in psychotherapy: Ethical and clinical explorations*. Washington, DC: American Psychological Association.

Author Index

Subject Index

About the DVD

SYSTEM REQUIREMENTS

- TV or computer DVD player
- Windows® XP, Vista, or 7; Mac OS® 10.4 or later
- 512 MB RAM
- A DVD drive

TIPS FOR PLAYING THE DVD

You can play this DVD using your computer's DVD drive or the DVD player connected to your television.

- **On a PC Running Windows® 7, Vista, or XP**: If you have more than one media player installed on your computer, Windows may ask you to choose one to play the DVD. After you do, the DVD should start in that media player.
- **On a Macintosh running Mac OS® X**: When you put the DVD into the drive on your Mac, the DVD player automatically opens—complete with onscreen remote control. You can use the on-screen remote controls, your keyboard's arrow keys, or your mouse to navigate through the DVD's menu system.
- **On a DVD player connected to your television**: Use your player's remote control to navigate through the DVD's menu system.

WHAT'S ON THE DVD

The following sections provide a summary of the software and other materials you'll find on the DVD.

The *Clinical Interviewing* DVD covers the following skills, techniques, and types of interviews:

- Nondirective Listening Responses (silence, clarifications, paraphrasing, reflection of feeling, summarizing, prompts, eye contact, body language)
- Directive Listening Responses (feeling validation, interpretive reflection of feeling, interpretation, reframe, confrontation)
- Directives and Action Responses (explanation, suggestion, agreement-disagreement, approval-disapproval, self-disclosure, urging, psychoeducational materials)
- General and Therapeutic Questions (indirect, open, swing, projective, closed)

- Intake Interview
- Mental Status Exam
- Suicide Assessment Interview

CUSTOMER CARE

If you have trouble with the DVD, please call the Wiley Product Technical Support phone number at (800) 762-2974. Outside the United States, call 1(317) 572-3994. You can also contact Wiley Product Technical Support at http:// support.wiley.com. John Wiley & Sons will provide technical support only for installation and other general quality control items. For technical support on the applications themselves, consult the program's vendor or author.

To place additional orders or to request information about other Wiley products, please call (877) 762–2974.